WADSWORTH
CENGAGE Learning™

ED PSYCH
Jack Snowman
Rick McCown

Executive Editor: Mark D. Kerr

Associate Developmental Editor: Caitlin Cox

Assistant Editor: Joshua Taylor

Editorial Assistant: Greta Lindquist

Media Editor: Ashley Cronin

Marketing Manager: Kara Kindstrom

Marketing Coordinator: Klaira Markenzon

Marketing Communications Manager:
Heather Baxley

Content Project Manager: Samen Iqbal

Design Director: Rob Hugel

Art Director: Jennifer Wahi

Print Buyer: Rebecca Cross

Rights Acquisitions Specialist: Roberta Broyer

Production Service: Mandy Walden, Lachina
Publishing Services

Photo Researchers: Linda Sykes and Mandy
Walden, Lachina Publishing Services

Text Researcher: Isabel Saraiva

Copy Editor: Jeff Anderson, Lachina Publishing
Services

Cover Designer: Kate Scheible

Cover Images: © Bart Coenders/iStock Photo;
© Bruce Lonngren/iStock Photo;
© sextoacto/Shutterstock Images

Compositor: Lachina Publishing Services

For product information and technology assistance, contact us at
Cengage Learning Customer & Sales Support, 1-800-354-9706.
For permission to use material from this text or product,
submit all requests online at **cengage.com/permissions**.
Further permissions questions can be emailed to
permissionrequest@cengage.com.

Library of Congress Control Number: 2011932853

ISBN-13: 978-1-111-84193-5

ISBN-10: 1-111-84193-4

Wadsworth
20 Davis Drive
Belmont, CA 94002-3098
USA

Cengage Learning is a leading provider of customized learning solutions with office locations around the globe, including Singapore, the United Kingdom, Australia, Mexico, Brazil, and Japan. Locate your local office at **www.cengage .com/global**.

Cengage Learning products are represented in Canada by Nelson Education, Ltd.

To learn more about Wadsworth, visit **www.cengage.com/wadsworth**. Purchase any of our products at your local college store or at our preferred online store **www.CengageBrain.com**.

Printed in the United States of America
1 2 3 4 5 6 7 15 14 13 12 11

© Robert Kneschke/Shutterstock Images

v

CHAPTER 3

Age-Level Characteristics 48

CHAPTER 4

Understanding Student Differences 70

© dpaint/Shutterstock Images

© Christopher Futcher/iStockphoto

© Pakhnyushcha/Shutterstock Images

CHAPTER 7

Behavioral Learning Theory: Operant Conditioning 148

CHAPTER 8

Information-Processing Theory 166

CHAPTER 9

Social Cognitive Theory 186

© Thomas M Perkins/Shutterstock Images

© de2marco/Shutterstock Images

© Skip ODonnell/iStockphoto

1

APPLYING PSYCHOLOGY TO TEACHING

LEARNING OBJECTIVES

After studying this chapter, you will be able to . . .

LO1 State the main focus of educational psychology.

LO2 Explain how learning about educational psychology will help make you a better teacher.

LO3 Describe the limitations of a nonscientific approach to solving education-related problems and the strengths of a scientific approach.

LO4 Describe how the limited focus of research, the complexity of teaching and learning, the differences in how educational psychologists select and interpret research findings, and revised ideas due to new research complicate the scientific study of behavior and thought processes.

LO5 Explain what it means to say that good teaching is partly an art and partly a science.

LO6 Define reflective teaching and explain how it contributes to a teacher's effectiveness.

visit 4ltrpress.cengage.com

As you begin to read this book, you may be asking yourself, "What will this book tell me about teaching and learning that I don't already know? After all, I've been in school for more than 12 years and have observed dozens of teachers. And teaching is nothing more than telling others what you know." What you may not realize—at least not yet—is that you likely have significant gaps in your knowledge about the factors that affect teaching and learning. You may also have formed incorrect beliefs about how to teach others and about how people learn in classroom settings. Our primary goal, then, is to help you fill in these gaps and create more accurate beliefs by explaining how you can use various psychological theories, concepts, and principles to become an effective classroom teacher. The purpose of this first chapter is to tell you a little bit about the field of educational psychology, why we think research on various aspects of teaching and classroom learning can help you become an effective teacher, and how you can best use research findings to achieve your teaching goals. So let's start with a comment and question that the two of us have heard from various people, including teachers, many, many times in our careers: "I've never heard of educational psychology. What is it all about?"

LO1 What Is Educational Psychology?

Educational psychology is a branch of psychology that is concerned with understanding and improving how students acquire a variety of capabilities through formal instruction in classroom settings. David Berliner (2006), for example, described educational psychology as a scientific discipline that uses psychological concepts and research methods to understand how the various characteristics of students, teachers, learning tasks, and educational settings interact to produce the everyday behaviors common in school settings. Since educational psychology is a scientific discipline, we will be describing one of its most important tools in just about every chapter: *theory*. Many people mistakenly think that a theory is nothing more than unproven, off-the-top-of-the-head speculation about some topic. Let's put that view to rest right now. In a scientific context, a theory is a proposed explanation of some phenomenon that is based in

part *on already existing facts*. Scientists then use what they already know to propose a tentative explanation of how something works that can be tested. The nature of theory and its relationship to research and practice should become clearer as you move through the book.

Some of the factors that psychological theories are concerned with and that affect how teachers teach and students learn include the learner's physical, social, emotional, and cognitive development; cultural, social, emotional, and intellectual differences; learning and problem-solving processes; self-esteem; motivation; testing; and measurement to formulate effective instructional lessons. In the next section, we'll explain why learning about these topics is worth your time and effort.

LO2 How Will Learning About Educational Psychology Help You Be a Better Teacher?

There's no question that knowledge of psychological concepts and their application to educational settings has the potential to help you be a better teacher. Whether that potential is ever fulfilled depends on how willing you are to maintain an open mind and a positive attitude. We say this because educational research is often described as being neither useful nor influential (Miller, Drill, & Behrstock, 2010). As you read through the next few paragraphs and the subsequent chapters, you'll see that criticisms like this are easily rebutted. We offer a three-pronged argument (teaching is a complex enterprise, research can inform teachers, and professional coursework contributes to competence) to explain how educational psychology can help you be a better teacher.

Teaching Is a Complex Enterprise

The first part of our argument is that teaching is not the simple, straightforward enterprise some people imagine it to be; in fact, it ranks in the top

David Young-Wolff/Photo Edit

The information in this book can help you be a better teacher for three reasons: Teaching is a complex activity that requires a broad knowledge base; many instructional practices are supported by research; and teachers who are knowledgeable about that research are better teachers.

quartile on complexity for all occupations (Rowan, 1994), and several analyses include teachers in the same occupational group as accountants, architects, computer programmers, counselors, engineers, and lawyers (Allegreto, Corcoran, & Mishel, 2004; U.S. Department of Labor, 2001). Marilyn Cochran-Smith, for many years the editor of the *Journal of Teacher Education*, has characterized teaching as "unforgivingly complex" (2003). There are several reasons why teaching is considered to be a complex activity. For one, teachers have daily responsibility for diverse populations of students with varied and sometimes contradictory needs. For another, teachers are constantly making decisions—before and after instruction as well as on the spot. If you are to be informed and effective, these decisions need to be based on a deep reservoir of knowledge and a wide range of skills. Here's a great observation on teaching that highlights its complexity: "Mathematicians need to understand a problem only for themselves; math teachers need both to know the math and to know how 30

Teaching is complex work because it requires a wide range of knowledge and skills.

different minds might understand (or misunderstand) it. Then they need to take each mind from not getting it to mastery. And they need to do this in 45 minutes or less" (Green, 2010).

Research Can Inform Teachers

The second part of our argument pertains to the potential usefulness of educational-psychology research. Contrary to the opinion noted above in the Miller et al. (2010) article, the research literature contains numerous studies that were conducted under realistic classroom conditions and offer useful ideas for improving instruction. There is consistent classroom-based support for the following instructional practices (Hattie, 2009; Marzano, Pickering, & Pollock, 2005; Simonsen, Fairbanks, Briesch, Myers, & Sugai, 2008; Walberg, 2006), all discussed in later chapters of this text:

1. Using more advanced students to tutor less advanced students.

2. Giving positive reinforcement to students whose performance meets or exceeds your objectives and giving corrective feedback to students whose performance falls short of your objectives.

3. Communicating to students what is expected of them and why.

4. Requiring students to respond to higher-order questions.

5. Providing students with cues about the nature of upcoming tasks by giving them introductory information and telling them what constitutes satisfactory performance.

6. Teaching students how to monitor and improve their own learning efforts and offering them structured opportunities to practice independent learning activities.

7. Knowing the misconceptions that students bring to the classroom that will likely interfere with their learning of a particular subject matter.

8. Creating learning situations in which students are expected to organize information in new ways and formulate problems for themselves.

9. Accepting responsibility for student outcomes rather than seeing students as solely responsible for what they learn and how they behave.

10. Showing students how to work in small, cooperative learning groups.

As much as we hope you will value the contribution that research can make to your effectiveness as a teacher, we also want you to be realistic about the nature of research and its use. You are probably familiar with the frustration many people experience when a new research finding, in medicine for example, contradicts an earlier finding. Indeed, you may have said out loud more than once, "Can't those scientists get it right once and for all?" As much as we would like the world to be simpler and more straightforward, most of the time it's not. Why not? Partly for reasons we have already mentioned. Classroom learning and teaching are complex processes that are influenced by many factors. And as we mention in a later section of this chapter, scientific research is limited in the number of factors it can investigate at one time. Consequently, the conclusions that are drawn about classroom learning and teaching are usually qualified and temporary.

This brief description of the nature of scientific research suggests that the insights you seek from research should be specific rather than general. So instead of asking, "Will my students benefit from approach A rather than approach B?" you need to ask, "For which students will this idea likely work best? Under what circumstances? With what kinds of tasks? And for what kinds of outcomes?" In other words, keep reminding yourself that nothing works for everybody in any and all circumstances. Notice also that we said research provides you with *insights* rather than *definitive answers*. Our choice of wording here is quite deliberate. Research in any field is a matter of adding to, taking away from, and revising an existing body of knowledge. For all practical purposes, we never get to the point where we say, "This is what we know and it will always be so." Instead, researchers say, "This is what we know for now." That's why we prefer that you treat research findings as providing you with insights or guidelines rather than hard and fast answers.

Coursework Contributes to Competence

The third part of our argument that educational psychology can help you be a better teacher concerns the courses you are currently taking, particularly this educational psychology course. Many researchers have asked, "How do the courses teachers take as students relate to how capable they perceive themselves to be as teachers?"

Surveys of beginning teachers (e.g., Brouwer & Korthagen, 2005; Maloch, Fine, & Flint, 2002/2003; National Comprehensive Center for Teacher Quality & Public Agenda, 2008a, 2008b; Ruhland & Bremer, 2002; Zientek, 2007) reveal a mixed picture. On the plus side, most beginning teachers reported that their training adequately prepared them to teach a specific subject, provide individualized instruction, manage the behavior of

Flash!Light/Stock Boston

The students of teachers who were trained in teacher education programs and certified by their states score higher on standardized achievement tests than do the students of noncertified teachers.

students in their classroom, and understand the impact of children's cognitive, social, and emotional development on learning (Maloch, Fine, & Flint, 2003/2003; National Comprehensive Center for Teacher Quality & Public Agenda, 2008a, 2008b; Zientek, 2007). On the minus side, beginning teachers felt that their teacher education programs did not do enough to prepare them to deal with children with special needs, children from ethnically and racially diverse backgrounds, assessment of learning, and interpretation of test results to students and parents (National Comprehensive Center for Teacher Quality & Public Agenda, 2008a, 2008b; Ruhland & Bremer, 2002; Zientek, 2007). This textbook will address all of these issues, including those about which teachers have reported discomfort. Our belief is that this course and this book will be one important means for helping you feel prepared to enter your first classroom.

Although it is reassuring to know that most beginning teachers have a generally favorable opinion of the quality of their preparation programs, researchers have also asked if the graduates of such programs provide high-quality instruction to their students. Two types of evidence shed some light on this issue.

> **Teachers who have had professional training are generally more effective.**

First, several studies (see, for example, American Educational Research Association, 2004; Berry, Hoke, & Hirsch, 2004; Darling-Hammond, Holtzman, Gatlin, & Heilig, 2005; Darling-Hammond & Youngs, 2002; Laczko-Kerr & Berliner, 2003; Wayne & Youngs, 2003; Wilson, Floden, & Ferrini-Mundy, 2002) found that the students of certified teachers scored higher on standardized achievement tests than did the students of teachers with nonstandard certification, even though teachers in the second group were judged to have had a good understanding of their subject matter. The value added by being trained in an accredited teacher education program and receiving standard certification is something called *pedagogical content knowledge*. It involves both knowing about and knowing how to use the contents of this book and those from other courses to present lessons in various subjects that are interesting, meaningful, and engaging. Research shows that the students of math teachers who were judged to have high levels of pedagogical content knowledge learned more than did students whose teachers lacked this characteristic but were considered nonetheless to be highly knowledgeable about mathematics (Baumert et al., 2010).

Second, the grades teachers earned in their teacher preparation program and their performance during student teaching were better predictors of how effective they were as teachers than were their scores on a standardized teacher certification test (D'Agostino & Powers, 2009).

But does it really matter in the long run if students who are exposed to high-quality teachers achieve higher grades and test scores? According to one study (Chetty et al., 2010), there is a payoff down the road. These researchers estimated that kindergarten students who were taught by above-average teachers (75th percentile and higher) earned $10,000 more in total lifetime earnings than did students taught by below-average teachers (25th percentile and lower). In Chapter 12, we'll explain what made these teachers above average.

The lesson to be learned from the research cited in this section should be obvious: Learn the material in this book until

© Olga Danylenko/Shutterstock Images

you know it like the back of your hand and you will have taken a major step to becoming a competent teacher! As we point out in Chapter 16, of all the variables that affect student achievement, the one that has the greatest impact is the teacher (Hattie, 2009).

LO3 The Nature and Values of Science

In an earlier section, we argued that teachers should use educational and psychological research to help them achieve their instructional goals. It's time to strengthen that argument by describing how common but nonscientific explanations of people's behavior lead to incorrect conclusions and poor decisions. Don't be surprised if you can remember times when you did what is described here. We'll follow that with a description of why scientific research is a superior approach.

Limitations of Nonscientific Observation

Making decisions on the basis of intuition, common knowledge, or informal observations of human behavior often leads to unsatisfactory outcomes. Suppose, for example, you have a foreign-language vocabulary assignment, a math assignment, and a reading assignment from your history book. You decide to work on all the assignments in one sitting. What could be more logical? you think. Focusing all your attention on each task until it's completed should produce a high level of learning. As a bonus, you'll be free for the next several days to do other things. But research suggests that a different approach will probably give you better results. Instead of working on one task until it's completed and then tackling the next one, you would be better off if you did less on each and spread the work over a few days. This is the phenomenon of massed versus distributed practice, which we discuss in Chapter 8.

The unfortunate consequences of nonscientific decision making can also be seen when educators decide to have a child repeat a grade for a second year because of poor achievement. This practice, which is commonly referred to as *grade retention*, has long been assumed to be an effective way of dealing with individual differences in learning rate, emotional development, and socialization skills. The percentage of students in grades K–12 in the United States who had ever been retained was 9.8% for 2007, with the highest rate

Grade retention policies are influenced by unsystematic observation.

(22.9%) occurring among students from low-income families (Planty et al., 2009). Retention is an expensive tactic: The average school spent $9,553 per retained student during the 2005–2006 school year (Planty et al., 2009). To some extent, retention rates are related to the growth of state learning standards and high-stakes testing programs (which we discuss in Chapter 15); school districts are often required to retain students whose test scores fall below a certain level.

The use of retention continues even though most research clearly shows that it has negative effects. Retained students are 40% to 50% more likely than nonretained students to drop out of school. And when you look at this practice from the other side of the coin—promoting low-achieving students who could just as easily have been retained—the results lead to the same conclusion. These students learn at least as much the following year, if not more, have a stronger self-concept, and are better adjusted emotionally than similar children who were retained (Duffrin, 2004a; Hong & Raudenbush, 2005; Jimerson, 2001; Jimerson, Anderson, & Whipple, 2002; Jimerson & Kaufman, 2003; Nagaoka & Roderick, 2004; Penfield, 2010; Ramirez & Carpenter, 2009).

So why does grade retention continue to be recommended by some parents, school boards, administrators, and teachers? Because the nonscientific reasons they invoke are intuitively appealing and have the ring of truth to them. One often-cited reason is that since practice makes perfect, students should do better with a second chance at a grade level. But this is a superficial analysis that ignores the role of many other variables, such as self-concept, motivation, and the social support of one's age-mates. Another nonscientific argument is generalizing from a single case or small number of cases. This takes the form of saying, "I remember when we retained Jimmy Smith and he turned out just fine." The problem with this argument is that it ignores all the factors that were specific to Jimmy's situation (Duffrin, 2004b; Graue & DiPerna, 2000; Owings & Kaplan, 2001; V. G. Thomas, 2000). As you can see, unsystematic observers are inclined to note only evidence that fits their expectations and ignore evidence that does not.

The reason retention does not work is simple: It does not address the causes of students' poor performance. These students typically begin school with more poorly developed academic skills, more serious health problems, and less stable home environments than their peers. In addition, retained students receive the same type of instruction and material the second time around. In short, retention is an attempt by policy makers, administrators, and some teachers to fit a short-term solution to a long-term problem. The best way to minimize, if not avoid, the use of retention is to provide developmentally, cognitively, and culturally appropriate forms of instruction (Darling-Hammond & Falk, 1997). The major goal of this text is to help you know how to provide such instruction as a teacher.

Because nonscientific thinking is often based on unexamined assumptions, we have included in this and subsequent chapters a feature called "Challenging Assumptions." In each instance we highlight a recommendation or practice that is based on one or more assumptions, offer a counterargument that challenges the assumption, and then invite you to respond. You may, of course, disagree with our position. That's fine, and we commend you for being an independent and critical thinker so long as your decision is based on credible evidence and logical thinking. The importance of this exercise is underscored by the finding that exemplary teacher education programs include specific strategies for helping students become aware of their assumptions about the nature of students and classroom learning (Darling-Hammond, 2006; Hattie, 2009).

Pause & Reflect *Imagine that you are a second-grade teacher. Your principal suggests that one of your students who performed poorly this year repeat second grade next year. Given what you know about the research on retention, how would you respond?*

Strengths of Scientific Observation

Now that we've described the major shortcomings of operating on the basis of common knowledge (or personal experience or intuition, if you prefer those terms), it's time to examine what makes a scientific approach to the study of behavior more useful. Most scientific studies have the following five characteristics, which we can designate with the labels *sampling*, *control*, *objectivity*, *publication*, and *replication*:

{ **Scientific characteristics: sampling, control, objectivity, publication, replication** }

1. Researchers study a representative sample of subjects so that individual idiosyncrasies are canceled out.

2. An effort is made to note all plausible hypotheses that can explain a given type of behavior, and each hypothesis is tested under controlled conditions. If all factors but one can be held constant in an experiment, the researcher may be able to trace the impact of a given condition by comparing the behaviors of those who have been exposed to it and those who have not.

3. Researchers make special efforts to be objective and guard against being misled by predetermined ideas, wishful thinking, or selected evidence. Observations are made in a carefully prescribed, systematic manner, which makes it possible for different observers to compare reactions.

4. Complete reports of experiments—including descriptions of subjects, methods, results, and conclusions—are published in professional journals.

5. Published findings let researchers learn what their colleagues have discovered, serve as a starting point for more ideas, and, most critically, let others replicate a study to see if they can obtain the same results. When several researchers working independently find pretty much the same thing, we can be more confident about saying that variables A, B, and C are related to each other and that A causes B.

LO4 Complicating Factors in the Study of Behavior and Thought Processes

We hope we've convinced you that using scientific tools to study what goes on in classrooms is far superior to relying on the unscientific methods mentioned before. Nevertheless, you should understand that scientific progress is, as we mentioned earlier, often slow and sometimes uncertain because classroom teaching and learning are incredibly complex processes. What follows is a brief description of several factors that sometimes frustrate both researchers and practitioners.

The Limited Focus of Research

Human behavior typically has many causes. A student may perform poorly on a history exam, for example, for one or more of the following reasons: poorly developed study skills, inattentiveness in class, low interest in the subject, a poorly written text, low motivation to achieve high grades, vaguely worded exam questions, and difficulty with a particular type of exam question (compare-and-contrast essays, for example).

> **Research focuses on a few aspects of a problem.**

To understand how these factors affect performance on school-related tasks, research psychologists study at most only a few of them at a time under conditions that may not be entirely realistic. Imagine that a researcher is interested in comparing lectures versus problem-solving exercises in terms of their effect on conceptual understanding. The researcher may recruit subjects who are equivalent in terms of social class, prior knowledge of the topic of the reading passage, and age; randomly assign them to either a teacher who mostly lectures or one who assigns problems to solve; and then examine each group's responses to several types of comprehension items. There's nothing inherently wrong with this approach; you just have to understand that the results relate most directly to the type of person who participated in the study and the circumstances under which the study was conducted. Change any of the variables and you might not get the same result. But by combining and interrelating separate studies that have looked at different aspects of the same problem, we can apply the findings to a wider range of people and circumstances.

The Complexity of Teaching and Learning

David Berliner (2002), a leading educational researcher, considers the scientific study of education to be "the hardest-to-do science of them all" for at least two reasons. First, it is difficult to implement research findings and programs uniformly because schools and classrooms differ from one another along such lines as characteristics of the students, quality and quantity of personnel, teaching methods, budget, leadership, and community support. Thus, a program or technique may work just as the research says it should in one district or teacher's class, but not in other classes or districts.

Second, the outcomes of schooling that teachers, students, and parents typically value are the result of complex interactions among numerous variables. Achievement may, for example, be the result of interactions among student characteristics (such as prior knowledge, interests, and socioeconomic levels),

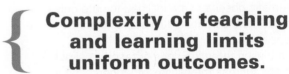

Complexity of teaching and learning limits uniform outcomes.

teacher characteristics (type of training, ideas about learning, interests, and values, for example), curriculum materials, socioeconomic status of the community, and peer influences. This complexity produces two outcomes that teachers find both frustrating and challenging: (1) Students exposed to the same materials and teaching methods are likely to vary in how much and what they learn (Daniel & Poole, 2009; Davis, 2007), and (2) a teacher's effectiveness is likely to vary from class to class and year to year (Kennedy, 2010).

The Selection and Interpretation of Data

Have you ever had an argument with a friend in which you supported your view with certain facts and figures, but your friend supported his or her position with a different set of facts and figures? Or perhaps both of you used the same set of facts but drew different conclusions from them. Well, researchers do exactly the same thing. Why? For the same reason you sometimes disagree with others. The amount of scientific information available on behavior and mental processes is so extensive that no individual could examine or interpret all of it. Accordingly, researchers learn to be highly selective in their reading. In addition, conclusions about the meaning of scientific results vary from one researcher to another. As you read this book, you will discover that there are differences of opinion among psychologists regarding certain aspects of development, motivation, and intelligence. Opposing views may be based on equally scientific evidence, but the way in which the evidence is selected and interpreted will vary. The fact that a topic is studied scientifically does not necessarily mean that opinions about interpretations of the data will be unanimous. Researchers, after all, are people too.

The Revision of Ideas Because of New Findings

Not only is there a mountain of scientific information that is subject to different interpretations, but it is also constantly being revised. A series of experiments may lead to the development of a new concept or pedagogical technique that is highly successful when it is first tried out. Subsequent studies, however, may reveal that the original research was incomplete, or repeated

Differences of opinion result from selection and interpretation of data.

Understanding and managing the teaching/learning process is a challenge for researchers and teachers because the process is affected by numerous variables that interact with one another.

© Suzie Fitzhugh

{ Accumulated knowledge leads researchers to revise original ideas. }

applications of a technique may show that it is less effective once the novelty has worn off. Frequent shifts of emphasis in education also reflect the basic nature of science. A quality of science that sets it apart from other intellectual endeavors is that the discoveries by one generation of scientists set the stage for more far-reaching discoveries by the next.

To repeat what we said earlier, as we learn more, it is inevitable that interpretations of how children learn and how we should teach will continue to change. We know more about development, learning, and teaching today than ever before, but because of the nature of some of the factors we have discussed and the complexity of human behavior, our answers are tentative and incomplete.

Take, for example, the case of neuroscience research. On the one hand, many educators (see, for example, E. P. Jensen, 2008) argue that enough is known about how the brain works under various circumstances to use those findings to create what are called brain-based approaches to education. On the other hand, critics (such as Sternberg, 2008; Varma, McCandless, & Schwartz, 2008; Willingham, 2008;

Challenging Assumptions

Show Me the Evidence!

When it comes to education, everybody has an opinion: Students should be spending more time on this subject or skill rather than that subject or skill; teachers should use this method and not that method; schools should make greater use of technology or lesser use of technology. Not that there's anything wrong with people expressing their views. Those who have a stake in our children's education should be willing to state what they see as public education's strengths and weaknesses and offer up potential solutions for those perceived weaknesses. But don't lose sight of the fact that some positions should be taken more seriously than others. So which ones deserve your attention and should be investigated further?

The answer to that question is easy if you've read and agreed with what we said earlier about the strengths and weaknesses of scientific versus nonscientific approaches to solving problems. Any suggestions for improving education should be based on the highest quality evidence rather than assumptions, untested theories, or an ideological point of view.

Here's a four-part test to apply to any claim or recommendation that's made: (1) Does the person making the claim provide one or more types of evidence? We've seen many suggestions that were based on little more than anecdotes or blind trust in a belief system. Look for various types of descriptive and/or experimental studies. (2) Does the evidence appear to be of high quality? Studies that have flawed designs and data analyses are of no value because they lead people down worthless paths. (3) Are the conclusions logically drawn from the data? Again, we've seen many studies that were fine up to this point, but then the authors made claims that were simply not supported by the data. (4) Are the suggestions for practice consistent with the conclusions? So the next time a friend or colleague at work says that educators should do so-and-so, say, "If you want to convince me, show me the evidence."

What Do You Think?

Some would argue that if educators always waited for conclusive evidence before deciding on a course of action, very little would change or be accomplished. If current practices are not producing desirable outcomes, then, so this argument goes, steps have to be taken on bases other than solid scientific evidence. Are you inclined to agree with this position? What unexamined assumptions, if any, is this argument based on?

Willis, 2008) argue that, while the results of neuroscience research are promising, those studies were not conducted under realistic classroom conditions and the results were not sufficiently consistent to serve as the basis for instructional tactics or programs. When and if a consensus develops among researchers that brain-based research has something of value to offer teachers (as happened with social cognitive theory, which we discuss at length in Chapter 9), future readers of this book will read about it here. One of our objectives in writing this text is to demonstrate the importance of basing your practices on principles that have solid research support.

Pause & Reflect *Think of a popular instructional practice. Would you classify it as a fad or as the outgrowth of scientific knowledge? Why? How can you tell the difference?*

LO5 Good Teaching Is Partly an Art and Partly a Science

Because teaching is a dynamic *decision-making process*, the science of psychology can provide you with a systematic, objective framework for making those decisions. But a scientific approach to teaching does have its limits. Complicating factors like the limited focus of research, the complexity of teaching and learning, and the need to revise old ideas in light of new findings mean that research cannot give you a prescription or a set of rules that specify how you should handle every situation. Often you will have to make on-the-spot, subjective decisions about how to present a lesson, explain a concept, handle mass boredom, or reprimand a student. Because teachers are often required to improvise (if they want to be effective), they are sometimes compared to stage actors. This contrast between an objective, systematic approach to planning instruction and the need to make immediate (yet appropriate) applications and modifications of those plans calls attention to a question that has been debated for years: Is teaching primarily an art or a science—or a combination of both?

The Argument for Teaching as an Art

Some educators have argued that teaching is an art that cannot be practiced or even studied entirely in an objective or scientific manner because of its inherent unpredictability (Eisner, 2002; Flinders, 1989; Hansgen, 1991;

Rubin, 1985; Wasserman, 1999). A good teacher draws as much from his or her motives, beliefs, values, and emotions as from a formal knowledge base.

So when we say that a good teacher knows when and how to improvise, we're talking about a teacher's ability and willingness to be flexible. Flexibility, which can be thought of as a "feel" for doing the right thing at the right time, can take several forms. First, it means being able to choose from among all the techniques and information at your disposal to formulate effective lesson plans that take the diverse needs and interests of all your students into consideration. It means knowing, for example, when to present a formal lesson and when to let students discover things for themselves, when to be demanding and when to make few demands, when and to whom to give direct help, and when and to whom to give indirect help. Bill Smoot, in his book *Conversations with Great Teachers* (2010), hit on this point by noting that while teaching is often done in groups, the teacher has to have the flexibility to understand that students are individuals who cannot all be approached in the same way.

Flexibility also means communicating emotions and interest in a variety of ways. There are times when eye contact and a facial expression are all that's needed to tell a student that you are pleased or displeased with what he or she is doing. At other times, you may feel it necessary to address a student's behavior in a stern, businesslike fashion or to say how pleased you are with a student's performance. In their book *Acting Lessons for Teachers: Using Performance Skills in the Classroom* (2006), Robert Tauber and Cathy Sargent Mester described the importance for successful teaching of such acting skills as voice animation (variations in pitch, volume, voice quality, and rate), body animation (facial expressions, gestures), and use of classroom space.

Pause&Reflect *The effective teacher-as-artist communicates enthusiasm. At some point, however, you may be asked to teach a grade level or subject for which you have little enthusiasm, or you may grow bored teaching the same grade level or subject year after year. How will you fulfill the role of teacher-artist in these situations?*

A third way in which teachers demonstrate flexibility is by their willingness and resourcefulness in working around impediments. Teaching does not always occur under ideal circumstances, and teachers must sometimes cope with inadequate facilities, insufficient materials, interruptions, and other difficulties.

Teacher educator Sharon Feiman-Nemser (2003) underscored the importance of flexibility to the art of teaching by noting what experienced educators said when asked what beginning teachers most needed to learn. One recommended that new teachers focus on helping students understand the essence of each lesson, even if that means going beyond or ignoring guidelines in a teacher's manual. Another noted that because teachers are essentially on stage, they need to develop a performing self that they are comfortable with. A third observation was that new teachers have to learn how to size up situations and think on their feet.

In sum, **teaching as an art** involves beliefs, emotions, values, and flexibility. Because these characteristics are intangible, they can be very difficult, if not impossible, to teach. Teachers must find these qualities within themselves. This chapter's Case in Print describes the intrinsic rewards that come from teaching in an environment that fosters the teacher-as-artist role.

The Argument for Teaching as a Science

The argument for **teaching as a science** is equally persuasive. Although many educational psychologists agree that the science of teaching, as such, does not exist, they contend that it is possible and desirable to have a scientific basis for the art of teaching (e.g., Hiebert, Gallimore, & Stigler, 2002; Kosunen & Mikkola, 2002;

teaching as an art A way of teaching that involves intangibles such as emotions, values, and flexibility.

teaching as a science A way of teaching based on applications of scientific research.

Part of the art of teaching is knowing when to introduce an unusual assignment or activity that captures students' interest.

Case in Print

The Joy of Being a Teacher-Artist: One Teacher's Tale

Some educators have argued that teaching is an art that cannot be practiced or even studied entirely in an objective or scientific manner because of its inherent unpredictability. . . . A good teacher draws as much from his or her motives, beliefs, values, and emotions as from a formal knowledge base. (p. 10–11)

Teaching Without a Script

MATTHEW KAY

The New York Times, 9/14/08

Three weeks ago, when my school asked 20 upperclassmen to help with a summer institute for freshmen, 80 showed up. At the end of August, our technology coordinator asked students to help her configure our laptops. Many kids spent the last free Saturday of summer vacation dragging icons across a screen. The school year at Science Leadership Academy here in Philadelphia has now begun, and our freshmen are noticing that the end of our school day stretches much longer than the end of the teachers' paid instructional time.

They are asking the same question that regularly stirs up our visitors. "Why do they stay?" Even as I write this, student laughter is floating up from our café—late on a Friday afternoon. Some have stepped out to get Chinese, and now they are back—to hang out with teachers in the principal's office. Given every opportunity to leave, both our educators and students regularly decide to stay.

All sides of every education debate agree that quality learning happens when knowledgeable, caring teachers use sound pedagogy. While theorists and politicians quibble over the definitions within this definition, most know that once a quality teacher is in an urban classroom, the biggest challenge is keeping them there. What keeps a dynamic, intelligent, young teacher in an urban classroom after they've built up enough experience to skip off to higher paying suburban pastures? How do you encourage them to build 30-year careers where many natives measure success by the ability to escape?

Many say the answer is money. And every election season candidates promise more of it. Whether they want to give it unilaterally, or only to teachers who somehow "merit" it, the theory is that you make the best stay by paying them more. (I treat this debate like so many barber shop disputes over slavery reparations. I don't expect a dime, but should the checks come, I'll be first in line.)

I am a good case study for this issue. I'm one of those young, dynamic teachers, and I want nothing more than to stay in Philadelphia's public schools for the rest of my career. And as my third teaching year begins, I'm wondering what this little downtown academy with big ideas has done to squelch my innate desire to move on. And I wonder why young teachers from all over the country are treating this Philly school like the Mecca of their craft. Why did they come, and why do they seem, like me, to want to stay around for a bit?

It's not money. Great teachers are deft managers, thirsty scholars, and empathetic people—and we would excel in careers that pay a whole lot more if cash was our driving ambition. The reason that the young teachers at S.L.A. are so excited to be here most likely mirrors my own—we are all treated like artists.

I've been a performance poet for the past three years, and though I enjoy the rush and buzz of a packed show, my favorite moments are the dark ones. The times that I spend in "the lab," reading, journaling, and spitting random punch lines to my reflection in the mirror. I give voice to real characters that I have recently been exposed to: an ill, pregnant woman, a Holocaust survivor, a drug runner from our local badlands. These people's scattered experiences are filtered through my brain and turned into something coherent, catchy, and meaningful to a larger audience.

So it is with the inquiry-based learning that we model for the other schools in Philadelphia. Our ninth graders come to us shy about asking questions that are often

Slavin, 2002, 2008). By drawing on established research findings, both prospective and practicing teachers can learn many of the prerequisites that make artistic teaching possible. Also, as Robert Slavin (2008) persuasively argues, working from a scientific basis helps teachers avoid the pitfall of subscribing to the latest fad.

The case for teaching as a science rests on the existence of a usable body of research findings. Fortunately, there is much here to work with. Research has identified dozens of instructional practices that improve student achievement. For example, at least 24 separate studies have found that giving teachers more instructional time—that is, giving students more time to learn—leads to higher achievement (Walberg, 2006; M. C. Wang, Haertel, & Walberg, 1993). This finding is

often used to support proposals for a longer school year. Other studies have demonstrated the benefits of alerting students to important material through the use of objectives and pretests, engaging students in a task through the use of questions and homework, and providing corrective feedback and reinforcement with written comments, verbal explanations, and praise.

The Teacher as Artistic Scholar: Combining the Art and Science of Teaching

To repeat a point we made earlier, teachers need to treat research findings not as absolute truths that will never change and that can be applied to all students at all times,

Chapter 1: Applying Psychology to Teaching

scattered and incoherent. When encouraged, they open up, and then incessantly offer their ideas. (I illustrate this for all classes on the first full day of every year, when I put a big rubber ball under my shirt and pretend to give laborious birth to it. We name this child "my idea." I pass it around nervously, and when someone drops it, I snatch it up and curl into the fetal position. They laugh. I eventually get over my shock and learn to trust again, slowly passing it, then throwing it around the room for everyone to touch. There are two morals: first, you can't protect your idea forever, and second, our ideas grow when, by dialogue and debate, others are allowed to get their fingerprints on them.)

This is when the S.L.A. teacher-artists go into the "lab." We show 32 young urban voices how to ask probing questions about a text, a formula, or a problem in their communities. We use those questions to flavor each unit plan that we prepare. The end product works much like that call-and-response piece that shouts "Listen!" and quiets all sidebar conversation. The audience owns the words too. The kids are more inspired to pay attention. The artist is more inspired to bring the noise.

I end each year with a speech unit. The kids dream up an injustice, question why it exists, and then seek to change some minds. They read powerful, controversial examples of oratory spanning from Frederick Douglass to Hitler to J.F.K. The idea for it came when, during a "To Kill a Mockingbird" unit two

years ago, students got a little excited during a mock jury deliberation. They did such a good job playing the relentlessly racist townspeople of Maycomb that I wondered aloud how such ignorance could be reasoned with. I challenged them to do so. With each child's fingerprint, the idea grew.

Last year, one of my students began her piece with, "I want an Iranian for president. I want a gay person for president. I want a person who has been stopped by the cops so many times because of the color of their skin that it's become a routine." A shyer kid spoke about gun violence. After listing many incidents that had been labeled "wake up calls," she shouted that, "the alarms have been relentless, but our response, again and again, has been to hit the snooze button. But there is no more need for a wake-up call. The need now is for action!" There was no fear.

If I hadn't been allowed to be an artist in the classroom, if my curriculum had been some stranger's standardized script, these girls may not have found their voices. To educate like this, a teacher shouldn't have to break the rules. Experiences like this should be the rule of any curriculum meant to engage this generation. If we want to convince dynamic, young educators to choose the inner city as the place to master their craft—we've got to remember that the best are artists. They like to create. And if they aren't allowed to do so, they will rebel—or they will leave. The chance to be an artist

has convinced me to stay—"merit pay" not withstanding.

Source: Matthew Kay, "Teaching without a script," from *The New York Times*, September 14, 2008. Copyright © 2008 The New York Times Co. Reprinted by permission.

Questions and Activities

1. The teacher who wrote this article is, by any measure, internally motivated, creative, and hardworking. Do you think these are characteristics that artistic teachers are born with or that they develop with experience? If you think such characteristics are at least partly learnable and if you think you might be lacking in one or more of these areas, what can you do to become an effective teacher-artist?

2. Regardless of whether you think the characteristics of a teacher-artist are innate or learned, what role does a school's environment play in facilitating this role? Do you believe this teacher would have been as creative and effective in any school?

3. This teacher claims that teachers from all over the country vie for teaching positions at the Science Leadership Academy for reasons other than money. What might those reasons be? Would you take a pay cut to teach at such a school? Why?

---

but as possibilities that they need to validate for a particular group of students at a particular point in time. That is why we chose to title this section "Good Teaching Is Partly an Art and Partly a Science." Our choice of wording indicates our belief that good teaching is a skillful blend of artistic and scientific elements. The teacher who attempts to base every action on scientific evidence is likely to come across as rigid and mechanical—perhaps even indecisive (when the scientific evidence is lacking or unclear). The teacher who ignores scientific knowledge about teaching and learning and makes arbitrary decisions runs the risk of using methods that are ineffective.

 Research provides a scientific basis for "artistic" teaching.

Pause & Reflect *How do good teachers strike a balance between the art and the science of teaching? Are they born with the right personality? Are they the products of good teacher education programs? If both factors play a role, which is more important?*

This analysis of teaching as a science and an art leads us to the conclusion that teachers need to learn how to play the role of artistic scholar in their own classrooms. That is, they need to figure out how to use research findings as ideas and guidelines to design potentially effective classroom practices. While playing this type of role is challenging, you will find yourself becoming better at it by using a valuable source of knowledge available to every teacher: your own classroom experiences. Although the knowledge that teachers gain from teaching actual lessons often lacks

reflective teaching A way of teaching that blends artistic and scientific elements through thoughtful analysis of classroom activity.

formative assessment A type of assessment that monitors a student's progress in order to facilitate learning rather than to assign a grade.

the broad generalizability that is characteristic of scientific knowledge, experience-based knowledge does have the following advantages (Hiebert, Gallimore, & Stigler, 2002):

- It is linked to a particular task and goal (such as teaching students how to discover the various themes embedded in a reading passage).

- It is sufficiently detailed, concrete, and specific that other teachers can use the same techniques with the same or highly similar material.

- It typically combines knowledge of the task, knowledge of teaching methods, and knowledge of students' characteristics.

LO6 Reflective Teaching: A Process to Help You Grow From Novice to Expert

The blending of artistic and scientific elements can be seen in discussions of what is called **reflective teaching** (see, for example, Eby, Herrell, & Jordan, 2006; Ellis, 2001; Henderson, 2001; McEntee et al., 2003). Reflective teachers are constantly engaged in thoughtful observation and analysis of their actions in the classroom before, during, and after interactions with their students.

Prior to instruction, reflective teachers may think about such things as the types of knowledge and skills that students in a democratic society need to learn, the kind of classroom atmosphere and teaching techniques that are most likely to produce this learning, and the kinds of assessments that will provide clear evidence that these goals are being accomplished. If, for example, you wanted students to sharpen their inquiry, reasoning, and decision-making skills, you might decide, after some reflection, to use debates, simulations, and laboratory experiments. If, on the other hand, you wanted students to memorize facts and information, you might decide to use worksheets and drill-and-practice exercises.

As they interact with students, reflective teachers are highly aware of how students are responding to what they are doing and are prepared to make minor but significant changes to keep a lesson moving

{ **Reflective teachers have particular attitudes and abilities.** }

toward its predetermined goal. Consider an elementary school classroom in which some students are having difficulty understanding the relationship between the orbits of the planets around the sun and their position in the night sky. The teacher knows there is a problem: Some students have puzzled expressions on their faces, and others cannot describe this phenomenon in their own words. Realizing that some students think in more concrete terms than others, the teacher decides to push the desks to the sides of the room and have the students simulate the planets by walking through their orbits. All in the moment, this teacher engages in thoughtful observation, spontaneous analysis, and flexible, resourceful problem solving.

To become a reflective teacher, you will need useful information about how well your students are responding to your lessons as well as several critical attitudes and abilities. Gaining insight into the effectiveness of your teaching is best accomplished by constantly monitoring your students' progress through a process known as **formative assessment**. As we discuss in Chapter 14, formative assessment involves a variety of informal and formal assessment techniques. Perhaps the simplest informal technique is observing how students respond during lessons. Other formative assessments include asking questions during lessons, having students read orally, assigning in-class worksheets and homework, and giving periodic quizzes. The important point to keep in mind is that formative assessment is not done for the purpose of giving students grades. Rather, it is done to provide you with the information you need to reflect on what you are doing and whether any changes need to be made. As for attitudes, three of the most important are an introspective orientation, an open-minded but questioning attitude about educational theories and practices, and the willingness to take responsibility for your decisions and actions. These attitudes need to be combined with the ability to view situations from the perspectives of others (students, parents, principal, other teachers), the ability to find information that allows an alternative explanation of classroom events and produces more effective instructional methods, and the ability to use compelling evidence in support of a decision (Eby, Herrell, & Hicks, 2002; D. D. Ross, Bondy, & Kyle, 1993).

Pause & Reflect *The reflective teacher sets aside regular blocks of time to think about teaching activities and make new plans. Most teachers complain about having insufficient time to reflect and plan. What would you do to make more time available?*

How Will This Book Help Prepare You to Meet Instructional Standards?

We live in an age of standards and accountability, particularly in education. Just as students, teachers, and administrators are held accountable for students' meeting various learning standards, prospective and beginning teachers are increasingly expected to demonstrate that they have met a set of knowledge standards that are believed to be the foundation of high-quality instruction. Among the standards that govern the preparation and licensing of teachers, two that are particularly prominent are a standardized test called the Praxis II and a set of 10 instructional principles and related standards called the InTASC (Interstate New Teacher Assessment and Support Consortium) standards. In this section, we briefly discuss the content of the Praxis II and the InTASC standards and show you how this text will help prepare you to meet the standards.

Praxis II and This Book

As part of recent educational reform efforts, many state boards of education and teacher education programs require that as a condition for licensure, beginning teachers demonstrate that they are knowledgeable about the psychological and educational factors that are likely to affect how well their students will perform in the classroom. A popular instrument used for this purpose is the Praxis II, published by the Educational Testing Service. The Principles of Learning and Teaching section of the Praxis II assesses a beginning teacher's knowledge of topics that are typically covered in an educational psychology course.

Because this textbook is closely aligned with the Principles of Learning and Teaching section of the Praxis II and emphasizes classroom applications, we believe it will help prepare you to do well on this important assessment. Although the Educational Testing Service offers separate sets of principles for grades K–6 and 7–12 (at

Ken Whitmore/Stone/Getty Images

Reflective teachers collect information about student performance and then use this information to think about what they do in class, why they do it, and how their methods affect student performance.

www.ets.org/Media/Tests/PRAXIS/taag/0522/topics_2 .htm and www.ets.org/Media/Tests/PRAXIS/taag/0524/ topics_1.htm, respectively), they are largely identical.

InTASC and This Book

In the early 1990s, the Interstate New Teacher Assessment and Support Consortium published a set of 10 instructional principles and related standards to guide the preparation of beginning teachers. These principles and standards represent the core knowledge, dispositions, and skills that InTASC believes are essential for all beginning teachers, regardless of their specialty or grade level. The InTASC standards are also designed to be compatible with the certification program for highly skilled veteran teachers developed by the National Board for Professional Teaching Standards.

An important part of the philosophy behind the InTASC standards is the belief that well-trained teachers have the knowledge, dispositions, and skills to help all students achieve at acceptable levels. That notion has also been a major part of the philosophy of this textbook.

WHAT ELSE? *RIP & REVIEW* **CARDS IN THE BACK**

2

THEORIES OF PSYCHOSOCIAL AND COGNITIVE DEVELOPMENT

LEARNING OBJECTIVES

After studying this chapter, you will be able to . . .

LO1 Explain how social interactions influence the development of one's personality, especially with regard to one's personal sense of industry and identity.

LO2 Provide examples of how Jean Piaget's stage theory of cognitive development can be used to guide learning experiences in and out of the classroom.

LO3 Explain how Lev Vygotsky's sociocultural theory of cognitive development connects social interaction in classrooms to the cognitive capacities of learners.

LO4 Provide examples of how technology can encourage cognitive development by challenging current conceptions and encouraging collaborative interactions.

LO5 Explain how cognitive development influences moral thinking and moral behavior.

In the opening chapter, we pointed out that individuals vary in how they perceive and think about the world around them. This commonplace observation implies that you need to be aware of the major ways in which students differ from one another in order to design potentially effective lessons. What may work well for one part of your class may not work quite so well for another part. The lesson that was a huge success with last year's class may be a disaster with this year's group if you fail to take into account critical differences between the two classes. The next five chapters of this book introduce you to how students may differ from one another in psychosocial development, cognitive development, age, mental ability, thinking style, achievement, ethnic background, and social class. You will also discover how those differences affect classroom learning.

This chapter focuses on Erik Erikson's psychosocial stages, Jean Piaget's cognitive stages, and Lev Vygotsky's views on the role of social interaction. It also describes Piaget's ideas about moral development, Lawrence Kohlberg's extension of Piaget's work, and Carol Gilligan's criticism and modification of Kohlberg's theory. The next chapter describes age-level characteristics of students at five levels: preschool, primary school, elementary school, middle school, and high school. Discussion at each age level focuses on four types of behavior: physical, social, emotional, and cognitive. The information in these chapters will help you adapt teaching techniques to the students who are in the age range that you expect to teach, as well as develop expectations of student behavior across age ranges. The patterns of behavior described in these chapters are ones that typical children and adolescents exhibit.

LO1 Erikson: Psychosocial Development

Of all the developmental theories that we could have chosen to discuss, why did we decide to open this chapter with Erik Erikson's theory of psychosocial development? There are several reasons for this choice:

© Jan Will/iStockphoto

© Superstock

- Erikson described psychological growth from infancy through old age. Thus, one can draw out instructional implications for every level of education from preschool through adult education.

- Erikson's theory portrays people as playing an active role in their own psychological development through their attempts to understand, organize, and integrate their everyday experiences.

- This theory highlights the important role that cultural goals, aspirations, expectations, requirements, and opportunities play in personal growth, a theme discussed in Chapter 5 (B. M. Newman & Newman, 2009).

epigenetic principle The notion that a child's personality develops through a series of genetically predetermined stages that interact with social interactions in the child's environment.

> { Erikson's theory encompasses the life span and highlights the role of the person and culture in development. }

Basic Principles of Erikson's Theory

Epigenetic Principle Erikson's theory of personality development is based on the **epigenetic principle.** According to the epigenetic principle, biological organisms develop sequentially, with various parts of the organism developing before others. An apple tree, for example, does not spring from the ground as a miniature version of a fully formed tree covered with fruit. Its various parts develop in a genetically predetermined sequence as it grows from a seed to a seedling to a sapling and eventually to a mature tree. But this genetic sequence interacts with the environment in which the organism grows. If a storm were to damage the seedling, for example, the tree's growth may be stunted, its trunk and branches may be misshaped, or it may even be destroyed. For the apple tree to grow into productive maturity, the environment must support rather than interfere with its sequentially determined

Personality grows out of successful resolution of psychosocial crises.

development. The interaction between sequentially determined development and the environment in which the genetic sequence emerges underlies Erikson's view of how the parts of child's personality develop as she or he grows.

Psychosocial Crisis In Erikson's view, personality development occurs as one successfully resolves a series of turning points, or psychosocial crises. Although the word *crisis* typically refers to an extraordinary event that threatens well-being, Erikson had a more benign meaning in mind. Crises occur when people feel compelled to adjust to the normal guidelines and expectations that society has for them but are not altogether certain that they are prepared to carry out these demands fully. For example, Western societies expect children of elementary and middle school age to develop a basic sense of industry, mostly through success in school. Adolescents are expected to come to terms with such questions as "Who am I?" and "Where am I going?" (B. M. Newman & Newman, 2009).

As you will see in the next section, Erikson described these crises in terms of opposing qualities that individuals typically develop. For each crisis, there is a desirable quality that can emerge and a corresponding undesirable characteristic. Erikson did not mean to imply that a healthy individual develops only positive qualities. He emphasized that people are best able to adapt to their world when they possess both the positive and negative qualities of a particular stage, provided the positive quality is significantly stronger than the negative quality. In the first stage, for example, it is important that the child learn trust, but a person who never experienced a bit of mistrust would struggle to understand the world. In Erikson's view, difficulties in development and adjustment arise when the negative quality outweighs the positive for any given stage or when the outcome for most stages is negative (B. M. Newman & Newman, 2009).

As you read through the following brief descriptions of the stages of psychosocial development, keep in mind that a positive resolution of the issue for each stage depends on how

well the issue of the previous stage was resolved. An adolescent who strongly doubts her own capabilities, for example, may have trouble making the commitments required for identity development in adulthood (Fadjukoff, Pulkkinen, & Kokko, 2005; Marcia, 2002, 2007). Lastly, Erikson's theory has eight stages that range from birth to old age. But because this book is written principally for those who will teach at the pre-K–12 levels, we will restrict our discussion to the first five stages.

Stages of Psychosocial Development

The following designations, age ranges, and essential characteristics of the stages of personality development were proposed by Erikson in *Childhood and Society* (1963).

Trust Versus Mistrust (Birth to 1 Year) Because infants are totally dependent on adults for their well-being, the first psychosocial crisis to be resolved concerns trust. Infants who consistently receive positive care will think of their world as safe and dependable. Conversely, children whose care is inadequate, inconsistent, or negative will approach the world with fear and suspicion.

Autonomy Versus Shame and Doubt (2 to 3 Years; Preschool) The main task for toddlers is to establish the beginnings of their independence. If they are permitted and encouraged to do what they are capable of doing at their own pace and in their own way—explore their environment, play with toys, and make progress with toilet training, for example—they will develop a sense of autonomy (willingness and ability to direct their own behavior). But if the adults around them are impatient and do too many things for young children or shame them for unacceptable behavior, feelings of self-doubt may occur.

Initiative Versus Guilt (4 to 5 Years; Preschool to Kindergarten) The ability to participate in many physical activities and to use language sets the stage for initiative, which "adds to autonomy the quality of undertaking, planning, and 'attacking' a task for the sake of being active and on the move" (Erikson, 1963). If 4- and 5-year olds are given freedom to decide what they will do, when they will do it, and how they will do it, and if parents and teachers take time to answer questions, tendencies toward initiative will be encouraged. Conversely, if children of this age are always told what to do and made to feel that their activities and questions have no point or are a nuisance to adults and older siblings, they will feel guilty about acting on their own.

Industry Versus Inferiority (6 to 11 Years; Elementary to Middle School) School is where children learn how to be productive with tasks that require mental effort over extended periods of time. If children at this stage are encouraged to make and do things well, helped to persevere, allowed to finish tasks, and praised for trying, industry results. If the children's efforts are unsuccessful or if children are criticized too often and too harshly, feelings of inferiority result. Children who feel inferior may never learn to enjoy intellectual work and take pride in doing at least one kind of thing really well. At worst, they may believe they will never excel at anything.

Identity Versus Role Confusion (12 to 18 Years; Middle Through High School) The goal at this stage is development of the roles and skills that will prepare adolescents to take a meaningful place in adult society. The danger at this stage is **role confusion**: having no clear conception of appropriate types of behavior that others will react to favorably. If adolescents succeed (as reflected by the reactions of others) in integrating roles in different situations to the point of experiencing continuity in their perception of self, identity develops. In common terms, they know who they are. If they are unable to establish a sense of stability in various aspects of their lives, role confusion results.

Of Erikson's eight stages, the two that we have chosen to highlight are industry versus inferiority and identity versus role confusion, because they are the primary psychosocial issues that students must resolve during their elementary, middle school, and high school years. The next two sections briefly describe the major factors that contribute to students' sense of industry and their grasp of who they are and what they might become.

Helping Students Develop a Sense of Industry

Between kindergarten and sixth grade, most children are eager to demonstrate that they can learn new skills and successfully accomplish assigned tasks. One factor that has long been known to have a detrimental effect on one's sense of industry is competition for a limited number of rewards. If you have ever taken a class where the teacher graded exams or projects "on a curve," you are familiar with the most common form that such competition takes in schools. What the teacher does is compare each student's score with the score of every other student in that class. The few students who achieve the highest scores receive the top

grade, regardless of the actual level of their scores. Then a predetermined number of Bs, Cs, Ds, and Fs are awarded. Because the resulting distribution of grades looks something like the outline of a bell, it is often referred to as a "bell-shaped curve" (which explains the origin of the term "grading on the curve").

There are at least two reasons that this practice may damage a student's sense of industry:

1. Grading on the curve limits the top rewards to a relatively small number of students, regardless of each student's actual level of performance. If the quality of instruction is good and students learn most of what has been assigned, the range of scores will be relatively small. Consider the impact to your sense of industry if you respond correctly to 85% of the questions on an exam but earn only a grade of C. The same problem exists when, for whatever reasons, all students perform poorly. How much pride can you have in a grade of A or B when you know it is based on a low success rate? The senior author of this book endured a college chemistry class in which the top grade on an exam went to a student who answered only 48% of the questions correctly.

2. Curve grading also guarantees that some students have to receive failing grades, regardless of their actual level of performance. Students who are forced into this unhealthy type of competition (there are acceptable forms of competition, which we describe in Chapter 13) may develop a sense of inadequacy and inferiority that will hamper them for the rest of their school career.

role confusion Uncertainty as to what behaviors will elicit a favorable reaction from others.

Pause & Reflect *Suppose you were an elementary school teacher. What kinds of things would you do to help your students attain a sense of industry rather than inferiority? How would you help them feel more capable and productive? What would you avoid doing?*

The solution to this problem is to base grades on realistic and attainable standards that are worked out ahead of time and communicated to the students. In Chapter 14 we describe how to do this.

> **{ Students' sense of industry can be hampered by unhealthy competition for grades. }**

psychosocial moratorium A period of identity development marked by a delay of commitment, ideally a time of adventure and exploration having a positive, or at least neutral, impact on the individual and society.

identity statuses A style of approach that adolescents adopt to deal with such identity-related issues as career goal, gender-role orientation, and religious beliefs. James Marcia identified four identity statuses: identity diffusion, moratorium, foreclosure, and identity achievement.

Helping Students Formulate an Identity

Erikson believed that our sense of who we are is the result of three factors: being comfortable with our physical self, knowing what we want to do with our life, and knowing that whatever our choice, we will be encouraged and reinforced by those who play a significant role in our life. As you may know from your own experience or the experiences of others, the process of identity formation is not always smooth, and it does not always follow the same path. But by being aware of the problems and uncertainties that adolescents may experience as they try to develop a sense of who they are, you can help them positively resolve this major developmental task.

Pause & Reflect American high schools are often criticized for not helping adolescents resolve identity problems. Do you agree? Why? How could schools improve?

A psychosocial moratorium delays commitment.

Taking a Psychosocial Moratorium One aspect of identity formation that often causes difficulty for adolescents is defining the kind of work they want to do—in other words, choosing a career. For individuals who are unprepared to make a career choice, Erikson suggested the possibility of a **psychosocial moratorium**. This is a period marked by a delay of commitment. Such a postponement occurred in Erikson's own life: After leaving high school, he spent several years wandering around Europe without making any firm decision about the sort of job he would seek. Under ideal circumstances, a psychosocial moratorium should be a period of adventure and exploration, having a positive, or at least neutral, impact on the individual and society.

Adolescent Identity Statuses

Erikson's observations on identity formation have been usefully extended by James Marcia's notion of **identity statuses** (1966, 1980, 2002, 2007). Identity statuses, of which there are four, are styles or processes "for

Challenging Assumptions

Promote Industry; Stamp Out Inferiority

Some educators, parents, and education policy makers act as if the most important purpose of education is to sort children into categories. They act on the assumption that only a few can take advantage of and, therefore, should receive the best educational opportunities. To cite only one example, consider how educational resources are distributed across and within communities. Consider also how assuming that only a few students are capable of high achievement influences a teacher's expectations for all students and how those expectations influence interactions in the classroom. Who were the students in your classrooms who were not expected to do well? We urge you to examine your own assumptions about student capabilities. If you expect students to fail, your interactions with those students are likely to promote a sense of inferiority and interfere with the development of such important characteristics as self-efficacy, self-worth, self-regulated learning skills, and intrinsic motivation. The evidence challenging

the assumption that students should be sorted can be found in most of the subsequent chapters in this book. We urge you to emphasize to students and others that a more relevant and useful goal is to help all students develop the attitudes, values, and cognitive skills that lead to high levels of meaningful learning.

What Do You Think?

As we challenge assumptions in this feature throughout the book, keep in mind that assumptions can be found not only in the statements that people make, but—more importantly—in their behavior. Have you seen behavior that has the effect of sorting kids according to their perceived or expected capability? Do you agree with the stand we have taken here? Why or why not? Go to the textbook's Education CourseMate website and select the "Challenging Assumptions" section to find out more about this and other controversial issues.

Adolescents exhibit a particular process, called an identity status, for establishing an identity.

handling the psychosocial task of establishing a sense of identity" (Waterman & Archer, 1990, p. 35). Marcia (1980) developed this idea as a way to test scientifically the validity of Erikson's notions about identity.

Marcia proposed that attainment of a mature identity depends on two variables: crisis and commitment. "Crisis refers to times during adolescence when the individual seems to be actively involved in choosing among alternative occupations and beliefs. Commitment refers to the degree of personal investment the individual expresses in an occupation or belief" (1967, p. 119). Subsequent research has shown that exploring and making commitments to interpersonal relationships also contribute to identity formation (Allison & Schultz, 2001; Marcia, 2001, 2002).

After analyzing interview records with these two criteria in mind, Marcia established four identity statuses, described in Table 2.1, that vary in their degree of crisis and commitment:

- Identity diffusion.
- Foreclosure.
- Moratorium.
- Identity achievement.

The moratorium and identity achievement statuses are generally thought to be more developmentally mature than the foreclosure and identity diffusion statuses because individuals exhibiting moratorium and identity achievement either have evaluated alternatives and made a commitment or are actively involved in obtaining and evaluating information in preparation for a commitment (Marcia, 2001, 2007). Support for the hypothesized superiority of the identity achievement status was provided by Anne Wallace-Broscious, Felicisima Serafica, and Samuel Osipow (1994). They found that high school students who had attained the identity achievement status scored higher on measures of career planning and career certainty than did students in the moratorium or identity diffusion statuses.

© John Henley/CORBIS

Identity, as Erikson defined it, involves acceptance of one's body, knowledge of where one is going, and recognition from those who count. A high school graduate who is pleased with his or her appearance, has already decided on a college major, and is admired by parents, other relatives, and friends is likely to experience a sense of psychosocial well-being.

TABLE 2.1 James Marcia's Identity Statuses

Identity Status	Crisis	Commitment	Characteristics
Identity diffusion	Not yet experienced. Little serious thought given to occupation, gender roles, values.	Weak. Ideas about occupation, gender roles, values are easily changed as a result of positive and negative feedback.	Not self-directed; disorganized, impulsive, low self-esteem, alienated from parents; avoids getting involved in schoolwork and interpersonal relationships.
Foreclosure	Not experienced. May never suffer doubts about identity issues.	Strong. Has accepted and endorsed the values of his or her parents.	Close-minded, authoritarian, low in anxiety; has difficulty solving problems under stress; feels superior to peers; more dependent on parents and other authority figures for guidance and approval than in other statuses.
Moratorium	Partially experienced. Has given some thought to identity-related questions.	Weak. Has not achieved satisfactory answers.	Anxious, dissatisfied with school; changes major often, daydreams, engages in intense but short-lived relationships; may temporarily reject parental and societal values.
Identity achievement	Fully experienced. Has considered and explored alternative positions regarding occupation, gender roles, values.	Strong. Has made self-chosen commitments to at least some aspects of identity.	Introspective; more planful, rational, and logical in decision making than in other identity statuses; high self-esteem; works effectively under stress; likely to form close interpersonal relationships. Usually the last identity status to emerge.

SOURCES: Cramer (2001); Hoegh & Bourgeois (2002); Kroger (2004); MacKinnon & Marcia (2002); Marcia (1999, 2002, 2007).

As you read the brief descriptions of each identity type in Table 2.1, keep a few points in mind. First, the more mature identity statuses are slow to evolve and are found in a relatively small percentage of individuals. Among one sample of sixth, seventh, and eighth graders, 12% were in the moratorium status and 9% had reached the identity achievement status (Allison & Schultz, 2001). Among adults, only about 33% undergo the exploration and identity construction process that characterizes the identity achievement status (Marcia, 1999).

Second, an identity status is not a once-and-for-all accomplishment; identity can continue to undergo developmental change in adulthood (Fadjukoff, Pulkkinen, & Kokko, 2005). If an ego-shattering event (loss of a job, divorce) occurs later in life, individuals who have reached identity achievement, for example, may find themselves uncertain about old values and behavior patterns and once again in crisis. But for most individuals, a new view of themselves is eventually created. This cycling between certainty and doubt as to who one is and where one fits in society may well occur in each of the last three of Erikson's stages, and is often referred to as a MAMA (moratorium–achievement–moratorium–achievement) cycle (Marcia, 1999, 2001, 2002).

Finally, after 40 years of research on identity, James Marcia (2007) reminded us that individuals are an amalgam of their experiences; thus, their identities reflect a mixture of identity statuses.

Cultural, Ethnic, and Gender Factors in Identity Status Although the foreclosure status is the historical norm for adolescents in Western societies, things can and do change. For example, individuals in moratorium were more numerous during the 1960s and 1970s than during the 1980s. This was a time of great social and cultural upheaval (opposition to the war in Vietnam, civil rights demonstrations, the women's movement), and many adolescents reacted to the uncertainty produced by these changes by not making a commitment to occupational, sexual, and political values (Scarr, Weinberg, & Levine, 1986; Waterman, 1988). Also, more recent evidence indicates that adolescents are now more likely to be in a moratorium status or an identity achievement status, or in transition between these two statuses,

than in the foreclosure status common to earlier generations (Branch & Boothe, 2002; Forbes & Ashton, 1998; M. F. Watson & Protinsky, 1991).

Gender differences in identity status are most apparent in the areas of political ideology, family and career priorities, and sexuality. With respect to political beliefs, males are more likely to exhibit a foreclosure process and females a diffusion process. With respect to family and career priorities and sexuality, males are likely to be foreclosed or diffuse, whereas females are likely to express an identity achievement or a moratorium status. These findings indicate that female adolescents are more likely than males to make developmentally advanced decisions in the areas of family and career roles and sexuality. A likely explanation has to do with how the female gender role has and has not changed over the past 20 years. Although most females now work outside the home, they are still expected to have primary responsibility for child rearing (Stier, Lewin-Epstein, & Braun, 2001).

A relevant question to ask about Marcia's identity statuses, particularly if you plan to teach in a foreign country or instruct students with different cultural backgrounds, is whether these identity statuses occur only in the United States. The answer appears to be no. Researchers in such diverse countries as Korea, India, Nigeria, Japan, Denmark, Netherlands, Colombia, and Haiti reported finding all four statuses, although the percentage of adolescents and young adults in each status did vary by culture (Portes, Dunham, & Del Castillo, 2000; Scarr, Weinberg, & Levine, 1986).

As you consider how diversity interacts with student identity, it is important not to confuse identity statuses with other aspects of identity. One example is ethnic identity. As the ethnic composition of the United States (where children of color will eventually outnumber white children) changes, more research is being done on the development of ethnic identity (e.g., French, Seidman, Allen, & Aber, 2006; Ghosh, Michelson, & Anyon, 2007). The work on identity status is one way to understand how identity can shift during the middle and high school years. In other chapters, we will discuss other aspects of background and environment that contribute to an important developmental outcome: one's sense of identity.

Criticisms of Erikson's theory: It is based largely on personal experience, not applicable to many cultures, and gender biased.

Chapter 2: Theories of Psychosocial and Cognitive Development

Criticisms of Erikson's Theory

Although Erikson's theory has in general been supported by research (Steinberg & Morris, 2001), several aspects have been criticized. For example, while Erikson occasionally carried out research investigations, most of his conclusions were based on personal and subjective interpretations that have been only partly substantiated by controlled investigations of the type that most psychologists value. Consequently, his theory is viewed by many as "a *descriptive* overview of social and emotional development that does not adequately *explain* how and why this development takes place" (Shaffer & Kipp, 2010, p. 46).

Other criticisms focus on Erikson's contention that one's identity is achieved by actively exploring alternatives regarding one's career, ideological beliefs, and interpersonal relationships, and then making choices. This is not, in all likelihood, a universal practice. In some societies and cultures, these decisions are for the most part made by adults and imposed on adolescents (Hoegh & Bourgeois, 2002; Marcia, 1999, 2001; Sorell & Montgomery, 2001). Recent work also suggests that one's sense of cultural identity is related to adaptive psychosocial functioning: what, in Erikson's theory, would be called positive resolution of the identity rather than role diffusion (Schwartz, Zamboanga, Weisskirch, & Wang, 2010).

Some critics, such as Carol Gilligan (1982, 1988), have argued that Erikson's stages reflect the personality development of males more accurately than that of females. We will encounter Gilligan's ideas later in this chapter.

If you keep these reservations in mind, you are likely to discover that Erikson's observations (as well as the identity statuses that Marcia described) clarify important aspects of development. The Suggestions for Teaching on the next page draw on Erikson's observations.

LO2 Piaget: Cognitive Development

Basic Principles of Piaget's Theory

Jean Piaget (1896–1980) earned his doctorate in biology in 1918 and began a program of research that has been called "the master plan" to address the question, "How does knowledge develop?" (L. Smith, 2002, p. 515). His theory of intellectual development, reflective of his basic interest in biology as well as knowledge, continues to spur research on the problem of how knowledge develops.

Piaget assumed that human beings are born with tendencies to organize and adapt. **Organization** is the human tendency to systematize, to pull together a variety of processes into an overall system. **Adaptation** is the human tendency to make adjustments to our environments. These tendencies—and the processes that operate when human beings engage them—are key to understanding Piaget's theory of cognitive development.

Organization *Organization* refers to the tendency of all individuals to systematize or combine processes into coherent (logically interrelated) systems. When we think of tulips and roses as subcategories of the more general category "flowers," instead of as two unrelated categories, we are using organization to aid our thinking process. This organizational capacity makes thinking processes efficient and powerful and allows a better fit, or adaptation, of the individual to the environment.

Schemes Children formulate organized patterns of behavior or thought, known as **schemes**, as they interact with their environment, parents, teachers, and age-mates. Schemes can be behavioral (throwing a ball) or cognitive (realizing that there are many different kinds of balls). Whenever a child encounters a new experience that does not easily fit into an existing scheme, adaptation is necessary.

Adaptation The process of creating a good fit or match between one's conception of reality (one's schemes) and the real-life experiences one encounters is called *adaptation*. According to Piaget, adaptation is accomplished by two subprocesses: **assimilation** and **accommodation**. A child may adapt by either interpreting an experience so that it fits an existing scheme (assimilation) or changing an existing scheme to incorporate the experience (accommodation).

Imagine a 6-year-old who goes to an aquarium for the first time and calls the goldfish "little fish" and the whales "big fish." In

"Little fish"

"Big fish"

> **organization** The tendency to systematize and combine processes into coherent general systems.

> **adaptation** The process, described by Piaget, of creating a good fit or match between one's conception of reality and one's real-life experiences.

> **scheme** An organized pattern of behavior or thought that children formulate as they interact with their environment, parents, teachers, and age-mates.

> **assimilation** The process of fitting new experience into an existing scheme.

> **accommodation** The process of creating or revising a scheme to fit a new experience.

Suggestions for Teaching

Applying Erikson's Theory of Psychosocial Development

1 **With younger preschool children, allow plenty of opportunities for free play and experimentation to encourage the development of autonomy, but provide guidance to reduce the possibility that children will experience doubt. Also avoid shaming children for unacceptable behavior.**

2 **With older preschool children, encourage activities that permit the use of initiative and provide a sense of accomplishment. Avoid making children feel guilty about well-motivated but inconvenient (to you) questions or actions.**

3 **During the elementary and middle school years, help children experience a sense of industry by presenting tasks that they can complete successfully.**
Arrange tasks so that students will know they have been successful. To limit feelings of inferiority, play down comparisons, and encourage cooperation and self-competition.

4 **At the secondary school level, keep in mind the significance of each student's search for a sense of identity.**
The American school system, particularly at the high school level, has been described as a place where individual differences are either ignored or discouraged and negative feedback greatly outweighs positive feedback (J. Johnson, Farkas, & Bers, 1997; Steinberg, 1996; Toch, 2003). Because you are important to your students, you can contribute to their sense of positive identity by recognizing them as individuals and praising them for their accomplishments. If you become aware that particular students lack recognition from peers because of abrasive qualities or ineptness, and if you have the time and opportunity, you might also attempt to encourage social skills.

Working with your school counselor, you may in some cases be able to help students make decisions about occupational choice by providing them with information (gleaned from classroom performance and standardized test results) about their intellectual capabilities, personality traits, interests, and values. Or you may be able to help students decide whether to apply for admission to college instead of entering the job market after high school graduation.

5 **Remain aware that adolescents may exhibit characteristics of different identity statuses.**
Some adolescents drift aimlessly; others may be distressed because they realize they lack goals and values. A few high school students may have arrived at self-chosen commitments; others may have accepted the goals and values of their parents.

If you become aware that certain students seem depressed or bothered because they are unable to develop a satisfactory set of personal values, consult your school psychologist or counselor. In addition, you might use the techniques just summarized to help these students experience at least a degree of identity achievement.

---

equilibration The tendency to organize schemes to allow better understanding of experiences.

both cases, the child is assimilating—attempting to fit a new experience into an existing scheme (in this case, the conception that all creatures that live in the water are fish). When her parents point out that even though whales live in the water, they are mammals, not fish, the 6-year-old begins to accommodate—to modify her existing scheme to fit the new experience she has encountered. Gradually (accommodations are made slowly, over repeated experiences), a new scheme forms that contains nonfish creatures that live in the water.

Relationships Among Organization, Schemes, and Adaptation To give you a basic understanding of Piaget's ideas, we have talked about them as distinct elements. But the concepts are all related. In their drive to be organized, individuals try to have a place for everything (accommodation) so they can put everything in its place (assimilation). The product of organization and adaptation is the creation of new schemes that allow individuals to organize at a higher level and adapt more effectively.

Equilibration, Disequilibrium, and Learning Piaget believed that people are driven to organize their schemes in order to achieve the best possible adaptation to their environment. He called this process **equilibration**, by which people achieve a kind of balance between how they experience the world and how they think about the world. But what motivates people to achieve this balance? It is a state of *disequilibrium*, or a perceived discrepancy between an existing scheme and something new. In other words, when people encounter something that is inconsistent with or contradicts what they already know or believe, this experience produces an imbalance, a disequilibrium that they are driven to eliminate (assuming they are sufficiently interested in the new experience to begin with).

A student may wonder why, for example, tomatoes and cucumbers are referred to as fruits in a science text, since she has always referred to them as vegetables and has distinguished fruits from vegetables

> **Experiencing a state of disequilibrium can be motivating.**

Activities that encourage children to create new ideas or schemes through experimentation, questioning, discussion, and discovery often produce constructive learning because of the inherent drive toward equilibration.

and discussing. This process of creating knowledge to solve a problem and eliminate a disequilibrium is referred to by Piagetian psychologists and educators as **constructing knowledge** (Brooks & Brooks, 2001; Elkind, 2005; Haney & McArthur, 2002; Yager, 2000). It is a powerful notion that has motivated a great deal of psychological research that can be applied to teaching and learning (S. P. Johnson, 2010). It will reappear in later chapters and in other forms. (The "Pause and Reflect" features in each chapter are intended to stimulate constructivist thinking.)

constructing knowledge The view that meaningful learning is the active creation of knowledge structures rather than a mere transferring of objective knowledge from one person to another.

Stages of Cognitive Development

Organization and adaptation are what Piaget called *invariant functions*. This means that these thought processes function the same way for infants, children, adolescents, and adults. Schemes, however, are not invariant; they undergo systematic change at particular points in time. As a result, there are real differences between the ways younger children and older children think and between the ways children and adults think. The schemes of infants and toddlers, for example, are sensory and motor in nature (and Piaget called the period of cognitive development for infants and toddlers the "sensorimotor stage"). They are often referred to as *habits* or *reflexes*. In early childhood, schemes gradually become more mental in nature; during this period, they are called *concepts* or *categories*. Finally, by late adolescence or early adulthood, schemes are complex and result in what we call *strategic* or *planful* behavior.

On the basis of his studies, Piaget concluded that schemes evolve through four stages. The *rate* at which a particular child proceeds through these stages varies, but Piaget believed that the *sequence* is the same in all children. To help you grasp the sequence of these stages, Table 2.2 briefly outlines the range of ages to which they generally apply and their distinguishing characteristics.

Although Piaget used this "stage" or stairstep metaphor to describe the pattern of cognitive development,

on the basis of sweetness. This discrepancy may cause the student to read the text carefully or ask the teacher for explanation. Gradually, the student reorganizes her thinking about the classification of fruits and vegetables in terms of edible plant roots, stems, leaves, and ovaries so that it is more consistent with the expert view. These processes are two sides of the learning coin: For equilibration to occur, disequilibrium must already have occurred. Disequilibrium can occur spontaneously within an individual through maturation and experience, or it can be introduced by someone else (such as a teacher).

Constructing Knowledge Meaningful learning, then, occurs when people *create* new ideas, or knowledge (rules and hypotheses that explain things), from existing information (for example, facts, concepts, and procedures). To solve a problem, we have to search our memory for information that can be used to fashion a solution. Using information can mean experimenting, questioning, reflecting, discovering, inventing,

TABLE 2.2 Piaget's Stages of Cognitive Development

Stage	Age Range	Characteristics
Sensorimotor	Birth to 2 years	Develops schemes primarily through sense and motor activities. Recognizes permanence of objects not seen.
Preoperational	2 to 7 years	Gradually acquires ability to conserve and decenter, but is not capable of operations or mentally reversing actions.
Concrete operational	7 to 11 years	Capable of operations but solves problems by generalizing from concrete experiences. Is not able to manipulate conditions mentally unless they have been experienced.
Formal operational	11 years and older	Able to deal with abstractions, form hypotheses, solve problems systematically, and engage in mental manipulations.

conservation The recognition that certain properties stay the same despite a change in appearance or positions.

perceptual centration The tendency to focus attention on only one characteristic of an object or aspect of a problem or event at a time.

decentration The ability to think of more than one quality of an object or problem at a time.

irreversibility The inability of a young child to mentally reverse physical or mental processes, such as pouring water from a tall, thin glass back into a short, squat one.

don't be misled into thinking that children jump from one stage to the next. In trying to understand certain concepts or solve certain problems, children may on some occasions use a more advanced kind of thinking but on other occasions revert to an earlier, less sophisticated form. Over time, the more advanced concepts and strategies supplant the less sophisticated ones. Because of this variability in how children think, some developmental psychologists (e.g., Siegler, 1996) prefer to use the metaphor of overlapping waves rather than stages to characterize the nature of cognitive development. But because Piaget spoke in terms of stages, we will as well. If you are interested in the cognitive development of infants and toddlers, you can consult any number of books and websites on the topic. We will focus of the stages that apply to learners from preschool through high school.

Preoperational Stage (Preschool and Primary Grades) When it comes to developing the capacity to think, mastering symbols and symbol systems (such as letters, words, and a language) is the key developmental task for students from preschool through the primary grades. Although the thinking at this stage is much more sophisticated than that of 1- and 2-year-olds, preschool children are limited in their ability to use their new symbol-oriented schemes. From an adult perspective, their thinking and behavior are illogical.

When Piaget used the term *operation*, he meant an action carried out through logical thinking. *Preoperational*, then, means prelogical. The main obstacles to logical thinking that preschoolers have to overcome are *perceptual centration*, *irreversibility*, and *egocentrism*. You

Preoperational stage: the child forms many new schemes but does not think logically

can see how these obstacles get in the way when children attempt to solve **conservation** problems—those that test their ability to recognize that certain properties stay the same despite a change in appearance or position.

One of the best-known conservation problems is conservation of continuous quantity. Imagine that you show a child two identical glasses of milk: same size, same shape, and same amount of milk in each glass. When you ask the child if there is the same amount of milk in each glass, she answers yes. Now imagine that you set a tall, thin glass cylinder next to the two identical glasses of milk (which are much shorter than the cylinder). You pour the milk from one of the short glasses into the tall cylinder and ask whether there is more milk in the glass or the cylinder. When Piaget did this sort of experiment, he found that children under 6 years of age usually said that there was more milk in the tall cylinder. When children around the age of 6 were asked, they were much more likely to say something like "They have the same amount."

One reason preoperational stage children have difficulty solving conservation problems (as well as other problems that require logical thinking) is **perceptual centration**: the strong tendency to focus attention on only one characteristic of an object or aspect of a problem or event at a time. The young child focuses only on the height of the milk in the two containers and ignores the differences in width and volume. Another way to put this is to say that the child has not yet mastered **decentration**—the ability to think of more than one quality at a time—and is therefore not inclined to contemplate alternatives.

The second obstacle to logical thinking is

Think of the stages of children's **cognitive development** as **overlapping waves**.

> ## Perceptual centration, irreversibility, and egocentrism are barriers to logical thought.

irreversibility. This means that young children cannot mentally pour the milk from the tall, thin cylinder back into the short, squat glass (thereby proving to themselves that the amount of milk is the same in two different containers). For the same reason, these youngsters do not understand the logic behind simple mathematical reversals (4 + 5 = 9; 9 – 5 = 4).

The third major impediment is **egocentrism**. When applied to preschool children, *egocentric* refers to how they understand and think about the world; it does not mean that they think of themselves as better than other people or that they don't care about others. It means that they have difficulty in seeing the world as other people see it. Egocentric thought means that preschool children are often incapable of thinking from the perspective of others (Piaget & Inhelder, 1956). It is as though they assume that others see things the same way they see them. As a result, attempts to explain the logic behind conservation are usually met with quizzical looks and the insistence (some would mistakenly call it stubbornness) that the tall, thin cylinder contains more milk.

Concrete Operational Stage (Elementary to Early Middle School) Through formal instruction, informal experiences, social contact, and maturation, children over the age of 7 gradually become less influenced by perceptual centration, irreversibility, and egocentrism (DeVries, 1997). Schemes develop that allow a greater understanding of such logic-based tasks as conservation (matter is neither created nor destroyed but simply changes shape, form, or position), class inclusion (the construction of hierarchical relationships among related classes of items), and seriation (the arrangement of items in a particular order).

But operational thinking is limited to objects that are actually present or that children have experienced

> ## Concrete operational stage: the child is capable of mentally reversing actions but generalizes only from concrete experiences

concretely and directly. For this reason, Piaget described the stage from approximately 7 to 11 years as that of *concrete operations*. The nature of the concrete operational stage can be illustrated by the child's mastery of different kinds of conservation.

Around the age of 7, as their schemes are evolving from preoperational thought to concrete operations, most children are capable of decentration and therefore can mentally conserve quantities even though those quantities may change shape and size. They can explain, for example, why the amount of milk in the short glass is equal to the amount of milk in the tall cylinder.

Even more, children in the concrete operational stage are often more capable of learning advanced concepts than most people realize. According to the National Research Council (2000), for example, the fundamental abilities that elementary students (K–4) are expected to acquire include asking questions about objects, conducting simple observations, using simple equipment (such as a magnifying glass) to gather data and extend the senses, and constructing and communicating explanations.

egocentrism
Difficulty in taking another person's point of view, a characteristic typical of young children.

Pause & Reflect

From Piaget's point of view, why is it incorrect to think of children as "small adults"?

Formal Operational Stage (Middle School, High School, and Beyond) The last stage is called *formal operational* because students at this stage can generalize from a particular instance to a general form. For example, a student who can recognize a particular algebra problem as belonging to the general class of "quadratic equations" is able to think about—or cognitively operate on—the general form of the problem. Students at the stage of formal operations can also mentally manipulate relationships and variables. For example, the formal operational thinker can read the analogies "5 is to 15 as 1 is to 3" and "penny is to dollar as year is to century" and realize that despite the different content, the form of the two analogies is identical (both are based on ratios). In the same way, the formal operational thinker can understand and use complex language forms: proverbs ("Strike while the iron is hot"), metaphor ("Procrastination is the thief of time"), sarcasm, and satire.

We can see the nature of formal operational thinking and how it differs from concrete operational thinking by looking at a simplified version of Piaget's rod-bending experiment. Adolescents are given a basin filled with water, a set of metal rods of varying lengths, and a set of weights. The rods are attached to the edge of the basin and the weights to the ends of the rods.

Students who are within Piaget's formal operational stage of cognitive development are capable of solving problems by systematically using abstract symbols to represent real objects.

The subject's task is to figure out how much weight is required to bend a rod just enough to touch the water. Let's say that our hypothetical subject picks out the longest rod in the set (which is 9 inches long), attaches it to the edge of the basin, and puts just enough weight on the end of it to get it to touch the water. This observation is then recorded. Successively shorter rods are selected, and the same procedure is carried out. At some point, the subject comes to the 4-inch rod. This rod does not touch the water even when all of the weights have been attached to it. There are, however, three more rods, all of which are shorter than the last one tested.

> **Formal operational stage: the child is able to deal with abstractions, form hypotheses, and engage in mental manipulations**

This is where the formal and concrete operators part company. The formal operational thinker reasons that if all of the available weights are not sufficient to bend the 4-inch rod enough to touch the water, the same will be true of the remaining rods. In essence, the rest of the experiment is done mentally and symbolically. The concrete operational thinker, however,

continues trying out each rod and recording each observation independent of the others. Although both subjects reach the same conclusion, the formal operator does so through a more powerful and efficient process.

But remember that new schemes develop gradually. Although adolescents can sometimes deal with mental abstractions representing concrete objects, most 12-year-olds solve problems haphazardly, using trial and error. It is not until the end of the high school years that adolescents are likely to approach a problem by forming hypotheses, mentally sorting out solutions, and systematically testing the most promising leads.

Some interpreters of Piaget (e.g., Wadsworth, 2004) note that a significant aspect of formal thought is that it causes the adolescent to concentrate more on possibilities than on realities. This is the ability that Erikson and others (e.g., Kalbaugh & Haviland, 1991) suggest is instrumental in the emergence of the identity crisis. At the point when older adolescents can become aware of all the factors that have to be considered in choosing a career and can imagine what it might be like to be employed, some may feel so threatened and confused that they postpone the final choice. Yet the same capability can also help resolve the identity crisis because adolescents can reason about possibilities in a logical manner. An adolescent girl, for example, may consider working as a pediatrician, teacher, or child psychologist in an underprivileged environment because she has always enjoyed and sought out activities that allowed her to interact with children and has also been concerned with the effects of deprivation on development.

Although mastery of formal thought equips the older adolescent with impressive intellectual skills, it may also lead to a tendency for the burgeoning formal thinker to become preoccupied with abstract and theoretical matters. Barry Wadsworth made this point in the following way:

> If motivated to do so, and if in possession of the necessary content, adolescents with formal reasoning can reason as logically as adults. The tools for an evaluation of intellectual arguments are formed and fully functional. One of the major affective differences between the thought of the adolescent and that of the adult is that, initially in their use of formal operations, adolescents apply a criterion of pure logic in evaluating reasoning about human events. If it is logical it is good, right, and so on. This is the nature of their egocentrism. Adolescents lack a full appreciation of the way in which the world is ordered. With the capability for generating endless hypotheses, an adolescent believes that what is best is what is logical. He or she does not yet differentiate between the logical

© Mike Booth/Alamy

world as she thinks it to be and the "real" world. (2004, p. 124)

This inability to differentiate between the world as the adolescent thinks it should be and the world as it actually is was referred to by David Elkind (1968) as **adolescent egocentrism**. This occurs when high school students use their emerging formal operational capabilities to think about themselves and the thinking of others. Because adolescents are preoccupied with themselves and how they appear to others, they assume that peers and adults are equally interested in what they think and do. This is why, in Elkind's view, the typical adolescent is so self-conscious. The major difference between the egocentrism of childhood and that of adolescence is summed up in Elkind's observation: "The child is egocentric in the sense that he is unable to take another person's point of view. The adolescent, on the other hand, takes the other person's point of view to an extreme degree" (1968, p. 153)

Elkind believes that adolescent egocentrism also explains why the peer group becomes such a potent force in high school:

Adolescent egocentrism . . . accounts, in part, for the power of the peer group during this period. The adolescent is so concerned with the reactions of others toward him, particularly his peers, that he is willing to do many things which are opposed to all of his previous training and to his own best interests. At the same time, this egocentric impression that he is always on stage may help to account for the many and varied adolescent attention-getting maneuvers. (1968, p. 154)

Although the concept of adolescent egocentrism is widely accepted among researchers, ascribing its cause to formal operational thinking gets mixed support. Some studies have found a relationship, while other studies have not (Rycek, Stuhr, & McDermott, 1998; Vartanian, 2000).

The Role of Social Interaction and Instruction in Cognitive Development

How Social Interaction Affects Cognitive Development
When it comes to social experiences, Piaget clearly believed that peer interactions do more to spur cognitive development than do interactions with adults. The reason is that children are more likely to

> **Piaget thought cognitive development to be more strongly influenced by peers than by adults.**

discuss, analyze, and debate the merits of another child's view of some issue (such as who should have which toy or what the rules of a game should be) than they are to take serious issue with an adult. The balance of power between children and adults is simply too unequal. Not only are most children quickly taught that adults know more and use superior reasoning, but also the adult always gets to have the last word: Argue too long, and it's off to bed with no dessert. But when children interact with one another, the outcome is more dependent on how well each child uses her wits (Light & Littleton, 1999).

It is the need to understand the ideas of a peer or playmate in order to formulate responses to those ideas that leads to less egocentrism and the development of new, more complex mental schemes. Put another way, a strongly felt sense of cognitive conflict automatically impels the child to strive for a higher level of equilibrium. Formal instruction by an adult expert simply does not have the same impact, regardless of how well designed it might be. That is why parents and teachers are often surprised to find children agreeing on some issue after having rejected an adult's explanation of the very same thing. Thus, educational programs that are patterned after Piaget's ideas usually provide many opportunities for children to interact socially and discover through these interactions basic ideas about how the world works (Crain, 2005; Rogoff, 1990; Tudge & Winterhoff, 1993). We will return to this idea later in the book when we discuss cooperative learning.

How Instruction Affects Cognitive Development
Although Piaget believed that formal instruction by expert adults will not significantly stimulate cognitive development, not all psychologists have been willing to accept this conclusion at face value. Over the past 30 years, dozens of experiments have been conducted to determine whether it is possible to teach preoperational stage children to understand and use concrete operational schemes, or to teach students in the concrete operational stage to grasp formal operational reasoning.

The typical conclusion of psychologists who have analyzed and evaluated this body of research ranges from uncertainty to cautious optimism (see, e.g., Case, 1975; T. L. Good & Brophy, 1995; Nagy & Griffiths, 1982; Sprinthall, Sprinthall, & Oja, 1998). The uncertainty results from shortcomings in the way some studies were carried out and disagreements about what constitutes evidence of true concrete operational thinking or formal operational thinking.

adolescent egocentrism The introspective, inward turning of a high school student's newly developed powers of thought, with a tendency to project one's self-analysis onto others.

The cautious optimism comes from the work of Michael Shayer and others (Adey, Shayer, & Yates, 2001; Shayer, 1999) in England. They found that schools that participated in a science instruction program called CASE (Cognitive Acceleration through Science Education), which combined aspects of the cognitive developmental theories of Piaget and Vygotsky, had a much greater percentage of 13- and 14-year-olds at or above the early formal operational stage than did non-CASE schools. Furthermore, after two years in the program, CASE students scored higher on national tests of mathematics, science, and English than did students in the non-CASE schools. CASE programs have also been implemented to help preoperational stage children acquire concrete operational schemes (Robertson, 2001) and to help teachers accelerate the cognitive development of students with various learning impediments (Simon, 2002).

The safest conclusion that can be drawn from this literature (see, for example, Sigelman & Shaffer, 1991; Sprinthall, Sprinthall, & Oja, 1998) is that children who are in the process of developing the schemes that will govern the next stage of cognitive functioning can, with good-quality instruction, be helped to refine those schemes a bit faster than would normally be the case. For example, teachers can teach the principle of conservation by using simple explanations and concrete materials and allowing children to manipulate the materials. This means that teachers should nurture the process of cognitive growth at any particular stage by presenting lessons in a form consistent with but slightly more advanced than the students' existing schemes. The objective here is to help students assimilate and accommodate new and different experiences as efficiently as possible.

Criticisms of Piaget's Theory

Underestimating Children's Capabilities Among the thousands of articles that have been published in response to Piaget's findings are many that offered critiques of his work. Some psychologists argued that Piaget underestimated children's abilities not only

© Nenov Brothers Photography/Shutterstock Images

Instruction can accelerate the development of schemes that have begun to form.

{ **Piaget's theory underestimates children's abilities.** }

because he imposed stringent criteria for inferring the presence of particular cognitive abilities, but also because the tasks he used were often complex and far removed from children's real-life experiences (Case, 1999). The term *preoperational*, for instance, stresses what is absent rather than what is present. Over the past two decades, researchers have focused more on what preoperational children *can* do. The results (summarized by Kamii, 2000; Siegler, 1998) suggested that preschoolers' cognitive abilities are more advanced in some areas than Piaget's work suggests.

Overestimating Adolescents' Capabilities Other evidence suggests that Piaget may have overestimated the formal thinking capabilities of adolescents. Norman Sprinthall and Richard Sprinthall (1987) reported that only 33% of a group of high school seniors could apply formal operational reasoning to scientific problem solving. Research summarized by Michael Shayer (1997) indicated that only 20% of children exhibit well-developed formal operational thinking by the end of adolescence. According to these studies, formal reasoning seems to be the exception, not the rule, throughout adolescence.

A study of French adolescents (Flieller, 1999) reported similar percentages but also sought to determine if a new pattern had emerged. The study used data collected at different times over a 20- to 30-year period. Of a group of 10- to 12-year-olds who were tested on formal operational tasks in 1972, only 9% were at the beginning of that stage and only 1% were mature formal operators. The percentages for a group of 10- to 12-year-olds tested in 1993 were just slightly higher: 13% and 3%, respectively. Significantly larger differences were noted, however, between two groups of 13- to 15-year-olds. Among those tested in 1967, 26% were early formal operators and 9% were mature formal operators. But among those tested in 1996, 40% were early formal operators and 15% were mature formal operators. The author of this study suggested that the increase in formal operational thinking among 13- to 15-year-olds may be attributable in part to teaching practices (such as creating tables to display information and using tree diagrams to clarify grammatical structure) that foster the development of formal operational schemes.

Vague Explanations for Cognitive Growth Piaget's theory has also been criticized for its vagueness in

Chapter 2: Theories of Psychosocial and Cognitive Development

> ## Most adolescents are not formal operational thinkers.

specifying the factors that are responsible for cognitive growth. Why, for example, do children give up conserving responses in favor of nonconserving responses at a particular age?

Robert Siegler (1996) suggested an explanation: He believes that variability in children's thinking plays an influential role. For example, it is not uncommon to hear children use on successive occasions different forms of a given verb, as in "I *ate* it," "I *eated* it," and "I *ated* it." Similar variability has been found in the use of memory strategies (5-year-old and 8-year-old children do not always rehearse information they want to remember), addition rules, time-telling rules, and block building tasks. Siegler's explanation is that variability gives the child a range of plausible options for dealing with a particular problem. The child then tries them out in an attempt to see which one produces the best adaptation. Note the use of the qualifying word *plausible*. Most children do not try out any and all possible solutions to a problem. Instead they stick to possibilities that are logically consistent with underlying principles of the problem. Once children have acquired a logical explanation for solving problems, they learn more and persist longer (Siegler & Svetina, 2006).

Cultural Differences Key assumptions underlying Piaget's theory, such as adaptation and constructivism, have fueled considerable cross-cultural research (Maynard, 2008). One question that has been raised is whether children from different cultures develop intellectually in the manner Piaget described. The answer at this point is both yes and no. The sequence of stages appears to be universal, but the rate of development may vary from one culture to another (Dasen & Heron, 1981; Hughes & Noppe, 1991; Leadbeater, 1991; Rogoff & Chavajay, 1995).

Although children in Western industrialized societies (like the United States) usually are not given babysitting responsibilities until they are at least 10 years old because their high level of egocentrism prevents them from considering the needs of the other child, Mayan children in Mexican villages as young as age 5 play this role because their culture stresses the development of cooperative behavior (Sameroff & McDonough, 1994).

Research conducted during the 1970s found that individuals living in non-Western cultures who had little

formal education did not engage in formal operational thinking. Although these same people used concrete operational schemes when tested with the kinds of tasks Piaget used, they usually did so at a later age than the Swiss children Piaget originally studied. This result was attributed to their lack of schooling, which left them unfamiliar with the language and conventions of formal testing. Researchers then conducted concrete operational tasks with materials that were part of these people's everyday lives; children from Zambia who were asked to reproduce a pattern with strips of wire rather than with paper and pencil performed as well as Western children who drew the patterns on paper (Rogoff & Chavajay, 1995).

Pause & Reflect *Noting that American schoolchildren score lower than many European and Asian children on standardized achievement tests, critics argue that U.S. formal schooling should begin earlier than age 5 and should focus on basic reading and math skills. In light of research on Piaget's theories, what do you think of this proposal?*

Now that you are familiar with Piaget's theory of cognitive development, you can use the Suggestions for Teaching on the next page to formulate specific classroom applications.

LO3 Vygotsky: Cognitive Development

From the time Piaget's work first became known to large numbers of American psychologists in the early 1960s until the 1980s, it was the dominant explanation of cognitive development. Not that Piaget didn't have his critics. As the previous section made clear, many psychologists challenged one aspect or another of his work. But there were no competing explanations of cognitive development. Beginning in the early 1980s, however, the ideas of Russian psychologist Lev Vygotsky began to appear in the psychological literature with increasing frequency. Vygotsky, who died from tuberculosis in 1934, was a contemporary of Piaget who had very different views about the major forces that shape learning and thinking, particularly with respect to the roles of culture, social interaction, and formal instruction (Rowe & Wertsch, 2002).

> ## { The sequence of stages is uniform across cultures but the rate of development varies. }

Suggestions for Teaching

Applying Piaget's Theory of Cognitive Development

1 Focus on what children at each stage can do, and avoid what they cannot meaningfully understand.

This application must be interpreted carefully, as recent research has shown that children at the preoperational and concrete operational levels can do more than Piaget believed. In general, however, it is safe to say that since preoperational stage children (preschoolers, kindergartners, most first and some second graders) can use language and other symbols to stand for objects, they should be given many opportunities to describe and explain things through the use of speech, artwork, body movement, role-playing, and musical performance. Although you can introduce the concepts of conservation, seriation, class inclusion, time, space, and number, attempts at mastering them should probably be postponed until children are in the concrete operational stage.

Concrete operational stage children (grades 3–6) can be given opportunities to master such mental processes as ordering, seriating, classifying, reversing, multiplying, dividing, subtracting, and adding by manipulating concrete objects or symbols. Although a few fifth and sixth graders may be capable of dealing with abstractions, most exercises that involve theorizing, hypoth-

esizing, or generalizing should be done with concrete objects or symbols.

Formal operational stage children (grade 7 through high school) can be given activities that require hypothetical-deductive reasoning, reflective thinking, analysis, synthesis, and evaluation.

2 Because individuals differ in their rates of intellectual growth, gear instructional materials and activities to each student's developmental level.

3 Because intellectual growth occurs when individuals attempt to eliminate a disequilibrium, instructional lessons and materials that introduce new concepts should provoke interest and curiosity and be moderately challenging in order to maximize assimilation and accommodation.

4 Although information (facts, concepts, procedures) can be efficiently transmitted from teacher to student through direct instruction, knowledge (rules and hypotheses) is best created by each student through the mental and physical manipulation of information.

Lesson plans should include opportunities for activity, manipulation, exploration, discussion, and application of information. Small-group science proj-

ects are one example of how to implement this goal.

5 Because students' schemes at any given time are an outgrowth of earlier schemes, point out to them how new ideas relate to their old ideas and extend their understanding. Memorization of information for its own sake should be avoided.

6 Begin lessons with concrete objects or ideas, and gradually shift explanations to a more abstract and general level.

Preschool, Elementary, and Middle School Grades[1]

1 Become thoroughly familiar with Piaget's theory so that you will be aware of how your students organize and synthesize ideas.

You may gain extra insight if you analyze your own thinking, since you are likely to discover that in some situations, you operate at a concrete rather than an abstract level.

2 If possible, assess the level and type of thinking of each child in your class. Ask individual children to perform some of Piaget's experiments, and spend most of your time listening to each child explain her reactions.

How Culture Affects Cognitive Development

Vygotsky's theory of cognitive development is often referred to as a sociocultural theory because it maintains that how we think is a function of both social and cultural forces. If, for example, you were given a list of nouns (such as *plate, box, peach, knife, apple, hoe, cup,*

and *potato*) and told to create groupings, you would probably put *plate, knife,* and *cup* in a group labeled "utensils" and *peach, apple,* and *potato* in a group labeled "food." Why? Is there something inherently compelling about those groupings? Not really.

We could just as logically have put *plate, knife,* and *apple* in a group, because we can use the first two to eat the third. But we are more likely to put objects in taxonomic categories than in functional categories because we have been taught by others who organize ideas taxonomically most of the time. And why do we think that way? Because we are the product of a culture that prizes the ability of its members to think at the most abstract levels (which is why Piaget saw formal operations as the most advanced stage of thinking).

Typically, then, parents and schools shape children's thought processes to reflect that which the culture values. So even when individuals are by themselves, what they think and do is the result of cultural

> **How we think is influenced by current social forces and historical cultural forces.**

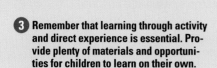

3 Remember that learning through activity and direct experience is essential. Provide plenty of materials and opportunities for children to learn on their own.

4 Arrange situations to permit social interaction, so that children can learn from one another.

Hearing others explain their views is a natural way for students to learn that not everyone sees things the same way. The placement of a few advanced thinkers with less mature thinkers is more likely to facilitate this process than is homogeneous grouping.

5 Plan learning experiences to take into account the level of thinking attained by an individual or group.

Encourage children to classify things on the basis of a single attribute before you expose them to problems that involve relationships among two or more attributes. Ask many questions, and give your students many opportunities to explain their interpretations of experiences, so that you can remain aware of their level of thinking.

6 Keep in mind the possibility that students may be influenced by egocentric speech and thought.

Consider the possibility that each child may assume that everyone else has the same conception of a word that he or she has. If confusion becomes apparent or if a child becomes impatient about failure to communicate, request an explanation in different terms. Or ask several children to explain their conception of an object or a situation.

Middle School and Secondary Grades[2]

1 Become well acquainted with the nature of concrete operational thinking and formal thought, so that you can recognize when your students are resorting to either type or a combination of the two.

2 To become aware of the type of thinking that individual students use, ask them to explain how they arrived at solutions to problems.

Ask for explanations as part of your classroom curriculum or in response to experimental situations similar to those that Piaget devised.

3 Teach students how to solve problems more systematically (suggestions for doing this will be provided in later chapters), and provide opportunities for hands-on science experiments.

4 Keep in mind that some high school students may be more interested in possibilities than in realities.

If class discussions become unrealistically theoretical and hypothetical, call attention to facts and practical difficulties. If students are contemptuous of unsuccessful attempts by adults to solve school, local, national, and international problems, point out the complexity of many situations involving conflicts of interest, perhaps by having students develop arguments for both sides.

5 Allow for the possibility that younger adolescents may go through a period of egocentrism that will cause them to act as if they are always on stage and to be extremely concerned about the reactions of peers.

---

[1]These guidelines are adapted from Elkind (1989); Ginsburg and Opper (1988); Kamii (2000); D. G. Singer and Revenson (1996); and Wadsworth (2004).

[2]Many of these suggestions are derived from points made in Chapter 2 of *Adolescence* (Steinberg, 2008).

---

values and practices, some of which may stretch back over hundreds or thousands of years, as well as recent social contacts (M. Cole, 2005; Wertsch & Tulviste, 1996).

The Importance of Psychological Tools Vygotsky believed that the most important things a culture passes on to its members (and their descendants) are what he called *psychological tools*. These are the cognitive devices and procedures with which we communicate and explore the world around us. They both aid and change our mental functioning. Speech, writing, gestures, diagrams, numbers, chemical formulas, musical notation,

 Psychological tools aid and change thought processes.

rules, and memory techniques are some examples of common psychological tools (Gredler & Shields, 2004).

Early explorers, for example, created maps to help them represent where they had been, communicate that knowledge to others, and plan future trips. Today we use the same type of tool to navigate efficiently over long distances or within relatively compact but complex environments (like large cities). Another example is the use of multiplication. If asked to solve the multiplication problem 343×822, you would, in all likelihood, quickly and easily come up with the answer 281,946 by using the following procedure:

$$
\begin{array}{r}
343 \\
\times\ 822 \\
\hline
686 \\
686 \\
2744 \\
\hline
281{,}946
\end{array}
$$

But you could have produced the same answer by adding 343 to itself 821 times. Why would you automatically opt for the first procedure? Because the culture in which you operate has, through the medium of formal instruction, provided you with a psychological tool called multiplication as a means of more efficiently and accurately solving certain types of complex mathematical problems (Wertsch, 1998).

Children are introduced to a culture's major psychological tools through social interactions with their parents and later through more formal interactions with classroom teachers. Eventually these social interactions are internalized as cognitive processes that are autonomously invoked. As Vygotsky so elegantly put it, "Through others we become ourselves" (quoted in Tudge & Scrimsher, 2003, p. 218).

How Social Interaction Affects Cognitive Development

The difference between Vygotsky's views on the origin and development of cognitive processes and those of other cognitive developmental psychologists is something like the old question, "Which came first: the chicken or the egg?" Influenced by Piaget, many developmental psychologists argue that as children overcome cognitive conflict through the internal processes of assimilation, accommodation, and equilibration, they become more capable of higher-level thinking, and so come to better understand the nature of the world in which they live and their place in it. In other words, cognitive development makes social development possible (see our discussion of Robert Selman's work on the social development of children in the next chapter).

Vygotsky, however, believed that just the opposite was true. He saw social interaction as the primary cause of cognitive development. Unlike Piaget, Vygotsky believed that children gain significantly from the knowledge and conceptual tools handed down to them by those who are more intellectually advanced,

> **Cognitive development is strongly influenced by those who are more intellectually advanced.**

whether they are same-age peers, older children, or adults.

Consider, for example, a simple concept like "grandmother." In the absence of formal instruction, a primary grade child's concept of grandmother is likely to be narrow in scope because it is based on personal experience ("My grandmother is 70 years old, has gray hair, wears glasses, and makes the best apple pie"). But when children are helped to understand the basic nature of the concept with such instructional tools as family tree diagrams, they understand the notion of "grandmother" (and other types of relatives) on a broader and more general basis. They can then use this concept to compare family structures with friends and, later, to do genealogical research (Tappan, 1998; Tudge & Scrimsher, 2003).

In order for social interactions to produce advances in cognitive development, Vygotsky argued, they have to contain a process called *mediation*. Mediation occurs when a more knowledgeable individual interprets a child's behavior and helps transform it into an internal and symbolic representation that means the same thing to the child as to others (Light & Littleton, 1999; Tudge & Winterhoff, 1993; Wertsch & Tulviste, 1996). Perhaps the following example will help clarify this point: Imagine a child who reaches out to grasp an object that is beyond her reach. A nearby parent thinks the child is pointing at the object, says, "Oh, you want the box of crayons," and retrieves the item for the child. Over time, what began as a grasping action becomes transformed, through the mediation of an adult, into an internalized sign ("I want you to give that object to me") that means the same thing to the child as it does to the adult (Driscoll, 2005). Thus, a child's potential level of mental development can be brought about only by introducing the more advanced thought processes of another person.

How Instruction Affects Cognitive Development

Vygotsky drew a distinction between the type of information that preschool children learn and the type of information that children who attend school learn (or should learn). During early childhood, children acquire what Vygotsky called **spontaneous concepts**. That is, they learn various facts and concepts and rules (such as how to speak their native language and how to classify objects in their environment), but they do so for the most part as a by-product of such other activities as engaging in play and communicating with parents and playmates. This kind of knowledge is unsystematic, unconscious, and directed at the child's everyday concrete experiences; hence, Vygotsky's use of the term *spontaneous*.

Chapter 2: Theories of Psychosocial and Cognitive Development

Teachers should help students learn how to use psychological tools.

Schooling, however, should be directed to the learning of what Vygotsky called **scientific concepts**. These are the psychological tools that allow us to manipulate our environment consciously and systematically. Vygotsky believed that the proper development of a child's mind depends on learning how to use these psychological tools, and that this will occur only if classroom instruction is properly designed. This means providing students with explicit and clear verbal definitions as a first step. The basic purpose of instruction, then, is not simply to add one piece of knowledge to another like pennies in a piggy bank but to stimulate and guide cognitive development (Crain, 2005; Rogoff, 1990).

Contemporary psychologists have extended Vygotsky's notions of spontaneous and scientific concepts. They use the term **empirical learning** to refer to the way in which young children acquire spontaneous concepts. The hallmark of empirical learning is that the most observable characteristics of objects and events are noticed and used as a basis for forming general concepts. The main limitation of this approach is that salient characteristics are not necessarily critical or defining characteristics, and it is the latter that form the basis of correct concept formation. For example, in the absence of formal instruction, children come to believe that any

scientific concepts
Vygotsky term for psychological tools as language, formulas, rules, and symbols that allow one to manipulate one's environment consciously and systematically.

empirical learning
The use of noticeable characteristics of objects and events to form spontaneous concepts; a form of learning typical of young children.

Jean Piaget believed that children's schemes develop more quickly when children interact with one another than when they interact with adults. But Lev Vygotsky believed that children learn from the instructional interactions they have with those who are more intellectually advanced.

theoretical learning
Learning how to use psychological tools across a range of settings and problem types to acquire new knowledge and skills.

zone of proximal development (ZPD)
Vygotsky's term for the difference between what a child can do on his or her own and what the child can accomplish with some assistance.

scaffolding
Supporting learning during its early phases through such techniques as demonstrating how tasks should be accomplished, giving hints to the correct solution to a problem or answer to a question, and providing leading questions. As students become more capable of working independently, these supports are withdrawn.

utterance that has two or more words is a sentence, that whales are fish, and that bamboo is not a type of grass.

Theoretical learning, on the other hand, involves using psychological tools to learn scientific concepts. As these general tools are used repeatedly with a variety of problems, they are gradually internalized and generalized to a wide variety of settings and problem types. Good-quality instruction, in this view, is aimed at helping children move from the very practical empirical learning to the more general theoretical learning and from using psychological tools overtly, with the aid of an adult, to using these tools mentally, without outside assistance (Karpov & Bransford, 1995; Morra, Gobbo, Marini, & Sheese, 2008).

Here's an example that compares the efficacy of the empirical and theoretical approaches: Two groups of 6-year-old children were taught how to write the 22 letters of the Russian alphabet. The first group was taught using the empirical approach. The teacher gave the students a model of each letter, showed them how to write each one, and gave a verbal explanation of how to write each letter. The students then copied each letter under the teacher's supervision. When they produced an acceptable copy of a letter, they were taught the next letter. The second group was taught using the theoretical approach. First, students were taught to analyze the shape of each letter so they could identify where the direction of the contour of each line changed. Then they were to place dots in those locations outlining the change in contour. Finally, they were to reproduce the pattern of dots on another part of the page and connect the dots with a pencil.

The speed with which the children in each group learned to accurately produce the letters of the alphabet differed by quite a large margin. The average student in the empirical group needed about 170 trials to learn the first letter and about 20 trials to write the last letter. The number of trials taken to learn all 22 letters was about 1,230. The average student in the theoretical group required only about 14 trials to learn how to write the first letter correctly, and from the eighth letter on needed only 1 trial per letter. The number of trials needed to learn all 22 letters for the second group was about 60. Furthermore, these students were able to

use the general method they were taught to help them learn to write the letters of the Latin and Arabic alphabets (Karpov & Bransford, 1995; Morra, Gobbo, Marini, & Sheese, 2008).

Instruction and the Zone of Proximal Development This discussion of empirical and theoretical learning illustrates Vygotsky's belief that well-designed instruction is like a magnet. If it is aimed slightly ahead of what children know and can do at the present time, it will pull them along, helping them master things they cannot learn on their own. We can illustrate this idea with an experiment that Vygotsky (1986) described. He gave two 8-year-olds of average ability problems that were a bit too difficult for them to solve on their own. (Although Vygotsky did not specify what types of problems they were, imagine that they were math problems.) He then tried to help the children solve the problems by giving them leading questions and hints. He found that one child, with the hints, was able to solve problems designed for 12-year-olds, whereas the other child, who also received the hints, could reach only a 9-year-old level.

Vygotsky referred to the difference between what a child can do on his or her own and what he or she can accomplish with some assistance as the **zone of proximal development (ZPD)**. The size of the first 8-year-old's zone was 4 (that is, the 8-year-old could, with help, solve the problem designed for a child 4 years older), whereas the second child had a zone of 1 (the child could solve the problem designed for a child 1 year older). According to Vygotsky, students with wider zones are likely to experience greater cognitive development when instruction is pitched just above the lower limit of their ZPD than will students with narrower zones because the former are in a better position to capitalize on the instruction. The ZPD, then, encompasses those abilities, attitudes, and patterns of thinking that are in the process of maturing and can be refined only with assistance (Holzman, 2009; Tappan, 2005; Tudge & Scrimsher, 2003).

Helping students answer difficult questions or solve problems by giving them hints or asking leading questions is an example of a technique called **scaffolding**.

> **Cognitive development is promoted by instruction in the zone of proximal development.**

Chapter 2: Theories of Psychosocial and Cognitive Development

{ Scaffolding techniques support student learning. }

Just as construction workers use external scaffolding to support their building efforts, Vygotsky recommended that teachers similarly support learning in its early phases. The purpose of scaffolding is to help students acquire knowledge and skills they would not have learned on their own. As the student demonstrates mastery over the content in question, the learning aids are faded and removed. Scaffolding techniques that are likely to help students traverse their ZPD include prompts, suggestions, checklists, modeling, rewards, feedback, cognitive structuring (using such devices as theories, categories, labels, and rules for helping students organize and understand ideas), and questioning (Gallimore & Tharp, 1990; Ratner, 1991). As students approach the upper limit of their ZPD, their behavior becomes smoother, more internalized, and more automatized. Any assistance offered at this level will likely be perceived as disruptive and irritating.

Mark Tappan (1998) proposed the following four-component model that teachers can use to optimize the effects of their scaffolding efforts and help students move through their ZPD:

1. *Model desired academic behaviors.* Children can imitate many behaviors that they do not have the capability to exhibit independently, and such experiences stimulate them to act this way on their own.

2. *Create a dialogue with the student.* A child's understanding of concepts, procedures, and principles becomes more systematic and organized as a result of the exchange of questions, explanations, and feedback between teacher and child within the child's ZPD. As with modeling, the effectiveness of this dialogue is determined, at least in part, by the extent to which the teacher and student are committed to creating and maintaining a relationship in which each makes an honest effort to satisfy the needs of the other.

3. *Practice.* Practice speeds up the internalizing of thinking skills that students observe and discuss with others (see Schmitz & Winksel, 2008).

4. *Confirmation.* To confirm others is to bring out the best in them by focusing on what they can do with some assistance; this process helps create a trusting and mutually supportive relationship between teacher and student. For example, you might say to a student, "I know this assignment seems difficult right now and that you have had some problems in the past with similar assignments, but with the help I'm willing to offer, I'm certain you'll do good-quality work."

Vygotsky's notion of producing cognitive development by embedding instruction within a student's ZPD is an attractive one that has many implications for instruction. In Chapter 9, on social cognitive theory, we will describe how this notion was used to improve the reading comprehension skills of low-achieving seventh graders.

Vygotsky's Zone of Proximal Development: Increasing Cognition in an Elementary Literacy Lesson

TeachSource Video Case

Go to the Education CourseMate website and watch the video, study the artifacts in the case, and reflect upon the following questions:

1. How does the video case illustrate the zone of proximal development as it is explained in this text? How does the video case bring this concept to life?
2. How does the classroom teacher in the video case (Dr. Hurley) scaffold instruction for the children? What kinds of hints and leading questions does she give them?

LO4 Using Technology to Promote Cognitive Development

Piaget and Vygotsky believed that people use physical, mental, and social experiences to construct personal conceptions (schemes) of what the world is like. Engagement with the environment and with others in the environment is critical to cognitive development. Although there are numerous opportunities throughout the course of each day to watch what other people do, try out ideas, and interact with others face-to-face, we are normally limited to the physical and social stimuli that make up our immediate environment. Factors such as distance, time, and cost keep us from wider-ranging interactions. Technology, however, has expanded the range of our experience. This is especially true with the advent of technologies that include interactive information sharing, collaboration, multiuser virtual environments, social networking, blogs, and the like.

The use of technology in both elementary and secondary schools continues to increase (J. A. Kulik, 2003a; Pullin, Gitsaki, & Baguley, 2010). Although classrooms

Technological learning environments can provide challenging problems that encourage social construction of knowledge.

Jose Luis Pelaez Inc/Blend Images/Jupiter Images

will likely remain, for some time to come, the primary place where students and teachers gather in person, technology allows students and teachers to engage people and information across time and space. So the classroom is no longer the only environment for learning; there are now numerous virtual environments that can be accessed through technology.

Technology Applied to Piaget

Central to Piaget's ideas of cognitive development is cognitive disequilibrium, when a student's understanding of the world does not match her or his experience. Situations that present problems for students to ponder and try to solve drive learning and development because they introduce disequilibrium. Technology gives students access to experiences that contribute to disequilibrium.

Microworlds, for example, are simulated learning environments that provide opportunities for students to think about problems for which there are not obvious solutions or situations that do not immediately "make sense." They also allow researchers to investigate how learners make decisions in contexts that can be more or less controlled (Elliott, Welsh, Nettelbeck, & Mills, 2007; Healy & Hoyles, 2001).

The Conservation of Area and Its Measurement (C.AR.ME) microworld provides a set of geometric tools to encourage students to create different ways to represent the concept of area measurement. A group of high school students created 11 ways to represent the measurement of area using C.AR.ME (Kordaki & Potari, 2002). Another microworld, Probability Explorer, allows students to design probability experiments that relate to such real-world activities as weather forecasting; it is intended to help students refine their intuitive understanding of chance (Drier, 2001). As these examples illustrate, microworlds foster cognitive development by encouraging student exploration, student control, and visual representation of abstract ideas. Some microworlds include sensors that are attached to a microcomputer to generate graphs of such physical phenomena as temperature, sound, motion, and electromotive force (Peña & Alessi, 1999; Trumper & Gelbman, 2000, 2002). Because such microworlds, also called **microcomputer-based laboratories**, provide an immediate link between a hands-on, concrete experience and a symbolic representation of that experience (a graph), their use may facilitate the shift from concrete to formal operational thinking (Trumper & Gelbman, 2000).

Opportunities to construct new understandings and conceptions (schemes) come not only from interacting with information and objects in an environment but from interacting with the people in that environment. Virtual learning allows students to engage environments and collaborate with people not otherwise accessible.

Technology Applied to Vygotsky

As you'll recall, Vygotsky believed that children gain significantly from the knowledge and conceptual tools handed down to them by those who are more intellectually advanced. Roy Pea (1985, 2004) and Gavriel Salomon (1988) were among the first to suggest that technology might play the same role as more capable tutors with such tasks as writing an essay and reading a book. Basically, the software provides prompts and expert guidance during reading and writing tasks. These supports, or scaffolds, are gradually faded as students become more competent at regulating their own behavior. According to some researchers (Cotterall & Cohen, 2003; Donovan & Smolkin, 2002), such support is vital in writing because young children often lack the cognitive resources and skills to move beyond simple knowledge telling in their compositions. Salomon, who helped develop both the Reading Partner and Writing Partner software tools, found that they improved children's reading comprehension, essay writing, effort, and awareness of useful self-questioning strategies (Salomon, Globerson, & Guterman, 1989; Zellermayer, Salomon, Globerson, & Givon, 1991). Some studies of the same period did not always report such positive results (Bonk & Reynolds, 1992; Daiute, 1985;

T. H. Reynolds & Bonk, 1996). However, as educators and researchers have gained experience with technologically based learning environments, Vygotsky's ideas have become better understood in that context and therefore more effectively applied (Alavi & Leidner, 2001; Borthick, Jones, & Wakai, 2003; W.-M. Roth & Lee, 2007). For example, Yelland and Masters (2007) found that within technological environments, children can support each other's learning, and the scaffolding that occurs in such environments supports learners cognitively, affectively, and technologically. Indeed, within the context of technologically driven learning environments, the technology itself, if it is designed to be supportive of the learner, is sometimes referred to as a scaffold (De Lisi, 2006).

Even so, Vygotsky viewed social interaction as the primary cause of cognitive development. Technology connects people to people, and it can do so in a variety of contexts that allow learners to gain knowledge and the psychological tools that help them to grow intellectually. One way in which technology connects people is in **multiuser virtual environments**. One such virtual learning environment, known as Quest Atlantis, has engaged over 20,000 students from four continents (Barab, Gresalfi et al., 2009; Gresalfi, Barab, Siyahhan, & Christensen, 2009). The Quest Atlantis

> **multiuser virtual environments**
> Online virtual worlds in which several people work together to solve various types of problems; one example is Quest Atlantis.
>
> **telementoring** The use of networking technologies by experts, mentors, instructors, and peers to demonstrate ideas, pose questions, offer insights, and provide relevant information that can help learners build new knowledge and effectively participate in a learning community.

> **Technology can act as and provide expert collaborative partners.**

TeachSource Video Case

Middle School Reading Instruction: Integrated Technology

Go to the Education CourseMate website and watch the video, study the artifacts in the case, and reflect upon the following questions:

1. How does the online chat room depicted in this video case illustrate Piaget's theory of cognitive conflict that is described in the chapter?
2. Describe the way that the online discussion group supports Vygotsky's notion of zone of proximal development and scaffolding.

project is examined in more detail in Chapter 10, and we see how students engage learning activities both online in the virtual environment and offline. The point here is that technology can support social interaction of many students in the same virtual environment.

A second way technology connects people is through online mentoring relationships, typically called **telementoring** (Duff, 2000; Murray, 2009; Rea, 2001; Scigliano, 2010). The education and technology literature is filled with examples of telementoring in pre-K–12 education. For instance, international weather projects such as the Kids as Global Scientists project (Mistler-Jackson & Songer, 2000) and the Global Learning and Observations to Benefit the Environment program (Barab & Luehmann, 2003; Finarelli, 1998) involve students in genuine scientific data collection and reporting. The collaborative relationships that students establish with peers and mentors create in students a strong sense of participation in what is called a community of practice. There are also telementoring opportunities for teachers (Whitehouse, McCloskey, & Ketelhut, 2010). The website of the International Telementor Program (www.telementor.org) provides volunteer mentors from around the world to teachers and students.

LO5 Piaget, Kohlberg, Gilligan, and Noddings: Moral Development

The theories of cognitive development that we examined previously focus on how thinking develops as humans grow and interact with their environments (including other people). One area in which that thinking is applied is to issues of right and wrong.

Piaget's Analysis of the Moral Judgment of the Child

Piaget was fascinated by children's learning in all its forms in all kinds of situations. As he watched children play games, he began to see differences in how children of different ages interpreted and applied the rules of the games.

Age Changes in Interpretation of Rules As he watched children playing games with each other, Piaget perceived that children of preschool and early elementary school age (roughly 4 to 7 years old) interpreted

rules as exemplars of how older children behaved when they played together. Children from 7 to 10 years old seemed to regard rules as sacred pronouncements handed down by older children or adults. Around middle school age (10 to 12 years old), rules became a set of agreements reached by mutual consent.

Moral Realism Versus Moral Relativism The way children of different ages responded to rules so intrigued Piaget that he decided to use the interview method to obtain more systematic information about moral development. He made up pairs of stories and asked children of different ages to discuss them. Here is a typical pair of stories (1965, p. 122):

A: There was a little boy called Julian. His father had gone out and Julian thought it would be fun to play with father's ink-pot. First he played with the pen, and then he made a little blot on the tablecloth.

B: A little boy who was called Augustus once noticed that his father's ink-pot was empty. One day that his father was away he thought of filling the ink-pot so as to help his father, and so that he should find it full when he came home. But while he was opening the ink-bottle he made a big blot on the table cloth.

Pause & Reflect *Remember our definition of decentration in the earlier discussion of Piaget's theory. How do you think the young child's lack of decentration might affect her moral reasoning?*

After reading these stories, Piaget asked, "Are these children equally guilty? Which of the two is naughtier, and why?" As was the case with interpretations of rules, Piaget found that younger children reacted to these stories differently from older children. The younger children maintained that Augustus was guiltier than Julian because he had made a bigger blot on the tablecloth. They took no account of the fact that Julian was misbehaving and that Augustus was trying to help his father. Older children, however, were more likely to base their judgment of guilt on the intent of each child. Piaget referred to the moral thinking of children up to the age of 10 or so as the **morality of constraint**, but he also called it *moral realism*. The thinking of children of 11 or older Piaget called the **morality of cooperation**. He also occasionally used the term *moral relativism*. Piaget concluded that the two basic types of moral reasoning differ in several ways. We summarize these differences in Table 2.3.

Reflecting on Table 2.3, it is not surprising that Piaget's ideas have led to more recent work that considers how the development of moral thinking informs and

TABLE 2.3 Morality of Constraint Versus Morality of Cooperation

Morality of Constraint (Typical of 6-Year-Olds)	Morality of Cooperation (Typical of 12-Year-Olds)
Holds single, absolute moral perspective (behavior is right or wrong)	Is aware of different viewpoints regarding rules
Believes rules are unchangeable	Believes rules are flexible
Determines extent of guilt by amount of damage	Considers the wrongdoers' intentions when evaluating guilt
Defines moral wrongness in terms of what is forbidden or punished	Defines moral wrongness in terms of violation of spirit of cooperation
Notice that these first four differences call attention to the tendency for children below the age of 10 or so to think of rules as sacred pronouncements handed down by external authority.	
Believes punishment should stress atonement and does not need to "fit the crime"	Believes punishment should involve either restitution or suffering the same fate as one's victim
Believes peer aggression should be punished by an external authority	Believes peer aggression should be punished by retaliatory behavior on the part of the victim*
Believes children should obey rules because they are established by those in authority	Believes children should obey rules because of mutual concerns for rights of others
Notice how these last three differences call attention to the tendency for children above the age of 10 or so to see rules as mutual agreements among equals.	

*Beyond the age of 12, adolescents increasingly affirm that reciprocal reactions, or "getting back," should be a response to good behavior, not bad behavior.
SOURCES: Freely adapted from interpretations of Piaget (1932) by Kohlberg (1969) and Lickona (1976).

is informed by experiences and observations of practices that affect conditions of social justice (Turiel, 2008).

Kohlberg's Description of Moral Development

Just as James Marcia elaborated Erikson's concept of identity formation, Lawrence Kohlberg elaborated Piaget's ideas on moral thinking. Kohlberg believed that (1) moral reasoning proceeds through fixed stages and (2) moral development can be accelerated through instruction.

Kohlberg's Use of Moral Dilemmas As a graduate student at the University of Chicago in the 1950s, Lawrence Kohlberg became fascinated by Piaget's studies of moral development. He decided to expand on Piaget's original research by making up stories involving moral dilemmas that would be more appropriate for older children. Here is the story that is most often mentioned in discussions of his work:

In Europe a woman was near death from cancer. One drug might save her, a form of radium that a druggist in the same town had recently discovered. The druggist was charging $2,000, ten times what the drug cost him to make. The sick woman's husband, Heinz, went to everyone he knew to borrow the money, but he could only get together about half of what it cost. He told the druggist that his wife was dying and asked him to sell it cheaper or let him pay later, but the druggist said "No." The husband got desperate and broke into the man's store to steal the drug for his wife. Should the husband have done that? Why? (1969, p. 376)

Kohlberg's Six Stages of Moral Reasoning After analyzing the responses of 10- to 16-year-olds to this and similar moral dilemmas, Kohlberg (1963) eventually developed a description of six stages of moral reasoning. The first two stages were labeled "preconventional morality" because young children (through age 8 or so) do not understand the conventions or rules of society. Stages 3 and 4 were labeled "conventional morality" because older children (beginning around age 10) and adolescents tend to conform to the rules of society bcause they are the convention. Stages 5 and 6 were labeled "postconventional morality" because the small proportion of adults thought to reach this stage understand the moral principles that underlie societal conventions. Be forewarned, however, that Kohlberg later revised some of his original stage designations and that descriptions of the stages have also been modified since he first proposed them. In different discussions of his stages, therefore, you may encounter varying descriptions.

The scoring system Kohlberg developed to evaluate a response to a moral dilemma is extremely complex. Furthermore, the responses of subjects are lengthy and may feature arguments about a particular decision. To help you understand a bit more about each Kohlberg stage, the following list offers simplified examples of responses to a dilemma such as that faced by Heinz. For maximum clarity, only brief typical responses to the question, "Why shouldn't you steal from a store?" are mentioned.

Stage 1: Punishment-obedience orientation. "You might get caught." (The physical consequences of an action determine goodness or badness.)

{ Preconventional morality: avoid punishment, receive benefits in return }

Stage 2: Instrumental relativist orientation. "You shouldn't steal something from a store, and the store owner shouldn't steal things that belong to you." (Obedience to laws should involve an even exchange.)

Stage 3: Good boy–nice girl orientation. "Your parents will be proud of you if you are honest." (The right action is one that will impress others.)

{ Conventional morality: impress others, respect authority }

Stage 4: Law-and-order orientation. "It's against the law, and if we don't obey laws, our whole society might fall apart." (To maintain the social order, fixed rules must be obeyed.)

Stage 5: Social contract orientation. "Under certain circumstances laws may have to be disregarded—if a person's life depends on breaking a law, for instance." (Rules should involve mutual agreements; the rights of the individual should be protected.)

{ Postconventional morality: mutual agreements, consistent principles }

Stage 6: Universal ethical principle orientation. "You need to weigh all the factors and then try to make the most appropriate decision in a given situation. Sometimes it would be morally wrong *not* to steal." (Moral decisions should be based on consistent applications of self-chosen ethical principles.)

Criticisms and Evaluations of Kohlberg's Theory Is Kohlberg's contention that moral reasoning proceeds through a fixed universal sequence of stages accurate? Based on analysis of research on moral development, Martin Hoffman (1980) concluded that although Kohlberg's sequence of stages may not be true of every individual in every culture, it may provide a useful general description of how moral reasoning develops in American society. Carol Gilligan (1979), whose position we discuss in detail later, has proposed two somewhat different sequences that reflect differences in male and female socialization.

Some have criticized Kohlberg's use of moral dilemmas on the grounds that they are too far removed from the kinds of everyday social interactions in which children and adolescents engage (e.g., Rest, Narvaez, Bebeau, & Thoma, 1999; Vitz, 1990). Individuals who are not adept at self-reflection or are without the vocabulary to express their thoughts clearly either would not be recruited into studies using moral dilemmas or would have little to contribute.

Another criticism concerns the type of moral issue that most interested Kohlberg. Kohlberg's theory deals primarily with what are called macromoral issues. These are broad social issues such as civil rights, free speech, the women's movement, and wilderness preservation. The focus is on how the behavior of individuals affects the structure of society and public policy. At this level, a moral person is one who attempts to influence laws and regulations because of a deeply held principle. For some psychologists (e.g., Rest, Narvaez, Bebeau, & Thoma, 1999), a limitation of Kohlberg's theory is that it does not adequately address micromoral issues. *Micromoral issues* concern personal interactions in everyday situations; examples include courtesy (not interrupting someone before that person has finished speaking), helpfulness (giving up your seat on a crowded bus or train to an elderly person), remembering significant events of friends and family, and punctuality for appointments. For micromoral issues, a moral person is one who is loyal and dedicated and cares about particular people.

Criticisms of Kohlberg's theory are that moral development is difficult to accelerate, moral dilemmas are not relevant to daily life, and the theory relies on macromoral issues and ignores characteristics other than moral reasoning.

Chapter 2: Theories of Psychosocial and Cognitive Development

Finally, Kohlberg's work has also been criticized because it places such a strong emphasis on the role of reasoning in moral behavior but says little about the nature of people who behave in moral ways (e.g., Arnold, 2000).

Pause & Reflect *How would you respond to a parent or colleague who argued that students have better things to do in class than discuss ways of resolving moral dilemmas?*

The Caring Orientation to Moral Development and Education

Carol Gilligan and Nel Noddings are pioneering educational scholars: They charted a new course in thinking about moral development and moral education. Each, in her own way, asked if our views of how we develop our identity, of how we think and act in moral situations, and of how we see ourselves and our relationships to others are more descriptive of males than females. We look first at Gilligan's objections to Erikson's and Kohlberg's theories and then at Noddings's care theory.

Gilligan's View of Identity and Moral Development

Carol Gilligan (1982, 1988) argued that Erikson's view of identity development and Kohlberg's view of moral development more accurately describe what occurs with adolescent males than with adolescent females. In her view, Erikson's and Kohlberg's ideas emphasize separation from parental authority and societal conventions. Instead of remaining loyal to adult authority, individuals as they mature shift their loyalty to abstract principles (for example, self-reliance, independence, justice, and fairness). This process of detachment allows adolescents to assume a more equal status with adults. It's almost as if adolescents are saying, "You have your life, and I have mine; you don't intrude on mine, and I won't intrude on yours."

But, Gilligan argued, many adolescent females have a different primary concern. They care less about separation and independence and more about remaining loyal to others through expressions of caring, understanding, and sharing of experiences. Detachment for these female adolescents is a moral problem rather than a sought-after developmental milestone. The problem for them is how to become autonomous while also being caring and connected.

Given this view, Gilligan believes that adolescent females are more likely to resolve Erikson's crises of identity versus role confusion and intimacy versus isolation concurrently rather than consecutively. The results of at least one study (Ochse & Plug, 1986) supported this view. With respect to Kohlberg's theory, Gilligan argued that because females are socialized to value

more highly the qualities of understanding, helping, and cooperation with others than that of preserving individual rights, and because this latter orientation is reflected most strongly in Kohlberg's two conventional stages (stages 3 and 4), females are more likely to be judged to be at a lower level of moral development than males.

Stephen Thoma (1986) offered a partial answer to Gilligan's criticism. After reviewing more than 50 studies on gender differences in moral development, he drew three conclusions:

1. The effect of gender on scores from the Defining Issues Test (DIT, a device that uses responses to moral dilemmas to determine level of moral reasoning) was very small. Less than one-half of 1% of the difference in DIT scores was due to gender differences.

2. Females almost always scored higher on the DIT. This slight superiority for females appeared in every age group studied (middle school, high school, college, adults).

3. Differences in DIT scores were strongly associated with differences in age and level of education. That is, individuals who were older and had graduated from college were more likely to score at the postconventional level than those who were younger and had less education.

Thoma's findings suggest that females are just as likely as males to use justice and fairness concepts in their reasoning about *hypothetical* moral dilemmas.

But there is one aspect of Gilligan's criticism that cannot be answered by Thoma's analysis. She argued that when females are faced with their own real-life moral dilemmas (abortion, civil rights, environmental pollution) rather than hypothetical ones, they are more likely to favor an orientation of caring, helping, and cooperation than one of justice, fairness, and individual rights.

Noddings's Care Theory The caring orientation advocated by Gilligan in the 1980s arose from her criticism that Erikson's and Kohlberg's theories did not provide the best account of the psychosocial and moral development of female adolescents. In 1984, the educational philosopher Nel Noddings published an important book entitled *Caring: A Feminine Approach to Ethics and Moral Education*. The book has remained an important source of ideas in matters of moral education—so much so that a second edition, with a new preface by Noddings that explained how some of her thinking had changed since the 1980s, was published in 2003. Noddings was careful to point out that her ideas were not descriptive only of females, but rather were framed from a feminine rather than a masculine perspective. She wrote: "The view here is a feminine view. This does not imply that all women will accept it or that men reject it; indeed, there is no reason why men should not embrace it." (Noddings, 1984/2003, p. 2). (Noddings does consider herself a feminist, but she was not familiar with the term when she wrote the first edition in the early 1980s.)

Noddings provided a different lens through which to view moral development. Rather than using moral reasoning as a starting point, as Kohlberg did, she started with the idea that there is a human desire for goodness, which she called a moral attitude. From that starting point, she developed care theory. Through the last three decades, care theory has come to focus clearly on the relationships and how those relationships function. In Noddings's view, it is not enough to say that we care, to simply express a concern for someone or some group of people. Care theory focuses on the whether a caring relationship exists. Noddings used an example to illustrate the point: Teachers in a school may claim that they care deeply for students and support their claim by citing the long hours and hard work they spend in service of students and their well-being. But if students genuinely feel as though nobody cares, then a caring relationship does not exist, no matter how hard teachers work or how often they express their concern for students and their desire to help them. In this case, the problem may be neither the teachers nor the students, but the conditions that prevent caring relations to exist and grow. As Noddings said in her 2003 preface to the second edition: "Our efforts should be directed to transforming the conditions that make caring difficult or impossible" (p. xiv). Noddings's care theory supports Gilligan's criticisms of Erikson and Kohlberg. Taken

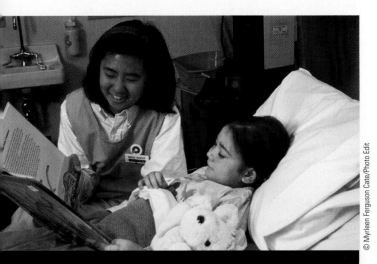

© Myrleen Ferguson Cate/Photo Edit

Carol Gilligan believes that Erikson's theory of identity development and Kohlberg's theory of moral development do not accurately describe the course of identity formation and moral reasoning in females. She argues that females are more likely to favor a caring-helping-cooperation orientation when dealing with real-life moral issues.

{ Although slight differences do exist, both males and females use caring and justice orientations to resolve real-life moral dilemmas. }

together, Noddings and Gilligan suggested that a "caring orientation" to social and moral development is an alternative to the orientation of justice, fairness, and individual rights that has emerged from Kohlberg's theory, and one that may lead to more socially just practices and policies (see Noddings, 2008).

Perhaps the best approach that educators can take when they involve students in discussions of moral issues is to emphasize the utility of *both* orientations. The recent research on gender differences supports the conclusion that females use both orientations to think about issues of right and wrong, and so do males. Emphasizing both orientations when classroom discussions focus on matters of right and wrong is one way of acknowledging student diversity. It also makes sense given a more recent review of many studies of gender differences in moral orientation. Jaffee, Hyde, and Shibley (2000) found that females as a group use a caring orientation to a slightly greater extent than a justice orientation. They found also that males as a group tend to use a justice orientation slightly more often than a caring orientation. The researchers found small differences between very large groups.

Does Moral Thinking Lead to Moral Behavior?

The Hartshorne and May Studies Over eight decades ago, researchers Hugh Hartshorne and Mark May conducted a series of studies in which they observed thousands of children at different age levels (1929, 1930a, 1930b).

Essentially, Hartshorne and May studied children in three ways. First, they observed how elementary-aged students responded in situations where a moral choice was made (e.g., students could be honest or dishonest in reporting their own performances). Second, they asked children to indicate right and wrong behaviors in hypothetical situations. Third, they compared children who received what in the 1920s and 1930s was called "moral instruction" with children who did not. The basic finding from the Hartshorne and May studies was that knowing the difference between right and wrong does not guarantee doing the right thing.

Recent research shows that Hartshorne and May's basic finding is still valid. Approximately 90% of high school students and 70% of college students admitted to engaging in academic cheating. At both grade levels, males cheated more often than females. Moreover, cheating was judged to be more or less acceptable depending on the reason. It was deemed more justifiable if it resulted in passing a class and getting a job that would help one's family. It was also seen as more justifiable if it was done because the student did not want to disappoint parents or receive academic probation, or because the instructor had treated the student unfairly (L. A. Jensen, Arnett, Feldman, & Cauffman, 2002). In another study on lying to parents, L. A. Jensen, Arnett, Feldman, and Cauffman (2004) found that both high school and college students lied to their parents across a range of real-life issues such as dating, parties, sex, and money. High school students tended to lie to parents more frequently than college students; the authors attributed the difference to factors related to the development of autonomy. They also found that students from cohesive, rather than controlling, family environments were less likely to report lying to parents and were less accepting of lying. As we will see in later chapters in the book, students' perceptions of their teachers can prove critical. In terms of cheating, students who perceive their teacher as less than effective facilitators of learning are more likely to cheat than students who view their instructors as effective teachers (Murdock, Miller, & Kohlhardt, 2004). Research has also shown that students are more likely to cheat when the culture of the classroom emphasizes good grades and high scores on tests (E. M. Anderman & Midgley, 2004; E. M. Anderman & Murdock, 2007.)

The insights from Piaget, Kohlberg, Gilligan, and Noddings are important for aspiring teachers. But as Hartshorne and May pointed out more than eight decades ago—and as researchers are still finding—there are gaps between moral reasoning and moral action or behavior. Mark Tappan (2006) has advocated a "sociocultural" approach to the study of moral development. You'll recall that Vygotsky's views on cognitive development helped to define the sociocultural approach. Tappan's approach takes into account the social culture of a classroom, such as the perceptions of students and an emphasis on grades and test scores, in attempting to connect reasoning and behavior in order to understand actions. Tappan's theoretical work may prove very helpful in judging the effectiveness of moral education programs aimed at improving students' ability not only to reason morally but to act in morally responsible ways.

Research on Character Education Programs Many parents, educators, and political leaders believe that today's students lack the moral values possessed by previous generations. Concerned adults cite violence in schools and widespread drug abuse, among other problems, as evidence of such a decline.

One commonly voiced solution to these problems is for the schools to institute moral education programs (also called character education programs). As this chapter's Case in Print demonstrates, these programs are attracting increasing attention. After reviewing the research on the effectiveness of character education programs, James Leming (1993) drew the following conclusions:

- Telling students what they should or should not do, through either slogans ("Just say no") or conduct codes, is unlikely to have significant or lasting effects on character.

- Helping students think about how to resolve moral dilemmas in higher-level ways does not automatically result in increases in morally acceptable behavior.

- Establishing an appropriate social environment plays an important role in the learning and exhibiting of virtuous behavior. When students have clear rules with which to guide their behavior, accept those rules as appropriate and worthwhile, and are rewarded for complying with those rules, they are more likely to exhibit morally acceptable behavior.

- Producing changes in moral behavior requires a commitment to a well-conceived, long-term program.

More recently, Leming (2008) advocated using a kind of engineering approach to design classroom environments that address what has been learned in effective character education programs. Many social critics recommend that, as part of character education programs or as an independent activity, children either read or have read to them stories with a moral theme (sometimes called virtue stories). Being exposed to such stories is supposed to help children develop a strong set of traditional moral values, such as honesty, trustworthiness, responsibility, and loyalty. Darcia Narvaez (2002) pointed out that such a claim, whether its advocates realize it, rests on five assumptions that are not supported by contemporary research findings on learning:

Assumption 1: Reading Is a Passive Activity The picture that emerges from thousands of research studies is that reading comprehension is not passive. Rather, it is the result of considerable cognitive activity. Children attempt to create a coherent, meaningful representation of a text by integrating the information in a text with prior knowledge.

Assumption 2: All Readers Extract the Same Information from a Text Because of individual differences in prior knowledge, interests, and reading skills, each reader constructs a somewhat unique representation of what a text is about. Furthermore, texts with

Teaching Students to be Good Characters

Many parents, educators, and political leaders believe that today's students lack the moral values possessed by previous generations. Concerned adults cite violence in schools and widespread drug abuse, among other problems, as evidence of such a decline. One commonly voiced solution to these problems is for the schools to institute moral education programs (also called character education programs). (p. 45)

Reading, Writing, and Character Education

CAROLYN BOWER

St. Louis Dispatch 11/28/03

A blue banner over the entrance to Ridgewood Middle School in Arnold reads "Character under construction."

Similar banners appear in the halls and gym. Once a week students take a half-hour to focus on a character education activity. Recently, Justin Schweiss, 12, and Conan Morrison, 14, dusted the lockers. A half dozen other seventh-graders gathered paper from classroom bins to recycle. Some students wrote messages about what they could do to promote peace.

"We don't have too many fights at this school," said Jacob Brydels, 14, an eighth-grade member of the Student Council. "We all get along."

Ridgewood, with about 530 students in grades seven and eight, is often singled out as an example of a school where character education works. Since focusing on character education a little more than three years ago, Ridgewood Principal Tim Crutchley has watched state test scores rise and discipline referrals drop by nearly 70 percent.

Hundreds of schools across the country use character education, defined as any initiative intended to develop student character. Missouri is one of 47 states that have received federal money for character education. Ridgewood is one of 111 school districts in Missouri and Illinois—and one of 38 in the St. Louis region—that take part in CHARACTERplus, a character education program.

Character education can improve academic achievement, behavior and attitudes, according to a study by Marvin Berkowitz and Melinda Bier, both at the University of Missouri at St. Louis. Berkowitz is the Sanford N. McDonnell Endowed Professor in Education at the university and Bier is an affiliate assistant professor.

The study was presented last month at a national forum of the Character Education Partnership, a nonpartisan coalition devoted to improving children's civic virtue and morals. The John Templeton Foundation financed the research.

Berkowitz found effective character education usually includes a number of strategies, requires staff training and needs parent and community involvement.

"We as a society have allowed an erosion of respect," Berkowitz said.

Students who act rudely to each other or cheat on tests reflect what has happened elsewhere in society with high profile scandals such as corporation executives cheating people of their money or celebrities cheating on their wives.

"In families we are not teaching or modeling how to treat other people with respect," Berkowitz said. "In schools we are not standing up to kids and saying, 'Look, this is the norm of civility in society.'"

At Jefferson Elementary School in Belleville, Principal Mark Eichenlaub began a push last year to involve parents and the community in character education.

Jefferson's 343 students in kindergarten through sixth grade have a reputation for strong academic achievement. But Eichenlaub wanted to make sure students, parents and those at the school were on the same page as far as intangible values.

The school adopted one rule for all students: "Be in the right place, at the right time, doing the right thing."

"There is no canned program," Eichenlaub said. "But creating a climate of character has to be the backbone of a school."

At Ridgewood, teachers study books such as Clifton Taulbert's "Eight Habits of the Heart," and talk about nurturing attitudes.

"The staff has to model good behavior, not just talk about it," said Kristen Pelster, assistant principal at Ridgewood. "Kids can't learn respect and responsibility by someone putting those words on paper on a wall. Character education is not a program. It is a way of life."

Source: Carolyn Bower, "Reading, writing, and character education," from *St. Louis Post-Dispatch*, November 28, 2003. Reprinted by permission of *St. Louis Post-Dispatch*.

Questions and Activities

1. Just on the basis of the information provided in the article, what factors might account for the success of the character education program at Ridgewood Middle School? What other factors might have played a role but not been mentioned?

2. Ridgewood Middle School has been identified as "a school where character education works" because state test scores increased and discipline referrals decreased. If you were responsible for designing and evaluating a character education program, would you be satisfied with these two outcomes as a basis for claiming that the program works? If not, what other outcomes would you want to measure? Why?

3. Professor Marvin Berkowitz, a character education researcher mentioned in the article, believes that there has been an erosion of respect in our society and that the cause is at least partly due to many parents' not teaching or modeling for their children how to treat other people with respect. Do you believe that people, including children, are unnecessarily rude toward and inconsiderate of others? If so, what other causes might there be besides parents who do a poor job of teaching their children?

4. Kristen Pelster, the assistant principal at Ridgewood Middle School, maintains that the teaching and administrative staff have to model good character and not just talk about it. How might you do that as a teacher?

Suggestions for Teaching

Encouraging Moral Development

1 Recognize that younger children respond to moral conflicts differently from older children.

2 Try to take the perspective of students, and stimulate their perspective-taking abilities.

3 Develop an awareness of moral issues by discussing a variety of real and hypothetical moral dilemmas and by using daily opportunities in the classroom to heighten moral awareness. (Moral education should be an integral part of the curriculum; it should not take place during a "moral education period.")

4 Create a classroom atmosphere that will enhance open discussion. For example, arrange face-to-face groupings, be an accepting model, foster listening and communication skills, and encourage student-to-student interaction.

Richard Hersh, Diana Paolitto, and Joseph Reimer (1979) offered the following specific suggestions for supervising classroom discussions:

- *Highlight the moral issue to be discussed.* Example: Describe a specific real or hypothetical moral dilemma.
- *Ask "why?" questions.* Example: After asking students what they would do if they were faced with the moral dilemma under discussion, ask them to explain why they would act that way.
- *Complicate the circumstances.* Example: After students have responded to the original dilemma, mention a factor that might complicate matters—for example, the involvement of a best friend in the dilemma.
- *Use personal and naturalistic examples.* Example: Invite students to put themselves in the position of individuals who are confronted by moral dilemmas described in newspapers or depicted on television.

---

unfamiliar ideas are likely to be recalled less well and have more distortions than texts with more familiar ideas.

Assumption 3: All Readers Understand the Author's Point

Once again, because of individual differences in prior knowledge, interests, and familiarity with the ideas presented in a text, some readers will "get" an author's point while others will construct something entirely different. (If you have ever argued with someone about the point of a movie or novel, you can appreciate this phenomenon.) Research on summarizing text passages shows that before the age of 10, children can accurately recount much of what they read but have great difficulty synthesizing that information to identify the author's main point.

Assumption 4: Moral Themes Are Readily Accessible to Readers

Because children have different conceptions (moral schemas, or prior moral knowledge) of how to get along with others and why such behavior is important, moral themes in a text are not necessarily accessible. As we noted earlier, people may base moral judgments on a variety of criteria, including personal interests (morally correct behavior is that which benefits me), norms (morally correct behavior is that which fosters law and order), and ideals (morally correct behavior is that which is consistent with higher-order principles). Older or more intellectually advanced children are more likely to grasp moral themes that reflect maintenance of norms and ideals than are younger or less advanced children. A recent study (Williams et al., 2002), although not done with morality stories, reinforced this point. Second and third graders who were trained to identify and comprehend story themes did better than noninstructed children, but they were unable to apply these themes to real-life situations or to identify and apply themes for which they received no instruction.

Assumption 5: Moral Themes Are Just Another Type of Information Conveyed by a Text

Because moral themes vary in their complexity and abstractness, and because children's comprehension of such themes develops through predictable stages, moral themes cannot be treated as the equivalent of fact-based information.

Despite the fact that character education programs have not received strong support in the research literature (probably because many programs are poorly designed or implemented), they are popular among parents and educators, and some appear to produce positive effects.

Whether or not your school has a character education program, there are certainly ways you can influence the moral development of your students. The Suggestions for Teaching above provide several ideas. But before you use any techniques of moral education in your classes, it is wise to check with your principal. In some communities, parents have insisted that they, not teachers, should take the responsibility for moral instruction.

WHAT ELSE? *RIP & REVIEW* **CARDS IN THE BACK**

3

AGE-LEVEL CHARACTERISTICS

LEARNING OBJECTIVES

After studying this chapter, you will be able to . . .

LO1 Describe one or more aspects of the physical, social, emotional, and cognitive development of preschool and kindergarten children.

LO2 Describe one or more aspects of the physical, social, emotional, and cognitive development of primary grade students.

LO3 Describe one or more aspects of the physical, social, emotional, and cognitive development of elementary grade students.

LO4 Describe one or more aspects of the physical, social, emotional, and cognitive development of middle school students.

LO5 Describe one or more aspects of the physical, social, emotional, and cognitive development of high school students.

visit **4ltrpress.cengage.com**

Having read and thought about the last chapter, you now have a basic understanding of children's psychosocial, cognitive, and moral development. To make this information even more useful, it needs to be supplemented by brief descriptions of how children think, feel, and behave at various age and grade levels.

To organize the points to be discussed, we have divided the developmental span into five levels, corresponding to common grade groupings in schools:

Preschool and kindergarten. Ages 3 through 5.

Primary grades. Grades 1 through 3; ages 6 through 8.

Elementary grades. Grades 4 and 5; ages 9 and 10.

Middle school. Grades 6 through 8; ages 11 through 13.

High school. Grades 9 through 12; ages 14 through 17.

Because the way grades are grouped varies, you may find yourself teaching in a school system in which the arrangement described in this chapter is not followed. In that case, simply refer to the appropriate age-level designations and, if necessary, concentrate on two levels rather than one.

At each of the five levels, behaviors are discussed under four headings: physical, social, emotional, and cognitive characteristics. Following each characteristic are implications for teachers. To help you establish a general conception of what children are like at each level, brief summaries of the types of behavior stressed by the theorists discussed in the preceding chapter are listed in a table in each section (Tables 3.1, 3.2, 3.3, 3.4, and 3.7).

LO1 Preschool and Kindergarten (3, 4, and 5 Years)

Physical Characteristics: Preschool and Kindergarten

1. *Preschool children are extremely active. They have good control of their bodies and enjoy activity for its own sake, but need rest periods.* Provide plenty of opportunities for children to run, climb, and jump. Arrange

these activities, as much as possible, so that they are under your control. If you follow a policy of complete freedom, you may discover that 30 improvising 3- to 5-year-olds can be a frightening thing. You might want to consider scheduling quiet activities after active ones, since preschoolers often don't recognize the need to slow down.

2. *Preschoolers' large muscles are more developed than those that control the fingers and hands. Therefore, preschoolers may be quite clumsy at, or physically incapable of, such skills as tying shoes and buttoning coats.* Avoid too many small-motor activities, such as pasting paper chains. Provide big brushes, crayons, and tools.

3. *The frontal lobes of the brain grow rapidly.* The frontal lobes govern such functions as planning, organizing, and focusing attention. As a result, most children of this age are capable of carrying out simple commands (such as putting away toys), focusing attention on the task at hand, and regulating their behavior (such as speaking softly instead of at the top of their voice) (Steinberg, Vandell, & Bornstein, 2011).

4. *Gender differences in physical development and motor skill proficiency are usually not noticeable until kindergarten and are fairly small in magnitude.* Differences that do manifest themselves are due in part to biological endowment and in part to differences in socialization (Berk, 2009). Consequently, you may want to encourage all children to participate in tasks that emphasize gross motor skills and tasks that emphasize fine motor skills.

Social Characteristics: Preschool and Kindergarten

1. *Most preschool and kindergarten children have one or more stable friendships.* How do you know if two children are friends?

© dpaint/Shutterstock Images

© Golden Pixels LLC/Alamy

TABLE 3.1 Applying Theories of Development to the Preschool and Kindergarten Years

Psychosocial development: Initiative vs. guilt. Children need opportunities for free play and experimentation, as well as experiences that give them a sense of accomplishment.

Cognitive development: Preoperational thought. Children gradually acquire the ability to conserve and decenter but are not capable of operational thinking and are unable to mentally reverse operations.

Moral development: Morality of constraint, preconventional level. Rules are viewed as unchangeable edicts handed down by those in authority. Punishment-obedience orientation focuses on physical consequences rather than on intentions.

General factors to keep in mind: Children are having their first experiences with school routine and interactions with more than a few peers, and are preparing for initial academic experiences in group settings. They need to learn to follow directions and get along with others.

The most direct method is to ask them whom they consider to be their friend. In addition, you can watch whom they talk to and play with the most. Kindergarten children who have a friend in class make a better adjustment to school than those who are social isolates (Steinberg, Vandell, & Bornstein, 2011), so it may be worth your while to try to foster friendships for students who appear to be unsuccessful at doing this on their own.

2. *Play activities are an important part of young children's development and should be encouraged.* Many adults believe that young children's play activities (meaning they are voluntary and self-organized) are relatively unimportant and so should be either ignored or deemphasized by educators. Nothing

© Petr Bonek/Alamy

Young children engage in a variety of types of play that have several developmental benefits.

Free play provides multiple benefits to young children.

could be more wrong. Research clearly shows that children of all ages profit socially, emotionally, and cognitively from engaging in play (Bergen & Fromberg, 2009).

The forms and types of play that young children exhibit are quite varied. Children may, for example, play by themselves with toys that are different from those being used by nearby children, play alongside but not with other children who are playing with the same toys, or play cooperatively with other children in an organized form of play. Common types of play include pretend play (mimicking the behavior of parents, siblings, and peers), exercise play (running, climbing, jumping, and other large-muscle activities), and rough-and-tumble play (mostly wrestling types of activities, as well as pretend fighting) (Bukatko, 2008; P. K. Smith, 2005).

3. *Preschool and kindergarten children show definite preferences for gender of play peers and for pair versus group play.* A 3-year study (Fabes, Martin, & Hanish, 2003) of more than 200 preschool children (average age 4.25 years) found the following play preferences:

- Same-sex play occurred more often than mixed-sex play.
- Girls were more likely than boys to play in pairs rather than groups, and boys were more likely than girls to play in groups rather than pairs. When girls did play in groups, they were more likely than boys to play in a group in which they were not the only member of their sex.
- When boys played with each other, whether in pairs or groups, they were more likely than girls who played with each other to engage in active-forceful play (no surprise here). This tendency was less apparent when a boy played in a group that was otherwise made up of all girls. But when a girl played in a group whose other members were boys, her level of active-forceful play tended to increase.

4. *Awareness of gender roles and gender typing is evident.* Late preschool and kindergarten children are very much aware that girls and boys dress and act differently from one another. This awareness of **gender roles** shows up very clearly in the toys

Gender differences in toy preferences and play activities are noticeable by kindergarten.

and activities that boys and girls prefer. Boys are more likely than girls to play outdoors, to engage in rough-and-tumble play, and to behave aggressively. Boys play with toy vehicles and construction toys, and they engage in action games (such as football). Girls prefer art activities, doll play, and dancing (D. B. Carter, 1987). By age 6, some children associate job titles that are considered to be gender neutral, such as doctor, librarian, and flight attendant, with either males (in the case of doctors) or females (in the case of librarians and waiters) (Liben, Bigler, & Krogh, 2002).

Emotional Characteristics: Preschool and Kindergarten

1. *Kindergarten children are aware of and can, to some extent, regulate their emotions.* In addition to being able to describe their own emotional states, 5-year-olds can tell when their peers are happy, sad, angry, surprised, or afraid. When they become angry at the behavior of a classmate, many kindergartners can suppress an impulse to hit or shove the other child. When they are faced with a situation or activity they are anxious about, they can nonetheless force themselves to act. The oldest grandchild of the senior author of this textbook, for example, was clearly anxious about getting on the school bus for his first day of kindergarten, but gamely got on anyway (and had such a wonderful time, he looked forward to going back the next day).

   Classroom teachers can contribute to a child's emotional development by explaining why we (meaning the child, classmates, the teacher) feel the way we do about various events or circumstances and how we should respond to those emotions. But because these children are likely to be in Piaget's preoperational stage of intellectual development, don't expect this approach to be successful the first time or every time. The egocentric orientation of 4- to 5-year-olds makes it difficult for them to reflect on the thoughts of themselves or others.

2. *Jealousy among classmates is likely to be fairly common, as kindergarten children have much affection for the teacher and actively seek approval. When there are 30 individuals competing for the affection and attention of just one teacher, some*

jealousy is inevitable. Try to spread your attention around as equitably as possible, and when you praise particular children, do it in a private or casual way. If one child is given lavish public recognition, it is only natural for the other children to feel resentful. Think back to how you felt about teachers' pets during your own school years.

Cognitive Characteristics: Preschool and Kindergarten

1. *By age 4, many children begin to develop a theory of mind.* Children's **theory of mind** concerns the ability of children around the age of 4 to be aware of the difference between thinking about something and experiencing that same thing; they also begin to understand that it is sometimes possible to predict the thoughts of others. These capacities are critical to understanding such aspects of social life as surprises, secrets, tricks, mistakes, and lies.

   By 3 years of age, most children realize the difference between thinking about something and actually experiencing that same something. But a significant change occurs around age 4, when children begin to realize that not everyone thinks the same things. If, for example, you put pencils in a box that was normally filled with candy, a 4-year-old would know that other children who were unaware of the switch would expect to see candy upon opening the box. Three-year-olds, on the other hand, would say that a peer would expect to see pencils because that's what they now saw (Astington, 1998).

gender roles Sets of behaviors typically identified with either males or females in a society; young children's awareness of these roles show up clearly in the different toys and activities that boys and girls prefer.

theory of mind The ability, typically developed by children around the age of 4, to be aware of the difference between thinking about something and experiencing that same thing and to predict the thoughts of others.

> **By age 4, children have a theory of mind: They are aware of their own mental processes and the possibility that others may think differently.**

Talking about different viewpoints will help children understand that people have beliefs about the world, that different people believe different things, and that beliefs may change when new information is acquired. Janet Astington (1998) offered the following example of how teachers can foster the development of children's theory of mind:

© carla francesca castagno/iStockphoto

In a 1st-grade classroom that I recently observed, the teacher often talked about her own thought processes, saying, for example, "I just learned something new" when she found out that one student had a pet rabbit at home. When she was surprised or made a mistake, she talked about her own wrong beliefs, and at story-time, she had the children talk about the motivations and beliefs of story characters. Her style of talk helped the class focus not just on the thought content, but also on the thinking process—yet the term theory of mind *was unknown to this teacher. (p. 48)*

2. *Kindergartners are quite skillful with language. Most of them like to talk, especially in front of a group.* Providing a sharing time gives children a natural opportunity for talking, but many will need help in becoming good listeners. Some sort of rotation scheme is usually necessary to divide talking opportunities between the gabby and the silent extremes. You might provide activities or experiences for less confident children to talk about, such as a field trip, a book, or a DVD. Make sure you know beforehand what each child intends to talk about, so that family secrets and other embarrassing topics are not given a public airing. Gently explain that there are some things that are only talked about at home.

3. *Many preschool and kindergarten children do not accurately assess their competence for particular tasks.* Preschool and kindergarten children typically think of themselves as being much more competent than they actually are, even when their performance lags behind that of their peers.

   Nevertheless, research suggests that under the right conditions, even some 4-year-olds can draw accurate conclusions about how well or poorly they have completed a task. In one study, children ages 4 and 5 were asked to do a simple maze-type task (tracing a winding path between an illustrated child and house) under one of two conditions: either in the presence of another child's work or in comparison with their own earlier attempt at the same task. About 40% of those who had another child's work available were able to use that to accurately assess their own performance. Most of the rest of this group could gauge their own performance by using the goal as a basis for comparison ("I only got halfway to the house") (Butler, 2005).

4. *Competence is encouraged by interaction, interest, opportunities, urging, limits, admiration, and signs of affection.* Studies of young children rated as highly competent (Burchinal, Peisner-Feinberg, Pianta, & Howes, 2002; Clawson & Robila, 2001; Schweinhart, Weikart, & Hohmann, 2002) show that to encourage preschoolers to make the most of their abilities, adults should

   - Interact with the child often and in a variety of ways.
   - Show interest in what the child does and says.
   - Provide opportunities for the child to investigate and experience many things.
   - Permit and encourage the child to do many things.
   - Urge the child to try to achieve mature and skilled types of behavior.
   - Establish firm and consistent limits regarding unacceptable forms of behavior, explain the reasons for these as soon as the child is able to understand, listen to complaints if the child feels the restrictions are too confining, and give additional reasons if the limits are still to be maintained as originally stated.
   - Show that the child's achievements are admired and appreciated.
   - Communicate love in a warm and sincere way.

{ **Four- and five-year-olds typically overestimate their capabilities.** }

Pause & Reflect *Given the characteristics of preschool and kindergarten children, what classroom atmosphere and instructional tactics would you use to foster learning and enjoyment of school?*

Chapter 3: Age-Level Characteristics

LO2 Primary Grades (Grades 1, 2, and 3; 6, 7, and 8 Years)

Physical Characteristics: Primary Grades

1. *Primary grade children are still extremely active. Because they are frequently required to participate in sedentary pursuits, energy is often released in the form of nervous habits—for example, pencil chewing, fingernail biting, and general fidgeting.* To minimize fidgeting, avoid situations in which your students must stay glued to their seats for long periods. Have frequent breaks, and try to work activity (such as bringing papers to your desk) into the lessons themselves. When children use computer software that contains sound effects, distribute headphones to ensure that they concentrate on their own work and to minimize distractions between students.

   One of the effects of the current emphasis on preparing students to meet state learning standards is the reduction or elimination of recess time, even for kindergarten and primary grade students. One survey, for example, found that 30% of kindergarten classrooms did not have a recess period (Pellegrini & Bohn, 2005). Are educators acting wisely in seeking to reduce the number and length of breaks young children receive to focus more intensively on teaching academic skills? Absolutely not! Research (Barros, Silver, & Stein, 2009; Pellegrini, 2009; Tomporowski, Davis, Miller, & Naglieri, 2008) clearly shows that children benefit cognitively from the physical activity and peer interactions that occur during recess breaks.

2. *Children still need rest periods; they become fatigued easily as a result of physical and mental exertion.* Schedule quiet activities after strenuous ones (story time after recess, for example) and relaxing activities after periods of mental concentration (art after spelling or math).

3. *Large-muscle control is still superior to fine coordination. Many children, especially boys, have difficulty manipulating a pencil.* Try not to schedule too much writing at one time. If drill periods are too long, skill may deteriorate and children may develop a negative attitude toward writing or toward school in general.

4. *Children tend to be extreme in their physical activities. They have excellent control of their bodies and develop considerable confidence in their skills. As a result, they often underestimate the danger involved in their more daring activities. The accident rate is at a peak in the third grade.* Try to prevent reckless play. During recess, for example, remind students not to stand on the seat as they swing back and forth and not to jump from the top of the monkey bars.

TABLE 3.2 Applying Theories of Development to the Primary Grade Years

Psychosocial development: Industry vs. inferiority. Students need to experience a sense of industry through successful completion of tasks. Failures should be minimized and corrected to prevent development of feelings of inferiority.

Cognitive development: Transition from preoperational to concrete operational thought. Students gradually acquire the ability to solve problems by generalizing from concrete experiences.

Moral development: Morality of constraint, preconventional level. Rules are viewed as edicts handed down by those in authority. Focus is on physical consequences, meaning that obeying rules should bring benefit in return.

General factors to keep in mind: Students are having their first experiences with school learning, are eager to learn how to read and write, and are likely to be upset by lack of progress. Initial attitudes toward schooling are being established. Initial roles in a group are being formed, roles that may establish a lasting pattern (for example, leader, follower, loner, athlete, or underachiever).

Social Characteristics: Primary Grades

The characteristics noted here are typical of both primary and elementary grade students, and underlie the elementary-level characteristics described in the next section.

1. *Children become somewhat more selective in their choice of friends and are likely to have a more or less permanent best friend.* Friendships are typically of the same sex, and are marked by mutual understanding, loyalty, cooperation, and sharing. Competition between friends should be discouraged because it can become intense and increase their dissatisfaction with each other. Although friends disagree with each other more often than with nonfriends, their conflicts are shorter, less heated, and less likely to lead to a dissolving of the relationship (Hartup, 1989; H. S. Ross & Spielmacher, 2005).

2. *Primary grade children often like organized games in small groups, but they may be overly concerned with rules or get carried away by team spirit.* Keep in mind that, according to Piaget, children at this age practice the morality of constraint: They find it difficult to understand how and why rules should be adjusted to special situations. When you divide a class into teams, you may be amazed at how intense the competition becomes. One way to reduce the rivalry is to rotate team membership frequently and promote games that require

Recess provides cognitive benefits for primary grade children.

more cooperation. *Cooperative Learning: Theory, Research, and Practice* (2nd ed., 1995), by Robert Slavin, describes several team learning games that emphasize cooperation.

3. *Quarrels are still frequent. Words are used more often than physical aggression, but many boys (in particular) may indulge in punching, wrestling, and shoving.* Occasional fights are to be expected at this age. If you can, give children a chance to work out their own solutions to disagreements; social conflict is effective in spurring cognitive growth (Howe, Rinaldi, Jennings, & Petrakos, 2002; B. C. Murphy & Eisenberg, 2002; Tudge & Rogoff, 1989). But there will be times when you have to intervene. If certain children, especially the same pair, seem to be involved in one long battle, you should probably try to negotiate a truce. And if a student is constantly the target of bullying (insults, threats, physical aggression, and exclusion from the peer group), you have to bring that to an immediate halt. Research has shown that third and fourth graders who were frequently victimized by classmates had lower scores on standardized achievement tests, lower grades, and higher levels of depression than their nonvictimized peers both at the time the incidents occurred and a year later (Schwartz, Gorman, Nakamoto, & Toblin, 2005).

Geoffrey Biddle/Time Life Pictures/Getty Images

Most primary grade students eagerly strive to obtain "helping" jobs around the classroom. Accordingly, you may wish to arrange a rotating schedule for such jobs.

Emotional Characteristics: Primary Grades

1. *Students are sensitive to criticism and ridicule and may have difficulty adjusting to failure.* Young children need frequent praise and recognition. Because they tend to admire or even worship their teachers, they may be crushed by criticism. Provide positive reinforcement as frequently as possible, and reserve your negative reactions for nonacademic misbehavior. Scrupulously avoid sarcasm and ridicule. Remember that this is the stage of industry versus inferiority; if you make a child feel inferior, you may make the development of a sense of industry more difficult.

2. *Most primary grade children are eager to please the teacher.* Children like to help, enjoy responsibility, and want to do well in their schoolwork. The time-honored technique for satisfying the urge to help is to assign jobs (pencil sharpener, wastebasket emptier, paper distributor, and the like) on a rotating basis.

3. *Children are becoming sensitive to the feelings of others.* Unfortunately, sensitivity permits children to hurt others deeply by attacking a sensitive spot without realizing how much damage is being done. It is not uncommon, for example, for one child to tease another about some characteristic like his or her appearance or a speech impediment. And when this happens, others sometimes join in. To reduce this type of behavior, you might explain to those doing the teasing how much it hurts the feelings of the target child and ask them to imagine how they would feel if the tables were turned.

Cognitive Characteristics: Primary Grades

1. *Children understand that there are different ways to know things and that some ways are better than others.* When an observation can be explained with either a possible (that is, a theoretical) explanation or an evidence-based explanation, preschoolers fail to see one as more compelling than the other, but primary grade children usually prefer the explanation based on evidence. This is the beginning of scientific thinking. When asked to identify from a

To encourage industry, use praise and avoid criticism.

picture which of two individuals had won a race, preschoolers tended to pick the one with the fancier running shoe and to claim that as the reason that runner won the race. Primary grade children, on the other hand, were more likely to choose the runner who was smiling and holding a trophy (Kuhn, 1999, 2002).

2. *Primary grade children begin to understand that learning and recall are caused by particular cognitive processes that they can control.* Not until children are about 7 or 8 years of age do they begin to realize that learning and memory stem from cognitive processes that are under their conscious control. When learning words, for example, younger children may need to be prompted or directed to group the words by category because they do not realize that such a technique aids recall. Likewise, they may not recognize their lack of comprehension when they read difficult or unfamiliar material and may need to be prompted to think about how well they are understanding what they read. By the primary grades, this awareness and monitoring of one's learning processes, called *metacognition*, begins to emerge (W. Schneider, 2002). We will return to the subject in Chapter 8.

3. *Talking aloud to oneself reaches a peak between the ages of 6 and 7 and then rapidly declines.* Don't be surprised or concerned if you observe students talking to themselves, either when they are by themselves or when they are with classmates. This is a well-documented phenomenon that Vygotsky (1962) called private speech. Vygotsky described private speech as a transition between speaking with others and thinking to oneself. Private speech is first noticeable around age 3 and may constitute anywhere from 20% to 60% of a child's utterances between the ages of 6 and 7. By age 8, however, it all but disappears and is replaced by silent, or inner, speech (Berk, 2009; Bukatko, 2008; Feigenbaum, 2002). One important purpose of private speech, which may consist of single words or phrases, is to help children clarify their thinking and solve difficult problems, such as those that arise in the course of doing math problems or reading unfamiliar material.

> { **Awareness of cognitive processes begins to emerge.** }

For example, a child may count on her fingers out loud while working on a math problem and then say, "The answer's 10."

LO3 Elementary School (Grades 4 and 5; 9 and 10 Years)

Physical Characteristics: Elementary Grades

1. *Both boys and girls become leaner and stronger.* In general, there is a decrease in the growth of fatty tissue and an increase in bone and muscle development. In a year's time, the average child of this age will grow about 2 to 3 inches and gain about 5 to 7 pounds. As a result, the typical child will tend to have a lean and gangly look. Although the average 9-year-old boy is slightly taller and heavier than the average 9-year-old girl, this difference all but disappears a year later. And from age 11 until about 14 and a half, girls are slightly heavier and taller than boys. Because secondary sex characteristics have not yet appeared, boys and girls can be mistaken for one another. This is particularly likely to happen when girls have close-cropped hair, boys have very long hair, and both genders wear gender-neutral clothing (Berk, 2009; Bukatko 2008; Hetherington & Parke, 1993).

2. *Obesity can become a problem for some children of this age group.* Because 9- and 10-year-olds have more control over their eating habits than younger children do, there is a greater tendency for them to overeat, particularly junk food. When this eating pattern is coupled with a relatively low level of physical activity (mainly because of watching television,

TABLE 3.3 Applying Theories of Development to the Elementary Grade Years

Psychosocial development: Industry vs. inferiority. Students should be kept constructively busy; comparisons between better and worse learners should be played down.

Cognitive development: Concrete operational thought. Except for the most intellectually advanced students, most will need to generalize from concrete experiences.

Moral development: Morality of constraint; transition from preconventional level to conventional level. A shift to viewing rules as mutual agreements is occurring, but "official" rules are obeyed out of respect for authority or out of a desire to impress others.

General factors to keep in mind: Initial enthusiasm for learning may fade as the novelty wears off and as the process of perfecting skills becomes more difficult. Differences in knowledge and skills of fastest and slowest learners become more noticeable. "Automatic" respect for teachers tends to diminish. Peer group influences become strong.

© Yuri Arcurs/Shutterstock Images

> ### Boys are slightly better at sports-related motor skills; girls are better at flexibility, balance, and rhythmic motor skills.

using the computer, and playing video games) and a genetic predisposition toward obesity, children become mildly to severely overweight. Between 1976 and 1980, 6.5% of children from 6 to 11 years of age were judged to be overweight. By 2004 that percentage increased more than one and one half times, to 17.5%. Not only do overweight children put themselves at risk for cardiovascular problems and type 2 diabetes later in life, but they also become targets for ridicule and ostracism from peers in the present (Eberstadt, 2003; Kelly & Moag-Stahlberg, 2002; National Center for Health Statistics, 2007).

3. *Although small in magnitude, gender differences in motor skill performance are apparent.* Boys tend to outperform girls on tasks that involve kicking, throwing, catching, running, broad jumping, and batting. Girls surpass boys on tasks that require muscular flexibility, balance, and rhythmic movements. These differences may be due in part to gender-role stereotyping; that is, because of socialization differences, girls are more likely to play hopscotch and jump rope, whereas boys are more likely to play baseball and basketball (Berk, 2009).

Both boys and girls attain mastery over large and small muscles; one benefit of this is a relatively orderly classroom. Fourth and fifth graders can sit quietly for extended periods and concentrate on whatever intellectual task is at hand (Hetherington & Parke, 1993). Another benefit is that children enjoy arts and crafts and musical activities.

Social Characteristics: Elementary Grades

1. *The peer group becomes powerful and begins to replace adults as the major source of behavior standards and recognition of achievement.* During the

avid Grossman/Photo Researchers Inc.

Junebug Clark/Photo Researchers Inc.

Elementary grade boys tend to be better than girls on motor skill tasks that involve large-muscle movement, whereas elementary grade girls tend to perform better than boys on motor skill tasks that involve muscular flexibility, balance, and rhythmic movements.

Chapter 3: Age-Level Characteristics

Peer group norms
for behavior begin to
replace adult norms.

early school years, parents and teachers set standards of conduct, and most children try to live up to them. But by grades 4 and 5, children are more interested in getting along with one another without adult supervision. Consequently, children come to realize that the rules for behavior within the peer group are not quite the same as the rules for behavior within the family or the classroom. Because children of this age are increasingly concerned with being accepted by their peer group and do not have enough self-assurance to oppose group norms, there is a noticeable increase, among both boys and girls, in gossip about others (Ross & Spielmacher, 2005).

2. *Friendships become more selective and gender based.* Elementary grade children become even more discriminating than primary grade children in the selection of friends and playmates. Most children choose a best friend, usually of the same gender. These relationships, based usually on common ideas, outlooks, and impressions of the world, may last through adolescence. Although children of this age will rarely refuse to interact with members of the opposite sex when directed to do so by parents and teachers, they will avoid the opposite sex when left to their own devices (Ross & Spielmacher, 2005).

3. *Play continues to make numerous contributions to children's development.* In describing some of the characteristics of preschool and kindergarten children earlier in the chapter, we noted the importance of play activities to several areas of development. Play is no less important at this age level. The benefits that elementary grade children reap when allowed to play their own games include refining the skills of self-direction and self-control, learning how to join the play activities of others, and developing such cognitive skills as planning and using symbols (Bergen & Fromberg, 2009).

Emotional Characteristics: Elementary Grades

1. *During this period, children develop a more global, integrated, and complex self-image.* There are several important facts to keep in mind about the formulation of a child's self-image. First, in elementary grade children self-image is more generalized or integrated than is the case for primary grade

children because it is based on information gained over time, tasks, and settings. A child may think of herself as socially adept not just because she is popular at school but because she has always been well liked and gets along well with adults, as well as peers, in a variety of situations. It is this generalized quality that helps make self-portraits relatively stable.

Second, comparison with others is the fundamental basis of a self-image during the elementary grades. This orientation is due in part to the fact that children are not as egocentric as they were a few years earlier and are developing the capability to think in terms of multiple categories. Also, because competition and individualism are highly prized values in many Western cultures, children will naturally compare themselves with one another ("I'm taller than my friend") and with broad-based norms ("I'm tall for my age") in an effort to determine who they are.

Third, in the elementary grades the self is described for the first time in terms of emotions (pride, shame, worry, anger, happiness) and how well they can be controlled.

Fourth, a child's sense of self is influenced by the information and attitudes that are communicated by such significant others as parents, teachers, and friends, and by how competent the child feels in areas in which success is important.

Pause & Reflect *The primary and elementary years correspond to Erikson's stage of industry versus inferiority. The implication is that educators should encourage a sense of industry and competence in each student. On a scale of 1 to 10, how well do you think schools accomplish this goal? What major factors account for your rating?*

2. *Disruptive family relationships, social rejection, and school failure may lead to delinquent behavior.* Gerald Patterson, Barbara DeBaryshe, and Elizabeth Ramsey (1989) marshaled a wide array of evidence to support their belief that delinquent behavior is the result of a causal chain of events that originates

Self-image becomes more generalized and stable; it is based primarily on comparisons with peers.

{ Delinquents have few friends, are easily distracted, are not interested in schoolwork, and lack basic skills. }

with dysfunctional parent–child relationships. In their view, poor parent–child relationships lead to behavior problems, which lead to peer rejection and academic failure, which lead to identification with a deviant peer group, which results in delinquent behavior. Parents of such children administer harsh and inconsistent punishment, provide little positive reinforcement, and do little monitoring and supervising of each child's activities. Because these children have not learned to follow adult rules and regulations but have learned how to satisfy their needs through coercive behavior, they are rejected by their peers, are easily distracted when doing schoolwork, show little interest in the subjects they study, and do not master many of the basic academic skills necessary for subsequent achievement.

Cognitive Characteristics: Elementary Grades

1. *The elementary grade child can think logically, although such thinking is constrained and inconsistent.* In terms of Piaget's stages, upper elementary grade children are concrete operational stage think-

ers. Most will have attained enough mastery of logical schemes that they can understand and solve tasks that involve such processes as class inclusion (understanding the superordinate–subordinate relationships that make up hierarchies), seriation, conservation, and symbolic representation (reading maps, for example), provided that the content of the task refers to real, tangible ideas that the child either has experienced or can imagine. But general and abstract ideas often escape the elementary age child. For example, sarcasm, metaphor, and allegory are usually lost on concrete stage thinkers.

2. *On tasks that call for simple memory skills, elementary grade children often perform about as well as adolescents or adults. But on tasks that require more complex memory skills, their performance is more limited.* When tasks call for recognizing previously learned information, such as vocabulary words or facts about a person or event, or for rehearsing several items for immediate use, elementary grade children can perform about as well as older students. But the same is not true for tasks that require such advanced memory processes as elaboration and organization. When asked to sort a set of pictures into categories, for example, elementary grade children created fewer and more idiosyncratic categories (which are generally less effective for later recall of the items in the category) than did older children or adults (Kail, 2010). Also bear in mind that elementary grade children need constant practice on a variety of tasks before they use such memory processes consistently and efficiently (W. Schneider, 2002).

LO4 Middle School (Grades 6, 7, and 8; 11, 12, and 13 Years)

In this section, we use the term *adolescent* for the first time in this chapter. Although it may strike you as odd to think of 11- and 12-year-olds as adolescents, developmental psychologists typically apply this term to individuals as young as 10. The reason they do is because adolescence involves a series of transitions (biological, social, emotional, and cognitive, for example) to a more mature life stage, some of which may begin in some

© 2010 Fancy/Jupiter Images Corporation

Although elementary grade children understand the logical basis for tasks such as classification, seriation, and conservation, they can solve such tasks only if those tasks are based on concrete objects and ideas.

Elementary grade students reason logically but concretely.

{Girls' growth spurt occurs earlier, so they look older than boys of the same age.}

individuals as early as 10 years of age (Steinberg, 2008). Although a variety of terms are used to denote the initial period of change that marks the adolescent years (ages 10 to 14), we use two of the more popular: *early adolescence* and *emerging adolescence*.

Physical Characteristics: Middle School

1. *Physical growth tends to be both rapid and uneven.* During the middle school years, the average child will grow 2 to 4 inches per year and gain 8 to 10 pounds per year. But some parts of the body, particularly the hands and feet, grow faster than others. Consequently, middle school children tend to look gangly and clumsy. Because girls mature more rapidly than boys, their **growth spurt** begins at about age 11, reaches a peak at about age 12, and is generally complete by age 15. The growth spurt for boys begins on average at about age 13, peaks at about age 14, and is generally complete by age 17. The result of this timing difference in the growth spurt is that many middle school girls look considerably older than boys of the same age. After the growth spurt, however, the muscles in the average boy's body are larger, as are the heart and lungs (Kail & Kavanaugh, 2010).

   Research on early and later maturation shows that differences in physical maturation are likely to produce specific differences in later behavior (see Table 3.5 on the next page). Because of their more adult appearance, **early-maturing boys** are likely to be more popular with peers, have more positive self-concepts, and have more friends among older peers. But friendships with older adolescents put early-maturing boys at greater risk for delinquency, drug and alcohol abuse, truancy, and increased sexual activity. In addition, recent studies suggested that early-maturing boys may be more susceptible to depression. As adults, early maturers were more likely to be responsible, cooperative, self-controlled,

conforming, and conventional. **Late-maturing boys**, by contrast, are likely to have relatively lower self-esteem and stronger feelings of inadequacy. Like their early-maturing counterparts, they may also be more susceptible to depression than their on-time peers. But later in adolescence, they showed higher levels of intellectual curiosity, exploratory behavior, and social initiative. As adults, late-maturing boys were more impulsive, assertive, insightful, and inventive (DeRose & Brooks-Gunn, 2009; Steinberg, 2008; Steinberg, Vandell, & Bornstein, 2011).

   Because **early-maturing girls** are taller and heavier than their peers and don't have a thin and "leggy" fashion-model look, they are likely to have lower self-esteem and are more likely to suffer from depression, anxiety, eating disorders, and panic attacks. They are more likely to be popular with boys, particularly older boys, and experience more pressure to date and become sexually active than their more normally developing peers. **Late-maturing girls**, whose growth spurt is less abrupt and whose size and appearance more closely reflect the feminine stereotype mentioned, share many of the characteristics (positive self-concept, popularity) of early-maturing boys.

> **Early-maturing boys are likely to draw favorable responses. Late-maturing boys may feel inadequate.**

growth spurt The rapid and uneven physical growth that besets adolescents during the middle school years.

early-maturing boys Boys whose early physical maturation typically draws favorable adult responses and promotes confidence and poise, thus contributing to leadership and popularity with peers.

late-maturing boys Boys whose delayed physical maturation typically causes inferiority feelings and leads to bossy and attention-getting behavior.

early-maturing girls Girls whose early physical maturation typically makes them socially out of step with their peers.

late-maturing girls Girls whose delayed physical maturation typically makes them more poised than others their age and elicits praise from elders, thus conferring leadership tendencies.

TABLE 3.4 Applying Theories of Development to the Middle School Years

Psychosocial development: Transition from industry vs. inferiority to identity vs. role confusion. Growing independence leads to initial thoughts about identity. There is greater concern about appearance and gender roles than about occupational choice.

Cognitive development: Beginning of formal operational thought for some. There is increasing ability to engage in mental manipulations and test hypotheses.

Moral development: Transition to morality of cooperation, conventional level. There is increasing willingness to think of rules as flexible mutual agreements, yet "official" rules are still likely to be obeyed out of respect for authority or out of a desire to impress others.

General factors to keep in mind: A growth spurt and puberty influence many aspects of behavior. An abrupt switch occurs (for sixth graders) from being the oldest, biggest, most sophisticated students in elementary school to being the youngest, smallest, least knowledgeable students in middle school. Acceptance by peers is extremely important. Students who do poor schoolwork begin to feel bitter, resentful, and restless. Awareness grows of a need to make personal value decisions regarding dress, premarital sex, and code of ethics.

interpersonal reasoning The ability to understand the relationship between motives and behavior among a group of people.

Late-maturing girls are more likely to be seen by peers as attractive, sociable, and expressive.

If late-maturing boys in your classes appear driven to seek attention or inclined to brood about their immaturity, you might try to give them extra opportunities to gain status and self-confidence by succeeding in schoolwork or other nonathletic activities. If you notice that early-maturing girls seem insecure, you might try to bolster their self-esteem by giving them extra attention and by recognizing their achievements.

2. *Pubertal development is evident in practically all girls and in many boys.* From ages 11 through 13, most girls develop sparse pubic and underarm hair and exhibit breast enlargement. In boys, the testes and scrotum begin to grow, and lightly pigmented pubic hair appears (McDevitt & Ormrod, 2010).

3. *Concern and curiosity about sex are almost universal, especially among girls.* For girls in the United States puberty can begin as early as age 7 or as late as age 13. For boys, the onset of puberty can be as early as age 9 or as late as age 13 and a half (Steinberg, Vandell, & Bornstein, 2011). Because sexual maturation involves drastic biological and psychological adjustments, children are concerned and curious. It seems obvious that accurate, unemotional answers to questions about sex

Average age of puberty: girls, 11; boys, 14

are desirable. However, for your own protection, you should follow the sex education policy at your school.

Social Characteristics: Middle School

1. *The development of interpersonal reasoning leads to greater understanding of the feelings of others.* As children become more cognitively sophisticated, they also become increasingly capable of understanding the complex nature of social relationships. This capability, which is called **interpersonal reasoning**, develops through a series of five stages and is based on the research of Robert L. Selman (1980). As you can see from Table 3.6, children gradually grasp the fact that a person's overt actions or words do not always reflect inner feelings, and that two people can have different interpretations of the meaning of a particular social interaction.

2. *The desire to conform reaches a peak during the middle school years.* Early adolescents find it reassuring to dress and behave like others, and they are likely to alter their own opinions to coincide with those of a group. When you encourage student participation in class discussions, you may need to be alert to the tendency for students at these grade levels to be reluctant to voice minority opinions. If you want them to think about controversial issues, it may be preferable to invite them to write their opinions anonymously rather than voice them in front of the class.

Early-maturing girls may suffer low self-esteem. Late-maturing girls are likely to be popular and carefree.

TABLE 3.5 The Impact of Early and Late Maturation

Maturational Stage	Characteristics as Adolescents	Characteristics as Adults
Early-maturing boys	Self-confident, high in self-esteem, likely to be chosen as leaders (but leadership tendencies more likely in low-SES boys than in middle-class boys), more likely to socialize with older peers and engage in substance abuse and delinquent behavior	Self-confident, responsible, cooperative, sociable; but also more rigid, moralistic, humorless, and conforming
Late-maturing boys	Energetic, bouncy, given to attention-getting behavior, having poor body image, low in self-esteem, aspiring lower for educational achievement, not popular	Impulsive and assertive; but also insightful, perceptive, creatively playful, able to cope with new situations
Early-maturing girls	More likely to date older boys, lower in self-esteem, lacking in poise (but middle-class girls more confident than those from low-SES groups), more likely to date, smoke, and drink earlier, more likely to develop eating disorders and depression	Self-possessed, self-directed, able to cope, emotionally stable, having a wide range of interests
Late-maturing girls	Confident, outgoing, assured, popular, likely to be chosen as leaders	Likely to experience difficulty adapting to stress, less agreeable, more likely to exhibit fluctuating moods

SOURCES: Harold, Colarossi, & Mercier (2007); Hetherington & Parke (1993); Steinberg (2008); Steinberg, Vandell, & Bornstein (2011); Weichold, Silbereisen, & Schmitt-Rodermund (2003).

TABLE 3.6 Stages of Interpersonal Reasoning
Described by Selman

Stage 0: Egocentric level (about ages 4 to 6). Children do not recognize that other persons may interpret the same social event or course of action differently from the way they do. They do not reflect on the thoughts of self and others. They can label the overtly expressed feelings of others but do not comprehend cause-and-effect relations of social actions.

Stage 1: Social information role taking (about ages 6 to 8). Children are able in limited ways to differentiate between their own interpretations of social interactions and the interpretations of others. But they cannot simultaneously think of their own view and those of others.

Stage 2: Self-reflective role taking (about ages 8 to 10). Interpersonal relations are interpreted in specific situations whereby each person understands the expectations of the other in that particular context. Children are not yet able to view the two perspectives at once, however.

Stage 3: Multiple role taking (about ages 10 to 12). Children become capable of taking a third-person view, which permits them to understand the expectations of themselves and of others in a variety of situations as if they were spectators.

Stage 4: Social and conventional system taking (about ages 12 to over 15). Each individual involved in a relationship with another understands many of the subtleties of the interactions involved. In addition, a societal perspective begins to develop. That is, actions are judged by how they might influence *all* individuals, not just those who are immediately concerned.

SOURCE: Adapted from discussions in Selman (1980).

Here's an interesting illustration of the power of group norms (Juvonen, 2000). Fourth, sixth, and eighth graders were asked to imagine that they had received a low score on an important exam and then to indicate how they would explain their performance to teachers and peers. The results may surprise you. The fourth and sixth graders were willing to explain their poor performance to both teachers and peers as being due to low ability rather than to low effort, whereas the eighth graders were much more likely to offer that explanation

> **Discussion of controversial issues may be difficult because of a strong desire to conform to peer norms.**

just to their peers. This seems counterintuitive. Why would adolescents want to portray themselves to their peers as being dumb (to put it crudely)? The answer is that ability is seen by many adolescents as something beyond their control. They therefore conclude that ascribing poor performance to low ability rather than to low effort will result in expressions of sympathy rather than contempt ("It wasn't Matthew's fault that he got a low grade on the last math exam; he just doesn't have a head for numbers").

Pause & Reflect *During the middle school years, the peer group becomes the general source for rules of behavior. Why? What advantages and disadvantages does this create?*

Emotional Characteristics: Middle School

1. *The view of early adolescence as a period of universal "storm and stress" appears to be an exaggeration.* The traditional view of adolescence, which is still widely held among nonpsychologists, is a dark one. Feelings of confusion, anxiety, and depression; extreme mood swings; and low levels of self-confidence are felt to be typical of this age group. Some of the reasons cited for this turbulence are

Social and Emotional Development: The Influence of Peer Groups

Go to the Education CourseMate website and watch the video, study the artifacts in the case, and reflect upon the following questions:

1. How do the middle school students in this Video Case illustrate Selman's theory of interpersonal reasoning?

2. How do the students in this Video Case illustrate the "desire to conform"?

rapid changes in height, weight, and body proportions; increases in hormone production; the task of identity formation; increased academic responsibilities; and the development of formal operational reasoning (Harold, Colarossi, & Mercier, 2007; R. W. Larson & Sheeber, 2009).

More recent studies (for example, those discussed by Harold, Colarossi, & Mercier, 2007; Larson & Sheeber, 2009; Steinberg & Morris, 2001) suggest a more complex picture. While it's true that adolescents typically experience more intense emotions than do adults, those emotions are both positive *and* negative (Larson & Sheeber, 2009). Second, even though many adolescents experience social and emotional problems from time to time and experiment with risky behavior, most do not develop significant social, emotional, or behavioral difficulties. For example, although most adolescents will have been drunk at least once before high school graduation, relatively few will develop drinking problems or allow alcohol to adversely affect their academic or social lives. But don't lose sight of the fact that some students do find this to be a difficult time and suffer from feelings of anxiety, low self-esteem, and depression.

2. *As a result of the continued influence of egocentric thought, middle school students are typically self-conscious and self-centered.* Because emerging adolescents are acutely aware of the physical and emotional changes that are taking place within them, they assume that everyone else is just as interested in, and is constantly evaluating, their appearance, feelings, and behavior. Consequently, they are deeply concerned about such matters as what type of clothing to wear for special occasions, with whom they should and should not be seen in public (they should never be seen with their parents at the mall, for example), and how they greet and talk with various people.

Another manifestation of adolescent egocentrism is the assumption that adults do not—indeed, cannot—understand the thoughts and feelings of early adolescence. It's as if the early adolescent believes she is experiencing things no one else has ever experienced before. Hence, a teen or preteen will likely say to a parent, "You just don't know what it feels like to be in love" (Wiles, Bondi, & Wiles, 2006).

Cognitive Characteristics: Middle School

1. *Because of the psychological demands of early adolescence, middle school students need a classroom environment that is open, supportive, and intellectually stimulating.* For the reasons we have

© Angela Hampton Picture Library/Alamy

Because of the importance of peer group values, middle school students often dress and behave similarly.

Challenging Assumptions

Meeting the Intellectual Needs of Middle School Students

Research from developmental and cognitive psychologists paints a consistent picture of middle school students. They can handle more abstract and complex tasks and work more independently of the teacher, and they have strong needs for both autonomy and social contact. Consequently, middle school teachers ought to minimize the use of lecture, independent seat-work, and competition for grades. Instead, teachers should design lessons around constructivist learning principles. For example, teachers should create assignments that relate to the issues and experiences adolescents are familiar with and care about, let students work cooperatively in small groups, provide whatever intellectual and emotional support students need to complete assignments, and foster the perception that the purpose of education is personal growth rather than competition for grades. Teachers who fail to provide this kind of environment may be doing more harm than good.

What Do You Think?

Do you agree that middle school teaching practices often leave much to be desired? As you consider this issue, check the additional resources available in the "Challenging Assumptions" section of the textbook's Education CourseMate website.

{ **The environment of middle schools should support adolescents' cognitive needs.** }

mentioned, early adolescence is an unsettling time for students. Partly because of these personal and environmental stresses, the self-concept, academic motivation, and achievement levels of adolescents decline, sometimes drastically. Analyses of middle school classrooms (e.g., Brinthaupt, Lipka, & Wallace, 2007; Gentry, Gable, & Rizza, 2002; Juvonen, 2007; Midgley, 2001; Midgley, Middleton, Gheen, & Kumar, 2002; Wigfield & Eccles, 2002) suggest the following:

- Take into account students' suggestions about such things as classroom rules, seating arrangements, homework assignments, and time spent on various tasks.

- Decrease competition and social comparisons among students by eliminating ability grouping, normative grading (also called grading on the curve, a practice we discuss in Chapter 14), and public evaluations of work.

- Provide more opportunities for small-group and individualized instruction.

- Avoid such motivation-destroying activities as copying information from the board or textbook onto worksheets and excessive verbatim recall of information.

- Create a friendly, supportive classroom environment.

2. *Self-efficacy becomes an important influence on intellectual and social behavior.* As we mentioned in point 1 under "Social Characteristics," middle school children become capable of analyzing both their own views of an interpersonal interaction and those of the other person. This newfound analytic ability is also turned inward, resulting in evaluations of one's intellectual and social capabilities. Albert Bandura (1986), a learning theorist whom we will

Elizabeth Crews Photography

Early adolescents are faced with several developmental challenges. Consequently, middle school teachers should make a special effort to establish a supportive classroom atmosphere in which students can meet their social, emotional, and cognitive needs.

Middle School Anxiety

For the reasons we have mentioned, early adolescence is an unsettling time for students. Partly because of these personal and environmental stresses, the self-concept, academic motivation, and achievement levels of adolescents decline, sometimes drastically. (p. 62–63)

Middle Ground

CAROLYN BOWER

St. Louis Dispatch 5/29/02

Getting lost. Not being able to open the combination lock to your locker. More homework. Less recess. Taunts from eighth-graders.

Those are among the fears some sixth-graders said they had when they first came to middle school from elementary school.

"Last year you got the advantage of being the oldest, but now you are the youngest," said Sara Klarfeld, a sixth-grader at Parkway Northeast Middle School in Creve Coeur. "Now you have to sit in the front of the bus. After a while you get used to it."

Sara and other students in Peggy Flynn's class recently wrote letters that Flynn will share with students entering sixth grade at Parkway Northeast in August. "I asked my students to give the new students advice about what it takes to survive in the sixth grade," Flynn said.

More than 88 percent of public school students nationwide change schools when they enter sixth grade. Some principals say that transition is one of the biggest of a student's school career.

From having one teacher and one classroom in elementary school, many middle-schoolers will change classes and have several teachers. And it's up to the student to find out what work to make up after an absence.

Flynn said teachers in middle school expect a lot of responsibility, independence and time management—things some students have not had to deal with.

"A comparable situation for an adult is changing jobs after working six years in the same place with the same people," said Jack Berckemeyer, assistant executive director of the National Middle School Association based in Columbus, Ohio.

Earlier this year, the middle school association and the National Association of Elementary School Principals issued a paper urging principals, teachers and parents to help ease the transition to middle school. Adults can help new middle school students recover that sense of belonging so common in elementary school, the groups said.

"When students feel more comfortable, they are more likely to perform well," said Nathan Bailey, principal at Ladue Middle School. Like principals in many area middle schools, Bailey meets with fifth-graders in the spring to answer their questions and give them a tour.

Triad Middle School Principal Max Pigg said fifth-graders in that district are invited to visit and to share classrooms with sixth-graders. "It seems to ease the anxiety," Pigg said.

In Parkway, at least one Parkway summer school offers a course in how to survive middle school.

Some of Flynn's students could teach that class.

"Future sixth-graders should never give out the combination to the lock on their locker because people will turn it upside down or take things and put them where you can't find them," Michael Holloran said.

Britt Banaszynski advised future sixth-graders to "get to classes on time, have your books and materials so you don't get in trouble."

"Teachers will say something if your shorts are too short or if you wear pajama pants," Claire Latham wrote to future sixth-graders.

Certain supplies are essential. Mike Caraffa, 12, recommends a calculator, a ruler, and "a focused mind."

Alena Armstrong said: "Let those butterflies out of your stomach and take a deep breath. Wish for the best. Be yourself, and don't try to impress others. It's really not that scary."

Source: Carolyn Bower, "Middle ground," from *St. Louis Post-Dispatch,* May 29, 2002. Reprinted by permission of *St. Louis Post-Dispatch.*

Questions and Activities

1. If the middle school years are especially challenging for 11- to 13-year-olds and their parents, then they certainly will be for teachers as well. What characteristics of this age group should you keep uppermost in mind, and what general approaches to instruction should you seek to implement?

2. Peggy Flynn, the sixth-grade teacher mentioned in this article, said that middle school teachers expect students to be more responsible and independent than they were in the elementary grades, yet she suggests that some students may have not had much experience or instruction in these capabilities. What steps can you take, as either an elementary grade or a middle school teacher, to help students learn to be more responsible and independent?

3. To find out for yourself what middle school students are like, arrange to visit several middle school classrooms and then interview some students and teachers.

discuss in Chapter 9, coined the term **self-efficacy** to refer to how capable people believe they are at dealing with one type of task or another. Thus a student may have a very strong sense of self-efficacy for math ("I know I can solve most any algebraic equation"), a moderate degree of self-efficacy for certain athletic activities ("I think I play baseball and basketball about as well as most other kids my age"), and a low sense of self-efficacy for interpersonal relationships ("I'm just not good at making friends").

These self-evaluative beliefs influence what activities students choose and how long they will persist at a given task, particularly when progress becomes difficult. Students with a moderate to strong sense of self-efficacy will persist at a task long enough to obtain the success or corrective feedback that leads to expectations of future success. Students with a low sense of self-efficacy, however, tend to abandon tasks at the first sign of difficulty, thereby establishing a pattern of failure, low expectations of future success, and task avoidance.

LO5 High School (Grades 9, 10, 11, and 12; 14, 15, 16, and 17 Years)

Physical Characteristics: High School

1. *Significant and large changes in physical development occur during adolescence.* Adolescent males and females add pounds and inches at a prodigious rate. The peak year for girls is about age 12, when the average girl adds 14 or so pounds and about 3 inches. The peak year for boys is about age 14, during which they can add 16 to 17 pounds and about 4 inches (Kail & Cavanaugh, 2010). Approximately 16% of students are considered to be overweight;

13% are obese (Centers for Disease Control and Prevention, 2008). The most significant glandular change accompanying puberty is arousal of the sex drive.

2. *Many adolescents become sexually active, although the long-term trend is down.* From 2001 through 2007, sexual intercourse among high school students trended up after having declined through the 1990s, as shown in Table 3.8. In 2007, close to two thirds of students reported having engaged in sexual intercourse by the end of grade 12. These findings illustrate the pressing need for sex education during the high school years.

self-efficacy The degree to which people believe they are capable or prepared to handle particular tasks.

Pause & Reflect *What are the advantages and disadvantages of sex education in school? For help with your answer, visit the websites of the National Campaign to Prevent Teen and Unplanned Pregnancy (www.thenationalcampaign.org) and the Sexuality Information and Education Council of the United States (www.siecus.org).*

Self-efficacy beliefs for academic and social tasks become strong influences on behavior.

TABLE 3.7 Applying Theories of Development to the High School Years

Psychosocial development: Identity vs. role confusion. Concerns arise about gender roles and occupational choice. Different identity statuses become apparent.

Cognitive development: Formal operational thought for many students. There is increasing ability to engage in mental manipulations, understand abstractions, and test hypotheses.

Moral development: Morality of cooperation, conventional level. There is increasing willingness to think of rules as mutual agreements and to allow for intentions and extenuating circumstances.

General factors to keep in mind: Achievement of sexual maturity has a profound effect on many aspects of behavior. Peer groups and reactions of friends are extremely important. There is concern about what will happen after graduation, particularly for students who do not intend to continue their education. Awareness grows of the significance of academic ability and importance of grades for certain career patterns. There is a need to make personal value decisions regarding use of drugs, premarital sex, and code of ethics.

TABLE 3.8 Trends in Sexual Activity Among High School Students

Percentage Who Reported Ever Having Sexual Intercourse		
	2001	2007
Gender		
Female	44.5	47.2
Male	49.4	51.2
Grade Level		
Ninth grade	34.8	33.2
Tenth grade	40.7	43.7
Eleventh grade	51.8	55.4
Twelfth grade	60.5	64.5
Ethnic Group		
Black	60.8	66.5
Hispanic	48.4	52.0
White	43.2	43.7

SOURCE: Centers for Disease Control and Prevention (2009).

sexually transmitted diseases Contagious diseases, such as HIV/AIDS, gonorrhea, and herpes, that are spread by sexual contact.

3. *Although the birthrate among unmarried adolescents has fallen in recent years, it remains unacceptably high, as does the rate of sexually transmitted diseases.* In 1991, the birthrate among teens ages 15 to 19 was 61.8 births per 1,000. By 2005, that figure had declined to 41.9. Pregnancy rates for teens 15 to 19 years old have also declined.

The relatively high levels of sexual activity and low levels of regular contraception among adolescents are particularly worrisome because they put adolescents at risk for contracting **sexually transmitted diseases**. According to the Centers for Disease Control and Prevention (2009), sexually transmitted diseases occur in the United States more frequently among adolescents than any other age group.

The worst of the sexually transmitted diseases is, of course, HIV/AIDS. *HIV* stands for *human immunodeficiency virus* and *AIDS* stands for *acquired immune deficiency syndrome*. HIV is the

Adamsmith/Taxi/Getty Images

Because many adolescents are sexually active, there is a strong need for sex education in the schools.

{ **Parents influence values and plans; peers influence immediate status.** }

viral cause of AIDS. In 2006, almost 12 adolescents for every 100,000 in the 15- to 19-year-old age group were diagnosed with HIV/AIDS (Centers for Disease Control and Prevention, 2009).

Social Characteristics: High School

1. *Parents and other adults are likely to influence long-range plans; peers are likely to influence immediate status.* When adolescents look for models and advice on such social matters as dress, hairstyle, speech patterns, friendships, and leisure activities, the peer group is likely to have the greatest influence (as a visit to any high school will reveal). Peer values can also influence academic performance. When the issues are which courses to take in school and what different careers are like, teachers, guidance counselors, and parents are likely to have more influence over decision making than peers. For questions about values, ethics, and future plans, the views of parents are usually sought (Steinberg, Vandell, & Bornstein, 2011).

Not surprisingly, most conflicts between parents and their adolescent children are about such peer-influenced issues as personal appearance, friends, dating, hours, and eating habits (Hill, 1987).

2. *Girls seem to experience greater anxiety about friendships than boys do.* Adolescent girls tend to seek intimacy in friendships. Boys, in contrast, often stress skills and interests when they form friendships, and their tendencies to be competitive and self-reliant may work against the formation of close relationships with male companions. Because adolescent girls often wish to form an intimate relationship with another girl, they are more likely than boys to experience anxiety, jealousy, and conflicts regarding friendships with same-sex peers (C. L. Hardy, Bukowski, & Sippola, 2002; Pleydon & Schner, 2001; Steinberg, Vandell, & Bornstein, 2011).

Girls are more likely than boys to experience anxiety about friendships.

3. *Many high school students are employed after school.* For any number of reasons, a fair percentage of high school students have part-time jobs during the school year. In 2007, 21% of 16- and 17-year-olds and 26% of 18- and 19-year-olds worked after school. These percentages have been trending lower, however, from their 2000 peak of 31% and 30%, respectively (Morisi, 2008). Most experts agree that students who work more than 20 hours per week are likely to have lower grades than students who work less or not at all (Steinberg, Vandell, & Bornstein, 2011).

Emotional Characteristics: High School

1. *Many psychiatric disorders either appear or become prominent during adolescence. Included among these are eating disorders, substance abuse, schizophrenia, depression, and suicide.* Eating disorders are much more common in females than in males. *Anorexia nervosa* is an eating disorder characterized by a preoccupation with body weight and food, behavior directed toward losing weight, peculiar patterns of handling food, weight loss, intense fear of gaining weight, and a distorted perception of one's body. This disorder occurs predominantly in females (more than 90% of cases) and usually appears between the ages of 14 and 17 (American Psychiatric Association, 2000).

    Bulimia nervosa is a disorder in which binge eating (uncontrolled rapid eating of large quantities of food over a short period of time) followed by self-induced vomiting is the predominant behavior. Binges are typically followed by feelings of guilt, depression, self-disgust, and fasting. As with anorexia, more than 90% of individuals with bulimia are female (American Psychiatric Association, 2000).

    A survey of high school students about substance abuse (Centers for Disease Control and Prevention, 2008) found that:
    * Twenty percent reported smoking on one or more of the 30 days before the survey, and about 8% reported smoking on 20 or more of the previous 30 days.
    * Twenty-four percent of female students and 27.8% of male students engaged in episodic heavy drinking (commonly known as binge drinking).
    * Thirty-eight percent had used marijuana at least once during their lifetimes, and 19.7% had used marijuana one or more times in the preceding 30 days.
    * A little more than 7% reported using some form of cocaine at least once during their lifetimes, and 4.33% reported using cocaine in the preceding 30 days.

© Richard Hutchings/Photo Edit

Many high school students, girls in particular, experience periods of depression, loneliness, and anxiety. Because severe depression often precedes a suicide attempt, teachers should refer students they believe to be depressed to the school counselor.

* About 4.5% of students reported using methamphetamine at least once during their lifetimes.

    Schizophrenia, a thinking disorder characterized by illogical and unrealistic thinking, delusions, and hallucinations, is relatively rare among adolescents, affecting less than 0.25% of all 13- to 19-year-olds. Early symptoms include odd, unpredictable behavior; difficulty communicating with others; social withdrawal; and rejection by peers (Beiser, Erickson, Fleming, & Iacono, 1993; Conger & Galambos, 1997; Gilberg, 2001).

2. *The most common type of emotional disorder during adolescence is depression.* Common symptoms of depression include feelings of worthlessness and lack of control over one's life, crying spells, and suicidal thoughts, threats, and attempts. Additional symptoms include moodiness, social isolation, fatigue, hypochondria, and difficulty in concentrating (Cicchetti & Toth, 1998; Peterson et al., 1993). In 2007, 35.8% of high school females and 21.2% of high school males reported feeling so sad and hopeless almost every day for two or more weeks in a row that they stopped engaging in some usual activities (Centers for Disease Control and Prevention, 2008).

3. *If depression becomes severe, suicide may be contemplated.* In 2007, 14.5% of high school students had seriously considered attempting suicide during

{ **Depression is most common among females.** }

> **Depression places adolescents at risk for suicide.**

the previous 12 months, 11.3% had made a suicide plan, and 6.9% had made one or more attempts. Many more females than males considered attempting suicide (18.7% versus 10.3%, respectively) and made one or more attempts (9.3% versus 4.6%). The only good news in these statistics is that they were lower than they had been in 2005. The single most important signal of a youth at risk for suicide is depression (National Center for Health Statistics, 2007).

Cognitive Characteristics: High School

1. *High school students become increasingly capable of engaging in formal thought, but they may not use this capability.* High school students are more likely than younger students to grasp relationships, mentally plan a course of action before proceeding, and test hypotheses systematically. Without supervision and guidance, however, they may not use such capabilities consistently (Harold, Colarossi, & Mercier, 2007).

2. *Between the ages of 12 and 16, political thinking becomes more abstract, liberal, and knowledgeable.* Many adolescents markedly change their thinking about political issues in the years between ages 12 and 16 (Adelson, 1972, 1986). The most significant changes are:

   - an increase in the ability to deal with such abstractions as freedom of speech, equal justice under law, and the concept of community;

   - a decline in authoritarian views;

   - an increase in the ability to imagine the consequences of current actions; and

   - an increase in political knowledge.

Selecting Technologies for Different Age Levels

As this chapter and the preceding one indicate, your teaching approaches will be influenced by the developmental level of your students. Your incorporation of educational technology will be no different. For kindergarten and primary grade teachers, tools to enhance student literacy are likely to be a priority. Elementary, middle school, and high school teachers will be more interested in tools that promote thinking, problem solving, and communication.

Using Technology to Reduce Egocentrism and Develop Interpersonal Reasoning

The main factor that contributes to the decline of egocentrism is exposure to different points of view through social interaction. Because these interactions do not have to be face-to-face, it is quite possible that sharing experiences and points of view by computer may produce the same result.

Social and Emotional Development: Understanding Adolescents

TeachSource Video Case

Go to the Education CourseMate website and watch the video, study the artifacts in the case, and reflect upon the following questions:

1. The text describes signs of adolescent students who might be "at risk." Based on your observations of the students in this Video Case, would you consider any of them to be at risk? Are there observable factors or characteristics that you can detect?

2. How does this Video Case illustrate the powerful influence of peer groups in adolescents' lives?

> ## Political thinking becomes more abstract, less authoritarian, and more knowledgeable.

One way to accomplish these exchanges is through Kidlink (www.kidlink.org), a nonprofit organization that helps teachers and students arrange electronic exchanges with students from around the world. The goal of Kidlink is to help children understand themselves, identify and define life goals, and collaborate with peers.

For schools that do not have the luxury of arranging real-time videoconferences, written asynchronous exchanges via e-mail have proven useful for accomplishing the same goal. One advantage of e-mail exchanges is that children who are outgoing and fluent speakers are less likely to discourage others from participating. In a test of this idea, fifth and sixth graders from two schools in the Netherlands worked on a biology project for several weeks, both among themselves and with students from the other school, by periodically exchanging e-mails about various aspects of the project. The researchers found that over the course of the study, the students became more reflective and aware of the different views of their peers (De Vries, Van der Meij, Boersma, & Pieters, 2005).

In recent years, new options for encouraging the decline of egocentrism and the growth of interpersonal reasoning have emerged. Referred to collectively as **Web 2.0**, these options include such tools as blogs, podcasts, and videos, such social networking websites as Facebook, MySpace, and Twitter, and such media sharing sites as YouTube and Flickr (see, for example, Bull, Hammond, & Ferster, 2008; Rosen & Nelson, 2008). These tools and websites allow individuals who share a common interest to work together to create, discuss, and modify a particular product, such as fiction or nonfiction stories, without having to purchase expensive software (B. Alexander & Levine, 2008; Berson, 2009; Greenhow, Robelia, & Hughes, 2010; Nebel, Jamison, & Bennett, 2009).

The Effect of Technology on Cognitive Development

One of the advantages of educational technology is that it can be readily used to support the development of such higher-level cognitive skills as inquiry, critical thinking, and problem solving. For example, **adventure learning** programs allow students to interact electronically with experts and explorers around the world. Students from various schools might get together for virtual field trips to places such as the Statue of Liberty for insights on immigration policies or the Civil War battlefield at Gettysburg for demonstrations of military tactics (M. A. Siegel & Kirkley, 1998).

Adventure learning explorations can be incorporated into the problem-based learning approach, a technique that promotes formal operational thought by emphasizing real-world problem solving. We discuss problem-based learning in Chapter 13. Two adventure learning websites that you might want to take a look at are the Adventure Learning Foundation at www.questconnect.org and ThinkQuest's Ocean Adventure site at http://library.thinkquest.org/18828.

WHAT ELSE? *RIP & REVIEW* **CARDS IN THE BACK**

Web 2.0 Social networking websites such as Facebook, Twitter, and Flickr that allow groups of students with a common interest to communicate with each other and work on shared projects by using such tools as blogs, podcasts, and videos.

adventure learning A type of learning wherein students might participate in real-life expeditions, virtual field trips, historical reenactments, and local adventures in their community, typically in structured activities with students from other schools.

UNDERSTANDING STUDENT DIFFERENCES

LEARNING OBJECTIVES

After studying this chapter, you will be able to . . .

LO1 Explain what intelligence tests are designed to do and how contemporary theories of intelligence differ from the traditional view.

LO2 Give some examples of how Robert Sternberg's and Howard Gardner's theories of intelligence can be used to guide classroom instruction.

LO3 Describe the learning styles of reflectivity/impulsivity, field dependence/field independence, and mental self-government.

LO4 Note where gender differences do and do not exist in cognition and achievement and explain how gender bias affects students.

visit **4ltrpress.cengage.com**

Sit back for a few minutes, and think about some of your friends and classmates from elementary and high school. Make a list of their physical characteristics (height, weight, visual acuity, and athletic skill, for example), social characteristics (outgoing, reserved, cooperative, sensitive to the needs of others, assertive), emotional characteristics (self-assured, optimistic, pessimistic, egotistical), and intellectual characteristics (methodical, creative, impulsive, good with numbers, terrible at organizing ideas). Now analyze your descriptions in terms of similarities and differences. In all likelihood, they point to many ways in which your friends and classmates have been alike but to even more ways in which they have differed from one another. Indeed, although human beings share many important characteristics, they also differ from one another in significant ways (and we tend to notice the differences more readily than the similarities).

Now imagine yourself a few years from now, when your job as a teacher is to help every student learn as much as possible despite all the ways in which students differ from one another. In one study of a group of first graders from a suburban school district, the number of words correctly read from a list of 100 words ranged from none to 100. By the middle grades, the least capable students will have read about 100,000 words, the average student will have read about one million words, and the most capable students will have read between 10 million and 50 million words (Roller, 2002).

Although it usually will be essential for you to plan lessons, assignments, and teaching techniques by taking into account typical characteristics, you will also have to expect and make allowances for differences among students. The practice of using different learning materials, instructional tactics, and learning activities with students who vary along such dimensions as intelligence, learning style, gender, ethnicity, and social class is commonly referred to as *differentiated instruction* (see, e.g., Benjamin, 2005; Tomlinson, Brimijoin, & Narvaez, 2008). The aim is for all students to meet the same goals.

Over the next two chapters, we examine five broad characteristics that distinguish one group of students from another and have a demonstrated effect on learning. In this chapter, we focus on differences in mental ability (usually referred to as *intelligence*), learning styles, and gender. In the next chapter, we explore two related

characteristics that are becoming more important every year: cultural and socioeconomic background. Teachers and researchers have demonstrated a strong interest in all five characteristics in recent years, and much has been written about them.

LO1 The Nature and Measurement of Intelligence

The Origin of Intelligence Testing

The form and content of contemporary intelligence tests owe much to the pioneering work of French psychologist Alfred Binet. In 1904, Binet was appointed to a commission of experts charged by the minister of public instruction for the Paris school system with figuring out an accurate and objective way of distinguishing between children who could profit from normal classroom instruction and those who required special education. Because the point of this project was to predict degree of future academic success, Binet created a set of questions and tasks that reflected the same cognitive processes as those demanded by everyday classroom activities. Thus Binet's first scale measured such processes as memory, attention, comprehension, discrimination, and reasoning.

In 1916, Lewis Terman of Stanford University published an extensive revision of Binet's test. This revision, which came to be known as the Stanford-Binet, proved to be extremely popular. One reason for its popularity was that Terman, following the 1912 suggestion of a German psychologist named William Stern, expressed a child's level of performance as a global figure called an intelligence quotient (IQ). Stern's original formula divided a child's mental age, which was determined by performance on the test, by the child's chronological age and multiplied

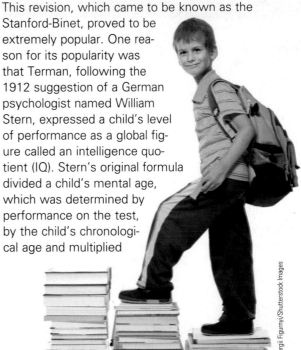

Individually administered intelligence tests (such as the one shown here) are usually given to determine eligibility for a special class. They were designed to predict—and are moderately good predictors of—academic performance.

was "to identify in order to help and improve, not to label in order to limit" (Gould, 1981, p. 152).

Later in this section, we will see that Binet's concern was well placed. First, however, we will turn to a more detailed consideration of what intelligence tests do and do not measure.

What Traditional Intelligence Tests Measure

In 1904, British psychologist Charles Spearman noticed that children given a battery of intellectual tests (such as the memory, reasoning, and comprehension tests that Binet and Terman used) showed a strong tendency to rank consistently from test to test: Children who scored high (or average or below average) on memory tests tended to score high (or average or below average) on reasoning and comprehension tests. Our use of the words *tendency* and *tended* indicates, of course, that the rankings were not identical. Some children scored well on some tests but performed more poorly on others.

Spearman explained this pattern by saying that intelligence is made up of two types of factors: a general factor (abbreviated as *g*) that affects performance on all intellectual tests and a set of specific factors (abbreviated as *s*) that affects performance on only specific intellectual tests. Spearman ascribed to the *g* factor the tendency for score rankings to remain constant over tests. That the rankings varied somewhat from test to test, he said, resulted from individual differences in specific factors. Not surprisingly, Spearman's explanation is called the *two-factor theory of intelligence*.

When you examine such contemporary intelligence tests as the Stanford-Binet Intelligence Scales, Fifth Edition (Roid, 2003), the Wechsler Intelligence Scale for Children—Fourth Edition (Wechsler, 2003), and the Wechsler Adult Intelligence Scale—Third Edition (Psychological Corporation, 2002; Wechsler, 1997), you will notice that the items in the various subtests differ greatly from one another. They may involve performing mental arithmetic, explaining the meanings of words, reproducing a pictured geometric design with blocks, or

the resulting figure by 100 to eliminate fractional values (Seagoe, 1975).

We have provided this abbreviated history lesson to illustrate two important points:

1. The form and function of contemporary intelligence tests have been directly influenced by the task Binet was given a century ago. Intelligence test items are still selected on the basis of their relationship to school success (Furnham, Monsen, & Ahmetoglu, 2009). Thus predictions about job success, marital bliss, happiness in life, or anything else made on the basis of an IQ score are attempts to make the test do something for which it was not designed. As some psychologists have pointed out, this type of test might better have been called a test of scholastic aptitude or school ability rather than a test of intelligence.

2. Stern and Terman's use of the IQ as a quantitative summary of a child's performance was not endorsed by Binet, who worried that educators would use a summary score as an excuse to ignore or get rid of uninterested or troublesome students. Binet's intent

Intelligence test scores most closely relate to school success, not job success, marital happiness, or life happiness.

{ IQ scores can change with experience and training. }

selecting from a larger set three pictures that share a common characteristic and form a group. These varied items are included because, despite their apparent differences, they relate strongly to one another and to performance in the classroom. In other words, intelligence tests still reflect Binet's original goal and Spearman's two-factor theory. In practice, the examiner can combine the scores from each subtest into a global index (the IQ score), offer a prediction about the tested individual's degree of academic success for the next year or so, and make some judgments about specific strengths and weaknesses.

Limitations of Intelligence Tests

So where does all this leave us in terms of trying to decide what traditional intelligence tests do and do not measure? Three points seem to be in order:

1. The appraisal of intelligence is limited by the fact that intelligence cannot be measured directly. Our efforts are confined to measuring the overt manifestations (responses to test items) of what is ultimately based on brain function and experience.

2. The intelligence we test is a sample of intellectual capabilities that relate to classroom achievement better than they relate to anything else. That is why, as stated earlier, many psychologists prefer the term *test of scholastic aptitude* or *test of school ability*.

3. Because current research demonstrates that the cognitive abilities measured by intelligence tests can be improved with systematic instruction (Sternberg, 2002a, 2002b, 2003; Sternberg, Jarvin, & Grigorenko, 2009), intelligence test scores should not be viewed as absolute measures of ability. Many people—parents, especially—fail to grasp this fact. An IQ score is not a once-and-for-all judgment of how bright a child is. It is merely an estimate of how successful a child is in handling certain kinds of problems at a particular time on a particular test as compared with other children of the same age.

Pause&Reflect *Imagine that a colleague tells you about one of her students, who has a C average and received an IQ score of 92 (low average) on a recent test. Your colleague says that because the student is working up to his ability level, he should not be encouraged to set higher goals because that would only lead to frustration. Your colleague then asks for your opinion. How do you respond?*

Because traditional theories of intelligence and their associated IQ tests view intelligence as being composed of a relatively small set of cognitive skills that relate best to academic success (Canivez, 2008), and because the results of such tests are used primarily to place students in special programs, contemporary theorists have proposed broader conceptions of intelligence that have more useful implications for classroom instruction.

intelligence The ability of an individual to use a variety of cognitive and non-cognitive capabilities to formulate goals, logically work toward achieving those goals, and adapt to the demands of the environment.

Contemporary Views of Intelligence

David Wechsler's Global Capacity View As David Wechsler (1975) persuasively pointed out, intelligence is not simply the sum of one's tested abilities. Wechsler defined **intelligence** as the global capacity of the individual to act purposefully, think rationally, and deal effectively with the environment. Given this definition, which many psychologists endorse, an IQ score reflects just one facet of a person's global capacity: the ability to act purposefully, rationally, and effectively on academic tasks in a *classroom* environment. However, people display intelligent behavior in other settings (at work, home, and play, for example), and other characteristics contribute to intelligent behavior (such as persistence, realistic goal setting, productive use of corrective feedback, creativity, and moral and aesthetic values). A true assessment of intelligence would take into account behavior related to these other settings and characteristics. Take, for example, a situation that has the potential to become confrontational and hostile. Wouldn't we be inclined to say that an individual who calms the emotions of others by being open-minded and pointing out potential solutions is behaving intelligently?

If recent formulations of intelligence by Robert Sternberg and Howard Gardner become widely accepted, future intelligence tests may be broader in scope than those in use today. Even before such tests are devised, these theories serve a useful purpose by reminding us that intelligence is multifaceted and can be expressed in many ways.

Intelligence involves more than what intelligence tests measure.

triarchic theory of intelligence
A theory formulated by Robert Sternberg that describes intelligence as being composed of practical, creative, and analytical components; also known as the theory of successful intelligence.

Robert Sternberg's Triarchic View: The Theory of Successful Intelligence Like David Wechsler, Robert Sternberg (2002a, 2002b, 2003) believes that most of the research evidence supports the view that intelligence has many facets, or dimensions, and that traditional mental ability tests measure just a few of these facets. Sternberg's **triarchic theory of intelligence** (which in later versions is called *the theory of successful intelligence*) has, as its name suggests, three main parts (see Figure 4.1):

- *Practical ability* involves applying knowledge to everyday situations, using knowledge and tools, and seeking relevance.

- *Creative ability* involves inventing, discovering, imagining, and supposing.

- *Analytical ability* involves breaking ideas and products into their component parts, making judgments, evaluating, comparing and contrasting, and critiquing.

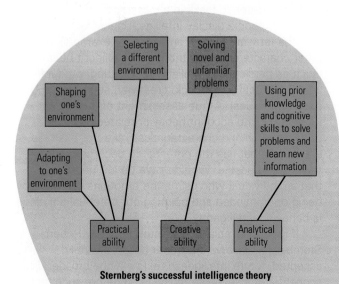

Sternberg's successful intelligence theory

FIGURE 4.1 The Three Components of Sternberg's Triarchic View of Successful Intelligence

SOURCES: Adapted from Sternberg (1985, 2003) and Stemler, Sternberg, Grigorenko, Jarvin, & Sharpes (2009).

{ **Triarchic view: part of intelligence is the ability to achieve personal goals** }

Because these abilities need information on which to operate, memory ability underlies each of them (Grigorenko, Jarvin, & Sternberg, 2002).

Sternberg's work is a break with tradition in two respects. First, it includes an aspect of intelligence that has been—and still is—largely overlooked: how people use practical intelligence to adapt to their environment. Second, Sternberg believes that each of these abilities can be improved through instruction and that students learn best when all three are called into play.

In describing the nature of practical intelligence, Sternberg argues that part of what makes an individual intelligent is the ability to achieve personal goals (for example, graduating from high school or college with honors, working for a particular company in a particular capacity, or having a successful marriage). One way to accomplish personal goals is to understand and adapt to the values that govern behavior in a particular setting. For example, if most teachers in a particular school (or executives in a particular company) place a high value on conformity and cooperation, the person who persistently challenges authority, suggests new ideas without being asked, or operates without consulting others will, in all likelihood, receive fewer rewards than those who are more willing to conform and cooperate. According to Sternberg's theory, this person would be less intelligent.

Where a mismatch exists and the individual cannot adapt to the values of the majority, the intelligent person explores ways to make the values of others more consistent with his own values and skills. An enterprising student may try to convince her teacher, for example, that short-answer questions are better measures of achievement than essay questions or that effort and classroom participation should count just as much toward a grade as test scores. Finally, where all attempts at adapting or attempting to change the views of others fail, the intelligent person seeks out a setting in which his behaviors are more consistent with those of others. For instance, many gifted and talented students will seek out private alternative schools where their particular abilities are more highly prized.

Sternberg's basic point is that intelligence should be viewed as a broad characteristic of people that is evidenced not only by how well they answer a particular set of test questions but also by how well they function in different settings. The individual with average test scores who succeeds in getting people to

Robert Sternberg's theory maintains that intelligence is composed of practical ability, creative ability, and analytical ability.

to improve analytical, creative, and practical thinking skills produced higher scores on tests of those abilities than did instruction that emphasized the learning and recall of factual information.

Howard Gardner's Multiple Intelligences Theory

Howard Gardner's conception of intelligence, like Sternberg's, is broader than traditional conceptions. It is different from Sternberg's, however, in that it describes eight separate types of intelligence. Accordingly, Gardner's work is referred to as the **theory of multiple intelligences** (or *MI theory*). The intelligences that Gardner describes are *logical-mathematical*, *linguistic*, *musical*, *spatial*, *bodily-kinesthetic*, *interpersonal* (understanding of others), *intrapersonal* (understanding of self), and *naturalist* (noticing the characteristics that distinguish one plant, mineral, or animal from another and creating useful classification schemes called *taxonomies*) (H. Gardner, 1999). Table 4.1 describes each of these intelligences and provides examples of the kind of person who best represents each one.

Because these intelligences are presumed to be independent of one another, an individual would likely exhibit different levels of skill in each of these domains. One student, for example, may show evidence of becoming an outstanding trial lawyer, novelist, or journalist because his linguistic intelligence produces a facility for vividly describing, explaining, or persuading. Another student may be able to manipulate aspects of sound (such as pitch, rhythm, and timbre) to produce musical experiences that people find highly

theory of multiple intelligences
A theory formulated by Howard Gardner that describes intelligence as being composed of eight mostly independent capabilities.

do what she wants is, in this view, at least as intelligent as the person who scores at the 99th percentile of a science test.

Research based on Sternberg's theory (e.g., Grigorenko, Jarvin, & Sternberg, 2002; Stemler, Sternberg, Grigorenko, Jarvin, & Sharpes, 2009; Sternberg & Grigorenko, 2004) supports his contention that its three main elements can be improved with the proper instruction. For example, a curriculum designed

TABLE 4.1 Gardner's Eight Intelligences

Intelligence	Core Components	End States
Logical-mathematical	Sensitivity to, and capacity to discern, logical or numerical patterns; ability to handle long chains of reasoning	Scientist Mathematician
Linguistic	Sensitivity to the sounds, rhythms, and meanings of words; sensitivity to the different functions of language	Poet Journalist
Musical	Abilities to produce and appreciate rhythm, pitch, and timbre; appreciation of the forms of musical expression	Violinist Composer
Spatial	Capacities to perceive the visual-spatial world accurately and to perform transformations on one's initial perceptions	Sculptor Navigator
Bodily-kinesthetic	Abilities to control one's body movements and handle objects skillfully	Dancer Athlete
Interpersonal	Capacities to discern and respond appropriately to the moods, temperaments, motivations, and desires of other people	Therapist Salesperson
Intrapersonal	Access to one's own feelings and the ability to discriminate among them and draw on them to guide behavior; knowledge of one's own strengths, weaknesses, desires, and intelligences	Person with detailed, accurate self-knowledge
Naturalist	Ability to recognize and classify the numerous plants and animals of one's environment and their relationships on a logical, justifiable basis; talent of caring for, taming, and interacting with various living creatures	Botanist Entomologist

SOURCE: Armstrong, 2009; Gardner (1999); Gardner & Hatch (1989).

pleasing. And the student who is adept at understanding her own and others' feelings and how those feelings relate to behavior would be exhibiting high intrapersonal and interpersonal intelligence. Like Sternberg's work, Gardner's theory cautions us against focusing on the results of IQ tests to the exclusion of other worthwhile behaviors.

Gardner's MI theory has become extremely popular among educators. As usually happens with such ideas, it is often misinterpreted. A number of misconceptions have arisen:

Misconception: A person who has a strength in a particular intelligence will excel on all tasks within that domain. Not so. A student with a high level of linguistic intelligence may be quite good at writing insightful essays on various topics but be unable to produce a good poem. Another student may excel at the kind of direct, fact-oriented style of writing that characterizes good newspaper reporting but be limited in her ability to write a long, highly analytical essay.

Misconception: Ability is destiny. If a child exhibits a high level of linguistic intelligence, she will not necessarily choose to major in English or journalism or seek a job as a writer. Not only do intelligences change over time in how they are used; decisions about a college major and career are influenced by many other factors. The student who wrote such interesting stories as a child may grow up to be a college professor who excels at writing journal articles and textbooks, or a noted politician, or a successful business leader (Hatch, 1997).

Misconception: Every child should be taught every subject in eight different ways to develop all of the intelligences. MI theory does not indicate or even suggest that such a step is necessary for learning to occur. In fact, it may be counterproductive if students are turned off by lessons that appear forced and contrived. And as a practical matter, there simply isn't enough time in the day to teach every lesson eight ways (H. Gardner, 1999; Hatch, 1997).

Pause & Reflect *Assuming that Robert Sternberg and Howard Gardner are correct in thinking that people can be intelligent in ways other than the traditional analytical, linguistic, and logical-mathematical modes, why do you think schools have been so reluctant to address other abilities?*

▶❚❚ Multiple Intelligences: Elementary School Instruction

Go to the Education CourseMate website and watch the video, study the artifacts in the case, and reflect upon the following questions:

1. Which of Gardner's eight intelligences, as described in Table 4.1, are depicted in the Video Case? How do specific students in the video illustrate these intelligences?

2. How does the teacher in this Video Case use MI theory to teach traditional academic skills and subject matter? Do you think his approach is effective? Why or why not?

Contemporary theories typically view intelligence as being composed of several types of capabilities. Howard Gardner's theory of multiple intelligence, for example, describes several different ways of expressing intelligent behavior.

LO2 Using the New Views of Intelligence to Guide Instruction

The various theories of intelligence that were formulated during the first half of the twentieth century are of limited value to educators because they do not allow teachers to match instructional approaches and learning assessments to abilities. For example, because traditional intelligence tests, such as the Stanford-Binet and the Wechsler Intelligence Scale for Children—Fourth Edition, are designed to rank students according to how they score rather than to assess how they think, their basic educational use is to determine eligibility for programs for the gifted and talented, learning disabled, and mentally disabled. What sets the theories of Sternberg and Gardner apart is their belief in a broad view of intelligence that can inform instructional practice and improve student performance (Armstrong, 2009; J.-Q. Chen, Moran, & Gardner, 2009; Sternberg, Jarvin, &

Grigorenko, 2009). The following are a few illustrations of how you can use Sternberg's and Gardner's ideas in your classroom.

Sternberg's Triarchic Theory of Successful Intelligence

Based on his triarchic view of successful intelligence, Sternberg proposed a teaching and assessment model (Stemler, Sternberg, Grigorenko, Jarvin, & Sharpes, 2009; Sternberg, 1996, 1997b). He suggested that for any grade level and for any subject, teaching and testing can be designed to emphasize the three abilities in his triarchic theory—analytical, creative, and practical—as well as memory. To take into account individual differences, instruction and testing should involve all four abilities. At some point, each student has an opportunity to excel because the task and related test match the student's ability. Table 4.2 shows how language arts,

TABLE 4.2 Teaching Different Subjects From a Triarchic Perspective

	Memory	Analysis	Creativity	Practicality
Language arts	Remember the name of Tom Sawyer's aunt.	Compare the personality of Tom Sawyer with that of Huckleberry Finn.	Write a very short story with Tom Sawyer as a character.	Describe how you could use Tom Sawyer's power of persuasion.
Mathematics	Remember the mathematical formula Distance = Rate × Time.	Solve a mathematical word problem using the $D = R \times T$ formula.	Create your own mathematical word problem using the $D = R \times T$ formula.	Show how to use the $D = R \times T$ formula to estimate driving time from one city to another.
Social studies	Remember a list of factors that led up to the U.S. Civil War.	Compare, contrast, and evaluate the arguments of those who supported slavery versus the arguments of those who opposed it.	Write a page of a journal from the viewpoint of either a Confederate or a Union soldier.	Discuss the applicability of the lessons of the Civil War to countries today.
Science	Name the main types of bacteria.	Analyze the means the immune system uses to fight bacterial infections.	Suggest ways to cope with the increasing immunity bacteria are showing to antibiotic drugs.	Suggest three steps that individuals might take to reduce the chances of bacterial infection.

SOURCE: Adapted from Sternberg (1997b) and Sternberg et al. (2009).

> **The triarchic view suggests that instruction and assessment should emphasize all types of ability.**

mathematics, social studies, and science can be taught so as to emphasize all four of these abilities. Notice that Sternberg did not suggest that *all* instruction and assessment match a student's dominant ability. Some attempts need to be made to strengthen abilities that are relatively weak.

Gardner's Multiple Intelligences Theory

Gardner's general recommendation for applying MI theory in the classroom were essentially the same as Sternberg's for applying the triarchic view. He believes that teachers should use MI theory as a framework for devising alternative ways to teach subject matter (J.-Q. Chen, Moran, & Gardner, 2009).

MI theory should lead to increased transfer of learning to out-of-school settings. Because MI theory helps students mentally represent ideas in multiple ways, students are likely to develop a better understanding of the topic and be able to use that knowledge in everyday life. For the same reason, MI theory also suggests that learning in out-of-school settings should lead to increased transfer of learning in school subjects. For example, musical experiences—both listening to music and taking music lessons—have been shown to have a positive relationship with scores on a variety of cognitive measures, including IQ tests (Schellenberg, 2006b). For preschool-age children, listening to music enhances creativity (Schellenberg, 2006a). Taking music lessons is positively related to academic ability, even when other factors, such as family income, parental education, and participation in activities other than music, are taken into account (Schellenberg, 2006b).

As we mentioned earlier, it is a mistake to think that every lesson has to be designed to involve all eight intelligences. But with a little thought, many lessons can be designed to include two or three. For example, a high school algebra teacher combined kinesthetic and logical-mathematical abilities to teach a lesson on graphing. Instead of using in-class paper-and-pencil exercises,

this teacher took the students outside to the school's courtyard. Using the large cement pavement squares as a grid, she had the students stand at various junctures of the grooves between squares and plot their own locations. Similarly, as part of a primary grade lesson on birds and their nesting habits, students designed and built birdhouses and then noted whether the birds used them, thereby using spatial, bodily-kinesthetic, and logical-mathematical abilities (Armstrong, 2009; L. Campbell, 1997).

Using Technology to Develop Intelligence

Because contemporary theories view intelligence as being made up of modifiable cognitive skills, you shouldn't be overly surprised that there are technology implications for the development of intelligence. In fact, technology education can support higher-level thinking such as metaphorical and analogical thinking; it provides students opportunities to "think outside the box" and, by doing so, to develop their cognitive capabilities (T. Lewis, 2005). Robert Sternberg (1997a) expressed that sentiment when he said, "Technology can enable people to better develop their intelligence—no question about it" (p. 13). Technological environments provide opportunities for students to engage their practical, creative, and analytical abilities in ways not always available in traditional classroom environments, and research (Howard, McGee, Shin, & Shia, 2001, for example) supports this contention.

Like Robert Sternberg, Howard Gardner believes that technology has a role to play in fostering the development of intelligence (or, from his perspective, intelligences). For example, he noted that computer programs allow students who cannot read music or play an instrument to create musical compositions and that interactive virtual environments can engage several intelligences (Gee, 2007; Weiss, 2000). In later chapters, especially Chapters 8 and 10, we will examine virtual learning environments, including multiuser virtual environments, in more detail.

For many educators, technology holds great promise in addressing the MI theory promoted by Gardner (McKenzie, 2002). For instance, web-based conferencing might promote students' interpersonal intelligence. Programs that make it easy to do concept mapping, flowcharts, photo editing, and three-dimensional imaging are closely tied to spatial intelligence (Lach, Little, & Nazzaro, 2003; McKenzie, 2002). Idea generation and prewriting software tools, such as Sunbuddy Writer, Imagination Express, and Inspiration, can assist verbal intelligence (Quenneville, 2001). Computer programming with tools such as LEGO/Logo can help students'

{ Various technology tools may strengthen different intelligences. }

problem-solving and logical-mathematical intelligence (Doppelt, 2009; Gillespie & Beisser, 2001; Suomala & Alajaaski, 2002). Other software addresses musical intelligence (for instance, by enabling students to see musical scores as the notes are played) and bodily-kinesthetic intelligence (by offering a visual breakdown of an athletic skill, such as a tennis swing). Clearly, there are technology tools for all the aspects of intelligence that Sternberg and Gardner described.

LO3 Learning Styles

Whether one conceives of intelligence as having one major component or several, psychologists agree that it is an *ability*. Typically, it is better to have more of an ability than less of it. In recent years, though, psychologists have also studied a characteristic for which what form it takes is more important than how much of it a person has. What we are referring to here is the concept of a *learning style* (*cognitive style* is an alternative term that you will also see in this literature). Unlike abilities, styles are considered to be value neutral—that is, all styles are adaptive under the right circumstances.

A **learning style** can be defined as a consistent preference over time and subject matter for perceiving, thinking about, and organizing information in a particular way (Moskvina & Kozhevnikov, 2011; L. Zhang & Sternberg, 2006, 2009). Some students, for example, prefer to think about the nature of a task, collect relevant information, and formulate a detailed plan before taking any action, whereas others prefer to run with the first idea they have and see where it leads. Some students prefer to work on several aspects of a task simultaneously, whereas others prefer to work on one aspect at a time in a logical sequence.

Notice that styles are referred to as *preferences*. They are not fixed modes of behavior that we are locked into. When the situation warrants, we can, at least temporarily, adopt different styles, although some people are better than others at switching styles.

Over the years, quite a few learning styles have been proposed. You will find, for example, articles about visual learners, verbal learners, assimilators, accommodators, global learners, analytic learners, abstract learners, and concrete learners (see, for example, Rayner & Cools, 2011). Of these many styles, we will examine three. Two of them (reflectivity/impulsivity and field dependence/field independence) were formulated more than 40 years ago and have a long history of research.

The third (mental self-government) is more recent in origin and contains some original elements but also includes styles that have been the subject of some research.

Reflectivity and Impulsivity

One of the first learning style dimensions to be investigated was reflectivity/impulsivity. During the early 1960s, Jerome Kagan (1964a, 1964b) found that some students seem to be characteristically **impulsive**, whereas others are characteristically **reflective**. Impulsive students were said to have a fast conceptual tempo (L. Zhang & Sternberg, 2009). When faced with a task for which there is no ready solution or a question for which the answer is uncertain, the impulsive student responds more quickly than the student who is more reflective. In problem-solving situations, the impulsive student collects less information, does so less systematically, and gives less thought to various solutions than does the more reflective student. The reflective student, in contrast, prefers to spend more time collecting information (which means searching one's memory as well as external sources) and analyzing its relevance to the solution before offering a response (Morgan, 1997).

Like IQ scores, these styles tend to be fairly stable, but they can, as we noted above, change in response to environmental demands. Decreases in television watching among a group of 6-year-olds resulted in decreased impulsivity, increased reflection, and more time spent reading (Greenfield, 2009).

Field Dependence and Field Independence

Another very popular learning style dimension, known as field dependence/field independence, was proposed

learning style A consistent tendency or preference to respond to a variety of intellectual tasks and problems in a particular fashion.

impulsive A learning style in which students respond relatively quickly to questions or tasks for which there is no obvious correct answer or solution.

reflective A learning style in which students collect and analyze information before offering an answer to a question or a solution to a problem.

> **Impulsive students prefer quick action; reflective students prefer to collect and analyze information before acting.**

During the elementary years it becomes apparent that students approach tasks in different ways. This preference for doing things in a particular way is often referred to as a cognitive style. Some students, for example, are impulsive thinkers who tend to react quickly when asked a question; other students are reflective thinkers who prefer to mull over things before answering.

field-dependent
A learning style in which a person's perception of and thinking about a task or problem are strongly influenced by such contextual factors as additional information and other people's behavior.

by Herbert Witkin (Witkin, Moore, Goodenough, & Cox, 1977) and refers to the extent to which a person's perception and thinking about a particular piece of information are influenced by the surrounding context. For example, when some individuals are shown a set of simple geometric figures and asked to locate each one (by outlining it with a pencil) within a larger and more complex display of intersecting lines, those with a field-dependent style take significantly longer to respond and identify fewer of the figures than individuals with a field-independent style. The former are labeled **field-dependent** because their perception is strongly influenced by the prevailing field. The latter are called **field-independent** because they are more

successful in isolating target information despite the fact that it is embedded within a larger and more complex context.

When we talk about individuals who have a field-dependent style and compare them with individuals who have a field-independent style, we do not mean to imply that there are two distinctly different types of individuals. That is like saying that people are either tall or short. Just as people's heights range over a measured span, students can vary in the extent to which they are field-dependent or field-independent. In fact, relatively few individuals exhibit a pure field-dependent or field-independent style (Morgan, 1997; L. Zhang & Sternberg, 2009).

In school, the notes that field-dependent students take are more likely to reflect the structure and sequence of ideas as presented by the teacher or textbook author, whereas the notes of field-independent

Chapter 4: Understanding Student Differences

students are more likely to reflect their own ideas about structure and sequence. When reading, field-independent students are more likely than field-dependent students to analyze the structure of the story. The significance of this difference in approach is clearly seen with materials and tasks that are poorly structured: Field-independent students usually perform better in these situations because of their willingness to create a more meaningful structure.

The positive effect of field independence on achievement is particularly noticeable in the sciences because of their emphasis on analyzing objects and ideas into their component parts, reorganizing ideas into new configurations, and identifying potential new uses of that information. Biology students, for example, need to be able to identify tissues, organs, and systems that are difficult to see at first glance because they are embedded in the surrounding tissue of an organism.

Mental Self-Government Styles

Robert Sternberg (1994), whose ideas on intelligence we discussed earlier in this chapter, proposed an interesting learning style theory that is roughly modeled on the different functions and forms of civil government. This theory of **mental self-government styles** has attracted considerable research (Black & McCoach, 2008; Nielsen, Kreiner, & Styles, 2007; L. Zhang, 2005). Although research to test the theory continues, it is viewed as a useful approach to understanding learning styles in a variety of settings.

In Table 4.3 we briefly describe the main characteristics of each style and suggest an instructional activity consistent with it. If you are wondering how to identify these styles, Sternberg offered a simple solution: Teachers can simply note the type of instruction that various students prefer and the test types on which they perform best.

Evidence that these styles can apply to various cultures came from Hong Kong, where instructional methods tend to emphasize rote learning and to be more regimented than is the case in many U.S. schools. High school students in Hong Kong who expressed a preference for the legislative, liberal, and judicial styles tended to have lower grades than did students who preferred

the conservative and executive styles (L. Zhang & Sternberg, 2001).

Using Awareness of Learning Styles to Guide Instruction

Because the typical classroom contains 25 or more students who may exhibit several styles, teachers must be flexible and learn to use a variety of teaching and assessment methods so that, at some point, every student's style is addressed (recall our discussion of the teacher-artist earlier in the book). An impulsive boy, for example, may disrupt a class discussion by blurting out the first thing that pops into his head, thereby upstaging the reflective types, who are still in the process of formulating more searching answers. To minimize this possibility, you may want to have an informal rotation scheme for recitation or sometimes require that everyone sit and think about a question for two or three minutes before answering.

To give the impulsive style its place in the sun, you might schedule speed drills or question-and-answer sessions covering previously learned basic material.

To motivate students with a legislative style of mental self-government, for example, have them describe what might have happened if a famous historical figure had acted differently than he or she did. For example, how might World War II have ended if President Harry Truman had decided *not* to drop the atomic bomb on Japan? To motivate students with a judicial style, have them compare and contrast the literary characters Tom Sawyer (from Mark Twain's novel of the same name) and Holden Caulfield (from J. D. Salinger's novel *The Catcher in the Rye*). As implied in these examples, a consideration of the diversity of intellectual styles has implications not only for designing instructional activities but also—as we will see in Chapter 14—for designing assessments (Sternberg, Grigorenko, & Zhang, 2008).

Using a variety of instructional techniques and assessments makes sense for several reasons. First, the ways in which students learn can change over time and situations (Compton-Lilly, 2009; Gutiérrez & Rogoff, 2003; Pacheco & Gutiérrez, 2009). Second, using various teaching techniques and testing formats may stimulate students to expand their own repertoire of learning styles (Sternberg, 1994; L. Zhang & Sternberg,

© mikeledray/Shutterstock Images

field-independent
A learning style in which a person's perception of and thinking about a task or problem are influenced more by the person's knowledge base than by the presence of additional information or other people's behavior.

mental self-government styles
A theory of learning style formulated by Robert Sternberg that is based on the different functions and forms of civil government. The theory describes 13 styles that can vary in terms of function, form, level, scope, and learning.

{ **Teachers should use various instructional methods to engage all styles of learning at one time or another.** }

TABLE 4.3 Matching Instructional Activities to Sternberg's Mental Self-Government Styles

Styles	Characteristics	Instructional Activities
Legislative	Prefers to formulate rules and plans, imagine possibilities, and create ideas and products.	Require students to design science projects, write stories, imagine how historical figures might have done things differently, organize work groups.
Executive	Prefers to follow rules and guidelines.	Present well-organized lectures, require students to prepare book reports, work out answers to problems.
Judicial	Prefers to compare things and make evaluations about quality, worth, effectiveness.	Require students to compare literary characters, critique an article, evaluate effectiveness of a program.
Monarchic	Prefers to work on one task at a time or to use a particular approach to tasks.	Assign one project, reading assignment, or homework assignment at a time. Allow ample time to complete all aspects of the assignment before assigning another.
Hierarchic	Prefers to have several tasks to work on, deciding which one to do first, second, and so on, and for how long.	Assign several tasks that vary in length, difficulty, and point value and are due at various times over several weeks.
Oligarchic	Prefers to have several tasks to work on, all of which are treated equally.	Assign several tasks that are equivalent in length, difficulty, and point value.
Anarchic	Prefers an unstructured, random approach to learning that is devoid of rules, procedures, or guidelines.	Assign tasks and problems that require nonconventional thinking and methods, self-directed form of study.
Global	Prefers to have an overall view of a task before beginning work.	Require students to scan a reading assignment to identify major topics, create an outline before writing, formulate a plan before beginning a complex task.
Local	Prefers to identify and work on the details of a particular part of a task before moving to another part.	Present a detailed outline or overview of a lecture or project. Require students to identify and interrelate particular details of each part of a reading assignment.
Internal	Prefers to work alone.	Require seatwork, projects, and assignments that do not depend on others for completion.
External	Prefers to work with others.	Assign group projects or reports, encourage study groups, create discussion groups.
Liberal	Prefers to work out own solution to problems.	Assign projects for which students must work out solution procedures. For example, identify and report on proposed legislation that concerns the environment.
Conservative	Prefers to do things according to established procedures.	Assign homework or projects that specify the steps, procedures, or rules for accomplishing the task.

SOURCE: Adapted from Sternberg (1994) and Zhang (2005).

2009). Finally, recent research suggests that, although students display learning style preferences, they can learn through a variety of instructional tasks (Krätzig & Arbuthnot, 2006). Table 4.3 can serve as a guide for varying your instructional tasks and, consequently, expanding your students' repertoires.

> **Teachers should use various test formats to expand students' repertoire of learning styles and measure accurately what students have learned.**

Using Technology to Accommodate Learning Styles

Just as technology can be used to strengthen different forms of intelligence, it can also be used to accommodate learning styles. Consider a recent study in which elementary students who used a web-based virtual science laboratory—one that integrated both information and communication in their science lessons—earned higher grades than students who engaged the lessons through traditional classroom instruction (Sun, Lin, & Yu, 2008). Although the students who used the web-based virtual lab exhibited different learning styles, there were no differences across learning styles. This finding allowed the authors to conclude that the web-based virtual lab accommodated the diversity of learning styles.

Aside from specific programs, such as a web-based virtual science lab, the range of technological tools that have become available in the Web 2.0 world can be used at all grade levels to address the varied learning styles that students bring to the classroom. Indeed,

Minjuan Wang and Myunghee Kang (2006) coined the term "cybergogy" to refer to ways in which information and communication technologies can be used to engage learners that vary in terms of not only their learning styles but their cultural backgrounds as well.

**Pause&
Reflect** *Analyze yourself in terms of the learning styles discussed in this chapter. Recall classroom situations that made you comfortable because they fit your style(s) and classroom situations in which you were uncomfortable because of a mismatch of style. Now imagine the students who will fill your classroom. Should you even try to design your lessons and assessments so that they match the styles of most students at least some of the time? If so, how will you do that?*

LO4 Gender Differences and Gender Bias

At the beginning of this chapter, we asked you to think about the ways in which friends and classmates from your elementary and high school years may have differed from one another. In all likelihood, you thought about how those people differed cognitively, socially, and emotionally. And with good reason. As we have seen so far in this chapter and in preceding ones, students' academic performance is strongly influenced by their cognitive, social, and emotional characteristics. But there is another major characteristic you may have ignored: gender. Although it may not be obvious, there are noticeable differences in the achievement patterns of males and females (some of which have essentially disappeared in recent years) and in how they are taught.

Gender Differences in Cognition and Achievement Test Scores

A large body of research shows that there are reliable gender differences in cognitive functioning and achievement. On some tests, boys outscore girls; on some tests girls have the upper hand; and on still others there are no discernible differences. Before we get into the specifics, let's make sure we're clear about what these differences mean. The findings that are summarized here are *average* differences. That means there will always be some females who outscore males even though most other females do not, and vice versa.

Generally, research on gender differences has found that males tended to outscore females on the following tests:

- *Visual-spatial ability*. This category includes tests of spatial perception, mental rotation, and spatial visualization. Although males, on average, outscored females on tests of all three of these visual-spatial abilities, the largest and most consistent differences have occurred on tests of spatial perception and mental rotation (Halpern & LaMay, 2000). On mental rotation tests, males were also better at judging how accurately they performed (Cooke-Simpson & Voyer, 2007).

- *College entrance*. Tests such as the SAT and ACT are designed to predict grade-point average at the end of the freshman year of college. The overall superiority of males in this category may be related to the fact that they outscore females on the math items by a larger margin than the females outscore them on the verbal items (Mau & Lynn, 2001).

Females tended to outscore males on the following tests:

- *Memory*. This is a broad category that includes memory for words from word lists, working memory (the number of pieces of information that one is aware of and that are available for immediate use), name–face associations, first name–last name associations, memory for spatial locations, and episodic memory (memories for the events in one's own life). This difference appears to persist throughout the life span (Halpern & LaMay, 2000).

- *Language use*. This is another broad category, encompassing tests of spelling, reading comprehension, writing, onset of speech, and rate of vocabulary growth. Although the gender disparity in language skills has moderated a bit over the years, females continue to outscore males on tests of spelling (Horne, 2007) and reading comprehension (National Center for Education Statistics, 2010a, 2010b). But before anyone in our audience starts tooting their horn, we need to point out one important fact. One of the major sources of data about gender differences in language skills comes from the National Assessment of Educational Progress (NAEP), a national test that is given to fourth, eighth, and twelfth graders in math and English. In 2009, females did outscore males on the language skills portion of the test at all three grade levels. The differences were 7 points, 9 points, and 12 points, respectively. But because this test is scored on a scale of 0 to 500, researchers treat such small differences as being essentially the same.

© Nina Shannon/iStockphoto

That brings us to test scores for which there is no gender difference. While there may seem to be no point in talking about a lack of difference, there is one that is worth mentioning because it represents the elimination of a long-standing difference. We're referring to math scores. On the 2009 NAEP test, average math scores for fourth, eighth, and twelfth grade males and females were essentially the same (National Center for Education Statistics, 2009, 2010a, 2010b). Likewise, state assessments that are used to satisfy the requirements of the No Child Left Behind Act have failed to demonstrate consistent gender differences. To counter the argument that state assessments are not difficult enough to capture the long-standing superiority of males for math reasoning, an analysis of the NAEP math test, which does contain higher-level items, also revealed no gender difference (Hyde, Lindberg, Linn, Ellis, & Williams, 2008).

Why do gender differences in cognition and achievement exist? No one knows for sure, although differences in hormones, brain structure, cognitive processes, and socialization are all thought to play a role. Despite increased awareness of how society reinforces gender role stereotyping and measures taken to ensure greater gender equity, girls and boys continue to receive different messages about what is considered to be appropriate behavior. Are gender differences the result of social pressures to participate in some activities and not others, or are socialization patterns the result of biological differences? Or do both factors play a role? We simply do not know yet.

Gender Differences in School Performance

In addition to gender differences on tests of cognitive skills and academic knowledge, males and females differ in the grades they receive in school and the emotions that accompany those grades. A study of more than 900 fourth, fifth, and sixth grade children (Pomerantz, 2002) showed that the girls on average received higher grades than the boys in language arts, social studies, science, and mathematics. But, somewhat unexpectedly, girls

© bonnie jacobs/iStockphoto

expressed greater worry about academic performance, higher levels of general anxiety, and higher levels of depression. The girls' perceived self-competence was lower than that of the boys for social studies, science, and math.

To put this picture in stark terms, girls achieve higher grades than boys but don't seem to be able to enjoy the fruits of their labors as much. One possibility is that girls are more concerned than boys with pleasing teachers and parents. Thus failure or lower-than-expected achievement is interpreted as disappointing those on whom they depend for approval. Another possibility is that girls are more likely than boys to use academic performance as an indicator of their abilities, spurring them to higher levels of learning as well as higher levels of internal distress because of the possibility of failure. Boys may be better able to maintain higher levels of self-confidence by denying the link between performance and ability.

A more recent study by Angela Duckworth and Martin Seligman (2006) offered an alternative, but related, explanation for the existence of gender differences in cognition and achievement. The authors noted that throughout the school-age years, girls earn higher grades than boys in all major subjects, even though girls do not perform better than boys on achievement or IQ tests. In a study of eighth graders in an urban magnet school, Duckworth and Seligman found that, as a group, females demonstrated more self-discipline than their male counterparts. In this study, eighth grade girls earned higher grade-point averages than boys but did only slightly better on an achievement test and less well on an IQ test. After extensive analyses, Duckworth and Seligman concluded that part of the reason girls had higher grade-point averages was their greater self-discipline. This superiority in self-discipline (or self-regulation, if you prefer that term) can be seen as early as kindergarten and may be at least a partial explanation of why girls earn higher grades than boys (Matthews, Ponitz, & Morrison, 2009). The more researchers learn about gender differences on standardized tests and in school achievement, the more a number of factors beyond cognitive and perceptual abilities seem either to account for those differences or to suggest that such differences are less significant than once thought.

Although you should be aware of the gender differences we have mentioned and should take steps to try to reduce them, you should also keep the following points in mind. First, there are many tasks for which differences do not exist. In fact, a recent review of research on gender differences, supported by the National Science Foundation, advanced the gender similarities hypothesis over the hypothesis of gender differences (Hyde, 2005; see also Marsh, Martin,

& Cheng, 2008). Second, some differences do not appear until later in development. For example, boys and girls have similar scores on tests of mathematical problem solving until adolescence, when boys begin to pull ahead. Third, what is true in general is not true of all individuals. Some boys score higher than most girls on tests of language use, and some girls score higher than most boys on tests of mathematical reasoning (Halpern, Wai, & Saw, 2005; Wigfield, Battle, Keller, & Eccles, 2002). Finally, as Robert Sternberg and Howard Gardner have argued, virtually all cognitive skills can be improved to some degree with the aid of well-designed instruction.

Gender Bias

If you asked your class a question and some students answered without waiting to be called on, how do you think you would react? Do you think you would react differently to male students than to female students? Don't be so sure that you would not. Studies have found that teachers are more willing to listen to and accept the spontaneous answers of male students than female students. Female students are often reminded that they are to raise their hands and be recognized by the teacher before answering. Boys also receive more extensive feedback than do girls, but they are punished more severely than girls for the same infraction. These consistent differences in responses to male and female students when there is no sound educational reason for them are the essence of **gender bias**.

Why do some teachers react differently to males and females? Probably because they are operating from traditional gender role stereotypes: They expect boys to be more impulsive and unruly and girls to be more orderly and obedient (American Association of University Women, 1999; Corbett, Hill, & St. Rose, 2008.)

Exposure to gender bias apparently begins early in a child's school life. Most preschool programs stress the importance of following directions and rules (impulse control) and contain many activities that facilitate small-muscle development and language skills. Because girls are typically better than boys in these areas before they go to preschool, the typical preschool experience does not help girls acquire new academically related skills and attitudes. For example, preschool age girls are usually not as competent as boys at large-motor activities (such as jumping, climbing, throwing, and digging) or investigatory activities (such as turning over rocks or pieces of wood to see what is under them). Lest you think that climbing, digging, and investigating one's environment are trivial behaviors, bear in mind that they are critical to the work of scientists who do field research, such as botanists, geologists, anthropologists, and oceanographers—occupations in which women are significantly underrepresented.

Gender bias is not a simple problem, and understanding it requires placing gender within the context of other social influences such as race, family structures, and socioeconomic class (Corbett, Hill, & St. Rose, 2008). Nevertheless, gender bias has been shown to affect students in a variety of ways.

gender bias The tendency of teachers to respond differently to male and female students when there is no educationally sound reason for doing so.

How Gender Bias Affects Students

Gender bias can affect students in at least three areas: the courses they choose to take, the careers they consider, and the extent to which they participate in class activities and discussions.

Course Selection Given what we have already said about gender bias, you might expect that high school girls would be less inclined than high school boys to take math and science courses. Twenty or so years ago you would have been right, but not anymore. According to the U.S. Department of Education (Freeman, 2004), a larger percentage of high school females in 2000 had taken geometry, algebra II, precalculus, biology, AP or honors biology, and chemistry. In some cases the differences were quite small (25% of males had taken precalculus vs. 28% of females), but in others they were larger (58% of males had taken chemistry vs. 66% of females). The only courses that attracted a greater percentage of males were calculus (12% vs. 11%) and physics (34% vs. 29%).

Pause & Reflect *Can you recall any instances of gender bias from teachers or friends? If so, do you think it had any effect on your choice of career?*

Career Choice As you may be aware because of numerous stories in the media, relatively few girls choose careers in science or mathematics. Wigfield, Battle, Keller, and Eccles (2002) found that a much smaller percentage of women than men held positions in such math- and science-oriented professions as chemistry and biological science (about 31%), engineering (about 18%), computer systems analysis (about 27%), and drafting, surveying, or mapping (about 17%). On the other hand, a much larger percentage of women than men were found in such nonmath and nonscience fields as educational administration (63%), educational and vocational counseling (69%), social work (68%), and public relations (68%).

Correcting Gender Bias

Gender bias can affect students in at least three areas: the courses they choose to take, the careers they consider, and the extent to which they participate in class activities and discussions. . . . As you may be aware because of numerous stories in the media, relatively few girls choose careers in science or mathematics. . . . Several factors are thought to influence the choice male and female students make to pursue a career in science or engineering. (p. 85)

Gender Still Hinders Women Scientists

THE ASSOCIATED PRESS
The Washington Post, 9/18/06

Gender bias—not any biological difference between the sexes—stifles the careers of female scientists at the nation's universities, says a new report that calls for wide-ranging steps to level the playing field.

The study is the latest since Harvard University's president ignited controversy last year by suggesting that innate gender differences may partly explain why fewer women than men reach top university science jobs. The comment eventually cost him his job.

Four times more men than women who hold doctorates in science and engineering have full-time faculty positions, the National Academy of Sciences reported Monday. Minority women are virtually absent from leading tenured positions.

Female scientists typically are paid less, promoted more slowly and receive less funding than male colleagues, discrepancies not explained by productivity, the scientific significance of their work or other performance measures, the report found.

"It is not lack of talent but unintentional biases and outmoded institutional structures that are hindering the access and advancement of women," the report said. "Neither our academic institutions nor our nation can afford such underuse of precious human capital in science and engineering."

University of Miami President Donna Shalala, chairwoman of the committee that wrote the report and a former Health and Human Services secretary, said today's bias is more subtle than she faced in the late 1960s. Shalala switched universities after a boss told her women scientists would never gain tenure because they were "a bad investment"—they might want time off to have babies.

The report calls on:

- The government to enforce existing anti-discrimination laws.

- University leaders to publicize the gender makeup of student enrollments and faculty ranks each year, and counteract bias in hiring and promotion.

- Funders of scientific research to allow grant money for dependent care, so scientists can attend work-related conferences or perform after-hours research.

Source: Associated Press, "Gender still hinders women scientists," as appeared in *The Washington Post,* September 18, 2006. Reprinted by permission of Associated Press.

Questions and Activities

1. This article shows how stereotyping operates—how group characteristics are assumed to be the same for every person belonging to a group. What are the effects of stereotyping cited in this article? How might those same effects operate in a classroom? Have you ever experienced stereotyping? As a teacher, how will you avoid the pitfalls of stereotyping?

2. The National Academy of Sciences report cited in the article makes recommendations to reduce gender bias. How might those recommendations be translated into actions that might be taken to reduce gender bias in classrooms?

3. Keeping in mind that research documents the existence of some gender differences while supporting the gender similarities hypothesis, what ideas can you come up with to ensure that girls think of themselves as equal in ability to boys in math and science?

4. In view of the facts that there are so few female scientists in universities and that a large percentage of education majors are female, what should be done to ensure that future teachers do not help perpetuate the gender bias described in the article?

Several factors are thought to influence the choice male and female students make to pursue a career in science or engineering. One is familiarity with and interest in the tools of science. In one study of middle school science classes in which instructors who were committed to increasing girls' active participation emphasized hands-on experiences, gender differences were still noted. Boys spent more time than girls manipulating the equipment, thereby forcing girls to participate in more passive ways (Jovanovic & King, 1998).

A second factor is perceived self-efficacy (how confident one feels in being able to meet the demands of a task). In the middle school science classes just mentioned (Jovanovic & King, 1998), even though end-of-year science grades were equal for girls and boys, only girls showed a significant decrease in their perception of their science ability over the school year. A 1996 survey found that although fourth grade boys and girls were equally confident about their math abilities, by twelfth grade only 47% of girls were confident about their math skills, as compared with 59% of the boys (Bae, Choy, Geddes, Sable, & Snyder, 2000).

A third factor is the competence-related beliefs and expectations communicated by parents and teachers. Girls who believe they have the ability to succeed in male-dominated fields were encouraged to adopt these

Chapter 4: Understanding Student Differences

Women who choose a career in math or science are likely to be those who do well in science classes, are encouraged to pursue math or science careers by parents or teachers, and have respected models available to emulate.

© Michael Newman/Photo Edit

in math or science, Amy Zeldin and Frank Pajares (2000) wanted to know what sets them apart from equally qualified women who choose other fields. Zeldin and Pajares found that these 15 women had very high levels of self-efficacy for math and science that could be traced to three sources: (1) early and consistent academic success, (2) encouragement to pursue math and science careers from such influential others as parents and teachers, and (3) the availability of respected models (both male and female) whom they could observe and model themselves after. All three sources working in concert appear necessary to persuade women to consider a career in math, science, or technology.

Class Participation As we pointed out earlier, many children tend to adopt the gender role that society portrays as the more appropriate and acceptable. Through the influence of parenting practices, advertising, peer norms, textbooks, and teaching practices, girls are reinforced for being polite, helpful, obedient, nonassertive, quiet, and aware of and responsive to the needs of others. Although views of girls' academic abilities are changing (Corbett, Hill, & St. Rose, 2008), boys, to a greater extent than girls, are reinforced for being assertive, independent, aggressive, competitive, intellectually curious, and achievement oriented. The degree

beliefs by parents and teachers (Wigfield, Battle, Keller, & Eccles, 2002). This chapter's Case in Print describes the findings of a report from the National Academy of Sciences and how those findings account for the gender bias we observe in scientific career fields.

Supporting evidence that factors such as self-efficacy influence career choice comes from a recent study of 15 women with established careers in math, science, or technology. Because there have always been women who have successfully carved out careers

{ **Gender bias can affect the courses students select, the career choices they make, and how much they participate in class.** }

 Gender Equity in the Classroom: Girls and Science

Go to the Education CourseMate website and watch the video, study the artifacts in the case, and reflect upon the following questions:

1. How does the Girls and Science program depicted in this Video Case try to address the problem of gender bias?

2. Describe some of the strategies used by the group leaders to promote gender equity and student interest in the material. Are these strategies effective?

TeachSource Video Case

Suggestions for Teaching

Addressing Student Differences

1 **Design lessons and test items that call for memory, analytical, creative, and practical abilities.**

Robert Sternberg (1997b; Sternberg, Grigorenko, & Zhang, 2008) pointed out that many teachers tend to emphasize memory and analytical abilities, which is fine for students—male or female—who are good at memorizing facts or breaking things down into their component parts and explaining how the parts relate to each other. But students whose abilities are in the creative or practical areas may appear to be less capable than they really are. You can get a better idea of each student's strengths and weaknesses and the degree to which students have learned the subject matter you just taught by using a variety of instructional cues and test items.

To emphasize students' memory abilities when you teach and test, use prompts such as "Who said. . .," "Summarize the ideas of. . .," "Who did. . .," "When did. . .," "How did. . .," and "Describe. . . ."

To emphasize students' analytical abilities, use prompts such as "Why, in your judgment, . . .," "Explain why. . .," "Explain what caused. . .," and "Critique. . . ."

To emphasize creative abilities, use prompts such as "Imagine. . .," "Design. . .," "Suppose that. . .," and "What would happen if. . . ."

To emphasize practical thinking, use prompts such as "Show how you can use. . .," "Implement. . .," and "Demonstrate how in the real world. . . ."

2 **Design lessons that emphasize different intelligences.**

As Howard Gardner and others pointed out, most of the tasks that we ask students to master reflect the linguistic and logical-mathematical forms of intelligence. But there are other ways that students can come to know things and demonstrate what they have learned. Potentially, lesson plans for any subject can be designed that incorporate each of Gardner's eight intelligences. Here are a few examples suggested by Thomas Armstrong (1994, 2009) and David Lazear (2003).

Elementary Grades: Punctuation Marks

- *Bodily-kinesthetic:* Students use their bodies to mimic the shapes of various punctuation marks.
- *Musical:* Students make up different sounds or songs for each punctuation mark.
- *Interpersonal:* In small groups of four to six, students teach and test one another on proper punctuation usage.

Middle School Grades: American History

- *Linguistic:* Students debate the pros and cons of key historical decisions (such as Abraham Lincoln's decision to use military force against the Confederate states, the Supreme Court decision in *Plessy v. Ferguson* that allowed separate facilities for Blacks and Whites, or President Harry Truman's decision to drop the atomic bomb on Japan).
- *Musical:* Students learn about and sing some of the songs that were popular at a particular point in the country's history.
- *Spatial:* Students draw murals that tell the story of a historical period.

High School Grades: Boyle's Law (Physics)

- *Logical-mathematical:* Students solve problems that require the use of Boyle's law: For a fixed mass and temperature of gas, the pressure is inversely proportional to the volume, or $PV = K$.
- *Bodily-kinesthetic:* Students breathe air into their mouths, move it to one side of their mouths (so that one cheek is puffed out), indicate whether the pressure goes up or down, distribute it to both sides of their mouths, and indicate again whether the pressure goes up or down.
- *Intrapersonal:* Students describe times in their lives when they felt they were under either a lot of psychological pressure or little pressure, and whether they felt as if they had either a lot of or a little psychological space.

---

loss of voice The tendency of adolescent females to suppress their true beliefs about issues and respond with claims that they have no opinion or state what they think others want to hear, because of socialization practices.

to which girls feel comfortable expressing themselves and their views is known as *level of voice*. According to Carol Gilligan and others, adolescent girls learn to suppress their true personalities and beliefs. Instead of saying what they really think about a topic, they either say that they have no opinion or say what they think others want to hear. Gilligan referred to this behavior as **loss of voice** (Harter, Waters, & Whitesell, 1997).

To measure the extent of loss of voice in different contexts, Susan Harter, Patricia Waters, and Nancy Whitesell (1997) gave questionnaires to several hundred students of both genders in grades 6 through 12.

The questionnaire items asked students to rate how honestly they voiced their ideas when they were in the presence of teachers, male classmates, female classmates, parents, and close friends. Their main findings were as follows:

- Males and females were most likely to speak their minds when they were with close friends and classmates of the same gender, and were less likely to do so when they were in the presence of members of the opposite gender, parents, and teachers.
- Loss of voice did not increase between grades 6 and 12.
- Equal numbers of males and females reported suppressing their true thoughts in certain circumstances.
- Girls who strongly identified with the stereotypical

3 **Recognize that different styles of learning call for different methods of instruction.**

Robert Sternberg's work on styles of mental self-government called for the same approach to instruction and testing as did his work on intellectual abilities: Use a variety of instructional methods and testing formats. Not only will you have a more accurate picture of what students know, but you will also be helping them learn how to shift styles to adapt to changing conditions. For example, students with a judicial style have a preference for "why" questions (for example, "Why did the United States go to war in Iraq in 2003?"), whereas students with a legislative style have a preference for "suppose" or "what if" questions (for example, "Suppose you were President George W. Bush; would you have gone to war in Iraq?"). Table 4.3 indicates which of Sternberg's learning styles are most compatible with particular methods of instruction.

4 **Help students become aware of the existence of gender bias.**

The following techniques have all been used by teachers to demonstrate that males often receive preferential treatment in our society in somewhat subtle ways (Bailey, 1996; Rop, 1998; Rutledge, 1997):

- Have students count how often in the space of a month male and female athletes are mentioned in the sports section of the local paper, and have them create a graph depicting the difference.
- Have students survey similar-aged friends and classmates about the size of their allowance and report the results by gender.
- Have students review several textbooks and record how often men and women are mentioned.
- Have students keep a record of who participates in class discussions, how often they speak, for how long, and how they respond to comments made by male versus female classmates.

5 **Encourage girls to consider pursuing a career in science.**

A female high school chemistry teacher offers the following suggestions to teachers interested in encouraging adolescent girls to consider a career in science (Rop, 1998):

- Invite female scientists to class to talk about science as a career, or arrange for an exchange through e-mail.
- Have students read articles written by female scientists, contact the authors with questions about the articles, and report the findings to the class.
- Contact recent female graduates who are majoring in science in college, and ask them to talk to the class about their experiences.

6 **Recognize that you will not be able to address the various abilities and cognitive styles of all of your students all of the time.**

Although this chapter has described three major ways in which students differ from one another and explained why it is important to gear instruction to these differences (the goal of differentiated instruction), we do not want you to get the impression that you should strive to accommodate the unique needs of each student every minute of the day. When you have 25 or more students in a class, such a goal is nearly impossible. But that does not mean you should make no attempt to get to know and work with students as individuals, either. You might, for example, adopt the practice of Lori Tukey (2002), a sixth grade teacher. She allowed students themselves to provide basic instruction on various aspects of writing. Each student listed aspects of writing, such as spelling, punctuation, and organization, that he or she wanted to improve. Then those who were proficient at one or more of these aspects were identified as "experts" to whom other students could go for help. This tactic gave the teacher enough extra time to work individually with each student twice a month.

female gender role were more likely than androgynous females (those who exhibit behaviors that are characteristic of both gender roles) to suppress their true thoughts when interacting with their teachers and male classmates. This difference between feminine and androgynous females disappeared with close friends and parents.

- Androgynous males and females who said they were frequently encouraged and supported by teachers for expressing their views were most likely to speak their minds in classroom and other settings.

These findings have major implications for the way in which teachers address female students, particularly those who have adopted a strong feminine gender role, and for the use of constructivist approaches to teaching (discussed in detail in Chapter 13). Because constructivism relies heavily on free and open discussion to produce its effects, teachers need to monitor carefully the verbal exchanges that occur among students and to intervene when necessary to ensure that all students feel that their opinions are getting a fair and respectful hearing.

Working Toward Gender Equity in the Classroom

Much of the literature on gender bias highlights the classroom obstacles that make it difficult for girls to take full advantage of their talents; but another important concept is gender equity, producing an educational experience that will be equally meaningful for students of both genders. Several authors (Bailey, 1996; Jobe, 2002/2003; D. Taylor & Lorimer, 2002/2003) have

Challenging Assumptions

Eliminate Gender Bias

Gender bias, or treating male students differently from female students when such differences are neither warranted nor desirable, should have no place in any teacher's classroom. Because such biases are typically based on stereotypes and prejudices (the type of nonsystematic data we criticized in Chapter 1), they are likely to have the negative impact on students' attitudes toward school, motivation for learning, classroom participation, course selection, and career choice that researchers have documented.

One way to avoid this undesirable practice is to think about the normally unconscious assumptions you make about the capabilities, motives, and interests of males and females, perhaps because of your own socialization. And when students, colleagues, or parents make broad-based, stereotypical statements such as "Girls aren't interested in technology" or "Boys don't like to display their emotions," respond by saying, "Oh, which girl [or boy]?" to get across the point that any given individual can deviate from whatever average trends might exist.

What Do You Think?

Do you believe that all teachers need to take specific steps to combat gender stereotypes? Look into the additional resources on this issue at the "Challenging Assumptions" section of the textbook's Education CourseMate website.

---

suggested the following techniques to benefit both genders:

1. Use work arrangements and reward systems that will encourage all students to value a thorough understanding of a subject or task and that emphasize group success as well as individual accomplishment. In Chapter 13 we describe how a technique called cooperative learning does just this.

2. Emphasize concrete, hands-on science, math, and technology activities.

3. Incorporate math, science, and technology concepts into such other subjects as music, history, art, and social studies.

4. Talk about the practical, everyday applications of math and science. Although girls seem more interested in science when they understand how such knowledge transfers to everyday life, so do many boys. Nobody suffers when the curriculum is made more meaningful and relevant.

5. Emphasize materials that highlight the accomplishments and characteristics of women (such as Hillary Rodham Clinton, Oprah Winfrey, and Sonia Sotomayor) and women's groups.

6. From the titles listed on the website Guys Read (www.guysread.com), create a reading list that appeals to boys.

Gender Differences and Technology: Overcoming the Digital Divide

In the 1980s, when desktop computers first started appearing in classrooms, surveys showed that females were less likely than males to use a computer either at school or at home. That difference disappeared by the beginning of the twenty-first century. A 2001 national survey of children and adolescents between the ages of 5 and 17 found that about 80% of males and females reported using a computer at school and about 65% of both sexes reported using a computer at home (DeBell & Chapman, 2003).

Although there is no overall difference between males and females in computer use, gender differences still exist. In a comparison of males and females of college age, females were shown to experience more

> **Females and males have equal access to computers, but differences in anxiety still exist.**

computer anxiety than males. This was the case even though females perceived themselves to be as capable or "fluent" in using the computer for communication and accessing the web (Bunz, 2009).

The greater anxiety that females experience in the use of computers is thought to be related to the continuing phenomenon of underrepresentation of women in technological fields such as engineering (Bunz, 2009; Kusku, Ozbilgin, & Ozkale, 2007). Among the steps that can be taken to continue to reduce the gender gap is using *telementoring* to put female students in touch with women professionals, especially in occupations in which women are under-represented (Murray, 2009; Whitehouse, McCloskey, & Ketelhut, 2010).

The Suggestions for Teaching in this chapter will help you better respond to differences in intelligence, learning styles, and gender.

WHAT ELSE? *RIP & REVIEW* **CARDS IN THE BACK**

5

ADDRESSING CULTURAL AND SOCIOECONOMIC DIVERSITY

LEARNING OBJECTIVES

After studying this chapter, you will be able to . . .

LO1 Define cultural pluralism and explain how immigration and birthrate patterns have made the United States more culturally diverse.

LO2 Describe how students' ethnicity and social class affect classroom learning and teacher expectancy.

LO3 Define multicultural education and name four basic approaches to multicultural education.

LO4 Describe the following types of bilingual education programs: transition, maintenance, and two-way bilingual.

visit 4ltrpress.cengage.com

To repeat a point we made earlier, if your instructional plans are to be effective, you have to take into account what your students are like. In previous chapters, we described students in terms of their age-related differences in psychosocial, cognitive, and moral development, and we discussed how students typically are similar to and different from one another in terms of physical, social, and cognitive characteristics. In this chapter, we will turn to two other important ways in which students differ: cultural background and language. In the next chapter, we will discuss still another dimension of diversity: the concepts of ability and disability.

Culture is a term that describes how a group of people perceives the world; formulates beliefs; evaluates objects, ideas, and experiences; and behaves. It can be thought of as a blueprint that guides the ways in which individuals within a group do such important things as communicate with others (both verbally and nonverbally), handle time and space, express emotions, and approach work and play. The concept of culture typically includes ethnic groups but can also encompass religious beliefs and socioeconomic status (Banks, 2009; Gollnick & Chinn, 2009).

As you may know from your own experience, from talking to others, and from various news accounts, people tend to identify with a particular group, and each group varies in its beliefs, attitudes, values, and behavior patterns because of differences in cultural norms. (By *norms*, we mean the perceptions, beliefs, and behaviors that characterize most members of a group.) Students who were raised with mainstream American values, for example, are quite comfortable with the practice of working individually and competing with others for academic rewards. The sentence (and forgive the sexist language, it's a saying from an earlier era), "It's every man for himself, so may the best man win" reflects this approach to life. Many Native American and Mexican American children, in contrast, have been taught to deemphasize competition and individual accomplishment in favor of cooperation and group solidarity (D. M. Sadker, Sadker, & Zittleman, 2008). This approach can be summed up by the sentence, "We're all in this together, so we have to help one another." To be an effective teacher in today's world, you need to be aware of the characteristics of various cultures.

The approach to teaching and learning that we will describe in this chapter, one that seeks to foster an understanding of and mutual respect for the values, beliefs, and practices of different cultural groups, is typically referred to as **multicultural education** (although the terms *culturally responsive schooling* and *culturally relevant education* are also used). Because culturally diverse children often come to school with different language backgrounds, another related issue is bilingual education, described at the end of this chapter.

culture A description of the ways a group of people perceives the world; formulates beliefs; evaluates objects, ideas, and experiences; and behaves.

multicultural education An approach to teaching and learning that seeks to foster an understanding of and mutual respect for the values, beliefs, and practices of different cultural groups.

LO1 THE RISE OF MULTICULTURALISM

From Melting Pot to Cultural Pluralism

More than most other countries, the United States is made up of numerous ethnic groups with widely diverse histories, cultural backgrounds, and values. In addition to the hundreds of thousands of Blacks who were brought to the United States as slaves, the United States was peopled by many waves of immigrants, mostly from Europe but also from Asia and Latin America. Throughout the 19th and 20th centuries, the United States needed large numbers of people to settle its western frontier, build its railroads, harvest its natural resources, and work in its growing factories. As Table 5.1 indicates, from 1820 to the end of 2007 just over 73 million immigrants entered the United States.

Throughout this period, the basic view of American society toward immigrants was that they should divest themselves of their old customs, views, allegiances, and rivalries as soon as possible and adopt English as their primary

> **Cultural pluralism assumes that societies should maintain different cultures, that every culture within a society should be respected, and that individuals have the right to participate in society without giving up cultural identity.**

melting pot
A term referring to the assimilation of diverse ethnic groups into one national mainstream.

cultural pluralism
A set of tenets based on three beliefs: (1) a society should strive to maintain different cultures within it; (2) each culture should be respected by others; and (3) individuals within a society should not have to give up their cultural identity.

language, along with mainstream American ideals, values, and customs. This assimilation of diverse ethnic groups into one national mainstream was known as the **melting pot** phenomenon, a term and viewpoint popularized in a 1909 play by Israel Zangwill, *The Melting Pot*. The main institution responsible for bringing about this assimilation was the public school (Ornstein, Levine, & Gutek, 2011).

The notion of America as a great melting pot was generally accepted until the social unrest of the late 1960s and early 1970s. As an outgrowth of urban riots and the civil rights movement, minority ethnic groups argued not only for bilingual education programs in public schools but also for ethnic studies. Since the early 1970s, factors such as discrimination, the desire to maintain culturally specific ideas and practices, and continued immigration from different parts of the world have served to maintain, if not accelerate, this trend toward cultural diversity—or **cultural pluralism**, to use the preferred term. Cultural pluralism rests on three beliefs: (1) that a society should strive to maintain the different cultures that reside within it; (2) that each culture within a society should be respected by others; and (3) that individuals within a society have the right to participate in all aspects of that society without having to give up their cultural identity (Sleeter & Grant, 2009). Our Case in Print for this chapter illustrates how all of these beliefs can be realized.

The Changing Face of the United States

The United States has always been a nation of immigrants. From the mid-1800s to the early 1900s, most immigrants came from European countries. In recent years, Asia (principally China, the Philippine Islands, and

TABLE 5.1 Number of Immigrants to the United States, by Decade

Years	Number	Years	Number
1820–1829	128,502	1920–1929	4,295,510
1830–1839	538,318	1930–1939	699,375
1840–1849	1,427,337	1940–1949	856,608
1850–1859	2,814,554	1950–1959	2,499,268
1860–1869	2,018,261	1960–1969	3,213,749
1870–1879	2,742,137	1970–1979	4,248,203
1880–1889	5,248,568	1980–1989	6,244,379
1890–1899	3,694,294	1990–1999	9,775,398
1900–1909	8,202,388	2000–2007	8,061,486
1910–1919	6,347,380		
		Total	**73,055,715**

SOURCE: U.S. Department of Homeland Security (2008).

India) and the Americas (principally Mexico and South America) have become the major contributors to U.S. immigration.

Adding to the change produced by immigration itself is the fact that immigrant mothers have a higher average birthrate than native-born mothers. As of 2006, native-born women averaged 52 births per 1,000, whereas foreign-born women averaged 70.8 per 1,000

> **The United States is becoming more culturally diverse because of changes in immigration and birthrates.**

FIGURE 5.1 Projected Change in Percentage of School-Age Children for Four Ethnic Groups Between 2010 and 2025

Because of rounding errors, percentages for each year do not add up to exactly 100%.

SOURCE: U.S. Census Bureau (2008b).

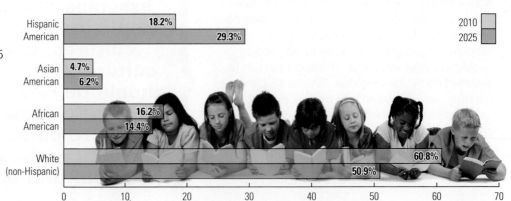

2010
2025

Hispanic American: 18.2% / 29.3%
Asian American: 4.7% / 6.2%
African American: 16.2% / 14.4%
White (non-Hispanic): 60.8% / 50.9%

0   10   20   30   40   50   60   70

Percentage of children from 5 through 18 years of age

Photo: © Christopher Futcher/iStockphoto

Chapter 5: Addressing Cultural and Socioeconomic Diversity

Case in Print

Cultural Diversity and E Pluribus Unum (Out of Many, One)

Since the early 1970s, factors such as discrimination, the desire to maintain culturally specific ideas and practices, and continued immigration from different parts of the world have served to maintain, if not accelerate, this trend toward cultural diversity—or cultural pluralism, to use the preferred term. Cultural pluralism rests on three beliefs: (1) that a society should strive to maintain the different cultures that reside within it; (2) that each culture within a society should be respected by others; and (3) that individuals within a society have the right to participate in all aspects of that society without having to give up their cultural identity. (p. 94)

Melting Pot Seems to Be Working Fine at This School

THERESA TIGHE

St. Louis Post-Dispatch, 10/20/06

This year students at Affton High School selected Selma Delic, a Bosnian refugee, to be senior class president and also homecoming queen.

Some people in the district say those honors mean that the tension that once existed between Bosnian and native-born Affton students has dissipated.

In the late 90s, Bosnian refugees began settling in the Affton area and sending their children to its schools. About 20 percent of the students in the district spoke a language other than English first. The majority of them are Bosnian.

Teri Blackburn, who teaches English as a second language at the school, said Selma's election couldn't have happened 10 to 12 years ago.

She said, "Native speakers were overwhelmed by people speaking a foreign language. People thought they were being talked about. There were cliques. They didn't sit together. If an argument were started by either side, neither side wanted to back down because of their differences."

Blackburn said the school didn't have any real trouble such as fights, which some districts experienced with the influx of Bosnian students. But she said it took four years before the two groups started to mingle.

Teachers at the high school say the tension there eased because of the passage of time. The youngsters have become accustomed to one another. The Bosnians

speak better English. Bosnians and Affton natives began to know one another by working together on class projects and in school activities.

Dzenita Horic, 20, lived through the change. A Bosnian, she began attending Affton district schools in the eighth grade. She said, "It was Bosnian kids on one side and American kids on another."

Horic said that by the time she graduated from Affton High, "we were all mixed together. I think we all grew up and realized we are all in the same boat. I think curiosity for each other's lifestyle helped."

She said it had irritated her that the other students didn't initially want to know about the Bosnian culture.

Horic said religion wasn't the reason for the division; rather, it helped break down the walls. She said other students would ask her about things such as the fast in Ramadan. She said she wanted to know what the Affton natives did after school and on Saturdays and about their values.

The success of Affton High's soccer team two years ago also helped. Five of the eleven starters were Bosnian, and the team won its district and went to the state finals. There was a little initial friction, but the players learned that wins weren't possible without team cooperation. The school cheered for the Affton High team, not the Bosnian or the American team.

Phil Beermann, the school's athletic director, said that when the Bosnians arrived in the school district, the players tended to play with their own nationalities. He said, "I really felt like we needed two soccer balls. It wasn't malicious. It was just that they were working with players of the same culture."

Admir Gledovic, an Affton graduate who played on that team, says Bosnians love soccer. He says that for Bosnian players, soccer is a link to their homeland and helps them build relationships with Americans.

The principal of Affton High, Jeff Morris, said, "Now it's just Affton High School. If we have trouble between kids, it's not because of ethnic differences."

Selma and her friends drew a blank when asked about ethnic divisions.

Selma said, "I never was picked on. It's not really like that."

Carl Stafford—a senior, a football player and an African-American at the school—said, "Bosnians hang with Bosnians, and

blacks with blacks, and white with white. But they don't only hang with each other."

Selma is a hardworking young woman with a winning smile and engaging manner. She divides the school into those who take part in school activities and those who don't. Her goal for the year is to unite them.

She said, "I want to make sure that everyone helps with class activities and goes to the dances."

Source: Teresa Tighe, "Melting pot seems to be working fine at this school," from *St. Louis Post-Dispatch*, October 20, 2006. Reprinted by permission of *St. Louis Post-Dispatch*.

Questions and Activities

1. Teri Blackburn, the English-as-a-second-language teacher at Affton High School, noted that for the first 4 years the Bosnian and native Affton students were suspicious of each other and remained in separate cliques. Based on what you read in Chapters 2 and 3, what characteristics of adolescence may also have contributed to this type of behavior?

2. After approximately 4 years, tension between the two groups eased, they began working together on class projects, and friendships formed. According to the teachers, this was due largely to the passage of time and the Bosnian students' becoming more fluent in English. Can you think of things the teachers might have done to help bring this goal about sooner? Here's a hint: A Bosnian student said she thought curiosity about each other's lifestyles helped.

3. A Bosnian student who attended Affton High School commented that because Bosnians love to play soccer, that sport was a link to their homeland and culture and helped them build relationships with the American students who also played soccer. How might you help students from different cultures that do not have a particular sport in common accomplish the same goal?

Suggestions for Teaching

Taking Account of Your Students' Cultural Differences

1 **Recognize that differences are not necessarily deficits.**

Students who subscribe to different value systems and exhibit different communication patterns, time orientations, learning modes, motives, and aspirations should not be viewed as incapable (García, 2002). Looking on ethnic and social class differences as deficits usually stems from an attitude called *ethnocentrism*. This is the tendency of people to think of their own culture as superior to the culture of other groups. You may be able to moderate your ethnocentric tendencies and motivate your students to learn by consciously using instructional tactics that are congruent with the different cultural backgrounds of your students.

2 **Recognize that the groups we and others describe with a general label are frequently made up of subgroups with somewhat different characteristics.**

These subgroups, in fact, may use different labels to refer to themselves. Among Native Americans, for example, Navajo differ from Hopi in physical appearance,

dress, and hairstyle. Individuals who are called Hispanic may trace their ancestry to one of a dozen or more countries and often refer to themselves as either Chicano, Latino, Mexicano, of Mexican descent, or of Spanish descent (Okagaki, 2006; Schmidt, 2003). One teacher, despite 18 years' experience, found herself ill prepared to teach children on a Chippewa-Cree reservation partly because she knew relatively little about the history, culture, and community in which she taught (Starnes, 2006). Learn as much as you can about the subgroups your students come from, and keep these specific qualities in mind as you teach.

3 **Above all, remember that each student is a unique person. Although descriptions of various ethnic groups and subgroups may accurately portray some general tendencies of a large group of people, they may apply only partly or not at all to given individuals.**

Rather than thinking of culture as a set of perceptions, thoughts, beliefs, and actions that are inherent in all individuals who nominally belong to a culture (perhaps

because of surname or country of origin), you will be far better served in working with students and their parents if you take the time to understand the extent to which individuals participate in the practices of their cultural communities. For example, some Latino students may prefer cooperative learning arrangements because such behavior is the norm at home and in their community, whereas others may prefer to work independently because that behavior is more typical for them (Gutiérrez & Rogoff, 2003). And although many Latino students earn lower grades and test scores than their White peers, there are also many who do not fit this pattern. Researchers found that Latino students who spoke English at home, who came from two-parent families, who spent more time on homework than their peers, and who had parents who supervised their homework not only significantly outscored their Latino peers who did not share these characteristics but also scored at the same level as White students who shared the same characteristics (Ramirez & Carpenter, 2005).

---

ethnic group A collection of people who identify with one another on the basis of such characteristics as ancestral origin, race, religion, language, values, political or economic interests, and behavior patterns.

(U.S. Census Bureau, 2008a). So what do these immigration and birthrate patterns mean to you and other future teachers? Classrooms will become increasingly culturally diverse (see Figure 5.1), and teachers will need to become familiar and comfortable with multicultural approaches to teaching.

Much of the rest of this chapter will focus on some of the major cultural characteristics of certain groups of students. But for you and your students to benefit from your knowledge of cultural diversity, you must view it in the proper perspective. The perspective we encourage you to adopt has three aspects, which are described in the Suggestions for Teaching above.

**Pause &
Reflect** How can you use the concept of constructivism (discussed in Chapter 2) to help students overcome any ethnocentrism they may have and understand the beliefs and practices of other cultures?

LO2 ETHNICITY AND SOCIAL CLASS

As we pointed out in the opening paragraphs of this chapter, culture refers to the ways in which a group of people perceives, thinks about, and interacts with the world. It provides a set of norms that guide what we say and how we say it, what we feel, and what we do in various situations. Two significant factors that most readily distinguish one culture from another are ethnicity and social class.

The Effect of Ethnicity on Learning

An **ethnic group** is a collection of people who identify with one another on the basis of one or more of the following characteristics: country from which one's ancestors came, race, religion, language, values, political interests, economic interests, and behavior

> **Ethnocentrism: belief that one's own culture is superior to other cultures**

patterns (Banks, 2009; Gollnick & Chinn, 2009). Viewed separately, the ethnic groups in the United States, particularly those of color, are numerical minorities; collectively, however, they constitute a considerable portion of American society (Banks, 2009). Most Americans identify with some ethnic group (Blacks, Chinese Americans, Latinos, German Americans, Irish Americans, and Italian Americans, to name but a few). As a teacher, you need to know how your students' ethnicity can affect student–teacher relationships.

Christine Bennett (2007) identifies five aspects of ethnicity that are potential sources of student–student and student–teacher misunderstanding: verbal communication patterns, nonverbal communication, time orientation, social values, and instructional formats and learning processes.

Verbal Communication Patterns Problems with verbal communication can occur when the values taught at home are different from those that govern classroom interactions. For example, in Latino families in which there are several siblings and the parenting style is authoritarian, children may be reluctant to enter into a teacher-led discussion in class. Because teachers, like parents, are viewed as authority figures, many children consider it inappropriate for them to offer their opinions. They are there to learn what the teacher tells them. But as with their siblings at home, they may be quite active in small-group discussions composed entirely of peers (García, 2002). American Indian culture provides another example. Some American Indian children prefer to work on ideas and skills in private until an acceptable degree of mastery is attained. Only then is a public performance considered appropriate (C. I. Bennett, 2007; K. Morrison, 2009).

Nonverbal Communication A form of nonverbal communication that mainstream American culture highly values is direct eye contact. Most people are taught to look directly at the person to whom they are speaking, because this behavior is believed to signify honesty on

the part of the speaker and interest on the part of the listener. Among certain American Indian, Latino, and Asian cultures, however, averting one's eyes is a sign of deference to and respect for the other person, whereas looking at someone directly while being corrected is a sign of defiance. Thus an Asian American, Latino, or American Indian student who looks down or away when being questioned or corrected about something is not necessarily trying to hide guilt or ignorance or to communicate lack of interest (C. I. Bennett, 2007; Castagno & Brayboy, 2008; Pewewardy, 2002).

Time Orientation Mainstream American culture is very time oriented, and people who know how to organize their time and work efficiently are praised and rewarded. We teach our children to value such statements as "Time is money" and "Never put off until tomorrow what you can do today." Nowhere else is this time orientation more evident than in our schools. Classes begin and end at a specified time regardless of whether one is interested in starting a project, pursuing a discussion, or finishing an experiment. But for students whose ethnic cultures are not so time bound (Latinos and American Indians, for example), such a rigid approach to learning may be upsetting. Indeed, it may also be upsetting to some students who reflect the mainstream culture (C. I. Bennett, 2007; Hansen, 2010).

Social Values Two values that lie at the heart of mainstream American society are competition ("Competition brings out the best in people") and rugged individualism ("People's accomplishments should reflect their own efforts"). Because schools tend to reflect mainstream beliefs, many classroom activities are competitive and done on one's own for one's personal benefit. However, students from some ethnic groups, such as Mexican Americans, are more likely to have been taught to value cooperative relationships and family loyalty. These students may thus prefer group projects; they may also respond more positively to praise that emphasizes family pride rather than individual glory (C. I. Bennett, 2007).

Instructional Formats and Learning Processes Finally, ethnic groups may differ in terms of the instructional formats and learning processes they prefer. The dominant instructional format, especially at the middle school and high school levels, is one in which all students work

encourage interpersonal interactions and the use of several sensory modalities, have produced positive results with Hawaiian children (Okagaki, 2001) and children of color (Sleeter & Grant, 2009).

But before you embrace a particular instructional format, make sure its demands are consistent with the cultural characteristics of your students. Here are two examples of why this factor needs to be carefully considered *before* instruction begins. In the first example, American college instructors found that freshman students at a Singapore university did not embrace such Web 2.0 applications as wikis, blogs, and Facebook as enthusiastically as did their American counterparts. The problem for Asian students is that reading, responding to, and modifying the work of classmates goes against such cultural norms as being loyal to your peers, not allowing them to lose face, and being cooperative rather than argumentative (Young, 2010). In the second example, Navajo students, who are taught by their culture to treat serious learning as private, may not fully participate in such traditionally Western activities as question-and-answer sessions, tests, debates, and contests (K. Morrison, 2009; Okagaki, 2001; Soldier, 1997).

With respect to learning processes, some researchers have found that many American Indians prefer, and learn more when they are prompted to use, visual imagery and drawing as a supplement to written and

Students from different ethnic groups often prefer different instructional formats and learning processes. Black students, for example, may favor cooperative learning over lecture and recitation, whereas American Indian students may dislike debates and contests.

from the same text, workbook, and worksheets. Rows of chairs face the front of the room, and the teacher governs exchanges with students by talking, asking questions, listening to answers, and asking for comments from specific students (Sleeter & Grant, 2009). Although we don't advocate totally abandoning this format, we do believe that it should be supplemented by other formats, such as role-playing, peer tutoring, small-group activities, and visual media (photographs and video, for example). These and other formats, which

{ **Ethnic group members may favor different learning arrangements and processes.** }

 Integrating Internet Research: High School Social Studies

Go to the Education CourseMate website and watch the video, study the artifacts in the case, and reflect upon the following questions:

1. Why is the computer-based assignment on the civil rights movement that is portrayed in this video clip likely to help high school students, especially those from minority groups, learn more about the topic than if they simply read about it or listened to their teacher lecture?

2. Elizabeth Sweeney, the teacher in this clip, says that as a relatively new teacher she was hesitant to use the computer lab because it meant allowing the task to become more student-centered and less teacher-directed. Do you think you will feel the same as a novice teacher? How did Ms. Sweeney get over her reluctance? Do you agree with her explanation?

TeachSource Video Case

Chapter 5: Addressing Cultural and Socioeconomic Diversity

spoken forms of instruction (Castagno & Brayboy, 2008; Marley & Levin, 2006; Marley, Levin, & Glenberg, 2007). Additional evidence that students' cultural backgrounds influence the learning processes they use comes from the work of Nola Purdie and John Hattie (1996). They found that Japanese students chose memorizing as their preferred learning processes, whereas a similar group of Australian students gave it a very low preference rating (18th out of 24 options). But it was a third group that produced the most surprising finding. A group of Japanese students who had been living in Australia for almost 3 years at the time of the study fell in between these two extremes (Li, 2002).

These findings suggest that although cultural background does influence choice of learning activity, the effects of culture seem to diminish as one becomes more accustomed to and comfortable with the values and practices of another culture.

The Effect of Social Class on Learning

The social class from which a student comes plays an influential role in behavior. **Social class** is an indicator of an individual's or a family's relative standing in society. It is determined by such factors as annual income, occupation, amount of education, place of residence, types of organizations to which family members belong, manner of dress, and material possessions. The first three factors are used by the federal government to determine the closely related concept of **socioeconomic status (SES)**.

For a variety of reasons, many members of such ethnic minority groups as Blacks, Latinos, and American Indians, as well as low-SES Whites, have fewer years of education, less prestigious occupations, and lower incomes than the average White person (Wiggan, 2007). Although most children who live in families with incomes below the poverty level are White (meaning of European ancestry), you can see from Figure 5.2 that

the poverty *rates* (meaning the percentage of people in a group who live below the official poverty line) among Black, American Indian, and Hispanic American families are usually about three times higher than those for White children (DeNavas-Walt, Proctor, & Smith, 2009; U.S. Census Bureau, 2009).

Ethnic minority children from low-SES families face a variety of obstacles that can negatively affect school achievement. In the next several pages, we describe some of these impediments.

Health Status Many low-SES Americans do not receive satisfactory health care (Stinson, 2003). For example, there is a greater incidence of premature births, birth defects, and infant mortality among low-SES children than among middle-SES children (Umar, 2003). Because poor children do not receive medical or dental care regularly, accurate statistics on general health are difficult to compile. It seems reasonable to assume, however, that the same inadequate nutrition and health care that leads to elevated infant mortality rates probably also leads to higher rates of illness in later years.

Another health-related factor in the development and intellectual performance of low-SES children is lead poisoning. Because many of these children live

FIGURE 5.2 Percentage of Families Within Ethnic Groups Living Below Poverty Level in 2008

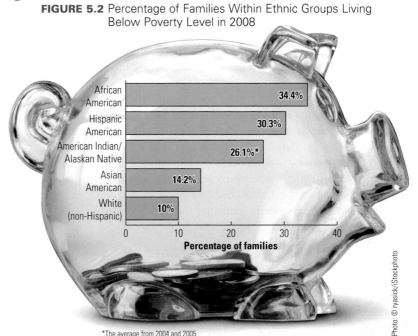

African American — 34.4%
Hispanic American — 30.3%
American Indian/Alaskan Native — 26.1%*
Asian American — 14.2%
White (non-Hispanic) — 10%

Percentage of families

*The average from 2004 and 2005.

SOURCES: DeNavas-Walt, Proctor, & Smith (2009); U.S. Census Bureau (2009).

Photo: © ryasick/iStockphoto

On average, ethnic minority and low-SES students do not perform as well as other groups in school because of such factors as poor health care, an unstable family environment, low motivation, negative attitudes toward school, and negative classroom environments.

© Catherine Karnow/CORBIS

in homes that were painted prior to the discontinuation of lead-based paint, their ingestion of paint dust and chips leads to elevated levels of lead in the blood. Exposure to lead, even in small amounts, is associated with low standardized test scores, attention deficits, and disruptive behavior in children.

Living Conditions Many low-SES students, especially those in urban areas, live in relatively small, and sometimes overcrowded, apartments. Adequate study space is often nonexistent, and parental supervision is spotty or absent. Their neighborhoods tend to be characterized by high levels of street crime and low levels of cohesion. That is, people often do not get along, are unwilling to help their neighbors, and do not watch over each other's property when they are away. Such adverse living conditions are associated with lower aspirations for attending college (Stewart, Stewart, & Simons, 2007). An additional burden for approximately 25% of Black and Latino primary grade children is changing schools due to a change in residence by the family. The challenge of new peers, instructional methods, and curricula may exacerbate whatever learning problems these students already have (R. Evans, 2005).

Family Environment Considerable research has shown that various aspects of family life, including those discussed in the following paragraphs, affect a child's cognitive development and school achievement (see, for example, Barton & Coley, 2007; Raudenbush, 2009). Low-SES students are more likely than middle-SES students to grow up in one-parent families. About

54% of Black students live with one parent versus approximately 19% of White students, with the father usually being the missing parent (Planty et al., 2008). Like many other risk factors, the effect of a one-parent family on the academic performance of a child is not straightforward. It depends on such factors as the duration and cause of the absent parent's separation, the age and sex of the child, and the type of interactions the child has with the remaining parent. But although one-parent families may not negatively affect a child's performance in school, two-parent families are likely to be more effective because both parents have the potential to exert a positive influence (Barton & Coley, 2007).

Some studies show that parents' support for their children's schooling varies by social class and ethnic group. For example, White and Asian American adolescents are more likely than Latino or Black adolescents to get support for academic achievement from parents as well as friends (Castagno & Brayboy, 2008; J. S. Lee & Bowen, 2006; Okagaki, 2001, 2006).

Because low-SES parents speak about 600 words per hour to their children, whereas middle- and upper-middle-SES parents speak about 2,100 words per hour to their children, many Black and Latino children start school with a vocabulary of about 5,000 words, whereas the average White student has a vocabulary of about 20,000 words (B. Hart & Risley, 1995). These experiences accumulate and make school learning easier and more familiar than it would otherwise be. A child who has not had such experiences is likely to be at a disadvantage when placed in competitive academic situations (Barton & Coley, 2007; Raudenbush, 2009).

Families from different SES levels also differ in home access to the Internet, producing what some call a technological underclass. In 2009, almost 80% of married couples with children had Internet access at home, as compared to 58% of single-parent families and 68% of families without children (Economics and Statistics Administration & National Telecommunications and Information Administration, 2010).

Overall, the interactions that occur between low-SES parents and their children tend to lack the characteristic of mediation (a concept we introduced earlier in the book in connection with Vygotsky's theory of cognitive development). When mediation occurs, someone who is more intellectually advanced than the learner presents, explains, and interprets stimuli in a way that produces a more meaningful understanding than the learner could have obtained working alone.

To illustrate this process, imagine a child walking alone through a hands-on science museum looking at the various exhibits, occasionally pushing the buttons of interactive displays, and listening to some of the prerecorded messages. What the child learns from this

Chapter 5: Addressing Cultural and Socioeconomic Diversity

experience is likely to be a haphazard collection of isolated fragments of information that are not meaningful. Now imagine another child of the same age looking at and interacting with the same exhibits but accompanied by a parent or older sibling who wants this to be a meaningful learning experience. The parent or sibling points out specific aspects of the displays, names them, describes their purpose, and explains how they work. This child is more likely than the first child to construct a set of cohesive, interrelated, and meaningful knowledge structures (Ben-Hur, 1998).

Beliefs and Attitudes About School As if the handicaps already mentioned weren't enough, some minority students, especially males, develop beliefs and attitudes that inhibit strong academic performance:

• In general, Black and Latino adolescents were more likely than Asian American or White adolescents to believe that they could get a good job without first getting a good education. But Asian American, White, and Latino adolescents who were doing well in school saw getting a good education as a prerequisite to getting a good job (Ogbu, 2003; Okagaki, 2001).

• Black and Hispanic girls in the second, fourth, and seventh grades were much more likely to admire, respect, and want to be like high-achieving female classmates than average- or low-achieving classmates. Although Black and Hispanic second- and fourth-grade boys responded similarly, the seventh-grade boys included many more low achievers on their list of admired and respected peers (A. Z. Taylor & Graham, 2007).

• Black students with a B+ or higher grade point average (GPA) and Latino students with a C+ or higher GPA were less popular with their peers than were Black and Latino students with lower grades (Fryer & Torelli, 2005).

• Personal experiences with racial discrimination (or even the suspicion that one has been discriminated against) have been linked to decreased perceptions of mastery, mistrust of teachers and school rules, and negative attitudes toward school (Graham & Hudley, 2005; A. Z. Taylor & Graham, 2007).

Why would minority students adopt such self-defeating attitudes and values? The surface explanation has to do with culture. In the peer culture of these students it is considered poor form to "act White" (work hard in school in order to achieve high grades), and one

risks rejection by doing so. The underlying reasons for the existence of this culture are a sense that one is not part of the larger school community, that school does not meet one's needs, that one is incapable of meeting academic demands, and that schoolwork is not part of who one wants to be (Fryer & Torelli, 2005; D. B. Jackson, 2003; Okagaki, 2006).

The frustration created by peers who do not share one's academic values was described by a Black female student who was attending a student conference of the Minority Student Achievement Network:

I'm a member from Amherst, Massachusetts, and it is predominantly White.... I'm able to get along with the White kids, but it's the Black kids that I find I have a hard time relating to.... In class, they're always thinking, "There goes that girl, trying to be smart, trying to 'act White.'" It seems like I can't relate to them, and I'm Black myself. How is that supposed to make me feel? I'm trying to fit in both worlds, and it's like I have no place. (C. Ash, 2000, p. 6)

Level of Motivation Many low-SES students (as well as some middle-SES students) may not be strongly motivated to do well in school because of one or more of several variables. One is lower levels of a characteristic called *need for achievement*. A need for achievement (which is discussed more fully in Chapter 11) is a drive to accomplish tasks and is thought to be one of the main reasons that people vary in their willingness to invest time and energy in the achievement of a goal. Research suggests that low-SES Black students score lower than comparable groups of White students on tests of need for achievement, but this racial difference is considerably smaller among middle-SES samples (Cooper & Dorr, 1995).

© Paul Tessier/iStockphoto

Achievement Levels All of the factors cited previously—health status, living conditions, family environment, school-related beliefs and attitudes, and motivation levels—can and do play a role in the poor academic performance of many students of color as compared to that of White students. Compared with White high school sophomores and seniors, Black, Latino, and American Indian students scored lower on standardized tests of vocabulary, reading, writing, mathematics, and science (Reardon, 2008; Reardon & Galindo, 2009). This difference in test scores is the often-mentioned *achievement gap*, and it has been found even among Black students who are members of relatively affluent middle-SES families (Ogbu, 2003; Rothstein, 2004). These differences appear during the preschool years and continue to grow during the primary and elementary grades. Between first and third grade, the gap in math achievement has been estimated to grow by 10% and the gap in reading by 40%. The gap continues to grow in subsequent grades, but at a slower rate (Reardon, 2008; Reardon & Galindo, 2009). Over the past 15 or so years, progress in narrowing the achievement gap (as measured by the National Assessment of Educational Progress test results) has been inconsistent. The gap was narrowed for some grade levels but not others, and for some minority groups but not others (National Center for Education Statistics, 2009). Obviously, much remains to be learned about why this gap exists and what can be done to consistently work toward its elimination.

At this point, we would like to repeat the advice we gave you at the beginning of this chapter: Don't fall into the trap of assuming that every student of color fits the portrait we've painted here. That's called stereotyping and it can have serious negative effects on your teaching effectiveness. To cite just one example, kindergarten children whose parents had recently emigrated from Mexico or Central America had lower scores on tests of reading and math skills than did students whose parents had recently emigrated from Cuba or South America (Reardon & Galindo, 2009).

© Tom Freeze/Shutterstock Images

> ## Children of color often score lower on tests and drop out of school sooner because of various social class factors.

Graduation Rates We now come to the last link in the chain of the effects of culture and SES on students—graduation from high school. It has been well documented for some time that significantly fewer Black, Latino, and American Indian adolescents graduate from high school than do Whites, thereby shortening their years of education and earning potential. What is not agreed upon is the exact percentage. Because researchers do not always use the same sets of data to determine the percentage of Black students who gradu-

ate from high school (some use data from the Census Bureau, whereas others use data published by the National Center for Educational Statistics), you can often find large differences in this statistic. Some researchers (such as C. B. Swanson, 2004) claim that almost half of all Black and Latino students do not receive a high school diploma; others (such as Mishel & Roy, 2007) claim that the figure is approximately 25% if one counts those who eventually obtain a GED (General Education Diploma). Investigations into the reasons that minority students fail to complete school have found that social class factors, economic factors, school environment factors, and individual factors may all play a role. Compared with White students who graduate, minority students have lower levels of motivation, lower self-esteem, and weaker academic skills; they are also more impulsive. In addition, students who do not graduate nearly always report a sense of alienation from school because of low teacher expectations (more on this in the next section), expressions of racial or ethnic group prejudice from teachers and students, and unfair discrimination. Students of any racial or ethnic group, whether White, Black, or Hispanic, who are required to repeat grades (recall our discussion of this topic in Chapter 1) are among the most likely to drop out of school and not graduate (Menzer & Hampel, 2009; Ramirez & Carpenter, 2009).

Pause & Reflect *What steps might you take to reduce or eliminate the sense of alienation that causes many students of color to drop out of school?*

The Effect of Ethnicity and Social Class on Teachers' Expectations

So far we have described how students' ethnic and social class backgrounds influence their approach to and success with various learning tasks. Now we would like to tell you how those and other characteristics often affect (consciously and unconsciously) the expectations that teachers have for student performance and how those expectations affect the quantity and quality of work that students exhibit. This phenomenon has been extensively studied since it was first proposed in 1968 and is typically referred to as the **teacher expectancy effect**. By becoming aware of the major factors that influence teachers' perceptions of and actions toward students, you may be able to reduce subjectivity to a minimum, particularly with students whose cultural backgrounds are very different from your own.

Teacher expectancy effect: students behave in ways that are consistent with expectations that teachers communicate

The teacher expectancy effect basically works as follows:

1. On the basis of such characteristics as race, SES, ethnic background, dress, speech pattern, and test scores, teachers form expectancies about how various students will perform in class.

2. They subtly communicate those expectancies to the students in a variety of ways.

3. Students come to behave in a way that is consistent with what the teacher expects.

Pause & Reflect *How have your experiences with members of ethnic or racial minority groups been similar to or different from what you have heard and read about those groups? Which source (personal experience or ideas derived from others) most affects your expectations for minority students?*

Research on the Effects of Teachers' Expectancies
Given the obvious implications of the teacher expectancy effect for shaping student behavior, researchers have been investigating its validity and limits for the last 40 years (see Spitz, 1999, for an excellent summary and analysis of the original and subsequent research, and Rosenthal, 2002, for the views of the senior author of the original study).

Research that has investigated the effect of teacher expectancy on classroom achievement and participation has generally found sizable positive *and* negative effects (Benner & Mistry, 2007; M. Chen & Bargh, 1997; T. L. Good & Nicholls, 2001; Jussim, Eccles, & Madon, 1996). For example, a study of several hundred low-income students between the ages of 9 and 16 (Benner

& Mistry, 2007) found that both mothers' and teachers' expectations were positively related to students' expectations and students' perceptions of their own ability, and that students' expectations and ability perceptions were positively related to achievement. Low expectations by both mother and teacher also had an impact on student achievement, albeit a negative one.

Teacher expectations are more likely to maintain already existing tendencies than to alter well-established behaviors drastically. When primary grade teachers work with the more proficient readers, they tend to smile, lean toward the students, and establish eye contact more often, and give criticism in friendlier, gentler tones than they use with the slow-track group. They often overlook the oral reading errors of proficient readers, and when they give corrections, they do so at the end of the sentence or other meaningful unit rather than in the middle of such units. And they ask comprehension questions more often than factual questions as a means of monitoring students' attention to the reading selection.

In contrast, teachers correct less proficient readers more often and in places that interrupt meaningful processing of the text, give these students less time to decode difficult words or to correct themselves, and ask low-level factual questions as a way of checking on students' attention. Teachers' body posture is often characterized by frowning, pursing the lips, shaking the head, pointing a finger, and sitting erect. As a result, initial differences between good and poor readers either remain or widen over the course of the school career (Graham & Hudley, 2005; Wuthrick, 1990).

{ Teacher expectancy has a strong effect on achievement and participation. }

Factors That Help Create Expectancies In addition to documenting the existence of teacher expectancy effects and the conditions under which they occur, researchers have sought to identify the factors that might create high or low teacher expectations. Here are some important factors taken from analyses by Thomas Good and Sharon Nicholls (2001), Vonnie McLoyd (1998), Sonia Nieto (2008), Harriet Tenenbaum and Martin Ruck (2007), and Yong Zhao and Wei Qiu (2009):

Teacher expectancies are influenced by social class, ethnic background, achievement, attractiveness, and gender.

Suggestions for Teaching

Promoting Classroom Achievement for All Students

1 **Use research findings for ideas about teaching educationally disadvantaged students.**

While you cannot do much, if anything, about a student's social class, health status, family dynamics, or peer group, you can, as the following study illustrates, do a great deal to encourage learning among students of all social classes. First-grade children who were judged to be at risk for academic failure scored at about the same level on a standardized achievement test as their not-at-risk peers when they experienced high levels of emotional and instructional support from their teachers. By contrast, at-risk children whose teachers were judged to provide lower levels of emotional and instructional support scored significantly below their not-at-risk peers (Hamre & Pianta, 2005).

What constitutes high levels of emotional and instructional support? Results from several studies (e.g., Burris & Welner, 2005; Denbo, 2002; D. Gardner, 2007; Hamre & Pianta, 2005; Mathis, 2005; Pogrow, 2009a) suggest the following characteristics:

- Being aware of students' needs, moods, interests, and capabilities.
- Establishing a classroom atmosphere characterized by pleasant conversations, spontaneous laughter, and exclamations of excitement.
- Having high but realistic expectations for one's students.
- Adopting mastery goals (an approach discussed later in this chapter and in Chapter 12).
- Never accepting low-quality work.
- Using scaffolded instruction (as discussed in Chapter 2).

- Teaching thinking skills (discussed more fully in Chapter 9).
- Aligning instruction with standards (discussed more fully in Chapter 13).
- Using formative evaluation (discussed more fully in Chapter 14).
- Eliminating ability grouping (in the elementary and middle school grades) and tracking (in the high school grades) systems and using heterogeneously grouped classes supplemented by extra support classes and after-school help. One New York high school that did this increased its graduation rate for Black and Latino students from 32% to 82%, and its graduation rate for White students from 88% to 97% (Burris & Welner, 2005). We discuss ability grouping and tracking more fully in Chapter 6.

2 **Follow the suggestions of teachers and students for producing high levels of motivation and achievement.**

The following lists overlap somewhat with the previous one, but that only serves to strengthen the validity of the suggestions.

David Gardner (2007), who taught for 33 years in schools that had high concentrations of low-income and ethnic minority students, was able to motivate his students and raise their achievement levels by doing the following:

- Setting high standards for students because he was convinced they were capable of meeting them.
- Telling students every day, both explicitly and implicitly, that he believed they were capable of high levels of achievement.

- Telling students that he would not accept poor-quality work and would return it to them to be redone.
- Avoiding helping students figure out how to meet the demands of a task when he was convinced they were capable of figuring it out for themselves.
- Telling students that failure was inevitable yet acceptable because that's how we learn.
- Making learning fun by using games and manipulables.

According to the responses of almost 400 low-income, inner-city middle school and high school students (D. Corbett & Wilson, 2002), good teachers do the following:

- Push students to learn by such actions as not accepting excuses for missed or late work, constantly checking homework, giving rewards, and keeping parents informed.
- Maintain an orderly and well-run classroom in which disruptions are kept to a minimum. (You will find more detailed information on how to create such an environment in Chapter 12.)
- Make themselves always available to provide a student with help in whatever form the student prefers. Some students, for example, want help after school, some during class, some individually, some by working with peers, and some through whole-class question-and-answer sessions. Some students may ask for help only if they are sure that no one besides the teacher knows they are receiving it.

- Middle-SES students are expected to receive higher grades than low-SES students, even when their IQ scores and achievement test scores are similar.
- Teachers have the highest achievement expectations for Asian American students, and more positive expectations for White students than for Black and Latino students.
- Teachers direct more neutral and positive statements (such as questions and encouragement) to White students than to minority students, but they criticize all students equally often.

- Teachers tend to perceive children from poor homes as less mature, less capable of following directions, and less capable of working independently than children from more advantaged homes.
- Teachers who think of intelligence as a fixed and stable capacity are more likely to formulate negative and positive expectations of students than are teachers who think of intelligence as a collection of skills that can be shaped.
- Teachers are more influenced by negative information about students (for example, low test

- Strive to have all students understand the material by not rushing through lessons and by offering explanations in a clear step-by-step fashion and in various ways.
- Use a variety of instructional tactics, such as group work, lecture, textbook reading, worksheets, whole-class instruction, and hands-on activities.
- Make an effort to understand students' behavior by trying to understand the personalities and after-school lives of students.

Since one of the observations made by students is that good teachers constantly check their homework, we'll address that issue now. The amount of homework assigned to students over the past 15 years has increased, largely because of the need for increasing numbers of students to achieve state-mandated standards and comply with the provisions of the No Child Left Behind Act of 2001. Educators believed that increasing the amount of homework assigned to students would lead to higher grades and test scores. Does it? Not surprisingly, the main conclusion to be drawn from the research literature (see, for example, Cooper, 2001; Cooper, Robinson, & Patall, 2006; R. J. Marzano & Pickering, 2007; Muhlenbruck, Cooper, Nye, & Lindsay, 2000) is that it depends on the student's grade level and how the homework is structured. Compared with peers who did no homework, there was a small benefit for late primary and elementary grade students and only a modest benefit for middle school students. The greatest benefit occurred among high school students. The benefits experienced by late primary and elementary

grade students occurred only when the homework was sufficiently easy that they could successfully complete all or most of it. As one former K–12 teacher pointed out (B. Jackson, 2007), there is still much to be learned about how such variables as students' skill levels, levels of parental involvement, and attitudes of parents and siblings toward school affect the benefits of doing homework, so keep an eye out for updates to this topic.

For those of you who are interested in the fortunes of athletic teams, think of yourself as modeling a successful coach. You should strive to make your classroom one where students respect and support one another, where students recognize that making mistakes is an inevitable part of learning, where each student's strengths are used to contribute to a larger group goal, where students receive constant feedback about their progress, and where students with more advanced knowledge and skills serve as models for and actively tutor classmates whose skills are not as well developed (Nasir, 2008).

3 **Be alert to the potential dangers of the teacher expectancy effect. Concentrate on individuals while guarding against the impact of stereotyping.**

Myrna Gantner (1997), an eighth-grade teacher in an inner-city middle school near the Mexican border, learned the following lessons about treating her Latino students as individuals:

- Treat Latino students the same as you would treat any other student. When teachers believe that inner-city Latino students are less capable than other

students, they tend to give them less time and attention. Students quickly notice these differences and may respond with lower-quality work and more disruptive behavior.
- Don't prejudge students. If you believe that most Latino children use drugs, belong to gangs, or have limited academic ability, students will eventually become aware of your prejudice and act accordingly. Gantner's students said they were most appreciative of teachers who were interested in them as individuals, had high expectations for them, and showed them how to achieve their goals.
- Don't ridicule or make fun of students' limited English proficiency. The best way to acquire proficiency in a second language is to use it frequently. Students will be less inclined to do so if they think teachers and other students will laugh at their mistakes.

4 **Remember that in addition to being a skilled teacher, you are also a human being who may at times react subjectively to students.**

Try to control the influence of such factors as name, ethnic background, gender, physical characteristics, knowledge of siblings or parents, grades, and test scores. If you think you can be honest with yourself, you might attempt to describe your prejudices so that you will be in a position to guard against them. (Do you tend to be annoyed when you read descriptions of the exploits of members of a particular religious or ethnic group, for example?) Try to think of a student independently of his or her siblings and parents.

scores) than they are by neutral or positive information.

- Attractive children are often perceived by teachers to be brighter, more capable, and more social than unattractive children.
- Teachers tend to approve of girls' behavior more frequently than they approve of boys' behavior.

It is important to bear in mind that these factors (plus others such as ethnic background, knowledge of siblings, and impressions of parents) usually operate in

concert to produce an expectancy. The Suggestions for Teaching above will give you some ideas for combating the damaging effects of teacher expectancies, as well as other problems often faced by low-SES and minority students.

LO3 MULTICULTURAL EDUCATION PROGRAMS

The concept of multicultural education has been around for some time. Many of the elements that constitute contemporary programs were devised 70 to 80 years ago as part of a then-current emphasis on international education (Gollnick & Chinn, 2009). In this section, we will give you some idea of what it might be like to teach today from a multicultural perspective by describing the basic assumptions, goals, approaches, and rationale of modern programs.

Assumptions and Goals

The various arguments in favor of multicultural education that are made by its proponents (for example, Banks, 2008, 2009; C. I. Bennett, 2007; Castagno & Brayboy, 2008; García, 2002; Gollnick & Chinn, 2009; A. Singer, 1994) stem from several assumptions. These assumptions and the goals that flow from them appear in Table 5.2.

Basic Approaches

James Banks (2009), a noted authority on multicultural education, describes four approaches to multicultural education. Most multicultural programs, particularly those in the primary grades, adopt what he calls the *contributions approach*. In this approach, ethnic historical figures whose values and behaviors are consistent with American mainstream culture (for example, Booker T. Washington and Sacagawea) are studied, whereas individuals who have challenged the dominant view (such as W. E. B. DuBois and Geronimo) are ignored.

A second approach, which incorporates the first, is called the *ethnic additive approach*. Here, an instructional unit composed of concepts, themes, points of view, and individual accomplishments is simply added

> **Multicultural programs aim to promote respect for diversity, reduction of ethnocentrism and stereotypes, and improved learning.**

to the curriculum. The perspective from which an ethnic group's contributions are viewed, however, tends to be that of the mainstream.

In a third approach, which Banks calls the *transformative approach*, the assumption is that there is no one valid way of understanding people, events, concepts, and themes. Rather, there are multiple views, and each has something of value to offer. For example, the view of the early pioneers who settled the American West could be summed up by such phrases as "How the West Was Won" and "The Westward Movement." But the Native American tribes who had lived there for thousands of years may well have referred to the same event as "How the West Was Taken" or "The Westward Plague."

Pause & Reflect *Think about the four approaches to multicultural education described in this section. What advantages and disadvantages do you see for each approach? Which approach would you use? Why?*

Finally, there is the *decision-making and social action approach*. It incorporates all of the components of the previous approaches and adds the requirement that students make decisions and take actions concerning a concept, issue, or problem being studied.

> **Multicultural education can be approached in different ways.**

TABLE 5.2 Common Assumptions and Goals of Multicultural Education Programs

Assumptions of Multicultural Education	Goals of Multicultural Education
U.S. culture has been formed by the contributions of different cultural groups	Promote understanding of the origins and lack of validity of ethnic stereotypes (e.g., Blacks are violent, Jews are stingy, Asian Americans excel at math and science, Latinos are hot tempered)
Individuals must have self-esteem and group esteem to work productively with people from other cultures	Give all students a sense of being valued and accepted by expressing positive attitudes, using appropriate instructional methods, and formulating fair disciplinary policies and practices
Learning about the achievements of one's cultural group will raise self- and group esteem	Promote self-acceptance and respect for other cultures by studying the impact ethnic groups have had on American society
American society benefits from positive interactions among members of different cultural groups	Reduce ethnocentrism and increase positive relationships among members of different ethnic groups by understanding the viewpoints and products of these groups
Academic performance is enhanced when teachers incorporate various cultural values and experiences into instructional lessons	Help students master basic reading, writing, and computation skills by embedding them in a personally meaningful (i.e., ethnically related) context

For children to understand and appreciate different cultural values and experiences, those values and experiences have to be integrated into the curriculum and rewarded by the teacher.

A Rationale for Multicultural Education

Some people seem to believe that multicultural education programs represent a rejection of basic American values and that this opposition to traditional values is the only rationale behind such programs. We feel this belief is mistaken on both counts. We see multicultural programs as being consistent with basic American values (such as tolerance of differences and equality of opportunity) and consider them to be justified in several ways.

1. *Multicultural programs foster teaching practices that are effective in general as well as for members of a particular group.* For example, expressing an interest in a student through occasional touching and smiling and allowing the child to tutor a younger student are practices likely to benefit most students, not just those of Latino origin.

2. *All students may profit from understanding different cultural values.* For example, the respect for elders that characterizes American Indian and Asian American cultures is likely to become increasingly desirable as the percentage of elderly Americans increases over the years. Similarly, learning the American Indian value of living in harmony with nature may come to be essential as we run out of natural resources and attempt to alleviate environmental pollution (Triandis, 1986).

3. *The United States is becoming an increasingly multicultural society, and students thus need to understand and know how to work with people of cultures different from their own.*

4. *Multicultural education programs expose students to the idea that "truth" is very much in the eye of the beholder.* From a European perspective, Christopher Columbus did indeed discover a new world. But from the perspective of the Arawak Indians who were native to the Caribbean, Columbus invaded territories that they had occupied for thousands of years. Similarly, one can describe the history of the United States as one in which continual progress toward democratic ideals has been made or as one in which progress has been interrupted by conflict, struggle, violence, and exclusion (Banks, 2009).

5. *Multicultural programs can encourage student motivation and learning.* These programs demonstrate respect for a child's culture and teach about the contributions that the student's group has made to American society. Proponents argue that these features both personalize education and make it more meaningful. Conversely, when children perceive disrespect for their cultural background, the result can be disastrous. Consider the following comment by a Mexican American student who realized for the first time that his teachers viewed him as both different and inferior:

One recreation period, when we were playing our usual game of soccer, I took time out to search

Advocates of multicultural education believe that ethnic minority students learn more effectively when some of their learning materials and assignments contain ethnically related content.

for a rest room. I spotted a building on the north side of the playground and ran for it. As I was about to enter, a teacher blew her whistle very loudly, freezing me on the spot. She approached me and demanded to know where I was going, who I was, and what I was doing on that side of the playground. I was dumbfounded and afraid to respond, so she took me by the ear and escorted me back across the playground to the south side. Her parting remark was a stern admonition not to cross the line and to stay with all the other Mexicans.

At that very moment I stopped, turned, and looked at the school as if for the first time. I saw a white line painted across the playground. On one side were the white children playing; on my side were the Mexicans. Then I looked at the building, which was divided in half. The office was in the center, with two wings spreading north and south—one wing for whites and the other for Mexicans. I was overwhelmed with emotions that I could not understand. I was hurt, disappointed, and frustrated. But more than anything else, I was profoundly angry. (Mendoza, 1994, p. 294)

Instructional Goals and Methods

Instructional Goals Teachers whose classes have a high percentage of children from ethnic minority and low-SES backgrounds often assume that they need to emphasize mastery of basic skills (such as computation, spelling, grammar, and word decoding) because minority and low-SES students are often deficient in those skills. Although this approach does improve children's

> **Peer tutoring, cooperative learning, and mastery learning are effective instructional tools.**

performance on tests of basic skills, some educators argue that it does so at the expense of learning higher-level skills and that it is possible for students from poverty backgrounds to acquire both basic and higher-level skills. Well, it's one thing to make a claim like this on logical or theoretical grounds, but it's something else to provide supportive empirical evidence.

Michael Knapp, Patrick Shields, and Brenda Turnbull (1995) did just that. They examined teaching practices in almost 140 first- through sixth-grade classrooms in 15 elementary schools that served large numbers of children from low-SES families to determine whether the assumption that low-SES children can acquire both basic and higher-level skills is true. Over a 2-year period, these authors studied classrooms in which the learning of basic skills was paramount, as well as classrooms that emphasized higher-level and more meaningful outcomes. Teachers in the first group made extensive use of drill and practice, tasks that were limited in their demands, and tasks that could be completed quickly. Teachers in the second group used classroom discussions to let students work out the reasons behind

TeachSource Video Case

Culturally Responsible Teaching: A Multicultural Lesson for Elementary Students

Go to the Education CourseMate website and watch the video, study the artifacts in the case, and reflect upon the following questions:

1. Does the "Coming to America" lesson shown in this Video Case meet any of the goals listed in Table 5.2? If so, which ones?

2. Do you find Mrs. Hurley to be an effective multicultural teacher? How does she meet the criteria listed?

mathematical procedures or explore alternative solutions to math problems, required students to read longer passages and gave them opportunities to discuss what they had read, taught them reading comprehension strategies, and gave them more extended writing assignments.

Knapp and his colleagues found that children whose instruction emphasized conceptual understanding and problem solving performed better on mathematics, reading comprehension, and writing test items that measured advanced skills than their counterparts whose instruction focused on mastery of basic skills. And their performance on basic skill items was either no worse or better than that of students whose teachers emphasized the learning of basic skills.

Instructional Methods The three instructional tactics that are recommended most often by proponents of multicultural education are peer tutoring, cooperative learning, and mastery learning. Although each of these techniques can be used with any group of students and for almost any purpose, they are so well suited to the goals of multicultural education that the phrase "culturally responsive teaching" has been used to describe them (Wlodkowski & Ginsberg, 1995).

Peer Tutoring As its name implies, **peer tutoring** involves the teaching of one student by another. The students may be similar in age or separated by one or more years. (The latter arrangement is usually referred to as *cross-age tutoring*.)

Researchers have consistently found that peer tutoring (also referred to as *peer-assisted learning*) aids achievement for a wide range of students and subject matters. On average, students who received peer tutoring scored 13 percentile ranks higher on a measure of achievement than students who did not receive peer tutoring. The strongest effects were obtained for younger students (grades 1–3), urban students, ethnic minority students, and low-SES students (Rohrbeck, Ginsburg-Block, Fantuzzo, & Miller, 2003). Peer tutoring also has positive effects on nonachievement outcomes. An analysis of 36 studies by the same researchers (Ginsburg-Block, Rohrbeck, & Fantuzzo, 2006) found positive effects for social outcomes (such as ability to make friends and cooperativeness) and self-concept for the same groups.

Students who provide the tutoring also reap substantial learning benefits, but only if they are trained and periodically reminded to provide what are called knowledge-building explanations and questions. Instead of merely telling the other student the answer, summarizing facts, or describing procedures, the tutor should, like any good teacher, also provide new examples, discuss underlying concepts, connect ideas, and pose questions that require integration and application (Roscoe & Chi, 2007).

Cooperative Learning Closely related to peer tutoring is cooperative learning. The general idea behind **cooperative learning** is that by working in small, heterogeneous groups (of four or five students total) and by helping one another master the various aspects of a particular task, students will be more motivated to learn, will learn more than if they had to work independently, and will forge stronger interpersonal relationships than they would by working alone.

David Johnson and Roger Johnson (1998, 2009a,b), who have been researching the effects of cooperative learning for over 25 years, made a basic observation about the relevance of cooperative learning to the goals of multicultural education programs: Students cannot learn everything they need to know about cultural diversity from reading books and articles. A deeper understanding of the nature and value of diversity is gained by learning how to work cooperatively with individuals from different cultural backgrounds.

Cooperative learning is a generally effective instructional tactic that is likely to be particularly useful with Latino, Black, and American Indian students. These cultures value a communal orientation that emphasizes cooperation and sharing. Thus these students may be more prepared than other individuals to work productively as part of a group by carrying out their own responsibilities, as well as helping others do the same (C. I. Bennett, 2007; Castagno & Brayboy, 2008; Nieto, 2008). One study found that small groups of Black fifth-grade students who were told that they had to help one another learn a reading passage recalled more of the text than did similar students who worked either in pairs or individually (Dill & Boykin, 2000). We will have more to say about cooperative learning and its effects on learning in Chapter 13.

Mastery Learning The third frequently recommended instructional tactic, **mastery learning**, is an approach to

peer tutoring
An approach to learning that involves the teaching of one student by another, based on evidence that a child's cognitive growth benefits from exposure to alternative cognitive schemes.

cooperative learning An approach that uses small heterogeneous groups for purposes of mutual help in the mastery of specific tasks.

mastery learning An approach that assumes most students can master the curriculum if certain conditions are established: (1) sufficient aptitude, (2) sufficient ability to understand instruction, (3) a willingness to persevere, (4) sufficient time, and (5) good-quality instruction.

© ARTappler/iStockphoto

Computer-based technology helps students learn more about other cultures and social classes by providing access to various reference sources and individuals from almost anywhere in the world.

Bridging the Cultural and SES Gap With Technology

As we stated earlier, a basic purpose of multicultural education is to give students the opportunity to learn about the characteristics of people from different cultures and to try to understand how those individuals view the world. For schools that draw from an ethnically, racially, and socioeconomically diverse population, acquiring firsthand experience with the history, beliefs, and practices of different cultures is not likely to be a major problem. But schools that draw from more homogeneous populations have traditionally been limited to such resources as books, magazines, and videotapes. This limitation on multicultural education is being surmounted, however, by the ability of technology to bring the world to the student, and in a very real sense.

Telecommunication projects allow students from different places and varied backgrounds to interact with one another, sharing ideas and experiences and learning new points of view. These exchanges can lead to a greater respect for diversity (Kontos & Mizell, 1997; Salmon & Akaran, 2001). Michaele Salmon and Susan Akaran (2001), for example, describe an e-mail exchange program between kindergarten students from New Jersey and first-grade Eskimo children from Alaska that produced greater respect for and understanding of each other's culture. For those teachers interested in providing their students with more in-depth knowledge about Alaskan Native culture and related approaches to instruction, a wealth of ideas and resources are available at the Alaska Native Knowledge Network (www.ankn.uaf.edu).

The 4Directions project is another significant example. Developed by a consortium of 19 American Indian schools in 10 states and 11 public and private universities and organizations, the project allows isolated, far-flung members of American Indian schools to share local customs and values with other American Indian tribes around the country. The students display their projects and achievements and participate in virtual communities through Internet teleconferencing. Although the 4Directions website (www.4directions .org) was created to facilitate communication among American Indian communities, the project welcomes other schools to participate in the project or use its resources (Allen et al., 1999). The Resources page contains several features, including culturally relevant lesson plans for eight subject areas and a virtual tour of the National Museum of the American Indian.

Earlier in this chapter, we indicated that many students from low-SES homes are considered to be at risk for educational failure because of adverse conditions

teaching and learning that assumes that most students can master the curriculum if the following conditions are established: that students (1) have sufficient aptitude to learn a particular task, (2) have sufficient ability to understand instruction, (3) are willing to persevere until they attain a certain level of mastery, (4) are allowed whatever time is necessary to attain mastery, and (5) are provided with good-quality instruction.

The basic mastery learning approach is to specify clearly what is to be learned, organize the content into a sequence of relatively short units, use a variety of instructional methods and materials, allow students to progress through the material at their own rate, monitor student progress to identify budding problems and provide corrective feedback, and allow students to relearn and retest on each unit until mastery is attained (J. H. Block, Efthim, & Burns, 1989; Gentile & Lalley, 2003).

Like the research on peer tutoring and cooperative learning, the research on mastery learning has generally been positive. On the basis of a comprehensive review of this literature, Chen-Lin Kulik, James Kulik, and Robert Bangert-Drowns (1990) conclude that mastery learning programs produce moderately strong effects on achievement. The average student in a mastery learning class scores about 20 percentile points higher on a classroom examination than a conventionally taught student. The positive effect of mastery learning was slightly more pronounced for lower-ability students. As compared with students in conventional classes, those in mastery classes had more positive feelings about the subjects they studied and the way in which they were taught.

surrounding their physical, social, emotional, and cognitive development. Technology may be an effective tool in combating this problem, as it has demonstrated its effectiveness at raising the achievement levels of at-risk, low-SES students. In one study (J. M. Cole & Hilliard, 2006), a group of low-SES third-grade students from an inner-city school who were two or more grade levels behind in reading were given 8 weeks of reading instruction using a web-based program called *Reading Upgrade*. This program uses music and video within an interactive environment to maintain student attention to and interest in lessons that focus on decoding, phonemic awareness, fluency, and comprehension. The *Reading Upgrade* group significantly outscored a similar group of students who received conventional reading instruction without the aid of computers; they gained the equivalent of one grade level on measures of decoding, fluency, and comprehension in just 8 weeks.

Now that you are familiar with the nature and goals of multicultural education programs and some of the instructional tools that are available to you, the Suggestions for Teaching beginning on the next page should help you get started.

LO4 BILINGUAL EDUCATION

As Table 5.1 shows, the 1990s set a U.S. record for the number of immigrants during a decade. Slightly more than 9.7 million legal immigrants arrived in the United States from 1990 through 1999. Not surprisingly, many of the school-age children of these families have either limited or no English proficiency. For 2006, 2.8 million K–12 students spoke a language other than English (most often Spanish) at home and spoke English with difficulty (Planty et al., 2008).

To address the needs of these students, the federal government provides financial support for the establishment of bilingual education programs. Because language is viewed as an important part of a group's culture, many school districts integrate bilingual education with multicultural education. In this section, we will examine the nature and effectiveness of bilingual education programs.

Goals and Approaches

Most bilingual education programs have a common long-term goal, but they differ in their approach to that goal. The goal is to help minority-language students acquire as efficiently as possible the English skills they will need to succeed in school and society. The approaches to that goal usually fall into

{ **Transition programs focus on a rapid shift to English proficiency.** }

one of three categories: *transition*, *maintenance*, or *two-way bilingual*.

Transition Programs Programs that take a transition approach teach students wholly (in the case of non-English-proficient students) or partly (in the case of limited-English-proficient students) in their native language so as not to impede their academic progress, but only until they can function adequately in English. At that point, students are placed in regular classes, in which all of the instruction is in English. To make the transition time as brief as possible, some programs add an English-as-a-second-language (ESL) component. ESL programs typically involve pulling students out of their regular classes and providing them with full-time intensive instruction in English (Gersten, 1999; Mora, Wink, & Wink, 2001; W. P. Thomas & Collier, 1999).

Maintenance Programs Programs that take a maintenance approach try to maintain or improve students' native-language skills. Instruction in the students' native language continues for a significant time before transition to English. Supporters of maintenance programs point to the results of psychological and linguistic studies that suggest that a strong native-language foundation

Some bilingual education programs emphasize using the student's native language competence to help the student learn English as quickly as possible. Other programs emphasize the maintenance or improvement of both the student's native language and English.

© Bob Daemmrich/Stock Boston

Suggestions for Teaching

Promoting Multicultural Understanding and Classroom Achievement

1 Use culturally relevant teaching methods.

To fulfill the goals of multicultural education, teachers should practice what is referred to as either culturally relevant pedagogy (Ladson-Billings, 2002) or culturally responsive pedagogy (Nieto, 2002/2003). This approach to instruction is based on two premises. First, all students, regardless of their ethnic, racial, and social class backgrounds, have assets they can use to aid their learning. Second, teachers need to be aware of and meet students' academic needs in any number of ways. In other words, simply adopting a multicultural basal reader is not culturally responsive pedagogy. In addition to adopting multicultural reading material, you should do everything possible to help all students learn to read. For example, successful teachers of Latino students in Arizona and California have high expectations for students, make their expectations clear, never accept low-quality work, scaffold students' learning, and use Spanish for instruction or allow students to speak Spanish among themselves when working in pairs or groups (Rolón, 2002/2003).

Gloria Ladson-Billings (2002), who has written extensively about working with minority and at-risk students, provides several examples of culturally relevant or responsive teaching. A second-grade teacher allowed her students to bring in lyrics from rap songs that both she and the students deemed to be inoffensive. The students performed the songs, and the teacher and students discussed the literal and figurative meanings of the words and such aspects of poetry as rhyme scheme, alliteration, and onomatopoeia. The students acquired an understanding of poetry that exceeded both the state's and school district's learning standards. Another teacher invited the parents of her students to conduct "seminars" in class for 2 to 4 days, 1 to 2 hours at a time. One parent who was famous for the quality of her sweet potato pie taught the students how to make one. In addition, the students were required to complete such related projects as a written report on George Washington Carver's research on the sweet potato, a marketing plan for selling pies, and a statement of the kind of education and experience one needed to become a cook or chef. Similar seminars were done by a carpenter, a former professional basketball player, a licensed practical nurse, and a church musician, all of whom were parents or relatives of the students.

2 Help make students aware of the contributions that specific ethnic groups have made to the development of the United States and the rest of the world.

As we noted earlier, James Banks (2009) has identified four approaches to multicultural education, the first of which is the contributions approach. This approach emphasizes the contributions that prominent individuals of various ethnic groups have made to the United States, as well as each group's major holidays, celebrations, and customs. One suggestion for implementing this approach is to invite family members of students (and other local residents) of different ethnic backgrounds to the classroom. Ask them to describe the values subscribed to by members of their group and explain how those values have contributed to life in the United States and the rest of the world.

3 Use instructional techniques and classroom activities that are consistent with the value system of students who share a particular cultural background and that encourage students to learn from and about one another's cultures.

Students from Latino cultures place a high value on the concept of collectivism, or the interdependence of family members. From an early age, children are taught to think first about fostering the success of any group to which they belong by seeking to work cooperatively with others (Rothstein-Fisch, Greenfield, & Trumbull, 1999). To capitalize on this value, consider doing some or all of the following:

- Assign two or three children rather than just one to a classroom task, such as cleaning up after an art period, and allow them to help one another if necessary.
- Increase the use of choral reading with students whose English proficiency is limited so they can practice their decoding and pronunciation skills without being the center of attention.
- After distributing a homework assignment, allow students to discuss the questions but not to write down the answers. Those who are more proficient in English and have better developed intellectual skills can help their less skilled classmates better understand the task. One third-grade teacher who used this technique was surprised to find that every student completed the assignment.

---

two-way bilingual (TWB) education An approach to bilingual education in which instruction is provided to all students in both the minority language and the majority language. Also called *bilingual immersion* or *dual language*.

supports the subsequent learning of both English and subject-matter knowledge. In addition, many proponents of multicultural education favor a maintenance approach because they see language as an important part of a group's cultural heritage (Mora, Wink, & Wink, 2001; Robledo & Cortez, 2002).

Two-Way Bilingual Programs Some bilingual education scholars (e.g., Caldéron & Minaya-Rowe, 2003; Pérez, 2004; W. P. Thomas & Collier, 1997/1998, 1999)

are critical of both transitional and maintenance bilingual education programs because they are remedial in nature and because students who participate in such programs tend to be perceived as inferior in some respect. These educators favor what is generally known as **two-way bilingual (TWB) education** (although the terms *bilingual immersion*, *two-way immersion*, and *dual language* are also used). In a TWB program, subject-matter instruction is provided in two languages to all students. This approach is typically used when English is the primary language of about half the students in a school and the other language (usually Spanish) is the primary language of the other half of the students.

Bear in mind, however, that students whose families have recently immigrated to the United States may not be familiar or comfortable with such student-centered techniques. In some cultures, for example, students are taught not to speak unless asked a direct question by the teacher, not to volunteer answers without being asked (so as not to appear boastful or conceited), and never to question what the teacher says, even when they know it to be wrong. These students will need time to become used to such practices as working with other students and asking the teacher for additional explanations (P. C. Miller & Endo, 2004).

4 At the secondary level, involve students in activities that explore cultural differences in perceptions, beliefs, and values.

A well-conceived multicultural education program cannot, and should not, avoid or minimize the issue of cultural conflict. There are at least two reasons for helping students examine this issue. One is that conflict has been a constant and salient aspect of relationships among cultural groups. Another is that cultural conflicts often produce changes that benefit all members of a society (a prime example is the civil rights movement of the 1960s, with its boycotts, marches, and demonstrations).

One technique for exploring cultural conflict is to have students search through newspapers, newsmagazines, and websites for articles that describe clashes. Ask them to identify the source of the conflict and how it might be positively resolved. Another technique is to involve students in games that simulate group conflict. Class members can, for example, play the role of state legislators who represent the interests of diverse ethnic groups and who have been lobbied to change the school funding formula so that poorer school districts receive more money (Appleton, 1983). The use of both simulations and the discussion of media reports will probably work best at the high school level because adolescents are better able than younger students to understand the abstract concepts involved in these activities.

5 Involve students, especially at the secondary level, in community service activities.

Service-learning programs, found in many school systems, serve several purposes. First, they afford students the opportunity to broaden the knowledge they acquire in school by working to solve real problems in a community setting. Second, they help students develop a sense of civic and social responsibility. Third, they help students become more knowledgeable about career options. And fourth, they provide a useful and needed service to the community (Billig, 2000). To cite one example, Natalie Russell (2007), who teaches English as a second language to high school students, described how she used service-learning projects, such as the creation of a Spanish/English phrasebook that was distributed free to community members, as a way to help students feel more connected to their community and to make their English lessons more meaningful and immediately useful. More detailed information about service-learning programs and organizations can be found on the website of the Corporation for National and Community Service (www.learnandserve.org).

6 Make every effort to contact and work with the parents of ethnic minority students.

To help students and their parents make a successful transition to a new country and school system, educators and multicultural education scholars (e.g., Castagno & Brayboy, 2008; Soldier, 1997) suggest trying the following:

- During the first week of the school year, hold parent–teacher–child conferences. Be willing to hold these meetings in the parents' home and during the evening hours if necessary.
- Recruit bilingual parent volunteers to help teachers and staff members talk with parents and students.
- When discussing classroom tasks and student performance with parents, avoid technical terminology and acronyms. Not only does this result in fewer misunderstandings, but it also lessens the sense of inferiority that some parents feel.
- Participate in the cultural events hosted by your students' community.
- Recruit community members to help your students with culture-specific projects that you would like the students to carry out.

Two-way bilingual education programs feature instruction in both languages.

TWB programs are used in 346 schools in 27 states in the United States (Center for Applied Linguistics, 2009). Although most of these programs are English–Spanish, other programs include Korean, French, Cantonese, Navajo, Japanese, Arabic, Portuguese, Russian, or Mandarin Chinese as the minority language. TWB programs differ from traditional transition and ESL programs in that they begin as early as kindergarten and continue throughout the elementary school years to maintain facility in the student's native language while building facility in the nonnative language.

Canada and Miami, Florida, have two of the oldest and largest TWB programs. Canada has always had a large French-speaking population, mostly in the province of Québec. Because many parents wanted their children to be proficient in both English and French, Canadian schools in the 1960s began a K–12 program. In kindergarten and first grade, 90% of the instruction is in French and the remaining 10% is in English. From grade 2 through grade 5, the proportion gradually shifts to 50/50. By grade 6, most students can work equally well on any subject matter in either language.

The impetus for a TWB program in the Miami area was the large number of residents who emigrated from Cuba. As with all other two-way programs, students whose primary language is Spanish *and* students whose primary language is English participate in the program together. Unlike the Canadian model, which has a strong immersion component in the early grades (80% to 90% of the instruction is in French), teachers in Miami's program teach in Spanish for half the day and in English for the other half of the day at all grade levels.

© Joseph Weber/iStockphoto

TWB programs typically include the following features:

- At least 6 years of bilingual instruction
- High-quality instruction in both languages
- Separation of the two languages for instruction (for example, by time of day, day of the week, or even by week)
- Use of the minority language for teaching and classroom discussion at least 50% of the time
- A roughly balanced percentage of students for whom each language is primary
- Use of peer tutoring

Despite the growth and success of TWB programs, as well as data showing that it takes most English language learners 7 to 10 years to become sufficiently fluent in English to compete academically with their peers (Lewis-Moreno, 2007), some states have eliminated all bilingual education programs. In 1998, Californians voted to eliminate their state's bilingual education program and provide instead a 1-year English-immersion program, in which minority-language students are taught only in English. In 2000, voters in Arizona approved a similar proposition (Thompson, DiCerbo, Mahoney, & MacSwan, 2002). An English-immersion program was approved in Massachusetts in 2002 but was later amended to allow TWB programs to continue to operate (Saltzman, 2003).

Research Findings

Much of the research on bilingual education has addressed one or the other of the following questions: Do English-language learners (ELLs) become proficient in English more quickly in bilingual programs or in English-only immersion programs? Do English-language learners score higher on subject-matter tests in bilingual programs or immersion programs? Before going further,

TeachSource Video Case

Bilingual Education: An Elementary Two-Way Immersion Program

Go to the Education CourseMate website and watch the video, study the artifacts in the case, and reflect upon the following questions:

1. The two teachers in this Video Case work together closely to teach students in two different languages. In your opinion, what are the pros and cons of this approach to bilingual education?

2. What are some of the specific challenges that teachers in a two-way program (such as the one depicted in the Video Case) might face?

Challenging Assumptions

Bilingual Education: Plus les choses changent, plus elles restent les mêmes

The preceding French phrase translates to "The more things change, the more they remain the same." So it is with the current dispute over the goals and methods of bilingual education. In the early part of the 20th century, prior to World War I, bilingual public schools were common, particularly in areas with large numbers of German immigrants. After the war, however, public financing of bilingual schools was abruptly withdrawn, partly as a reaction against Germany (which lost the war and was seen as the aggressor) and partly because of increasing nationalism and isolationism. American society strongly endorsed a one country/one culture policy and stressed once again the idea of America as a melting pot. As a result, English-immersion programs for immigrant students became the norm.

But during and after World War II, as now, American students' deficiencies in foreign-language fluency became noticeable and a source of concern. This situation contributed to the first Bilingual Education Act in 1965, which emphasized the maintenance of one's native language, as well as mastery of English.

As a future educator whose decisions will rest partly on scientific evidence, you should ignore as much as possible both the pro and con arguments about bilingual education that appear to be based on biases and political beliefs. Focus instead on what the research has to say. Our reading of the current research leads us to conclude that bilingual education, particularly in the form of two-way bilingual programs, benefits both limited-English-proficient and native English-speaking students. Given the ease with which technology allows students from different countries to communicate and work collaboratively, as well as the trend toward international commerce, programs that increase students' bilingual fluency should be encouraged and strongly supported.

What Do You Think?

Have you ever taken part in bilingual education? What is your position on expanding its use in U.S. schools? For more material on this subject, go to the "Challenging Assumptions" section of the textbook's Education CourseMate website.

{ **Bilingual education programs produce moderate learning gains.** }

a word of caution: bilingual versus immersion programs is a hot button issue. The arguments on both sides are both passionate and strident. We think you will find it interesting to compare the emotional appeals that are made with the data summarized here.

- Despite heated arguments about whether immersion programs or transition programs (the most common form of bilingual instruction) help ELLs acquire English proficiency more quickly, the answer, at least for now, seems to be that it may not matter very much. In one large-scale study (Tong, Lara-Alecio, Irby, Mathes, & Kwok, 2008), about 800 kindergarten Spanish-speaking ELLs were randomly assigned to one of four types of programs: regular transition, enhanced transition, regular immersion, or enhanced immersion. The main difference between the regular and enhanced versions of the transition and immersion programs

was additional daily English instruction activities. After 2 years, students in the two enhanced groups were equally proficient in English, and both groups were more proficient than students in the traditional transition group.

- In comparison with immersion (English-only) programs, participation in bilingual education programs produces small to moderate gains in reading, language skills, mathematics, and total achievement when measured by tests in English. When measured by tests administered in the student's native language, participation in bilingual education leads to significantly better performance on tests of listening comprehension, reading, writing, total language, mathematics, social studies, and attitudes toward school and self. Thus, increasing the amount of time devoted to instruction in English (as is done in immersion programs) does not necessarily lead to higher levels of achievement (Cummins, 1999; Slavin & Cheung, 2005; Willig, 1985). Early analysis of California's immersion program indicated that although ELL students improved their scores on the Stanford 9 (a standardized achievement test), the scores of non-ELL students increased by a similar amount. Consequently, the achievement gap between ELL and non-ELL students remained unchanged (Thompson, DiCerbo, Mahoney, & MacSwan, 2002).

- Students who participate in TWB programs score at or above grade level on subject-matter tests and score higher on reading and mathematics tests than ELL students who are taught only in English (Pérez, 2004; Slavin & Cheung, 2005).

TECHNOLOGY AND BILINGUAL EDUCATION

Multimedia, hypermedia, e-mail, and other technologies are enhancing opportunities for bilingual students and ELL students to more efficiently acquire English language skills and other subject matter. Former ESL teacher Jan Lacina described, for example, how Internet chat sessions, discussion boards, and computer programs can be used to help students refine their language skills. Chat rooms and discussion boards have the advantage of letting students review and possibly revise what they have written before sending it off and may be particularly beneficial for students who are shy or are anxious about mispronunciations (Lacina, 2004/2005). A computer program that may be worth investigating is the Reading Assistant from Scientific Learning (www .scilearn.com/products/reading-assistant). Students read aloud into a headset microphone, and the program provides audio and visual help for words the student mispronounces or has trouble pronouncing.

There are also numerous web resources that support bilingual instruction. One site that serves both teachers and students is Dave's ESL Cafe (www.eslcafe.com). A menu called "Stuff for Students" contains the following pages: Help Center (a discussion forum), Hint-of-the-Day, Idioms, Phrasal Verbs, Pronunciation Power, Quizzes, Slang, and Student Forums. The website Science Fair Assistant (www.iteachilearn .com/teach/tech/science.htm), written in both English and Spanish, is designed to help children in grades K–8 find experiments and ideas for a science project. Finally, a number of publications describe how to use websites in creating lessons to improve ELL students' listening, oral proficiency, reading comprehension, and writing skills (e.g., Feyten et al., 2002).

WHAT ELSE? *RIP & REVIEW* **CARDS IN THE BACK**

6

ACCOMMODATING STUDENT VARIABILITY

LEARNING OBJECTIVES

After studying this chapter, you will be able to . . .

LO1 Explain the various forms of ability grouping, the findings from evaluation studies, and the practices that are suggested by the research.

LO2 Describe the key features of the Individuals with Disabilities Education Act (IDEA) and the ways those features influence teaching practice.

LO3 Describe the characteristics of learners with intellectual disability and explain how their learning can be supported.

LO4 Describe the characteristics of students with learning disabilities and attention deficit/hyperactivity disorder (ADHD) and explain how their learning can be supported.

LO5 Describe the characteristics of students with emotional disturbance and explain how their learning can be supported.

LO6 Describe the characteristics of students who are gifted and talented and explain how their learning can be supported.

LO7 Explain how the universal design for learning (UDL) approach and the use of assistive technology support learners.

visit 4ltrpress.cengage.com

Prior to the twentieth century, few educators had to deal with the challenge of teaching extremely diverse groups of students. Most communities were fairly small, and students in a given school tended to come from similar backgrounds. Many children, especially those of low socioeconomic status (SES), attended school irregularly or not at all. In 1900, for example, only 8.5% of eligible students attended high school (Boyer, 1983), and these students were almost entirely from the upper and middle classes (Gutek, 1992). In addition, children with mental, emotional, or physical disabilities were sent to special schools, educated at home, or not educated at all. In comparison with today's schools, earlier student populations were considerably less diverse.

In the preceding chapter, you read about the varieties of cultural and socioeconomic diversity among today's students. This chapter focuses on another dimension of diversity: the twin (but often somewhat fuzzy) concepts of ability and disability. Before explaining how educators attempt to meet the needs of diverse students, we take a brief look at historical developments that helped shape current educational practices.

Historical Developments

The Growth of Public Education and Age-Graded Classrooms

By 1920, public education in the United States was no longer a small-scale and optional enterprise, largely because of three developments. First, by 1918 all states had passed compulsory attendance laws. Second, child labor laws had been enacted by many states, as well as by Congress in 1916, to eliminate the hiring of children and adolescents in mines and factories. Third, large numbers of immigrant children arrived in the United States from 1901 through 1920. The result was a vast increase in the number and diversity of children attending elementary and high school.

Educators initially dealt with this growth in student variability by forming age-graded classrooms. Introduced in schools in Quincy, Massachusetts, in the mid-1800s, these classrooms grouped all students of a particular age together each year to master a certain portion of the school's curriculum (Gutek, 1992). The main assumptions behind this approach were that teachers could be more effective in helping

students learn and that students would have more positive attitudes toward themselves and school when classrooms were more homogeneous than heterogeneous (Oakes, 2005; Peltier, 1991). Regardless of whether these assumptions were well founded (an issue we will address shortly), they were (and still are) so widely held by educators that two additional approaches to creating even more homogeneous groups were eventually implemented: ability grouping and special class placement.

Ability-Grouped Classrooms

Ability grouping involved the use of standardized mental ability or achievement tests to create groups of students who were considered very similar to each other in learning ability. In elementary and middle schools, students typically were (and frequently still are) placed in low-, average-, or high-ability groups. At the high school level, students were placed into different tracks that were geared toward such different post–high school goals as college, secretarial work, and vocational school.

Ability grouping was another means for school authorities to deal with the large influx of immigrant students. Because many of these children were not fluent in English and had had limited amounts of education in their native countries, they scored low on standardized tests when compared with American test norms. In addition, many of these children came from poor homes and were in poor health. At the time, their assignment to a low-ability group seemed both logical and appropriate (Wheelock, 1994). In the next major part of this chapter, we will look at current applications of ability grouping, which now takes several forms and is still used to reduce the normal range of variability in cognitive ability and achievement found in the typical classroom.

Special Education

For children whose abilities and disabilities fell within the normal range, age grading and ability testing were seen as workable approaches to creating more homogeneous classes. However, compulsory attendance laws also brought to school many children with mild to severe mental and physical disabilities. These students were deemed incapable of profiting from any type of normal classroom instruction and so were assigned to special schools. Unfortunately, as Alfred Binet

between-class ability grouping Assigning students of similar learning ability to separate classes based on scores from standardized intelligence or achievement tests.

regrouping A form of ability grouping that brings together students of the same age, ability, and grade from different classrooms for instruction in a specific subject, usually reading or mathematics.

feared, the labeling of a student as "mentally retarded" or "physically disabled" often resulted in a vastly inferior education. Early in the twentieth century, special schools served as convenient dumping grounds for all kinds of children who could not adapt to the regular classroom (Vallecorsa, deBettencourt, & Zigmond, 2000).

In the latter two thirds of this chapter, we will detail the varied types and degrees of special class placement for children whose intellectual, social, emotional, or physical development falls outside (above as well as below) the range of normal variation. In discussing this approach, we pay particular attention to Public Law 101-476, the Individuals with Disabilities Education Act (IDEA), which was enacted to counter past excesses of special class placement and to encourage the placement of children with disabilities in regular classes.

LO1 Ability Grouping

Ability grouping is a widespread practice (Dornbusch & Kaufman, 2001; Lleras & Rangel, 2009). In the elementary grades, virtually all teachers form separate groups within their classrooms for instruction in reading, and many do so for mathematics as well. At the middle school level, approximately two thirds to three fourths of schools assign students to

In ability grouping, students are selected and placed in homogeneous groups with other students who are considered to have very similar learning abilities.

different self-contained classes in one or more subjects on the basis of standardized test scores. This proportion rises to about 85% at the high school level, where students are assigned to different classes (e.g., honors, college preparatory, basic) on a subject-by-subject basis (Dornbusch & Kaufman, 2001). At the middle and high school levels, the term *tracking* rather than *ability grouping* is typically used. In this section, we will describe the most common ways in which teachers group students by ability, examine the assumptions that provide the rationale for this practice, summarize research findings on the effectiveness of ability grouping, and look at alternative courses of action.

Types of Ability Groups

Four approaches to ability grouping are popular among educators today: between-class ability grouping, regrouping, the Joplin Plan, and within-class grouping. You may be able to recall a few classes in which one or another of these techniques was used. If not, you will no doubt encounter at least one of them during your first year of teaching.

Between-Class Ability Grouping The goal of **between-class ability grouping** is for each class to be made up of students who are homogeneous in standardized intelligence or achievement test scores. Three levels of classes are usually formed: high, average, and low. Students in one ability group typically have little or no contact with students in other ability groups during the school day. Although each group covers the same subjects, a higher group does so in greater depth and breadth than lower groups. At the high school level, as we mentioned, this approach is often called *tracking*.

Regrouping The groups formed under a **regrouping** plan are more flexible in assignments and narrower in scope than between-class groups. Students of the same age, ability, and grade from different classrooms come together for instruction in a specific subject, usually reading or mathematics. If a student begins to outperform the other members of the group significantly, a change of group assignment is easier because it involves just that particular subject.

Regrouping has two major disadvantages, however. First, it requires a certain degree of planning and cooperation among the teachers involved. They must agree, for example, to schedule reading and arithmetic during the same periods. Second, many teachers are uncomfortable working with children whom they see only once a day for an hour or so.

Joplin Plan Although regrouping (as described in the previous section) combines students from different classes, the students are all in the same grade level. The **Joplin Plan**, in contrast, combines students across grade levels. For example, all third, fourth, and fifth graders whose grade-equivalent scores in reading are 4.6 (fourth grade, sixth month) would come together for reading instruction. The same would be done for mathematics. The Joplin Plan has the same advantages and disadvantages as simple regrouping, and it is the basis for a successful reading program called Success for All (J. A. Kulik, 2003b; Slavin, Madden, Chambers, & Haxby, 2009).

> **Ability grouping assumes that intelligence is inherited, unchangeable, and reflected by IQ, and that instruction in ability groups will be superior.**

Within-Class Ability Grouping The most popular form of ability grouping, occurring in almost all elementary school classes, **within-class ability grouping** involves the division of a single class of students into two or three groups for reading and math instruction. Like regrouping and the Joplin Plan, within-class ability grouping has the advantages of being flexible in terms of group assignments and being restricted to one or two subjects. One disadvantage of this approach is that the teacher needs to be skilled at keeping the other students in the class productively occupied while working with a particular group. Other disadvantages will be seen as we examine the research later in this section.

Pause & Reflect *You probably experienced ability grouping in one form or another at the elementary and secondary levels. Think about whether it might have been between-class grouping, regrouping, the Joplin Plan, or within-class grouping. Could you tell which group you were in? Did you have feelings about being in that group?*

Assumptions Underlying Ability Grouping

When ability grouping was initiated early in the twentieth century, much less was known about the various factors that affect classroom learning. Consequently, educators simply assumed certain things to be true.

Two of those assumptions were that intelligence, which affects the capacity to learn, was a fixed, inherited trait and that little could be done to change the learning capacity of individuals. A third assumption was that intelligence was adequately reflected by an intelligence quotient (IQ) score. A fourth assumption was that all students would learn best when grouped with those of similar ability (G. Hong & Hong, 2009; Ornstein, Levine, & Gutek, 2011). Although many educators still believe these assumptions are true, the research evidence summarized here and elsewhere in this book casts doubt on their validity.

Joplin Plan An ability grouping technique that combines students of different grade levels according to their standardized test scores.

within-class ability grouping A form of ability grouping that involves the division of a single class of students into two or three groups for reading and math instruction.

Evaluations of Ability Grouping

Because ability grouping occurs in virtually all school districts, its effects have been intensively studied (Abrami, Lou, Chambers, Poulsen, & Spence, 2000; Applebee, Langer, Nystrand, & Gamoran, 2003; R. M. Callahan, 2005; G. Hong & Hong, 2009; J. A. Kulik, 2003b; Lleras & Rangel, 2009; Lou, Abrami, & Spence, 2000; Robinson, 2008; Yonezawa, Wells, & Serna, 2002). The main findings of these analyses were as follows:

1. There was little to no support for between-class ability grouping. Students assigned to low-ability classes generally performed worse than comparable students in heterogeneous classes. Students assigned to average-ability classes performed at about the same level as their nongrouped peers. High-ability students sometimes performed slightly better in homogeneous classes than in heterogeneous classes. A report by the Carnegie Corporation on educating adolescents noted: "Instruction in tracked classes thus falls short on measures of both equity and excellence. Tracking affects students unequally, both by grouping students of color and economically disadvantaged students in lower tracks and by providing unequal educational opportunities to students. Instruction in lower-track classes is typically far from excellent, often depending on rote memorization and recall, isolated facts, worksheets, and a slow pace" (see A. W. Jackson & Davis, 2000, p. 66). A study of high school students in California learning English as a second

> **No research supports between-class ability grouping.**

language supported the Carnegie report. The academic track in which the high school students were placed was a better predictor of a variety of academic performances—including grades and scores on standardized achievement tests—than was the students' proficiency in English. Lower-track placement meant also that students took fewer classes that would qualify them for college admission (R. M. Callahan, 2005; see also Robinson, 2008).

2. Research on the effect of regrouping for reading or mathematics was inconclusive. Some of the relatively few studies that have been done on this form of ability grouping suggested that it can be effective if the instructional pace and level of the text match the student's actual achievement level rather than the student's nominal grade level. In other words, a fifth grader who scores at the fourth grade level on a reading test should be reading out of a fourth grade reading book.

3. The Joplin Plan yielded moderately positive effects compared with instruction in heterogeneous classes.

4. Within-class ability grouping in mathematics and science in grades 1 through 12 produced modestly positive results (about 8 percentile ranks) compared with whole-class instruction and an even smaller positive effect (about 4 percentile ranks) compared with mixed-ability groups. Average-achieving students benefited most from being placed in homogeneous ability groups, whereas low-achieving students benefited most from being placed in mixed ability groups.

> **Joplin Plan and within-class ability grouping for math and science produce moderate increases in learning.**

Research also showed that some within-class grouping practices were more effective than others. The largest positive effects were found in classrooms that had the following two conditions: (1) Students were assigned to groups not only on the basis of ability but also on the basis of other factors that contributed to group cohesiveness and (2) cooperative learning techniques were used that included the features of positive interdependence and individual accountability (Abrami, Lou,

Chambers, Poulsen, & Spence, 2000; Lou, Abrami, & Spence, 2000). (See Chapter 13, for a discussion of these and other features of cooperative learning.)

5. Students in homogeneously grouped classes scored the same as students in heterogeneously grouped classes on measures of self-esteem.

6. Students in high-ability classes had more positive attitudes about school and higher educational aspirations than did students in low-ability classrooms (Ireson & Hallam, 2009).

7. Between-class ability grouping affected the quality of instruction received by students. The best teachers in a school were often assigned to teach the highest tracks, whereas the least experienced or weakest teachers were assigned to teach the lowest tracks. As a consequence, the students who were most in need of critical thinking, self-direction, creativity, and active participation received less instruction in those areas. Instead, students engaged in lower-track classes were expected to do well in academics. This was particularly true in science and math.

> **Between-class ability grouping negatively influences teaching goals and methods.**

Despite the evidence against between-class ability grouping, students of color and low-SES students are frequently assigned to the lowest tracks, where they fall further behind White, middle-SES students (Lleras & Rangel, 2009). This situation has prompted accusations of discrimination, and some districts have responded by adopting policies that specifically allow low-track students to enroll in honors courses. However, this technique (sometimes called a "freedom of choice program") does not necessarily increase the participation of students of color in higher-level courses. An examination of this practice in four middle schools and six high schools indicated that it was largely ineffective in encouraging students of color and low-SES students to enroll in honors classes (Yonezawa, Wells, & Serna, 2002). Low-track students were not always informed or encouraged to request honors classes. Even when the low-track students requested a high-track class, they often learned that they had not taken the prerequisite classes.

To Group or Not to Group?

The findings we have summarized suggest three courses of action. The first course is to discontinue the use of full-day, between-class ability groups or tracks.

Challenging Assumptions

Ability Grouping and Tracking: A Practice That Fails to Deliver What It Promises

At the beginning of this book, we stated that an advantage of using scientific methods to study education is that it helps us avoid drawing false conclusions about an idea or practice because of subjective and unsystematic thinking. When people make assumptions based on personal values and experience for systematic research findings, educational decisions that are detrimental to students are usually the result. So it is with between-class ability grouping and rigid tracking systems at the middle school and high school levels. Many educators fervently believe that teachers are more effective and students learn more when classrooms are more homogeneous in ability than heterogeneous. But almost all of the research conducted on ability grouping and tracking over the past several decades refutes these beliefs. Consequently, this is a practice that should rarely, if ever, be used. Among other detriments, it destroys the motivation of students and stunts their intellectual growth.

We believe that teachers should speak out forcefully against between-class ability grouping and in favor of effective instructional practices that can be used with all students, especially cooperative learning and peer tutoring. When the opportunity arises, let your colleagues know that the assumptions they carry about the benefits of ability grouping are not supported by the scientific literature.

What Do You Think?

Do you share our opposition to ability grouping and tracking? Do you think such practices aided or hindered your own educational progress? Explore this subject further in the "Challenging Assumptions" section of the textbook's Education CourseMate website.

Most middle and high schools continue to use this form of ability grouping, but students do not learn more or have more positive feelings about themselves and school. This is a case in which even widely held beliefs must be modified or eliminated because the weight of evidence goes against them.

The second course of action is to use only those forms of ability grouping that produce positive results: within-class grouping and the Joplin Plan, especially for reading and mathematics. It is unclear why these forms of ability grouping work. It has been assumed (Tieso, 2003) that the increase in group homogeneity allows for more appropriate and potent forms of instruction (for example, greater effort by the teacher to bring lower-achieving groups up to the level of higher-achieving groups). If this assumption is correct, within-class ability grouping and the Joplin Plan must be carried out in such a way that homogeneous groups are guaranteed to result. The best way to achieve similarity in cognitive ability among students is to group them on the basis of past classroom performance, standardized achievement test scores, or both. The least desirable (but most frequently used) approach is basing the assignments solely on IQ scores.

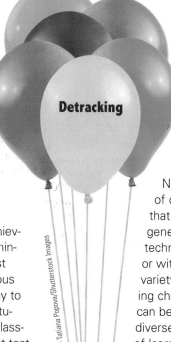
© Tatiana Popova/Shutterstock Images

The third course of action is to dispense with all forms of ability grouping, a practice called *detracking*. Detracking practices vary widely. When implemented well, however, detracking has been shown to support learning of all students in heterogeneous classrooms (Burris, Wiley, Welner, & Murphy, 2008; Rubin, 2006; Watanabe, 2008). In keeping with the concept of differentiated instruction mentioned in Chapter 4 (Tomlinson, Brimijoin, & Narvaez, 2008), teachers can use a variety of organizational and instructional techniques that will allow them to cope with a heterogeneous class, or they can use these same techniques in conjunction with the Joplin Plan or within-class grouping. As you encounter the variety of instructional techniques in the remaining chapters, keep in mind how each technique can become one more tool for addressing the diverse learning needs of a heterogeneous group of learners.

LO2 The Individuals With Disabilities Education Act (IDEA)

Many of the criticisms and arguments marshaled against ability grouping have come to be applied as well to special classes for students with disabilities. In addition, the elimination of racially segregated schools by the U.S. Supreme Court in the case of *Brown v. Board of Education* (1954) established a precedent for providing students with disabilities with an equal opportunity for a free and appropriate education (Ornstein, Levine, & Gutek, 2011). As a result, influential members of Congress were persuaded in the early 1970s that it was time for the federal government to take steps to correct the perceived inequities and deficiencies in our educational system. The result was a landmark piece of legislation: Public Law 94-142, the Education for All Handicapped Children Act of 1975. This law was revised and expanded in 1986 as the Education of the Handicapped Act Amendments of 1986 (Public Law 99-457) and again in 1990 as the Individuals with Disabilities Education Act (IDEA, Public Law 101-476). IDEA was amended in 1997 to broaden and clarify a number of its provisions ("Individuals with Disabilities," 1997; Ysseldyke, Algozzine, & Thurlow, 2000). It was amended again in 2004 to enhance parental involvement resulting from the No Child Left Behind Act of 2001 (Dardig, 2005) and to provide a method of identifying students with disabilities, called response to intervention, or RTI (Fuchs & Fuchs, 2006, 2009). The most recent regulations governing the implementation of IDEA were issued in 2006. (The U.S. Department of Education statistics reported later in the chapter come

{ **Before placement, a student must be given a complete, valid, and appropriate evaluation.** }

from its 2006 annual report to Congress on the implementation of IDEA.)

Major Provisions of IDEA

A Free and Appropriate Public Education The basic purpose of IDEA is to ensure that all individuals from birth through age 21 who have an identifiable disability, regardless of how severe, receive at public expense supervised special education and related services that meet their unique educational needs. These services can be delivered in a classroom, at home, in a hospital, or in a specialized institution, and may include physical and vocational education as well as instruction in the typical academic subjects (U.S. Department of Education, 2004).

Preplacement Evaluation Before a child with a disability can be placed in a program that provides special education services, "a full and individual initial evaluation" must be conducted (see http://idea.ed.gov [IDEA Regulations, Part 300/D/Sec. 300.301(a)]). Such an evaluation must conform to the following IDEA rules:

1. Tests must be administered in the child's native language.

2. Tests must be valid for the specific purposes for which they are used.

 ## Inclusion: Grouping Strategies for Inclusive Classrooms

Go to the Education CourseMate website and watch the video, study the artifacts in the case, and reflect upon the following questions:

1. In the Video Case, we see a class that groups students in a heterogeneous fashion. What are the pros and cons of this grouping strategy?

2. What are some of the strategies that the teachers in the Video Case use to ensure that all students participate in their various learning groups?

Chapter 6: Accommodating Student Variability

3. Tests must be administered by trained individuals according to the instructions provided by the test publishers.

4. Tests administered to students who have impaired sensory, manual, or speaking skills must reflect aptitude or achievement rather than the impairment.

5. No single procedure (such as an IQ test) can be the sole basis for determining an appropriate educational program. Data should be collected from such nontest sources as observations by other professionals (such as the classroom teacher), medical records, and parental interviews.

6. Evaluations must be made by a multidisciplinary team that contains at least one teacher or other specialist with knowledge in the area of the suspected disability.

7. The child must be assessed in all areas related to the suspected disability.

When you deal with students whose first language is not English, it is important to realize that standardized tests are designed to reflect cultural experiences common to the United States and that English words and phrases may not mean quite the same thing when translated. Therefore, these tests may not be measuring what they were developed to measure. In other words, they may not be valid. The results of such assessments should therefore be interpreted very cautiously (Kubiszyn & Borich, 2010; Robinson, 2008).

Individualized Education Program According to the IDEA regulations published in 2006 by the U.S. Department of Education (www.idea.ed.gov), every child who is identified as having a disability and who receives special education services must have an **individualized education program (IEP)** prepared by an IEP team. The IEP team includes parents, at least one regular classroom teacher, at least one special education teacher, a school district representative with expertise in providing or supervising the instruction of students with special learning needs, and—whenever appropriate—the child with the disability. Others may join the IEP team if they bring additional knowledge of the child, evaluations of the child's capacities, or

> **An IEP must include objectives, services to be provided, and criteria for determining achievement.**

resources of the school district. The IEP generated by the team is a written statement that describes the educational program they have designed to meet the child's unique needs. The IEP must include the following elements (which have been edited and numbered to make them clearer):

1. A statement of the child's current levels of academic achievement and functional performance.

2. A statement of measurable annual goals, including academic and functional goals designed to:

  2a. Meet the needs that result from the child's disability;

  2b. Enable the child to be involved in and make progress in the general education curriculum; and

  2c. Meet each of the child's other educational needs that result from the child's disability.

3. For children with disabilities who take alternate assessments aligned to alternate achievement standards, a description of benchmarks or short-term objectives.

4. A description of how the child's progress toward meeting the annual goals will be measured, and when periodic reports on progress will be provided.

5. A statement of the special education and related services and supplementary aids and services, based on peer-reviewed research to the extent practicable, to be provided to or for the child.

6. A statement of any individual appropriate accommodations that are necessary to measure the academic achievement and functional performance of the child on state and district-wide assessments. If the IEP team determines that the child must take an alternate assessment the following statements are required:

  6a. A statement of why the child cannot participate in the regular assessment; and

  6b. A statement of why the particular alternate assessment selected is appropriate.

Least Restrictive Environment According to the federal regulations that govern the implementation of IDEA, educational services must be provided to children with disabilities in the **least restrictive environment** that their disability will allow. A school district must identify a

individualized education program (IEP) A written statement describing an educational program designed to meet the unique needs of a child with a particular disability.

least restrictive environment A requirement (under the 1994 Code of Federal Regulations governing the implementation of IDEA) that disabled children be provided with education in the least restrictive setting possible, usually by including them in regular classrooms.

mainstreaming
The policy of placing students with disabilities in regular classes.

inclusion
An extension of the "least restrictive environment" provision of IDEA in which students with disabilities are placed in regular classrooms for the entire school day and receive some instruction and support from a special education teacher.

full inclusion
The practice of eliminating pullout programs (those outside the classroom) and providing regular teachers with special training so as to keep special-needs students in regular classrooms. Also called *inclusion*.

continuum of increasingly restrictive placements (instruction in regular classes, special classes, home instruction, instruction in hospitals and institutions) and, on the basis of the multidisciplinary team's evaluation, select the least restrictive setting that will best meet the student's special educational needs. This provision has often been referred to as **mainstreaming** because the goal of the regulation is to have as many children with disabilities as possible, regardless of the severity of the disability, enter the mainstream of education by attending regular classes with nondisabled students. In recent years, mainstreaming has frequently evolved into *inclusion*, a practice we discuss later in this chapter. The practice becomes controversial when mainstreaming is applied unequally to different ethnic groups, a controversy that mirrors the achievement gap and that continues in schools today (Blanchett, Klingner, & Harry, 2009). The controversy is addressed in this chapter's Case in Print.

The "least restrictive environment" provision of IDEA has led to mainstreaming—the policy that children with disabilities should attend regular classes to the maximum extent possible. Some special education proponents argue that full-time regular classroom placement should be the only option for such students.

© Bob Daemmrich/Photo Edit

The Policy of Inclusion

Although IDEA calls for children with disabilities to be placed in the least restrictive environment, the law clearly allows for more restrictive placements than those of the regular classroom "when the nature or severity of the disability is such that education in regular classes with the use of supplementary aids and services cannot be achieved satisfactorily" (U.S. Department of Education, 2004, Sec. 612(a)(5)). Nevertheless, there has been a movement in recent years to eliminate this option. Known as **inclusion** and **full inclusion**, these extensions of the mainstreaming provision have become one of the most controversial outgrowths of IDEA.

As most proponents use the term, *inclusion* means keeping special education students in regular classrooms and bringing support services to the children rather than the other way around. *Full inclusion* refers to the practice of eliminating all pullout programs *and* special education teachers and of providing regular classroom teachers with training in teaching special-needs students so that they can teach these students in the regular classroom (Kirk, Gallagher, Coleman, & Anastasiow, 2009; D. D. Smith & Tyler, 2010).

The Debate About Inclusion Because of the challenges presented by inclusion, teachers often question the practice. Proponents of inclusion and full inclusion often raise four arguments to support their position:

1. Research suggests that special-needs students who are segregated from regular students performed more poorly academically and socially than comparable students who were included (Kavale, 2002).

2. Given the substantial body of evidence demonstrating the propensity of children to observe and imitate more competent children (see, for example, Schunk, 1987), it can be assumed that students with disabilities will learn more by interacting with nondisabled students than by attending homogeneous classes (see Kleinert, Browder, & Towles-Reeves, 2009; Sapon-Shevin, 2003).

3. The Supreme Court in *Brown v. Board of Education* declared the doctrine of "separate but equal" to be unconstitutional. Therefore, pullout programs are a violation of the civil rights of children with special needs because these programs segregate them from their nondisabled peers in programs that are assumed to be separate but equal (Kavale, 2002; Mock & Kauffman, 2002).

4. Disproportionate numbers of students of color are placed in special education (Artiles, Klingner, & Tate, 2006; Harry & Klingner, 2006). As one example, according to the National Research Council (2002), Black students are disproportion-

ately placed in special education categories, such as "intellectual disabilities" and "learning disabilities" (these and other types of special needs are described later in this chapter). Black students who are placed in special education achieve at lower levels and are less likely to leave special education placements than their White counterparts (U.S. Department of Education, 2004). The gap in special education not only mirrors the achievement gap discussed in Chapter 5 but also results in the separation of Black students with special needs from the curriculum that their nondisabled peers experience (Blanchett, 2006). This harkens back to the violations from segregation addressed in *Brown v. Board of Education* (see Oakes, 2005) and can also contribute to a lack of tolerance among groups (Sapon-Shevin, 2003).

{ **An inclusion policy aims to keep students with disabilities in regular classrooms for the entire day.** }

Opponents of inclusion often cite cases of special-needs students disrupting the normal flow of instruction or of teachers being inadequately prepared to assist learners with special needs (Kavale, 2002; Mock & Kauffman, 2002).

Response to Intervention When the original Individuals with Disabilities Education Act (IDEA) was updated in 2004 to the Individuals with Disabilities Education Improvement Act (called "IDEA, 2004"), an important change occurred. Prior to IDEA, 2004, school professionals were encouraged to identify children with learning disabilities on the basis of the discrepancy between a student's IQ and achievement. Those whose achievement levels were considerably lower than one would predict on the basis of IQ were identified as having a learning problem. IDEA, 2004 introduced an additional method of identifying students with learning problems: **response to intervention (RTI)** (Bocala, Mello, Reedy, & Lacireno-Paquet, 2009; Fuchs & Fuchs, 2006, 2009; S. Jackson, Pretti-Frontczak, Harjusola-Webb, Grisham-Brown, & Romani, 2009; Stepanek & Peixotto, 2009; Zirkel & Thomas, 2010).

RTI was introduced as a way to determine how much students benefit from—or are responsive to—the instructional interventions they experience in the classroom. Students who respond to instruction are successful learners. Those who have difficulties with the instruction they encounter, especially in the early grades, have learning problems, placing them at-risk.

The idea is to discover problems early because if they go unchecked, the child's difficulties can multiply from grade to grade to the point that the student drops out of school. Thus, one of the purposes of RTI was to assess students early, to discover learning problems that students may be having, and to provide support through appropriate, research-based instructional interventions (Fletcher & Vaughn, 2009). A second purpose was to help teachers document each instructional intervention with a student and how well that student responded to each intervention; this documentation would help teachers assess how effective their instructional practices were in advancing student learning (Daly, Martens, Barnett, Witt, & Olson, 2007).

As we will see in later chapters, RTI has evolved as a means of collecting data on student learning and using those data to address learning difficulties that all students will, from time to time, experience. If we think about RTI in the context of the dynamic interactions that constitute teaching and learning, it suggests a continuous cycle of teaching: testing for learning–teaching–testing for learning . . .a cycle that repeats and repeats (Fuchs et al., 2007), and that moves the purpose of assessment beyond simply the identification of students who may be at risk to helping all students in all classrooms (Griffiths, VanDerHeyden, Skokut, & Lilles, 2009; VanDerHeyden, Witt, & Gilbertson, 2007). As mentioned, we will revisit RTI again in other chapters. For now, we return to IDEA and the disabling conditions that are addressed in it.

What IDEA Means to Regular Classroom Teachers

By the time you begin your teaching career, the original legislation governing the delivery of educational services to students with disabilities will have been in effect for more than 30 years. In the last three decades, departments of education in the various states and school districts have developed their own policies and procedures for implementing the requirements of IDEA. Schools and school districts typically provide new teachers with professional development opportunities to help them learn the local ins and outs of working with students with disabilities. But to be hired as a new teacher, you must demonstrate knowledge of some key implications of IDEA, such as the kinds of disabling conditions that your students may present, your responsibilities under IDEA, and an understanding of disabling conditions beyond IDEA.

response to intervention (RTI) A diagnostic technique that assesses how well students respond to instructional interventions in order to identify the type of instruction and special education services that they require to succeed.

The Kinds of Disabling Conditions Included Under IDEA According to the U.S. Department of Education (2009b), during the 2004–2005 academic year, 5.72 million children and youths ages 6 through 17 (11.6% of the total number of individuals in this age group) received special education services under IDEA.

For individuals between the ages of 3 and 20, IDEA recognizes 12 categories of disability. A 13th category, developmental delay, applies only to children ages 3 through 9 and is optional for state programs. The first 12 categories described in the legislation are listed here in alphabetical order, with brief definitions of each type.

Autism. Significant difficulty in verbal and nonverbal communication and social interaction that adversely affects educational performance.

Deaf-blindness. Impairments of both hearing and vision, the combination of which causes severe communication, developmental, and educational problems. The combination of these impairments is such that a child's educational and physical needs cannot be adequately met by programs designed for only deaf children or only blind children.

Emotional disturbance. Personal and social problems, exhibited in an extreme degree over a period of time, that adversely affect a child's ability to learn and get along with others. (Prior to the 1997 amendments to IDEA, this category was called "serious emotional disturbance.")

Hearing impairment. Permanent or fluctuating difficulty in understanding speech that adversely affects educational performance.

Mental retardation. (This is the term used in the IDEA legislation, but as we will see shortly, professional educators now speak of "intellectual disability.") Significant subaverage general intellectual functioning accompanied by deficits in adaptive behavior (how well a person functions in social environments).

Multiple disabilities. Two or more impairments (such as mental retardation–blindness and mental retardation–orthopedic, but not deaf–blindness) that cause such severe educational problems that a child's needs cannot be adequately met by programs designed solely for one of the impairments.

Orthopedic impairments. Impairment in a child's ability to use arms, legs, hands, or feet that significantly affects that child's educational performance.

Other health impairments. Conditions such as asthma, hemophilia, sickle-cell anemia, epilepsy, heart disease, and diabetes that so limit the strength, vitality, or alertness of a child that educational performance is significantly affected.

Specific learning disability. A disorder in one or more of the basic psychological processes involved in understanding or using language that leads to learning problems not traceable to physical disabilities, mental retardation, emotional disturbance, or cultural-economic disadvantage.

Speech or language impairment. A communication disorder such as stuttering, impaired articulation, or a language or voice impairment that adversely affects educational performance.

Foundations: Aligning Instruction With Federal Legislation

Go to the Education CourseMate website and watch the video, study the artifacts in the case, and reflect upon the following questions:

1. After reading about the inclusion debate and listening to the school professionals in this Video Case, what are your thoughts and position on this important educational issue?

2. Based on both the teacher interviews in this Video Case and the material you have read about IDEA, what do you think your responsibilities as a regular classroom teacher might be? Explain your answer.

TeachSource Video Case

Case in Print

Who Swims in the Mainstream?

A school district must identify a continuum of increasingly restrictive placements. . . . This provision has often been referred to as mainstreaming because the goal of the regulation is to have as many children with disabilities as possible, regardless of the severity of the disability, enter the mainstream of education by attending regular classes with nondisabled students. In recent years, mainstreaming has frequently evolved into inclusion. . . . The practice becomes controversial when mainstreaming is applied unequally to different ethnic groups, a controversy that mirrors the achievement gap and that continues in schools today (p. 125–126).

Study Finds Special Ed Disparities

LINDA PERLSTEIN

The Washington Post, 12/18/03

African American and Hispanic students in special education were far more likely than white and Asian students in recent years to be educated in special classrooms instead of integrated into the general population, according to a study of special education in Montgomery County Public Schools.

The study also found that students who live in poverty were almost 2½ times more likely than higher-income students to be labeled emotionally disturbed, and African Americans were almost three times more likely than whites to be identified as mentally retarded, a ratio that lowers only slightly when controlling for income.

The report was prepared by Margaret J. McLaughlin and Sandra Embler of the University of Maryland School of Education under the auspices of the county's Continuous Improvement Team. The Board of Education had directed the team to come up with a set of indicators for measuring the status of special education in the county. The report was completed in the summer but presented to the board last week as part of an update on special education services.

"Most of it was anticipated, but to get anything done you have to have a baseline for improvement," said Ricki Sabia, a co-chairman of the Continuous Improvement Team. "The whole point of the report was to bring up these issues, and the next step is to drill down what to do about it."

Black students received an average of 16.8 hours of special education services in total weekly compared with 14.8 for Hispanics and 12.4 hours for whites. Low-income students received 16.3 hours weekly, compared with 12 hours for the rest of the population.

For students with and without disabilities, a gap in academic performance exists by race and by income. Brian Bartels, Montgomery County's director of special education, said this correlation may partially explain why black, Hispanic and low-income disabled students are receiving more intensive services in less integrated environments, not just in Montgomery County but elsewhere in the state as well.

Educators may recommend more intensive services—not necessarily in separate settings—because of the greater instructional needs of students with lower achievement levels, Bartels said.

Attendance rates for special education students were, depending on school level, from 1 percentage point to 3 percentage points lower than rates for students in regular programs. Disparity in absences was greatest in high schools. Students with emotional disabilities and low-income students were most likely to have many absences.

Bartels said depression and behavioral problems may be keeping some emotionally disturbed students home, though he also said the attendance rate may have been skewed by a small number of students with very large numbers of absences.

Regardless of income, Asian American students were less likely than those in any other racial or ethnic group to receive special education services. They were, however, more likely to receive assistance in speech and language.

Thirteen percent of students with disabilities received no scores on the Comprehensive Test of Basic Skills. The CTBS is not used to comply with the federal No Child Left Behind Act, but test participation is a concern because the law requires that 95 percent of students in any group, including special education, take standardized tests.

Of the students who took the test, 70 percent received extra time to complete it, and more than 50 percent of sixth-graders and

25 percent of second-graders used a calculator—both permitted accommodations.

In surveys, special education teachers said parents do not support them in discipline or instruction or recognize their accomplishments, while parents and special education teachers felt that teachers in regular classrooms have low expectations for disabled students.

Source: Linda Perlstein, "Study finds special ed disparities," from *The Washington Post*, December 18, 2003. Copyright © 2003 *The Washington Post.* Reprinted by permission.

Questions and Activities

1. The study of special education placements in the Montgomery County (Maryland) school system that is described in this article replicates the findings of other, more recent, studies: Compared with White, middle-SES students, a larger percentage of ethnic minority, students of color, and low-income students are placed in special education classes. What factors (one of which was mentioned in the article) might account for this difference?

2. Assuming for the moment that all of these students met IDEA guidelines for receiving special education services, how likely is it that a special education class is the most appropriate placement (that is, the least restrictive environment) for all or most of these students? Why?

3. The last paragraph of the article indicates that special education teachers, regular education teachers, and parents of students with disabilities are not in agreement about how to handle students with disabilities. Form your own opinion by talking to individuals from these three groups about their views on special education class placement versus mainstreaming. If there are differences, try to identify their basis.

Traumatic brain injury. A brain injury due to an accident that causes cognitive or psychosocial impairments that adversely affect educational performance.

Visual impairment including blindness. A visual impairment so severe that even with corrective lenses a child's educational performance is adversely affected.

The percentages of each type of student who received special educational services during the 2004–2005 school year are indicated in Table 6.1. As you can see, the children with disabilities who most commonly received services (90% of the total) were those classified as having a specific learning disability, a speech or language impairment, mental retardation, or an emotional disturbance.

The Teacher's Responsibilities Under IDEA Regular classroom teachers may be involved in activities required directly or indirectly by IDEA in four possible ways: referral, assessment, preparation of the IEP, and implementation and evaluation of the IEP.

Referral Most referrals for assessment and possible special instruction are made by a child's teacher or parents because they are the ones most familiar with the quality of the child's daily work and progress as compared with other children.

Suzie Fitzhugh

The decision whether a child qualifies for special education services under IDEA is made largely on the basis of information supplied by the multidisciplinary assessment team. Classroom teachers typically contribute information about the child's academic and social behavior.

Assessment The initial assessments are combined with other data (e.g., teachers' and parents' observations) and evaluated by a multidisciplinary assessment team—including a classroom teacher—to determine if special education services or accommodations are needed. Because IDEA requires that classroom teachers be part of the multidisciplinary assessment team and potentially use RTI, you should be prepared to provide such information as the child's responsiveness to instructional interventions, homework quality and test scores, ability to understand and use language, ability to perform various motor functions, alertness at different times of the day, and interpersonal relationships with classmates (Fuchs & Fuchs, 2006, 2009; Kubiszyn & Borich, 2010).

Preparation of the IEP Earlier in the chapter we described the required membership of the IEP team for

TABLE 6.1 Students Receiving Special Education Services, 2004–2005

Disabling Condition	Percentage of Total School Enrollment[a]	Percentage of Students With Disabilities Served[b]
Specific learning disabilities	5.42	46.4
Speech or language impairments	2.32	18.8
Mental retardation	1.00	9.3
Other health impairments	1.00	8.4
Emotional disturbance	0.93	7.9
Autism	0.32	2.7
Multiple disabilities	0.23	2.2
Hearing impairments	0.14	1.2
Orthopedic impairments	0.12	1.1
Visual impairments	0.05	0.4
Traumatic brain injury	0.04	0.4
Deaf-blindness	0.00	0.0
Total	11.57	98.8[c]

[a]Percentages are based on children with disabilities ages 6–17 as a percentage of total school enrollment for kindergarten through 12th grade.
[b]Percentages are based on children with a disability ages 6–21 as a percentage of the total number of students receiving special education.
[c]Percentage does not add up to 100 percent because of rounding.
SOURCE: U.S. Department of Education (2009a, 2009b).

Students with learning disabilities, speech impairments, mental retardation, or emotional disturbance are most likely to be served under IDEA.

Chapter 6: Accommodating Student Variability

FIGURE 6.1 Example of an Individualized Education Program (IEP)

INDIVIDUAL EDUCATIONAL PLAN	11/2011
	DATE

STUDENT: Last Name _____ First _____ Middle 5.3 _____ 8-4-01

School of Attendance _____ Home School _____ Grade Level _____ Birthdate/Age

School Address _____ School Telephone Number

Child Study Team Members

_____ L D Teacher

Name Homeroom Title | Case Manager Parents

Name Facilitator Title | Name Title

Name Speech Title | Name Title

Summary of Assessment results

IDENTIFIED STUDENT NEEDS: _Reading from last half of DISTAR II - present performance level_

LONG TERM GOALS: _To improve reading achievement level by at least one year's gain. To improve math achievement to grade level. To improve language skills by one year's gain._

SHORT TERM GOALS: _Master Level 4 vocabulary and reading skills. Master math skills in basic curriculum. Master spelling words from Level 3 list. Complete units 1-9 from Level 3 curriculum._

MAINSTREAM MODIFICATIONS: _____

White Copy—Cumulative Folder | Goldenrod Copy—Case Manager
Pink Copy—Special Teacher | Yellow Copy—Parent

Description of Services to Be Provided

Type of Service	Teacher	Starting Date	Amt. of time per day	OBJECTIVES AND CRITERIA FOR ATTAINMENT
SLD level III	LD Teacher	11-11-99	2½ hrs	Reading: will know all vocabulary through the "Honeycomb" level. Will master skills as presented through Distar II. Will know 1 2 3 second-symbols presented in "Sound Way to Reading." Math: will pass all tests at Basic 4 level. Spelling: 5 words each week from level 3 lists. Language: will complete Units 1-9 of the 4th grade language program. Will also complete supplemental units from "Language Step by Step."

Mainstream Classes	Teacher	Amt. of time per day	OBJECTIVES AND CRITERIA FOR ATTAINMENT
		3½ hrs	Out of seat behavior: Sit attentively and listen during mainstream class discussions. A simple management plan will be implemented if he does not meet this expectation. Mainstream modifications of Social Studies: will keep a folder in which he expresses through drawing the topics his class will cover. Modified district Social Studies curriculum. No formal testing will be made.

The following equipment and other services in personnel, transportation, curriculum methods, and educational services will be provided: _Distar II Reading Program, Spelling Level 3, "Sound Way to Reading" Program, Vocabulary tapes_

Substantiation of least restrictive alternatives: _The planning team has determined academic needs are best met with direct SLD support in reading, math, language, and spelling_

ANTICIPATED LENGTH OF PLAN _1 yr._ The next periodic review will be held: _May 2012_
DATE/TIME/PLACE

☐ I approve this program placement and the above IEP
☐ I do not approve this placement and/or the IEP
☐ I request a conciliation conference

_____ PARENT/GUARDIAN

Form 2011 _____ Principal or Designee

a student with disability. (We described the required elements of an IEP as well.) It is not unusual for the members of the multidisciplinary assessment team to join the IEP team. Figure 6.1 provides an example of an IEP.

{ The classroom teacher, parents, and several specialists prepare an IEP. }

Implementation and Evaluation of the IEP Given the efforts to make inclusion the common practice in schools, it is likely that you will have students with disabilities as learners in your classroom. Because the IEP is planned by a multidisciplinary team, you will be given direction and support in providing regular class instruction for students who have a disabling condition as defined under IDEA. The advent of the RTI approach—not only for purposes of early assessment of disability but for helping all learners—means you will be expected to collect data and use those data to monitor how well your student is responding to the interventions specified in the IEP.

Section 504: A Broader View of Disabling Conditions

The civil rights movement of the 1960s led to the Rehabilitation Act of 1973. Section 504 of that act prevents discrimination against people with disabilities who participate in any federally funded program, which includes public schools. The ADA Amendments Act of 2008 (ADAAA), which became effective on January 1, 2009, broadened the interpretation of disability as it is applied in Section 504. The ADAAA dealt with the possibility that some students in your class who are not covered by IDEA may have a condition that, if not addressed, could limit their access to and participation in learning opportunities. In such cases, under ADAAA, the school must provide a plan to overcome the limitation. For example, a student with diabetes may need accommodations to monitor and control her blood sugar levels. A 504 plan for the student with diabetes may include a "private space" in the school or classroom for testing. Most 504 plans cover students with health or medical challenges or those with attention deficit/hyperactivity disorder who are not already covered by IDEA.

Regardless of whether a disability is covered legally through IDEA or through ADAAA changes to Section 504, the types of students you will sometimes be expected to teach in your classroom will vary. Some will be special education students who are included in your classroom for part of the school day. Others, although different from many students in some noticeable respect, will not qualify for special education services under IDEA. The remainder of this chapter will describe students from both categories and techniques for teaching them. Students with intellectual disability, learning disabilities, and emotional disturbance often require special forms of instruction, and we will focus on these categories. In addition, though not mentioned in IDEA or Section 504, students who are gifted and talented require special forms of instruction, as we will also discuss.

Pause & Reflect

Many teachers say that although they agree with the philosophy behind IDEA, they feel that their training has not adequately prepared them to meet the needs of students with disabling conditions. Would you say the same about your teacher education program? Why? What might you do to prepare yourself better?

LO3 Students With Intellectual Disability (Formerly Called Mental Retardation)

Definition of Intellectual Disability

On January 1, 2007, the American Association on Mental Retardation became the American Association on Intellectual and Developmental Disabilities, and in 2009, the premier research journal of the 130-year-old organization changed from the *American Journal on Mental Retardation* to the *American Journal on Intellectual and Developmental Disabilities*. The name changes were made to reflect the scope of the work that is done by researchers and the organization, to better advocate for political and social change, and to find a more socially acceptable way of addressing people with an intellectual disability. AAIDD defines **intellectual disability** as "a disability characterized by significant limitations both in intellectual functioning and in adaptive behavior, which covers many everyday social and practical skills. This disability originates before the age of 18" (American Association on Intellectual and Developmental Disabilities, 2009).

Although we will use the term *intellectual disability* from this point on in the chapter, you will recall earlier

references to mental retardation as one of the disabling conditions included under IDEA and in Table 6.1. Our reason for using the old term is that the language of IDEA still refers to it. Indeed, the percentages and the disabling conditions reported in Table 6.1 are taken directly from the annual report on IDEA submitted by the U.S. Department of Education to Congress in 2009. It will undoubtedly take some time for the term *mental retardation* to disappear from educational discourse, and so we expect that educators will have to live with both terms for some period to come. Nevertheless, the name change is not purely cosmetic: The term *intellectual disability* differs from *mental retardation* in important, albeit subtle, ways.

Older notions of mental retardation used IQ score as the key criterion. An individual whose score is two or more standard deviations below the mean (a score of 75 or below) on a standardized test of intelligence is considered to have a significant limitation in intellectual functioning. (If you're not sure what a standard deviation is, take a look now at Chapter 15, in which we discuss this statistical concept.)

The new definition of intellectual disability is documented in the 11th edition of the AAIDD definition manual, titled *Intellectual Disability: Definition, Classification, and Systems of Supports* (Schalock et al., 2010). The book, 7 years in the writing, was authored by 18 experts[*] and focuses on both intellectual functioning and adaptive behavior in three areas: conceptual skills, social skills, and practical, everyday living skills. Thus, understanding intellectual disability is not simply interpreting a number on a test but interpreting how well a person develops adaptive behaviors that allow the person to live successfully within her or his environment. Perhaps this new view reminds you of Sternberg's triarchic theory of intelligence, also known as the theory of successful intelligence. Sternberg's idea that intelligence manifests itself in a variety of ways in a variety of contexts is consistent with the effort to replace the idea of mental retardation with the concept of intellectual disability. That concept includes a multifaceted evaluation and ties evaluation to a system for planning and providing supports that helps the student with intellectual disability participate successfully in daily life.

Characteristics of Children With Intellectual Disability

IQ tests are still used as a tool for determining intellectual disability, but they are only one tool that measures

[*]Schalock, R., Borthwick-Duffy, S., Bradley, V., Buntinx, W., Coulter, D., Craig, E., Gomez, S., Lachapelle, Y., Luckasson, R., Reeve, A., Shogren, K., Snell, M., Spreat, S., Tassé, M., Thompson, J., Verdugo-Alonso, M., Wehmeyer, M., & Yeager, M. (2010).

> ## Students with intellectual disability may frustrate easily and lack confidence and self-esteem.

intellectual capacity. Other tools are just as important; one example is the Diagnostic Adaptive Behavior Scale. This tool assesses limitations in conceptual skills (such as understanding language, number concepts, money, and time), social skills (such as establishing and maintaining relationships, obeying rules or laws, and avoiding being victimized by others), and practical skills (such as maintaining personal care, using public transportation, and establishing schedules and routines). It is important to understand that the limitations in intellectual functioning (which can be informed by IQ tests) become more noticeable as a person tries to do everyday things. Experiencing difficulty in meeting everyday needs can lead to feelings of confusion and frustration. These feelings, in conjunction with the cognitive deficits outlined in the next paragraph, sometimes make it difficult for a child with intellectual disability to make friends and get along with peers.

Cognitively, learners with intellectual disability tend to have difficulty grasping complex concepts or ideas, memorizing, paying attention for extended periods, and formulating learning strategies that fit particular situations. Typically, they are delayed in their language development and show a limited amount of *metacognition*, that is, knowledge about how they learn and the factors that affect learning. (This concept will be discussed more fully in Chapter 8.)

Several of these cognitive deficits often operate in concert to produce or contribute to the learning problems of students with intellectual disability. Consider, for example, the problem of generalization (also known as *transfer*). This refers to the ability of a learner to take something that has been learned in one context, such as paper-and-pencil arithmetic skills, and use it to deal with a similar but different task, such as knowing whether correct change has been received after making a purchase at a store. Students with mild intellectual disability may not spontaneously exhibit transfer because (1) their metacognitive deficits limit their tendency to look for signs of similarity between two tasks, (2) their relatively short attention span prevents them from noticing similarities, and (3) their limited memory capacity and skills lessen their ability to recall relevant knowledge.

As you consider the characteristics of learners with intellectual disability, it is important to realize that while they may exhibit certain limitations or weaknesses, they also have strengths—just like everyone else.

The Suggestions for Teaching on the next page take into account the characteristics just described, as well as points made by Michael Hardman, Clifford Drew, and M. Winston Egan (2011); Nancy Hunt and Kathleen Marshall (2006); William L. Heward (2009); Samuel Kirk, James Gallagher, Mary Ruth Coleman, and Nicholas Anastasiow (2009); and Deborah Deutsch Smith and Naomi Chowdhuri Tyler (2010).

learning disabilities
Problems in otherwise mentally fit students who are unable to respond to certain aspects of the curriculum presented in regular classrooms because of disorders in one or more basic psychological processes.

LO4 Students With Learning Disabilities

By far the greatest number of students who qualify for special education under IDEA are those classified as having **learning disabilities**. According to U.S. Department of Education figures (2009a), the number of students identified as learning disabled increased from approximately 800,000 in 1976–1977 to more than 2.5 million in 2004–2005. In the 1976–1977 school year, students with learning disabilities accounted for about 24% of the disabled population. By the 2004–2005 school year, that estimate had grown to nearly 50%. Especially because so many students are now classified as learning disabled, it is important to define and explore the characteristics of students with learning disabilities.

Characteristics of Students With Learning Disabilities

According to IDEA, an individual who has a specific learning disability can be described as follows:

1. The individual has a *disorder in one or more of the basic psychological processes*. These processes refer to intrinsic prerequisite abilities such as memory, auditory perception, and visual perception.

2. The individual has *difficulty in learning*, specifically in the areas of speaking, listening, writing, reading (word recognition skills and comprehension), spelling, and mathematics (calculation and reasoning).

> ## { Students with intellectual disability tend to oversimplify and have difficulty generalizing. }

Suggestions for Teaching

Instructing Students With Intellectual Disability

1 Do your homework.

As you plan how you are going to help a student with intellectual disability succeed in your classroom, make sure that you learn as much about your student's specific strengths and weaknesses as possible. Remember, you are teaching a unique individual, not a disabling condition category.

As can be seen in Table 6.1, intellectual disability is a condition that affects about 1 in 100 school children. Of those in school who receive special education services, students with intellectual disability number around 1 in 10. The point is that the number of students with disabilities that will be included in regular classes is likely to be fairly small. Before you plan learning activities for your students with intellectual disability, make sure that you consult all of the data that have been gathered by the multidisciplinary assessment team and how those data have been used to formulate the IEP for each student. And keep in mind that adaptive behavior includes not only conceptual skills that help students attain academic success, but social and practical skills that will help them function more effectively in their day-to-day lives.

2 Engage in and model positive social interactions.

The general cognitive characteristics of *learners with intellectual disability* make it difficult for them to deal with complex ideas, concepts, and situations. Social interactions in classrooms—where students are not only interacting with others but often doing so in an attempt to accomplish a task or negotiate some conceptual understanding—can be quite complex. It is important, therefore, that you attend to the quality of the interactions in your classroom. The best place to start is with your own social interactions in the classroom. Make a point of interacting with your students with intellectual disability and try to make each interaction a positive one. You might, for example, greet a student by saying something like, "I'm so glad you're here today. You make the classroom a nicer place to be in." Even in situations where the student is experiencing confusion or frustration, you can communicate positively. For example, you might say something like, "I know this assignment feels difficult, but that

is a good thing. When you are trying to learn something and it feels hard, that means you are really learning something new. And if we can work together so that you stick with it, it means you will be able to do something that you couldn't do before." If you get into the habit of interacting positively with your students with intellectual disability you will model such interaction for the other students in your class and communicate high expectations to all learners in your classroom.

Recall Erikson's theory of psychosocial development. The nature of their social interactions with others influences children's sense of self. Positive social experiences lead to feelings of industry rather than inferiority for younger children and contribute to a sense of identity rather than role confusion for adolescents.

3 Keep assignments and other learning tasks short and build on what students already know.

A student's exhibiting intellectual disability does not mean the student is incapable of completing substantial, multielement assignments, such as term papers. It does mean, however, that you should not assume that students with intellectual disability will be able to complete a complicated, multitask assignment on their own. By planning small, clearly defined learning tasks that build on what students already know and are able to do, you can facilitate their success. Rather than giving a student with intellectual disability the assignment to write a term paper on some aspect of the legislative process, you might begin by having the student record a short video on a law that she or he knows and understands. From that beginning, you can move on to more short videos that can be combined and that build toward a statement about where laws come from. In Chapter 7 we will learn about the theoretical basis for this kind of "successive approximation" of complex behaviors and the ways technology can support such teaching efforts.

4 Teach simple techniques for improving memory, and consistently point out how use of these techniques leads to more accurate recall.

In Chapter 9 we will describe a set of memory aids called *mnemonic devices*. Used for thousands of years by scholars and teach-

ers in different countries, most are fairly simple devices that help a learner organize information, encode it meaningfully, and generate cues that allow it to be retrieved from memory when needed. The simplest mnemonic devices are rhymes, first-letter mnemonics (also known as acronyms), and sentence mnemonics. For example, a first-letter mnemonic or acronym for the Great Lakes is *HOMES*: Huron, Ontario, Michigan, Erie, Superior.

5 Assess how well your students respond to intervention and use the data to try new teaching ideas.

Remember that RTI is not only a way to measure whether students have special learning needs or require accommodations; it is an approach to teaching that can serve you and your students with intellectual disabilities well. (As we will see, it is an approach that can serve all learners, with or without disabling conditions.)

The IEP will provide you with guidance as you plan ways to help your students succeed. But just because the IEP suggests an intervention that is thought to be effective doesn't mean that intervention will be effective. Think about your teaching efforts as research and development. You try to intervene in some way to help your student, you collect data (e.g., quiz scores, discussions, assignments, personal observations), and you evaluate whether and how well the intervention is working. Based on what you learn from the data you collect from your assessments, you make changes in an attempt to improve or develop effective ways of facilitating student learning. As we will see in Chapter 14, the data from assessments can be shared with students to help them see their own progress and to encourage them to keep trying when the going gets tough.

3. The problem is *not due primarily to other causes*, such as visual or hearing impairments, motor disabilities, mental retardation, emotional disturbance, or economic, environmental, or cultural disadvantage.

In addition to problems with cognitive processing and learning, many students with a learning disability (as well as students with intellectual disability and students with emotional disturbance) have more poorly developed social skills than their nondisabled peers. Such students are more likely to ignore the teacher's directions, cheat, use profane language, disturb other students, disrupt group activities, and start fights. Consequently, they are often rejected by the rest of the class, which contributes to lowered self-esteem and poor academic performance (Gresham & MacMillan, 1997; Toth & King, 2010).

Some people dismiss the notion of learning disabilities as a fiction because, they say, everyone at one time or another has misread numbers, letters, and words; confused pronunciations of words and letters; and suffered embarrassing lapses of attention and memory. But students with learning disabilities really are different from others—mostly in degree rather than in kind. Although the individual without a disability may occasionally exhibit lapses in basic information processing, the individual with a learning disability does so consistently and with little hope of self-correction. The important point to keep in mind is that you need to know what a student with a learning disability (as well as a low-achieving student without a learning disability) can and cannot do so that you can effectively remediate those weaknesses (Lerner & Johns, 2009; Spear-Swerling & Sternberg, 1998).

Identifying Students With Learning Disabilities

The major criterion used by most school districts to identify children with learning disabilities is at least an average score on a standardized test of intelligence and a significantly below average score (one standard deviation or more) on a standardized achievement test. In other words, districts typically look for a discrepancy between achievement and IQ scores.

Because about 80% of children with learning disabilities have difficulty with reading (Meyer, 2000), a considerable amount of research has been done to determine whether a discrepancy between IQ and reading comprehension scores is a valid indicator of a learning disability. One approach to this problem has been to compare children who exhibit the discrepancy we just described with children whose IQ and reading scores are both below average. Researchers often refer to students in the first group as IQ discrepant and students

© Mike Goldwater/Alamy

Students with a learning disability learn more slowly than other students because of difficulties in perception, attention, and memory.

in the second group as IQ consistent. Two analyses of almost four dozen studies that have examined this issue (Meyer, 2000; Steubing et al., 2002) concluded that IQ-consistent students are indistinguishable from IQ-discrepant students in terms of reading skills (such as phonological awareness and word naming) and behavior (such as social skills and fine motor skills).

This research casts doubt on the usefulness of the discrepancy criterion. Learning disabilities certainly exist, but educators may need to develop a more sophisticated means of identifying them.

Students with learning disabilities have problems with perception, attention, memory, and metacognition.

Problems With Basic Psychological Processes

The fundamental problem that underlies a learning disability is, as the IDEA statute states, "a disorder in one or more of the basic psychological processes" (http://idea.ed.gov [Title I/Part/Sec. 602(30)(A)]). Although this phrase is somewhat vague, it generally refers to problems with how students receive information, process it, and express what they have learned. Specifically, many students with learning disabilities have deficits in perception, attention, memory encoding and storage, and metacognition.

Some students with learning disabilities have great difficulty perceiving the difference between certain sounds (*f* and *v*, for example, or *m* and *n*) or the appearance of letters (*m* and *n*, or *b*, *p*, and *d*, for example). As a result, words that begin with one letter (such as *vase*) are sometimes perceived and pronounced as if they begin with another letter (as in *face*). As you can no doubt appreciate from this simple example, this type of deficit makes learning to read and comprehend during reading long and frustrating for some students.

Many students with learning disabilities also have difficulty with attention and impulse control: focusing on a task, noticing important cues and ideas, and staying with the task until it is completed. The source of the distraction may be objects and activities in the classroom, or it may be unrelated thoughts. In either case, the student misses much of what the teacher says or what is on a page of text, or misinterprets directions.

Because so many students with learning disabilities have problems with perception and attention, they also have problems with accurate recall of information. Accurate recall is heavily dependent on what is stored in memory in the first place and where information is stored in memory (Hunt & Marshall, 2006), so students who encode partial, incorrect, or unimportant information have memory problems.

Like students with intellectual disability, many students with learning disabilities have a deficit in metacognitive skills (Hunt & Marshall, 2006). As a result, their learning activities are chaotic, like those of young children. For example, they may begin a task before they have thought through all of the steps.

Students with learning disabilities tend to be characterized as passive and disorganized: passive in the sense that they take few active steps to attend to relevant

information, store it effectively in memory, and retrieve it when needed; and disorganized in the sense that their learning activities are often unplanned and subject to whatever happens to capture their attention at the moment.

Given these problems with basic processes, researchers have studied ways to help students structure the way they learn. For example, one approach to improving the reading skills of students with learning disabilities that has shown some promise is teaching students how to use reading comprehension strategies (Gersten, Fuchs, Williams, & Baker, 2001). One such program that was tested on middle school students with reading disabilities (Bryant et al., 2000) contained the following components:

1. *Word identification*. Students used a first-letter mnemonic to help them recall the seven steps involved in decoding multisyllabic words.

2. *Partner reading*. To improve reading fluency (reading whole words in text accurately and at an appropriate speed), pairs of students modeled fluent reading for one another and helped each other decode unfamiliar words.

3. *Collaborative strategic reading*. This technique is aimed at improving reading comprehension and combines two proven instructional techniques—reciprocal teaching and cooperative learning (we discuss both techniques in detail in later chapters). Students first learned how to use the four comprehension-aiding techniques that are part of reciprocal teaching: (a) previewing a reading passage to help students make predictions about what they will read and already know about the topic, (b) monitoring reading to identify and fix comprehension failures, (c) identifying main ideas, and (d) asking questions and reviewing. Students then applied the techniques by working either in pairs or small cooperative groups.

Compared with pretest scores, students using these reading comprehension strategies achieved higher posttest scores on word identification, reading fluency, and reading comprehension tests. The differences for word identification and reading fluency were statistically significant (meaning they were not likely due to chance).

Attention Deficit/Hyperactivity Disorder

Many children who have a learning disability are also diagnosed as having **attention deficit/hyperactivity disorder (ADHD)**. Estimates of the extent to which these two conditions co-occur range from 25% to 40% (Lerner, 2003; Lerner & Johns, 2009). Approximately 3.3% of 6- to 11-year-old children have ADHD alone, with boys outnumbering girls by at least 3 to 1

> ## Symptoms of ADHD include inattention, hyperactivity, and impulsivity.

(Bowman, 2002). In addition, some studies have found that as many as 30% of children with ADHD exhibit aggressive behaviors (such as fighting, stealing, lying about others, and vandalism) that are consistent with the psychiatric diagnosis of conduct disorder (Connor, 2002). The co-occurrence of ADHD and conduct disorder (called *comorbidity*) is seen more frequently among children from urban homes than middle-SES suburban homes and is associated with significant social, behavioral, and academic problems (Bloomquist & Schnell, 2002).

The American Psychiatric Association recognizes three types of children with ADHD: (1) children who are predominantly inattentive, (2) children who are predominantly hyperactive and impulsive, and (3) children who exhibit a combination of all three behaviors. For a student to be judged as having ADHD, the symptoms have to appear before the age of 7; have to be displayed in several settings, such as at home, at school, and at play; and have to persist over time (American Psychiatric Association, 2000). Although ADHD is not mentioned in IDEA as a separate disability category, services for children with ADHD can be funded under the "specific learning disability" category, the "emotional disturbance" category, or the "other health impairments" category of IDEA (Lerner, 2003).

In general, the treatments for ADHD fall into one of the following three categories (Lerner, 2003; Purdie, Hattie, & Carroll, 2002):

1. *Prescribed stimulant medication.* The most popular class of drugs prescribed for children with ADHD is psychostimulants. The psychostimulants that are prescribed most often are Ritalin, Dexedrine, Cylert, and Adderall. The effect of these medications is highly specific. Some children do better on one drug, others on another, and still others do not respond to any of them.

2. *School-based psychological/educational programs.* These programs typically involve behavior management, cognitive behavioral therapy, or classroom environment restructuring. Behavior management programs (which we describe in more detail in Chapter 7) involve the systematic use of reinforcement and punishment to increase the frequency of desired behaviors and decrease the frequency of undesired behaviors. Cognitive behavioral therapy programs involve teaching students to remind themselves to use effective learning skills, monitor their progress, and reinforce themselves. Classroom environment restructuring programs use such techniques as reducing classroom noise, assigning students permanent seats, seating students with ADHD at the front of the class, and providing frequent breaks between tasks.

3. *Multimodal programs.* Multimodal programs involve combinations of one or more of the preceding treatments, typically stimulant medications and cognitive behavioral programs.

An analysis of 74 research studies (Purdie, Hattie, & Carroll, 2002) found, not surprisingly, that an overall best treatment for ADHD does not exist. Rather, different treatments had stronger effects depending on the outcome that was being examined. For example, stimulant medications were more effective than other treatments in minimizing impulsivity, hyperactivity, and attentional deficits; multimodal programs were most effective in reducing classmates' dislike and fostering more effective prosocial skills and positive peer interactions; and school-based programs were most effective in aiding the growth of cognitive skills.

The Suggestions for Teaching on the next page will give you some ideas about how to help students with learning disabilities and ADHD improve their learning skills and feel better about themselves.

LO5 Students With Emotional Disturbance

Estimates of Emotional Disturbance

In the 2009 report to Congress on the implementation of IDEA, the U.S. Department of Education noted that 453,795 students between the ages of 6 and 17 were classified as emotionally disturbed in the 2004–2005 school year (U.S. Department of Education, Office of Special Education and Rehabilitative Services, Office of Special Education Programs, 2009a). This figure accounted for 8% of all school children with disabilities and slightly less than 1% of the general school-age population. Not everyone agrees that these figures accurately reflect the scope of the problem; other scholars believe that 3% to 5% of all school-age

Suggestions for Teaching

Instructing Students With Learning Disabilities and ADHD

1 Structure learning tasks to help students with learning disabilities and ADHD compensate for weaknesses in psychological processes.

Because of their weaknesses in basic psychological processes, students with learning disabilities and ADHD are often distractible, impulsive, forgetful, disorganized, poor at comprehension, and unaware of the factors that affect learning. Research findings indicate that the most effective instructional approach in such cases is one that combines direct instruction with social constructivist approaches to strategy learning (both methods are described in Chapter 13). This combined approach has produced substantial improvements in reading comprehension, vocabulary, word recognition, memory, writing, cognitive processing, and self-concept (Lerner & Johns, 2009; Rotter, 2009; H. L. Swanson & Hoskyn, 1998). The following examples are consistent with an instructional approach that is based on both direct instruction and strategy instruction:

- For students who have difficulty distinguishing between stimuli (such as letters, words, or phrases) that look or sound similar, point out and highlight their distinguishing characteristics. For example, highlight the circular part of the letters *b, p,* and *d* and place a directional arrow at the end of the straight segment to emphasize that they have the same shape but differ in their spatial orientation. Or highlight the letters *t* and *r* in the words *though, thought,* and *through* to emphasize that they differ from each other by the absence or presence of one letter.
- For students who are easily distracted, instruct them to place only the materials being used on top of the desk or within sight.
- For students who seem unable to attend to important stimuli such as significant sections of a text page, show them how to underline or outline in an effort to distinguish between important and unimportant material. Or suggest that they use a ruler or pointing device under each line as they read, so that they can evaluate one sentence at a time. To help them attend to important parts of directions, highlight or write keywords and phrases

in all capitals. For especially important tasks, you might want to ask students to paraphrase directions or repeat them verbatim.
- For students who have a short attention span, give brief assignments and divide complex material into smaller segments. After each short lesson segment, provide both immediate positive feedback and tangible evidence of progress. (Many sets of published materials prepared for use with students with learning disabilities are designed in this way.)
- To improve students' memory for and comprehension of information, teach memorization skills and methods for relating new information to existing knowledge schemes to improve long-term storage and retrieval. Also, make frequent use of simple, concrete analogies and examples to explain and illustrate complex, abstract ideas. (We will describe several techniques for enhancing memory and comprehension in Chapter 9.)
- To improve organization, suggest that students use a notebook to keep a record of homework assignments, a checklist of materials needed for class, and a list of books and materials they need to take home for studying and homework.
- To improve general awareness of the learning process, emphasize the importance of thinking about the factors that could affect one's performance on a particular task, of forming a plan before actually starting to work, and of monitoring the effectiveness of learning activities.
- Consider the variety of learning environments available through multimedia software programs. Some students with learning disabilities may respond better to a combination of visual and auditory information, whereas others may learn best in a hands-on setting. Multimedia programs provide options to address these different styles and also allow the student to control the direction and pace of learning. Examples of such programs can be found on the Special Needs page of the Educational Software Directory website (www.educational-software -directory.net).

2 Capitalize on the resources in your classroom to help students with learning disabilities and ADHD improve academically, socially, and emotionally.

Although you and the resource teacher will be the main sources of instruction and support for mainstreamed students, recognize that other sources of classroom support are almost always available. The other students in your class, for example, can supplement your instructional efforts. As we pointed out in the previous chapter, peer tutoring typically produces gains in achievement and improvements in interpersonal relationships and attitudes toward subject matter. These effects have been documented for students with learning disabilities as well as for low-achieving students without learning disabilities (Fuchs, Fuchs, Mathes, & Simmons, 1997). And do not overlook the benefits of having students with learning disabilities play the role of tutor. Giving a student with a disability the opportunity to tutor either a low-achieving classmate in a subject that is not affected by the student's disability or a younger student in a lower grade can produce a noticeable increase in self-esteem.

Another way to make use of the other students in your class is through cooperative learning. This technique was described in the last chapter and is explored in more detail in Chapter 13. Like peer tutoring, which it incorporates, cooperative learning also produces gains in achievement, interpersonal relationships, and self-esteem.

Finally, make use of the various ways in which information can be presented to students and in which students can respond. In addition to text material and lecturing, you can use films, computer-based presentations, picture charts, diagrams, and demonstrations. As well as having students demonstrate what they have learned through paper-and-pencil tests and other written products, you can have them make oral presentations, produce pictorial products, create an actual product, or give a performance. Hands-on activities are particularly useful for students with ADHD.

children qualify for special education services under IDEA's emotional disturbance criteria (Heward, 2009).

Definitions of Emotional Disturbance

Two reasons that estimates of **emotional disturbance** vary are the lack of clear descriptions of such forms of behavior and different interpretations of the descriptions that do exist. Children with *emotional disturbance* are defined in IDEA in this way (IDEA, 2004, Sec. 300.8 (c) (4)(i)):

(I) The term means a condition exhibiting one or more of the following characteristics over a long period of time and to a marked degree that adversely affects a child's educational performance:

(A) An inability to learn that cannot be explained by intellectual, sensory, or health factors.

(B) An inability to build or maintain satisfactory interpersonal relationships with peers and teachers.

(C) Inappropriate types of behavior or feelings under normal circumstances.

(D) A general pervasive mood of unhappiness or depression.

(E) A tendency to develop physical symptoms or fears associated with personal or school problems.

Several special education scholars (Heward, 2009; Kirk, Gallagher, Coleman & Anastasiow, 2009; Smith & Tyler, 2010) have pointed out the difficulties caused by vague terminology in distinguishing between students who have emotional disturbance and students who do not. The phrase "a long period of time," for example, is not defined in the law (although many special education experts use 6 months as a rough rule of thumb). Indicators such as "satisfactory interpersonal relationships," "inappropriate types of behavior or feelings under normal circumstances," and "general pervasive mood" are difficult to measure objectively and can often be observed in nondisturbed individuals. Because long-term observation of behavior is often critical in making a correct diagnosis of emotional disturbance, you can aid the multidisciplinary assessment team in this task by keeping a behavioral log of a child you suspect may have this disorder.

That many educators and psychologists use such terms as *emotionally disturbed*, *socially maladjusted*, and *behavior disordered* synonymously makes matters even more confusing. The term **behavior disorder** has many adherents and has been adopted by several states for two basic reasons. One reason is that it calls attention to the actual behavior that is disordered and needs to be changed. The second reason is that behaviors can be directly and objectively assessed. Although there are subtle differences between the terms *emotionally disturbed* and *behavior disorder*, they are essentially interchangeable, and you can probably assume that those who use them are referring to children who share similar characteristics. Because of the nature of bureaucracies, however, it may be necessary for anyone hoping to obtain special assistance for a child with what many contemporary psychologists would call a behavior disorder to refer to that child as emotionally disturbed, as that is the label used in IDEA.

Characteristics of Students With an Emotional Disturbance

The most frequently used classification system of emotional disturbance (or behavior disorder) involves two basic patterns: externalizing and internalizing (Heward, 2009; Wicks-Nelson & Israel, 2003).

emotional disturbance
An emotional condition in which inappropriate aggressive or withdrawal behaviors are exhibited over a long period of time and to a marked degree, adversely affecting a child's educational performance.

behavior disorder
An emotional condition in which inappropriate aggressive or withdrawal behaviors are exhibited over a long period of time and to a marked degree, adversely affecting a child's educational performance. Also called *emotional disturbance*.

Frank Siteman/Stock Boston

Students who have an emotional disturbance tend to be either aggressive or withdrawn. Because aggressive students disrupt classroom routines, teachers need to focus on classroom design features and employ behavior management techniques to reduce the probability of such behaviors.

- Externalizing students are often aggressive, uncooperative, restless, and negativistic. They tend to lie and steal, defy teachers, and be hostile to authority figures. Sometimes they are cruel and malicious.

- Internalizing students, by contrast, are typically shy, timid, anxious, and fearful. They are often depressed and lacking in self-confidence.

Students who act out in aggressive or other socially inappropriate ways attract attention: It is hard to ignore such behavior. Quiet students who withdraw from social interaction with others may not be very noticeable, but they may be more prone to depression and risk of suicide during the adolescent years. The Suggestions for Teaching on the facing page will help you teach both the withdrawn student and the aggressive student.

LO6 Students Who Are Gifted and Talented

Unlike students with intellectual disability, learning disabilities, and emotional disturbance, students who are considered gifted and talented are not covered by IDEA. Instead, the federal government provides technical assistance to states and local school districts for establishing programs for superior students. Although most states have such programs, some experts in special education (Colangelo & Davis, 2003; J. J. Gallagher, 2003) have argued that school systems are not given the resources they need to meet the needs of all gifted and talented students adequately. The Suggestions for Teaching that follow a bit later reflect this situation. All of the suggestions are inexpensive to implement and require few additional personnel.

A definition of the term **gifted and talented** was provided in the Jacob Javits Act, part of the Elementary and Secondary Education Act passed by Congress in 1988:

The term gifted and talented children and youth *means children and youth who give evidence of high performance capability in areas such as intel-*

lectual, creative, artistic, or leadership capacity, or in specific academic fields, and who require services or activities not ordinarily provided by the school in order to fully develop such capabilities.

Identification of Gifted and Talented Students

Eligibility for gifted and talented programs has traditionally been based on standardized test scores, particularly IQ tests. It was not uncommon in years past for students to have to achieve an IQ score of at least 130 to be admitted to such programs. But criticisms about the narrow range of skills covered by such tests (and their heavy reliance on multiple-choice items) have led most states to deemphasize or eliminate the use of traditional intelligence tests and a numerical cutoff score for identification (Reid, Romanoff, & Algozzine, 2000; Renzulli, 2002).

> **Gifted and talented students show high performance in one or more areas.**

Evidence that alternative assessments can do a better job of identifying gifted and talented children does exist. In one study (Reid, Romranoff, & Algozzine, 2000), 434 second grade students who were recommended for a gifted education program were tested with both traditional and nontraditional measures. The traditional assessment was a nonverbal test of analogical reasoning. The nontraditional assessment, which combined aspects of both Gardner's and Sternberg's theories of intelligence, was a set of linguistic, logical-mathematical, and spatial problem-solving tasks that called for analytical, synthetic, and practical thinking. For example, students were given a bag of small items, each of which had to be used as the basis of a 5-minute story. For another task, students were given a set of colored cardboard pieces and told to make a variety of objects, such as an animal, a building, something that moves, and whatever they wanted. On the basis of analogical reasoning scores, about 17% of the sample would have been recommended for placement in the gifted program. That percentage rose to 40% when scores from the problem-solving assessment were used. Another interesting statistic is that almost 70% of the students recommended on the basis of their problem-solving performances would not have been recommended on the basis of their analogical reasoning scores.

Joseph Renzulli (2002), a leading researcher of giftedness and gifted education, believes that the concept of giftedness should be expanded beyond the dimensions examined in the study we just described to include students who can channel their assets into

> **Students with behavior disorders tend to be either aggressive or withdrawn.**

Suggestions for Teaching

Instructing Students With Emotional Disturbance

Most of these suggestions are derived from points made in Chapters 7, 8, and 9 of *Strategies for Addressing Behavior Problems in the Classroom* (6th ed., 2010), by Mary Margaret Kerr and C. Michael Nelson.

1 Design the classroom environment and formulate lesson plans to encourage social interaction and cooperation.

Students whose emotional disturbance manifests itself as social withdrawal may stay away from others on purpose (perhaps because they find social contacts threatening), or they may find that others stay away from them (perhaps because they have poorly developed social skills). Regardless of the cause, the classroom environment and your instructional activities can be designed to foster appropriate interpersonal contact:

- Preschool and elementary school teachers can use toys and materials, as well as organized games and sports, that encourage cooperative play and have a reduced focus on individual performance. Activities might include dress-up games or puppet plays; games might include soccer, variations of tag, and kickball or softball modified so that everyone on the team gets a turn to kick or bat before the team plays in the field.

- Elementary and middle school teachers can use one or more of several team-oriented learning activities. *Cooperative Learning* (1995) by Robert Slavin provides details on using such activities as student teams-achievement divisions, jigsaw, and team-accelerated instruction (see also Slavin, Lake, & Groff, 2009).

2 Prompt and reinforce appropriate social interactions.

Prompting and positive reinforcement are basic learning principles that will be discussed in Chapter 7. Essentially, a prompt is a stimulus that draws out a desired response, and positive reinforcement involves giving the student a positive reinforcer (something the student wants) immediately after a desired behavior. The aim is to get the student to behave that way again. Typical reinforcers are verbal praise, stickers, and small prizes.

For example, you can set up a cooperative task or activity: "Marc, I would like you to help Carol and Raquel paint the scenery for next week's play. You can paint the trees and flowers, Carol will paint the grass, and Raquel will do the people." After several minutes, say something like, "That's good work. I am really pleased at how well the three of you are working together." Similar comments can be made at intervals as the interaction continues.

3 Train other students to initiate social interaction.

In all likelihood, you will have too many classroom responsibilities to spend a great deal of time working directly with a withdrawn child. It may be possible, however, using the steps that follow, to train other students to initiate contact with withdrawn students.

First, choose a student as a helper who interacts freely and well, can follow your instructions, and can concentrate on the training task for at least 10 minutes. Second, explain that the goal is to get the withdrawn child to work or play with the helping student but that the helper should expect rejection, particularly at first. Role-play the actions of a withdrawn child so that the helper understands what you mean by rejection. Emphasize the importance of making periodic attempts at interaction. Third, instruct the helper to suggest games or activities that appeal to the withdrawn student. Fourth, reinforce the helper's attempts to interact with the withdrawn child.

4 Design the classroom environment to reduce the probability of disruptive behavior.

The best way to deal with aggressive or antisocial behavior is to nip it in the bud. This strategy has at least three related benefits. One benefit of fewer disruptions is that you can better accomplish what you had planned for the day. A second benefit is that you are likely to be in a more positive frame of mind than if you spend half the day acting as a ref-

eree. A third benefit is that because of fewer disruptions and a more positive attitude, you may be less inclined to resort to permissible or even impermissible forms of physical punishment (which often produces undesirable side effects).

- With student input, formulate rules for classroom behavior and penalties for infractions of rules. Remind all students of the penalties, particularly when a disruptive incident seems about to occur, and consistently apply the penalties when the rules are broken.

- Place valued objects and materials out of reach when they are not needed or in use.

- Minimize the aggressive student's frustration with learning by using some of the same techniques you would use for a child with intellectual disability: Break tasks down into small, easy-to-manage pieces; provide clear directions; and reinforce correct responses.

5 Reinforce appropriate behavior, and, if necessary, punish inappropriate behavior.

In suggestion 2, we described the use of positive reinforcement to encourage desired behavior. Reinforcement has the dual effect of teaching the aggressive student which behavior is appropriate and reducing the frequency of inappropriate behavior as it is replaced by desired behavior. Disruptive behavior will still occur, however. Three effective techniques for suppressing it while reinforcing desired behaviors are contingency contracts, token economies and fines, and time-out. Each of these techniques will be described in Chapter 7.

6 Use group contingency management techniques.

You may want to reward the entire class when the aggressive student behaves appropriately for a certain period of time. Such rewards, which may be free time, special classroom events, or certain privileges, should make the aggressive student the hero and foster better peer relationships.

twice exceptional
A term that describes students who are exceptional because they are both gifted and talented and challenged in some physical, social, emotional, or cognitive way.

constructive social actions that benefit others. As an example, he described Melanie, a fifth grade girl who befriended Tony, a visually impaired first-grade boy who was ignored by most other students and teased by a few. Melanie persuaded some of the school's most popular students to sit with Tony in the lunchroom, and she recruited other students to create and illustrate large-print books on topics of interest to Tony. Over the course of several months, Tony was accepted by many of the school's students, and his attitude toward school markedly improved. According to Howard Gardner's multiple intelligences theory, Melanie's gift likely stems from an above-average interpersonal (and possibly intrapersonal) intelligence. In the adult world, two examples of this type of person are Mother Teresa and Martin Luther King Jr.—and, as Renzulli pointed out, no one really cares what their test scores or grade-point averages were.

Broadening the definition and instruments used to assess giftedness is necessary, given the diversity of students who are identified as gifted and talented (B. Harris, Plucker, Rapp, & Martínez, 2009; Reis & Renzulli, 2009). Even so, students of color and those from poverty are underrepresented in programs for the gifted and talented. The same can be said of students whose first language is something other than English (B. Harris, Plucker, Rapp, & Martínez, 2009).

Characteristics of Gifted and Talented Students

In one sense, gifted and talented students are like any other group of students. Some are healthy and well-coordinated, whereas others are not. Some are extremely popular and well-liked, but others are not. Some are well-adjusted; others are not (Kirk, Gallagher, Coleman, & Anastasiow, 2009). Some formulate strong identities (Marcia's identity achievement status) and are successful later in life, whereas others are not (Zuo & Cramond, 2001). But as a group, gifted and talented students are often noticeably different (Hardman, Drew, &

> **Students of color are underrepresented in gifted classes because of overreliance on test scores.**

Egan, 2011). Here are some of the main characteristics that many gifted and talented students share:

- They excel at tasks that involve language, abstract logical thinking, and mathematics.
- They are faster at encoding information and retrieving it from memory.
- They are highly aware of how they learn and the various conditions that affect their learning. As a result, they excel at transferring previously learned information and skills to new problems and settings.
- They exhibit such high levels of motivation and task persistence that the phrase "rage to master" is sometimes used to describe their behavior.
- They tend to be more solitary and introverted than average children.
- They tend to have very intense emotional lives. They react with intense emotions, such as joy, regret, or sorrow, to a story, a piece of music, or a social encounter.

> **Gifted and talented students differ from their nongifted peers intellectually and emotionally.**

A final point about the characteristics of gifted and talented students is that some of the students are challenged with learning disabilities, attention disorders, or autism spectrum disorders—such as Asperger syndrome—which means they have difficulty with social relations. Such students are identified as **twice exceptional**: They are exceptional because they are gifted and talented and they are exceptional because they are challenged in some intellectual, social, physical, or emotional way (e.g., Assouline, Nicpon, & Doobay, 2009). If you find yourself working with twice exceptional students, you may need to combine the following instructional options with Suggestions for Teaching from earlier sections.

Instructional Options

Gifted and talented students constantly challenge a teacher's skill, ingenuity, and classroom resources. While trying to instruct the class as a whole, the teacher is faced with the need to provide more and more interesting and challenging materials and ideas to gifted students. In this section, we will examine three possible ways to engage these students.

Accelerated Instruction Accelerated instruction is often suggested as one way to meet the academic needs of gifted and talented students. For many people, the phrase *accelerated instruction* means allowing the student to skip one or more grades, which, although not as common as in years past, does occasionally occur. But there are at least three other ways of accomplishing the same goal: (1) The curriculum can be compressed, allowing gifted and talented students to complete the work for more than one grade during the regular school year; (2) the school year can be extended by the use of summer sessions; and (3) students can take college courses while still in high school. As with all other informed educational decisions, the unique needs of the individual and the situation must be considered before the best course of action can be determined.

Gifted and Talented Classes and Schools Some public school districts offer separate classes for gifted and talented students as either an alternative to accelerated instruction or something that follows accelerated instruction. In addition, so-called magnet schools are composed of students whose average level of ability is higher than that found in a typical elementary, middle, or high school. Finally, many states sponsor high-ability high schools, particularly in mathematics and science.

Recent findings have suggested that such placements do not produce uniformly positive results and should be made only after the characteristics of the student and the program have been carefully considered. The effects of separate class or school placement on measures of academic self-concept have been inconsistent; some researchers found them to be higher than those of students who remain in heterogeneous classes, whereas other researchers found either no differences or declines (Hoge & Renzulli, 1993; J. A. Kulik & Kulik, 1991; Seaton, Marsh, & Craven, 2010).

Enrichment and Differentiated Instruction Because of the potential negative effects of grade skipping, the limited availability of special classes and schools, and the fact that such classes and schools are not good options for some gifted and talented students, teach-

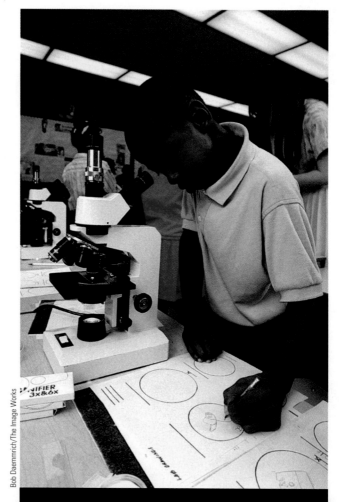

Bob Daemmrich/The Image Works

Because gifted and talented students understand and integrate abstract ideas more quickly than do their nongifted classmates, they are capable of successfully completing tasks that older students routinely carry out.

> **Separate classes for gifted and talented students aid achievement but may lower the academic self-concept of some students.**

ers may find themselves with one or two gifted and talented students in a regular classroom. A solution for meeting the special needs of these students (as well as those with disabilities) is a practice often referred to as *differentiated instruction*, a technique we have mentioned earlier. Basically, this means using different learning materials, instructional methods, assignments, and tests to accommodate differences in students' abilities, learning styles, prior knowledge, and cultural background (Benjamin, 2005; Gregory, 2003; Gregory & Kuzmich, 2005; Tomlinson, Brimijoin, & Narvaez, 2008).

One scheme for delivering differentiated instruction to gifted and talented learners has been developed by Sally Reis and Joseph Renzulli (Reis & Renzulli, 1985, 2009; Renzulli, Gentry, & Reis, 2003). Based on their view that giftedness is a combination of above-average cognitive ability, creativity, and task commitment, Reis and Renzulli described three levels of curriculum enrichment for gifted and talented learners:

Type I enrichment: Exploratory activities that are designed to expose students to topics, events, books, people, and places not ordinarily covered in the regular curriculum. The basic purpose of these activities is to stimulate new interests. Among the many suggestions Reis and Renzulli offer are having students view and write reports on films and videos and having local residents make presentations on their occupations or hobbies.

Type II enrichment: Instructional methods and materials aimed at the development of such thinking and feeling processes as thinking creatively, classifying and analyzing data, solving problems, appreciating, and valuing.

Type III enrichment: Activities in which students investigate and collect data about a real topic or problem. For example, a student may decide to document the history of her school, focusing on such issues as changes in size, instructional materials and methods, and curriculum.

Numerous sites on the Internet are devoted to long-distance education, enrichment, and tutoring. The website of the Talent Identification Program at Duke University (www.tip.duke.edu) contains information about online teaching and learning opportunities and various telementoring programs. The Suggestions for Teaching on the facing page provide further ideas for working with gifted and talented students.

Pause&Reflect *Relatively little money is spent on programs for the gifted and talented compared with the amounts made available for the disabled. Defenders of this arrangement sometimes argue that because gifted students have a built-in advantage, we should invest most of our resources in services for those with disabilities. Do you agree or disagree? Why?*

LO7 Using Technology to Assist Exceptional Students

There is perhaps no other area in education today in which technology is making as significant an impact as in the field of special education. This is largely due to the notion of universal design for learning (UDL) and the use of assistive technology (Hitchcock & Stahl, 2003; Scott, McGuire, & Shaw, 2003).

Universal Design for Learning

Universal design for learning (UDL) is an approach that seeks to eliminate the barriers to learning for all students, no matter what challenges they bring with them to school. According to the Center for Applied Special Technology (2008), UDL is guided by three principles: (1) providing multiple means of representing

TeachSource Video Case

Academic Diversity: Differentiated Instuction

Go to the Education CourseMate website and watch the video, study the artifacts in the case, and reflect upon the following questions:

1. What did the teacher in this Video Case do to make the lesson work for all of her students? Describe some of the strategies and tools that she used.

2. Based on reading the chapter and watching the Video Case, what do you think would be most challenging for a classroom teacher about "doing" differentiated instruction?

Suggestions for Teaching

Instructing Gifted and Talented Students

1 Consult with gifted and talented students regarding individual study projects, perhaps involving a learning contract.

It is important that individualized assignments be clearly aligned with curriculum standards. One way to make that alignment is to work collaboratively with students to design assignments that yield the required learning outcomes. Collaboratively designing the work allows students to engage their own interests and talents. For example, a student with a deep interest in film might decide to make a documentary; another with an interest in the theater might decide to write a play; another might decide to generate an interactive computer game or use social media to coordinate a national or international public service campaign. One key consideration is to avoid rewarding gifted and talented students publicly so that other students are discouraged and the student who is gifted and talented is possibly embarrassed.

Encouraging students who are gifted and talented to pursue their own interests through extracurricular reading and writing can certainly benefit students. Care must be taken, however, to avoid students getting the impression that this is just "extra credit." Keep in mind the Type III enrichment activities discussed earlier. If the reading and writing are connected to something the students want to research or help them develop research proposals or research studies, the supplementary work may be seen as an opportunity rather than just an additional assignment to earn extra points for a grade.

2 Consider carefully before asking gifted and talented students to serve as peer tutors.

Students who are gifted and talented are often considered viable candidates to serve as tutors for other students. This can be tricky. Some students may welcome the opportunity, and the students who receive the tutorial assistance may be very happy to have it. But that will not always be the case, and it is important to determine ahead of time that the arrangement will work before implementing it. One possibility is to invite the gifted and talented student to serve as a consultant and respond to those who ask for the help. There are programs, for example, in which gifted and talented students provide help via the school public access television station; they receive questions via phone, text messages, or e-mail and then respond to those questions. Under such circumstances, it is possible for such "homework help" programs to respond to questions without revealing who asked for help. Such "broadcast tutoring" via television, podcasts, or webinars can help other students who have similar questions.

---

what is to be learned, (2) providing multiple means of action and expression (the "how" of learning), and (3) providing multiple means of engagement (the "why" of learning). The underlying assumption of UDL is that students represent a continuum of differences rather than falling into one of the two categories of "normal" and "disabled." Furthermore, UDL assumes that this diversity is the norm rather than the exception and that the norm of diversity, if embraced in schools and classrooms, strengthens the learning environment (Grabinger, Aplin, & Ponnappa-Brenner, 2008; Meo, 2008).

Although UDL has application for face-to-face learning environments such as classrooms, it has also been used to enable the addition of "Web 2.0 tools into the mix for teaching and learning" (Grabinger, Aplin, & Ponnappa-Brenner, 2008, p. 68). Following the UDL principles of the Center for Applied Special Technology, Scott Grabinger and his colleagues identified Web-based tools that can provide access and support for learners with problems in attention and memory, language, executive functions, problem solving, and social functioning.

Mandated by IDEA for any need related to the learning or development of a child with a disability, **assistive technology** is defined as "any item, piece of equipment, or product system, whether acquired commercially off the shelf, modified, or customized, that is used to increase, maintain, or improve functional capabilities of a child with a disability" (IDEA, 2004, Sec. 602 (1); see also Maanum, 2009). We turn now to assistive technologies for students with disabilities.

> **assistive technology** Any item, device, or piece of equipment, from low-tech equipment such as taped stories to more sophisticated technologies such as voice-recognition and speech-synthesis devices, that is used to increase, maintain, or improve the functional abilities of persons with disabilities.

{ **Federal legislation has led to the development of various assistive technologies.** }

Assistive Technologies

Technology for Students With Hearing Impairments
Hearing-impaired students can be assisted with technology tools in a number of ways, including closed captioning, audio amplification, and cochlear implants. Closed captioning (presenting spoken words

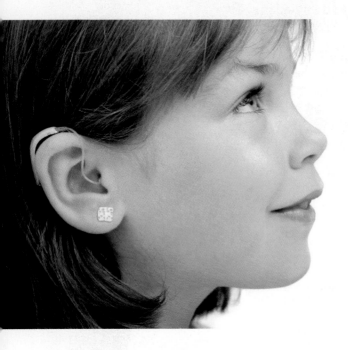

© Carmen Martinez Banús/iStockphoto

as text on a screen) occurs most often in connection with television programs; but this technology can also be used in classrooms to help hearing-impaired students follow a teacher's lectures or explanations. Audio amplification usually requires the teacher to wear a small microphone and transmitter, whose signal is amplified and sent to a student wearing a lightweight receiver (Camp & Stark, 2006). A third option for students with severe to profound hearing loss is a cochlear implant (Compton, Tucker, & Flynn, 2009). This system involves several external components (microphone, speech processor, transmitter, power pack) and a surgically implanted receiver-stimulator. The website for Gallaudet University—a well-known school in Washington, DC, for people who are deaf—includes a page that describes its assistive technologies for people with hearing impairment (http://tap.gallaudet.edu).

Technology for Students With Visual Impairments
Speech synthesizers and magnification devices provide technological assistance to those who are visually impaired. With speech synthesis, the user can select a word, sentence, or chunk of information from any written or scanned text and hear it pronounced by a speech synthesizer. For example, the Kurzweil Reader scans printed material and converts it into high-quality speech. Braille can also be converted in standard text (to be read aloud) or into synthesized speech. Optical devices or software can magnify enormously the content on computer screens; head-mounted magnifiers allow students to see over various distances (Gold & Lowe, 2009; Griffin, Williams, Davis, & Engleman, 2002). The website of the National

Federation of the Blind (www.nfb.org) describes screen readers and other digital devices that are available for individuals with visual impairments.

Technology for Students With Orthopedic Impairments
For students who have physical limitations, electronics can be controlled by pointing devices that are held in the mouth, attached to the head, or voice activated. Keyboards and touch pads that vary in relation to the strength and dexterity of the user are also available (Duhaney & Duhaney, 2000). Software for helping individuals with physical and other disabilities use computers more effectively can be found at the Virtual Assistive Technology Center website (http://vatc .freeservers.com).

Technology for Students With Speech or Language Impairments
Technology can also help individuals with communication impairments. Research has shown positive effects of computer training on vocabulary, early grammar skills, and social communication among toddlers with Down syndrome as well as young children with severe language and behavioral disabilities (Westwood, 2009). Computer programs designed to help students with speech or language impairments acquire language and communication skills can be found on the website of the International Society for Augmentative and Alternative Communication (www .isaac-online.org).

Technology for Students With Learning Disabilities
As we saw earlier in this chapter, learning disabled students typically have problems with reading, writing, and mathematics. But research has shown that the extent of these obstacles can be reduced by using software programs designed for students with learning problems (Westwood, 2009).

In the area of writing, there are many tools for students with learning disabilities that can help them—and other students—with basic sentence generation, transcription, and revision. Spelling, style, and grammar checkers can help raise student focus from mechanical demands and surface-level concerns to higher-level

> **Research has shown that obstacles can be reduced by using software programs designed for students with learning problems.**

issues of text cohesion and integration. Word prediction software can help students write more coherent and meaningful sentences by offering a choice of several words based on what the student has already written (Duhaney & Duhaney, 2000). Additional information about resources and teaching strategies for students with learning disabilities can be found on this book's Education CourseMate website.

Technology for Gifted and Talented Students Gifted students can also benefit

WHAT ELSE? *RIP & REVIEW* **CARDS IN THE BACK**

from advances in instructional technology. Stanford University, for instance, has been experimenting with providing year-round accelerated instruction in mathematics, physics, English, and computer science to gifted high school students through the Education Program for Gifted Youth (Ravaglia, Alper, Rozenfeld, & Suppes, 1998; Ravaglia, Sommer, Sanders, Oas, & DeLeone, 1999). The website for the program—which contains recent evaluation reports—can be found at http://epgy.stanford.edu.

7

BEHAVIORAL LEARNING THEORY: OPERANT CONDITIONING

LEARNING OBJECTIVES

After studying this chapter, you will be able to . . .

LO1 Define operant conditioning and at least five of its basic principles.

LO2 Describe at least three educational applications of operant conditioning principles.

Why do we have schools? No, that's not a trick question. We suspect you know the answer, at least intuitively: The primary reason that we have schools is to help children acquire the knowledge and skills that adults consider necessary for successful functioning in society. Seems obvious, doesn't it? And if you accept that premise, then it logically follows that the instructional and curricular decisions that teachers make should be based on an understanding of how people learn (as well as on developmental factors and sources of individual differences, since they influence how and how well people learn). But you would be surprised how often discussions about improving education either ignore or only briefly consider the nature of the learning process. Over the next four chapters we will show you how complex the learning process is and how it has been studied from different perspectives.

{ Operant conditioning: voluntary response is strengthened or weakened by consequences that follow }

This chapter is devoted to what is generally called behavioral learning theory. More precisely, the chapter describes a theory called operant conditioning and some of its implications. Operant conditioning focuses on the factors in a person's external environment that influence the types of behaviors the person exhibits and the extent to which the person is likely to exhibit those behaviors in the future. Subsequent chapters will examine the roles that other people and our own thought processes play in learning.

LO1 Operant Conditioning

To give you a fuller appreciation of what operant conditioning is all about and why, we need to go back to the early part of the twentieth century, when psychology was just getting started as a separate discipline. In 1913, with the publication of an article titled "Psychology as the Behaviorist Views It," the influential American psychologist John Watson argued that psychology would quickly lose credibility as a science if it focused on internal mental and emotional states that

could not be directly observed or accurately measured. The solution was to study what could be directly observed and objectively and accurately measured: the external stimuli that people experienced and what people did in response—in a word, behavior.

From that point until the late 1960s, behavioral theories of one sort or another dominated the psychology of learning. Although they are considerably less popular today, they still offer many useful ideas for classroom teachers.

The Basic Idea

Behavioral learning theories culminated in the work of B. F. Skinner. Skinner put together a theory that not only successfully combines many different ideas but also serves as the basis for a variety of applications to human behavior. Skinner's theory, **operant conditioning**, takes as its starting point something that most of us have noticed at one time or another: The voluntary responses of animals and humans are more likely to be repeated when they are rewarded (although psychologists prefer the technical term *reinforced*) and less likely to be repeated when they are either ignored or punished. In this way, organisms learn new behaviors and when to exhibit them and "unlearn" existing behaviors. The term *operant conditioning* refers to the fact that organisms learn to "operate" on their environment (make a particular response) to obtain or avoid a particular consequence.

Most of the experiments on which the principles of operant conditioning are based involved an ingenious apparatus that Skinner invented, which is almost always referred to as a *Skinner box.* This is a small enclosure that contains only a bar (or lever) and a small tray. Outside the box is a hopper holding a supply of food pellets that are dropped into the tray when the bar is pressed under certain conditions.

A hungry rat is placed in the box, and when in the course of exploring its new environment the rat approaches and then presses the bar, it is rewarded with a food pellet. The rat then presses the bar more frequently than it did before being rewarded. If food pellets are supplied under some conditions when the bar is pushed

operant conditioning The theory of behavior developed by B. F. Skinner based on the fact that organisms respond to their environments in particular ways to obtain or avoid particular consequences.

© Pakhnyushcha/Shutterstock Images

© Jose Luis Pelaez Inc./Blend Images/Photolibrary.com

down—for example, when a tone is sounded—but not under others, the rat learns to discriminate one situation from the other, and the rate of bar pressing drops noticeably when the tone is not sounded. If a tone is sounded that is very close in frequency to the original tone, the rat generalizes (treats the two tones as equivalent) and presses the bar at the same rate for both. But if the food pellets are not given after the rat presses the bar, that behavior stops, or is extinguished.

Does this description mean that we are no different from laboratory animals? No, not at all. What it does mean is that the environmental forces that affect how an animal behaves in a laboratory setting are the same ones that affect how we behave in various real-life settings. But for reasons that will become apparent when we get into Chapters 8 and 9, we are not nearly as predictable as lab rats.

Basic Principles of Operant Conditioning

To repeat the basic idea behind operant conditioning: All behaviors are accompanied by certain consequences, and these consequences strongly influence (some might say determine) whether the behaviors are repeated and at what level of intensity. In general, the consequences that follow behavior are either pleasant and desirable (getting a promotion, receiving an A on an exam) or unpleasant and aversive (being fired, receiving an F on an exam). Depending on conditions that we will discuss shortly, these consequences either increase (strengthen) or decrease (weaken) the likelihood that the preceding behavior will recur under the same or similar circumstances.

When consequences strengthen a preceding behavior, *reinforcement* has taken place. When consequences weaken a preceding behavior, *punishment* and *extinction* have occurred. There are two forms of reinforcement and two forms of punishment that we describe next, along with several related principles.

Pause & Reflect *Operant conditioning holds that we learn to respond or not respond to certain stimuli because our responses are followed by desirable or aversive consequences. How many of your own behaviors can you explain in this fashion? Why, for example, are you reading this book and pondering these questions?*

Positive Reinforcement The concept of positive reinforcement is easy to understand. If you can recall spending more time studying for a certain subject because of a compliment from the teacher or a high grade on an examination, you have experienced positive reinforcement. Specifically, **positive reinforcement** involves strengthening a target behavior—that is, increasing and maintaining the probability that a particular behavior will be repeated—by presenting a stimulus (called a *positive reinforcer*) immediately after the behavior has occurred. Praise, recognition, and the opportunity for free play are positive reinforcers for many (but not all) students.

> **Positive reinforcement: strengthen a target behavior by presenting a positive reinforcer after the behavior occurs**

Negative Reinforcement People frequently have difficulty understanding the concept of negative reinforcement, most often confusing it with punishment, so we will examine it carefully here. The goal of **negative reinforcement** is the same as that of positive reinforcement: to *increase* the strength of a particular behavior. The method, however, is different. Instead of supplying a desired

Yellow Dog Productions/Getty Images

Students are likely to be motivated to learn if they are positively reinforced for completing a project or task. Awards and praise from the teacher and from peers are strong positive reinforcers for many students.

> **Negative reinforcement: strengthen a target behavior by removing an aversive stimulus after the behavior occurs**

stimulus, *one removes an unwanted stimulus* whenever a target behavior is exhibited. As you study this definition, pay attention to both the action and the effect on behavior. Just as *positive* refers to adding, *negative* refers to the act of *removing* a stimulus. By removing something unwanted, you encourage the student to learn new behaviors.

In everyday life, negative reinforcement occurs quite frequently. A child picks up his clothes or toys to stop his parents' nagging. A driver uses a seat belt to stop the annoying buzzer sound. A gardener pulls weeds to avoid a shabby looking garden (something the senior author has experienced countless times). Later in the chapter, we will describe how educators use negative reinforcement. We will also discuss its desirability relative to positive reinforcement.

Punishment Operant psychologists define **punishment** as reducing the frequency of an undesired behavior through the use of an aversive stimulus. This goal can be accomplished in one of two ways. The first is by using what is known as *Type I punishment*

© Jakub Krechowicz/Shutterstock Images

I will not chew gum in class.
I will not chew gum in class.
I will not chew gum in class.
I will not chew gum in class.
I will not chew gum in class.

or *presentation punishment*. Type I punishment involves administering such time-honored stimuli as scolding, paddling, ridiculing, or an assignment to write 500 times "I will not chew gum in class" in an attempt to get the student to stop doing something. But just because you present someone with what you consider to be an aversive stimulus does not, by itself, mean that you have punished that person. It does happen that some children are so starved for attention that scolding or ridiculing them actually *reinforces* the undesired behavior. The proof, as the saying goes, is in the pudding. You have to see a decline in the undesired behavior.

Many people confuse negative reinforcement with punishment. Let's clear that up right now. Both involve the use of an aversive stimulus, but the effects of each are opposite. Remember that negative reinforcement strengthens a target behavior, whereas punishment weakens or eliminates a behavior.

Time-Out The second procedure that decreases the frequency of or eliminates a target behavior is another form of punishment that is called **time-out** (or sometimes *Type II punishment* or *removal punishment*). Instead of presenting an aversive stimulus, time-out *temporarily removes the opportunity to receive positive reinforcement*. For instance, a student who frequently disrupts the classroom routine to get attention may be sent to sit in an empty room for 5 minutes. Removal from a reinforcing environment (as well as the angry tone of voice and

© hans.slegers/Shutterstock Images

Punishment: weaken a target behavior by presenting an aversive stimulus after the behavior occurs

extinction Causing a target behavior to cease by ignoring it.

generalization The learned ability to respond in similar ways to similar stimuli.

facial expression that normally accompany the order to leave the classroom) is usually looked on as an aversive consequence by the individual being removed. Suspension of an athlete from competition is another example of this form of punishment.

Because punishment has such a negative connotation, you may be wondering if it is effective and if its use is ethical. Those are excellent questions that we will take up later in this chapter.

Extinction A third consequence that weakens undesired behavior but is not considered to be a type of punishment is extinction. **Extinction** occurs when a previously reinforced behavior decreases in frequency, and eventually ceases altogether, because reinforcement is withheld. Examples of extinction include a mother's ignoring a whining child or a teacher's ignoring a student who spontaneously answers a question without waiting to be called on. Both extinction and time-out are most effective when combined with other consequences, such as positive reinforcement. To help yourself define and remember the distinguishing characteristics of positive reinforcement, negative reinforcement, punishment, and extinction, study Figure 7.1

Before we look at a few other basic principles, we're going to repeat a point we made earlier to make sure your understanding of reinforcement, punishment, and extinction is perfectly clear. From an operant perspective, you can claim to have punished someone else *only* if the target behavior occurs less often in response to what you thought was an aversive stimulus. Too many teachers who are unfamiliar with operant conditioning principles say, "I punished Jason for teasing Marla, but it didn't work." Guess what? If Jason continues to tease Marla, then he wasn't punished. The same is true for positive and negative reinforcement. Heaping praise on a student or stopping a stream of criticisms of your significant other is considered to be reinforcement only if a particular behavior then occurs more frequently.

Generalization When an individual learns to make a particular response to a particular stimulus and then makes the same or a similar response in a slightly different situation, **generalization** has occurred. For

The time-out procedure recommended by behavior modification enthusiasts involves weakening an undesirable form of behavior (such as shoving on the playground) by temporarily removing positive reinforcement (by having the misbehaving student remain in a corner of the classroom for 5 minutes while the rest of the class continues to enjoy another activity).

FIGURE 7.1 Conditions That Define Reinforcement, Punishment, and Extinction

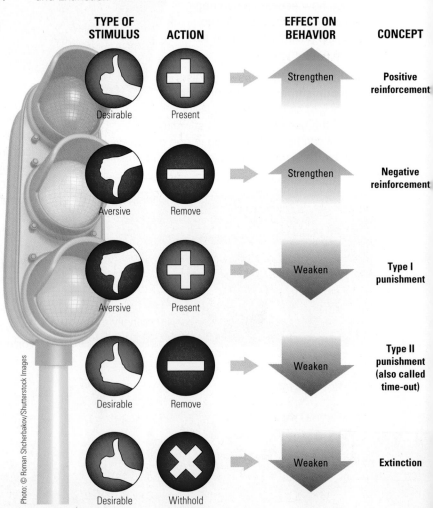

TYPE OF STIMULUS	ACTION	EFFECT ON BEHAVIOR	CONCEPT
Desirable	Present	Strengthen	Positive reinforcement
Aversive	Remove	Strengthen	Negative reinforcement
Aversive	Present	Weaken	Type I punishment
Desirable	Remove	Weaken	Type II punishment (also called time-out)
Desirable	Withhold	Weaken	Extinction

example, students who were positively reinforced for using effective study skills in history then go on to use those same skills in chemistry, social studies, algebra, and other subjects. Or, to use a less encouraging illustration, students ignore or question a teacher's every request and direction because they have been reinforced for responding that way to their parents at home. The less similar the new stimulus is to the original, however, the less similar the response is likely to be.

Generalization: responding in similar ways to similar stimuli

Discrimination When inappropriate generalizations occur, as in the preceding example, they can be essentially extinguished through discrimination training. In **discrimination**, individuals notice the unique aspects of seemingly similar situations (for example, that teachers are not parents, although both are adults) and respond differently to each situation. Teachers can encourage this process by reinforcing only the desired behaviors (for instance, attention, obedience, and cooperation) and withholding reinforcement following undesired behaviors (such as inattention or disobedience).

Shaping Up to now, we have not distinguished relatively simple learned behaviors from more complex ones. A bit of reflection, however, should enable you to realize that many of the behaviors human beings learn (such as playing a sport or writing a term paper) are complex and are acquired gradually. The principle of **shaping** best explains how complex responses are learned.

In shaping, actions that move progressively closer to the desired *terminal behavior* (to use Skinner's term) are reinforced. Actions that do not represent closer approximations of the terminal behavior are ignored. The key to success is to take one step at a time. The movements must be gradual enough that the person becomes aware that each step in the sequence is

Discrimination: responding in different ways to somewhat similar stimuli

essential. This process is typically called *reinforcing successive approximations to the terminal behavior.*

Schedules of Reinforcement If you have been reading this section on basic principles carefully, you may have begun to wonder whether the use of operant conditioning principles, particularly positive reinforcement, requires you as the teacher to be present every time a desired response happens. If so, you might have some justifiable reservations about the practicality of this theory. The answer is yes, up to a point, but after that, no. As we have pointed out, when you are trying to get a new behavior established, especially if it is a complex behavior that requires shaping, learning proceeds best when every desired response is positively reinforced and every undesired response is ignored. This is known as a *continuous reinforcement schedule.*

Once the behavior has been learned, however, positive reinforcement can be employed on a noncontinuous, or intermittent, basis to perpetuate the behavior. There are four basic *intermittent reinforcement schedules:* fixed interval, variable interval, fixed ratio, and variable ratio. Each schedule produces a different pattern of behavior.

Fixed Interval Schedule In a fixed interval schedule, a learner is reinforced for the first desired response that occurs after a predetermined amount of time has elapsed (for example, 5 minutes, 1 hour, or 7 days). Once the response has occurred and been reinforced, the next interval begins. Any desired behaviors that are made during an interval are ignored. The reinforced behavior occurs at a lower level during the early part of the interval and gradually rises as the time for reinforcement draws closer. Once the reinforcer is delivered, the frequency of the relevant behavior declines, then gradually rises toward the end of the next interval.

Complex behaviors are shaped by reinforcing closer approximations to the terminal behavior.

discrimination A process in which individuals notice the unique aspects of seemingly similar situations and thus learn different ways of responding.

shaping Promoting the learning of complex behaviors by reinforcing successive approximations to the terminal behavior.

© Alex Slobodkin/iStockphoto

Fixed interval schedules of reinforcement occur in education when teachers schedule exams or projects at regular intervals. The grade or score is considered to be a reinforcer. As you are certainly aware, it is not unusual to see little studying or progress occur during the early part of the interval. However, several days before an exam or due date, the pace quickens considerably.

Variable Interval Schedule If you would like to see a more consistent pattern of behavior, you might consider using a variable interval schedule. With this schedule, the length of time between reinforcements is essentially random but averages out to a predetermined interval. Thus four successive reinforcements may occur at the following intervals: 1 week, 4 weeks, 2 weeks, 5 weeks. The average interval is 3 weeks. Teachers who give surprise quizzes or call on students to answer oral questions on the average of once every third day are invoking a variable interval schedule.

{ **Variable interval schedule: reinforce after random time intervals** }

Fixed Ratio Schedule Within a fixed ratio schedule, reinforcement is provided whenever a predetermined number of responses is made. A rat in a Skinner box may be reinforced with a food pellet whenever it presses a lever 50 times. A factory worker may earn $20 for every five electronic circuit boards assembled. A teacher may reinforce a student with praise for every 10 arithmetic problems correctly completed. Fixed ratio schedules tend to produce high response rates because the faster the learner responds, the sooner the reinforcement is delivered. However, a relatively brief period of no or few responses occurs immediately after the reinforcer is delivered.

Variable Ratio Schedule Like a variable interval schedule, a variable ratio schedule tends to eliminate irregularities in response rate, thereby producing a more consistent rate. This is accomplished through reinforcement after a different number of responses from one time to the next, according to a predetermined average. If you decided to use a VR 15 schedule, you might reinforce a desired behavior after 12, 7, 23, and 18 occur-

rences, respectively (that is, after the 12th, 19th, 42nd, and 60th desired behaviors). If you add 12, 7, 23, and 18 together and divide by 4, you get 15, which means that you're reinforcing the behavior after an average of 15 responses. Because the occurrence of reinforcement is so unpredictable, learners tend to respond fairly rapidly for long periods of time. If you need proof, just watch people play the slot machines in gambling casinos.

Fixed ratio schedule: reinforce after a set number of responses

LO2 Educational Applications of Operant Conditioning Principles

In the late 1940s, when Skinner's daughter was in elementary school, he observed a number of instructional weaknesses that concerned him. These included the excessive use of aversive consequences to shape behavior (students studying to avoid a low grade or embarrassment in the classroom), an overly long interval between taking tests or handing in homework and getting corrective feedback, and poorly organized lessons and workbooks that did not lead to specific goals. So being a loving and concerned parent, he decided to do what many concerned parents do: take matters into his own hands and create a solution. Skinner became convinced that if the principles of operant conditioning were systematically applied to education, all such weaknesses could be reduced or eliminated. That belief, which he reiterated consistently until his death in 1990 (see, for example, Skinner, 1984), is based on four prescriptions that come straight from his laboratory research on operant conditioning:

1. Be clear about what is to be taught.
2. Teach first things first.
3. Present subsequent material in small, logical steps.
4. Allow students to learn at their own rate.

This straightforward formulation became the basis for two educational applications: an approach

to teaching that we now call computer-based instruction; and a set of procedures for helping students learn appropriate classroom behaviors, referred to as behavior modification. The next few sections will describe the nature of these applications and assess the extent to which they improve classroom learning.

Computer-Based Instruction

Does Computer-Based Instruction Aid Learning?

When desktop computers and the instructional programs that were created for them were introduced into public schools in the early 1980s, many educators and psychologists believed that students would learn significantly more through this medium than through traditional teacher-led, text-based instruction. This approach to instruction has been referred to mostly as **computer-based instruction (CBI)**, although the term *technology-enhanced instruction* is being used with increasing frequency.

{ **Types of CBI programs include drill and practice, tutorials, and simulations and games.** }

Instructional programs designed for computers generally fall into one of the categories described in Table 7.1. The research that has been done on the effectiveness of these varieties of CBI paints an interesting picture.

computer-based instruction (CBI) Teaching methods that use interactive software as an aid to learning.

Research on the Effects of CBI Computer-based instruction is such a widely researched topic that several authors from time to time have attempted to summarize what has been learned about one aspect or another of this matter. In the typical experiment, one group of students receives instruction either partly or entirely via computer while an equivalent group receives either conventional instruction (a text assignment supplemented by classroom lecture and discussion) or an alternative form of CBI. Here is a brief summary of the main findings from several of these analyses:

1. Studies conducted during the 1970s and 1980s on the effect of tutorial programs found that, on average, CBI-taught students scored 14 percentile ranks higher on an achievement test than conventionally taught students. For studies on tutorial programs conducted during the 1990s, the effect was even

TABLE 7.1 Major Types of CBI Programs

Type of Program	Purpose	Main Features*
Drill and practice	Practice knowledge and skills learned earlier to produce fast and accurate responses.	Presents many problems, questions, and exercises.
		Checks answers and provides feedback.
		Provides cues when student is not sure of correct responses.
		Keeps track of errors.
		Adjusts difficulty level of problems and questions to the proficiency level of the student.
Tutorial	Teach new information (e.g., facts, definitions, concepts) and skills.	Presents new material in linear, branching, or dialogue format.
		In linear format, requires all students to begin with first frame and work through subsequent frames in given sequence. Minimizes incorrect responses through brief answers, small steps, and frequent prompts.
		In branching format, allows students to respond to different sets of frames depending on correctness of responses. For incorrect responses, provides supplementary material that attempts to reteach.
		In dialogue format, mimics teacher–student interactions by presenting material, evaluating responses, and adjusting subsequent instruction by presenting either more difficult or easier material.
Simulations and games	Teach new information and skills and provide an opportunity to apply what was learned in a meaningful context that would otherwise be unavailable because of cost, physical danger, or time constraints.	Allows students to use newly learned and existing information to solve a realistic problem.
		Can offer realistic (e.g., piloting a plane), historical/adventure (e.g., guiding a wagon train across the Oregon Trail), or imaginary (e.g., colonizing a new world) settings.
		Enables students to practice creating and testing hypotheses about the effects of different variables on achieving a goal.

*Not all programs contain all of the listed features.
SOURCE: Grabe & Grabe (2007).

Computer-based instruction has been shown to produce moderate increases in learning, particularly tutorial and simulation programs.

3. Students whose beginning reading skills (e.g., phonological awareness, word reading, text reading, reading and listening) were supported by CBI outscored students whose instruction was not computer based on reading tests by about 10 percentile ranks (Blok, Oostdam, Otter, & Overmaat, 2002). Interestingly, the findings of this review were about the same as those from reviews conducted 10 to 15 years earlier. Despite the introduction of more sophisticated computer programs in recent years (providing verbal feedback, for example), their effect on the learning of beginning reading skills has remained fairly constant.

CBI is no substitute for high-quality teaching.

4. An analysis of 78 studies that were published between 1998 and 2007 reported some of the strongest positive effects to date. On average, students given CBI scored 33 percentile ranks higher on achievement tests than their non-CBI counterparts (Camnalbur & Erdogan, 2008).

5. An analysis of data collected from tens of thousands of students in 31 countries found that performance in school was positively related to the use of a computer at home for accessing the Internet, to the availability of educational software at home, and to *moderate* computer use at school. Both low and high levels of use at school were associated with lower levels of achievement (Bielefeldt, 2005).

stronger: CBI-taught students scored 22 percentile ranks higher than their conventionally taught peers (J. A. Kulik, 2003a; Liao, 2007).

2. The average effect of simulation programs on achievement for studies conducted during the 1990s was a positive average effect of about one third of a standard deviation (whose meaning we discuss in Chapter 15). This means that students who worked on simulation programs scored 13 percentile ranks higher than their conventionally taught peers (J. A. Kulik, 2003a).

TeachSource Video Case

Integrating Technology to Improve Students' Learning: A High School Simulation

Go to the Education CourseMate website and watch the video, study the artifacts in the case, and reflect upon the following questions:

1. Is Mr. Bateman's biology lesson and use of technology in class a good example of Skinner's approach to instruction?

2. According to current educational research, computer-based simulation programs like the one depicted in this Video Case greatly improve student achievement in science. Using the Video Case and the text's discussion of behavioral theory, explain why this might be true.

Evaluation of CBI So, what to make of these analyses of over three decades of research on CBI? At least three conclusions seem to be in order.

First, CBI is not the equivalent of a wonder drug. That means you should take with a grain of salt overly enthusiastic, pie-in-the-sky claims about how technology-enhanced instruction will revolutionize classroom instruction. There's no question that CBI enhances student learning, but the effect is a moderate one. Given all of the factors that affect learning—and you'll get a better appreciation of this as you get further into the book—that conclusion should surprise no one.

Second, like so many other things in life, technology is subject to the "too much of a good thing can be bad for you" principle. Look again at the last finding we mentioned, about high levels of computer use.

Third, these findings reaffirm what we suggested in the opening chapter about good teaching being partly an art and partly a science. Whenever you as a teacher apply any psychological principle in your classroom, you will need to ask yourself: For whom is this instructional technique likely to be beneficial? With what materials? For what outcome? In other words, as effective as computer-based instruction may be in certain circumstances, it should never be looked upon as a substitute for high-quality instruction. Talented teachers will always be needed to create a positive classroom environment, monitor student progress, and orchestrate the sequence and pace of instructional events.

Pause & Reflect *Many educators feel that operant conditioning presents a cold, dehumanizing picture of human learning and ignores the role of such factors as free will, motives, and creativity. Do you feel that way while reading this chapter? Do you think positive attributes of operant conditioning balance out possible negative aspects?*

Behavior Modification

Although applied in many ways, the term **behavior modification** basically refers to the use of operant conditioning techniques to (as the phrase indicates) modify behavior. Because those who use such techniques attempt to manage behavior by making rewards contingent on certain actions, the term *contingency management* is also sometimes used. Our Case in Print for this chapter illustrates how several school systems are trying to modify students' attendance and studying behaviors with attractive positive reinforcers.

After Skinner and his followers had perfected techniques of operant conditioning in modifying the behavior of animals, they concluded that similar techniques could be used with humans. In this section we will briefly discuss several techniques that teachers may use to

strengthen or weaken specific behaviors. Techniques applied in education to strengthen behaviors include shaping, token economies, and contingency contracts. Techniques that aim to weaken behaviors include extinction and punishment.

behavior modification The use of operant conditioning techniques to modify behavior, generally by making rewards contingent on certain actions. Also called *contingency management*.

Shaping You may want to take a few minutes now to review our earlier explanation of shaping. Most attempts at shaping important classroom behaviors should include at least the following steps (Alberto & Troutman, 2009; Miltenberger, 2008):

1. Select the target behavior.
2. Obtain reliable baseline data (that is, determine how often the target behavior occurs in the normal course of events).
3. Select potential reinforcers.
4. Reinforce successive approximations of the target behavior each time they occur.
5. Reinforce the newly established target behavior each time it occurs.
6. Continue reinforcing the target behavior on a variable reinforcement schedule.

To illustrate how shaping might be used, imagine that you are a third grade teacher (or a middle or high school teacher) with a chronic problem: One of your students rarely completes more than a small percentage of the arithmetic (or algebra) problems on the worksheets you distribute in class, even though you know the student possesses the necessary skills. To begin, you decide that a reasonable goal would be for the student to complete at least 85% of the problems on a given worksheet. Next, you review the student's work for the past several weeks and determine that, on average, the student completed only 25% of the problems per worksheet. Your next step is to select positive reinforcers that you know or suspect will work.

{ **Behavior modification: shape behavior by ignoring undesirable responses and reinforcing desirable responses** }

Reinforcers come in a variety of forms. Most elementary school teachers typically use such things as stickers, verbal praise, smiles, and classroom privileges (for example, feeding the gerbil or cleaning the erasers). Middle school and high school teachers can use letter or numerical grades, material incentives (such as board

Premack principle
A shaping technique that allows students to indulge in a favorite activity after completing a set of instructional objectives. Also called *Grandma's rule.*

token economy
A behavior-strengthening technique that uses items of no inherent value to "purchase" other items perceived to be valuable.

games and computer games, as long as school policy and your financial resources allow it), and privately given verbal praise. With certain reservations, public forms of recognition can also be used. The reservations include the following:

- Because many adolescents are acutely self-conscious, any public display of student work or presentation of awards should be made to several students at the same time, to avoid possible embarrassment (Emmer & Evertson, 2009).

- Awards should be made without letter grades.

- Awards should be given with an awareness that public displays of recognition are not appropriate or comfortable for all cultures.

Premack principle: required work first, then chosen reward

One popular shaping technique that has stood the test of time involves having students list favorite activities on a card. Then they are told that they will be able to indulge in one of those activities for a stated period of time after they have completed a set of instructional objectives. This technique is sometimes called the **Premack principle** after psychologist David Premack (1959), who first proposed it. It is also called *Grandma's rule* because it is a variation of a technique that grandmothers have used for hundreds of years ("Finish your peas, and you can have dessert").

Once you have decided on a sequence of objectives and a method of reinforcement, you are ready to shape the target behavior. For example, you can start by reinforcing the student for completing five problems (25%) each day for several consecutive days. Then you reinforce the student for completing five problems and starting a sixth (a fixed ratio schedule). Then you reinforce the student for six completed problems, and so on. Once the student consistently completes at least 85%

Then

If . . .

A token economy is a flexible reinforcement system.

of the problems, you provide reinforcement after every fifth worksheet, on average (a variable ratio schedule).

Token Economies A second technique used to strengthen behavior in the classroom, the **token economy**, was introduced first with people who had been hospitalized for emotional disturbances and then with students in special education classes. A token is something that has little or no inherent value but that can be used to "purchase" things that do have perceived value. In society, money is our most ubiquitous token. Its value lies not in what it is made of but in what it can purchase—a car, a house, or a college education. By the same token (if you will excuse the pun), students can accumulate check marks, gold stars, or happy faces and "cash them in" at some later date for any one of several reinforcers. Such instructional activities as doing math worksheets, working at the computer, engaging in leisure reading, and playing academic games have proven to be effective reinforcers in token economies (Higgins, Williams, & McLaughlin, 2001). Token economies have even been proven effective in getting college students to increase their degree of in-class participation (Boniecki & Moore, 2003).

One reason for the development of the token economy approach was the limited flexibility of more commonly used reinforcers. Candies and cookies, for instance, tend to lose their reinforcing value fairly quickly when supplied continually. It is not always convenient to award free time or the opportunity to engage in a highly preferred activity immediately after a desired response. And social rewards may or may not be sufficiently reinforcing for some individuals. Tokens, however, can always be given immediately after a desirable behavior, can be awarded according to one of the four schedules mentioned earlier, and can be redeemed for items or activities that have high reinforcing value.

Token economies—especially when combined with classroom rules, appropriate delivery of reinforcers, and response cost (a concept we describe a bit later in the chapter)—are effective in reducing such disruptive classroom behaviors as talking out of turn, being out of one's seat, fighting, and being off-task. Reductions of 50 percent or more in such behaviors are not uncommon. Token economies have also been effective in improving academic performance in a variety of subject areas (Higgins, Williams, & McLaughlin, 2001; Kehle, Bray, Theodore, Jenson, & Clark, 2000; Naughton & McLaughlin, 1995). Token economies have been used successfully with individual students, groups of students, entire classrooms, and even entire schools.

Contingency contracting: supply reinforcement after student completes mutually agreed-on assignment

Contingency Contracting A third technique teachers use to strengthen behavior is **contingency contracting**. A contingency contract is simply a more formal method of specifying desirable behaviors and consequent reinforcement. The contract, which can be written or verbal, is an agreement worked out by two people (teacher and student, parent and child, counselor and client) in which one person (student, child, client) agrees to behave in a mutually acceptable way and the other person (teacher, parent, counselor) agrees to provide a mutually acceptable form of reinforcement. For example, a student may contract to sit quietly and work on a social studies assignment for 30 minutes. When the student is done, the teacher may reinforce the child with 10 minutes of free time, a token, or a small toy.

Contracts can be drawn up with all members of a class individually, with selected individual class members, or with the class as a whole. As with most other contracts, provisions can be made for renegotiating the terms. Moreover, the technique is flexible enough to incorporate the techniques of token economies and shaping. It is possible, for example, to draw up a contract that provides tokens for successive approximations to some target behavior (Bushrod, Williams, & McLaughlin, 1995).

Extinction, Time-Out, and Response Cost The primary goal of behavior modification is to strengthen desired behaviors. Toward that end, techniques such as shaping, token economies, and contingency contracts are likely to be very useful. There will be times, however, when you have to weaken or eliminate undesired behaviors because they interfere with instruction and learning. For these occasions, you might consider some form of extinction. Research has demonstrated that

extinction is effective in reducing the frequency of many types of problem behaviors (Miltenberger, 2008).

The most straightforward approach is to ignore the undesired response. If a student bids for your attention by clowning around, for instance, you may discourage repetition of that sort of behavior by ignoring it. It is possible, however, that classmates will not ignore the behavior, but laugh at it. Such response-strengthening reactions from classmates will likely counteract your lack of reinforcement. Accordingly, you need to observe what happens when you try to extinguish behavior by not responding.

If other students are reinforcing a youngster's undesired behavior or if a behavior becomes disruptive, you may want to apply the time-out procedure. Suppose a physically active third grade boy seems unable to keep himself from shoving classmates during recess. If verbal requests, reminders, or warnings fail to limit shoving, the boy can be required to take a 5-minute time-out period immediately after he shoves a classmate. He must sit alone in the classroom for that period of time while the rest of the class remains out on the

{ **Time-out works best with disruptive, aggressive children.** }

Jim Pickerell/Stock Boston

One useful method for positively reinforcing desired behavior is a token economy—supplying students with objects that have no inherent value but can be accumulated and redeemed for more meaningful reinforcers.

Going to School Can Be a Rewarding Experience

Although applied in many ways, the term behavior modification *basically refers to the use of operant conditioning techniques to (as the phrase indicates) modify behavior. Because those who use such techniques attempt to manage behavior by making rewards contingent on certain actions, the term* contingency management *is also sometimes used. (p. 157)*

Attendance Prize: Schools Offer Kids Big Rewards Just to Get Them to Show Up

MEAD GRUVER
Associated Press, 12/01/06

CASPER, Wyo.—Sixteen-year-old Kaytie Christopherson was getting ready to do her homework on a Friday when she got a call that made a big improvement in her life: She had won a brand-new pickup truck for near-perfect school attendance.

The truck was a $28,000 Chevrolet Colorado crew cab, in red, that included an MP3 player.

"I take it everywhere," the high school junior said. "I pay attention to where I park it, though."

Public schools commonly reward excellent attendance with movie tickets, gas vouchers and iPods. But some diligent students like Kaytie are now hitting the ultimate teenage jackpot for going to school: They have won cars or trucks.

School districts in Hartford, Conn., Pueblo, Colo., South Lake Tahoe, Calif., and Wickenburg and Yuma, Ariz., are also giving away vehicles this school year.

In most cases the car or truck is donated by a local dealership, and the prizes typically are awarded through drawings open only to students with good attendance.

So does bribing students with the possibility of winning a car or truck actually get them to think twice about staying home from school? Some educators think so, and say their giveaways have boosted attendance. But the evidence is not clear-cut.

Kaytie—who has a 4.0 average at Natrona County High, Dick Cheney's alma mater—won her truck last spring, in the school system's first such drawing. But she said that wasn't what motivated her to keep up her attendance; she just didn't want to fall behind.

District attendance officer Gary Somerville said he hopes to raise attendance and also reduce the district's 29 percent dropout rate, which he blames in part on Wyoming's booming gas-and-oil industry.

"These kids can go out and earn $15, $16, $17 an hour swinging a hammer. It's kind of hard to keep them in school past their 16th birthday," he said.

Hartford has been holding a drawing—for either a car or $10,000—for the past six years. Five of those times the winning family chose the money.

"I can't tell you that it's increased attendance," district spokesman Terry D'Italia said. "But what it has done over the years is just kept a focus on it and kept it at the top of kids' minds."

Jack Stafford, associate principal at South Tahoe High School, said changing times call for such incentives. "My mom had the three-B rule: There'd better be blood, bone or barf, or I was going to school," Stafford said. But "that's not the case now."

Districts have a lot to gain and little to lose by holding car drawings. The vehicles are usually free. And in Wyoming, even a one-student increase in average daily enrollment means another $12,000 in state funding for the year.

Source: "Attendance prize: Schools offer kids big rewards just to get them to show up," *Associated Press,* December 1, 2006. Reprinted by permission of Associated Press.

Questions and Activities

1. Assume that you are an expert on operant conditioning and behavior modification techniques and have been asked to defend a school board's decision to award a $28,000 vehicle to the high school student with the best yearly attendance record. What are the strongest arguments that you think you could make? Now assume that you have been asked to criticize the very same practice. Again, what would be your strongest arguments?

2. Gary Somerville, the district attendance officer quoted in this article, expressed the hope that the prospect of winning an expensive truck would discourage students from dropping out of school to take jobs that pay $15 an hour or more working for Wyoming's oil and gas industry. If you wanted to argue that Mr. Somerville is overlooking more important variables that influence both attendance and dropping out of school, what points would you make?

3. Make a judgment as to how successful you think this positive reinforcement program is likely to be, particularly over the long term, by evaluating how closely it meets accepted guidelines for shaping behavior through positive reinforcement.

4. Jack Stafford, an associate principal at a California high school, claimed that changing times call for larger and more attractive reinforcers to strengthen school attendance. Using your own high school experience as a guide, do you agree or disagree with this assessment? Interview at least six of your peers for their reactions.

playground. Time-out is an effective means of reducing or eliminating undesired behaviors, particularly those that are aggressive or disruptive, for both regular and mainstreamed children (Alberto & Troutman, 2009; Miltenberger, 2008). The rules for the procedure should be clearly explained, and after being sentenced to time-out (which should last no more than 5 minutes), a child should be given reinforcement for agreeable, helpful behavior—for example, "Thank you for collecting all the playground balls so nicely, Tommy."

Another technique, **response cost**, is similar to time-out in that it involves the removal of a stimulus. It is often used with a token economy. In this procedure, a certain amount of positive reinforcement (for example, 5% of previously earned tokens) is withdrawn every time a child makes an undesired response. If you have ever been caught exceeding the speed limit and been fined at least $50, you can probably attest to the power of response cost as a modifier of behavior. As with extinction and time-out, research has confirmed that response cost helps reduce a variety of problem behaviors (such as getting off task, not following directions, and engaging in disruptive behavior) for a wide range of children (Miltenberger, 2008).

Punishment Punishment is one of the most common behavior modification techniques, particularly when it takes the form of corporal punishment. It is also one of the most controversial. One factor that makes this issue controversial is that many parents believe in corporal punishment and spank their children, whereas lobbying groups (such as End Physical Punishment of Children and the National Coalition to Abolish Corporal Punishment in Schools) work to persuade state and federal officials to pass laws that forbid the practice, partly

on the basis of moral grounds and partly because there is no scientific evidence that corporal punishment helps children develop more effective social and self-control skills (Dupper & Dingus, 2008; Gershoff, 2002).

> **response cost**
> The withdrawal of previously earned positive reinforcers as a consequence of undesired behavior, often used with a token economy.

Pause & Reflect *Skinner argued that society too frequently uses aversive means (particularly punishment) to shape desired behavior rather than the more effective positive reinforcement. As you think about how your behavior has been shaped, would you agree or disagree? Why do you think we use punishment so frequently?*

A second factor is that researchers have different views about what the existing research means. For example, Elizabeth Gershoff (2002) analyzed 88 studies conducted over the past 60 years and concluded that corporal punishment was strongly associated with such negative behaviors and experiences as low internalization of moral rules, aggression, delinquent and antisocial behavior, low-quality parent–child relationships, and receipt of physical abuse. The definition of corporal punishment used by Gershoff was "the use of physical force with the intention of causing a child to experience pain but not injury for the purposes of correction or control of the child's behavior" (p. 540).

Gershoff's conclusions were challenged by Diana Baumrind, Robert Larzelere, and Philip Cowan (2002) on several grounds, one of which concerned the definition Gershoff chose to work from. These researchers argued that Gershoff's findings were due in part to the fact that

Classroom Management: Handling a Student With Behavior Problems

TeachSource Video Case

Go to the Education CourseMate website and watch the video, study the artifacts in the case, and reflect upon the following questions:

1. Which basic principles of operant conditioning did Mrs. Henry use when trying to help the troubled student in the Video Case? Explain your answer.

2. What are some examples of positive reinforcement that the teachers could use with this student (to decrease his negative behavior)?

Suggestions for Teaching

Applying Operant Conditioning in the Classroom

1 Remain aware that behavior is the result of particular conditions.

Unlike the controlled environment of a Skinner box, many causes of behavior in a real-life classroom may not be observable or traceable. Nevertheless, there will be times when you and your students may benefit if you say to yourself, "Now, there have to be some causes for that behavior. Can I figure out what they are and do something about changing things for the better?" When you are engaging in such speculations, keep in mind that reinforcement strengthens behavior. Check to see whether you are inadvertently rewarding students for misbehavior (by calling attention to them, for example, or by failing to reinforce those who engage in desirable forms of behavior).

Examples

- If you become aware that it takes a long time for your students to settle down at the beginning of a period and that you are reacting by addressing critical remarks specifically to those who dawdle the longest, ignore the dawdlers and respond positively to those who are ready to get to work.
- Let's say that you have given students 30 minutes to finish an assignment. To your dismay, few of them get to work until almost the end of the period, and you find that you have to do a lot of nagging. When you later analyze why this happened, you conclude that you actually encouraged the time-killing behavior because of the way you set up the lesson. The next time you give a similar assignment, tell the students that as soon as they complete it they can have class time to work on homework, and that you will be available to give help or advice to those who want it.

2 Use reinforcement, and use it appropriately to strengthen behaviors you want to encourage.

Why would we remind you to do something as obvious as reinforce behaviors you want students to acquire and exhibit in the future? Wouldn't you do that almost automatically? Well, we certainly hope so, but statistics suggest otherwise. A large team of researchers (Goodlad, 1984) observed the classroom behavior of 1,350 teachers and 17,163 students in 38 schools from seven sections

of the country. What they found may surprise you. Teachers' praise of student work occurred about 2% of the observed time in the primary grades and about 1% of the time in high school!

Once you have resolved to reinforce desired behavior systematically, you need to be sure that you do it appropriately. Although reinforcement is a simple principle that can be readily understood at an intuitive level, it has to be used in the right way to produce desired results. Paul Chance (1992) offered seven guidelines for the effective use of positive reinforcement:

- Use the weakest reward available to strengthen a behavior. In other words, do not use material rewards when you know that praise will be just as effective a reinforcer. Save the material rewards for that special behavior for which praise or other reinforcers may not be effective.
- When possible, avoid using rewards as incentives. What Chance means is not to get into the habit of automatically telling the student that if she does what you want, you will provide a specific reward. Instead, sometimes ask the student to do something (like work quietly or help another student), and then provide the reinforcer.
- Reward at a high rate in the early stages of learning, and reduce the frequency of rewards as learning progresses.
- Reward only the behavior you want repeated. Although you may not realize it, students are often very sensitive to what is and is not being reinforced. If you decide that one way to encourage students to be more creative in their writing is to tell them not to worry about spelling and grammar errors, then do not be surprised to see a number of misspelled words and poorly constructed sentences. Or if you decide to reward only the three highest scorers on a test, reasoning that competition brings out the best in people, be prepared to deal with the fact that competition also brings out some of the worst in people (like cheating and refusing to help others).
- Remember that what is an effective reinforcer for one student may not be for another. For some students, comments such as "Very interesting point," "That's right," or "That was a big help" will strengthen the target behavior. But

One of the basic principles of instruction derived from operant conditioning experiments is that teachers should provide elementary grade students with immediate reinforcement for correct responses.

for others, something less overt, such as smiling encouragingly, may be just right. This is what we meant in Chapter 1 when we said that part of the art of teaching is knowing your students well enough that you know what to do with which student for any particular situation.

- Set standards so that success is a realistic possibility for each student. You may have students whose English proficiency is limited or who have disabilities related to learning and intellectual functioning. One way to deal with such diversity is to reward students for making steady progress from whatever their baseline level of performance was at the beginning of the term.
- An often-mentioned goal of teachers is to have students become intrinsically motivated or to take personal pride and satisfaction in simply doing something well. You can use natural instructional opportunities to point this out—for example, explore with students as they are writing how satisfying it is to write a clear and interesting story.

3 Take advantage of knowledge about the impact of different reinforcement schedules to encourage persistent and permanent learning.
a. When students first attempt a new kind of learning, supply frequent reinforcement. Then supply rewards less often.

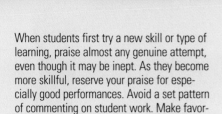

When students first try a new skill or type of learning, praise almost any genuine attempt, even though it may be inept. As they become more skillful, reserve your praise for especially good performances. Avoid a set pattern of commenting on student work. Make favorable remarks at unpredictable intervals.

b. If you want to encourage periodic spurts of activity, use a fixed interval schedule of reinforcement.

Occasionally, you will want to encourage students to engage in spurts of activity, as steady output might be too demanding or fatiguing. In such cases, supply reinforcement at specified periods of time. For example, when students are engaging in strenuous or concentrated activity, circulate and provide praise and encouragement by following a set pattern that will bring you in contact with each student at predictable intervals.

4 Give students opportunities to make overt responses, and provide prompt feedback.

a. Require students to make frequent, overt, and relevant responses.

The tendency of teachers is to talk, and for large chunks of time. Those who advocate an approach to teaching based on operant conditioning principles recommend that teachers limit the amount of information and explanation they give to students and instead substitute opportunities for students to respond overtly. In addition, the responses should be directly related to the objectives. If your objectives emphasize the application of concepts and principles, then most of the responses students are asked to make should be about applications. The reason for this suggestion is that the delivery of corrective feedback and other forms of positive reinforcement can be increased when students make frequent responses, thereby accelerating the process of shaping.

Examples

- Instead of lecturing for 20 to 30 minutes at a time about the development of science and technology in the twentieth century, present information in smaller chunks, perhaps 8 to 10 minutes at a time, and then ask students to describe how an everyday product or service grew out of a particular scientific principle.
- Periodically ask students to summarize the main points of the material you presented over the past several minutes.

b. Provide feedback so that correct responses will be reinforced and students will become aware of and correct errors.

Research clearly shows that students who study material about a topic, answer a set of questions about that material, and are then told whether their responses are correct and why score significantly higher on a subsequent test of that material than do students who receive no feedback. The difference was about three fourths of a standard deviation, meaning that students who received feedback scored about 27 percentile ranks higher than students who received no feedback. Here are a couple of examples of how you can provide timely and useful feedback to students (Bangert-Drowns, Kulik, Kulik, & Morgan, 1991).

Examples

- Immediately after students read a chapter in a text, give them an informal quiz on the key points you listed. Then have them pair off, exchange quizzes, and correct and discuss them.
- As soon as you complete a lecture or demonstration, ask individual students to volunteer to read to the rest of the class what they wrote about the points they were told to look for. Indicate whether the answer is correct; if it is incorrect or incomplete, ask (in a relaxed and nonthreatening way) for additional comments. Direct students to amend and revise their notes as they listen to the responses.

5 When students must struggle to concentrate on material that is not intrinsically interesting, use special forms of reinforcement to motivate them to persevere.

For a variety of reasons, some students may have an extraordinarily difficult time concentrating on almost anything. And, as we all know, to master almost any skill or subject we have to engage in a certain amount of tedious effort. Here are some behavior modification procedures that may help:

a. Select, with student assistance, a variety of reinforcers.

A behavior modification approach to motivation appears to work most successfully when students are aware of and eager to earn a payoff. Because students react differently

to rewards and because any reward is likely to lose effectiveness if used to excess, it is desirable to list several kinds of rewards and permit students to choose. Some behavior modification enthusiasts (for example, Alberto & Troutman, 2009) have even recommended that you make up a *reinforcement preference list* for each student. If you allow your students to prepare individual reinforcement menus themselves, they should be instructed to list school activities they really enjoy doing. It would be wise, however, to stress that the students' lists must be approved by you so that they will not conflict with school regulations or interfere with the rights of others. A student's reward menu might include activities such as reading a self-chosen book, working on an art or craft project, or viewing a DVD in another room.

b. Establish, in consultation with individual students, an initial contract of work to be performed to earn a particular reward.

Once you have established a list of payoffs, you might consult with students (on an individual basis, if possible) to establish a certain amount of work that must be completed for students to obtain a reward selected from the menu. (Refer to Chapter 13 for Robert Mager's suggestions on preparing specific objectives.) To ensure that students will earn the reward, the first contract should not be too demanding. For example, it might be something as simple as "Successfully spell at least 7 out of 10 words on a list of previously misspelled words" or "Correctly answer at least 6 out of 10 questions about the content of a textbook chapter."

c. Once the initial reward is earned, establish a series of short contracts leading to frequent, immediate rewards.

The results of many operant conditioning experiments suggest that the frequency of reinforcement is of greater significance than the amount of reinforcement. Therefore, having students work on brief contracts that lead to frequent payoffs immediately after the task is completed is preferable to having them work toward a delayed, king-sized reward.

Challenging Assumptions

Positive Reinforcement Versus Punishment as a Classroom Management Tool

Common sense suggests that when one pedagogical technique is shown to be largely effective for achieving a particular objective and a second technique is shown to be largely ineffective, the former would be used by at least a sizable minority of teachers while the latter would be ignored by most. Well, common sense does not always prevail, particularly in the case of using positive reinforcement and punishment as classroom management tools. As we've documented on these pages, few teachers use positive reinforcement in their classrooms despite its demonstrated effectiveness in promoting desired behaviors. Various forms of punishment, which have numerous disadvantages, are more popular.

One reason for this contrary state of affairs undoubtedly has to do with the decline in popularity of operant conditioning theory in educational psychology textbooks and courses. It is not unusual these days for students in teacher education programs to have learned little or nothing about operant conditioning principles and their classroom applications. As a result, many teachers fall into what is called the negative reinforcement trap. Here's how it works: A student's misbehavior instinctively elicits a punishing response from a teacher because punishment can be administered quickly and easily and often produces a rapid (albeit temporary) suppression of the undesired behavior. Let's say the teacher sends the offending student to the principal's office. Having obtained at least temporary relief, the teacher is now more inclined to send the next misbehaving student to the office. Now let's examine this situation from the student's perspective. Some students may misbehave because they find the work boring or, even worse, threatening because of a fear of failure. Sending such a student out of the room removes the student from a punishing environment. This is a form of negative reinforcement, which increases the likelihood that the student will engage in subsequent misbehavior.

The best way to deal with this problem is to avoid it in the first place by using a combination of effective teaching methods and positive reinforcement, an approach that is referred to in the literature as positive behavior support (see Gettinger & Stoiber, 2006; Marquis et al., 2000). In the Suggestions for Teaching in this chapter, we discuss several ways in which positive reinforcement can be used appropriately and effectively.

What Do You Think?

Have you seen the type of situation described here during your own schooling? What do you think about it? For more on this topic, go to the "Challenging Assumptions" section of the textbook's Education CourseMate website.

---

the definition she used allowed her to include studies whose forms of punishment were more severe than most parents administer. Baumrind et al. advocated limiting the analysis to studies in which the form of corporal punishment used was the more common mild to moderate spanking. They defined spanking as a "subset of the broader category of corporal punishment that is a) physically non-injurious; b) intended to modify behavior; and c) administered with an opened hand to the extremities or buttocks" (p. 581). A reanalysis of those studies examined by Gershoff that were more consistent with this narrower definition produced a considerably weaker (but still positive) relationship between spanking and aggressive behavior. For this reason, as well as limitations in many of the studies, Baumrind and colleagues concluded that a blanket condemnation of spanking cannot be made on the basis of the existing research (although it may be made on other bases).

A final word of caution before leaving this topic: As Gershoff pointed out, the studies she reviewed were correlational in nature. That is, researchers simply sought to determine whether a relationship exists between corporal punishment and aggressive behaviors exhibited by children. Consequently, one cannot draw the conclusion from this research that spanking children *causes* them to be more aggressive. It is just as plausible, until additional research proves otherwise, that the behavior of children who are inherently more aggressive than others causes their parents and other adults to administer more corporal punishment. Another possibility is that a third variable, such as inconsistent discipline, is responsible for both increased use of corporal punishment and aggressive behavior in children.

> **Research is unclear about the strength of negative effects of corporal punishment.**

Should You Use Behavior Modification? This may seem a strange question to ask, given the number of pages we have just spent covering behavior modification methods. Obviously, we feel that the results of decades of research on these techniques justify their use by teachers. Nevertheless, there are criticisms of behavior modification that are not adequately addressed by research findings and that you should carefully consider.

One criticism of using behavior modification over an extended period of time is that students may develop a "What's in it for me?" attitude and learning may come to an abrupt halt when no one is around to supply reinforcement (Kohn, 1993).

A second major criticism is that behavior modification methods, because of their potential power, may lend themselves to inappropriate or even unethical uses. For example, teachers may shape students to be quiet and obedient because it makes their job easier, even though such behaviors do not always produce optimum conditions for learning.

In response to these criticisms, Skinner and other behavioral scientists (see, for example, Chance, 1993; Flora, 2004; Maag, 2001) have argued that students' behaviors are going to be shaped one way or another regardless of what we do or do not do. It would be far better, so this argument goes, to use behavior modification tools in such a way that almost everyone acquires behaviors that support meaningful learning. This response suggests that educators could be accused of being unethical for not making use of an effective learning tool. The challenge, of course, is to use it wisely. The Suggestions for Teaching on the previous pages will give you additional ideas for putting operant conditioning principles into practice.

WHAT ELSE? *RIP & REVIEW* **CARDS IN THE BACK**

8

INFORMATION-PROCESSING THEORY

LEARNING OBJECTIVES

After studying this chapter, you will be able to . . .

LO1 Explain what is meant by the information-processing view of learning.

LO2 Describe the various components and processes that make up the multistore model of information processing.

LO3 Define metacognition and explain how it affects the learning process.

LO4 Describe the ways technology can help students improve how much and how well they learn different subjects.

visit 4ltrpress.cengage.com

In Chapter 7 we noted that operant conditioning emphasizes the role of external factors in learning. Behavioral psychologists focus on the nature of a stimulus to which a student is exposed, the response that the student makes, and the consequences that follow the response. They see no reason to speculate about what takes place in the student's mind before and after the response. The extensive Suggestions for Teaching presented in Chapter 7 serve as evidence that conclusions and principles based on analyses of external stimuli, observable responses, and observable consequences can be of considerable value to teachers.

But cognitive psychologists, meaning those who study how the mind works and influences behavior, are convinced that it is possible to study nonobservable behavior, such as thought processes, in a scientific manner. Some of these cognitive psychologists are especially interested in an area of study known as **information-processing theory**, which seeks to understand how people acquire new information, how they create and store mental representations of information, how they recall it from memory, and how what they already know guides and determines what and how they will learn.

Before getting into the nuts and bolts of information-processing theory, we need to repeat the same caveat that we mentioned in Chapter 1: Don't look for explanations of how people encode, store, and retrieve information from memory that can be applied to all types of people, tasks, and settings. For all of its sophistication, research on memory has not progressed to the point where general laws can be formulated (Roediger, 2008). The interactions between people and the settings in which they function are too numerous and complex to allow for that kind of predictability. Once again, you will have to slip into the role of teacher-artist and figure out how to apply these insights to a given group of students, studying a particular part of the curriculum, who will be given a particular type of test to assess what they have learned.

LO1 The Information-Processing View of Learning

Information-processing psychologists assume three things about how people learn: Information is processed in stages, there are limits on how much information can be processed at any stage, and previously learned information affects how and what people currently learn (Dehn, 2008; Linnell, 2007). Because learning is seen as the result of an interaction between the information to be learned and a learner who processes that information on the basis of existing knowledge schemes, this is a *constructivist* view of learning (Ashcraft & Radvansky, 2010; Winne, 2001). If you're not sure what a constructivist theory is, no need to worry; we give you a full explanation in Chapter 10.

A careful reading of this chapter is important because the information-processing decisions you make affect when you learn, how much you learn, how well you learn—indeed, whether you learn at all. To give you an appreciation of the information-processing approach to learning and how it can help teachers and students do their jobs, the next section will describe several basic cognitive processes and their role in the storage and retrieval of information.

> ## { Information processing: how humans attend to, recognize, transform, store, and retrieve information }

LO2 A Model of Information Processing

Many psychologists think of information as being held in and transferred among three memory stores: a sensory register, a short-term store, and a long-term store. Each store varies as to what processes are required to move information into and out of it, how much information it can hold, and how long it can hold information. A symbolic representation of these memory stores and their associated processes appears in Figure 8.1; called a *multistore* model, it is based on the work of several theorists (for example, Atkinson & Shiffrin, 1968; Norman & Rumelhart, 1970). Note that our use of the term *memory stores* is not meant to suggest specific locations in the brain where information is held; it is simply a metaphorical device for classifying different memory phenomena.

information-processing theory An area of study that seeks to understand how people acquire, store, and recall information, and how their current knowledge guides and determines what and how they will learn.

© Thomas M Perkins/Shutterstock Images

© Leonard McLane/Photolibrary.com

sensory register (SR) The primary memory store that temporarily records (for 1 to 3 seconds) an incoming flow of data from the sense receptors.

recognition A cognitive process that involves noting key features of a stimulus and relating them to previously stored information in an interactive manner.

Pause& Reflect

Can you think of any personal experiences that illustrate one or more of the three memory stores? Have you recently, for instance, retrieved a long-dormant memory because of a chance encounter with an associated word, sound, or smell?

As shown in Figure 8.1, *control processes* govern both the manner in which information is encoded and its flow between memory stores. These processes include *recognition*, *attention*, *maintenance rehearsal*, *elaborative rehearsal* (also called *elaborative encoding*), and retrieval. Each control process is associated primarily with a particular memory store.

The control processes are an important aspect of the information-processing system for two reasons. First, they determine the quantity and quality of information that the learner stores in and retrieves from memory. Second, it is the learner who decides whether, when, and how to employ them. That the control processes are under our direct, conscious control will take on added importance when we discuss educational applications a bit later. Before we get to applications, however, we need to make you more familiar with the three memory stores and the control processes specifically associated with each of them.

The Sensory Register and Its Control Processes

The Sensory Register A description of how human learners process information typically begins with environmental stimuli. Our sense receptors are constantly stimulated by various sights, sounds, textures, odors, and tastes. These experiences are initially recorded in the **sensory register (SR)**, the first memory store. It is called the sensory register because the information it stores is thought to be encoded in the same form in which it is originally perceived—that is, as raw sensory data.

The purpose of the SR is to hold information just long enough (about 1 to 3 seconds) for us to decide whether we want to attend to it further. Information not selectively attended to and recognized decays or disappears from the system. At the moment you are reading these words, for example, you are being exposed to the appearance of letters printed on paper, sounds in the place where you are reading, and many other stimuli. The sensory register might be compared to an unending series of instant camera snapshots or video segments, each lasting from 1 to 3 seconds before fading away. If you recognize and attend to one of the snapshots, it will be "processed" and transferred to short-term memory.

The Nature of Recognition The process of **recognition** involves noting key features of a stimulus and relating them to already stored information. This process is interactive in that it depends partly on information extracted from the stimulus itself and partly on information stored in long-term memory. The ability to recognize a dog, for example, involves noticing those physical features of the animal that give it "dogness" (for example, height, length, number of feet, type of coat) and combining the results of that analysis with relevant information from long-term memory (such as that dogs are household pets, are walked on a leash by their owners, and are used to guard property).

To the degree that an object's defining features are ambiguous (as when one observes an unfamiliar breed of dog from a great distance) or that a learner lacks relevant prior knowledge (as many young children do), recognition and more meaningful processing will suffer. Recognition of words and sentences during reading, for example, can be aided by such

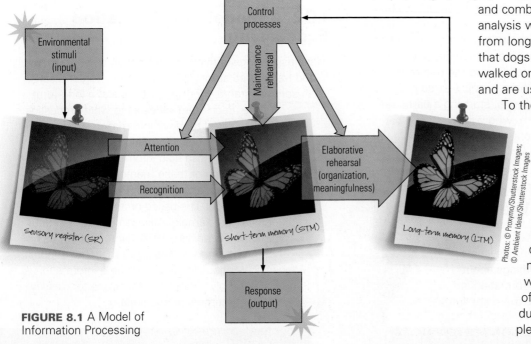

FIGURE 8.1 A Model of Information Processing

Photos: © Proxymo/Shutterstock Images; © Ambient Ideas/Shutterstock Images

Chapter 8: Information-Processing Theory

factors as clear printing and knowledge of spelling patterns, letter sounds, and the frequency with which words appear in natural language. The important point to remember is that recognition and meaningful processing of information are most effective when we make use of all available sources of information (Ashcraft & Radvansky, 2010; Leacock & Nesbit, 2007).

One implication of this information-processing view is that elementary school students need more structured learning tasks than middle school or high school students. Because of their limited store of knowledge in long-term memory and narrow ability to relate what they do know logically to the task at hand, younger students should be provided with clear, complete, explicit directions and learning materials (Doyle, 1983; Palmer & Wehmeyer, 2003).

The Impact of Attention The environment usually provides us with more information than we can deal with at one time. From the multitude of sights, sounds, smells, and other stimuli impinging on us at a given moment, we notice and record in the sensory register only a fraction. At this point, yet another reduction typically occurs. We may process only one third of the already-selected information recorded in the SR. We continually focus on one thing at the expense of something else. This selective focusing on a portion of the information currently stored in the sensory register is what we call **attention**.

> ## Information in long-term memory influences what we attend to.

What governs what we attend to? According to one of the pioneers of cognitive psychology, Ulric Neisser, "Perceivers pick up only what they have schemata for, and willy-nilly ignore the rest" (1976, p. 79). In other words, we choose what we will see (or hear) by using our prior knowledge and experiences to anticipate the nature of incoming information. Students daydream, doodle, and write text messages rather than listen to a lecture because they anticipate hearing little of value.

Now, you may believe that you're more aware of what is going on around you than most other people. And you may be, but we doubt it. So what makes us think that your ability to attend to several things at

Dog

Dog???

© Michael Pettigrew/Shutterstock Images; © artemisphoto/Shutterstock Images

once is probably no better than average? The results of the following experiment, which was conducted on college students much like you. If you were one of the subjects in this study (Chabris & Simons, 2010), you would be asked to watch a brief video of three people in white shirts passing a basketball to one another and three people in black shirts doing the same thing. Your task is to count how often the ball gets passed among the three participants in white shirts and ignore how often the three people in the black shirts pass the ball to one another. Not a particularly hard task, but it does require you to focus your attention on the people in the white shirts. At some point during this ball-passing activity, another person, dressed in a gorilla suit, walks into the scene, stops, faces the camera, beats on his chest, turns, and walks out of the other side of the scene. The gorilla is visible for 9 seconds.

After viewing the video, the experimenter then asks you to report what you saw. You're probably thinking that the first words out of your mouth would be something like, "You probably won't believe me, but I saw a gorilla!" We hate to disappoint you, but since half the subjects in this study said they didn't "see" a gorilla, you probably wouldn't have either. We put "see" in quotation marks because the gorilla did fall within each subject's field of vision. We know this because the researchers also tracked their eye movements, and knew whether an image of the gorilla appeared on each person's retina. This phenomenon is called *inattentional blindness* and explains why people who text and drive or talk on a cell phone while driving are more likely to have an accident than people who focus entirely on their driving. If you're meaningfully processing a phone conversation, you're not attending to and processing the conditions on the road.

© Yuri Arcurs/Shutterstock Images

Short-Term Memory and Its Control Processes

Short-Term Memory Once information has been attended to, it is transferred to **short-term memory (STM)**, the second memory store. Short-term memory can hold anywhere from five to nine (seven is the average) unrelated bits of information for approximately 20 seconds. Although the capacity of STM is relatively small, we can expand this limit a bit by using a technique called *chunking*, which we describe in this chapter's Suggestions for Teaching. The brief amount of time that information remains available in STM may seem surprising, but it can be easily demonstrated. Imagine that you look up and dial an unfamiliar phone number and receive a busy signal. If something or someone else then distracts you for 15 to 20 seconds, chances are you will have forgotten the number.

Short-term memory is more than just a place to temporarily store whatever we are currently thinking about (ideally, this page of the textbook rather than last night's party). It is also where we encode, organize, and retrieve information. Psychologists use the term *working memory* to refer to the aspect of STM that actively processes information. So when we try to figure out how to compose a sentence, solve a math problem, or recall a scientific formula, those activities take place in working memory.

Working memory is increasingly being viewed as a critical component in our information-processing system (Klingberg, 2009; Rose, Myerson, Roediger, & Hale, 2010; Thorn & Page, 2009). Logic suggests, and research has confirmed, that differences in working memory are strongly related to differences in such basic skills as reading comprehension, listening comprehension, oral expression, writing, math calculation, and math reasoning (Dehn, 2008). Preschool and first grade children, for example, who scored higher than their peers on a test of working memory were better able to complete a card sorting task that required keeping track of several pieces of information (Marcovitch, Boseovski, Knapp, & Kane, 2010). This finding does not, however, mean that students with a smaller working memory are doomed to be underperformers. The same researchers cited evidence that children can be trained to use their working memory more effectively.

Rehearsal A severe limitation of short-term memory is how quickly information disappears or is forgotten in the absence of further processing. This problem can be dealt with through *rehearsal*. Most people think of rehearsal as repeating something over and over either in silence or out loud. The usual purpose for such behavior is to memorize information for later use, although occasionally we simply want to hold material in short-term memory for immediate use (for example, to redial a phone number after getting a busy signal). Rehearsal can serve both purposes, but not in the same way. Accordingly, cognitive psychologists have found it necessary and useful to distinguish two types of rehearsal: maintenance and elaborative.

Maintenance rehearsal (also called *rote rehearsal* or *repetition*) has a mechanical quality. Its only purpose is to use mental and verbal repetition to hold information in short-term memory for some immediate

TeachSource Video Case

Cooperative Learning in the Elementary Grades: Jigsaw Model

Go to the Education CourseMate website and watch the video, study the artifacts in the case, and reflect upon the following questions:

1. How do the students in this Video Case demonstrate the information-processing concepts of attention and elaborative rehearsal?

2. What are some ways that students in this Video Case demonstrate how their prior knowledge (information in long-term memory) influences their preparation in expert groups, their peer teaching to their home groups, and their assessments?

Case in Print

A Head for Numbers

Elaborative rehearsal (also called elaborative encoding) consciously relates new information to knowledge already stored in long-term memory. Elaboration occurs when we use information stored in long-term memory to add details to new information, clarify the meaning of a new idea, make inferences, construct visual images, and create analogies (Dunlosky & Bjork, 2008a). In these ways, we facilitate both the transfer of information to long-term memory and its maintenance in short-term memory.

A Small Number With a Big Following

DON TROOP

Chronicle of Higher Education, 3/7/10

At precisely 1:59 a.m. on Sunday, Joe Anderson will arise at his parents' home and begin reciting, by memory, the first thousand digits of pi: "3.14159265358979323846. . . ."

Mr. Anderson has performed this exercise previously on Pi Day, an informal holiday that math lovers observe every March 14 in honor of their favorite irrational number: pi—so tiny (it's closer to three than four) yet random and infinite (as far as anyone knows).

Mr. Anderson, 17, is a student at the Texas Academy of Mathematics and Science, a two-year residential program at the University of North Texas that allows exceptional students to complete their freshman and sophomore years of college while earning the equivalent of a high-school diploma. His interest in the function of memory led

him to take on the challenge of reciting pi. He visualizes the numbers in groups of five or 10 and practices by typing the digits into his calculator, which is programmed to tell him if he's made a mistake. When he performs his trick in front of an audience—it takes about 10 minutes, he says—he imagines punching the numbers into an invisible keypad.

"My plan for this year is to rememorize the thousand I know, but learn them better," says Mr. Anderson, an aspiring physicist who will be on spring break this Pi Day. "I will memorize them while doing something with my hands so I can't utilize the muscle memory. I'm thinking of doing Chinese yo-yo tricks while I recite the numbers so I won't be able to type out imaginary keys with my hands."

Mr. Anderson's talent for remembering might seem superhuman, but his thousand-number feat is dwarfed by that of a Chinese graduate student, Lu Chao, who captured the world record in 2005 by reciting pi to 67,890 digits over 24 hours, according to PhysOrg.com. The world record for calculating pi is even more daunting. A computer scientist in France, Fabrice Bellard, recently carried out the value of pi to 2.7 trillion decimal points. Mr. Bellard, PhysOrg reports, ran his own software algorithms on a personal computer, completing his 131-day task on December 31, 2009.

When it comes to memorization, those of us who struggle to retain even the basic numbers of life—birthdays, anniversaries, ATM passcodes—would do well to use a popular mnemonic device, a sentence in which the letter counts of each word signify

the first 15 numbers of pi: "How I want a drink, alcoholic of course, after the heavy lectures involving quantum mechanics!"

Source: Don Troop, "A small number with a big following," from *Chronicle of Higher Education*, March 7, 2010. Copyright 2010, the *Chronicle of Higher Education*. Reprinted with permission.

Questions and Activities

1. The elaborative encoding techniques used by Joe Anderson to memorize the first thousand digits of pi obviously account for a large part of his success in performing this task. But the article suggests other contributing factors. What might they be?

2. Given how effective elaborative encoding techniques are at helping us process information, why don't more people use them? Use yourself as a case study to answer this question.

3. Would you be willing to memorize a large amount of information as a way to demonstrate to your students how powerful elaborative encoding techniques are and to motivate them to emulate your feat?

purpose. Although this is a useful and often-used capability (as in the telephone example), it has no effect on long-term memory storage.

Elaborative rehearsal (also called *elaborative encoding*) consciously relates new information to knowledge already stored in long-term memory. Elaboration occurs when we use information stored in long-term memory to add details to new information, clarify the meaning of a new idea, make inferences, construct visual images, and create analogies (Dunlosky & Bjork, 2008a). In these ways, we facilitate both the transfer of information to long-term memory and its maintenance in short-term memory. For example, if you wanted to learn the lines for a part in a play, you might try to relate the dialogue and behavior of your character to similar personal experiences you remember. As you strive to

memorize the lines and actions, your mental "elaborations" will help you store your part in long-term memory so that you can retrieve it later. Our Case in Print for this chapter illustrates how people can memorize what seem to be impossibly large amounts of information through the skilled use of elaborative encoding.

Elaborative rehearsal, whereby information from long-term memory is used in learning new information, is the rule rather than the exception. Mature learners don't often employ maintenance rehearsal by itself. The decision to use one or the other, however, depends on the demands you expect the environment to make

> **elaborative rehearsal** A process that consciously relates new information to knowledge already stored in long-term memory. Also called *elaborative encoding*.

on you. If you need to remember things for future use, use elaborative rehearsal; if you want to keep something in consciousness just for the moment, use rote rehearsal.

So far, we have explained the effect of elaborative rehearsal in terms of relating new information to information already stored in long-term memory. That's fine as a very general explanation. But to be more precise, we need to point out that elaborative rehearsal is based on *organization* (for example, grouping several items together on some common basis and rehearsing them as a set) and *meaningfulness* (relating the lines in a play to similar personal experiences, for example).

Organizing material reduces the number of chunks and provides recall cues.

Organization Quite often the information we want to learn is complex and interrelated. We can make this type of material easier to learn by organizing multiple pieces of information into a few "clumps," or "chunks," of information, particularly when each part of a chunk helps us remember other parts (Cowan, 2005). The value of organizing material was illustrated by a classic experiment (Bower, Clark, Lesgold, & Winzenz, 1969) in which two groups of participants were asked to learn 112 words in four successive lists but under different conditions. One group was given each of the four lists for four trials in the hierarchical or "blocked" arrangement displayed in Figure 8.2. The other group was given the same lists and the same hierarchical tree arrangement, but the words from each list were randomly arranged over the four levels of the hierarchy.

As you can see, through the first three trials, the group given the word lists in a blocked arrangement recalled more than twice as many words as the group given the words in a random arrangement and achieved perfect recall scores for the last two trials. The organized material was much easier to learn not only because there were fewer chunks to memorize but also because each item in a group served as a cue for the other items. When you decide to store pertinent material from this chapter in your long-term memory in preparation for an exam, you will find the job much easier if you organize what you are studying.

Meaningfulness The meaningfulness of new information that a person is about to learn has been charac-

terized as "potentially the most powerful variable for explaining the learning of complex verbal discourse" (R. E. Johnson, 1975, pp. 425–426). According to David Ausubel (Ausubel, Novak, & Hanesian, 1978), **meaningful learning** occurs when a learner encounters clear,

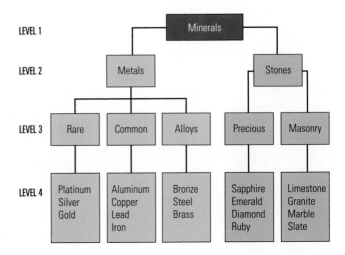

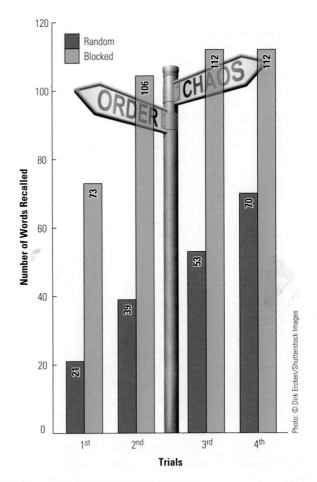

FIGURE 8.2 Hierarchical Arrangement of Words Produces Superior Recall
SOURCE: Bower, Clark, Lesgold, & Winzenz (1969).

logically organized material and consciously tries to relate the new material to ideas and experiences stored in long-term memory. To understand learning theory principles, for example, you might imagine yourself using them to teach a lesson to a group of students. Or you might modify a previously constructed flowchart on the basis of new information. The basic idea behind meaningful learning is that the learner actively attempts to associate new ideas with existing ones (Loyens & Rikers, 2011; Thorn & Page, 2009). As another example, many of the Pause & Reflect questions in this book are designed to foster meaningful encoding by getting you to relate text information to relevant prior experience. As you will see in Chapter 10, instructional approaches that are based on the principle of meaningfulness emphasize such active forms of learning as doing projects and solving problems that relate to students' everyday lives (as well as to state standards).

> **Meaningful learning occurs when organized material is associated with stored knowledge.**

This brief description of meaningfulness and its role in learning contains a strong implication for teaching in culturally diverse classrooms: You can foster meaningful learning for students from other cultures by pointing out similarities between ideas presented in class and students' culture-specific knowledge. For example, you might point out that September 16 has the same significance to the people of Mexico as July 4 has to U.S. citizens because the former date commemorates Mexico's revolution against and independence from Spain.

Visual Imagery Encoding Like pictures, images can be said to be worth a thousand words because they contain a wealth of information in a compact, organized, and meaningful format. Consider Benjamin Banneker (1731–1806), who has been called the first Black intellectual. Banneker was a self-taught mathematician, astronomer, and surveyor (Cothran, 2006). He predicted a solar eclipse in 1789, published tide tables, and was appointed by President George Washington to the commission that established the boundaries of Washington, DC. His accomplishments (such as building a wooden clock based just on an earlier examination of the workings of a pocket watch) suggest that mental imagery was critical to his thinking. Other notable individuals, such as Albert Einstein (physics), Michael Faraday (physics), James D. Watson (biochemistry), and Joan Didion

To help students encode information, teach them how to group objects and ideas according to some shared feature.

(literature) have described how mental imagery played a significant role in their thinking and problem-solving efforts (Shepard, 1978).

Research has consistently shown that students who are directed to generate visual images as they read lists of words or sentences, several paragraphs of text, or lengthy text passages attain higher levels of comprehension and recall than students who are not so instructed. Also, text passages that contained many concrete words and phrases were more easily

Meaningful learning occurs when a learner relates, either spontaneously or with help, clearly written and logically organized information to existing networks of information stored in long-term memory.

dual coding theory A theory of elaboration that states that concrete objects and words are remembered better than abstract information because they are coded in memory as both visual images and verbal labels, whereas abstract words are only encoded verbally.

long-term memory (LTM) The storehouse of permanently recorded information in an individual's memory.

understood and more accurately recalled than passages that contained more abstract than concrete ideas (J. M. Clark & Paivio, 1991). In one study (Sadoski, Goetz, & Rodriguez, 2000), the beneficial effect of concreteness was obtained for several passage types (such as expository text, persuasive text, stories, and narratives). The more concrete the passage was, the more it was rated comprehensible by students, and students who read concrete passages recalled 1.7 times as much information as students who read abstract passages. As we will see in the next chapter, concreteness and visual imagery are an integral part of several effective study skills.

The theory that these findings support is Allan Paivio's dual coding theory (Clark & Paivio, 1991; Meilinger, Knauff, & Bülthoff, 2008; Sadoski & Paivio, 2007). According to the **dual coding theory**, concrete material (such as pictures of familiar objects) and concrete words (such as *horse, bottle,* and *water*) are remembered better than abstract words (such as *deduction, justice,* and *theory*) because the former can be encoded in two ways—as images and as verbal labels—whereas the latter are encoded only verbally. This makes retrieval easier because a twice-coded item provides more potential retrieval cues than an item that exists in only one form.

Before you go on to read about long-term memory, look at Table 8.1, which summarizes some important points about the control processes of short-term memory and the implications for teachers. Later in the chapter, the Suggestions for Teaching will help you put these ideas into practice.

Long-Term Memory

We have already referred in a general way to the third memory store, **long-term memory (LTM)**, which is perhaps the most interesting of all. On the basis of

neurological and experimental, evidence, most cognitive psychologists believe that the storage capacity of LTM is unlimited and that it contains a permanent record of everything an individual has learned, although some doubt exists about the latter point (see, for example, W. A. Rogers, Pak, & Fisk, 2007; Schunk, 2004).

The neurological evidence comes from the work of Wilder Penfield (1969), a Canadian neurosurgeon who operated on more than 1,000 patients who experienced epileptic seizures. To determine the source of the seizures, Penfield electrically stimulated various parts of the brain's surface. During this procedure, many patients reported vivid images of long-dormant events from their past. It was as if a neurological video had been turned on.

The experimental evidence, although less dramatic, is just as interesting, and it too has its origins in the early days of information-processing theory. In a typical memory study (such as Tulving & Pearlstone, 1966), participants receive a list of nouns to learn. After giving them ample opportunity to recall as many of the words as possible, researchers provide retrieval cues—for instance, category labels such as "clothing," "food," or "animals." In many cases, participants who are given the cues quickly recall additional items. Experiments on how well people recognize previously seen pictures have produced some startling findings. Thirty-six hours after viewing more than 2,500 pictures, a group of college students correctly identified an average of about 2,250, or 90% (Standing, Conezio, & Haber, 1970).

Before we move on to a discussion of how information is organized in long-term memory, let's make sure we understand what the research mentioned in the previous two paragraphs does and does not imply. It does suggest that there is more information in long-term memory than we can get to on a given occasion. How many of you have had the experience of not being able to recall a piece of information that you knew was in long-term memory, only to be able to recall it some time later? What this research does not suggest, however, is that everything we have ever experienced is stored there in something like a photographic or videographic record. As you now know, information that is not noticed or linked with previously learned information never gets beyond the short-term store. What you will learn shortly is that quite a bit of what is stored in long-term memory is different from when it was first learned. In other words, we often operate on the basis of distorted knowledge. Read on to find out why.

How Information Is Organized in Long-Term Memory

As you have seen, long-term memory plays an influential role throughout the information-processing system. The interests, attitudes,

"theory"

TABLE 8.1 Implications for Instruction: How Findings About the Control Processes of Short-Term Memory Should Influence Your Teaching

Research Finding	Implications
Recognition involves relating a stimulus to information from long-term memory.	Compared with older students, elementary school students have less knowledge stored in long-term memory, and therefore they need structured learning tasks in which one step leads clearly to the next.
Attention is influenced by previous experience stored in long-term memory—we notice what we expect to be important.	Teachers should develop techniques for capturing students' attention and convincing them that the information being presented will be important to them.
Rehearsal prevents the quick disappearance of information from short-term memory. Most children do not begin to rehearse on their own until about age seven.	All children, especially younger ones, can benefit from being taught rehearsal techniques.
Organization of material into chunks makes it much easier to remember.	Teachers can aid students by presenting material in logical chunks and by showing students how to organize information on their own.
Meaningful learning occurs when the learner relates new information to prior ideas and experiences.	Teachers should mediate learning by relating new information to students' cultural knowledge and by helping students to learn techniques of self-mediation.
Visual imagery is easier to recall than abstractions.	Teachers should help students develop learning skills that incorporate visual imagery and other memory-aiding techniques.

skills, and knowledge of the world that reside there influence what we perceive, how we interpret our perceptions, and whether we process information for short-term or long-term storage. In most instances, retrieval of information from long-term memory is extremely rapid and accurate, like finding a book in a well-run library. Accordingly, we can conclude that information in long-term memory must be organized. The nature of this organization is a key area in the study of memory. The insights it provides help to illuminate the encoding and retrieval processes associated with long-term memory.

{ **Information in long-term memory is organized as schemata.** }

Many cognitive psychologists believe that our store of knowledge in long-term memory is organized in terms of **schemata** (which is the plural of *schema* and is related in meaning to Jean Piaget's *scheme*). A schema is typically defined as an abstract structure of information. It is abstract because it summarizes information about many different cases or examples of something, and it is structured because it represents how its own informational components are interrelated. Schemata give us expectations about objects and events (dogs bark, birds fly, students listen to their teachers and study industriously). When our schemata are well formed and a specific event is consistent with our expectation, comprehension occurs. When schemata are poorly structured or absent, learning is slow and uncertain (Bruning, Schraw, Norby, & Ronning, 2004; Lewandowsky & Thomas 2009; Moreno, 2006; Schunk, 2004).

The effect of schemas on memory and comprehension was first investigated during the early 1930s by Sir Frederic Bartlett (1932), an English psychologist. In one experiment, Bartlett had participants read and recall a brief story, titled "The War of the Ghosts," that was based on North American Indian folklore. Because Bartlett's participants had little knowledge of American Indian culture, they had difficulty accurately recalling the story; they omitted certain details and distorted others. The distortions were particularly interesting because they

schemata Plural of *schema*; abstract information structures by which our store of knowledge is organized in long-term memory. *Schemas* is another plural form.

Because people interpret new information and experiences on the basis of existing memory schemes, and because no two people's schemes are identical, each person is likely to represent the same idea or experience in a unique fashion.

© Jeff Greenberg/Photo Edit

reflected an attempt to interpret the story in terms of the logic and beliefs of Western culture. Similar studies, conducted more recently with other kinds of reading materials, reported similar results (Derry, 1996; T. L. Griffiths, Steyvers, & Tenenbaum, 2007). The conclusion that Bartlett and other researchers have drawn is that remembering is not simply a matter of retrieving a true-to-life record of information. People often remember their *interpretations* or *constructions* of something read, seen, or heard (Lampinen & Odegard, 2006). In addition, when they experience crucial gaps in memory, they tend to fill in these blanks with logical reconstructions of what they think must have been. People then report these reconstructions as memories of actual events (Derry, 1996).

Why We Forget

Forgetting is a fact of life. We all do it and will continue to do it for as long as we live. But before we get into the possible reasons why forgetting occurs, we need to clarify exactly what we mean by the term. Forgetting is the inability, often temporary but possibly permanent, to retrieve *previously learned information*. That deliberate choice of wording eliminates from consideration a very common experience that is often referred to as forgetting by the average person: failing to recall something that was never learned in the first place. If a student complains that she can't recall what the teacher said in class, it may be because she was busy checking her e-mail or Facebook page. This is an attention and motivation problem, not a forgetting problem (Wixted, 2010).

So if experimental, neurological, and clinical evidence suggest that long-term memory is a limitless, permanent, and organized storehouse of previously learned information, then why do we sometimes have difficulty getting at that information when we want it? If you're looking for one simple answer, sorry, you've come to the wrong place. There are several possible reasons why forgetting occurs (see Roediger, Weinstein, & Agarwal, 2020). Which explanation best explains a failed recall attempt will depend on the circumstances.

Inadequate Consolidation Sometimes forgetting occurs because the material wasn't adequately learned in the first place. When learning new material, many students will try to learn as much of it as possible in as little time as possible. Students call this *cramming*. Psychologists call it *massed practice*. Whatever the label, it's a terrible tactic because it typically produces a disorganized and poor-quality representation in LTM that is hard to retrieve. A better option is to engage

in *distributed practice*: Study and then restudy smaller chunks of material at regular intervals. This is thought to strengthen the representation of the material in memory and to distinguish it from material learned later, a process memory researchers call *consolidation*. We discuss massed and distributed practice in more detail in the Suggestions for Teaching on pages 178 and 179.

Nonmeaningful Learning A second reason why forgetting occurs is that the information is so different from anything we already know that we can't connect it to existing knowledge schemes in a meaningful way. Recall of this information is marked by omissions and distortions. A good example of how nonmeaningful material negatively affects retrieval from LTM is our discussion in the previous section of Bartlett's research with the "War of the Ghosts" passage. We suggest ways to deal with this problem in the Suggestions for Teaching in this chapter and the next.

Few Opportunities for Retrieval Our third reason is one you probably don't want to hear: You don't take enough tests as you are learning new material! Yes, we know you don't like tests, but that's because they usually have high stakes attached to them (they're used to determine your grade). But tests (short quizzes, actually) can also be used to give you feedback about how well you are learning and, by stimulating you to recall what you learned, strengthen those representations in LTM.

Interference From Other Material Being a student means having to cope with a constant stream of learning material. Inevitably, we encounter ideas that are similar to those we learned earlier but call for different responses. In such cases, interference from material learned earlier, whether in school or out, can make it difficult to come up with the correct response. This happens quite frequently in learning a foreign language because words that look alike mean different things. Take, for example, the French words for hair (*cheveux*) and horse (*cheval*). Students frequently make the wrong choice because of the similarity in spelling and pronunciation. Another example is when a teacher tries to learn the names of a new group of students at the beginning of the year and calls some of them, at least for a while, by the names of the students in the previous class.

Lack of Retrieval Cues Our last explanation concerns the availability of retrieval cues. A retrieval cue can be any information, such as a word, phrase, image, sound, and so on, that is associated with the learned material. Learning does not take place in a vacuum; it occurs in a specific context that includes aspects of the

© Four Oaks/Shutterstock Images

cheveux or cheval?

physical environment, characteristics of the learning material, and associated thoughts. Let's say that as you read this chapter you also take note of the headings and subheadings and create analogies (like thinking of short-term memory as a funnel that's seven chunks wide). If that additional information is present when you want to recall the chapter's content, either because it's given to you or because you can generate it yourself, you're more likely to recall the target information. This is known as the **encoding specificity principle**: Retrieval is more likely to be successful when material that was part of the original encoding is present at the time of recall. The power of retrieval cues is such that one researcher said, "If the right retrieval cue does not come along, the corresponding memory trace might as well not even be there as it will never be retrieved again" (Wixted, 2010, p. 287).

The previous several sections vividly demonstrate the interactive nature of memory. What we know influences what we perceive and how we interpret and store those perceptions. And because our memories of specific events or experiences are assembled, constructed, and sometimes reassembled by the brain over time, accurate and complete recall of information we once stored is not always possible. As a teacher, then, you should pay deliberate attention to how your students use their background knowledge, helping them to use it as accurately and completely as possible to process new information.

LO3 Metacognition

The discussion up to this point has focused on how people attend to, encode, store, and retrieve information. In other words, we have described some basic cognitive processes. But there's another dimension to

Challenging Assumptions

Students Are Learners, Not Just Performers

Visit a school in the last 2 months of winter and you will see teachers preparing their students to perform as well as they possibly can on the state exams in April and May. Ask teachers why they are so focused on the state exams, and they will tell you that the administration has made student performance on the exams a top priority. Ask the administrators why student performance on the exams deserves so much time and energy, and they will tell you that poor student performance on the exams can decrease property values in the community, can mean the replacement—at considerable expense—of an entire curriculum, and can even cost teachers and administrators their jobs. As you will see in Chapter 15, a lot is riding on students' performance on the state exams. And so teachers guide students through the material they expect to be on the tests; teachers go over and over it in an effort to ensure that every student gets every possible test item correct. The teachers lead the students through seemingly endless drill and practice. (Some teachers—and some students—call it "drill and kill.") The teachers work very hard, the students work very hard, and the administrators feel the pressure and keep the pressure on.

Days and weeks of drill and practice, focused on rote learning that serves only to make students perform better on a test, goes against what research tells us about effective learn-

ing. In focusing on discrete information or skills, students have few opportunities to draw on their prior knowledge, to learn in authentic settings, and to explore and investigate so as to understand new information in meaningful contexts. Research shows us that prior knowledge is critical for student learning. Drilling students to perform can kill learning. We believe educational professionals must be held accountable, but they should be held accountable for student learning, not just test performance. If we are content simply to focus on performance, then let's continue to devote each winter to test preparation. But if we value our students as learners instead of performers, then the time has come to end the winter of our discontent. And we should do it now.

What Do You Think?

Does our position accord with your own experience? That is, did you feel as if you were learning material solely for the purpose of answering questions correctly on a state-mandated test and not for any future meaningful use? If so, how can you prepare your students for these exams and still make the learning experience relevant to their lives? Explore this issue further at the "Challenging Assumptions" section of the textbook's Education CourseMate website.

Suggestions for Teaching

Helping Your Students Become Efficient Information Processors

1 **Develop and use a variety of techniques to attract and hold attention, and give your students opportunities to practice and refine their skills in maintaining attention.**

a. Be aware of what will capture your students' attention.

The ability to capture your students' attention is affected by characteristics of the information itself and the learners' related past experiences. Learners are more likely to attend to things they expect to find interesting or meaningful. It is also true that human beings are sensitive to abrupt, sudden changes in their environment. Thus anything that stands out, breaks a rhythm, or is unpredictable is almost certain to command students' attention.

Examples

- Print key words or ideas in extra-large letters on the board.
- Use colored chalk to emphasize important points written on the board.
- When you come to a particularly important part of a lesson, say, "Now really concentrate on this. It's especially important." Then present the idea with intensity and emphasis.
- Start off a lesson with unexpected remarks, such as, "Imagine that you have just inherited a million dollars.. . ."

b. To maintain attention, emphasize the possible utility of learning new ideas.

Although it is possible to overdo attempts at making the curriculum relevant, it never hurts to think of possible ways of relating school learning to the present and future lives of students. When students realize that the basic purpose of school is to help them adapt to their environment, they are more likely to pay close attention to what you are trying to do.

Example

- Teach basic skills—such as arithmetic computation, arithmetic reasoning, spelling, writing, and reading—as part of class projects that relate to students' natural interests (for example, keeping records of money for newspaper deliveries; measuring rainfall, temperature, and wind speed; writing letters to local television stations to express opinions on or request information about television shows).

2 **Point out, and encourage students to recognize, that certain bits of information are important and can be related to what they already know.**

Attention is one control process for the sensory register; the other is recognition. Sometimes the two processes can be used together to induce students to focus on important parts of material to be learned. Sometimes you can urge your students to recognize key features or familiar relationships on their own.

Examples

- Say: "This math problem is very similar to one you solved last week. Does anyone recognize something familiar about this problem?"
- Say: "In this chapter, the same basic point is made in several different ways. As you read, try to recognize and write down as many variations on that basic theme as you can."
- Give students opportunities to express ideas in their own words and relate new knowledge to previous learning.
- Have students practice grouping numbers, letters, or classroom items according to some shared feature, such as odd numbers, multiples of five, letters with circles, or things made of wood.

3 **Show students that they can become more efficient learners by combining previously unrelated facts and concepts into larger chunks.**

Do you recall our description of short-term memory being limited to about five to nine items, or chunks, of information at any point in time? (If you don't, perhaps you should take that as a cue to pay particularly close attention to the contents of this chapter.) We also said that this limit could be fudged somewhat by taking advantage of the principle of chunking. Basically, this involves creating associations between what you're trying to learn and what you already have in long-term memory. In this way, you can take what may have been four or five separate pieces of information and reduce them to one piece.

The power of chunking information into meaningful units was dramatically demonstrated in a study conducted with a single college student of average memory ability and intelligence (Ericsson, Chase, & Faloon, 1980). Over 20 months, he was able to improve his memory for digits from seven to almost 80! Being a track and field buff, he categorized three- and four-digit groups as running times for imaginary races. Thus 3,492 became "3 minutes and 49.2 seconds, near world-record time." Number groups that could not be encoded as running times were encoded as ages. These two chunking techniques accounted for almost 90% of his associations. Part of the reason why chunking works is that it reduces the load on memory. Through combining previously unrelated bits of information into larger units, we actually have less to learn. The other part of the reason is that it creates more coherent and meaningful units, which are easier to recall. If at all possible, try to include lessons on, and opportunities for students to practice, chunking.

---

massed practice
An approach to learning that emphasizes a few long, infrequently spaced study periods.

this story that you need to know about: a more general level of thinking that makes it possible for us to control memory and other cognitive processes. That level of thinking, which is called *metacognition*, refers to the ways that what we know about the nature of our own thought processes affects how we learn and solve problems.

The Nature and Importance of Metacognition

The notion of metacognition was proposed by developmental psychologist John Flavell (1976) to explain why children of different ages deal with learning tasks in different ways. For example, when 7-year-olds are taught how to remember pairs of nouns using both a less effective technique (simply repeating the words) and a

4 **Take advantage of the power of distributed practice.**

If you knew you were going to be tested over the contents of this chapter a few days from now, would you wait until the day before the test and then read the entire chapter a few times, or would you read about one third of the chapter each day, with a quick review several hours later of what you had read, for each of three days before the exam? If you opted for the first approach, you would be engaging in what psychologists call **massed practice**. If you chose the second approach, you would be engaging in **distributed practice**. Would your choice make any difference in your test score? Almost certainly. The superiority of distributed over massed practice for a wide range of materials and learners is well established in the research literature (see, for example, Cepeda et al., 2009; Dempster, 1988; Rohrer & Pashler, 2010; Seabrook, Brown, & Solity, 2005).

Now turn this example around and picture yourself as a primary grade teacher who is writing out a lesson plan to teach the beginning reading skill of grapheme–phoneme (letter–sound) correspondences for 30 minutes each day for the coming week. Your students will perform better on a subsequent test if you divide your lessons into three 10-minute sessions a day rather than one 30-minute session. Distributed practice works for the same reason that chunking works: It reduces the demand on memory.

If your students are intellectually ready to direct their own learning, you should tell them about the relative merits of distributed versus massed practice. Most students not only are unaware of the benefits of distributed study periods but also go to considerable lengths to block or mass the study time devoted to a particular subject, even when that tactic is a hindrance rather than a help (Rohrer & Pashler, 2010).

5 **Organize what you ask your students to learn, and urge older students to organize material on their own.**

At least some items in most sets of information that you ask your students to learn will be related to other items, and you will find it desirable to call attention to interrelationships. The experiment by Bower, Clark, Lesgold, and Winzenz (1969) described earlier, in which one group of students was given a randomly arranged set of items to learn and another group was presented the same items in logically ordered groups, illustrates the value of organization. By placing related items in groups, you reduce the number of chunks to be learned and also make it possible for students to benefit from cues supplied by the interrelationships between items in any given set. And by placing items in logical order, you help students grasp how information at the beginning of a chapter or lesson makes it easier to learn information that is presented later.

Examples

- If students are to learn how to identify trees, birds, rocks, or something similar, group items that are related (for example, deciduous trees and evergreen trees). Call attention to distinctive features and organizational schemes that have been developed.
- Print an outline of a chapter on the board, or give students a duplicated outline, and have them record notes under the various headings. Whenever you give a lecture or demonstration, print an outline on the board. Call attention to the sequence of topics, and demonstrate how various points emerge from or are related to other points.

6 **Make what students learn more meaningful by presenting information in concrete, visual terms.**

To avoid blank stares and puzzled expressions from students when you explain an idea in abstract terms, try using representations that can more easily be visualized. Concrete analogies, for example, offer one effective way to add meaning to material. Consider someone who has no knowledge of basic physics but is trying to understand a passage about the flow of electricity through metal. For this person, statements about crystalline lattice arrays, free-floating electrons, and the effects of impurities will mean very little. However, such abstract ideas can be explained in more familiar terms. You might compare the molecular structure of a metal bar to a Tinkertoy arrangement, for example, or liken the effect of impurities to placing a book in the middle of a row of falling dominoes. Such analogies increase recall and comprehension (Royer & Cable, 1975, 1976).

You should also consider using what are called graphical displays. These are visual-symbolic spatial representations of objects, concepts, and their relationships. Examples of graphical displays include diagrams, matrices, graphs, concept maps, and charts.

Examples

- When you explain or demonstrate, express complex and abstract ideas in several different ways. Be sure to provide plenty of examples.
- Use illustrations, diagrams, and concept maps.
- Make sure the type of visual display used is consistent with the goal of a lesson. For example, when the goal is to understand a cause-and-effect relationship, diagrams that show relationships among objects or concepts should be used; but when the goal is to learn about changes over time, as in plant or animal growth, animation is a better choice than a static display.

more effective technique (imagining the members of each pair doing something together), most of these children will use the less effective technique when given a new set of pairs to learn. Most 10-year-olds, however, will opt to use the more effective method. The explanation for this finding is that the 7-year-old has not had enough learning experiences to recognize that some problem-solving methods are better than others. To the younger child, one means is as good as another.

This lack of metacognitive knowledge makes true strategic learning impossible for young children (Ornstein, Grammer, & Coffman, 2010).

One way to grasp the essence of metacognition is to contrast it with cognition. The term *cognition* is used to describe

> **distributed practice**
> The practice of breaking up learning tasks into small, easy-to-manage pieces that are learned over several relatively brief sessions.

metacognition
Knowledge about the operations of cognition and how to use them to achieve a learning goal.

the ways in which information is processed—that is, the ways it is attended to, recognized, encoded, stored in memory for various lengths of time, retrieved from storage, and used for one purpose or another. **Metacognition** refers to our knowledge about those operations and how they might best be used to achieve a learning goal. As Flavell put it:

> I am engaging in metacognition . . . if I notice that I am having more trouble learning A than B; if it strikes me that I should double-check C before accepting it as a fact; if it occurs to me that I had better scrutinize each and every alternative in any multiple-choice type task situation before deciding which is the best one; if I become aware that I am not sure what the experimenter really wants me to do; if I sense that I had better make a note of D because I may forget it; if I think to ask someone about E to see if I have it right. Such examples could be multiplied endlessly. (1976, p. 232)

Metacognition is obviously a very broad concept. It covers everything an individual can know that relates to how information is processed (see W. Schneider, 2010; Van Overschelde, 2008). To get a better grasp of this concept, you may find it helpful to think of metacognition as being made up of *declarative, conditional,* and *procedural* components.

Declarative knowledge can be thought of as "knowing that" and is composed of

- *Knowledge-of-person variables*: for example, knowing that you are good at learning verbal material but poor at learning mathematical material, or knowing that you quickly forget information that is not rehearsed or encoded.

- *Knowledge-of-task variables*: for instance, knowing that passages with long sentences and unfamiliar words are usually harder to understand than passages that are more simply written.

- *Knowledge-of-strategy variables*: for example, knowing that mnemonic devices (we describe these in the next chapter) make it easier to store and retrieve information from LTM in verbatim form, but that concept maps (also described in the next chapter) aid comprehension of a reading passage.

Conditional knowledge concerns knowing when and why we use certain learning processes in certain circumstances. Knowing that good readers first skim a reading passage to learn about its length and structure and to gain some familiarity with it, and that effective study requires a certain minimum amount of time with no distractions present are examples of conditional knowledge.

Metacognition refers to the knowledge we have about how we learn. It is a key component of our ability to regulate our learning processes.

Procedural knowledge involves knowing how to use various cognitive processes. Examples include knowing how to skim a passage versus reading it for comprehension, knowing how to test one's comprehension of a passage, and knowing how to create effective concept maps.

Age Trends in Metacognition

Because metacognitive knowledge develops gradually throughout childhood and adolescence, there are significant differences in what younger and older children know about their cognitive processes and how to control them. The following summary of research findings (see Duell, 1986; Larkin, 2010; W. Schneider, 2010; B. Schwartz, 2011; Waters & Kunnmann, 2010) should give you some idea of what to expect with children of different ages:

- In terms of diagnosing task difficulty, most 6-year-olds know that more familiar items are easier to remember than less familiar items and that a small set of items is easier to recall than a large set of items. What 6-year-olds do not yet realize is that the amount of information they can recall immediately after they study it is limited.

- Similar findings have been obtained for reading tasks. Most second graders know that interest, familiarity, and story length influence comprehension and recall. However, they are relatively unaware of the effect of how ideas are sequenced,

Chapter 8: Information-Processing Theory

the introductory and summary qualities of first and last paragraphs, and the relationship between reading goals and tactics. Sixth graders, by contrast, are much more aware of the effects of these variables on comprehension and recall.

- Most young children know very little about the role their own capabilities play in learning. For example, not until about 9 years of age do most children realize that their recall right after they study something is limited. Consequently, children through the third grade usually overestimate how much they can store in and retrieve from short-term memory.

- Many kindergarten and first grade children try to remember a set of objects by using such techniques as naming them, grouping them in categories, arranging them in alphabetical order, or creating a story about them. But fewer of them can explain why these techniques work. Many fourth and fifth graders, however, do understand how these tactics aid recall.

- In terms of monitoring the progress of learning, most children younger than 7 or 8 are not very proficient at determining when they know something well enough to pass a memory test. Also, most first graders typically don't know what they don't know. When given multiple opportunities to study and recall a lengthy set of pictures, 6-year-olds chose to study pictures they had previously seen and recalled, as well as ones they hadn't. Third graders, by contrast, focused on previously unseen pictures.

Insight into one's learning processes improves with age.

The general conclusion that emerges from these findings is that the youngest school-age children have only limited knowledge of how their cognitive processes work and when to use them. Consequently, primary grade children do not systematically analyze learning tasks, formulate plans for learning, use appropriate techniques of enhancing memory and comprehension, or monitor their progress because they do not (some would say cannot) understand the benefits of doing these things. But as the two studies we are about to discuss indicate, even primary grade children are capable of using what they know under the right circumstances to enhance their learning and of benefiting, both immediately and years later, from metacognitive instruction and feedback.

In the first study (Waters & Kunnmann, 2010), first graders were asked to learn the names of eight pictured items and were told that pairs of items belonged to the same category (e.g., pants and hat are clothing, shovel and rake are tools). The children were then told to arrange the items in any way that would make it easier for them to recall later. Not only did they arrange most of the items in category pairs, but they were able to explain that they did so to make it easier for them to recall as many items as possible (on average, about 87%). Now here's the interesting part of this study: When these same children were given a set of 16 items (four per category), their performance and metacognitive awareness dropped off considerably. The classroom implication is that young children can be prompted to demonstrate metacognitive awareness, but only on tasks that are well within their working-memory capabilities.

The second study (Ornstein, Grammer, & Coffman, 2010) demonstrated the value of providing first graders with both memory instruction ("Remember to read out loud what you wrote to see if it makes sense"; "To help you remember which number is in the tens place, write a T above it, and to help you remember which number is in the ones place, write an O above it") and metacognitive feedback ("Tell me how you solved that problem"; "Let me explain why labeling the place values of a number is a good way to remember them"). By the fourth grade, these same students were more likely to use such study skills as note taking, rereading, and self-testing than were students whose first grade teachers provided very little memory instruction and metacognitive feedback.

The main implication for classroom instruction that flows from the research on metacognition is that you can encourage your students to develop their metacognitive skills and knowledge by thinking about the various conditions that affect how they learn and remember. The very youngest students (through third grade) should be told periodically that such cognitive behaviors as describing, recalling, guessing, and understanding mean different things, produce different results, and vary in how well they fit a task's demands. For older elementary school and middle school students, explain the learning process and focus on the circumstances in which different learning tactics are likely to be useful. Then have students keep a diary or log in which they note when they use learning tactics, which ones, and with what success. Look for cases in which good performance corresponds to frequent reported use of tactics and positively reinforce those individuals. Encourage greater use of tactics among students whose performance and reported use of them are below average.

Next we examine several ways in which you can use computer-based technology to improve your students' information-processing skills for a variety of learning tasks.

LO4 Technology as an Information-Processing Tool

Many school tasks place strenuous demands on students' information-processing skills because they involve a considerable amount of new and somewhat abstract information. Computer-based technology can lighten this burden by representing information in meaningful ways and letting students manipulate ideas in realistic settings. For instance, software programs can help a learner grasp an idea for a musical composition, see the structure of her writing plans, watch chemical molecules react, or provide complex environments, complete with problems that need solutions.

But as you read through this section, please keep in mind what we said earlier about technology and other teaching tools: There is no one-size-fits-all solution to the challenge of teaching others. Technology, as useful as it can be for helping you achieve certain goals, has potential costs. Here's one example of what we mean. Because human beings are limited in how much information we can process at any point in time, students

Web 2.0 technologies can enable children from different cultures to share experiences in shared virtual environments.

can easily become overloaded, lose track of the point of an assignment, and be unable to recall much of the material they encounter as they read and click on the links of web pages and hypermedia programs (Carr, 2010). How do we know this is so? Research (e.g., Greenfield, 2009; Ophir, Nass, & Wagner, 2009) has demonstrated this outcome many times. In one case, a group of students watched a news anchor read stories while headlines about sports, weather, and other news of the day slowly crawled along the bottom of the screen. The other group watched the same broadcast but with the news crawl taken out. Students in the first group recalled significantly fewer facts about the stories read by the anchor than did students in the second group (Greenfield, 2009). The solution for teachers is twofold. First, teach students how to be disciplined and purposeful users of technology. Second, choose hypermedia programs (those that contain print, pictorial, and/or animated sources of information with links to other pages that can be examined in any order the learner chooses) that have the smallest number of features that will still allow you to accomplish your instructional goal.

Technology Tools for Writing

Because of its flexibility, technology can be used in a variety of ways to make writing less threatening and to increase both the quantity and quality of students' writing. Here's just one example: In classrooms where computers are networked, teachers can use a technique called an electronic read-around. Sitting at separate computers, each student writes on a topic the teacher gives. Each student then clicks on an icon representing another student's computer, reads what that student wrote, and provides feedback in a different font at the end of the document. This process is repeated until each student has read and commented on each other student's text. Students then use the comments to revise and edit their own pieces (Strassman & D'Amore, 2002).

Technology Tools for Reading

As with writing, the use of electronic support systems to increase students' reading skills has increased around the world (Lai, Chang, & Ye, 2006; Llabo, 2002). In comparison with primary grade students who read a print version of a story, students who listened to a story from a CD-ROM storybook significantly increased their sight word vocabulary, reading level, and ability to retell the story accurately and completely (K. I. Matthew, 1996; McKenna, Cowart, & Watkins, 1997). When third graders had to read a CD story themselves but were able to use such other features as clicking on words and illustrations to obtain pronunciations and definitions, their retelling scores did not differ from those of children who read a print version, but they did score significantly higher on comprehension questions (Doty, Popplewell, & Byers, 2001).

Technology Tools for Science and Math

In mathematics and science, Marcia Linn (1992) and other prominent researchers have argued that students should spend less time manually calculating and plotting data and more time using technology to summarize and interpret data, look for trends, and predict relationships. To help teachers put this philosophy into practice, Linn and others created the Web-Based Inquiry Science Environment (WISE) Project (http://wise.berkeley.edu). Based largely on constructivist learning principles and 15 years of classroom research (Slotta & Linn, 2009), the WISE website contains a variety of science projects that teachers can adapt to local curricula and to state and national standards. The overarching goal of the WISE learning environment is to help students make connections among science ideas rather than memorize isolated facts whose relevance is not understood and that are soon forgotten. For each project, students have to locate relevant information on the web, record and organize their findings in an electronic notebook, and participate in online discussions to refine their procedures and conclusions. The Houses in the Desert project, for example, requires pairs of middle school students to design a desert house that will be comfortable to live in. Using resources available on the web, students have to (among other things) analyze the suitability of various materials for walls, roofs, and windows and perform a heat-flow analysis. The WISE site also allows students to compare climate data in a desert with climate data from their own community (M. C. Linn & Slotta, 2000).

Technology Tools for Art and Music

As you may be aware, computer tools are also being used in the fine and performing arts. Art education, for instance, benefits from electronic tools such as the draw and paint modules that quickly erase or alter ideas. Students can use these tools to mimic the branching, spiraling, and exploding structures of nature (as seen, for example, in trees, vines, and flowers) (Lach, Little, & Nazzaro, 2003), and they can create abstract patterns by repeating, changing the horizontal and vertical orientation, and changing the alignment of a basic pattern

(Yoerg, 2002). With these tools, students can also draw objects in two-point perspective (B. Patterson, 2002) and create stylized portraits by using shadows, contour lines, stippling, and cross-hatching (Mathes, 2002).

For the music classroom, there are tools such as digital oscilloscopes that help students understand relationships between pitch and wavelength. In addition, CD technology can be used to present graphical representations of notes as they are played, sections of which can be saved and compared with other verses of the same song or with other songs, thereby helping students understand themes and patterns in music. Moreover, computer tools such as musical instrument digital interface and formal instrumental music tuition allow students to compose at the keyboard, play a musical instrument and record it on a computer, and play one part of a multi-instrument piece while the program plays the other instruments (Peters, 2001; Reninger, 2000; Seddon & O'Neill, 2006). Students can explore concepts of pitch, duration, sound combination, repetition, and melody and engage in the process of musical thinking.

© Sander Hulberts/iStockphoto

> **Virtual environments provide rich content and context that can support collaborative learning.**

Multimedia, Hypermedia, and Virtual Environments

As mentioned in previous chapters, multimedia encyclopedias, databases, and libraries provide students with a wide variety of information resources.

Multimedia Tools Multimedia tools offer multiple views (text, photographs, digitized video, animation, sound) of difficult concepts that can enrich student understanding of the topic. The use of multimedia tools is related to such information-processing concepts as meaningful learning, the dual coding of information, the use of visual imagery, and elaborative rehearsal (Leacock & Nesbit, 2007; R. E. Mayer & Moreno, 2002, 2003; S. K. Reed, 2006).

Hypermedia Tools Hypermedia technology exists when multimedia information can be nonsequentially accessed, examined, and constructed by users, thereby enabling them to move from one information resource to another while controlling which options to take (Grabe & Grabe, 2007). There are clear advantages to hypermedia, such as the richness of the network of ideas, the compact storage of information, the rapid nonlinear access to information, the flexible use of information, and the learner's control over the system. Not surprisingly, it has been suggested that hypermedia tools radically alter the way people read, write, compute, and perhaps even think (Keengwe, Onchwari, Wachira, 2008; S. C. Yang, 2001).

Virtual Environments By combining multimedia and hypermedia capabilities, researchers and designers have developed rich, complex virtual environments in which multiple learners can engage individual or collaborative learning experiences. (We mentioned these environments, called multiuser virtual environments, in Chapter 2.) One such environment is Quest Atlantis (http:// atlantis.crlt.indiana.edu), which has been well researched and documented (Barab, Gresalfi, et al., 2009; Barab, Scott et al., 2009; M. Thomas, Barab, & Tuzun, 2009) and continues

WHAT ELSE? *RIP & REVIEW* **CARDS IN THE BACK**

to attract much attention from researchers, teachers, parents, and organizations such as the National Science Foundation, the MacArthur Foundation, and NASA. We will revisit Quest Atlantis in Chapter 10, but it is mentioned here as an example of how information across a variety of content areas can be engaged by students.

The virtual world of Quest Atlantis includes various kinds of learning experiences for students: quests, missions, and units. Quests are tasks that are tied to particular areas of the curriculum to ensure that students acquire content knowledge. Missions combine a number of tasks and other learning opportunities that are integrated through general problem-solving exercises and driven by a narrative or story line. Units provide teachers with lesson plans that combine virtual and face-to-face learning activities. For example, the Taiga Water Quality Unit in Quest Atlantis challenges students to address an ecological situation that has resulted in dead and dying fish in Taiga Park. Students acquire information by navigating through the park to collect data and evidence to make a recommendation about how to solve the problem. After deciding what action to take, students then travel 20 years into the future to see the consequences of their decisions.

9

SOCIAL COGNITIVE THEORY

LEARNING OBJECTIVES

After studying this chapter, you will be able to . . .

LO1 Define and provide examples of self-regulation and self-efficacy, and describe how they contribute to achievement.

LO2 Explain what it means to be a self-regulated learner and note how teachers can help students acquire this capability.

LO3 Summarize research findings on various aspects of social cognitive theory.

LO4 Note how technology can be used to promote self-regulated learning.

In the last two chapters, we looked at two very different descriptions of how learning occurs. Operant conditioning focuses exclusively on the role of observable, external events on learning new behaviors and strengthening or weakening existing ones. The strength of operant conditioning is the insight it provides about how environmental consequences affect learning. Its main weakness is that it offers no insights into what people do with that information.

Information-processing theory, on the other hand, focuses almost exclusively on the role of internal processes in learning. In this view, people are exposed to stimuli, and whether and how they attend to, encode, store, and retrieve that information influences what they know and can do. But information-processing theory has very little to say about how the social setting in which behavior occurs influences what people learn.

That brings us to this chapter, where we will examine a third approach that shares common ground with operant conditioning and information-processing theory but goes beyond both. Known initially as *social learning theory* and more recently as **social cognitive theory**, this explanation of learning was based on the premise that neither spontaneous behavior nor reinforcement is necessary for learning to occur. New behaviors could also be learned by observing and imitating a model. The current version of social cognitive theory incorporates elements of both operant conditioning and information processing, and it emphasizes how behavioral and personal factors interact with the social setting in which behavior occurs.

Albert Bandura (1986, 1997, 2001, 2002) is generally considered to be the driving force behind social cognitive theory. His goal is to explain how learning results from interactions among three factors: (1) personal characteristics, such as the various cognitive processes covered in Chapter 8 as well as self-perceptions and emotional states; (2) behavioral patterns; and (3) the social environment, such as interactions with others. Bandura calls the process of interaction among these three elements **triadic reciprocal causation**. This impressive-sounding mouthful is not as difficult to understand as it sounds. *Triadic* simply means having three elements, and *reciprocal* indicates that the elements influence one another. The entire term means that one's internal processes, behavior, and social environment (the "triadic" part of the term) can affect one another (the "reciprocal" part) to produce learning (the "causation" part). To simplify our writing and your reading, we will refer to Bandura's model of triadic reciprocal causation as the *triadic model*.

Bandura and others (e.g., Pajares, 2009; Schunk, 1998, 2001; Zimmerman, 2000) are particularly interested in using social cognitive theory to describe how people become *self-regulated* learners.

LO1 Self-Regulation and Self-Efficacy, and How They Affect Learning

Social cognitive theory assumes that people, and not environmental forces, are the predominant cause of their own behavior. Bandura uses the term **personal agency** to refer to the potential control we have over our own behavior, and he believes that our capacity for personal agency grows out of two capabilities: *self-regulation* and *self-efficacy* (J. Martin, 2004).

The Nature of Self-Regulation

What does self-regulation mean? Basically, it refers to the ways in which we alter our behavior in order to achieve a goal in response to different forces without being prompted to do so. The cruise control feature in your car is a simple nonhuman example. You set it at, say, 65 miles per hour, and the computer adjusts the throttle to maintain that speed as the car travels up and down hills or encounters strong winds. In similar fashion, people regulate their own behavior as they encounter different forces. A teacher who modifies a particular day's lesson plan to capitalize

social cognitive theory An explanation of how people learn to become self-regulated learners through the interactive effects of their personal characteristics, behaviors, and social reinforcement.

triadic reciprocal causation The conceptual foundation of social cognitive theory, which specifies that learned capabilities are the product of interactions among an individual's personal characteristics, behaviors, and social environment.

personal agency The idea of people (rather than environmental forces) as the primary cause of their own behavior.

{ **Triadic reciprocal causation: behavior is the result of interactions among personal characteristics, behavior, and environmental factors** }

on students' interest in a major news story, monitors students' reaction to the new lesson, compares her students' and her own performance against an internal standard, and rewards herself if she feels that standard has been met is illustrating the essence of self-regulation. But students who have to be constantly reminded to set aside sufficient time for homework and to eliminate distractions are not demonstrating self-regulated behavior. In essence, self-regulation involves spontaneously bringing appropriate personal resources to bear on a problem.

Self-regulation: consistently and spontaneously using various capabilities in new situations

When applied to the classroom, **self-regulated learning** involves, among other things, knowing under what circumstances to use particular learning techniques and why they work (part of the metacognition concept we introduced in the previous chapter), analyzing the characteristics of learning tasks, using various techniques for learning new information, using various techniques for remaining calm and confident, estimating how much time it will take to complete a task, monitoring one's progress, knowing when and from whom to seek help, and feeling a sense of pride and satisfaction about accomplishing one's learning goals (Paris & Paris, 2001; Pressley & Hilden, 2006; Schunk, 2001; Zimmerman & Kitsantas, 2005).

Being able to regulate one's cognitive processes is a critically important capability for students to acquire for at least three reasons:

1. As students get older, and especially when they get into the middle and high school grades, they are expected to assume greater responsibility for their learning than in earlier grades; thus, they receive less prompting and guidance from teachers and parents.

2. As students move through the primary, elementary, middle school, and high school grades, they

have to learn and be tested over increasingly larger amounts of more complex material. With less parental and teacher supervision, the temptation to put off studying or to do it superficially increases. Unfortunately, the damaging long-term consequences of poorly regulated academic behavior (low grades and diminished opportunities for higher education and employment) are not immediately apparent.

3. Because of the rapid pace of change in today's world, individuals increasingly need to be self-directed, autonomous learners not just during their school years but over their lifetimes (Zimmerman, 1990, 2002).

Although the skill of self-regulation is important to academic success, some students are better at it than others. The characteristic that is most strongly related to and best explains differences in self-regulation is perceived self-efficacy. In the next section, we describe self-efficacy and its relationship to self-regulation.

Pause& Reflect *Should the development of self-regulated learning skills be left to parents and out-of-school experiences, or should this be a primary goal of our education system? If the latter, when should it begin?*

The Role of Self-Efficacy in Self-Regulation

Self-efficacy refers to how capable or prepared we believe we are to handle particular kinds of tasks (Bandura, 1997, 2001, 2002). For example, a student may have a high level of self-efficacy for mathematical reasoning—a feeling that she can master any math task she might encounter in a particular course—but have a low level of self-efficacy for critical analysis of English literature.

Self-regulation is important because students are expected to become increasingly independent learners as they progress through school.

Self-efficacy beliefs occupy a central role in social cognitive theory because of their widespread and significant effects. They help influence whether people think optimistically or pessimistically, act in ways that are

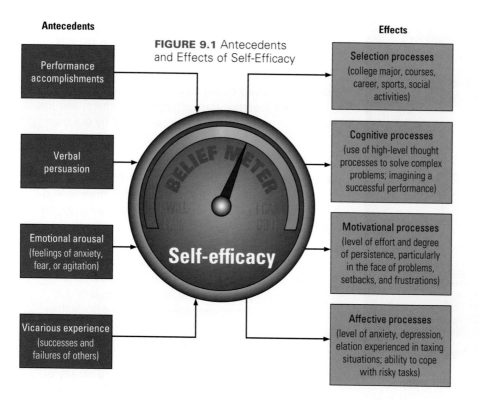

Antecedents

- Performance accomplishments
- Verbal persuasion
- Emotional arousal (feelings of anxiety, fear, or agitation)
- Vicarious experience (successes and failures of others)

BELIEF METER

I WILL FAIL — I CAN DO IT

Self-efficacy

FIGURE 9.1 Antecedents and Effects of Self-Efficacy

Effects

- Selection processes (college major, courses, career, sports, social activities)
- Cognitive processes (use of high-level thought processes to solve complex problems; imagining a successful performance)
- Motivational processes (level of effort and degree of persistence, particularly in the face of problems, setbacks, and frustrations)
- Affective processes (level of anxiety, depression, elation experienced in taxing situations; ability to cope with risky tasks)

beneficial or detrimental to achieving goals, approach or avoid tasks, engage tasks with a high or low level of motivation, persevere for a short or lengthy period of time when tasks are difficult, and are motivated or demoralized by failure. These beliefs are often called the single most important factor that affects the strength of a person's sense of agency.

> **Self-efficacy: how capable one feels to handle particular kinds of tasks**

Students who believe they are capable of successfully performing a task are more likely than students with low levels of self-efficacy to use such self-regulating skills as concentrating on the task, creating strategies, using appropriate tactics, managing time effectively, monitoring their own performance, and making whatever adjustments are necessary to improve their future learning efforts. By contrast, students who do not believe they have the cognitive skills to cope with the demands of a particular subject are unlikely to do much

serious reading or thinking about the subject or to spend much time preparing for tests. Such students are often referred to as lazy, inattentive, lacking initiative, and dependent on others. They often find themselves in a vicious circle as their avoidance of challenging tasks and their dependence on others reduces their chances of developing self-regulation skills and a strong sense of self-efficacy (Bandura, 1997; Pajares, 2009).

Self-efficacy can be affected by one or more of several factors and, in turn, can affect one or more of several important self-regulatory behaviors (see Figure 9.1).

Factors That Affect Self-Efficacy Four factors that affect self-efficacy are shown on the "Antecedents" side of Figure 9.1.

1. *Performance accomplishments.* One obvious way in which we develop a sense of what we can and cannot do in various areas is by thinking about how well we have performed in the past on a given task or a set of closely related tasks. If, for example, my friends are always reluctant to have me on their team for neighborhood baseball games, and if I strike out or ground out far more often than I hit, I will probably conclude that I just do not have whatever skills it takes to be a competitive baseball player. Conversely, if my personal history of performance in school includes mostly grades of A and I consistently rank among the top 10 students, my sense of academic self-efficacy is likely to be quite high.

2. *Verbal persuasion.* A second source of influence mentioned by Bandura—verbal persuasion—is also fairly obvious. We frequently try to convince a child, student, relative, spouse, friend, or coworker that he or she has the ability to perform some task at an acceptable level. Perhaps you can recall feeling somewhat more confident about handling some task (such as college classes) after having several family members and friends express their confidence in your ability.

 Self-efficacy beliefs influence the use of self-regulating skills.

A person's self-efficacy for a particular task is influenced primarily by past performance but also by encouragement from others, emotional reactions, and observation of others.

© Paul Barton/CORBIS

3. *Emotional arousal.* A third source of influence is more subtle. It is the emotions we feel as we prepare to engage in a task. Individuals with low self-efficacy for science may become anxious, fearful, or restless prior to attending chemistry class or taking an exam in physics. Those with high self-efficacy may feel assured, comfortable, and eager to display what they have learned. Some individuals are acutely aware of these emotional states, and their emotions become a cause as well as a result of their high or low self-efficacy.

4. *Vicarious experience.* Finally, our sense of self-efficacy may be influenced by observing the successes and failures of individuals with whom we identify. This is what Bandura referred to as vicarious experience. If I take note of the fact that a sibling or neighborhood friend who is like me in many respects but is a year older has successfully adjusted to high school, I may feel more optimistic about my own adjustment the following year. We will have more to say a bit later in this chapter about the role of observing and imitating a model.

Pause& Reflect *On the basis of your own experience, do you agree that personal experience is the most important factor affecting self-efficacy? What steps can you take to raise the probability that your students will experience more successes than failures?*

Of these four self-efficacy factors, personal accomplishment is the most important because it carries the greatest weight. As important as it is to feel calm and be free of crippling fear or anxiety, to have parents, peers, and teachers express their confidence in us, and to have successful models to observe, actual failures are likely to override these other influences. In other words, our feelings, the comments of others, and the actions of models need to be confirmed by our own performance if they are to be effective contributors to self-efficacy.

Types of Behavior Affected by Self-Efficacy The four types of behavior that are at least partly influenced by an individual's level of self-efficacy are shown on the "Effects" side of Figure 9.1.

1. *Selection processes.* By the term *selection processes*, we mean the way a person goes about selecting goals and activities. Individuals with a strong sense of self-efficacy, particularly if it extends over several areas, are more likely than others to consider a variety of goals and participate in a variety of activities. They may, for example, think about a wide range of career options, explore several majors while in college, take a variety of courses, participate in different sporting activities, engage in different types of social activities, and have a wide circle of friends.

Self-efficacy influences goals and activities, cognitive processes, perseverance, and emotions.

2. *Cognitive processes.* Individuals with high self-efficacy, compared with their peers who are low in self-efficacy, tend to use higher-level thought processes (such as analysis, synthesis, and evaluation) to solve complex problems. Thus, in preparing a classroom report or a paper, students with low self-efficacy may do little more than repeat a set of facts found in various sources. In contrast, students with high self-efficacy often discuss similarities and differences, inconsistencies and contradictions, and make evaluations about the validity and usefulness of the information they have found. Another cognitive difference is that people high in self-efficacy are more likely to visualize themselves being successful at some challenging task, whereas individuals low in self-efficacy are more likely to imagine disaster. This leads to differences in the next category of behaviors—motivation.

FIGURE 9.2 Phases and Categories of the Self-Regulation Cycle
SOURCES: Zimmerman (2000, 2008); Zimmerman & Kitsantas (2005).

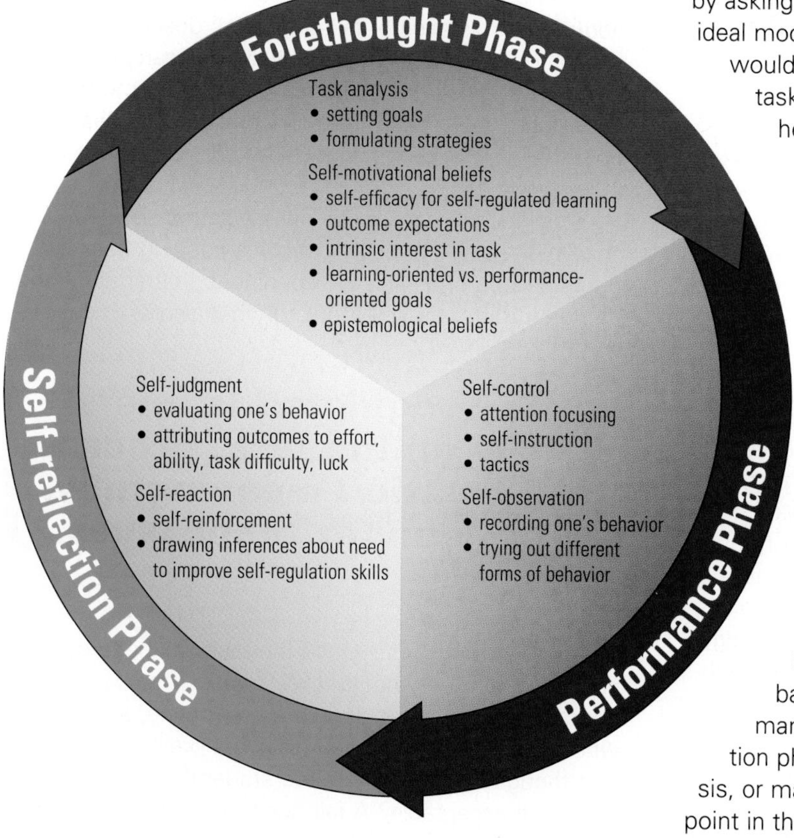

Forethought Phase

Task analysis
- setting goals
- formulating strategies

Self-motivational beliefs
- self-efficacy for self-regulated learning
- outcome expectations
- intrinsic interest in task
- learning-oriented vs. performance-oriented goals
- epistemological beliefs

Self-control
- attention focusing
- self-instruction
- tactics

Self-observation
- recording one's behavior
- trying out different forms of behavior

Self-judgment
- evaluating one's behavior
- attributing outcomes to effort, ability, task difficulty, luck

Self-reaction
- self-reinforcement
- drawing inferences about need to improve self-regulation skills

Self-reflection Phase

Performance Phase

Now that we have established the importance of self-efficacy to self-regulation, we can turn our attention to the nuts and bolts of self-regulation. Let's do this by asking the following question: If we were to build an ideal model of a self-regulated learner, what capabilities would it include and at what points in dealing with a task would they be used? The model we describe here comes largely from the work of Barry Zimmerman (2000, 2002), a leading social cognitive theorist and researcher.

The Components of a Self-Regulatory System

Self-regulatory processes and their related beliefs can be grouped into one of three categories, each of which, ideally, comes into play at different points in time in the course of pursuing a goal (see Figure 9.2). Notice how we qualified the first sentence of this paragraph by saying that the various categories of self-regulatory processes *ideally* come into play at different points during the process. Keep in mind that learners can, for example, cycle back to the forethought phase from the performance phase before going on to the self-reflection phase, begin a task without doing a task analysis, or make self-judgments and self-reactions at any point in the process (Muis, 2007).

Forethought Phase As its name implies, the forethought phase occurs prior to the beginning of a task. At this point we would like to see learners think about what they want to accomplish (set goals) and how they are going to achieve their goals (formulate strategies).

These initial steps, as well as the ones to come later, will be of little value to learners if they aren't motivated to use them. This is why self-motivational beliefs are part of this phase. Self-efficacy beliefs, as you can probably guess from what you read earlier, pertain to how capable people believe themselves to be about using self-regulatory processes. Outcome expectations refer to predictions about the consequences of achieving a goal (such as praise, prestige, increased responsibility). Intrinsic interest can maintain motivation for self-regulated learning in situations in which external rewards are either unavailable or unattractive. Goal orientations can be learning oriented or performance oriented. Individuals who have a learning orientation are interested in learning primarily for its internal rewards (better understanding of the world in which they live, increased competence) and are more apt to be motivated to use self-regulation processes than are performance-oriented individuals, whose goal is

3. *Motivational processes.* Those who rate their capabilities as higher than average can be expected to work harder and longer to achieve a goal than those who feel less capable. This difference should be particularly noticeable when individuals experience frustrations (poor-quality instruction, for example) and setbacks (such as a serious illness).

4. *Affective processes.* Finally, when faced with a challenging task, the individual with high self-efficacy is more likely to experience excitement, curiosity, and an eagerness to get started rather than the sense of anxiety, depression, and impending disaster that many individuals with low self-efficacy feel.

Before leaving this discussion of self-efficacy, we would like to make one last point about its role in self-regulated behavior. As important as self-efficacy is, you should realize that other factors play a role as well. In addition to feeling capable of successfully completing a particular task, students also need to possess basic knowledge and skills, anticipate that their efforts will be appropriately rewarded, and value the knowledge, skill, or activity that they have been asked to learn or complete (Pajares, 2009).

to achieve a higher score or grade than others. Epistemological beliefs refer to what a person believes about the nature of knowledge and how we come to know things. We can believe, for example, that knowledge is certain (there is a correct, clear-cut answer for every question or problem that, once known, does not change) or that it evolves as scholars conduct further inquiries. We can believe that the acquisition of knowledge occurs either quickly or gradually. We can believe that authority figures are the sole source of all knowledge or that knowledge is also acquired through personal observation, experimentation, and reasoning. And we can believe that knowledge is composed of mostly unrelated pieces or that it is organized, like schemas, into integrated and interrelated bodies.

The significance of epistemological beliefs is that they have been shown to affect all aspects of self-regulated learning. For example, students who believe that knowledge is a collection of mostly unrelated facts are more likely to use rote rehearsal tactics than are students who believe that knowledge is best thought of as interrelated bodies of information whose structure is likely to change over time. In the course of doing a research project, students who believe that knowledge is certain and unchanging may see nothing wrong with consulting out-of-date reference materials. Students who believe that learning either occurs quickly or not at all are less likely to persevere with difficult tasks or to try a different approach when their first approach fails than are students who believe that learning occurs gradually and with effort (Muis, 2007).

Performance Phase At this point, the learner is faced with the task and actually has to do something (sound familiar?). The first part of this phase is to approach the task in a disciplined manner. This involves focusing attention on the task (ignoring distractions, executing the task at a slower pace than normal, and not thinking about prior mistakes or failed efforts), describing either silently or out loud the steps involved in carrying out the task, and using specific *tactics* to either memorize information in verbatim form or comprehend ideas and how they relate to one another (we discuss these later in this chapter).

The second part of this phase, self-observation (also known as self-monitoring), involves keeping track of one's performance and the conditions that affect it and trying out different self-regulatory behaviors.

{ **Self-regulated learners focus on the task, process information meaningfully, and monitor themselves.** }

Self-Reflection Phase Once the task has been completed, the learner should take stock of what was done, whether the results were acceptable, and whether changes are called for. In all likelihood, the first thought that will cross the student's mind is, was the result acceptable? A fair question, but one that can be answered in different ways. One answer may be in terms of how well the student mastered the teacher's objectives. Another answer may involve a comparison with the student's past performance. A third answer

TeachSource Video Case

Performance Assessment: Student Presentation in a High School English Class

Go to the Education CourseMate website and watch the video, study the artifacts in the case, and reflect upon the following questions:

1. How do the class presentations in this Video Case allow students to practice their self-regulation skills?

2. How does the peer assessment component of this literature lesson illustrate the self-reflection phase of Zimmerman's model?

Chapter 9: Social Cognitive Theory

may involve a comparison with classmates. If the task involved a group effort, a fourth answer may be in terms of the student's contribution to the group. The next step in this self-evaluation process may be a consideration of the factors that played a major role in one's success or failure. This involves identifying what are called *causal attributions*. Whether we judge our performance to be a success or a failure will likely be attributed to one or more of the following causes: ability, effort, task difficulty, and luck (we describe these in more detail in Chapter 11). Self-reinforcement refers to whatever positive thoughts and feelings we experience as a result of meeting or exceeding our expectations. Lastly, the ideal learner draws some conclusions about whether and how to improve his or her self-regulatory skills.

As we noted earlier, learning to become a self-regulated learner (the terms *self-directed*, *autonomous*, and *strategic* learner are also used) is one of the most important outcomes of schooling. These skills are essential to achieving success in school and in life. That being the case, it's time to examine what *you* can do to help students acquire this critical capability.

LO2 Helping Students Become Self-Regulated Learners

How Well Prepared Are Students to Be Self-Regulated Learners?

We would like to be able to tell you that most students possess the self-regulated learning (SRL) skills we have discussed, but unfortunately, we cannot. Although evidence exists that students are more likely to use effective learning skills as they get older (Greene & Azevedo, 2009; W. Schneider, Knopf, & Stefanek, 2002) and that some students behave strategically by using different learning skills for different tasks (Hadwin, Winne, Stockley, Nesbit, & Woszczyna, 2001), many do not do so either systematically or consistently. Their attempts at encoding rarely go beyond rote rehearsal (for example, rereading a textbook chapter), simple organizational schemes (outlining), and various cuing devices (underlining or highlighting), and they have a poor sense of how well prepared they are to take a test (Bond, Miller, & Kennon, 1987; Callender & McDaniel, 2009; Karpicke,

Students who are self-regulated learners tend to achieve at high levels by using appropriate cognitive and metacognitive skills for particular tasks in the right way and at the right time.

Butler, & Roediger, 2009; Kornell & Bjork, 2007; McDaniel, Howard, & Einstein, 2009; Peverly, Brobst, Graham, & Shaw, 2003; Winne & Jamieson-Noel, 2002, 2003). Because of its complexity, you can expect expertise in SRL to develop gradually over many years. Based on research on the development of related skills, it is estimated that students will need at least several years of systematic strategy instruction to become highly proficient self-regulated learners (K. R. Harris, Alexander, & Graham, 2008; Pressley & Hilden, 2006; Winne & Stockley, 1998). This chapter's Case in Print reveals that many students still seem to lack SRL skills when they reach college.

One reason for this state of affairs is that very little instructional time (about 10%) is devoted to teaching SRL skills (Hamman, Berthelot, Saia, & Crowley, 2000; Moely et al., 1992). Another reason is that teachers sometimes make it difficult for students to formulate and use effective strategies by not aligning course

Self-regulated learners evaluate their performance, make appropriate attributions for success and failure, reinforce themselves, and make decisions about where improvements are needed.

learning strategy
A general plan that a learner formulates for achieving a somewhat distant academic goal.

learning tactic
A specific technique that a learner uses to accomplish an immediate learning objective.

concept mapping
A comprehension-directed tactic for identifying and visually representing on paper the ideas that comprise a section of text and the ways in which they relate to each other.

mnemonic device
A memory-directed tactic that helps a learner transform or organize information to enhance its retrievability.

goals, classroom instruction, test content, and test demands. That is, teachers may tell students that their goal is for students to understand concepts, integrate ideas, and apply what they have learned to other tasks and subjects, but then emphasize the memorization and recall of facts both in class and on tests. Under these circumstances, students are likely to be unsure as to which type of demand should govern how they study, so they settle on a "middle-of-the-road" approach that does justice to neither (Broekkamp & van Hout-Wolters, 2007).

Pause& Reflect *Many teachers have said that they would like to teach their students more about the nature and use of learning processes but don't have time because of the amount of subject material they must cover. What can you do to avoid this pitfall?*

To help students become effective self-regulated learners, you will obviously need to teach them the skills that are part of the self-regulation cycle that we described earlier. A good place to start is with some of the more useful tactics for memorizing and comprehending information.

The Nature of Learning Tactics and Strategies

A **learning strategy** is a general *plan* that a learner formulates for achieving a somewhat distant academic goal (such as getting an A on the next exam). Like all strategies, it specifies what will be done to achieve the goal, where it will be done, and when it will be done. **Learning tactics** are specific *techniques* (such as a memory aid or a form of note taking) that a learner uses to accomplish an immediate objective (such as understanding the concepts in a textbook chapter and how they relate to one another). Tactics are the "what" part of a strategy.

As you can see, tactics have an integral connection to strategies. They are the learning tools that move you closer to your goal. Thus they have to be chosen so as to be consistent with the goals of a strategy. If you had to recall verbatim the preamble to the U.S. Constitution, for example, would you use a learning tactic that would help you understand the gist of each phrase or one that

would allow accurate and complete recall? It is surprising how often students fail to consider this point.

Types of Tactics

Most learning tactics can be placed in one of two categories based on the tactic's primary purpose:

- Memory-directed tactics, which contain techniques that help produce accurate storage and retrieval of information, and

- Comprehension-directed tactics, which contain techniques that aid in understanding the meaning of ideas and their interrelationships (Levin, 1982).

Because of space limitations, we cannot discuss all the tactics in each category. Instead, we have chosen to briefly discuss a few that either are very popular with students or have been shown to be reasonably effective. The first two, *rehearsal* and *mnemonic devices*, are memory-directed tactics. Both can take several forms and are used by students of almost every age. The last two, *self-questioning* and **concept mapping**, are comprehension-directed tactics used frequently by students from the upper elementary grades through college.

> **Strategy: plan to achieve a long-term goal**
> **Tactic: specific technique that helps achieve an immediate objective**

Rehearsal The simplest form of rehearsal—rote rehearsal—is one of the earliest tactics to appear during childhood, and almost everyone uses it on occasion. It is not a particularly effective tactic for long-term storage and recall because it doesn't produce distinct encoding or good retrieval cues. But it is a useful tactic for purposes of short-term memory. A slightly more advanced version, *cumulative rehearsal*, involves rehearsing a small set of items for several repetitions, dropping the item at the top of the list and adding a new one, giving the set several repetitions, dropping the item at the head of the set and adding a new one, rehearsing the set, and so on (Pressley & Hilden, 2006; Schlagmüller & Schneider, 2002). Even among college students (yes, reader, this means you), rehearsal, in the form of rereading sections of text, is a very popular tactic (Callender & McDaniel, 2009).

Mnemonic Devices A **mnemonic device** is a memory-directed tactic that helps a learner transform or organize information to enhance its retrievability. Such devices can be used to learn and remember individual items of information (a name, a definition, a date), sets of information (a list of names, a list of vocabulary definitions, a

TABLE 9.1 Five Types of Mnemonic Devices

Mnemonic	Description	Examples	Uses
Rhyme	The items of information that one wants to recall are embedded in a rhyme that may range from one to several lines. A rhyme for recalling the names of the first 40 U.S. presidents, for example, contains 14 lines.	• Thirty days hath September, April, June, and November • Fiddledeedum, fiddledeedee, a ring around the moon is π times d; if a hole in your sock you want repaired, use the formula πr squared (the formulas for circumference and area of a circle)	Recalling specific items of factual information
Acronym	The first letter from each item to be remembered is used to make a word. Often called the *first-letter mnemonic*.	• HOMES (the names of the Great Lakes—Huron, Ontario, Michigan, Erie, Superior)	Recalling a short set of items, particularly abstract items, in random or serial order
Acrostic	The first letter from each item to be remembered is used to create a series of words that forms a sentence. The first letters of the words in the sentence correspond to the first letters of the items to be remembered.	• Kindly Place Cover Over Fresh Green Spring Vegetables (the taxonomic classification of plants and animals—kingdom, phylum, class, order, family, genus, species, and variety) • A Rat In The House May Eat The Ice Cream (the spelling of the word *arithmetic*)	Recalling items, particularly abstract ones, in random or serial order
Loci method	First, visual images of a set of well-known locations that form a natural series (such as the furniture in and the architectural features of the rooms of one's house) are generated and memorized. Second, images of the items to be memorized (objects, events, or ideas) are generated and "placed" each in a separate location. Third, the learner mentally walks through each location, retrieving each image from where it was placed and decoding into a written or spoken message. *Loci* (pronounced *low sigh*) is the plural of *locus*, which means "place."	• To recall the four stages of Piaget's theory: For the sensorimotor stage, picture a car engine with eyes, ears, nose, and a mouth. Place this image in your first location (fireplace mantel). For the preoperational stage, picture Piaget dressed in a surgical gown scrubbing up before an operation. Place this image in your second location (bookshelf). For the concrete operational stage, picture Piaget as a surgeon cutting open a piece of concrete. Place this image in your third location (chair). For the formal operational stage, picture Piaget as a surgeon dressed in a tuxedo. Place this image in your fourth location (sofa).	Recalling lists of discrete items or ideas from text passages. Works equally well for free recall and serial recall, abstract and concrete items.
Keyword method	Created to aid the learning of foreign language vocabulary, but applicable to any task in which one piece of information has to be associated with another. First, some part of the foreign word is isolated that, when spoken, sounds like a meaningful English word. This is the keyword. Then a visual image of the keyword is created. Finally, a compound visual image is formed using the keyword and the translation of the foreign word.	• The Spanish word *pato* (pronounced *pot-o*) means "duck." The Keyword is *pot*. Imagine a duck with a pot over its head or a duck simmering in a pot. • English psychologist Charles Spearman proposed that intelligence was composed of two factors—*g* and *s*. The keyword is *spear*. Imagine a spear being thrown at a gas (for *g* and *s*) can.	Can be used to recall cities and their products, states and their capitals, medical definitions, and famous people's accomplishments. For kindergarten through fourth grade, works best when children are given the keywords and pictures.

SOURCES: Atkinson (1975); Atkinson & Raugh (1975); Bellezza (1981); Carney, Levin, & Levin (1994); Raugh & Atkinson (1975); Yates (1966).

sequence of events), and ideas expressed in text. These devices range from simple, easy-to-learn techniques to somewhat complex systems that require a fair amount of practice.

Although mnemonic devices have been described and practiced for more than 2,000 years, they were rarely made the object of scientific study until the 1960s (see Yates, 1966, for a detailed discussion of the history of mnemonics). Since that time, mnemonics have been frequently and intensively studied by researchers, and several reviews of mnemonics research have been done (for example, Bellezza, 1981; Carney & Levin, 2002; Levin, 1993; Snowman, 1986). Table 9.1 provides descriptions, examples, and uses of five mnemonic devices: rhymes, acronyms, acrostics, the loci method, and the keyword method.

Why Mnemonic Devices Are Effective Mnemonic devices work so well because they enhance the encodability and retrievability of information. First, they provide a context (such as acronyms, sentences, mental walks) in which apparently unrelated items can be organized. Second, the meaningfulness of material to be learned is enhanced through associations with more familiar meaningful information (for example, memory pegs or loci). Third, they provide distinctive retrieval cues that must be encoded with the material to be learned. Fourth, they force the learner to be an active participant in the learning process (Morris, 1977).

Here's an example taken from a study conducted with college students (Rummel, Levin, & Woodward, 2003). Let's imagine that your instructor scheduled a quiz over the contents of Chapter 4. To remember that Charles Spearman formulated a theory of intelligence that is composed of a general factor and several specialized factors, you picture in your mind a man holding a general-purpose spear (he's a spear man) in one hand and several smaller, more specialized spears in the other hand. If you're like the students in the study, you should have more success recalling this information than a classmate who simply read the material one or more times.

> **Mnemonic devices meaningfully organize information and provide retrieval cues.**

Why You Should Teach Students How to Use Mnemonic Devices Despite the demonstrated effectiveness of mnemonic devices, many people argue against teaching them to students. They feel that students should learn the skills of critical thinking and problem solving rather than ways to recall isolated bits of verbatim information reliably. When factual information is needed, one can always turn to a reference source. Although we agree with the importance of teaching students to be critical thinkers and problem solvers, we feel this view is shortsighted for three reasons.

- It is very time consuming to be constantly looking things up in reference books.

- The critique of mnemonic training ignores the fact that effective problem solving depends on ready access to a well-organized and meaningful knowledge base. Indeed, people who are judged to be expert in a particular field have an impressive array of factual material at their fingertips.

- Critics of mnemonics education focus only on the "little idea" that mnemonic usage aids verbatim recall of bits of information. The "big idea" is that students come to realize that the ability to learn and remember large amounts of information is an acquired capability. Too often students (and adults) assume that an effective memory is innate and requires high intelligence. Once they realize that learning is a skill, students may be more inclined to learn how to use other tactics and how to formulate broad-based strategies.

> **Self-questioning improves comprehension and knowledge integration.**

Self- and Peer-Questioning Because students are expected to demonstrate much of what they know by answering written test questions, self-questioning can be a valuable learning tactic. The key to using questions profitably is to recognize that different types of questions make different cognitive demands. Some questions require little more than verbatim recall or recognition of simple facts and details. If an exam is designed to stress factual recall, then it may be helpful for a student to generate such questions while studying. Other questions, however, assess comprehension, application, or synthesis of main ideas or other high-level information.

To ensure that students fully understood how to write comprehension-aiding questions, Alison King (1992) created a set of question stems (see Table 9.2) that were intended to help students identify main ideas and think about how those ideas related to each other and to what the students already knew. This tactic produces better recall and comprehension of material than simple reviewing for middle school, high school, and college students (A. King, 1992, 1994, 1998).

Self-questioning works for two reasons:

- To answer the kinds of question stems King suggested, students have to engage in such higher-level thinking processes as translating ideas into their own words ("What is the meaning of . . .?" "Explain why . . . ."), looking for similarities and differences ("What is the difference between . . . and . . .?" "How are . . . and . . . similar?"), thinking about how ideas relate to one another ("Compare . . . and . . . with regard to . . . .") and to previously learned information ("How does . . . tie in with what we learned before?"), and evaluating the quality of ideas ("What are the strengths and weaknesses of . . .?").

- It helps students to monitor their comprehension. If too many questions cannot be answered or if the

TABLE 9.2 Self-Questioning Stems

What is a new example of . . .?	How would you use . . . to . . .?
What would happen if . . .?	What are the strengths and weaknesses of . . .?
What do we already know about . . .?	How does . . . tie in with what we learned before?
Explain why	Explain how . . ..
How does . . . affect . . .?	What is the meaning of . . .?
Why is . . . important?	What is the difference between . . . and . . .?
How are . . . and . . . similar?	What is the best. . ., and why?
What are some possible solutions to the problem of . . .?	Compare . . . and . . . with regard to . . ..
How does . . . cause . . .?	What do you think causes . . .?

SOURCE: From A. King. (1992). Facilitating elaborative learning through guided student-generated questioning. *Educational Psychologist, 27*(1), 111–126. Reprinted by permission of Lawrence Erlbaum Associates, Inc. (Taylor & Francis Group), http://www.informaworld.com

answers appear to be too superficial, this provides clear evidence that the student has not achieved an adequate understanding of the passage.

Studies examining the effect of responding to question stems have reported very strong effects. The average student who responded to question stems while reading a passage scored about 37 percentile ranks higher on a subsequent teacher-made test than students who did not answer question stems. Differences of this magnitude do not appear in research studies very often; in this case, it argues strongly for providing students with question stems and teaching them how to construct their own questions and answers (Rosenshine, Meister, & Chapman, 1996).

Concept Mapping One technique that helps students identify, visually organize, and represent the relation-

ships among a set of ideas is concept mapping. (We mention concept maps again and provide an example in Chapter 13.) Considerable research documents the positive effect of concept mapping on students' recall and comprehension when compared with just reading text. These benefits are stronger for students with low verbal ability or low prior knowledge, and for middle school students as compared to high school students (Nesbit & Adesope, 2006; Novak, 2009; O'Donnell, Dansereau, & Hall, 2002; Romance & Vitale, 1999). But should you provide students with ready-made concept maps or let them construct their own? The answer to that question is that it depends, at least in part, on two factors. First, students who have no familiarity with concept mapping will probably learn more when they are provided with concept maps. Second, if you intend to test students simply on their ability to store and retrieve the information they

 Metacognition: Helping Students Become Strategic Learners

TeachSource Video Case

Go to the Education CourseMate website and watch the video, study the artifacts in the case, and reflect upon the following questions:

1. To help her students better understand the newspaper article she has assigned them to read, the teacher in this video, Julie Craven, has them write in the margins whatever questions and reactions come to mind as they read. How might such a tactic improve students' comprehension?

2. Earlier in this chapter we noted that expertise in self-regulated learning develops gradually. Ms. Craven makes the same observation, as do her students. This slow progress may cause some students to give up on becoming self-regulated learners. How might you keep students motivated while they gradually acquire and refine their self-regulation skills?

3. There are several benefits to becoming a strategic learner, one of which has to do with self-efficacy. Can you identify where in the video this benefit is mentioned?

read, it probably won't make much of a difference. But if you intend to test them on their ability to transfer what they have learned to similar but new contexts, you should probably give them concept maps that you have created (Stull & Mayer, 2007).

Conclusions Regarding Learning Tactics On the basis of this brief review, we can draw two conclusions. One is that students need to be systematically taught how to use learning tactics to make connections among ideas contained in text and lecture, as well as between new and previously learned information. No one expects students to teach themselves to read, write, and compute. So why should they be expected to teach themselves how to use a variety of learning tactics?

The second conclusion is that learning tactics should not be taught as isolated techniques, particularly to high school students. If tactics are taught that way, most students probably will not keep using them for very long or recognize that as the situation changes, so should the tactic. Therefore, as we implied earlier, students should be taught how to use tactics as part of a broader learning strategy.

Supporting Students' Strategy Use

As noted earlier, a learning strategy is a plan for accomplishing a learning goal that takes into account various internal and external conditions. As such, it is the product of the forethought phase of the self-regulation cycle outlined in Figure 9.2. The pertinent internal and external conditions may include the knowledge and skills that the teacher wants students to acquire, the amount of time allotted to learn certain amounts of material, the types of tests students take, the type of information teachers give students about test content, and the students' goals, motives, and level of self-regulated learning skills (see Broekkamp & van Hout-Wolters, 2007 for a detailed discussion of these and other conditions).

To help your students create good-quality strategies, you should use the three-phase self-regulation model as a guide for teaching those self-regulation skills. But you should also remind yourself and your students of the following four points: First, learning conditions constantly change. Subject matters contain different types of information and structures, teachers use different instructional methods and have different styles, exams differ in the kinds of demands they make, and the interests, motives, and capabilities of students change over time. Accordingly, strategies must be *formulated* or constructed anew as one moves from task to task rather than *selected* from a bank of previously formulated strategies. The true strategist, in other words, exhibits a characteristic that is referred to as *mindfulness* (P. A. Alexander, Graham, & Harris, 1998). A mindful learner is aware of the need to be strategic,

With the teacher's help, students can learn how to formulate strategic learning plans by identifying and analyzing the important aspects of a task. Then they can tailor these plans to their own strengths and weaknesses as learners.

attends to the various elements that make up a learning task, and thinks about how to use the learning skills he or she possesses to greatest effect. For example, a mindful learner would be aware that the age-old read-recite-review study technique produces higher levels of free recall than either taking notes or reading a passage twice, but would also know that for multiple-choice or short-answer tests, there is no appreciable difference among these three tactics (McDaniel, Howard, & Einstein, 2009).

The second point you and your students should know about good-quality learning strategies is that because this is a new skill that will take some time to master, you will need to provide students with what is called metacognitive feedback. If you expect students to continue to create strategies and use various tactics for different types of tasks, you will need to explain why they work and the circumstances under which

Challenging Assumptions

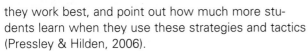

Teach Students How to Be Self-Regulated Learners

A perennial complaint among educators is that many students lack the skills and knowledge to function as self-regulated learners. This is a strange complaint because everyone from politicians to parents endorses the goals of self-directed learning and lifelong learning. Like motherhood and apple pie, they are easy goals to endorse because nobody could be against them. But when it comes to putting one's resources where one's rhetoric is, much of this support disappears like the morning mist. The following reasons account for a large part of this inconsistency:

1. Many people (including teachers, parents, and students) believe that self-regulation is a natural process that students will figure out and master if they just work at it long and hard enough. This leads to the ubiquitous but mostly useless advice to "study harder."

2. School is thought of as a place where students acquire bodies of information about various subject matters and the so-called basic skills of reading, writing, and computing. There is simply not enough room in the curriculum to teach students how to be self-directed learners.

3. Teachers and administrators are held accountable for how well students score on state-mandated tests. Consequently, school curricula and classroom instruction emphasize those skills and bodies of knowledge that relate most directly to state learning standards and test items, and SRL skills either are ignored or take a back seat.

If this situation is to change, everyone involved in education needs to realize that there is nothing more basic than learning how to be a self-regulated learner. These skills allow students to become proficient at reading, writing, and computing and to direct their learning long after they finish school. Consequently, SRL skills should be as much a part of the curriculum as the three Rs.

The place to start is the individual classroom. At the very least, you should teach students that a relationship exists between the cognitive processes they use and the outcomes they observe, how and when to use various learning tactics, how to determine whether learning is proceeding as planned, and what to do if it is not.

What Do You Think?

What's your response to this argument? Is SRL so "basic" that teachers should not even have to teach it? At the "Challenging Assumptions" section of the textbook's Education CourseMate website, you can find out more about this important issue.

---

they work best, and point out how much more students learn when they use these strategies and tactics (Pressley & Hilden, 2006).

The third point follows from the second and concerns both your motivation and that of your students. Becoming a self-regulated or strategic learner requires concentrated effort over an extended period of time. Consequently, you may be inclined to believe that such a goal is beyond the reach of most elementary, middle school, and possibly even high school students. In the next section we will summarize research that we hope convinces you that even elementary school youngsters can be trained to use a variety of self-regulation skills in context-appropriate ways. We hope you will use this evidence to remind your students that with persistence and effort they can indeed become effective self-regulated learners.

Finally, because strategic learners tailor their learning processes to the perceived demands of a task, teachers need to clearly convey to students such critical information as what tasks or parts of tasks (such as certain parts of a reading assignment) are sufficiently important that they will be tested and what form the tests will take. Students, in turn, need to accurately perceive those demands (Beishuizen & Stoutjesdijk, 1999). A study conducted in the Netherlands (Broekkamp, van Hout-Wolters, Rijlaarsdam, & van den Bergh, 2002) showed that this process occurs less frequently than one would desire. The study examined how 22 history teachers and their 11th grade students rated the importance of sections of an 8,000-word textbook passage on U.S. presidents. In brief, here is what the researchers found:

1. There was only limited agreement among teachers about which sections of the text students should focus on in preparation for a test.

2. There was only limited agreement among students, as well as between students and their teacher, as to which sections of the text were most important.

In other words, teachers had only limited success in communicating to students what parts of the passage were more important than others, and students were as apt to focus on the less important parts as the more important ones.

Wanted: Self-Regulated Learners

We would like to be able to tell you that most students possess the self-regulated learning (SRL) skills we have discussed, but unfortunately, we cannot. Although evidence exists that students are more likely to use effective learning skills as they get older (Greene & Azevedo, 2009; W. Schneider, Knopf, & Stefanek, 2002) and that some students behave strategically by using different learning skills for different tasks (Hadwin, Winne, Stockley, Nesbit, & Woszczyna, 2001), many do not do so either systematically or consistently. (p. 193)

Students Unprepared for Rigors of College

FREDREKA SCHOUTEN
Gannett New Service, 10/30/03

High school graduates in Nevada with at least a B average can win $10,000 college scholarships—enough to guarantee them free rides at any public university in the state.

But that ride has proved rough for many. Nearly one-third of the kids who get the scholarships, created to keep the state's most promising students in Nevada, have to take remedial classes when they start college.

They are not alone. Around the country, students, even those with stellar high school records, have discovered they don't have all the skills to survive in college. In Georgia, for instance, four out of 10 students who earn the popular Hope Scholarships to the state's university system lose the scholarship after they earn about 30 credits—roughly one year's worth of work—because they can't keep their grades up.

Student performance on college-admissions tests also point to possible grade inflation. Fifteen years ago, students with A averages accounted for 28 percent of SAT test takers, said Wayne Camara, who oversees research for the College Board.

Today, a whopping 42 percent of college-bound seniors have A averages, but they score no better on the college admissions tests than did "A" students a decade earlier.

Some education experts say the trend is a clear sign that high school teachers are handing out high grades for weak work. But many argue the real culprit is the typical high school course load. Students just aren't taking the rigorous math, science and writing classes in high school that they need to succeed in college and the workplace.

Only one in three 18-year-olds is even minimally prepared for college, according to a recent report by the Manhattan Institute, a New York–based think tank. The picture was even bleaker for minority students. Only 20 percent of blacks in the class of 2001 were college-ready.

Lack of Preparation

Researchers defined minimum preparation as having a regular high school diploma—instead of merely passing the General Educational Development test—the GED—and taking at least four years of English, three years of math, and two years each of social studies, science and a foreign language in high school. They also counted students who performed at least at the basic level on a national reading test.

The preparation gap is particularly acute for graduates of inner-city and rural high schools, said Gary Henry, a Georgia State University professor who studies the Hope Scholarships.

Schools in those areas "can't hire really qualified math and science teachers so the course gets lowered to the level that the teacher is capable of teaching," he said.

"The students have no way of knowing whether the algebra class was decent. All they know is that they passed it."

Ivrekia Stanley thought her prospects were bright when she graduated from Forest Park High School in suburban Atlanta in 1999. Her 3.6 grade-point average earned her a Hope Scholarship and a ticket to college. But when she entered Georgia Perimeter College, a two-year community college, she had to take remedial classes in reading and math.

"You get very discouraged. You don't want to tell anybody you're in these classes," Stanley recalled. She said she kept telling herself, "I have a Hope Scholarship. I'm smarter than this."

But she said the classes taught her some lessons she hadn't learned in high school, like stopping to look up unfamiliar words in the dictionary and quickly determining the main point of a written passage.

This fall, the 22-year-old transferred to Georgia State, where she majors in criminal justice. She has a 3.8 grade-point average and has retained the Hope Scholarship.

observational learning The part of the triadic model of social cognitive theory that describes the role of observing and imitating the behavior of models in learning new capabilities. Also called *modeling*.

These findings suggest that teachers should provide students with clear and comprehensive information about the relative importance of various parts of a reading passage, instruct students in how to identify the important parts of a reading passage, and avoid dwelling on or overemphasizing aspects of a reading assignment that they have no intention of testing students on.

Modeling and Self-Regulated Learning

What little students know about the nature and use of self-regulatory skills has usually been acquired through direct instruction (by teachers, parents, and peers) and trial-and-error learning. But there is another way to strengthen self-efficacy beliefs and learn how to use self-regulatory skills: observing and imitating the behavior of a skilled model. This form of learning is often referred to as **observational learning** or *modeling*.

Observational learning can play an especially strong role in the acquisition of self-regulatory skills.

40% Lose Scholarships

About 40 percent of Hope Scholars who entered Georgia schools as freshmen in fall 2000 failed to maintain the minimum 3.0 GPA in their first 30 credit hours of college work and lost the scholarships.

Statistics like those from Georgia have inspired officials in Nevada to set up strong mentoring programs to help their Millennium Scholarship recipients and students from the state's rural areas stay in school, said Barbara King, who oversees tutoring programs at the Reno campus of the University of Nevada.

King runs an Internet listserv for the students where she posts reminders about finding tutors and deadlines for dropping classes. She also tries to improve their study habits.

"I tell them to pay attention to repetition during lectures," King said. "The second time a professor says something, underline it. The third time, put a 'T' for 'test' next to it. It probably will be on the test."

Other King tips: Set aside two to three hours of study for every hour spent in class, keep that time commitment in mind when considering taking on a part time job, and read the review questions at the end of a chapter first.

She advises students to try and answer those questions before tackling the reading assignment, because that will help pinpoint important material.

"We're not just assuming that because students got a 3.0 in high school that they come in here knowing what to do," King said.

Class Choice Important

Researchers say that when it comes to college success, what students study in high school is as important as their study skills.

Those who continue studying math for a fourth year in high school—taking classes such as trigonometry and calculus that are harder than second-year algebra—double their chances of earning a bachelor's degree, said Clifford Adelman, a U.S. Department of Education researcher who has examined thousands of high school and college transcripts.

His advice to parents: "Encourage your kids to be challenged in (high) school, and worry less about grades." Before granting merit-based scholarships like Hope, more states now demand that students demonstrate they passed rigorous classes in high school.

Under the Texas Grant program, which pays college tuition for financially needy students, eligible students must take the state's basic college-prep curriculum. That includes four years of English and three years of math, along with three years of science classes.

Starting with the high school freshman class of 2004, all Texas public high schools automatically will enroll students in the college-prep curriculum unless their parents or guardians formally object.

Source: Fredreka Schouten, "Students unprepared for rigors of college," Gannett News Service, October 30, 2003.

Questions and Activities

1. This article notes that many high school students in Nevada have to take remedial classes during their first year of college, and 40% of students in Georgia with state scholarships lose them after the first year of college because of low grades. Two explanations that are offered for students' difficulty in coping with the academic demands of college are grade inflation in high school and students' avoidance of rigorous math, science, and writing courses. A third, and more likely, explanation for students' lack of preparedness for college is poorly developed self-regulation skills. Explain why this factor, and not grade inflation or course selection, is likely to be the primary cause of so many students' academic difficulties in college.

2. One student quoted in the article, Ivrekia Stanley, said that despite her 3.6 grade-point average in high school, she had to take remedial math and reading courses at a community college, where she learned such valuable skills as looking up unfamiliar words in a dictionary and figuring out the main point of a passage. Do you think these basic SRL skills were not learned in high school because they weren't taught or because Ms. Stanley simply didn't learn them at the time? Try using your own high school experience and those of your friends to justify your answer.

3. The first sentence of the last section of the article states, "Researchers say that when it comes to college success, what students study in high school is as important as their study skills." The reporter backs up this claim with the finding by Clifford Adelman, a researcher with the U.S. Department of Education, that students who take 4 years of math in high school, and who take advanced math classes during their senior year, are twice as likely to graduate from college. Given what we said earlier in the book about how several plausible causal explanations can be generated from correlational data, come up with another explanation of the finding cited by Mr. Adelman.

Evidence suggests that these skills are learned best when they are acquired according to the following four-level model: observation, emulation, self-control, and self-regulation (Zimmerman, 2000, 2002; Zimmerman & Kitsantas, 2002, 2005). In the description that follows, note how the high levels of support and guidance (or *scaffolding*, to use the constructivist terminology) that are present for the observation and emulation levels are reduced at the self-control level and eliminated at the self-regulation level. Table 9.3 on the next page summarizes the cognitive and behav-

ioral requirements of the learner and the source of the learner's motivation for each level.

Observation At the observation level, learners pick up the major features of a skill or strategy, as well as performance standards, motivational beliefs, and values, by watching and listening as a model exhibits the skill and explains the reasons for the behavior: for example, a model who persists at trying to solve a problem and expresses the belief that he is capable of solving the problem. What would motivate a student to observe

TABLE 9.3 A Social Cognitive Model of Self-Regulated Skill Learning

Level	Main Requirement of the Learner	Source of Motivation
Observation	Attend to actions and verbalizations of the model and discriminate relevant from irrelevant behaviors	Vicarious: note rewards received by the model and anticipate receiving similar rewards for exhibiting similar behavior
Emulation	Exhibit the general form of the modeled behavior	Direct: feedback from the model or others
Self-control	Learn to exhibit the modeled behavior automatically through self-directed practice (focus on the underlying rule or process that produces the behavior and compare the behavior with personal standards)	Self-satisfaction from matching the standards and behavior of the model
Self-regulation	Learn to adapt the behavior to changes in internal and external conditions (such as the reactions of others)	Self-efficacy beliefs and degree of intrinsic interest in the skill

SOURCES: Zimmerman (2000, 2002); Zimmerman & Kitsantas (2002).

vicarious reinforcement The strengthening of a particular behavior in an observer who anticipates receiving a reward for the behavior because someone else has been so rewarded.

and then try to emulate a model's behavior? At least four factors do so:

1. Being unfamiliar with the task at hand or feeling incapable of successfully carrying it out.

2. Having a model available that you admire and respect because he or she has the knowledge, skills, and attributes that you would like to have.

3. Having a model available whose behavior you consider to be acceptable and appropriate. Thus students will often model a peer's behavior.

4. Seeing a model reinforced for exhibiting a particular behavior, and anticipating that you will be similarly reinforced (Schunk, 2001). This type of reinforcement is referred to as **vicarious reinforcement**

> **Self-regulation skills are learned best in a four-level process: observation, emulation, self-control, and self-regulation.**

because you're experiencing the effect of the reinforcement through another person.

Emulation At the emulation level, learners reproduce the general form of the model's behavior. Because learners rarely copy the exact behaviors of a model, the term *emulation* is used here instead of the word *imitation*. Social cognitive theorists identify four types

Modeling: Social Cognitive Theory in a High School Chemistry Lesson

Go to the Education CourseMate website and watch the video, study the artifacts in the case, and reflect upon the following questions:

1. Do you find this teacher's use of modeling and observational learning to be effective? Explain why or why not.

2. Based on the teacher and the Video Case, give some ideas of subject areas or lessons in which modeling and observational learning would work especially well.

TeachSource Video Case

of emulation effects that result from observing models: inhibition, disinhibition, facilitation, and true observational learning.

Inhibition occurs when we learn not to do something that we already know how to do because a model we are observing refrains from behaving in that way, is punished for behaving in that way, or does something different from what we intended to do.

Disinhibition occurs when we learn to exhibit a behavior that is usually disapproved of by most people because a model does the same thing without being punished.

Facilitation occurs whenever we are prompted to do something (usually because we see others doing the same thing) that we do not ordinarily do because of insufficient motivation rather than social disapproval.

Pause& Reflect *Can you recall a teacher you admired so much that you emulated some aspect of her or his behavior (either then or later)? How might you have the same effect on your students?*

The last of the four types of emulation effects, *true observational learning*, occurs when we learn a new behavioral pattern by watching and imitating the performance of someone else.

Self-Control The self-control level of observational learning is marked by the learner's being able to exhibit the modeled behavior in the absence of the model. Self-control is achieved through self-directed practice. The learner focuses on the underlying rule or process that produces the behavior and compares the behavior with personal standards.

Self-Regulation The self-regulation level is attained when learners can adapt the modeled behavior to changes in internal and external conditions (such as a low level of interest in a topic or negative reactions of others). The motivation for self-regulated behavior comes from one's perceived self-efficacy and degree of intrinsic interest in the modeled behavior.

LO3 What Research Says About Social Cognitive Theory

There is no question that social cognitive theory offers a compelling explanation of learning. But as with all theories, its value to teachers and others depends on the extent to which its concepts and their proposed relationships are supported by research findings. The research that has been conducted over the past several decades is both broad and deep. The effect of social cognitive theory on learning has been examined in a number of

© Stephen McBrady/Photo Edit

Social cognitive theory holds that one way students acquire self-regulated learning skills is by observing and imitating the behavior of admired models, such as teachers, siblings, and peers.

different subject areas and under a variety of conditions. The vast majority of these studies have produced positive findings. Teachers should feel quite comfortable about creating instructional tactics that are based on social cognitive theory. What follows is a brief summary of some of that research.

- As social cognitive theory predicts, self-efficacy, epistemological beliefs, and self-regulation processes are positively related to each other, and each characteristic is positively related to achievement (Lodewyk, 2007; Lodewyk & Winne, 2005; Schommer-Aikins, Duell, & Hutter, 2005; Swalander & Taube, 2007; Trautwein & Lüdtke, 2007; Usher & Pajares, 2008a).

- Middle school students who watched peers solve math problems scored higher on a test of similar problems and had higher levels of self-efficacy for mathematical problem solving than did children who either watched an adult model or worked from written instructions (Schunk & Hanson, 1985; Schunk, Hanson, & Cox, 1987).

Suggestions for Teaching

Applying Social Cognitive Theory in the Classroom

1 **Include the development of self-regulated learning skills in your objectives and lesson plans.**

The research that we summarized clearly shows that SRL skills make a significant contribution to students' achievement. But this same research also suggests that students should not be given responsibility for their own learning without adequate preparation (Greene & Azevedo, 2007). Consequently, the development of students' SRL skills should be included in your instructional objectives and lesson plans. You can help students become more effective self-regulated learners by incorporating the following elements into your classroom instruction (Ley & Young, 2001; Randi & Corno, 2000; Schunk, 2001):

a. Emphasize how important SRL skills are to learning and when they should be used.

In all likelihood, you will want students to attain some degree of proficiency in goal setting, planning, use of tactics and strategies, monitoring of their actions and progress, self-evaluation, and self-reinforcement. When teaching planning skills, for example, point out that students who are good planners know the conditions under which they learn best and choose or arrange environments that eliminate or decrease distractions. To raise students' awareness of the value of a good learning environment, you can have them keep a log of how much time they spend studying in various places and at various times, what internal and external distractions they experience, and how they deal with those distractions. On the basis of this information, they can draw conclusions about when and under what circumstances they learn best. To help students choose or create a hospitable learning environment, you can prepare and distribute a checklist of desirable features. Likely features of a good learning environment would include

relative quiet, good lighting and ventilation, and comfortable furniture; it would be best to not include other people, a television set, or alternative reading material such as comic books or magazines.

Self-regulated learners commonly use many types of memory and comprehension tactics. You can help students appreciate the value of these skills by using such techniques as mnemonic devices, outlines, concept maps, previews, graphs, flowcharts, and tables as you teach and by explaining how they are used and how they aid learning. To increase the probability that students will use such techniques themselves, teach them how to make outlines before they write essays and show them how to create concept maps, graphs, flowcharts, and tables after they have read a section of text.

Lastly, continually remind students that self-regulated behavior is the product of self-motivational beliefs as well as various cognitive skills. The success of any instruction you will provide on SRL skills will greatly depend on students' beliefs about their self-efficacy and the basic nature of their learning ability.

b. Model SRL skills, including the standards you use to evaluate your performance and reinforce yourself.

You can enhance the learning of SRL skills by having students observe and imitate what you and other skilled learners do. As noted, when you demonstrate a skill or process, you should first explain what you are going to do. Then take time to describe why you are going to do it and how you will evaluate the quality of your performance. Then demonstrate the behavior, evaluate your performance, and, if you feel your behavior has met your standards, verbally administer some self-praise. The importance of modeling thought processes that are normally hidden from observation was noted by Margaret Metzger (1998), a high school English teacher. To

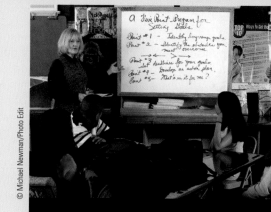

Teachers can help students acquire and refine regulated learning skills by providing direct in tion in such skills as goal setting, planning, us learning tactics, monitoring, and self-evaluatio

help students better understand the process of literary interpretation and criticism, she recommended a procedure in which she led some students through a discussion of a story while other students observed and took notes on the process.

2 **Teach students how to use both memory-directed and comprehension-directed tactics.**

a. Teach students how to use various forms of rehearsal and mnemonic devices.

We have at least two reasons for recommending the teaching of rehearsal. One is that maintenance rehearsal is a useful tactic for keeping a relatively small amount of information active in short-term memory. The other is that maintenance rehearsal is one of a few tactics that young children can learn to use. If you do decide to teach rehearsal, we have two suggestions. First, remind young children that rehearsal is something that learners consciously decide to do when they want to remember things. Second, remind

• Primary and elementary grade students who were taught a self-regulating writing strategy and got to observe a classmate implement the strategy wrote longer and higher-quality essays than did students who received either normal writing instruction or just the writing strategy instruction alone (Glaser & Brunstein, 2007; K. R. Harris, Graham, & Mason,

2006). On average, this approach to writing instruction produced an advantage of 14 percentile ranks on tests of writing quality as compared to other forms of writing instruction (Graham & Perin, 2007).

• Elementary grade students produced higher-quality written products when they had the opportunity to observe a model who was similar to themselves

Rhoda Sidney/Stock Boston

Research findings demonstrate that note taking in one form or another is an effective tactic for improving comprehension of text and lecture material. Consequently, students should be taught the basic principles that support effective note taking.

students to rehearse no more than seven items (or chunks) at a time.

As you prepare class presentations or encounter bits of information that students seem to have difficulty learning, ask yourself if a mnemonic device would be useful. You might write up a list of the devices discussed earlier. Part of the value of mnemonic devices is that they make learning easier. They are also fun to make up and use. Moreover, rhymes, acronyms, and acrostics can be constructed rather quickly.

b. Teach students how to formulate comprehension questions.

We concluded earlier that self-questioning could be an effective comprehension tactic if students were trained to write good comprehension questions and given opportunities to practice the technique. We suggest you try the following instructional sequence:

1. Discuss the purpose of student-generated questions.
2. Point out the differences between knowledge-level questions and different types of comprehension-level questions (such as analysis, synthesis, and evaluation). An excellent discussion of these types can be found in the *Taxonomy of Educational Objectives, Handbook I: Cognitive Domain* (B. S. Bloom, Englehart, Furst, Hill, & Krathwohl, 1956).
3. Explain and illustrate the kinds of responses that should be given to different types of comprehension-level questions.
4. Provide students with a sample paragraph and a set of high-level question stems. Have students formulate questions and responses either individually or in pairs.
5. Provide corrective feedback.
6. Give students short passages from which to practice.
7. Provide corrective feedback (Hattie & Timperley, 2007; A. King, 1994).

❸ Establish the foundation for self-regulated learning in kindergarten and the primary grades.

As we noted earlier, becoming a proficient self-regulated learner requires systematic instruction and experience spread over many years. Consequently, the foundation for SRL should be established in kindergarten and the primary grades. Observations of teachers in kindergarten through third grade (Perry, VandeKamp, Mercer, & Nordby, 2002) have provided some insight as to how this might be accomplished. In general, teachers whose classrooms were rated as high-SRL

classrooms emphasized student choice of activities, support in meeting academic challenges (a technique we referred to earlier in the book as scaffolding), and evaluation of oneself and classmates in a nonthreatening, mastery-oriented environment. Here are some specific examples of how SRL-oriented instruction was carried out:

- Prior to an oral reading of the story "The Three Little Pigs," students were allowed to decide whether to track the text with their fingers or their eyes.
- When a student had trouble decoding a word during an oral story reading, the teacher asked the other children in the group to suggest a solution. They then tried each suggestion to see which one worked.
- Students were asked to create an alternate story ending for "The Three Little Pigs." To help them meet this challenge, the teacher allowed students to share their ideas with a classmate and, later, with the teacher. The teacher recorded each child's idea on chart paper so everyone in class could see everyone else's ideas.
- Kindergarten and first grade children who had trouble writing out their ideas for a writing assignment were encouraged to start with drawings as a way to plan and organize their ideas.
- In preparation for student/parent–teacher conferences, students were asked to select samples of their work to share with parents and reflect on what they could do now that they could not do earlier in the school year.
- To help second grade students choose and carry out a research topic, the teacher asked them to answer three questions: Am I interested in this topic? Can I find books about this topic? Can I read the books by myself, or will I need help from a friend or an adult?

(Braaksma, Rijlaarsdam, & van den Bergh, 2002; Schunk, Hanson, & Cox, 1987).
- Students who were taught a multicomponent strategy (summarize, question, clarify, predict) called *reciprocal teaching* scored markedly higher on tests of reading comprehension than did students who were given standard reading instruction (Alfassi,

1998; C. J. Carter, 1997; Kim, Baylor, & PALS Group, 2006; Rosenshine & Meister, 1994b).

Now that you are familiar with social cognitive theory and research, it is time to examine several Suggestions for Teaching (above) derived from these principles and research findings.

LO4 Using Technology to Promote Self-Regulated Learning

Teaching students to become proficient self-regulated learners will require thousands of hours of instruction spread over many years. With the many instructional responsibilities teachers have, you stand a better chance of contributing to this goal if you can use technology to supplement and reinforce your efforts. The studies we summarize in this section suggest that, with certain qualifications, this is a real possibility.

Modeling

Modeling, as you now know, is an effective way to help students acquire important SRL skills. It can also strengthen students' self-efficacy for computer-based learning (Moos & Azevedo, 2009). But what if a teacher does not have sufficient time to perform this function or cannot always supply the modeling just when students need it? Might not a computer-based video model serve as an effective substitute? This was the driving question behind a study conducted with sixth grade students (Pedersen & Liu, 2002).

> **Computer programs that include models can improve students' problem-solving skills.**

Three groups of students worked on a computer-based hypermedia problem-solving simulation over the course of fifteen 45-minute class periods. Called Alien Rescue, the simulation had students play the role of scientists on an international space station whose mission was to rescue alien life forms. They encountered a ship that contained six species of aliens, survivors of a distant solar system that was destroyed by the explosion of a nearby star. The life-support system of the alien ship had been damaged, and its members were in suspended animation. The students' task was to figure out which planets or moons of our solar system might serve as suitable homes for each of the alien species by using existing databases and a simulation within the program that let them design and launch probes. They recorded their notes and solutions in an online notebook.

The group that watched video segments of an expert scientist describing the process he used to solve the same problem for one of the alien species out-scored the group that received the same basic instruction but did not observe a model and the group that watched a model who provided no clues as to how he solved the problem on several measures of problem solving.

Subsequent research (e.g., Pedersen & Liu, 2002/2003; Wouters, Paas, & van Merriënboer, 2009) has shown that watching a computer-based model, even an animated one, produces better learning and transfer of problem-solving skills than watching no model.

Providing Cognitive and Metacognitive Feedback

As you undoubtedly know from your own experience (although we do mention it in later chapters) efficient and effective learning of new skills requires timely feedback. Because teachers may not always be in a position to offer feedback precisely when it is needed, computer programs have been created to fill this need. One such program, Summary Street, was designed to help students improve their ability to summarize text by giving them many opportunities to summarize different types of text, by providing feedback, and by having them revise their summaries (with more feedback) as often as necessary until they meet the standards built into the program. Eighth grade students who worked with Summary Street for 4 weeks showed greater improvement both in the amount of relevant information contained in their summaries and in the quality of their summaries than did a comparable group of students who summarized the same passages but did not receive feedback. Low- and medium-performing students made the largest improvements (Franzke, Kintsch, Caccamise, Johnson, & Dooley, 2005).

As we noted earlier in the chapter, self-regulated learners monitor their thinking as they work through a task to ensure a high level of learning. Teachers and parents often help students develop and strengthen this skill by reminding them to think about key operations, such as appropriately defining the problem or issue at hand and recalling relevant prior knowledge. This type of support is often referred to as *metacognitive feedback*. The type of feedback students more commonly receive, called *results feedback*, takes the form of such cautionary and positive statements as "Try again," "Check once more," and "Very good, wonderful job!"

One study (Kramarski & Zeichner, 2001) compared computer-provided instruction and metacognitive feedback with computer-provided instruction and results feedback on 11th graders' mathematical problem solving. As students in the metacognitive feedback group worked through the program, the computer would prompt them to think about the nature of the problem, the relevance of prior knowledge, and the use of appropriate problem-solving techniques by posing such questions as "What is the problem all about?" "What are the similarities and differences between the problem at hand and problems you have solved in the past?" and "What tactics or principles are appropriate for solving this problem and why?" Students in the results feedback group received comments such as "Think about it, you made a mistake," "Try again," "Check it once more," "Very good," and "Wonderful job!"

On a 27-item test that required students to explain their reasoning behind their solutions to each problem, students who received metacognitive feedback significantly outscored students who received results feedback. The explanations of the metacognitive feedback group were of a significantly higher quality (they included both algebraic formulas and verbal arguments) than the explanations of the results feedback group.

Providing Scaffolded Instruction

Earlier in the book we described Vygotsky's theory of cognitive development and his recommendation that teachers use various instructional aids, called scaffolds, to help students acquire the knowledge and self-regulatory skills that they would probably not otherwise acquire. But as busy as most classrooms are, it is not always possible for teachers to maximize the use of scaffolded instruction. Many advocates of computer-based instruction believe that computer programs that have various types of scaffolds built into them can accomplish what some teachers cannot. A study designed to assess that belief (Brush & Saye, 2001) examined the extent to which 11th-grade students used the features of a hypermedia database called Decision Point! that contained both information about the civil rights movement in the United States during the 1960s and several types of scaffolds designed to encourage students to make optimal use of the database.

Each student was assigned to a four-person group. The students in each group were told to assume that they were civil rights leaders in 1968 shortly after the assassination of Martin Luther King Jr. They were asked to develop a solution

to the following problem: What strategies should be used to continue pursuing the goal of the civil rights movement? Using the Decision Point! database, each group was assigned to gather relevant information on particular aspects of the civil rights movement (e.g., the legal system, desegregation, voting rights, the Student Nonviolent Coordinating Committee, and the rejection of integration).

The Decision Point! database contained four types of scaffolds. The first was a set of interactive essays. Each essay provided an overview of a historical event, such as the March on Washington to secure voting rights for all Blacks, with hyperlinks to related documents within the database. If you have seen online encyclopedias in which certain names, places, events, and concepts of an essay are highlighted and linked to related documents, you can visualize how these interactive essays worked. The second scaffold was a set of recommended documents for each event. The program suggested that students first examine 8 to 10 recommended documents for an event before exploring any other information sources. The third scaffold was a student guide that provided categories that might be used by a professional historian to organize and synthesize information about an event (such as groups involved in the event, goals of each group, and strategies used by each group). The final scaffold was a journal in which students could note the effectiveness of their daily information-gathering strategies, the problems they had encountered, and the progress they had made toward completing the task. The purpose of the journal was to help students monitor their efforts.

Of the four scaffolds designed into the database, the interactive essays were used the most. Each group examined at least one of the essays, and two of the four groups read the essays for each event they were assigned. A third group examined all but one of the essays. The hyperlinks, however, were used much less frequently. Only 39% of the total number of documents available were accessed. Although students ignored most of the available documents, the ones they did examine were usually those recommended by the program. Consequently, this was felt to be a somewhat effective scaffold. Only two groups used the student guide scaffold to summarize their analyses for each event they were assigned to research. Moreover, the students' responses to this scaffold were judged to be inadequate. Most contained just a single phrase or sentence for each category. The student journals were used least of all. No group completed a journal for each day of data collection, and the entries were brief and superficial.

The results of this study provide limited support for embedding self-regulatory scaffolds in computerized databases. Students are most likely to use those scaffolds that they perceive to be most relevant to the successful completion of a task and ignore those that appear less relevant or require more time to complete than they have available.

Conclusions About Computer Technology and Self-Regulated Learning

The studies we have summarized, and many others, indicate that computer-based instructional programs can play a productive role in the development and support of students' SRL skills. They can provide students with concrete examples of self-regulation skills and explanations of how those skills relate to achieving a goal. They can support and strengthen the skill of self-monitoring by reminding students at critical points to think about the nature of the problem being solved, similar problems encountered in the past, and appropriate problem-solving tactics. They can also provide a variety of scaffolds.

In short, technology can do for SRL many of the things that teachers do, giving teachers more time to work individually with students who need additional help. But (to repeat a point we made earlier in the book) the use of technology to promote SRL has its limits. Without teacher guidance and oversight, some students will profit from such open-ended tools as simulations, databases, the Internet, and the various social networking tools that are part of what is called Web 2.0, whereas others will likely feel overwhelmed and confused. Part of the art of teaching is figuring out which technology tools to use, with which students, and for which purposes.

WHAT ELSE? *RIP & REVIEW* **CARDS IN THE BACK**

10

CONSTRUCTIVIST LEARNING THEORY, PROBLEM SOLVING, AND TRANSFER

LEARNING OBJECTIVES

After studying this chapter, you will be able to . . .

LO1 Explain how the cognitive, social, and critical variations of constructivism contribute to the conditions that foster constructivist learning.

LO2 Contrast and compare how different types of problems engage constructivist learning, and explain how the 5-step approach can be used to build students' problem solving skills.

LO3 Explain why transfer of learning is critical to sound teaching and learning.

LO4 Explain technologically-based learning environments support knowledge construction and problem solving.

When you begin to teach, you may devote a substantial amount of class time to having students learn information discovered by others. But the acquisition of a storehouse of facts, concepts, and principles is only part of what constitutes an appropriate education. Students must also learn how to *find*, *evaluate*, and *use* what they need to know to accomplish whatever goals they set for themselves. In other words, students need to learn how to be effective problem solvers.

One justification for teaching problem-solving skills in *addition* to ensuring mastery of factual information is that life in technologically oriented countries is marked by high-speed change. New products, services, and social conventions are rapidly introduced and integrated into our lifestyles. Computers, cellular telephones, portable music players—once separate devices and now combined in a single object that fits in your hand—anticancer drugs, and in vitro fertilization, to name just a few examples, are relatively recent innovations that significantly affect the lives of many people.

But change, particularly rapid change, can be a mixed blessing. Although new products and services can make life more convenient, efficient, and enjoyable, they can also make it more complicated and problematic. The green revolution promises new jobs, but requires major changes in how companies earn profits and employees earn livings. Advances in medical care promise healthier and longer lives, but they introduce a host of moral, ethical, legal, and economic problems.

The educational implication that flows from these observations is clear: If we are to benefit from our ability to produce rapid and sometimes dramatic change, our schools need to invest more time, money, and effort in teaching students how to be effective problem solvers. As Lauren Resnick, a past president of the American Educational Research Association, argued, "We need to identify and closely examine the aspects of education that are most likely to produce ability to adapt in the face of transitions and breakdowns. . . . School should focus its efforts on preparing people to be good adaptive learners, so that they can perform effectively when situations are unpredictable and task demands change" (1987, p. 18).

Resnick's argument, which echoes many others, is not without some justification. A survey by the American Management Association (Greenberg, Canzoneri, & Joe, 2000) found that 38% of job applicants lacked sufficient skills for the positions they sought. Rather than blaming "a 'dumbing down' of the incoming workforce," the authors attributed the problem to "the higher skills required in today's workplace" (p. 2).

Good problem solvers share two general characteristics: a well-organized, meaningful fund of knowledge and a systematic set of problem-solving skills. Historically, cognitive learning theories have been particularly useful sources of ideas for imparting both. In this chapter, then, we will examine the issue of meaningful learning from the perspective of a cognitive theory that we introduced previously in the book: constructivism. We will then go on to describe the nature of the problem-solving process and what you can do to help your students become better problem solvers. We will conclude by describing the circumstances under which learned capabilities are applied to new tasks, a process known as transfer of learning.

LO1 Meaningful Learning Within a Constructivist Framework

Constructivism, as you may recall, holds that meaningful learning occurs when people actively try to make sense of the world—when they construct an interpretation of how and why things are—by filtering new ideas and experiences through existing knowledge structures (referred to in previous chapters as schemes or schemata). For example, an individual who lives in a country that provides, for little or no cost, such social services as medical care, counseling, education, job placement and training, and several weeks of paid vacation a year is likely to have constructed a rather different view of the role of government in people's lives from that of someone who lives in a country with a more market-oriented economy. To put it another way, meaningful learning is the active creation of knowledge structures (such as concepts, rules, hypotheses, and associations) from personal experience. In this section, we'll take a brief look at an early constructivist-oriented approach to learning, examine the nature of the constructivist model, and then put it all in perspective by considering the limits, as well as the advantages, of the constructivist viewpoint.

constructivism
The view that meaningful learning is the active creation of knowledge structures rather than a mere transfer of objective knowledge from one person to another.

Discovery Learning: An Early Constructivist Perspective

Constructivist explanations of learning are not new. Over the past 75 years, they have been promoted by such notable scholars as John Dewey, Jean Piaget, Lev Vygotsky, and Jerome Bruner, who in the 1960s contributed the concept of **discovery learning**.

Bruner's ideas about learning through discovery were in reaction to what he argued was a regimented approach to classroom teaching and learning that focused too much on drill and practice and following predetermined, prescribed procedures for solving problems. True learning, said Bruner, involves "figuring out how to use what you already know in order to go beyond what you already think" (1983, p. 183). Bruner argued that students need and deserve opportunities to try to determine for themselves what the problems are and then explore ways to solve the problems, both independently and with others. The kind of teaching that fosters discovery learning aligns quite closely with Piaget's concept of *disequilibrium* (discussed in Chapter 2). Introducing challenges that encourage students to stop and think, to consider and reconsider, and to ask questions and seek additional information is what is meant by constructive learning theory. Much of what Bruner advocated as discovery learning is today referred to as *inquiry* or *inquiry learning* (Guccione, 2011).

Bruner did not suggest that students should discover every fact, principle, or formula they may need to know. Discovery is simply too inefficient a process to be used that widely, and learning from others can be as meaningful as personal discovery (R. E. Mayer, 2004; 2009). Rather, he argued that certain types of outcomes—understanding the ways in which ideas connect with one another, the possibility of solving problems on our own, and how what we already know is relevant to what we are trying to learn—are the essence of education and can best be achieved through personal discovery.

{ **Bruner: discover how ideas relate to each other and to existing knowledge** }

Constructivism Today

Constructivism is an umbrella term. It covers several views of learning that share common claims (Rikers, van Gog, & Paas, 2008; Tobias & Duffy, 2009). After a brief examination of the claims that unite the various views of learning under the classification of constructivism, we will describe three variations of constructivist learning theory and look at the conditions that foster constructivist learning.

Common Claims That Frame Constructivism We identify four claims that, taken together, provide a frame through which to view learning and learners. Looking through the constructivist frame we see four key ideas: prior knowledge, multiple perspectives, self-regulation, and authentic learning (Loyens, Rikers, & Schmidt, 2007). The claim that captures each idea is described briefly in turn.

TeachSource Video Case

Elementary School Language Arts: Inquiry Learning

Go to the Education CourseMate website and watch the video, study the artifacts in the case, and reflect upon the following questions:

1. How does this Video Case illustrate the concepts of constructivism and discovery learning?

2. How does the classroom teacher in this Video Case encourage students to construct their own knowledge? What strategies and instructional approaches does she use?

1. *Meaningful learning is the active creation of knowledge structures from personal experience.* Constructivists view the learner as an active agent in the construction of knowledge (Cunningham, 1992; Gijbels, van de Watering, Dochy, & van den Bossche, 2006; Loyens, Rikers, & Schmidt, 2008). Each learner builds a personal view of the world by using existing knowledge, interests, attitudes, goals, and the like to select and interpret the information she encounters (Koohang, Riley, Smith, & Schreurs, 2009; R. E. Mayer, 2008). This assumption highlights the importance of what educational psychologists call prior knowledge—the previously learned knowledge and skill that students bring to the classroom (Ozuru, Dempsey, & McNamara, 2009).

Construction of ideas is strongly influenced by the student's prior knowledge.

The knowledge that learners bring with them to a learning task has long been suspected of having a powerful effect on subsequent performance. In 1978, David Ausubel wrote on the flyleaf of his textbook *Educational Psychology: A Cognitive View,* "If I had to reduce all of educational psychology to just one principle, I would say this: the most important single factor influencing learning is what the learner already knows. Ascertain this and teach him [or her] accordingly" (Ausubel, Novak, & Hanesian, 1978).

2. *Social interaction and the negotiation of understanding with others can help learners construct knowledge.* One person's knowledge can never be identical to another person's because knowledge is the result of a personal interpretation of experience, which is influenced by such factors as the learner's age, gender, race, ethnic background, and knowledge base. By interacting with others, learners have the opportunity to gain a perspective different from their own. Thus, the additions to, deletions from, and modifications of individuals' knowledge structures result from the sharing of multiple perspectives. Systematic, open-minded discussions and debates are instrumental in helping individuals create personal views (Azevedo, 2009; Paavola, Lipponen, & Hakkarainen, 2004).

3. *Self-regulation by learners is a key to successful learning.* Self-regulated learning, as you will recall from the previous chapter, occurs when a person generates and controls thoughts, feelings, and actions in an effort to achieve a learning goal. Reflecting on the discussions of self-regulated learning in the previous chapter—and the first two claims mentioned here—this third claim of constructivists should come as no surprise. Constructivists view learners not as passive recipients of new information but as active agents who use their prior knowledge and experiences to engage their environments (including other people) in order to enhance their existing knowledge structures (Piaget's concept of assimilation) and to build new knowledge structures (accommodation). Self-regulation skills allow learners to take charge: to function as the agents of their own learning rather than objects of instruction.

4. *Authentic problems provide realistic contexts that contribute to the construction and transfer of knowledge.* When students encounter problems that are realistic, they are able to use what they already know about the problem situation (Driscoll, 2005). For example, imagine that a middle school class in Juneau, Alaska, needs to learn how to use mathematical formulas to make predictions. They need to understand what variables are, how some variables can be used or combined to predict other variables, and what to do with the values of predictor variables in order to make their predictions. One way to approach the task would be to memorize the formulas, plug in values that are provided on a test or in a problem workbook, generate their predictions, and find out if the predictions match the "correct answers." Another way to approach the task would be to pose the question: What might happen to the economy of Juneau as the nearby Mendenhall Glacier (which is a major tourist attraction) shrinks? Such a question provides rich opportunities to identify variables that affect the ecology of the glacier and its changing distance from the town and its tourists, to conduct research in order to build predictive models. What are the variables involved? It would help to know the number of tourist visits to Mendenhall Glacier per year, jobs supported by tourism, hotel and cruise ship fees, customers in restaurant and shops, and tax dollars. How do we find out that information? How do the variables influence the economy? How do we measure that influence?

In addition to allowing students to engage their prior knowledge, authentic tasks often provide opportunities for learners to work collaboratively, thus providing opportunities for social interaction and the negotiation of meaning through multiple perspectives (Kordaki, 2009).

cognitive constructivism
A form of constructivist learning theory that emphasizes the role of assimilation and accommodation in constructing an understanding of the world in which one lives.

social constructivism A form of constructivist learning theory that emphasizes how people use such cultural tools as language, mathematics, and approaches to problem solving in social settings to construct a common or shared understanding of the world in which they live.

Taken together, these constructivist claims provide a frame for understanding meaningful learning as the construction of knowledge. When we look through the constructivist frame, our view is directed toward the key concepts of prior knowledge, multiple perspectives, self-regulation, and authentic learning. As mentioned earlier, however, constructivist theory has several variations. We can think of those variations as lenses that can be placed in the frame. The frame keeps our attention directed toward the common constructivist claims and the key concepts they represent. But each lens slightly changes how we focus among the key concepts. One lens, for example, brings prior knowledge into relief; another places the multiple perspectives of social interaction in the foreground. Each lens represents a variation on the constructivist theme. We look briefly through the three lenses: cognitive, social, and critical constructivism.

The constructivist variation known as **social constructivism** holds that meaningful learning occurs when people are explicitly taught how to use the psychological tools of their culture (such as language, mathematics, and approaches to problem solving) and are then given the opportunity to use these tools in authentic, real-life activities to create a common, or shared, understanding of some phenomenon (Burton, Lee, & Younie, 2009; McInerney, 2005). Students are encouraged to engage in open-ended discussion with peers and teachers about such things as the meaning of terms and procedures, the relationships among ideas, and the applicability of knowledge to specific contexts. This process is often referred to by social constructivists as *negotiating meaning*. This view has its roots in the writings of such individuals as the psychologist Lev Vygotsky and the educational philosopher John Dewey

> **In addition to prior knowledge, construction of ideas is aided by multiple perspectives, self-regulation, and authentic tasks.**

Three Variations on a Constructivist Theme One view of meaningful learning that we have described, Jean Piaget's, holds that it is the natural result of an intrinsic drive to resolve inconsistencies and contradictions—that is, always to have a view of the world that makes sense in the light of what we currently know. One variation of constructivism, **cognitive constructivism**, is an outgrowth of Piaget's ideas because it focuses on the cognitive processes that take place within individuals. In other words, an individual's conception of the truth of some matter (for example, that both birds and airplanes can fly because they use the same aerodynamic principles) is based on her ability, with guidance, to assimilate information effectively into existing schemes and develop new schemes and operations (the process Piaget called *accommodation*) in response to novel or discrepant ideas (Fosnot & Perry, 2005; Windschitl, 2002).

Most constructivist theories take one of three forms: cognitive constructivism, social constructivism, or critical constructivism. The first emphasizes the effect of one's cognitive processes on meaningful learning, whereas the latter two emphasize the effect of other people's arguments and cultural points of view.

Chapter 10: Constructivist Learning Theory, Problem Solving, and Transfer

(M. Cole & Gajdamaschko, 2007; Postholm, 2008; Windschitl, 2002). This variation has also given rise to an increasing focus by researchers on how culture and history influence people's thoughts and actions as they engage with others and with their environment.

A framework that guides this focus is called cultural-historical activity theory, or CHAT for short (M. Cole, 1996; W.-M. Roth & Lee, 2007; Saka, Southerland, & Brooks, 2009; Yamagata-Lynch & Haudenschild, 2008, 2009). CHAT provides a way of analyzing and understanding activity in complex, real-life situations. For example, Lisa Yamagata-Lynch (2007) used activity systems analysis (see Engeström, 1999) to investigate an effort to integrate technology in a school district in hopes that increased use of technology would enhance student learning. The analysis of the activities of individual teachers, teacher groups, and technology staff in the school and the district, and the activities in a professional development program, allowed Yamagata-Lynch to observe how the activities of various individuals and groups interacted. By using activity systems analysis, she was able to identify obstacles to attaining the goal of technology integration and the tensions that were created as people in various roles worked toward the goal (some tensions can contribute positively to attaining the goal).

CHAT evolved from the social constructivism of Vygotsky. As it has evolved, the importance of culture and one's history within a culture have been brought into clearer focus by the third lens through which we can view the constructivist view of meaningful learning.

The third variation on the constructivist theme is referred to as **critical constructivism** (Fok & Watkins, 2009; Jean-Marie, Normore, & Brooks, 2009; Stears, 2009). The label "critical" was applied to constructivism as some researchers began to incorporate a critical theory perspective to study how learners constructed knowledge. According to philosopher James Bohman, "a theory is critical to the extent that it seeks human emancipation." Bohman goes on to say that "a critical theory provides the descriptive and normative bases for social inquiry aimed at decreasing domination and increasing freedom in all their forms" (Bohman, 2009, para. 1). Thus, critical constructivists seek (1) to understand why learners from some cultural or social groups more easily construct knowledge in school environments than others and (2) to liberate the learning of learners who experience difficulty in school environments, so that all students can successfully construct knowledge (Harrington & Enochs, 2009).

As we discussed in Chapter 5, two important factors that distinguish one culture from another are ethnicity and social class. We learned also that cultural differences can mean differences in communication patterns that lead to misunderstandings among students and between students and teachers. Finally, we learned that teacher expectations can influence how students perform in school. Critical constructivism focuses on what the social aspects are of learning environments that teachers create in their classrooms, whether those environments perpetuate cultural myths (for example, "children from lower socioeconomic groups do not have sufficient prior knowledge to construct knowledge"), and how learners' cultural backgrounds influence how they interact with others and with the content they are being asked to learn (G. Goodman, 2008; Loyens & Gijbels, 2008; P. Taylor, 1996).

Although the cognitive, social, and critical constructivist perspectives emphasize different aspects of learning, they are not incompatible. The cognitive approach does not deny the value of learning in group activities nor the influence of one's cultural background; the social approach does not deny the value of working independently of others; and the critical approach acknowledges that cognitive processing and social negotiation are key to constructing knowledge.

Putting Constructivist Learning Practice in Perspective There are conditions that foster constructivist learning practices and there are conditions that discourage them. The fostering conditions include a cognitive apprenticeship between student and teacher, a use of realistic problems and conditions, and an emphasis on multiple perspectives.

Cognitive Apprenticeship The practice of cognitive apprenticeship is related to the strategy of reciprocal teaching discussed in Chapter 9 (Palincsar & Brown, 1984). The main feature of cognitive apprenticeship is that the teacher models a cognitive process that students are to learn and then gradually turns responsibility for executing the process over to students as they become more skilled (Seezink, Poell, & Kirschner, 2009). As you may recall from our earlier discussions—in Chapter 2, for example—providing such environmental supports as modeling, hints, leading questions, and suggestions and then gradually removing them as the learner demonstrates increased competence is called *scaffolding*.

Situated Learning By establishing the condition of **situated learning** (or situated cognition), students are

critical constructivism
A form of constructivism that seeks (1) to understand why learners from some cultural or social groups more easily construct knowledge in school environments than others and (2) to liberate the learning of students who experience difficulty in school environments, so that all students can successfully construct knowledge.

situated learning
The idea that problem-solving skills, cognitive strategies, and knowledge are closely linked to the specific context or environment in which they are acquired; hence, the more authentic, or true to life, the task, the more meaningful the learning. Also called *situated cognition*.

given learning tasks set in realistic contexts. A realistic context is one in which students must solve a meaningful problem by using a variety of skills and information. The rationale for this condition is twofold:

1. Learning is more likely to be meaningful (related to previously learned knowledge and skills) when it is embedded in a realistic context (Duffy & Cunningham, 1996; Hung, 2002).

2. Traditional forms of classroom learning and instruction, which are largely decontextualized in the sense that what students learn is relevant only to taking tests and performing other classroom tasks, leads to a condition that has been referred to as *inert knowledge* (Gentner, Loewenstein, Thompson, & Forbus, 2009). Inert knowledge is what some might refer to as "useless trivia." We will return to the idea of inert knowledge when we address helping students become good problem solvers later in this chapter.

As an example of situated learning, the game of baseball can be used as a vehicle for middle school or high school students to apply aspects of science, mathematics, and sociology. Students could be asked to use their knowledge of physics to explain how pitchers are able to make the ball curve left or right or drop down as it approaches home plate. They could be asked to use their mathematical skills to figure out how far home runs travel or whether the distance between bases is optimal. They could also be asked to read about the Negro Leagues and Jackie Robinson and discuss why it took until the late 1940s for major league baseball to begin integration.

A more formal way of implementing situated learning is to use problem-based learning (Hung, 2002; Jeong & Hmelo-Silver, 2010). Unlike a traditional approach to instruction in which students first learn a body of knowledge and then use that knowledge to solve problems, problem-based learning presents students with complex, authentic problems (such as creating a water management plan for the desert Southwest) and requires them to identify and locate the information they need to solve the problem. This chapter's Case in Print provides an account of how technology is being combined with problem-based learning, a topic we will return to again in the technology section at the end of the chapter.

Multiple Perspectives The third practice that fosters constructivist learning is the use of multiple perspectives. The rationale, again, is twofold: most of life's problems are multifaceted, and the knowledge base of experts is a network of interrelated ideas. The complex process of

becoming an effective teacher is a good example of the need for multiple perspectives, including the perspectives of other teachers (Chan & Pang, 2006).

Although constructivism has much to offer teachers, like any other theory it does have its limitations, and there may be problems with its implementation (Kirschner, Sweller, & Clark, 2006; R. E. Mayer, 2009). Here are a few you should keep in mind:

- Constructivist practices emphasize guiding rather than telling, seeking diverse perspectives, modifying previous conceptions in the light of new information, and creating an atmosphere that encourages active participation. Such practices make it difficult to create highly detailed or scripted lesson plans. Much of what teachers do depends on how students respond. Teaching from this perspective will place a premium on your teacher-artist abilities.

- Teaching from a constructivist perspective is more time consuming and places higher demands on learners than a typical lecture format (Perkins, 1999; Schwartz, Lindgren, & Lewis, 2009).

- There are competing expectations for students to demonstrate that they "know the right answer" (on annual achievement tests, for example) and that they can think beyond the right answer, using what they know to understand and solve novel problems (Samuelson, 2006). Teachers who believe that their primary responsibility is to prepare students for high-stakes tests are less likely to use a constructivist approach (Haney & McArthur, 2002; Nichols & Berliner, 2007). For those who see the benefit of constructivist learning practices, it is critical to find a balance between helping students demonstrate what they know and helping them develop their capacities to think deeply and creatively about problems and issues. We will see how critical in later chapters that address how to plan, assess, and manage learning.

Pause& Reflect *Can you recall a class in which the instructor used constructivist techniques? What did the instructor do? How did you react? Was the learning outcome more meaningful for you than in other classes?*

The extent to which teachers engage in constructivist teaching practices is determined in large part by how completely they accept its underlying principles (e.g., knowledge is situated, knowledge is the result of discussions among students and between students and the teacher, students have input into the curriculum, learning is grounded in real-life tasks and settings to make it relevant to students' lives).

© deva/Shutterstock Images

Chapter 10: Constructivist Learning Theory, Problem Solving, and Transfer

The Suggestions for Teaching on pages 220–221 provide a closer look at constructivist learning practices.

LO2 The Nature of Problem Solving

As with most of the other topics covered in this book, an extensive amount of theorizing and research on problem solving has been conducted over the years. We will focus our discussion on the types of problems that students are typically required to deal with, the cognitive processes that play a central role in problem solving, and various approaches to teaching problem solving in the classroom.

Let's begin by asking what we mean by the terms *problem* and *problem solving*. Most, if not all, psychologists would agree that "a problem is said to exist when one has a goal and has not yet identified a means for reaching that goal" (Gagné, Yekovich, & Yekovich, 1993, p. 211). **Problem solving**, then, is the identification and application of knowledge and skills that result in goal attainment (Kruse, 2009; Martinez, 1998). Although this definition encompasses a wide range of problem types, we will focus on three types that students frequently encounter both in and out of school.

Three Common Types of Problems

In the first category are the well-structured problems of mathematics and science—the type of problems that students from kindergarten through middle school are typically required to solve. **Well-structured problems** are clearly formulated, can be solved by recall and application of a specific procedure (called an *algorithm*), and result in a solution that can be evaluated against a well-known, agreed-on standard (Kapur & Kinzer, 2009)—for example:

$$5 + 8$$
$$732 - 485$$
$$8 + 3x = 40 - 5x$$

© Bob Daemmrich/Photo Edit

Well-structured problems have a clear structure, can be solved by using a standard procedure, and produce solutions that can be evaluated against an agreed-on standard. They are the type of problem that students are asked to solve most frequently.

problem solving The identification and application of knowledge and skills that result in goal attainment.

well-structured problem A clearly formulated problem with known solution procedures and known evaluation standards.

TeachSource Video Case

Middle School Science Instruction: Inquiry Learning

Go to the Education CourseMate website and watch the video, study the artifacts in the case, and reflect upon the following questions:

1. Does Robert Cho's science class meet the criteria for a constructivist classroom?

2. Based on this Video Case and the discussion on constructivism in this section of the text, why do you think that teaching using a constructivist approach is more time consuming for teachers (as opposed to other teaching methods)? Cite some possible reasons.

Combining Technology and Problems to Construct Knowledge

The fostering conditions include a cognitive apprenticeship between student and teacher, a use of realistic problems and conditions, and an emphasis on multiple perspectives. . . . By establishing the condition of situated learning (or situated cognition), students are given learning tasks set in realistic contexts. . . . A more formal way of implementing situated learning is to use problem-based learning (Hung, 2002; Jeong & Hmelo-Silver, 2010). Unlike a traditional approach to instruction in which students first learn a body of knowledge and then use that knowledge to solve problems, problem-based learning presents students with complex, authentic problems (such as creating a water management plan for the desert Southwest) and requires them to identify and locate the information they need. (pp. 215–216)

At School, Technology Starts to Turn a Corner

STEVE LOHR

The New York Times (www.nytimes.com), 8/17/08

Count me a technological optimist, but I have always thought that the people who advocate putting computers in classrooms as a way to transform education were well intentioned but wide of the mark. It's not the problem, and it's not the answer.

Yet as a new school year begins, the time may have come to reconsider how large a role technology can play in changing education. There are promising examples, both in the United States and abroad, and they share some characteristics. The ratio of computers to pupils is one to one. Technology isn't off in a computer lab. Computing is an integral tool in all disciplines, always at the ready.

Web-based education software has matured in the last few years, so that students, teachers and families can be linked through networks. Until recently, computing in the classroom amounted to students doing Internet searches, sending e-mail and mastering word processing, presentation programs and spreadsheets. That's useful stuff, to be sure, but not something that alters how schools work.

The new Web education networks can open the door to broader changes. Parents become more engaged because they can monitor their children's attendance, punctuality, homework and performance, and can get tips for helping them at home. Teachers can share methods, lesson plans and online curriculum materials.

In the classroom, the emphasis can shift to project-based learning, a real break with the textbook-and-lecture model of education. In a high school class, a project might begin with a hypothetical letter from the White House that says oil prices are spiking, the economy is faltering and the president's poll numbers are falling. The assignment would be to devise a new energy policy in two weeks. The shared Web space for the project, for example, would include the White House letter, the sources the students must consult, their work plan and timetable, assignments for each student, the assessment criteria for their grades and, eventually, the paper the team delivers. Oral presentations would be required.

The project-based approach, some educators say, encourages active learning and produces better performance in class and on standardized tests.

The educational bottom line, it seems, is that while computer technology has matured and become more affordable, the most significant development has been a deeper understanding of how to use the technology.

"Unless you change how you teach and how kids work, new technology is not really going to make a difference," said Bob Pearlman, a former teacher who is the director of strategic planning for the New Technology Foundation, a nonprofit organization.

The foundation, based in Napa, Calif., has developed a model for project-based teaching and is at the forefront of the drive for technology-enabled reform of education. Forty-two schools in nine states are trying the foundation's model, and their numbers are growing rapidly.

ill-structured problem A vaguely stated problem with unclear solution procedures and vague evaluation standards.

What constitutes a problem to be solved varies with the age and experience of the learner and the nature of the problem itself (Martinez, 1998). The second of the mathematical examples is likely to be a genuine problem for some first or second graders who are used to seeing subtraction exercises arrayed vertically (minuend on top, subtrahend beneath, horizontal line under the subtrahend). Fifth graders, however, who have had experience with arithmetic assignments in a variety of formats, would be able to retrieve and use the correct algorithm automatically. Because the fifth graders know the means to reach their goal, they do not face a problem-solving task according to our definition, just a type of exercise or practice.

In the second category are the ill-structured problems often encountered in everyday life and in disciplines such as economics and psychology. **Ill-structured problems** are more complex, provide few cues pointing to solution procedures, and have less definite criteria for determining when they have been solved (Choi & Lee, 2009; Kapur & Kinzer, 2007). Examples of ill-structured problems are how to identify and reward good teachers, how to improve access to public buildings and facilities for people with physical disabilities, and how to increase voter turnout for elections.

The third category includes problems that are also ill structured but that differ from the examples just

Behind the efforts, of course, are concerns that K–12 public schools are falling short in preparing students for the twin challenges of globalization and technological change. Worries about the nation's future competitiveness led to the creation in 2002 of the Partnership for 21st Century Skills, a coalition whose members include the Department of Education and technology companies like Apple, Cisco Systems, Dell and Microsoft.

The government-industry partnership identifies a set of skills that mirror those that the New Technology Foundation model is meant to nurture. Those skills include collaboration, systems thinking, self-direction and communication, both online and in person.

State officials in Indiana took a look at the foundation's model and offered travel grants for local teachers and administrators to visit its schools in California. Sally Nichols, an English teacher, came away impressed and signed up for the new project-based teaching program at her school, Decatur Central High School in Indianapolis.

Last year, Ms. Nichols and another teacher taught a biology and literature class for freshmen. (Cross-disciplinary courses are common in the New Technology model.) Typically, half of freshmen fail biology, but under the project-based model the failure rate was cut in half.

"There's a lot of ownership by the kids in their work instead of teachers lecturing and being the givers of all knowledge," Ms. Nichols explained. "The classes are just much more alive. They don't sleep in class."

In Indiana, the number of schools using the foundation model will increase to six this year, and an additional dozen communities have signed up for the next year, said David Shane, a member of the state board of education. "It's caught fire in Indiana, and we've got to have this kind of education to prepare our young people for the future in a global economy that is immersed in technology."

The extra cost for schools that have adopted the New Technology model is about $1,000 per student a year, once a school is set up, says Mr. Pearlman of the foundation. After the first three years, the extra cost should decline considerably, he said.

In England, where the government has promoted technology in schools for a decade, the experiment with technology-driven change in education is further along.

Five years ago, the government gave computers to students at two schools in high-crime neighborhoods in Birmingham. For the students, a Web-based portal is the virtual doorway for assignments, school social activities, online mentoring, discussion groups and e-mail. Even students who are suspended from school for a few days beg not to lose their access to the portal, says Sir Mark Grundy, 49, the executive principal of Shireland Collegiate Academy and the George Salter Collegiate Academy. Today, the schools are among the top in the nation in yearly improvements in students' performance in reading and math tests.

Sir Mark says he is convinced that advances in computing, combined with improved understanding of how to tailor the technology to different students, can help transform education.

"This is the best Trojan horse for causing change in schools that I have ever seen," he said.

Source: Steve Lohr, "At school, technology starts to turn a corner," from *The New York Times* (www.nytimes.com), August 17, 2008. Copyright © 2008 The New York Times Co. Reprinted by permission.

Questions and Activities

1. What principles of constructivist learning theory are reflected in the instructional activities described in this story?
2. What other problem-based projects can you think of that could take advantage of technology? Describe a problem, what you would have students do, and what you would hope they accomplish.

---

mentioned in two respects. First, these problems tend to divide people into opposing camps because of the emotions they arouse. Second, the primary goal, at least initially, is not to determine a course of action but to identify the most reasonable position. These problems are often referred to as **issues** (Ruggiero, 2009; Troyer & Youngreen, 2009). Examples of issues are capital punishment, gun control, and nondenominational prayer in classrooms. High school students typically have more opportunities than younger students to deal with ill-structured problems and issues of the type cited here. That does not mean, however, that younger students have no opportunities to deal with ill-structured problems or issues. Consider self-regulated learning, discussed in the previous chapter. Goal orientation plays a role in the development of self-regulated learning and self-efficacy. Performance goals provide clear, easily specified outcomes; they are similar to well-structured problems. Learning goals, however, are more similar to ill-structured problems or issues. Suppose you have young students who desire to become politicians or firefighters. They will see value in establishing goals that will help them learn the knowledge and skills they need to become politicians or firefighters. Generating personally valued goals can be an opportunity for younger students to solve ill-structured problems (R. Miller & Brickman, 2004).

issue An ill-structured problem that arouses strong feelings.

Suggestions for Teaching

Using a Constructivist Approach to Meaningful Learning

There are four key ideas that frame constructivist views of learning. The suggestions for teaching that follow are based on each of those ideas. A fifth suggestion is provided to address concerns that are sometimes expressed about constructivism and standards.

1 **Help students create knowledge from personal experience.**

At the crux of the constructivist view of learning is the idea that learners use what they already know (sometimes called prior knowledge) to build new understanding. The basic idea is to *arrange* the elements of a learning task and *guide* student actions so that students discover, or construct, a personally meaningful conception of a problem or issue (as opposed to someone else's conception). For example, you might introduce a lesson on persuasive writing by asking students to think about the memorable advertisements they have seen in magazines on television. You could then have students discuss their selections in small groups and have each group generate a list of principles of persuasive writing based on their discussion.

Another suggestion for helping students access what they already know in order to construct meaningful conceptions is to "preview" their assigned reading. One way this can be done is to engage students in an activity before they read an assigned chapter, story, book, website. If they are given opportunities to use what they already know in the context of the kinds of concepts, issues, or problems they will encounter in the reading assignment, they are more likely to construct meaningful interpretations of what they read. Here are two ideas for previewing:

One way to preview is to give students a list of concepts, issues, or questions that will be addressed in the assigned reading. Have students write down what they know about the concepts or issues or have them answer the questions. After individuals have responded, they can share what they know (or think they know) with other students and then with the entire class. At this point, you can respond to the "prereading knowledge" the students have shared and do so with the coming reading assignment in mind.

A second way to preview is to give students the opportunity to engage in activity that is relevant to the reading. Imagine that you are about to assign a chapter on the legislative process. As a preview activity, you might have students work in small groups to generate a list of rules that should govern some school or social function (e.g., library use, a class party or school dance, volunteer efforts in the community, homework policies). Have students reflect on the process by which their group tried to develop and agree on the rules. Such an exercise gives them an experience that could help them make meaning of the chapter they are going to read.

2 **Allow students to construct knowledge by negotiating their understanding with others.**

In the examples in the first suggestion, you might have noticed the idea of allowing students to discuss their views or collaborate with others. Constructivists assume that because people have different experiences, they construct different meanings and understandings from those experiences. By encouraging students to share their ideas and use the ideas of others to inform and test their own views, you help a richer learning environment emerge.

There is an instructional practice that is known widely among practicing teachers as "think-pair-share." A variation on that technique works as follows:

1. Students are presented with a problem or asked a question and given time to formulate a response by themselves (typically they jot down their ideas in a "1- or 2-minute write").
2. Students are then paired. Students in each pair take turns sharing while the other listens carefully.
3. Together the pair of students collaborate to create an answer that is "better" than either individual response.
4. If time permits, two pairs of students can form a group of four. The group of four can now follow the steps of sharing, listening, and creating.

5. The "better" responses that emerged from either the pairs or the pairs of pairs are then shared with the entire class (they can be shared orally in a whole-group discussion, or written versions can be projected for the whole class to see or posted on a class discussion board).

The class can argue the merits of the various responses and try to arrive at a whole-class consensus. This kind of learning activity can also be used to trace how the consensus was reached: What were the first responses to be generated by individuals? How did the responses change as pairs collaborated? The paired pairs (groups of four)? The whole class? In this way, students can see how interaction and negotiation can influence learning.

3 **Encourage students to take responsibility not only for what they learn, but also how they learn.**

From a constructivist perspective, one of the most important outcomes of learning is the development of self-regulation. Typically, when people think about school learning, they think about acquiring information, content, and knowledge. But there are also skills to be learned and self-regulation is a critical skill for student success. The question here is, how can you help your students take responsibility for their own learning, become better monitors of their learning, and determine and use effective strategies with confidence?

© Kenneth C. Zirkel/iStockphoto

© Leah-Anne Thompson/iStockphoto

Reflect back on the previous suggestion for a moment. If you use the think-pair-share technique as a way of helping students see how their thinking changes as they engage with other students, you are helping them see how they learn and giving them a chance to reflect on what they can do differently to make the process more effective or efficient. Engaging your students in this kind of reflection on how they approach and engage a learning task and what they can do better is one way to help them develop the skills needed for self-regulation.

Another way is to give students plenty of opportunities to evaluate their own work. For example, suppose your students are to complete a short report on some observations they made in their neighborhood as part of a social studies unit. You might have them complete and submit a "final draft" that is presented and discussed in a small group. (Group members can be given the responsibility for suggesting changes to each author.) After the discussion, students are then given the opportunity to use what they learned from the discussion—including improvements that come from simply presenting their work to others—to evaluate their final draft and submit a revision. Another variation might be to have students submit their revision with an author's note. In the note, the writer identifies the improvements that were made between the final draft and the final revision and the reasons those improvements were made.

The more opportunities students have to evaluate and improve their own learning products and performances, the more likely it is that they will improve their capacity for self-regulation. And as their self-regulatory skills improve, so will their sense of self-efficacy as learners. (Recall the discussion in Chapter 9 of the connection between self-regulation and self-efficacy.)

4 Provide real-life problems that challenge and "stretch" your students' thinking.
Using real-world problems helps situate learning and helps students engage in meaningful learning in several ways. First, because the problems are real instead of hypothetical, students can use what they already

know—their prior knowledge—about the problems. Second, they can talk with their fellow students about their perceptions of the problem and to people who are affected by the problem. Third, they can collect data to understand the nature of the problem from multiple perspectives. Fourth, because the problems exist, they have not yet been solved: No one has printed the solution in the back of a textbook. Part of the learning that authentic problems provide is the opportunity to first understand the problem before trying to solve it. As we will see later in this chapter, problem understanding is critical to becoming a good problem solver.

We will have more to say about the nature of problems later in this chapter and in Chapter 13, particularly in the context of problem-based learning. For now, consider how, say, local environmental or social issues—from recycling and water conservation to food banks and transportation—might provide opportunities for students to construct and apply their understanding of math, history, or science and develop their skills in research, writing, and oral communication. Grappling with real problems gives students a chance to demonstrate their learning in ways that have consequences beyond submitting an assignment to one teacher and receiving a grade.

© xpixel/Shutterstock Images

5 Use guided experiences to satisfy both constructivist principles and state learning standards.
Because constructivism is strongly student centered and emphasizes high-level outcomes, it is sometimes perceived as being incompatible with the need for teachers to prepare students for high-stakes tests that are based on state learning standards. But through the use of guided experiences, teachers can do both. The trick is to embed standards in learning experiences that students care about. Geoffrey Caine, Renate Nummela Caine, and Carol McClintic (2002) described how this was done for eighth grade classes studying the U.S. Civil War.

To satisfy state learning standards, students needed to learn such things as the nature of slavery, the causes of the war, important dates and the sequence of events, major battles, and significant individuals who affected the course of the war. The first step

was to teach students how to listen to one another and express disagreements in a non-judgmental way.

An introductory event was then used to spark students' interest in the topic. They were read a story about a woman who disguised herself as a man, enlisted in the Union Army, and worked as a coal handler on a canal boat. They were then shown a short segment from the motion picture *Gettysburg* in which Confederate soldiers marched directly into cannon and rifle fire. The last part of the introduction involved telling students that over 400 women disguised themselves as men and participated in the war and that the 51,000 soldiers who were killed during the 3-day Battle of Gettysburg exceeded the number of U.S. soldiers who were killed during the entire Vietnam War. When invited to raise questions, the students wanted to know such things as why women fought in the war, how it was that nobody knew they were women, why the North and South went to war, and why soldiers would walk into enemy gunfire.

The students were assigned to groups based on the similarity of the questions they raised and were told to seek answers from library resources, the Internet, and interviews with war veterans. The teachers used the subsequent reports each group made to the class and the discussions that followed to ensure that such standards-related issues as the different groups involved in the war and the nature of slavery were introduced and discussed.

© Nikola Nastasic/iStockphoto

problem representation The process of finding ways to express a problem so as to recall the optimal amount of solution-relevant information from long-term memory. Also called *problem framing*.

Helping Students Become Good Problem Solvers

Despite the differences that exist among well-structured problems, ill-structured problems, and issues, recent theory and research suggest that good problem solvers employ the same general approach when solving one or another of these problem types (Bransford & Stein, 1993; Gagné, Yekovich, & Yekovich, 1993; C. Matthew & Sternberg, 2009; Pretz, Naples, & Sternberg, 2003; Ruggiero, 2009). This approach consists of five steps or processes:

1. Realize that a problem exists.
2. Understand the nature of the problem.
3. Compile relevant information.
4. Formulate and carry out a solution.
5. Evaluate the solution.

Well-structured problems may call only for the implementation of steps 2, 4, and 5, but the other two problem types require all five steps. We will discuss each of these steps in the next few pages, along with some specific techniques that you can use to help your students become good problem solvers.

> **Problem finding depends on curiosity and dissatisfaction with the status quo.**

Step 1: Realize That a Problem Exists Most people assume that if a problem is worth solving, they won't have to seek it out; it will make itself known. Like most other assumptions, this one is only partly true. Well-structured problems are often thrust on us by teachers, in the form of in-class exercises or homework, or by supervisors at work. Ill-structured problems and issues, however, often remain hidden from most people. It is a characteristic of good problem solvers that they are more sensitive to the existence of problems than most of their peers (Kruse, 2009; Pretz, Naples, & Sternberg, 2003).

The keys to problem recognition, or *problem finding* as it is sometimes called, are curiosity and dissatisfaction. You need to question why a rule, procedure, or product is the way it is, or feel frustrated or irritated because something does not work as well as it might.

The organization Mothers Against Drunk Driving, for example, was begun by a woman who, because her daughter had been killed in a traffic accident by a drunk driver, was dissatisfied with current, ineffective laws. This organization has been instrumental in getting state legislatures to pass laws against drunk driving that mandate more severe penalties.

Problem finding does not come readily to most people, possibly because schools emphasize solving well-structured problems and possibly because most people have a natural tendency to assume that things work as well as they can. Like any other cognitive process, however, problem recognition can improve with instruction and practice. Students can be sensitized in a number of ways to the absence or flaws and shortcomings of products, procedures, rules, or whatever else. We will make some specific suggestions about improving problem recognition and the other problem-solving processes a bit later.

> **Problem framing depends on knowledge of the subject matter and familiarity with problem types.**

Step 2: Understand the Nature of the Problem The second step in the problem-solving process is perhaps the most critical. The problem solver has to construct an *optimal* representation, or understanding, of the nature of a problem or issue. The preceding sentence stresses the word *optimal* for two reasons. First, most problems can be expressed in a number of ways. Written problems, for example, can be recast as pictures, equations, graphs, charts, or diagrams. Second, because the way we represent the problem determines the amount and type of solution-relevant information we recall from long-term memory, some representations are better than others. For obvious reasons, problem-solving researchers often refer to this process as **problem representation** or *problem framing* (Derry et al., 2005; Giaccardi, 2005; P. Miller, Fagley, & Casella, 2009).

To achieve an optimal understanding of a problem, an individual needs two things: a high degree of knowledge of the subject matter (facts, concepts, and principles) on which the problem is based and a familiarity with that particular type of problem. This background will allow the person to recognize important elements (words, phrases, and numbers) in the problem statement and patterns of relationships among the problem elements. This recognition will activate one or more solution-relevant schemes from long-term memory. It is this level of knowledge of subject matter and problem types that distinguishes the high-quality problem representations of the expert problem solver from the low-quality representations of the novice. Experts typically represent problems in terms of one or more basic patterns or underlying principles, whereas novices focus on limited or superficial surface features of problems.

To give you a clearer idea of the nature and power of an optimal problem representation, consider the following situation: When novices are given a set of physics problems to solve, they sort them into categories on the basis of some noticeable feature. For example, they group together all problems that involve the use of an inclined plane or all the ones that involve the use of pulleys. Then novices search their memories for previously learned information. The drawback to this approach is that although two or three problems may involve the use of an inclined plane, their solutions may depend on the application of different laws of physics. Experts, in contrast, draw on their extensive and well-organized knowledge base to represent groups of problems according to a common underlying principle, such as conservation of energy or Newton's third law (Pretz, Naples, & Sternberg, 2003; Stemler, Sternberg, Grigorenko, Jarvin, & Sharpes, 2009; Sternberg, 2009).

An important aspect of problem solving is the ability to activate relevant schemes (organized collections of facts, concepts, principles, and procedures) from long-term memory when they are needed. The more relevant and powerful the activated scheme is, the more likely it is that an effective problem solution will be achieved. But as many observers of education have pointed out, acquiring this ability is often easier said than done. John Bransford argues that standard educational practices produce knowledge that is *inert*. As mentioned earlier

in the chapter, inert knowledge can be accessed only under conditions that closely mimic the original learning context (Bransford, Sherwood, Vye, & Rieser, 1986). Richard Feynman, a Nobel Prize–winning physicist, made the same observation in describing how his classmates at the Massachusetts Institute of Technology failed to recognize the application of a previously learned mathematical formula: "They didn't put two and two together. They didn't even know what they 'knew.' I don't know what's the matter with people: they don't learn by understanding; they learn by some other way— by rote, or something. Their knowledge is so fragile!" (1985, p. 36). To overcome this limitation of inert and fragile knowledge, teachers need to present subject matter in a highly organized fashion, and students need to learn more about the various conditions under which their knowledge applies.

> **Inert knowledge results from learning isolated facts under limited conditions.**

Step 3: Compile Relevant Information For well-structured problems that are relatively simple and familiar (such as arithmetic drill problems), this step in the problem-solving process occurs simultaneously with problem representation. In the process of defining a simple problem, we very quickly and easily recall from long-term memory all the information needed to achieve a solution. As problems and issues become

Constructivist Teaching in Action: A High School Classroom Debate

Go to the Education CourseMate website and watch the video, study the artifacts in the case, and reflect upon the following questions:

1. Why is the classroom debate an excellent example of constructivism in action? Do you find the classroom debate format to be an example of social constructivism or cognitive constructivism?

2. How does the classroom teacher in this Video Case arrange the elements of this lesson and guide students so that their constructivist learning experience is effective? Please cite specific examples.

heuristic A general approach to solving problems, such as studying worked examples or breaking problems into parts, that can be applied to different subject areas.

more complex, however, we run into two difficulties: The amount of information relevant to the solution becomes too great to keep track of mentally, and there is an increasing chance that we may not possess all the relevant information. As a result, we are forced to compile what we know in the form of lists, tables, pictures, graphs, diagrams, and so on, and to seek additional information from other sources.

The key to using oneself as an information source is the ability to accurately retrieve information from long-term memory that will aid in the solution of the problem. We need to think back over what we have learned in other, somewhat similar situations, make a list of some other form of representation of those ideas, and make a judgment as to how helpful that knowledge might be. Techniques for ensuring accurate and reliable recall were discussed in Chapter 8.

In addition to relying on our own knowledge and experience to solve problems, we can draw on the knowledge and experience of friends, colleagues, and experts. The main purpose of soliciting the views of others about solutions to problems and positions on issues is to identify the reasons and evidence those people offer in support of their positions. This skill of asking questions and analyzing responses is quite useful in debates and classroom discussions of controversial issues.

Step 4: Formulate and Carry Out a Solution When you feel that you understand the nature of a problem or issue and possess sufficient relevant information, you are ready to attempt a solution. The first step is to consider which of several alternative approaches is likely to be most effective. The literature on problem solving mentions quite a few solution strategies. Because these solution strategies are very general in nature—they can apply to different kinds of problems in different content areas and offer only a general approach to solving a problem—they are referred to as *heuristics* (Martinez, 1998). We will discuss seven **heuristics** that we think are particularly useful.

- *Study worked examples.* This approach may strike you as so obvious that it hardly merits attention, but it is worth mentioning for two reasons. First, obvious solution strategies are the ones that are most often overlooked. Second, it is a very effective solution strategy (Renkl, Hilbert, & Schworm, 2009). The beneficial effect is thought to be due to the learners' acquisition of a general problem schema. To get the most out of this heuristic, use multiple examples and different formats for each

problem type and encourage learners to explain to themselves the problem-solving strategy illustrated by the examples (R. K. Atkinson, Derry, Renkl, & Wortham, 2000; Kalyuga, 2009).

- *Work on a simpler version of the problem.* This is another common and very effective approach. Geometry offers a particularly clear example of working on a simpler problem. If you are having difficulty solving a problem of solid geometry (which involves three dimensions), work out a similar problem in plane geometry (two dimensions) and then apply the solution to the three-dimensional example (Nickerson, 1994; Polya, 1957). Architects and engineers employ this approach when they construct scaled-down models of bridges, buildings, experimental aircraft, and the like. Scientists do the same thing by creating laboratory simulations of real-world phenomena.

- *Break the problem into parts.* The key to this approach is to make sure you break the problem into manageable parts. Whether you can do this will depend largely on how much subject-matter knowledge you have. The more you know about the domain from which the problem comes, the easier it is to know how to break a problem into logical, easy-to-handle parts.

  At least two benefits result from breaking a problem into parts: (1) It reduces to a manageable level the amount of information you have to keep in short-term memory, and (2) the method used to solve one part of the problem can often be used to solve another part (Hilbert & Renkl, 2009). Bransford and Stein (1993) used the following example to illustrate how this approach works:

  Problem: What day follows the day before yesterday if two days from now will be Sunday?

  1. What is today if two days from now will be Sunday? (Friday)

  2. If today is Friday, what is the day before yesterday? (Wednesday)

  3. What day follows Wednesday? (Thursday)

- *Work backward.* This is a particularly good solution strategy to use whenever the goal is clear but the beginning state is not. Bransford and Stein (1993) offered the following example: Suppose you arranged to meet someone at a restaurant across town at noon. When should you leave your office to be sure of arriving on time? By working backward from your destination and arrival time (it takes about 10 minutes to find a parking spot and walk to the restaurant; it takes about 30 minutes to drive to the area where you would park; it takes about 5 minutes to walk from your office to your car), you

To figure out the solution to a problem, good problem solvers often work first on a simpler version of the problem.

© Suzie Fitzhugh

would more quickly and easily determine when to leave your office (about 11:15) than if you had worked the problem forward.

- *Study successively partial solutions (backward fading).* Students vary in how much they know about the subject matter on which the problems are based, and students with more prior knowledge do better on problem-solving tests when they are given problem-solving instruction and practice than when they are given worked examples to study (R. K. Atkinson, Derry, Renkl, & Wortham, 2000; Paas & van Gog, 2009). For these reasons, a good procedure to use with all students is something called *backward fading*. Backward fading is basically a combination of studying worked examples, working backward, and practicing solving problems. First, a completely worked-out example (such as one that requires three steps to complete) is provided. Then a similar problem is presented with only the first two steps worked out. The last step has to be completed by the learner. A third problem provides the solution to the first step and requires the learner to determine the solution for steps two and three. Finally, the fourth problem requires the learner to solve all three steps. Compared with peers who saw ordinary worked examples and practiced solving problems, a group of college students who were exposed to the backward fading procedure scored significantly better on problems that were both similar to and different from the practice problems (R. K. Atkinson, Renkl, & Merrill, 2003).

- *Solve an analogous problem.* If you are having difficulty solving a problem, possibly because your knowledge of the subject matter is incomplete, it may be useful to think of a similar problem about a subject in which you are more knowledgeable (B. Hoffman & Schraw, 2009). Solve the analogous problem, and then use the same method to solve the first problem. In essence, this is a way of making the unfamiliar familiar.

    Although solving analogous problems is a very powerful solution strategy, it can be difficult to employ, especially for novices. In our previous discussion of understanding the problem, we made the point that novices represent problems on the basis of superficial features, whereas experts operate from knowledge of underlying concepts and principles. The same is true of analogies. Most of us know that DNA is somehow related to the image of a "twisted ladder" called the *double helix*, but there is much more to mapping the human genome than visualizing a twisted ladder. Novices are more likely than experts to use superficial analogies (Gick, 1986). Analogous problems are discussed in the upcoming Suggestions for Teaching.

- *Create an external representation of the problem.* This heuristic is doubly useful because it also aids in problem framing. Many problems can be represented as pictures, equations, graphs, flowcharts, and the like (Mueller, 2009). The figures in the next Suggestions for Teaching section illustrate how a pictorial or symbolic form of representation can help in both understanding and solving the problem (Martinez, 1998).

Step 5: Evaluate the Solution The last step in the problem-solving process is to evaluate the adequacy of the solution. For relatively simple, well-structured problems in which the emphasis is on producing a correct response, two levels of evaluation are available:

- The problem solver can ask whether, given the problem statement, the answer makes sense. For example, if the problem reads "$75 \times 5 = ?$" and the response is 80, a little voice inside the problem solver's head should say that the answer cannot possibly be right. This signal should prompt a reevaluation of the way the problem was represented and the solution procedure that was used (for example, "I misread the times sign as a plus sign and added when I should have multiplied").

- The problem solver can use an alternative algorithm to check the accuracy of the solution. This is necessary because an error in carrying out an algorithm can produce an incorrect response that is still in the ballpark. For example, a common error

Suggestions for Teaching

Teaching Problem-Solving Techniques

1 Teach students how to identify problems.

Because the notion of finding problems is likely to strike students as an unusual activity, you may want to introduce this skill in gradual steps. One way to start is to have students list different ways in which problems can be identified. Typical responses are to scan newspaper and magazine articles, observe customer and employee behavior in a store, watch traffic patterns in a local area, and interview local residents, including, for instance, teachers, business owners, police, clergy, and government officials. A next step is to have students carry out these suggested activities in order to gain an understanding of the status quo and to find out how people identify problems. They may learn, for example, that a principal periodically has lunch with a teacher in order to learn of conditions that decrease the teacher's effectiveness.

2 Teach students how to represent problems.

Problem representation involves transforming the words that express a problem into an internal representation of those words. To do this, students must understand the concepts embedded in the problem statement and the relationships among those concepts. Consequently, the ability to construct a good representation of a problem is based on a command of the subject matter surrounding the problem and familiarity with the particular type of problem.

As the work of Jerome Bruner and David Ausubel indicates, students need to acquire a genuine understanding of many of the associations, discriminations, concepts, and rules of a discipline before they can effectively solve problems in that subject-matter area. Too often, students are taught to state principles on cue, but they reveal by further responses that they do not understand what they are saying. The recommendations we make in this book about presenting information in an organized fashion and in meaningful contexts will go a long way toward helping students understand the subject matter on which problems are based; see the specific suggestions in Chapters 8 and 11.

The classic illustration of what can occur when information is not learned meaningfully was given over a century ago by William James in his *Talks to Teachers*:

A friend of mine, visiting a school, was asked to examine a young class in geography. Glancing at the book, she said: "Suppose you should dig a hole in the ground, hundreds of feet deep, how should you find it at the bottom—warmer or colder than on top?" None of the class replying, the teacher said: "I'm sure they know, but I think you don't ask the question quite rightly. Let me try." So, taking the book, she asked: "In what condition is the interior of the globe?" and received the immediate answer from half the class at once: "The interior of the globe is in a condition of igneous fusion." (1899, p. 150)

If these students had genuinely understood concepts and principles regarding the composition of the earth (such as the relationship between igneous fusion and heat), instead of having simply memorized meaningless phrases, they would have been able to answer the original question.

Once you are satisfied that students meaningfully understand the elements of a problem, you can demonstrate methods to represent those elements and how they interrelate. One frequent recommendation is to use visual forms of problem representation (concept maps, Venn diagrams, flowcharts, and drawings, for example). Visual representations of ideas foster comprehension because of their concreteness. The following two examples illustrate how a Venn diagram (a set of intersecting circles) and a flow diagram can represent a particular type of problem.[1]

Example Problem

The government wants to contact all druggists, all gun store owners, and all parents in a town without contacting anyone twice. Based on the following statistics, how many people must be contacted?

Druggists	10
Gun store owners	5
Parents	3,000
Druggists who own gun stores	0
Druggists who are parents	7
Gun store owners who are parents	3

Example Problem

Sally loaned $7.00 to Betty. But Sally borrowed $15.00 from Estella and $32.00 from Joan. Moreover, Joan owes $3.00 to Estella and $7.00 to Betty. One day the women got together at Betty's house to straighten out their accounts. Which woman left with $18.00 more than she came with?

3 Teach students how to compile relevant information.

Good problem solvers start with themselves when compiling information to solve a problem or evidence to support a position on an issue. They recognize the importance of recalling earlier-learned information (metacognitive knowledge) and are adept at doing so (cognitive skill). Poor problem solvers, by contrast, lack metacognitive knowledge, cognitive skills, or both. If their deficiency is metacognitive, they make little or no effort to recall solution-relevant memories, even when the information was recently learned, because they do not understand the importance of searching long-term memory for potentially useful knowledge. Even if a student poor in problem solving recognizes the value of searching long-term memory for relevant infor-

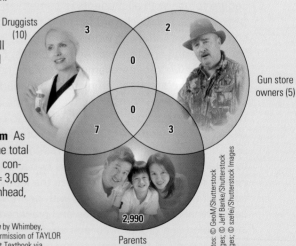

Druggists (10)

Gun store owners (5)

Parents (3,000)

Solution Using Venn Diagram As the Venn diagram illustrates, the total number of people who must be contacted is 2,990 + 7 + 3 + 3 + 2 = 3,005 (adapted from Whimbey & Lochhead, 1999, p. 104).[1]

[1] Source: *Problem Solving & Comprehension* by Whimbey, Arthur. Copyright 1999. Reproduced with permission of TAYLOR 7 FRANCIS GROUP LLC-BOOKS in the format Textbook via Copyright Clearance Center.

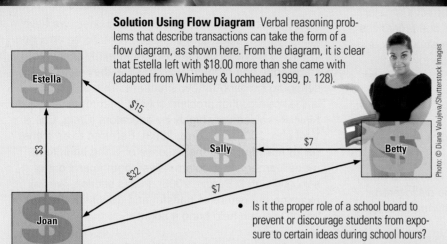

Solution Using Flow Diagram Verbal reasoning problems that describe transactions can take the form of a flow diagram, as shown here. From the diagram, it is clear that Estella left with $18.00 more than she came with (adapted from Whimbey & Lochhead, 1999, p. 128).

Photo: © Diana Valujeva/Shutterstock Images

mation, he may still be handicapped because of inadequate encoding and retrieval skills.

To minimize any metacognitive deficiency, make sure your instruction in problem solving methods emphasizes the importance of retrieving and using previously learned knowledge. To minimize retrieval problems, make sure you recall and implement the Suggestions for Teaching that we offered in Chapter 8.

If a student does not possess all the relevant information needed to work out a solution or analyze an issue, you will have to guide her toward individuals and sources that can help. In referring students to individuals, select people who are judged to be reasonably knowledgeable about the subject, are careful thinkers, and are willing to share their ideas (Ruggiero, 1988, 2009). As an example, consider the issue of whether certain books (such as *The Catcher in the Rye* by J. D. Salinger, *I Know Why the Caged Bird Sings* by Maya Angelou, *Native Son* by Richard Wright, and *The Adventures of Huckleberry Finn* by Mark Twain) should be banned from a school's reading list. In interviewing a knowledgeable person, students might ask questions such as the following because they allow some insight into the individual's reasoning process and the evidence used to support a position:

- What general effects do you think characters in novels who rebel against adult authority have on a reader's behavior?
- Are certain groups of people, such as middle and high school students, likely to be influenced by the motives and actions of such characters? Why do you think so?
- Does a ban on certain books violate the authors' right to free speech?
- Does a book ban violate the principle of academic freedom? Why?

- Is it the proper role of a school board to prevent or discourage students from exposure to certain ideas during school hours?

If a reasonably informed person is not available, recognized authorities can often be interviewed by phone. In the case of a student's choosing this tactic, Ruggiero suggested calling or writing in advance for an appointment, preparing questions in advance, and asking permission to record the interview.

Obviously, in addition to (or in lieu of) personal interviews, students can find substantial information in a good library. For example, you can steer them toward books by recognized authorities, research findings, court cases, and interviews with prominent individuals in periodicals. Although the Internet potentially contains a vast amount of information on any topic, you should warn students about indiscriminately using material gathered there. As with any other medium, there are more and less reliable sources, and only material from reputable sources should be gathered. One additional benefit is that an extra layer of problem-solving activity is introduced when students must decide how to gather and evaluate online information.

④ Teach several methods for formulating problem solutions.

Previously, we mentioned seven methods for formulating a problem solution: study worked examples, work on a simpler version of the problem, break the problem into parts, work backward, study successively partial solutions, solve an analogous problem, and create an external representation of the problem.

In *The Art of Thinking* (9th ed., 2009), Vincent Ruggerio provides a wealth of suggestions for helping students become better problem solvers. We encourage you to consult such sources so that you will be well prepared to teach each of these seven methods.

⑤ Teach students the skills of evaluation.

Solutions to well-structured problems are usually evaluated through the application of an estimating or checking routine. Such procedures can be found in any good mathematics text. The evaluation of solutions to ill-structured problems and analyses of issues, however, is more complex and is less frequently taught. Ruggiero (1988, 2009) discussed the following 10 habits and skills that contribute to a person's ability to evaluate complex solutions and positions:

- Being open-minded about opposing points of view.
- Selecting proper criteria of evaluation. Faulty applications of this skill abound; a current example is the use of standardized achievement test scores to evaluate the quality of classroom instruction.
- Understanding the essence of an argument. To foster this skill, Ruggiero recommended that students be taught how to write a précis, which is a concise summary of an oral argument or a reading passage.
- Evaluating the reliability of sources.
- Properly interpreting factual data (for example, recognizing that an increase in a state's income tax rate from 4% to 6% is an increase not of 2% but of 50%).
- Testing the credibility of hypotheses. On the basis of existing data, hypotheses can range from highly improbable to highly probable.
- Making important distinctions (for instance, between preference and judgment, emotion and content, appearance and reality).
- Recognizing unstated assumptions (for example, that because two events occur close together in time, one causes the other; that what is clear to us will be clear to others; that if the majority believes something, it must be true).
- Evaluating the validity and truthfulness of one's arguments (by, for example, checking that conclusions logically follow from premises and that they have not been influenced by such reasoning flaws as either-or thinking, overgeneralizing, or oversimplifying).
- Recognizing when evidence is insufficient. All of these 10 skills can be modeled and taught in your classroom.

in multiple-column subtraction problems is to subtract a smaller digit from a larger one regardless of whether the small number is in the minuend (top row) or the subtrahend (bottom row) (Mayer, 1987), as in

$$
\begin{array}{r}
522 \\
-\ 418 \\
\hline
116
\end{array}
$$

Because this answer is off by only 12, it "looks right." The flaw can be discovered, however, by adding the answer to the subtrahend to produce the minuend.

Pause & Reflect

Critics of American education argue that students are poor problem solvers because they receive little systematic instruction in problem-solving processes. How would you rate the instruction you received in problem solving? In terms of the five steps discussed over the preceding pages, which ones were you taught? What can you do to ensure that your students become good problem solvers?

The evaluation of solutions to ill-structured problems is likely to be more complicated and time consuming for at least two reasons. First, the evaluation should occur both before and after the solution is implemented. Although many flaws and omissions can be identified and corrected beforehand, some will slip through. There is much to be learned by observing the effects of our solutions. Second, because these ill-structured problems are complex, often involving a dozen or more variables, some sort of systematic framework should guide the evaluation. Vincent Ruggiero (1988, pp. 44–46) suggested a four-step procedure:

1. Ask and answer a set of basic questions. Imagine, for example, that you have proposed a classroom incentive system (a token economy, perhaps) to enhance student motivation. You might ask such questions as, How will this program be implemented? By whom? When? Where? With what materials? How will the materials be obtained?

2. Identify imperfections and complications. Is this idea, for example, safe, convenient, efficient, economical, and compatible with existing policies and practices?

3. Anticipate possible negative reactions from other people. For instance, might parents or the school principal object?

4. Devise improvements.

LO3 Transfer of Learning

Throughout this chapter and preceding ones, we have indicated that classroom instruction should be arranged in such a way that students independently apply the knowledge and problem-solving skills they learn in school to similar but new situations. This capability is the main goal of problem-solving instruction and is typically valued very highly by educators (Craig, Chi, & VanLehn, 2009; De Corte, 2003). Referred to as **transfer of learning**, it is the essence of being an autonomous learner and problem solver, both in and out of school (Pugh & Bergin, 2005). In this section, we will examine the nature of transfer and discuss ways in which you can help bring it about.

The Nature and Significance of Transfer of Learning

For over a century, psychologists have investigated how learning in one context is transferred to learning in other contexts. Early on, psychologists acknowledged that in some cases, prior learning aids in subsequent learning (this is called *positive transfer*). In some cases, prior learning interferes with subsequent learning (*negative transfer*). In yet other cases, prior learning has no effect on subsequent learning (*zero transfer*) (Osman, 2008). Our primary interest here is in finding ways to foster positive transfer, thus eliminating negative and zero transfer as outcomes. We begin by examining two distinctions that will help us understand the conditions that foster positive transfer: (1) specific and general transfer and (2) near and far transfer.

Specific and General Transfer When examining how positive transfer occurs, it is sometimes unclear whether transfer from one task to another is due to specific similarities or to more general similarities (Cornoldi, 2010). Psychologists decide whether transfer is due to specific or general factors by setting up learning tasks such as the following for three different but equivalent groups of learners.

	Initial Task	Transfer Task
Group 1	Learn French	Learn Spanish
Group 2	Learn Chinese	Learn Spanish
Group 3	Learn Spanish	

If on a Spanish test, group 1 scores higher than group 2, the difference is attributed to **specific transfer** of similarities between French and Spanish (such as vocabulary, verb conjugations, and sentence structure). If groups 1 and 2 score the same and both outscore group 3 on the Spanish test, the difference is attributed

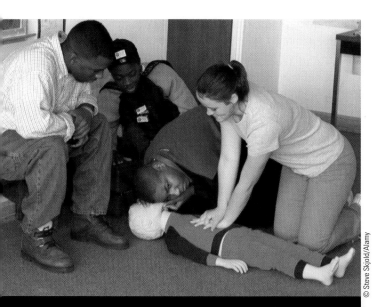

If teachers want students to apply what they learn in the classroom in other settings in the future, they should create tasks and conditions that are similar to those that students will encounter later.

to nonspecific transfer, or **general transfer**, of similarities between the two tasks, since Chinese shares no apparent specific characteristics with French or Spanish (both Romance languages). In this case, it is possible that learners use cognitive strategies—such as imagery, verbal elaboration, and mnemonic devices—when learning a foreign language and that these transfer to the learning of other foreign languages. Such nonspecific transfer effects have also been demonstrated for other classroom tasks, such as problem solving and learning from text (Cornoldi, 2010; Royer, 1979).

Near and Far Transfer Another common distinction, similar to the specific/general distinction, is based on the perceived similarity of the original learning task to the transfer task. **Near transfer** refers to situations in which the knowledge domains are highly similar, the settings in which the original learning and transfer tasks occur are basically the same, and the elapsed time between the two tasks is relatively short. **Far transfer** occurs when the knowledge domains and settings are judged to be dissimilar and the time between the original learning and transfer tasks is relatively long (Y. Rosen, 2009). Thus using math skills acquired over the past several weeks to solve the problems at the end of the current chapter in a textbook is an example of near transfer. Using those same skills several years later to determine which of several investment options is most likely to produce the highest rate of return is an example of far transfer.

You may have noticed our use of such imprecise and subjective terms as "highly similar," "basically the same," "relatively long," and "judged to be dissimilar." This is done for a good reason. At present, there is no way to precisely measure the similarity between a learning task and a transfer task. The best we can do is identify the major dimensions that two tasks share (such as subject matter, physical setting, time between two tasks, and conditions under which each is performed) and subjectively decide that the two dimensions are sufficiently similar or dissimilar to warrant the label *near transfer* or *far transfer*. Sometimes this approach produces a high degree of agreement, but at other times one person's far transfer is another person's near transfer (Barnett & Ceci, 2002).

Contemporary Views of Specific/Near and General/Far Transfer

Gavriel Salomon and David Perkins (1989) combined aspects of specific and near transfer and general and far transfer under the labels *low-road transfer* and *high-road transfer*, respectively.

Low-Road Transfer **Low-road transfer** refers to a situation in which a previously learned skill or idea is almost automatically retrieved from memory and applied to a highly similar current task. For example, a student who has mastered the skill of two-column addition and correctly completes three-column and four-column addition problems with no prompting or instruction is exhibiting low-road transfer. Another example is a student who learns how to tune up car engines in an auto shop class and then almost effortlessly and automatically carries out the same task as an employee of an auto repair business. Low-road transfer is basically a contemporary version of the first explanation of transfer given by Edward Thorndike and Robert Woodworth in 1901. Their explanation—called the theory of identical elements—was that the degree of transfer depended on the similarity of the original task in which a skill or knowledge was

general transfer
A situation in which prior learning aids subsequent learning due to the use of similar cognitive strategies.

near transfer
A situation in which knowledge and skills learned at an earlier point in time in a particular context are used to help one learn new information or solve a problem in a very similar context and soon after the original learning.

far transfer
A situation in which knowledge and skills learned at an earlier point in time in a particular context are used to help one learn new information or solve a problem in a very different context at a much later point in time.

low-road transfer
A situation in which a previously learned skill or idea is almost automatically retrieved from memory and applied to a highly similar current task.

high-road transfer
A situation involving the conscious, controlled, somewhat effortful formulation of an "abstraction" (that is, a rule, schema, strategy, or analogy) that allows a connection to be made between two tasks.

acquired and the task to which the skill or knowledge must be transferred (D. King, Bellocchi, & Ritchie, 2008).

Two conditions need to be present for low-road transfer to occur:

1. Students have to be given ample opportunities to practice using the target skill.

2. Practice has to occur with different materials and in different settings. The more varied the practice is, the greater is the range of tasks to which the skill can be applied.

If, for example, you want students to be good note takers, give them instruction and ample practice at taking notes from their biology, health, and English textbooks. Once they become accomplished note takers in these subjects, they will likely apply this skill to other subjects in an almost automatic fashion.

In essence, what we are describing is the behavioral principle of generalization. Because the transfer task is similar in one or more respects to the practice

task and tends to occur in similar settings, low-road transfer is similar to specific and near transfer.

High-Road Transfer **High-road transfer** refers to the ways people transfer prior knowledge and skills over longer time periods to new situations that look rather different from the original task. High-road transfer involves the conscious, controlled, somewhat effortful formulation of an "abstraction" (that is, a rule, schema, strategy, or analogy) that allows a connection to be made between two tasks (King, Bellocchi, & Ritchie, 2008). For example, an individual who learns to set aside a certain number of hours every day to complete homework assignments and study for upcoming exams formulates the principle that the most efficient way to accomplish a task is to break it down into small pieces and work at each piece according to a set schedule. As an adult, the individual uses this principle to deal successfully with complex tasks at work and at home.

As another example, imagine a student who, after much observation and thought, has finally developed a good sense of what school is and how one is supposed to behave there. This student has developed a school schema. Such a schema would probably be made up of actors (teachers and students), objects (desks, books,

Challenging Assumptions

When It Comes to Transfer, Be Careful What You Wish For

In January 2002, President George W. Bush signed into law the reauthorization of the Elementary and Secondary Education Act, more popularly known as No Child Left Behind (NCLB). The implementation of NCLB—including consequences for schools and school districts whose students' test scores fail to show what is called *adequate yearly progress*—has ushered in an unprecedented focus on testing. The original intentions were good: NCLB was an effort to ensure that all children learned, that no child was left behind in the crucial areas of math and reading/language arts. The consequences, however, have not been good. The yearly tests carry high stakes for schools and districts. Many schools and districts exert enormous effort and spend a great deal of time preparing their students to perform well on the annual state tests. One concern is that there is so much focus on learning to perform well on state tests that other learning opportunities are missed. Of greater concern are cases in which the pressure placed on students, teachers, and school administrators has yielded ethical breaches, psychological harm, and physical stress and illness (Nichols & Berliner, 2007). Such consequences are at odds with what we have learned about

the transfer of learning. The negative consequences of NCLB may have been unintended, but when unattended consequences occur, faulty assumptions are often the culprit.

From a transfer of learning perspective (as well as other perspectives that we will mention later in the book), we question the assumptions that underlie NCLB and how it is implemented. We wonder, for example, how extensive and intensive preparation focused on each student performing as well as possible on one yearly test helps students construct knowledge by negotiating meaning with others, solve authentic and ill-defined problems, and engage in the critically important process of mindful abstraction.

What Do You Think?

What have been your own student experiences with annual yearly tests? Given your understanding of low-road and high-road transfer—both of which can lead to meaningful learning—how would you challenge or change the current emphasis on high-stakes testing? To investigate this subject further, see the "Challenging Assumptions" section of the textbook's Education CourseMate website.

Chapter 10: Constructivist Learning Theory, Problem Solving, and Transfer

computers), and events (reading, listening, writing, talking, drawing). Because this is an idealized abstraction, actual classrooms may contain fewer or greater numbers of these characteristics in varying proportions. Even so, with this schema, a student could walk into any instructional setting (another school classroom, a training seminar, or a press briefing, for example) and readily understand what was going on, why it was going on, and how to behave. Of course, with repeated applications of schemata, rules, strategies, and the like, the behaviors become less conscious and more automatic. What was once a reflection of high-road transfer becomes low-road transfer.

Researchers (e.g., Bereiter, 1997; Lim, Reiser, & Olina, 2009; Salomon & Perkins, 1989) have referred to this deliberate, conscious, effortful formulating of a general principle or schema that can be applied to a variety of different-looking but fundamentally similar tasks as *mindful abstraction*. The *mindful* part of the phrase indicates that the abstraction must be thought about and fully understood for high-road transfer to occur. That is, people must be aware of what they are doing and why they are doing it. This is essentially training in metacognition, the capacity to think about one's own thinking.

> **Low-road and high-road transfer are produced by varied practice at applying skills, rules, and memory retrieval cues.**

Teaching for Low-Road and High-Road Transfer As we noted at the beginning of this section, transfer of previously learned knowledge and skills to new tasks and settings is a goal that is high on almost every teacher's list. Yet one study of classroom activity found that only 7% of tasks required students to use information they had learned previously (Bennett, Desforges, Cockburn, & Wilkinson, 1984). Perhaps most teachers feel they simply don't know how to teach for transfer. That need not be your fate. The following guidelines (based on Cox, 1997; De Corte, 2003; Lim, Reiser, Olina, 2009; Salomon & Perkins, 1989) should produce greater levels of both low-road and high-road transfer:

1. Provide students with multiple opportunities for varied practice to help them develop a rich web of interrelated concepts.

2. Give students opportunities to solve problems that are similar to those they will eventually have to solve, and establish conditions similar to those they will eventually face.

3. Teach students how, for a variety of tasks, to formulate general rules, strategies, or schemes that they can use in the future with a variety of similar problems.

4. Give students cues that will allow them to retrieve from memory earlier-learned information that can be used to make current learning easier.

5. Teach students to focus on the beneficial effects of creating and using rules and strategies to solve particular kinds of problems.

LO4 Technology Tools for Knowledge Construction and Problem Solving

The use of computer-based technology to support a constructivist approach to learning is often called learning *with* computers (Jonassen, Howland, Marra, & Crismond, 2008; Y. Rosen, 2009). Students learn with computers when computers support knowledge construction, exploration, learning by doing, learning by conversing, and learning by reflecting.

The term *mindtools* refers to computer applications that lend themselves to these types of activities. Mindtools include databases, semantic networks (concept mapping programs), spreadsheets, expert systems (artificial intelligence), microworlds, search engines, visualization tools, hypermedia, and computer conferencing (Jonassen, Howland, Moore, Marra, & Crismond, 2008). Rather than using computer programs just to present and represent information more efficiently, which is what drill and tutorial programs do, mindtools allow learners to construct, share, and revise knowledge in more open-ended environments. In effect, learners become producers, designers, and authors of knowledge (Moos & Azevedo, 2009). In this section we provide two examples. The first is a brief example of an environment that has evolved through a considerable period of research and development. The second, which we examine in great detail, points us to the future: the use of gaming in the design of online learning environments.

> **Technology can help students construct knowledge and become better problem solvers.**

Computer-Supported Intentional Learning Environments/Knowledge Forum

Marlene Scardamalia and Carl Bereiter asked us to "imagine a network of networks—people from schools, universities, cultural institutions, service organizations, businesses—simultaneously building knowledge within their primary groups while advancing the knowledge of others. We might call such a community network a knowledge-building society" (1996, p. 10). Since the 1980s these researchers have developed and tested aspects of such a network with the Computer-Supported Intentional Learning Environments (CSILE) project (Scardamalia, 2004; Scardamalia & Bereiter, 1991).

The CSILE project was built around the concept of intentional learning (Scardamalia & Bereiter, 1991). In an intentional learning environment, students learn how to set goals, generate and interrelate new ideas, link new knowledge to old, negotiate meaning with peers, and relate what they learn to other tasks. The product of these activities, like the product of any scientific inquiry, is then made available to other students (Watkins, 2005).

The CSILE project allows students to create informational links, or "notes," in several ways (for example, text notes, drawings, graphs, pictures, time lines, and maps). CSILE also contains designated "cooperation" icons that encourage students to reflect on how their work links to others, as well as idea browsing and linking tools for marking notes that involve or intend cooperation. Using this database system, students comment on the work of others, read responses to their hypotheses, or search for information posted by their peers under a particular topic title.

Studies have shown that students who used CSILE performed better on standardized language and reading tests, asked deeper questions, were more elaborate and coherent in their commentaries,

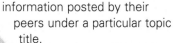

demonstrated more mature beliefs about learning, and engaged in discussions that were more committed to scientific progress (Scardamalia & Bereiter, 1996).

A version of CSILE for the web, called Knowledge Forum, has since emerged. The goal of Knowledge Forum is to have students mimic the collaborative knowledge-building process that characterizes the work of expert learners. Consequently, students must label their contribution to a communal database topic prior to posting it by using such labels as "My Theory," "I Need to Understand," "New Information," "This Theory Cannot Explain," "A Better Theory," and "Putting Our Knowledge Together." So if in the course of helping to build a knowledge base about human vision, a student wrote, "I need to understand why we have two eyes instead of one or three," another member of this community could post a "New Information" note that discussed the relationship between binocular vision and depth perception. The resulting knowledge base would then be subject to modifications and additions from others. A recent 3-year study of fourth graders suggested that Knowledge Forum supports the development of collective responsibility for learning and effective participation in a "knowledge-creating culture" (J. Zhang, Scardamalia, Reeve, & Messina, 2009, p. 7).

Quest Atlantis: Gaming and Consequential Engagement

The first decade of the twenty-first century may well be remembered as the decade of what we call—at the time we are writing this—"new media." We may not call it "new media" for long, however, because *newer* new media are being created all the time. Our terminology has a hard time keeping up with the technology. But one thing is certain: The first decade of the twenty-first century is when we began to see serious, extensive scholarship, research, and development on how new media influence learning and socialization. The MacArthur Foundation funded a large-scale, influential study that was documented in a book entitled, *Hanging Out, Messing Around, and Geeking Out: Kids Living and Learning with New Media* (Ito et al., 2010). Among other issues, the book examines the generational and "digital divide" between school-age learners and the adults who make decisions about how schools should operate: "The discourse of digital generations and digital youth posits that new media empower youth to challenge the social norms and educational agendas of their elders in unique ways" (p. 2).

Among the issues raised by new media is gaming. Many educators worry that online games are a bad influence on today's youth. They worry that those who spend hours and hours in difficult, often

© Özgür Donmaz/iStockphoto

frustrating, effort to gain access to the next level are wasting time that could be better spent reading books. Others worry that the content of online games sends negative social messages steeped in violence and sexual exploitation. But there are voices emerging from the worry that suggest that games provide effective learning environments (Barab & Dede, 2007). James Paul Gee (2007) published a collection of essays titled *Good Video Games and Good Learning*. Steven Johnson (2006) wrote a best seller arguing that popular culture—including gaming and other new media—enhances rather than diminishes intellectual development. His book is called *Everything Bad Is Good for You*.

Among the increasing number of online games is one that we have mentioned in previous chapters and that deserves a closer look in the context of constructivist learning theory and problem solving: Quest Atlantis (QA) (see Barab, Gresalfi et al., 2009; Barab, Scott et al., 2009; Gresalfi, Barab, Siyahhan, & Christensen, 2009). Sasha Barab (a core founder of the QA project) and other QA colleagues described some of the key design features of QA as follows:

Quest Atlantis is chiefly a virtual world housed on a central Internet server, accessible from school or home to children with online access, password permission, and the client software. As a multiuser virtual environment, Quest Atlantis immerses children in educational tasks in an adventure to save a fictional Atlantis from impending disaster. Participating as "Questers," children engage in the virtual environment and respond to associated inquiry-based challenges called Quests, and through these challenges, they help the Atlantian Council restore the lost wisdom of their civilization, one much like our own. The story line, associated structures, and governing policies constitute what is referred to in the commercial gaming sector as the metagame. Specifically, the Quest Atlantis metagame consists of several key elements:

- *A shared mythological context that establishes and supports program activities.*
- *A set of online spaces in which children, mentors, and the Atlantian Council can interact with each other.*
- *A well-defined advancement system centered on pedagogically valid activities that encourage academic and social learning.*

- *Regalia and rewards associated with advancement and wisdom.*
- *An individual homepage for each child, showing their advancement and serving as a portfolio of their work.*

Through this metacontext, the primary function of which is both structural (providing a cohesive framework) and motivational (providing an engaging context to stimulate participation and learning), Quests and member behaviors are targeted and instilled with meaning. However, in contrast to traditional role-playing games, one's game identity and activity depend on the child exiting the virtual environment to respond to Quests in the physical world. In this way, Quest Atlantis is not simply a "computer game" but incorporates "real-world" activities as well. (Barab, Dodge, Thomas, Jackson, & Tuzun, 2007, pp. 268–269)

Although the design of QA has taken advantage of what has been learned from other online games, it has also incorporated other features that are consistent with constructivist learning in all of its variations. Looking through a cognitive lens, video and online games engage users. Players spend many hours—often long stretches of time—in problem-solving mode: cognitively processing information and testing hypotheses in order to achieve a goal. QA's design takes advantage of the cognitive engagement that online games provide, but it also has features that are constructivist when we look at QA through social and critical constructivist lenses.

Unlike most video and online games, QA forms a community through both its virtual space and its face-to-face interaction at Quest Atlantis Centers. In order for students to participate, they must be part of a particular QA Center, such as a school, a museum, or an after-school program. Students and their teachers are registered formally as participants online and have access to materials that are

consequential engagement
A situation that occurs when learners choose certain tools (a procedure or concept, for example) to understand and solve problems *and* when they evaluate the effectiveness of the tools they have chosen.

used for "real-world" learning activities in which they engage offline. The learning environments of "Questers" include collaboration with others at distance and with teachers and students in their local QA Center.

One of the criticisms of commercial video and online games is that they advocate violence and other antisocial behavior. QA was designed to help learners develop an awareness of seven dimensions that, taken together, address constructivism in its social and critical forms. The seven dimensions, which are part of QA's "Project Mission," are:

- Compassionate Wisdom: "Be Kind"

- Creative Expression: "I Create"

- Environmental Awareness: "Think Globally, Act Locally"

- Personal Agency: "I Have Voice"

- Healthy Communities: "Live, Love, Grow"

- Social Responsibility: "We Can Make a Difference"

- Diversity Affirmation: "Everyone Matters" The dimensions—in the form above—are given on the QA website (see http://atlantis.crlt.indiana.edu; they are discussed more formally in Barab et al, 2007).

> **Consequential engagement contributes to the active participation of learners' knowledge construction.**

Constructivist learning requires that students be engaged actively in creating their own understanding of concepts and procedures as well the development of their own problem-solving skills. As educational practice continues to evolve via the design and development of technological innovations, researchers are asking an essentially constructivist question: What are the features of an effective instructional design to support collaborative, creative learning? (H.-Y. Hong & Sullivan, 2009). Quest Atlantis—which has been well researched throughout its design and development—provides one answer to the question: *consequential engagement.*

As we have seen from the overview, QA offers learners ways to engage actively in their learning. From a design standpoint, QA has sought to engage students at three levels: procedural, conceptual, and consequential. Procedural engagement refers to using procedures accurately, but using procedures does not necessarily mean that students understand why the procedures are important. (Have you ever memorized a formula for a test without really understanding why the formula was developed in the first place?) Conceptual engagement means more than rote use of a procedure; it involves understanding why the procedure works, under what conditions it works, and why it has value. **Consequential engagement** occurs when learners choose certain tools (a procedure or concept, for example) to understand and solve problems *and* when they evaluate the effectiveness of the tools they have chosen. QA invites students to "inhabit roles and assume identities as they adopt conceptually-relevant intentions in a virtual world in which they make choices." (Gresalfi, Barab, Siyahhan, & Christensen, 2009, p. 24). Having made choices of what to do, how to do it, and what tools to use, learners influence the situation in which they are learning. Building on an example from Gresalfi and her colleagues, suppose that you compared and contrasted Piaget's stages of cognitive development with Vygotsky's notion of scaffolding and decided to use heterogeneous grouping for a particular lesson. Using the procedure of comparing and contrasting the concepts of Piaget and Vygotsky, you made a decision. Now, what happens with that decision? If you are writing or answering a test question, you engage the procedure and the concepts in order to justify the decision in writing. But suppose you had the opportunity to implement that decision in a real or virtual classroom environment. By implementing your decision, you change the environment, but you also have the opportunity to observe the effects of your decision within the environment. Did the heterogeneous grouping work? What were the consequences of your decision?

Designing learning experiences that enhance consequential engagement contributes significantly to the active participation of learners in the construction of their own knowledge. QA is designed for "engaged participation" that affords learners procedural, conceptual, and—most critically—consequential engagement in contextually and conceptually rich learning environments. It has emerged as an exemplar of game-based curricula that are likely to influence the learning environments you will experience in your teaching career. Research on QA has shown significant learning gains on assessments that are oriented toward established standards and that are entirely independent of the QA curriculum. Perhaps even more importantly, both teachers and students who have participated in QA report "transformative personal experiences" that have led to increased motivation to pursue the curricular issues raised in QA outside of school. You can learn more about Quest Atlantis at http://atlantis.crlt.indiana.edu.

WHAT ELSE? *RIP & REVIEW* **CARDS IN THE BACK**

Pause& Reflect *This chapter argues that if teachers want transfer, they should teach for transfer. Go to the Quest Atlantis website and investigate overview materials, including the available videos. Do you think the "student quests" are likely to produce transfer? Why?*

11

MOTIVATION

LEARNING OBJECTIVES

After studying this chapter, you will be able to . . .

LO1 Explain the effects of reinforcement on both extrinsic and intrinsic motivation.

LO2 Provide examples of influences on self-efficacy and how self-efficacy serves motivation to learn.

LO3 Describe how beliefs frame students' thinking and how that thinking and personal interests affect motivation.

LO4 Explain how basic human needs serve as the foundation for choice making and are prerequisite to personal and academic growth.

LO5 Provide examples of the ways in which self-perceptions influence student motivation.

LO6 Describe how technology can increase students' intrinsic motivation.

visit **4ltrpress.cengage.com**

Teaching is very much like putting together a puzzle. You first have to identify the pieces and then figure out how to construct them into a meaningful whole. This book is designed to help you identify the relevant pieces that make up the puzzle of effective teaching and give you some ideas for using them in a coordinated fashion. In Chapters 2 and 3, for example, you learned how important it is to understand how students develop socially, emotionally, and cognitively; what students are like at different ages; and how they differ from one another. In Chapters 4–6, you were introduced to those pieces of the puzzle that pertain to the learning process and how different views of learning can be used to guide the type of instruction you provide. The puzzle pieces in this and the two subsequent chapters deal with the importance of establishing a classroom environment that will motivate students to learn and of maintaining that positive atmosphere over time.

In this chapter, we address the question of why students strive (or don't strive) for academic achievement—that is, what motivates students? The importance of motivation was vividly pointed out by Larry Cuban, a Stanford University professor of education who returned to teach a high school class for one semester after a 16-year absence. He said, "If I wanted those students to be engaged intellectually, then every day—and I *do* mean *every* day—I had to figure out an angle, a way of making connections between whatever we were studying and their daily lives in school, in the community, or in the nation" (1990, pp. 480–481).

The senior author of this book remembers an instance from his days as a school psychologist that reinforces Cuban's observation. A teacher referred a 10-year-old student for testing and possible placement in a special education class (this was before the advent of inclusive classrooms) because the student's classroom performance, particularly in math, was very poor. On almost every test and homework assignment he received grades of D or F. Two pieces of evidence led to the conclusion that this student suffered more from lack of motivation than from intellectual deficits. First, his score on an individually administered intelligence test was average. Second, and most significant, he made pocket money in the evenings by keeping score for several bowling teams at the neighborhood bowling alley. Obviously, there was nothing wrong with this student's ability to learn or with his arithmetic skills!

Motivation can be defined as the selection, persistence, intensity, and direction of behavior (Fulmer & Frijters, 2009). In practical terms, motivation is simply the willingness of a person to expend a certain amount of effort to achieve a particular goal under a particular set of circumstances. Nevertheless, many teachers have at least two major misconceptions about motivation that prevent them from using this concept with maximum effectiveness. One misconception is that some students are unmotivated. Strictly speaking, that is not an accurate statement. As long as a student chooses goals and expends a certain amount of effort to achieve them, she is, by definition, motivated. What teachers really mean is that students are not motivated to behave in the way teachers would like them to behave. In other words, their motivation is negatively, rather than positively, oriented. The second misconception is that one person can directly motivate another. This view is inaccurate because motivation comes from within a person. What you *can* do—with the help of the various motivation theories discussed in this chapter—is learn how to create the circumstances that *influence* students to do what you want them to do (A. Martin & Dowson, 2009; Matos, Lens, & Vansteenkiste, 2009).

LO1 The Behavioral View of Motivation

Earlier in the text we noted that some psychologists explain learning from a theoretical perspective that focuses exclusively on the effects of observable stimuli, responses, and consequences on our propensity to exhibit particular behaviors. This approach is called operant conditioning, and its application to motivation has focused on the effect of reinforcement.

The Effect of Reinforcement

In Chapter 7 we discussed Skinner's emphasis on the role of reinforcement in learning. Skinner's theory is called operant conditioning because it is an explanation of how learners operate on their environment and how the environment operates on learners. Operant conditioning theory is a description and explanation of how contingencies between learners' behaviors and environmental consequences are established.

Let's try a small thought experiment. Think about what happens each time you walk into a new class: You want to know how the class is going to operate, don't you? You want to know what you have to do in order to do well in the class: *How many tests? What kinds of tests? Is there a final? Is it comprehensive? Is there a research paper? How long does it need to be? How many references are required?* In general, what you want to know is: *What's the deal in this class?* If we translate that question into the language of operant conditioning we get the following: *What are the contingencies that are going to operate in this environment?* Learning the contingencies that operate in a particular environment allows you to behave in ways that lead to desirable consequences, and to avoid behaving in ways that lead to undesirable consequences. When your students enter your class, they will need to learn the contingencies that will operate in the environment you will create for them.

Some may think it a bit strange to use a thought experiment with operant conditioning theory. The reason is that operant conditioning is a behavioral theory because it focuses on observable behavior and observable aspects of the environment in which learners behave, not on what learners believe or think. Even so, Skinner thought very carefully about how the environment influences behavior and how behavior influences the environment. As we saw in Chapter 7, the most effective tool in the operant conditioning arsenal, by far, is positive reinforcement. If students behave in ways that bring about consequences that they desire, they are likely to continue such behavior. If students study and, as a consequence, succeed in a class, they are likely to continue studying. Clearly, there are positive motivational effects of positive reinforcement; but there are also limitations.

Limitations of the Behavioral View

Although approaches to motivation based on positive reinforcement are often useful, you should be aware of the disadvantages that can come from overuse or misuse of such techniques. Most of the criticisms of the use of reinforcement as a motivational incentive stem from the fact that it represents **extrinsic motivation**. That is, the learner decides to engage in an activity (such as participate in class, do homework, study for exams) to earn a reward that is not inherently related to the activity (such as praise from the teacher, a high grade, or the privilege of doing something different). By contrast, students under the influence of **intrinsic motivation** study a subject or acquire a skill because it produces such inherently positive consequences as becoming more knowledgeable, competent, and independent.

Pause & Reflect *What percentage of your behavior do you think stems from intrinsic motivation? From extrinsic motivation? Is it possible to change this ratio? How?*

Although extrinsic motivation is widespread in society (individuals are motivated to engage in many activities because they hope to win certificates, badges, medals, public recognition, prizes, or admiration from others), this approach has at least three potential dangers (Covington, 2009; Kaufman & Beghetto, 2009; Kohn, 1999, 2006):

1. Changes in behavior may be temporary. As soon as the extrinsic reward has been obtained, the student may revert to such earlier behaviors as studying inconsistently, turning in poor-quality homework, and disrupting class with irrelevant comments and behaviors.

2. Students may develop a materialistic attitude toward learning. They may think (or say), "What tangible reward will I get if I agree to learn this information?" If the answer is "none," they may decide to make little or no effort to learn.

3. Giving students extrinsic rewards for completing a task may lessen whatever intrinsic motivation they may have for that activity.

> **Excessive use of external rewards may lead to only temporary behavior change, materialistic attitudes, or decreased intrinsic motivation.**

This last disadvantage, which is referred to as the *undermining effect*, has been extensively investigated by researchers (Akin-Little, Eckert, Lovett, & Little,

2004; Deci, Koestner, & Ryan, 1999, 2001; Marinak & Gambrell, 2008; Wiechman & Gurland, 2009). It appears that giving students rewards may indeed decrease their intrinsic motivation for a task, but only under certain conditions. Under other conditions, external rewards may enhance intrinsic motivation. Figure 11.1 summarizes recent research on this subject. Notice, in particular, that intrinsic motivation falls when students must compete for a limited supply of rewards. In contrast, intrinsic motivation rises when the reward consists of positive verbal feedback and is available to all who meet the standard.

Making students compete against each other for limited rewards (the "grading on a curve" practice we first mentioned in our discussion of Erik Erikson's psychosocial theory of development) is particularly damaging to intrinsic motivation because of its impact on self-worth. Whether intended or not, children in our society base their sense of self-worth on their accomplishments. When we artificially limit opportunities to attain the highest level of accomplishment, intrinsic motivation declines in an effort to protect one's sense of self-worth (Covington, 2009; Wiechman & Gurland, 2009).

FIGURE 11.1 Conditions Determining the Effect of External Rewards on Intrinsic Motivation

INCREASE

EFFECT ON INTRINSIC MOTIVATION

CONDITION

Initial interest in task is low because task is perceived as boring or irrelevant.

Initial interest in task is high and reward takes the form of positive verbal feedback.

Most desirable or highest reward (such as grade of A) is available to all who meet a predetermined set of criteria.

CONDITION

Initial interest in task is very high.

Rewards used are tangible (such as candy, toys, stickers).

Rewards are held out in advance as incentives.

Rewards are given simply for engaging in the task.

Students must compete against one another for limited supply of rewards.

DECREASE

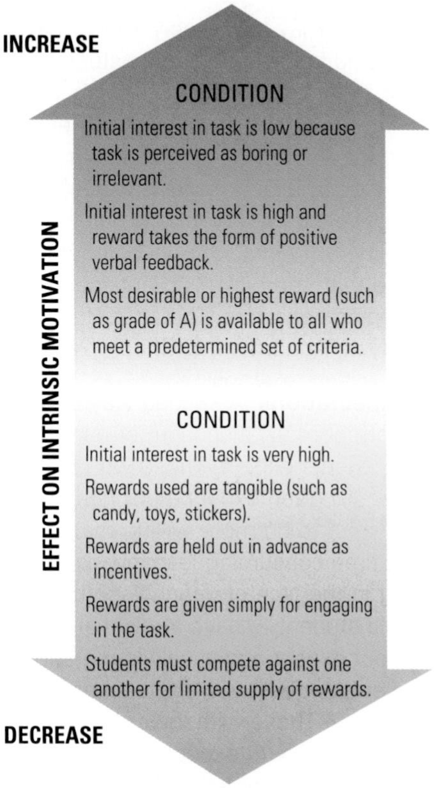

SOURCES: Cameron (2001); Cameron, Banko, & Pierce (2001); Covington (2009); Deci, Koestner, & Ryan (2001); Marinak & Gambrell (2008).

Taken as a whole, these results strongly suggest that teachers should avoid the indiscriminate use of rewards for influencing classroom behavior, particularly when an activity seems to be naturally interesting to students. Instead, rewards should be used to provide students with information about their level of competence on tasks they have not yet mastered and to encourage them to explore topics in which their initial interest is low.

> **Intrinsic motivation is enhanced when the reward consists of positive feedback and is available to all who qualify.**

LO2 The Social Cognitive View of Motivation

Social cognitive theorists, such as Albert Bandura, Dale Schunk, and Barry Zimmerman, emphasize two factors that strongly influence motivation to learn: (1) the models to which people are exposed and (2) people's sense of self-efficacy, or how capable they believe they are to handle a particular task.

The Power of Persuasive Models

One factor that positively affects students' self-efficacy and motivation to learn certain behaviors is the opportunity to see other people exhibiting those behaviors and to observe the consequences that occur. Social cognitive theorists refer to this as observation, imitation, and vicarious reinforcement. As we pointed out in Chapter 9, *vicarious* reinforcement means that we expect to receive the same reinforcer that we see someone else get for exhibiting a particular behavior.

A student who observes an older brother or sister reaping benefits from earning high grades may strive to do the same, with the expectation of experiencing the same or similar benefits. A student who notices that a classmate receives praise from the teacher after acting in a certain way may decide to imitate such behavior to win similar rewards. A student who identifies with and admires a teacher may work hard partly to please the admired individual and partly to try to become like that individual. Both vicarious reinforcement and direct

When students admire and identify with classmates who are positively reinforced for their behavior, the observing students' self-efficacy and motivation to exhibit the same behavior may be strengthened.

© Bob Daemmrich/Photo Edit

reinforcement can raise an individual's sense of self-efficacy for a particular task, which in turn leads to higher levels of motivation.

The Importance of Self-Efficacy

An individual's sense of self-efficacy can affect motivation to learn through its influence on the learning goal the individual chooses, the outcome the individual expects, and the reasons (or attributions) the individual gives to explain successes and failures.

Choice of Learning Goals Analyses of learning goals suggest that a student may choose a task mastery goal, a performance-approach goal, a performance-avoidance goal, or a combination of task mastery and performance-approach goals (Britner & Pajares, 2006; Murayama & Elliot, 2009; Pintrich & Schunk, 2002; Urdan & Mestas, 2006; Usher & Pajares, 2008b; C. Walker & Greene, 2009).

- *Task mastery goals* involve doing what is necessary to learn meaningfully the information and skills that have been assigned. Students with high levels of self-efficacy choose this goal more often than do students with low levels of self-efficacy. In pursuit of task mastery goals, students with high self-efficacy will use a variety of encoding techniques, do more organizing of information to make it meaningful, review and practice more frequently, monitor their understanding more closely, formulate more effective learning strategies, and treat mistakes as part of learning.

- *Performance-approach goals* involve demonstrating to teachers and peers one's superior intellectual

ability by outperforming most others in class. If the best way to accomplish this goal is to do assignments neatly and exactly according to directions, or to memorize large amounts of information to get a high grade on a test without necessarily understanding the ideas or how they relate to one another, then these tactics will be used. Students who adopt performance-approach goals often do well on tests, but they are less likely than students who adopt mastery goals to develop a strong interest in various subjects. On the other hand, students who choose performance-approach goals tend to have high levels of self-efficacy.

- *Performance-avoidance goals* involve reducing the possibility of failure so as not to appear less capable than other students. Students can reduce their chances of failure by avoiding novel and challenging tasks or by cheating. They can also engage in *self-handicapping behaviors* such as putting off homework or projects until the last minute, studying superficially for an exam, and getting involved in many in-school and out-of-school nonacademic activities. The purpose of self-handicapping is to be able to blame poor performance on circumstances rather than on one's ability. Students most likely to choose performance-avoidance goals are boys and those with low grades and low academic self-efficacy.

  Teachers may unwittingly encourage self-handicapping behaviors, even in students whose sense of self-efficacy is at least adequate, by using a norm-referenced grading system. Because students are compared with one another to determine the top, middle, and low grades, this system encourages students to attribute their grades to a fixed ability. Students who have doubts about their ability are then more likely to engage in self-handicapping behaviors (Thrash & Hurst, 2008; Urdan, Ryan, Anderman, & Gheen, 2002).

Outcome Expectations A second way in which self-efficacy can affect motivation is in terms of the outcomes that students expect. Those with high levels of self-efficacy more often expect a positive outcome. As a result, they tend to be more willing to use the more complex and time-consuming learning skills and to persist longer in the face of difficulties. (It is possible, however, for a student to have a relatively high level of self-efficacy but expect a relatively low grade on a test because the student believes the teacher is prejudiced or grades unfairly.) Those with lower levels of self-efficacy are more likely to expect a disappointing outcome, tend to use simpler learning skills, and are likely to give up more quickly when tasks demand greater cognitive efforts (Pajares, 2007).

Attributions A third way in which self-efficacy influences motivation is through the reasons students cite to explain why they succeeded or failed at a task. Those with a high level of self-efficacy for a subject are likely to attribute failure to insufficient effort (and so vow to work harder the next time) but credit their success to a combination of ability and effort. Their peers who are lower in self-efficacy are likely to explain their failures by saying that they just don't have the ability to do well, but they will chalk their successes up to an easy task or luck. As we point out a bit further on in this chapter, this latter attribution pattern undercuts motivation (Graham & Williams, 2009).

LO3 Other Cognitive Views of Motivation

In addition to social cognitive theorists, researchers who take other cognitive approaches to learning have done extensive studies of motivation. The views described in this section emphasize how the following five characteristics affect students' intrinsic motivation to learn: the inherent need to construct an organized and logically consistent knowledge base, one's expectations for successfully completing a task, the factors that one believes account for success and failure, one's beliefs about the nature of cognitive ability, and one's interests.

hard work vs. luck

> Self-efficacy affects choice of goals, expectations of success, and attributions for success and failure.

You should also be aware that intrinsic motivation for school learning is fairly well developed by about 9 years of age (fourth grade) and becomes increasingly stable through late adolescence. Thus it is important to develop intrinsic motivation in students in the primary grades, as well as to identify students with low levels of academic motivation (Marinak & Gambrell, 2008).

Cognitive Development and the Need for Conceptual Organization

As we learned in Chapter 2, Piaget's theory of cognitive development assumes that humans have an inherited need to organize their experiences into coherent intellectual schemes or knowledge structures. This need to make sense of experiences is what drives humans to *assimilate* experiences into existing knowledge structures or—when experience runs counter to what they know—to *accommodate* by changing their intellectual scheme, the way they understand. The need to organize our experiences, through either assimilation or accommodation, can be a powerful motivator.

When new experiences require accommodation, individuals will repeatedly use new schemes because of an inherent desire to master their environment. This explains why young children can, with no loss of enthusiasm, sing the same song, tell the same story, and play the same game over and over, and why they repeatedly open and shut doors to rooms and cupboards with no apparent purpose. It also explains why older children take great delight in collecting and organizing almost everything they can get their hands on and why adolescents who have begun to attain formal operational thinking will argue incessantly about all the unfairness in the world and how it can be eliminated (Stipek, 2002).

The Need for Achievement

Have you ever decided to take on a moderately difficult task (such as taking a course on astronomy even though you are a history major and have only a limited background in science) and then found that you had somewhat conflicting feelings about it? On the one hand, you felt eager to start the course, confident that you would be pleased with your performance. But on the other hand, you also felt a bit of anxiety because of the small possibility of failure. Now try to imagine the opposite situation. In reaction to a suggestion to take a course outside your major, you refuse because the probability of failure seems great, whereas the probability of success seems quite small.

In 1964, John Atkinson proposed that such differences in achievement behavior are due to differences in something called the *need for achievement*. Individuals

> Cognitive development view of motivation: strive for equilibration; master the environment

attribution theory
A body of research into the ways that students explain their success or failure, usually in terms of ability, effort, task difficulty, and luck.

with a high need for achievement have a stronger expectation of success than they do a fear of failure for most tasks and therefore anticipate a feeling of pride in accomplishment. When given a choice, high-need achievers seek out moderately challenging tasks because they offer an optimal balance between challenge and expected success. By contrast, individuals with a low need for achievement avoid such tasks because their fear of failure greatly outweighs their expectation of success and they therefore anticipate feelings of shame. When faced with a choice, low-need achievers typically choose either relatively easy tasks because the probability of success is high or very difficult tasks because there is no shame in failing to achieve a lofty goal. Atkinson's theory was an early version of what is currently called *expectancy-value theory* (Pekrun, Elliot, & Maier, 2009; Wigfield, Tonks, & Klauda, 2009). An individual's level of motivation for a particular task is governed by that person's expectation of success and the value placed on that success (J. Cole, Bergin, & Whittaker, 2008).

> **High-need achievers prefer moderately challenging tasks. Low-need achievers prefer very easy or very hard tasks.**

Explanations of Success and Failure: Attribution Theory

Thinking back on tests you have taken or presentations you have made, try to recall those tests or performances on which you did well and those on which you performed less well. Were there instances in which your performances (good or bad) were exactly what you expected? Were you ever surprised by a performance? Did you ever "luck out" on an exam? Were you ever puzzled that you did poorly because you thought you had "aced it"?

The reasons people give for their successes and their failures—or, put another way, the factors to which they attribute their successes and failures—have been studied extensively and have yielded a perspective on motivation called **attribution theory** (Graham & Williams, 2009; McCrea, 2008; Weiner, 2010). Although

the specific statements that people make to explain what caused an outcome may vary, it turns out that the underlying attributions can be reliably categorized as *ability*, *task difficulty*, *effort*, or *luck*. To illustrate, imagine that a group of students took a biology test. Some did very well and some very poorly. What follows are some statements that students might make about their performance and how those statements align with the categories of attributions:

Type of Attribution	Typical Explanation of Success	Typical Explanation of Failure
Ability	"I have always been good at biology."	"Science is not my strong point."
Task difficulty	"That was easier than I expected."	"That was a really hard test."
Effort	"I really studied hard for this test."	"I didn't read two chapters for this test."
Luck	"Whew! My guesses were right!"	"None of my guesses were right."

Keeping in mind the kinds of attributions that learners make, take a look at Table 11.1 for a few moments and try to make some sense of it. We will then discuss how understanding learner's attributions of their successes and their failures can help you understand your students' motivation to learn in your class.

The causal dimensions in Table 11.1 refer to the nature of the causes of each kind of attribution. Consider for example, ability attributions. Ability, in Table 11.1, is both internal and stable. One's ability in a particular area resides within one's self, not outside. Thus, the causal locus (i.e., the location of the cause of success or failure) of ability is internal. One's ability is also fairly stable. Certainly a person's ability can change, but the change happens over time. When one says, "Science is not my strong point," that person does not wake up the next day feeling that she or he is suddenly a scientific genius. When someone cites ability as the reason why she succeeded or failed on a task, she is attributing the outcome to a cause that is both internal and stable. Task difficulty is fairly stable as well, but the task is outside the person—a part of the person's environment—and, therefore, an external cause.

Turning to the unstable causes in Table 11.1, we see effort and luck. Both are unstable because they can

TABLE 11.1 Causal Properties of Attributions

		Causal Locus (Is the cause of the outcome inside or outside the learner?)	
		Internal	External
Causal Stability (Is the cause consistent or variable?)	Stable	Ability	Task difficulty
	Unstable	Effort	Luck

SOURCE: Adapted from Weiner, 2010, p. 32.

change quickly. Students can decide to spend more time studying for the next test and so do, no matter whether they consider themselves to have high or low ability. Effort is something under the student's control and, therefore, internal. Luck—the other unstable category of attribution—is not under the student's control. When students attribute either their successes or their failures to luck, it is because they perceive what happens to them as being neither predictable or under their control.

Note that Table 11.1 focuses on the kinds of reasons students give for the outcomes they experience, not whether students succeed or fail. And yet, we know from our study of self-efficacy and other views of motivation that success boosts and failure erodes motivation to learn. We also know, however, that some students who succeed nearly all of the time are not highly motivated in school. Let's consider success for a moment. Using the perspective of attribution theory—and taking into account the notion of expectancy value mentioned previously—we can explain why not all success is equal.

Task difficulty, as a category of attributions, is an external causal locus. But the level of difficulty is in the eye of the beholder: Some tasks that are perceived as difficult by some students are perceived by others to be easy. Imagine that you are working on a task that you consider difficult; imagine also that you succeed in completing the difficult task. Now imagine that you succeed on a task that you consider to be easy. How do you feel about each success? According to Bernard Weiner (2010), if a task is perceived to be difficult, success is more likely to be attributed to an internal causal locus (effort or ability in Table 11.1). We tend to reason as follows: We don't succeed on difficult tasks because they are difficult; we succeed on difficult tasks because we are smart or have worked hard. When a task is easy, we are more likely to attribute our success to the ease of the task. One reason we perceive tasks to be easy is that they do not require a great deal of ability or a great deal of effort. Because we attribute success on difficult tasks to internal reasons and success on easy tasks to external reasons, we tend to feel more pride when we succeed on difficult tasks than on easy tasks. Pride that comes from one's abilities and one's efforts breeds self-confidence, self-efficacy, a sense of industry rather than inferiority, and a positive academic self-perception.

A clear implication of attribution theory is that understanding students' explanations for their successes and failures can give us insights into their

motivation to learn. To understand our students' attributions, we must give them opportunities to reflect on their successes and their failures, and we must listen closely to what they have to say. As teachers, the outcomes we want for our students include acquiring the knowledge and skills in particular content areas. But we should also help them learn to have confidence in their abilities to overcome obstacles that get in the way of constructing knowledge and building skills. We want them to learn biology, but in order for them to do so, they must also learn that they are capable of learning biology. As students become more confident and convinced that their own efforts—even in the face of difficult tasks—will lead to success, they grow more in control and more self-assured (Graham & Williams, 2009).

Pause & Reflect *Do you fit the pattern of most successful students, attributing success to effort and ability, and failure to lack of effort? If so, how did you get this way? Is there anything you can draw from your own experiences to help students develop this pattern?*

The typical attribution pattern of high-achieving students highlights an important point: Both effort and ability should be credited with contributing to one's success. Students who attribute their success mostly to effort may conclude that they have a low level of ability because they have to work harder to achieve the same level of performance as others (McCrea, 2008).

Beliefs About the Nature of Cognitive Ability

Children's motivation for learning is affected by their beliefs about the nature of ability. During the primary and elementary grades, children create and refine their conception of ability. By the time they reach middle school, most children start to think of themselves and others as belonging to particular categories in terms of ability.

Changes in Beliefs About Ability

According to Carol Dweck (2002a, 2002b; see also Dweck & Master, 2009), a leading theorist and researcher on this subject, noticeable changes in children's ability conceptions occur at two points in time: between 7 and 8 years of age and between 10 and 12 years of age. Compared with kindergarten and early primary grade children, 7- and 8-year-olds are more likely to do the following:

- Show an increased interest in the concept of ability and take greater notice of peer behaviors that are relevant to achievement comparisons.

- Distinguish ability from such other characteristics as social skills, likability, and physical skills, and believe that the same person can have different levels of ability for different academic skills (such as reading, writing, and mathematics).

- Think of ability as a more internal and less observable characteristic that is defined normatively (that is, by comparing oneself to others).

- Think of ability as a characteristic that is stable over time and can therefore be used to make predictions about future academic performance.

- Engage in self-criticism related to ability and compare their performance with that of others.

Compared with 7- and 8-year-olds, 10- to 12-year-old children are more likely to do the following:

- Distinguish between effort and ability as factors in performance. Consequently, some are more likely to say of two students who receive the same grade on a test or assignment that the one who exerted more effort has less ability.

- Evaluate their academic ability more accurately, although more begin to underestimate their ability.

- Think of ability as being both a stable characteristic and a fixed capacity that explains the grades they currently receive and will receive in the future. It is not uncommon to hear older children and adolescents talk about peers who do or do not have "it" (Anderman & Maehr, 1994). Consequently, students who believe their ability in a particular subject is below average seek to avoid additional courses in that subject. Girls, especially high-achieving ones, are more likely than boys to adopt this view of ability, and this may partly explain their greater reluctance to take advanced science and math classes in high school.

- Value performance goals (getting the highest grade possible) over learning goals (making meaningful connections among ideas and how they relate to the world outside of school).

> { **Students with incremental beliefs tend to have mastery goals and be motivated to learn meaningfully and improve their skills.** }

Why these changes occur, and why they occur in some individuals but not others, is not entirely known, but comparing the performance of a student with the performance of every other student in a class to determine who gets which grades (the practice of grading on a curve) is suspected of playing a major role. One casualty of this belief, as we've indicated, is motivation for learning (J. A. Chen & Pajares, 2010; Lepper, Corpus, & Iyengar, 2005).

Types of Beliefs About Ability According to the work of Dweck (2002a) and others (e.g., Chen & Pajares, 2010; Dweck & Master, 2009; Quihuis, Bempechat, Jimenez, & Boulay, 2002), students can be placed into one of three categories based on their beliefs about the nature of cognitive ability:

1. *Entity theorists.* Some students subscribe solely to what is called an entity theory; they talk about intelligence as if it were a thing, or an entity, that has fixed characteristics.

2. *Incremental theorists.* Other students subscribe solely to what is called an incremental theory, believing that intelligence can be improved gradually by degrees or increments as they refine their thinking skills and acquire new ones. Entity and incremental theorists hold to their respective views for all subjects.

3. *Mixed theorists.* Students in this group subscribe to both entity and incremental theories, depending on the subject. A mixed theorist may, for example, be an entity theorist for math but an incremental theorist for science, whereas the opposite (or some other) pattern may prevail for another student.

Students with incremental beliefs tend to be motivated to acquire new and more effective cognitive skills and are said to have *mastery goals.* They seek challenging tasks and do not give up easily, because they see obstacles as a natural part of the learning process. They often tell themselves what adults have told them for years: "Think carefully," "Pay attention," and "Try to recall useful information that you learned earlier." They seem to focus on the questions "How do you do this?" and "What can I learn from this?" Errors are seen as opportunities for useful feedback. Not surprisingly, these students are more likely than entity theorists to attribute failure to insufficient effort and ineffective learning skills.

Students who believe that intelligence is an unchangeable entity are primarily motivated to appear smart to others by getting high grades and praise and by avoiding low grades, criticism, and shame. Such students are said to have *performance goals.* When confronted with a new task, their initial thought is likely to be "Am I smart enough to do this?" They may forgo

Students who believe that intelligence is a collection of cognitive skills that can be refined are likely to adopt mastery goals and attribute failure to insufficient effort, whereas students who believe that intelligence is an unchangeable capacity are likely to adopt performance goals and attribute failure to low ability.

opportunities to learn new ideas and skills if they think they will become confused and make mistakes, and they tend to attribute failure to low ability rather than insufficient effort.

> **Among students with entity beliefs, those with high confidence seek challenges, and those with low confidence avoid them.**

However, among students who subscribe to the entity theory, there is a difference between those with high confidence in their ability and those with low confidence. High-confidence entity theorists are likely to demonstrate such mastery-oriented behaviors as seeking challenges and persisting in the face of difficulty. Those with low confidence, in contrast, may be more interested in avoiding failure and criticism—even after achieving initial success—than in continuing to be positively reinforced for outperforming others. Because of their anxiety over the possibility of failure, these low-confidence entity theorists are less likely than students who have an incremental view of ability to exhibit subsequent motivation for a task (Cury, Da Fonseca, Zahn,

& Elliot, 2008; Rawsthorne & Elliot, 1999). If avoidance is not possible, they become discouraged at the first sign of difficulty. This, in turn, produces anxiety, ineffective problem solving, and withdrawal from the task (as a way to avoid concluding that they lack ability and thereby maintain some self-esteem). According to attribution theory, entity theorists should continue this pattern because success is not attributed to effort but failure is attributed to low ability.

The Effect of Interest on Intrinsic Motivation

Interest can be described as a psychological state that involves focused attention, increased cognitive functioning, persistence, and emotional involvement (Ainley, Hidi, & Berndorff, 2002; R. Miller & Brickman, 2004; Schraw & Lehman, 2001). A person's interest in a topic can come from personal or situational sources:

- *Personal interest* (also referred to as *individual* or *topic interest*) is characterized by an intrinsic desire to understand a topic, a desire that persists over time and is based on preexisting knowledge, personal experience, and emotion.

- *Situational interest* is more temporary and is based on context-specific factors, such as the unusualness of information or its personal relevance. For example, baseball teams that qualify for or win league championships or World Series after many years of not doing so (think the Chicago Cubs or Boston Red Sox) often spark temporary interest in the players and the games among people who live in those cities. Similarly, people who buy a company's stock often become interested, albeit temporarily, in the company's activities.

The degree of personal interest a student brings to a subject or activity has been shown to affect intrinsic motivation for that task. Personally interested students pay greater attention to the task, stay with it for a longer period of time, learn more from it, and enjoy their involvement to a greater degree (R. Miller & Brickman, 2004; Schraw & Lehman, 2001; Tabachnick, Miller, & Relyea, 2008).

It is possible, of course, that situational interest in a topic can grow into a personal interest. Consider, for example, a high school student who knows nothing of how information is stored in and retrieved from memory but learns about it when she has to read a chapter on memory in her psychology textbook. Fascinated with the description of various forms of encoding and retrieval cues because of her own problems with being able to accurately recall information for tests, she searches for additional books and articles on the topic and even thinks about majoring in psychology in college (Renninger & Hidi, 2002; Schraw & Lehman, 2001).

Factors That Influence Personal Interest A long-term interest in a particular subject or activity may be influenced by one or more of the following factors (Hidi, 2001; R. Miller & Brickman, 2004; Schraw & Lehman, 2001; Tabachnick, Miller, & Relyea, 2008):

- *Ideas and activities that are valued by one's culture or ethnic group.* As we discussed in Chapter 5, culture is the filter through which groups of people interpret the world and assign values to objects, ideas, and activities. Thus, inner-city male youths are likely to be strongly interested in playing basketball and following the exploits of professional basketball players, whereas a rural midwestern male of the same age is likely to be interested in fishing and hunting.

- *The emotions that are aroused by the subject or activity.* Students who experience extreme math anxiety, for example, are less likely to develop a strong interest in math-related activities than those who experience more positive emotions.

- *The degree of competence one attains in a subject or activity.* People typically spend more time pursuing activities that they are good at than activities at which they do not excel.

- *The degree to which a subject or activity is perceived to be relevant to achieving a goal.* As we will note in Chapter 13, many students fail to perceive such relevance, partly because teachers rarely take the time to explain how a topic or lesson may affect students' lives.

- *Level of prior knowledge.* People are often more interested in topics they already know something about than in topics they know nothing about.

- *A perceived hole in a topic that the person already knows a good deal about.* A person who considers himself to be well informed about the music of Mozart would likely be highly interested in reading the score of a newly discovered composition by Mozart.

Factors That Influence Situational Interest Some of the factors that spark a spontaneous and short-term interest in a topic or activity include (Hidi, 2001; Montalvo, Mansfield, & Miller, 2007; Reeve & Halusic, 2009; Schraw & Lehman, 2001):

- *A state of cognitive conflict or disequilibrium.* Teachers can sometimes spark students' interest in a topic by showing or telling them something that is discrepant with a current belief. Consider, for example, a high school class on government. The teacher has a lesson planned on government spending and wants to avoid the usual lack of interest that this topic produces. One tactic would be to ask students

if they believe that the money they contribute to Social Security from their part-time jobs (or the full-time jobs they will eventually have) is placed in an account with their name on it, where it remains until they become eligible for benefits in their mid-60s. Most will probably believe something like that. The teacher could then tell them that the contributions they make today are actually used to pay the benefits of current retirees and that their Social Security benefits will come from the Social Security taxes levied on a future generation of workers.

- *Well-written reading material.* Texts and other written materials that are logically organized and engaging are rated as more interesting by students and produce higher levels of comprehension than more poorly written material.

- *The opportunity to work on a task with others.* As we saw earlier in the book, cooperative arrangements are highly motivating and produce high levels of learning.

> { **Teachers can spark students' interest by introducing cognitive conflict or disequilibrium.** }

- *The opportunity to engage in hands-on activities.* The point here is that the activities should engage students; putting one's hands on something does not guarantee that students will be engaged.

- *The opportunity to observe influential models.* As we saw in Chapter 9, models can serve to focus students on important behaviors and encourage students to emulate those behaviors, such as self-regulation.

- *The teacher's use of novel stimuli.* Rather than use the same kind of materials—for example, always having students work the problems at the end of the chapter—teachers should employ a variety of materials and set different kinds of challenges for students. The use of authentic problems can be helpful in this regard.

- *The teacher's use of games and puzzles.* This finding is an extension of some others: games and puzzles are the kinds of hands-on activities that can engage students. Introducing games and puzzles can also serve as novel stimuli.

These findings have a number of clear instructional implications. Given that some students may develop a strong interest in a topic as a result of a classroom activity or assignment and that this initial interest may grow into a personal interest and the adoption of mastery goals, a general recommendation is for teachers to do what constructivist learning theory implies: Involve students in a variety of subject matters and meaningful activities (Zhu et al., 2009). If you think about it, the purpose of exposing students to a wide variety of topics during their school years is not simply to provide them with basic knowledge of all of those topics but also to increase the likelihood that students will encounter those topics in situations that engage them, perhaps to the point at which topics grow into personal interests. Many of us have "discovered" our personal interests, and indeed our careers, as a result of situational interest growing into personal interest.

This chapter's Case in Print illustrates how a program to help children in China learn to read uses personal and situational interest to develop intrinsic motivation. The Suggestions for Teaching offer further recommendations.

Flow and Engagement The concept of flow has been championed for more than three decades by Mihaly Csikszentmihalyi. Flow is the mental state of high engagement in an activity. It is characterized by intense concentration, sustained interest, and enjoyment of the activity's challenge (Csikszentmihalyi, 1975, 1996, 2000, 2002; Nakamura & Csikszentmihalyi, 2009). If you have ever been engaged in an activity (e.g., playing a video game or reading a novel) that captured your interest so completely that you lost track of time and had trouble

breaking away from the activity, you have experienced something like the state of flow. Factors that influence either personal or situational interest can result in students' experiencing flow and developing intrinsic motivation. For example, researchers in China have seen how flow influences engagement in instant messaging behavior and the selection of the particular messaging product (Lu, Zhou, & Wang, 2008).

> **Flow is experienced as intense engagement or absorbed concentration.**

Research has used the concept of flow as a way of investigating the effects of student engagement in classrooms (Inal & Cagiltay, 2007; Owston, Wideman, Sinitskaya, & Brown, 2009). Rathunde and Csikszentmihalyi (2005) compared the academic experiences of nearly 300 middle school students divided into two groups: those who were enrolled in a program that took advantage of the factors that influence both personal and situational interest (called a Montessori program) and students in a traditional middle school program. The students in the two groups were matched on a number of demographic factors to help ensure that any differences between the groups were most likely due to the kind of program they attended. The study produced two major findings. First, the students in both types of middle school programs reported very similar experiences when engaged in nonacademic

TeachSource Video Case

Motivating Adolescent Learners: Curriculum Based on Real Life

Go to the Education CourseMate website and watch the video, study the artifacts in the case, and reflect upon the following questions:

1. What are the concepts of personal and situational interest? How do these concepts relate to the school store project depicted within this Video Case?

2. For the students in this Video Case, is working in the school store an extrinsic or an intrinsic motivator? Explain your answer.

deficiency needs
The first four levels (physiological, safety, belongingness and love, and esteem) in Maslow's hierarchy of needs, so called because they cause people to act only when they are unmet to some degree.

growth need
A yearning for personal fulfillment that people constantly strive to satisfy.

self-actualization
The movement toward the full development of one's potential talents and capabilities.

activities at school. Second, when engaged in academic activities, the Montessori students reported more flow experiences, more energetic engagement, and greater intrinsic motivation than the students in the traditional middle school.

Another study by Csikszentmihalyi and his colleagues used the concept of flow to examine how high school students spent their time in school and the conditions under which they felt engaged (Shernoff, Csikszentmihalyi, Schneider, & Shernoff, 2003). The researchers studied a longitudinal sample of more than 500 high school students from across the United States. The students reported increased engagement in academic activities when both the challenge of the activity and their own skill were high, when the instruction was perceived as relevant, and when they felt control over the learning environment. In more concrete terms, the students were more engaged in participating in individual and group learning activities than in listening to lectures, watching videos, or taking exams. The researchers concluded that a sense of flow (i.e., intense engagement) is more likely when students feel a sense of control over their own learning and when the learning activities challenge students at a level appropriate to their skills.

Limitations of Cognitive Views

Cognitive views of motivation rest on understanding what students think, how they think, and what inferences and conclusions their thinking yields. Some may suggest that because cognitive views of motivation tend to focus on what happens within a student's mind—on disequilibrium, intrinsic curiosity, engagement, and personal interest rather than extrinsic rewards—the teacher's job is made more difficult. It is certainly true that teachers do not always find the provocative question or challenging task that creates cognitive disequilibrium for every student. We do not possess efficient and objective instruments for measuring students' need for achievement. And it can take considerable time and effort to change students' faulty attributions and beliefs, especially if they perceive themselves to be of low ability. While some may claim that these obstacles are limitations to applying cognitive views of motivation in the classroom, others—and we include ourselves among this group—suggest that understanding the role that cognition plays in student motivation

offers teachers opportunities to gather information and better understand the human beings they are teaching.

Now that you are familiar with some of the approaches to motivation, it is time to consider Suggestions for Teaching that show how these ideas can be converted into classroom practice.

LO4 A Humanistic View of Motivation

To this point in our discussion of motivation, we have reviewed the behavioral perspective (a perspective that was addressed extensively in Chapter 7), the social cognitive perspective, and other cognitive views. We now turn briefly to a humanistic view of motivation, so called because it is based on the idea that, as human beings, our state of mind and the motives that drive us to achieve are based on needs that span the human condition.

Maslow's Theory of Growth Motivation

Abraham Maslow's theory of human motivation was built on the idea that humans have different kinds of needs: Some are very basic to our existence; others are more intellectual or even, some would say, spiritual. Maslow elaborated on this idea by proposing a five-level hierarchy of needs (Maslow, 1987). *Physiological* needs are at the bottom of the hierarchy, followed in ascending order by *safety*, *belongingness and love*, *esteem*, and *self-actualization* needs (see Figure 11.2). This order reflects differences in the relative strength of each need. The lower a need is in the hierarchy, the greater is its strength, because when a lower-level need is activated (as in the case of extreme hunger or fear for one's physical safety), people will stop trying to satisfy a higher-level need (such as esteem or self-actualization) and focus on satisfying the currently active lower-level need.

The first four levels of needs (physiological, safety, belongingness and love, and esteem) are often referred to as **deficiency needs** because they motivate people to act only when they are unmet to some degree. Self-actualization, by contrast, is often called a **growth need** because people constantly strive to satisfy it. Basically, **self-actualization** refers to the need for self-fulfillment—the need to develop all of one's potential talents and capabilities. For example, an individual who felt she had the capability to write novels, teach, practice medicine, and raise children would not feel self-actualized until she had accomplished all of these goals to some minimal degree. Because it is at the top of the hierarchy and addresses the potential of the whole person, self-actualization is discussed more frequently than the other needs.

Case in Print

Taking an Interest in Learning

Interest can be described as a psychological state that involves focused attention, increased cognitive functioning, persistence, and emotional involvement. . . . A person's interest in a topic can come from personal or situational sources: Personal interest (also referred to as individual or topic interest) is characterized by an intrinsic desire to understand a topic, a desire that persists over time and is based on preexisting knowledge, personal experience, and emotion. Situational interest is more temporary and is based on context-specific factors, such as the unusualness of information or its personal relevance. . . . Factors that influence either personal or situational interest can result in students' experiencing flow and developing intrinsic motivation. (pp. 245, 247)

Program Aims to Make Reading Easier, More Fun, for Children in China

CRAIG CHAMBERLAIN

News Bureau, University of Illinois, 10/18/06

CHAMPAIGN, Ill.—What could an English-speaking American reading expert hope to discover from studying how Chinese learn their language? And what might he and his colleagues have to offer as a result?

For one thing: A new program to make books and reading more fun for Chinese children, and a publishing company started in order to produce the materials and train teachers how to use them.

The company is just 4 years old, but its "shared book" program already is in use with 250,000 children ages 3 to 5 in more than 8,000 kindergarten classrooms across urban China. There are about 60 million Chinese in that age group.

"Chinese is not an easy language to learn to read," says Richard Anderson, who has led a research project at the University of Illinois at Urbana-Champaign since the early 1990s on the process and psychology of learning to read Chinese. He also is the director of the U. of I. Center for the Study of Reading.

For most Chinese children, Anderson said, the process of learning to read begins in the first grade with the hard work of learning Chinese characters, largely through drill and practice. They are expected to memorize 1,200 characters by the end of the second grade and 2,500 by the end of the sixth grade.

And the Chinese don't have a strong tradition of reading to their preschool-age children or doing other activities connected with books, said Anderson, who also is a U. of I. professor of educational psychology. Their books for young children tend to be heavily moralistic and "not designed to be really exciting fiction," he said. They are not books young children can learn to read themselves.

Anderson and his research colleagues, from both the U. of I. and Beijing Normal University, sought to design a program that would not only lay the foundation for literacy, but also would encourage young children to read more and to read for pleasure.

"We wanted them to feel it was worth the trouble. We wanted to build in them an intrinsic motivation for reading. . . . We wanted children to become really excited by reading so that they can hang in there during those tough first several years of school."

China is fertile ground for a program such as this because literacy is becoming essential for many jobs in the nation's growing economy. In addition, most couples now have only one child, the result of the country's population policies, Anderson said. "Making sure your child gets a good education is a very, very high priority."

The seeds for the research project in China were planted in the early 1980s, as the nation was opening up to the West. Anderson visited China with a group of educators. Connections made then eventually led to doctoral students and researchers from Beijing Normal coming to work with Anderson and his Illinois colleagues.

What they've found, along with other researchers in the field, are surprising similarities in the way children learn to read each language, Anderson said. "It's amazing the extent to which the fundamental processes are the same, or at least highly similar, between Chinese and English, considering that everything is different," he said.

The shared book approach being promoted by the publishing company, which Anderson started with Chinese investors, grew out of another line of research studying Chinese schools and their approach to teaching reading. They saw some strengths in the Chinese approach, but were concerned about an over-reliance on rewards and punishments, and too much emphasis on intensive reading aimed at learning fundamentals, Anderson said.

"We discovered not much extensive reading," he said, meaning reading for pleasure and practice.

Through the shared book approach, "we want to lay a foundation for reading in an easy, natural way—one that will build children's excitement about reading," Anderson said. "In this approach, we're trying to make progress on all aspects of Chinese reading, but we're especially trying to build oral language facility, which is very important."

The program involves significant time spent reading stories with students, using large illustrated books. Children are able to learn quite a few Chinese characters simply from reading the stories again and again, he said.

In one key activity, each child is encouraged to do his or her own "book," which requires the child to create a story, do the drawings, and then explain the story to a parent (usually the mother), who writes out the story below the pictures.

In doing these activities, "we get a huge amount of parent collaboration, which is also good for the development of literacy," Anderson said.

Source: Craig Chamberlain, "Program aims to make reading easier, more fun, for children in China," *News Bureau*, University of Illinois, 10/18/06. Reprinted by permission.

Questions and Activities

1. According to this chapter, interest in learning is influenced by several individual and situational factors. Review the lists of these factors and then identify which factors were probably operating in the program described in this article.
2. Explain how the approach to motivation taken by the researchers in the Chinese reading project is consistent with a constructivist view of learning.
3. What insights into intrinsic and extrinsic motivation are provided by this cross-cultural glimpse into educational practices?

Suggestions for Teaching

Facilitating Students' Motivation to Learn

1 **Give praise as positive reinforcement, but do so effectively.**

A number of operant conditioning techniques were described in Chapter 7 and its Suggestions for Teaching. In this chapter, we focus using praise as a form of positive reinforcement.

Think about the times when you've been praised for a job well done, particularly when you weren't sure about the quality of your work. In all likelihood, it had a strong, maybe even dramatic, effect on your motivation. That being the case, you might think that effective positive reinforcement in the form of verbal praise is a common occurrence in the classroom. But you would be wrong. Observations of classrooms have revealed that verbal praise is given infrequently and is often given in ways that limit its effectiveness (Brophy, 1981; Reinke, Lewis-Palmer, & Merrell, 2008). In an effort to help teachers administer praise more effectively, Brophy drew up the guidelines for effective praise listed in Table 11.2.

2 **Make sure that students know what they are to do, how to proceed, and how to determine when they have achieved goals.**

One way to structure students' learning efforts is to follow the suggestions offered by Raymond Wlodkowski for drawing up a personal contract. He recommended that such a contract contain four elements. A sample contract (Wlodkowski, 1978, p. 57) is presented here, with a description of each element in brackets.

Date _____

1. Within the next two weeks I will learn to multiply correctly single-digit numbers ranging between 5 and 9, for example, 5 ? 6, 6 ? 7, 7 ? 8, 8 ? 9, 9 ? 5. [What the student will learn]

2. When I feel prepared, I will ask to take a mastery test containing 50 problems from this range of multiplication facts. [How the student can demonstrate learning]

3. I will complete this contract when I can finish the mastery test with no more than three errors. [The degree of proficiency to be demonstrated]

4. My preparation and study will involve choosing work from the workbook activi-

TABLE 11.2 Guidelines for Effective Praise

Effective Praise	Ineffective Praise
1. Is delivered contingently	1. Is delivered randomly or unsystematically
2. Specifies the particulars of the accomplishment	2. Is restricted to global positive reactions
3. Shows spontaneity, variety, and other signs of credibility; suggests clear attention to the student's accomplishment	3. Shows a bland uniformity, which suggests a conditional response made with minimal attention
4. Rewards attainment of specified performance criteria (which can include effort criteria)	4. Rewards mere participation, without consideration of performance process or outcomes
5. Provides information to students about their competence or the value of their accomplishments	5. Provides no information at all or gives students information about their status
6. Orients students toward better appreciating their own task-related behavior and thinking about problem solving	6. Orients students toward comparing themselves with others and thinking about competing
7. Uses students' own prior accomplishments as the context for describing new accomplishments	7. Uses the accomplishments of peers as the context for describing students' present accomplishments
8. Is given in recognition of noteworthy effort or success at tasks that are difficult (for *this* student)	8. Is given without regard to the effort expended or the meaning of the accomplishment (for *this* student)
9. Attributes success to effort and ability, implying that similar successes can be expected in the future	9. Attributes success to ability alone or to external factors such as luck or easiness of the task
10. Leads students to expend effort on the task because they enjoy the task or want to develop task-relevant skills	10. Leads students to expend effort on the task for external reasons—to please the teacher, win a competition or reward, etc.
11. Focuses students' attention on their own task-relevant behavior	11. Focuses students' attention on the teacher as an external authority figure who is manipulating them
12. Fosters appreciation of and desirable attributions about task-relevant behavior after the process is completed	12. Intrudes into the ongoing process, distracting attention from task-relevant behavior

SOURCES: Brophy (1981); Hester, Hendrickson, & Gable (2009); Reinke, Lewis-Palmer, & Merrell (2008).

ties, number games, and filmstrip materials. [How the student will proceed]

Signed _____

3 **Encourage low-achieving students to attribute success to a combination of ability and effort, and failure to insufficient effort.**

Should you decide to try to alter the attributions of a student who is having difficulty with one or more subjects, here are three suggestions based on an analysis of 20 attribution training studies (Robertson, 2000):

• Make sure the student has the ability to succeed on a task before telling the

student to attribute failure to insufficient effort. Students who try hard but lack the cognitive skills necessary for success are likely to become convinced not only that they lack the ability but also that they will never become capable of success on that type of task.

• Tell students that having the ability for a subject is the same as knowing how to formulate and use a learning strategy for that subject. Thus success is attributable to an appropriate strategy (which is controllable), whereas failure is attributable to insufficient effort at formulating the strategy (also controllable).

- Combine attribution training with strategy instruction for students who don't understand the relationship between strategy use and success and failure.

④ Encourage students to think of ability as a set of cognitive skills that can be added to and refined, rather than as a fixed entity that is resistant to change, by praising the processes they use to succeed.

The work that Carol Dweck (2002a, 2002b; Dweck & Master, 2009) has done on students' beliefs about ability clearly shows that those who adopt an entity view are more likely to develop a maladaptive approach to learning than are those who adopt an incremental view. One way to help students develop incremental rather than entity beliefs is to praise them for their effort and use of effective skills rather than for their ability after they do well on a task.

Avoid comments that encourage entity beliefs, such as:

"You did very well on this test; you certainly are smart."
"You're really good at this."

A better alternative is to offer what Dweck calls process praise. Examples of process praise are:

"That's a really high score; you must have worked really hard at these problems."
"Now that you've mastered this skill, let's go on to something a bit harder that you can learn from."
"You did a fine job on this paper because you started early and used the writing skills we practiced in class."

⑤ Encourage students to adopt mastery learning goals.

As we noted earlier, students may adopt task mastery goals, performance-approach goals, or performance-avoidance goals. To briefly review, students who have task mastery goals are motivated to use effective learning tactics to acquire new knowledge and skills even if it means an occasional disappointing performance. Students who adopt performance-approach goals, on the other hand, are principally motivated to outscore others on exams and assignments in order to demonstrate their ability. Students who adopt performance-avoidance goals are prin-

cipally motivated to avoid failure and appearing less capable than their peers by engaging in such behaviors as self-handicapping, avoiding novel and challenging tasks, and cheating.

The following suggestions for helping students adopt mastery goals (Urdan & Midgley, 2001) were designed with middle school students in mind but are just as applicable to both lower and higher grades:

- Group students by topic, interest, or their own choice rather than by ability.
- Use a variety of assessment techniques (discussed in Chapter 14) rather than just one, and make the top grade potentially achievable for all students by evaluating performance according to a predetermined set of criteria.
- Provide students with feedback about their progress rather than feedback about how they scored relative to the rest of the class.
- Recognize students who demonstrate progress rather than focusing just on students who have achieved the highest grades.
- Provide students with opportunities to choose what projects they will do, what electives they will take, and how long they wish to study a particular subject, rather than having these decisions made exclusively by administrators and teachers.
- Treat mistakes as a part of learning, encourage students to take academic risks, and allow students to redo work that does not meet some minimum satisfactory standard.
- Provide students with complex and challenging tasks that require comprehension and problem solving rather than tasks that require little more than rote learning and verbatim recall.
- Use cross-age tutoring, peer tutoring, and enrichment activities rather than grade retention with students who are falling behind.
- Use cooperative learning methods rather than competition. Because so much has been written about the use of cooperative learning techniques and their demonstrated effectiveness in raising motivation and learning, we discuss this recommendation in more detail in Chapter 13.

⑥ Maximize factors that appeal to both personal and situational interest.
  a. Find out what your students' interests are and design as many in-class and out-of-class assignments as possible around those interests.
  b. Try to associate subjects and assignments with pleasurable rather than painful experiences by using such techniques as cooperative learning and constructivist approaches to teaching, as well as providing students with the information-processing tools they need to master your objectives.
  c. Link new topics to information students are already likely to have or provide relevant background knowledge in creative yet understandable ways.
  d. Select reading materials that are logically organized and written in an engaging style.

Well-designed projects can often be a vehicle for students to engage personal interests. Even when some students do not have a personal interest, situational interest can drive their learning. For example, Diane Curtis (2002) describes a fifth grade project that helped students fulfill state curriculum standards in social studies, math, writing, and technology. Building on their interest in architecture, the students completed a project on several of the major memorial buildings in Washington, DC (such as those honoring Presidents Washington and Jefferson, as well as the Vietnam Veterans Memorial). They gathered information from books, the web, and architects about the memorials, drew computer models of them, created a timeline of construction, and researched the contributions of Jefferson and others to the writing of the U.S. Constitution. This was followed by a field trip to Washington, DC, and a presentation of their work to community members.

As we know, project-based learning can be time consuming. To help teachers overcome that barrier, several websites offer project-based programs that provide curriculum materials, assignments, resources, and contact with experts. See, for example, the JASON Project (www.jason.org), Journey North (www.learner.org/jnorth), and ThinkQuest (www.thinkquest.org).

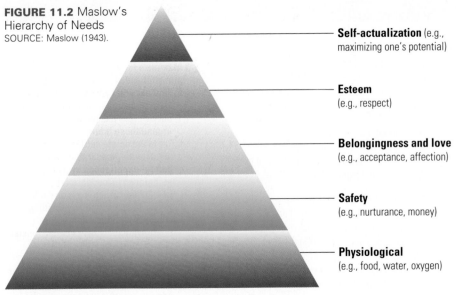

FIGURE 11.2 Maslow's Hierarchy of Needs
SOURCE: Maslow (1943).

- **Self-actualization** (e.g., maximizing one's potential)
- **Esteem** (e.g., respect)
- **Belongingness and love** (e.g., acceptance, affection)
- **Safety** (e.g., nurturance, money)
- **Physiological** (e.g., food, water, oxygen)

Maslow originally felt that self-actualization needs would automatically be activated as soon as esteem needs were met, but he changed his mind when he encountered individuals whose behavior did not fit this pattern. He concluded that individuals whose self-actualization needs became activated and met held in high regard such values as truth, goodness, beauty, justice, autonomy, and humor (Feist & Feist, 2001).

Pause&Reflect *Maslow stated that for individuals to be motivated to satisfy self-actualization needs, deficiency needs have to be satisfied first. Has this been true in your experience? If not, what was different?*

In addition to the five basic needs that compose the hierarchy, Maslow described cognitive needs (such as the needs to know and to understand) and aesthetic needs (such as the needs for order, symmetry, or harmony) (Maslow, 1987). Although not part of the basic hierarchy, these two classes of needs play a critical role in the satisfaction of basic needs. Maslow maintains that such conditions as the freedom to investigate and learn and fairness, honesty, and orderliness in interpersonal relationships are critical because their absence makes satisfaction of the five basic needs impossible. (Imagine, for example, trying to satisfy your belongingness and love needs or your esteem needs in an atmosphere characterized by dishonesty, unfair punishment, and restrictions on freedom of speech.)

{ **Self-actualization depends on satisfaction of lower needs and belief in certain values.** }

Implications of Maslow's Theory

Maslow's theory of growth motivation (or need gratification, if you prefer) holds important implications for educators. Clearly, one implication is that students who are hungry, do not feel safe, or do not feel they are accepted as part of a group or a community are unlikely to be motivated to maximize their potential academically. What are the effects on children who are homeless or come from poverty? What are the effects for students whose cultural backgrounds may differ from the predominant culture of the school? Aside from physiological needs, how do the basic needs of safety, belongingness, and esteem from others impact academic opportunity and achievement? Consider, for a moment, the disproportionate numbers of students of color and students from poverty who are designated for special education (the subject of Chapter 6's Case in Print; see also Blanchett, Klingner, & Harry, 2009).

Maslow's theory suggests that not all academic problems are traceable to intellectual deficiencies; there could well be deficiency needs that are going unmet. When we think of deficiency needs in Maslow's hierarchy, we are not just thinking about difficult living conditions that accrue from a life in severe poverty (although those are clearly important to consider). We are also thinking of students from a wide range of socioeconomic backgrounds who may feel isolated or unaccepted. Several researchers have reported that low-achieving students have reported that they would like to get better grades but don't make more of an effort because, in their eyes, teachers don't care about them or what they do (Glasser, 1998; Montalvo, Mansfield, & Miller, 2007).

You may very well have students in your classes who have needs that will be difficult for you to identify, let alone meet. Imagine a high school student who appears to have all of the economic and social advantages necessary for a well-adjusted teen, but who feels that her parents do not love her and her peers do not accept her. If, according to Maslow, her needs for love, belonging, and esteem are not satisfied, she is less likely to be in the mood to learn and to respond to your efforts to help her do so.

Then again, there will be times when you can be quite instrumental in helping to satisfy certain deficiency needs. The development of self-esteem, for example,

Theorists such as Abraham Maslow, who argued that deficiency needs such as belongingness and self-esteem must be satisfied before students will be motivated to learn, call attention to the importance of positive teacher–student relationships in the classroom.

John Lei/Stock Boston

LO5 The Role of Self-Perceptions in Motivation

Current interest in the effects of self-perceptions on school motivation and achievement runs high and seems to have been prompted by such developments as a better understanding of the nature of self-concept and self-esteem, Albert Bandura's introduction of the self-efficacy concept, advances in the measurement of self-perceptions, and the consistent finding of a positive relationship among self-perceptions, motivation, and school achievement (Trautwein, Lüdtke, Köller, & Baumert, 2006). Much of this interest can be traced to ideas published during the 1960s and 1970s by psychologists such as Abraham Maslow, Carl Rogers, and Arthur Combs. These individuals stressed that how students see and judge themselves and others plays an important part in determining how motivated they are and how much they learn.

In the next section we focus on the relationship of academic self-concept to motivation and learning. As we noted earlier in the book, self-concept is somewhat different from self-esteem, self-efficacy, and identity. Table 11.3 offers a quick review of these terms.

The Role of Academic Self-Concept in Motivation and Learning

Over the years, researchers have consistently found a moderately positive relationship (called a correlation) between measures of academic self-concept and school achievement. Students who score relatively high on

is closely tied to successful classroom achievement for almost all students. Although you may not be able to feed students when they are hungry or always protect them from physical danger, you can always take steps that will help them.

TABLE 11.3 Comparing Identity, Self-Esteem, Self-Concept, and Self-Efficacy

Type of Self-Perception	Major Characteristics	Examples
Identity	• The largely nonevaluative picture people have of themselves and the groups to which they belong	• "I am an animal lover." • "I am female." • "I am going to be a writer."
Self-esteem (self-worth)	• The global evaluative judgments people make of themselves • An indication of how you feel about your identity	• "I am a good person." • "I am happy with myself the way I am." • "I feel inferior to most people."
Self-concept	• The evaluative judgments people make of their competence in specific areas or domains and their associated feelings of self-worth • Past-oriented • May be hierarchically arranged for older students; for example, academic self-concept is verbal self-concept plus mathematical self-concept plus science self-concept, etc.	• "I'm pretty good at sports." • "I have always done well in math." • "My academic skills are about average." • "I get tongue-tied when I have to speak in public."
Self-efficacy	• The beliefs people have about their ability to carry out a specific course of action • Future-oriented	• "I believe I can learn how to use a computer program." • "I don't think I'll ever figure out how to solve quadratic equations." • "I'm sure I can get at least a B in this course."

SOURCES: Bong & Skaalvik (2003); Harter (1999); Kaplan & Flum (2009); Kernis (2002); Schunk & Pajares (2002).

measures of academic self-concept tend to have higher-than-average grades. But correlation does not imply causation. The fact that students with high academic self-concept scores tend to have high grades is not sufficient grounds for concluding that high academic self-concept causes high achievement. It is just as plausible that high achievement causes increased academic self-concept or that increases in both variables are due to the influence of a third variable, for example, the extent of ability grouping in a student's high school (Ireson & Hallam, 2009). Recent work on the relationship between academic self-concept and achievement has begun to shed some light on what causes what.

> **Academic self-concept and achievement can positively affect each other.**

On the basis of their own research with children in grades 2, 3, and 4 and of the research of others, Frédéric Guay, Herbert Marsh, and Michel Boivin (2003) proposed the causal explanation depicted in Figure 11.3. They maintained that academic self-concept and achievement have what are called reciprocal effects. That is, not only does prior achievement affect children's academic self-concept, but also the current strength of a child's academic self-concept influences subsequent achievement. In addition, prior achievement has a significant positive relationship with subsequent achievement, and prior self-concept has a significant positive relationship with subsequent self-concept.

Although the role of motivation was not directly tested in this study, related research suggests that the effect of academic self-concept on subsequent achievement is likely to be influenced by motivation. So a

student with a strong academic self-concept for, say, social studies is likely to be highly motivated to take additional courses in that subject and to use effective learning skills, which produce higher levels of achievement. At the same time, high levels of achievement strengthen the student's academic self-concept, which supports a high level of motivation, which supports high levels of achievement, and so on.

The instructional implication that flows from this research is fairly clear: Teachers should design instructional programs that are aimed directly at improving both academic self-concept and achievement. The former can be accomplished by, for example, pointing out to students how well they have learned certain skills and bodies of knowledge, and the latter can be accomplished by teaching students the information-processing and self-regulation skills we discussed in Chapters 8 and 9.

Motivation and Identity

Generally speaking, the relationship between motivation and identity is seen as the links between a person's goal-directed behavior and that person's perception of who she or he is or may become (Kaplan & Flum, 2009). Jacquelynne Eccles (2009), for example, argued that identity can be conceptualized as two sets of self-perceptions: 1) perceptions of skills, characteristics, and competencies and 2) perceptions of personal values and goals. In combination, these two sets of self-perceptions determine a person's expectations for success and the kinds of tasks she or he views as important. Thus, identity influences behavioral actions: what one chooses to do and how one chooses to engage in what they do. Think back to our earlier discussions of self-efficacy and how efficacy perceptions are context specific: One may feel confident in science class, but not as confident in a literature class.

K. Ann Renninger (2009) saw the connection between motivation and identity as the interaction of interest and identity. In her view, a student who is "interested" in science "identifies with" the content of science. In this view, understanding a student's motivation means understanding what kinds of content and activities attract a student. Renninger's conception is consistent with what we have examined as intrinsic motivation. The instructional implication here is that enhancing motivation in a particular area is a matter of creating opportunities for students to develop their interest in various academic pursuits. Interest can be "triggered" by a

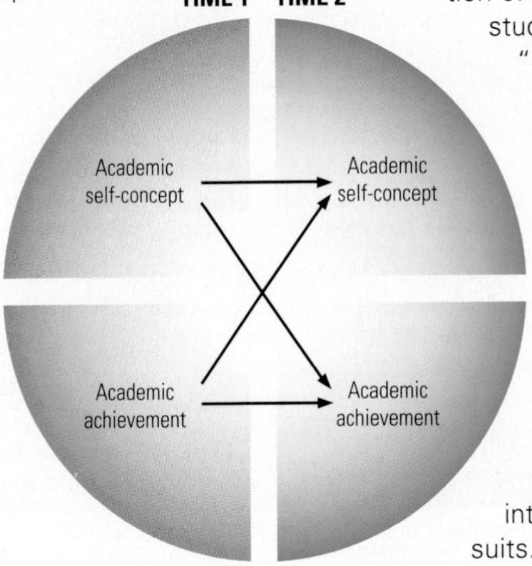

TIME 1   TIME 2

Academic self-concept → Academic self-concept

Academic self-concept → Academic achievement

Academic achievement → Academic achievement

FIGURE 11.3 Relationship Between Academic Self-Concept and Achievement

SOURCE: Adapted from Guay, Marsh, & Boivin (2003).

Challenging Assumptions

Rigor in Teaching and Learning

Rigor in teaching and learning is a good thing; on that there is general agreement. But what is rigor? Some people assume that rigor means material that is inherently hard or difficult to learn. There is no getting around the fact that some concepts and skills are harder to learn than others, that they require students to struggle. Indeed, as we have learned, some of the most interesting learning challenges create a state of cognitive conflict or disequilibrium in students. Engaging students in ways that challenge their capacities, that require them to think differently than they have thought previously, that call for the use of scaffolding to help students make significant breakthroughs is something to which teachers should aspire. The problem comes when an assumption is made that not every student is capable of learning difficult concepts, solving complex problems, or persisting long enough to develop sophisticated skills. That assumption tends to be accompanied by the following reasoning: If it is true that not every student can struggle successfully, then it must be true that students should receive different grades; if grades are the way of signaling those differences, then it must be the case that only a very best few will earn the very best grades; thus, the grading system should be set up so that only a few students can earn the highest grade. From a behavioral point view, a contingency is established and that contingency is that every student must compete with every other student for limited rewards. As a consequence, many people—inside and outside of education—argue that grades are an indicator of rigor. But deciding before learning starts how many high grades will be awarded is not rigorous teaching, it is just an easy way to ensure that not all of the students will earn the highest grade. Our argument here is that rigor is better assumed to be diligence in helping all students demonstrate high levels of learning. Here is our claim: Compared to a teacher who predetermines how many students will receive high grades, the teacher who holds high standards for her students and then finds ways to help almost every student attain those high standards is the more rigorous teacher.

What Do You Think?

Using what you have learned about self-perceptions and motivation to this point, how would you defend the claim we have made? What theory and research support our claim? How will you apply the argument you have just made in your classroom? To delve further into this issue, see the "Challenging Assumptions" section of the textbook's Education CourseMate website.

Students who have strong academic self-concepts often are more highly motivated and earn higher grades than students with weaker academic self-concepts.

John Howard/Jupiter Images

situation that attracts their attention. That interest can be maintained through interactions with others that help students connect skills and prior knowledge to the situation. Seeing their own skills and experiences as connected to the situation helps students "identify with" that situation to the point where they began to engage and reengage similar situations on their own. A student who sees a teacher hold a plastic bag filled with water and then pierce that bag with a sharp pencil—without bursting the bag or spilling even a drop of water—may reenact the event for family and friends outside the classroom and eventually develop a personal interest in investigating the elastic properties of various substances. This view helps teachers think about the instructional events they plan for their students as opportunities for students to "identify with" those events and, thus, develop an interest that will motivate in the future. We will consider instructional planning in Chapter 13.

As we learned in Chapter 2, identity is a crucial issue during adolescence. Middle and high school students are consumed with many questions: "Who am

Suggestions for Teaching

Satisfying Deficiency Needs and Strengthening Self-Perceptions

1 Make learning inviting to students.

Motivation researchers (e.g., Riggs & Gholar, 2009; Tomlinson, 2002) maintain that students care about learning when they are invited to learn. Teachers extend such invitations when they do the following:

- Meet Maslow's safety and belonging needs. Examples of meeting students' safety and belonging needs include never ridiculing a student for lack of knowledge or skills or letting other students do the same, praising students when they do well and inquiring about possible problems when they do not, relating lessons to students' interests, and learning students' names as quickly as possible.

- Provide opportunities for students to make meaningful contributions to their classroom. Examples here include having students help classmates master instructional objectives through short-term tutoring or cooperative learning arrangements and inviting students to use personal experiences and background as a way to broaden a lesson or class discussion. One classroom teacher created overhead transparencies of students' work for use as an instructional tool; this gave students the sense that they were a contributing part of a community (Gilness, 2003).

- Create a sense of purpose for the material students are required to learn. As we point out in Chapter 13, students rarely ask "Why do I have to learn this?" (although it is uppermost in their minds), and teachers rarely offer an explanation without being prompted. One way to create purpose for a reading lesson is to engage the students in a discussion of an issue they are interested in that is at the heart of a story or novel they are about to read.

- Allow students to develop a sense of power about their learning. Students who believe that the knowledge and skills they are learning are useful to them now (using history as a tool for thinking about the present, for example), who know what constitutes good-quality work and believe themselves capable of producing it, and who know how to set goals and meet them are more likely than other students to believe they are in control of their learning.

- Create challenging tasks for students. Students who work hard, who feel they are being stretched, yet who succeed more often than not are more likely to enjoy learning and to approach future tasks with increased motivation than are students whose work is routine and consistently at a low level of difficulty.

2 Direct learning experiences toward feelings of success in an effort to encourage an orientation toward achievement, high self-esteem, and a strong sense of self-efficacy and academic self-concept.

To feel successful, an individual must first establish goals that are neither so low as to be unfulfilling nor so high as to be impossible, and then be able to achieve them at an acceptable level.

a. Make use of learning goals and objectives that are challenging but attainable and, when appropriate, that involve student input.

As we will discussed in Chapter 13, although you will have primary responsibility for choosing the learning objectives for your students, you can use this process to heighten motivation by inviting them to participate in selecting objectives or at least in thinking along with you as you explain why the objectives are worthwhile. This will tend to shift the emphasis from extrinsic to intrinsic motivation.

To help students suggest appropriate objectives, you may want to use the techniques recommended by Robert Mager (1997). You might assist your students in stating objectives in terms of a time limit, a minimum number of correct responses, a proportion of correct responses, or a sample of actions.

b. Help students master your objectives.

As you have seen, a student's past accomplishments on a particular task influence his or her self-efficacy and academic self-concept. Consequently, you should do whatever you can to help students achieve at an acceptable level. One important recommendation for helping students become better learners was made earlier: Teach them how to create and use learning strategies. Another procedure that will help them get the most out of their strategies is to assign moderately difficult tasks and provide the minimum amount of assistance necessary to complete the task successfully (think of Vygotsky's zone of proximal development and the concept of scaffolding).

I?" "What am I going to do with my life?" "How do I fit in with others in my group?" (Eccles, 2009). The perceptions that each of your students develops—her or his self-concept, self-esteem, sense of self-efficacy, identity—are part of what they will learn in and out of school and in and out of your classroom. The learning opportunities you provide will influence not only their academic skills and knowledge but how they come to perceive and understand themselves.

Now that you are familiar with approaches to motivation based on humanistic theories and on self-perceptions, consider the additional Suggestions for Teaching.

Many of the motivational techniques we have suggested in this chapter can be enhanced by the appropriate use of technology. To conclude the chapter, we discuss research on the link between technology and motivation, and we survey a number of kinds of technology that have been shown to be useful.

LO6 Motivating Students With Technology

Extrinsic Versus Intrinsic Motivation

Previously in this chapter, we contrasted the behavioral, or extrinsic, approach to motivation with various cognitive, or intrinsic, approaches. Our goal was not to demonstrate that one approach is inherently superior to the other but to point out how and when both approaches can profitably be used to support classroom learning.

A parallel situation exists with regard to the motivating effects of technology. Behavioral psychologists, for example, argue that students who work on computer-based drill-and-practice programs are motivated by the immediate feedback they receive and the steady progress they make. Cognitive psychologists argue that involving students in fantasy environments or authentic tasks that are directed to audiences besides the teacher is intrinsically motivating because such programs and tasks give students a sense of confidence, personal responsibility, and control over their own learning (Fok & Watkins, 2009; Hewitt, 2002; Moreno & Mayer, 2002, 2005).

Technology can be used to support both extrinsic and intrinsic motivation.

Despite the differences in these two approaches to motivation, they are not mutually exclusive. Some of the most innovative and effective technological aids to learning combine both approaches (Shin, 2009). Consider, for example, the Quest Atlantis project we mentioned in Chapter 10.

Using Technology to Increase Motivation to Learn

Computer-based technology can accommodate both extrinsic and intrinsic approaches to motivation, But does it, in fact, increase students' motivation to learn?

Critics of computer-based learning argue that any observed increases in student motivation are likely to be short-term and due largely to the novelty when students engage new programs, games, or virtual environments. But several studies have demonstrated that the use of computer-based instruction increases students' intrinsic motivation and performance:

- First graders in urban schools who were at risk of failing to learn basic literacy skills engaged in computer-assisted literacy instruction. Not only did the technology engage the students in ways that enhanced their listening, reading, and writing skills, but it did so in ways that made the students less anxious about difficulties they encountered and more likely to persist when they encountered difficulties (Blachowicz et al., 2009).

- Eighth graders who were judged to be candidates for dropping out of school because of academic and

social problems received 2 weeks of instruction on the Bill of Rights. Those who were given a chance to create and present a multimedia project on the subject scored better on tests of both subject matter and attitudes toward learning than peers who engaged in traditional classroom projects (Woodul, Vitale, & Scott, 2000).

- High school seniors working in cooperative learning groups created PowerPoint presentations about poets of the Romantic period. Compared with previous classes, this group showed a much higher level of motivation for learning about this subject matter (Marr, 2000).

- High school students in Israel—where engineering education is part of the high school curriculum—have used technology, including creating their own computer programs, to design and build Lego robots, cars, cranes, and even a system that would allow a boat to cross a waterfall in both directions (Doppelt, 2009). According to the researchers, "The laboratory became a second home to the pupils. They came to work on their projects during breaks and free hours, and even after school" (Doppelt & Barak, 2002, p. 26).

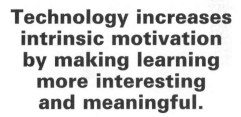

{ Technology increases intrinsic motivation by making learning more interesting and meaningful. }

Computer-based or augmented programs are often used to improve students' literacy skills and motivation for reading and writing. For example, a technology-enhanced summer program designed to help low-achieving inner-city middle school children improve their reading and writing skills produced noticeable improvements in motivation. Students used data-gathering tools, data management tools, and presentation tools to complete inquiry projects and present the results to an audience of parents, peers, and siblings. As the students shared their efforts with one another and noticed the impact of such features as computer graphics, web pages, PowerPoint slide shows, and videotaped interviews, they quickly and eagerly revised their own projects to incorporate one or more of these features (Owens, Hester, & Teale, 2002).

A survey of elementary grade teachers who published students' writing projects on a classroom website revealed a similar motivating effect. Students were more inclined to complete their projects and to do

Integrating Internet Research: High School Social Studies

Go to the Education CourseMate website and watch the video, study the artifacts in the case, and reflect upon the following questions:

1. Does the Civil Rights Scrapbook Project promote extrinsic motivation, intrinsic motivation, or both? What evidence can you cite based on observing the students in this Video Case?

2. If you were a student in this class, would you find this technology project motivating? Why or why not? What aspects of the lesson are especially motivating? What ideas do you have to make the lesson more motivating for students?

high-quality work when they knew it would be seen by a wider audience (Karchmer, 2001). According to one fourth grade teacher:

> *Before the Internet, my children did not write as much, as writing without a purpose was not fulfilling. We have a purpose now and that makes the work more interesting for the children. They are really proud to see their work on the Internet. . . . I believe the students are being more careful with their language arts skills. Their errors are pretty easy to see, and they do not seem to have any problem with changing them. In paper and pencil writing, it is very difficult to get them to change what they are writing. (Karchmer, 2001, p. 459)*

E-mail and other messaging systems are often used to heighten student interest and motivation. Pen-pal projects can link students in different locales or countries. Rebecca Sipe (2000) described a project in

WHAT ELSE? *RIP & REVIEW* **CARDS IN THE BACK**

which her preservice teacher education undergraduates corresponded with tenth grade English students, who helped the preservice students formulate realistic classroom beliefs and practices. Carole Duff (2000) described how female high school students use e-mail to get career advice, academic guidance, and personal support from a professional woman mentor. Diane Friedlaender (2009) described how, at the onset of the Iraq War, a teacher arranged for middle school students in Oakland, California, to become pen pals with students in Iraq. The Oakland students "studied the reasons given for the war, listened to and spoke with guest speakers on a weekly basis, and wrote, directed, and acted in a play about the impact of war on families. Students even marched down Market Street in San Francisco holding up pictures of their pen pals" (Friedlaender, 2009, p. 10). Connecting students to real people and real events provides extrinsic and releases intrinsic motivation to learn.

12

CLASSROOM RULES

1. Be Prepared

2. Be Respectful

* Show respect to others and their property
* Respect YOURSELF!

CLASSROOM MANAGEMENT

LEARNING OBJECTIVES

After studying this chapter, you will be able to . . .

LO1 Compare and contrast the authoritarian, permissive, and authoritative styles of teaching.

LO2 Describe the techniques identified by Jacob Kounin for preventing classroom behavior problems.

LO3 Give examples of how at least five of the techniques identified by Redl and Wattenberg for dealing with classroom behavior problems would be used.

LO4 Discuss the prevalence of violence, including bullying, in American schools and identify the major reasons that have been proposed as its cause.

LO5 Describe a classroom-based program and a school-wide program for reducing violence.

... ally or physically ... urt anyone! ... re you do !!!

... ur Hand
... eak when others ... king... Classmates, tea...
Best !!!

By now you have no doubt begun to realize what we pointed out at the beginning of the book: Teaching is a complex enterprise. If not managed properly, an endeavor as complex as teaching can easily become chaotic. When that happens, students are likely to become confused, bored, uninterested, restless, and perhaps even disruptive. But a well-managed classroom is not what many people think: students working silently at their desks (or in front of their computers), speaking only when spoken to, and providing verbatim recitations of what the teacher and textbook said. Such a classroom is incompatible with the contemporary views of learning and motivation described in the preceding chapters. If some of your goals are for students to acquire a meaningful knowledge base, become proficient problem solvers, and learn how to work productively with others, then you have to accept the idea that these goals are best met in classrooms that are characterized by a fair amount of autonomy, physical movement, and social interaction (Emmer & Stough, 2001). And you'll be helping your students out financially if you think of classroom management in these terms. In Chapter 1 we mentioned a study (Chetty et al., 2010) in which students of above-average kindergarten teachers were estimated to have earned more money as adults than peers who were in the classrooms of below-average teachers. A large part of that benefit was due to the teachers' above-average classroom management skills. Those teachers helped students acquire such personal management skills as getting along with classmates, listening to and following directions, and focusing on a task until it's completed, which contribute to a classroom atmosphere that is productive and nonthreatening.

To help you accomplish these goals *and* keep student behavior within manageable bounds, we describe in this chapter various techniques that you can use to prevent behavior problems from occurring, and a set of techniques for dealing with misbehavior once it has occurred. In addition, we analyze the issue of school violence and bullying, summarize approaches to reducing its frequency, and note how technology has been used to encourage underachieving and disruptive students to stay in school.

LO1 Authoritarian, Permissive, and Authoritative Approaches to Classroom Management

Managing the behavior of a classroom full of students is similar to parenting a child: Some approaches are better than others at producing competent and self-regulated individuals. In investigating the relationship between parenting styles and competent children, Diana Baumrind (1971, 1991) identified three dominant styles that parents use to manage the behavior of their children: authoritarian, permissive, and authoritative. Because teachers use the same three styles, we'll briefly summarize them for you.

Authoritarian parents establish rules for their children's behavior and expect them to be blindly obeyed. Explanations of the reason for a particular rule are almost never given. Instead, rewards and punishments are given for following or not following rules. *Permissive* parents represent the other extreme. They impose few controls; they allow their children to make many basic decisions (such as what to eat, what to wear, when to go to bed) and provide advice or assistance only when asked. *Authoritative* parents provide rules but discuss the reasons for them, teach their children how to follow them, and reward children for exhibiting self-control. Authoritative parents also cede more responsibility for self-governance to their children as the children demonstrate increased self-regulation skills. This style, more so than the other two, leads to children's internalizing the parents' norms and maintaining intrinsic motivation for following them in the future.

You can probably see the parallel between Baumrind's work and classroom management. Teachers who adopt an authoritarian style are likely to have student compliance rather than autonomy as their main goal ("Do what I say because I say so") and make heavy use of rewards and punishments to produce that compliance. Teachers who adopt a permissive style are likely to rely heavily on students' identifying with and respecting them as their main approach to classroom management ("Do what I say because you like me and respect my judgment"). Teachers who adopt an authoritative style are likely to want

ripple effect The response of an entire class to a reprimand directed at only one student.

withitness An attribute of teachers who prove to their students that they know what is going on in a classroom and as a result have fewer discipline problems than teachers who lack this characteristic.

their students to learn to eventually regulate their own behavior. By explaining the rationale for classroom rules and adjusting those rules as students demonstrate the ability to govern themselves appropriately, authoritative teachers hope to convince students that adopting the teacher's norms for classroom behavior as their own will lead to the achievement of valued academic goals ("Do what I say because doing so will help you learn more"). The students of authoritative teachers better understand the need for classroom rules and tend to operate within them most of the time (J. M. T. Walker & Hoover-Dempsey, 2006).

{ **An authoritative approach to classroom management is superior to permissive or authoritarian approaches.** }

Two studies support the extension of Baumrind's parenting styles to classroom teachers. In one, middle school students who described their teachers in terms that reflect the authoritative style (for example, the teacher sets clear rules and explains the penalty for breaking them, trusts students to carry out certain tasks independently, treats all students fairly, does not criticize students for not having the right answer, and has high expectations for academic achievement and behavior) scored higher on measures of motivation, prosocial behavior, and achievement than did students who described their teachers in more authoritarian terms (Wentzel, 2002).

The other study demonstrated that a teacher's decision to either support student autonomy or be more controlling of what students do in class is very much a function of the environment in which the teacher works. When teachers have curriculum decisions and performance standards for which they will be held accountable imposed on them, and when they feel that students are not highly motivated to learn, their intrinsic motivation for teaching suffers. This lowered intrinsic motivation, in turn, leads them to be less supportive of student autonomy and more controlling (Pelletier, Séguin-Lévesque, & Legault, 2002).

The next part of this chapter will describe guidelines you might follow to establish and maintain an authoritative classroom environment.

© HomeStudio/Shutterstock Images

LO2 Preventing Problems: Techniques of Classroom Management

Kounin's Observations on Group Management

The modern era of research on classroom management can be said to have started with the publication of a book by Jacob Kounin titled *Discipline and Group Management in Classrooms* (1970). Kounin noticed that when he reprimanded a college student for blatantly reading a newspaper in class, the entire class responded as if the reprimand had been directed at all of them. He subsequently called this the **ripple effect**. Chances are you can recall a situation in which you were paying attention to a lesson or working on an assignment and the teacher suddenly became quite upset with the behavior of a disruptive classmate. If you felt a bit tense after the incident, you can appreciate the power of the ripple effect.

Teachers who show they are "with it" head off discipline problems.

Kounin went on to supervise a series of observational and experimental studies of student reactions to techniques of teacher control. In analyzing the results of these various studies, he came to the conclusion that the following classroom management techniques appear to be most effective:

Pause & Reflect *Would you use the ripple effect deliberately? Why or why not?*

1. *Show your students that you are "with it."* Kounin coined the term **withitness** to emphasize that teachers who prove to their students that they know what is going on in a classroom (the legendary teacher with "eyes in the back of her head") usually have fewer behavior problems than teachers who appear to be unaware of potentially disruptive behavior. "With it" teachers will prevent small problems from becoming large ones by staring at a misbehaving student with a firm facial expression or by making a quick comment about focusing on the task at hand (we describe these and other techniques later in the chapter). Teachers who aren't "with it," on the

other hand, either don't notice such behavior or hope that it will just disappear of its own accord.

2. *Cope with overlapping situations.* Kounin found that some teachers were better than others at addressing more than one situation at a time. One primary grade teacher, for example, was working with a reading group when she noticed two boys on the other side of the room poking each other. She abruptly got up, walked over to the boys, criticized them at length, and then returned to the reading group. By the time she returned, however, the children in the reading group had become bored and off task. Another teacher who was faced with a similar situation told a student in her reading group to continue reading aloud, and that she was listening, while she also told two nearby students to stop talking and finish their seatwork exercise.

{ Being able to handle overlapping activities helps maintain classroom control. }

3. *Maintain smoothness and momentum in class activities.* Being a classroom teacher is a bit like being a traffic cop: Both need to keep things moving smoothly. Because teachers and students are constantly moving from one lesson to another, smooth transitions help students maintain their focus and

Bob Daemmrich/Bob Daemmrich Photography

Jacob Kounin found that teachers who were "with it" could deal with overlapping situations, maintained smoothness and momentum in class activities, used a variety of activities, kept the whole class involved, were decisive in handling misbehavior, and had few discipline problems.

motivation levels. Try to avoid the following sequence that Kounin observed: A teacher ends a math lesson, directs the students to take out their reading books, remembers she forgot to have the children score their math workbooks, interrupts the reading lesson, and has them take out their math workbooks again. Other impediments to instructional momentum include abruptly ending one lesson and, with little warning or preparation, starting another, and spending an inordinate amount of time commenting on such relatively trivial incidents as a student losing a pencil.

Teachers who continually interrupt activities have discipline problems.

4. *Keep the whole class involved.* When conducting recitations or question-and-answer sessions, some teachers make the mistake of calling on students in a predictable order and in such a way that the rest of the class serves as a passive audience. As a result, some students are likely to tune out until it is their turn to respond. Here are two suggestions for keeping all students involved in a lesson:

   • Ask a question, and after pausing a few seconds to let everyone think about it, pick out someone at random to answer it.

   • When dealing with lengthy or complex material, call on several students in quick succession (and in unpredictable order) and ask each to handle one section. In a primary grade reading group, for example, have one child read a sentence; then pick someone at the other side of the group to read the next sentence, and so on.

5. *Introduce variety and be enthusiastic, particularly with younger students.* Some of the teachers Kounin observed were, to put it bluntly, dull and boring, because they followed the same procedure day after day and responded with the same, almost reflexive comments. At the other end of the scale were teachers who introduced variety, responded with enthusiasm and interest, and moved quickly to new activities when they sensed that students either had mastered a particular lesson or had reached the limits of their attention span. It seems logical to assume that students will be less inclined to sleep, daydream, or engage in disruptive activities if they are exposed to an enthusiastic teacher who varies the pace and type of classroom activities.

6. *Be decisive in handling misbehavior.* When criticizing student behavior, be clear and firm, focus on behavior rather than on personalities, and try to avoid angry outbursts. Here are some examples of how you can be decisive yet fair:

- Identify the misbehaver and state what the unacceptable behavior is. ("Jorge! Don't flip that CD at Jamal.")
- Specify a more constructive behavior. ("Please put the CD back in the storage box.")
- Explain why the deviant behavior should cease. ("If the CD gets broken or dirty, no one else will be able to use it, and we'll have to try to get a new one.")
- Be firm and authoritative and convey a no-nonsense attitude. ("All infractions of classroom rules will result in an appropriate punishment—no ifs, ands, or buts.")
- Do not resort to anger, humiliation, or extreme punishment. Kounin concluded that extreme reactions did not seem to make children behave better. Instead, anger and severe reprimands (such as "Roger, that was an incredibly stupid thing to do. Do it again and you'll be sorry") upset them and made them feel tense and nervous. Not only is this recommendation consistent with common sense, but it is also supported by research. Students who were consistently the target of verbal abuse from teachers, such as ridicule, name-calling, shaming, yelling, and negative comparisons to other students, were more likely than students who were not treated this way to exhibit subsequent behavior problems and to achieve at lower levels (Brendgen, Wanner, Vitaro, Bukowski, & Tremblay, 2007).
- Focus on behavior, not on personality. (Say, "Ramona, staring out the window instead of reading your textbook is unacceptable behavior in my classroom" rather than "Ramona, you're the laziest student I have ever had in class.")

{ **Identify misbehavers and firmly specify constructive behavior.** }

Contemporary Studies of Classroom Management

Kounin's pioneering work, as well as the thousands of studies that followed, leave no doubt that students in classrooms (indeed, any group in any setting) require a structure to channel and guide their behavior (see, for example, Emmer & Evertson, 2009; Evertson & Emmer, 2009; Kraft, 2010; D. D. Ross, Bondy, Gallingane,

& Hambacher, 2008; Simonsen, Fairbanks, Briesch, Myers, & Sugai, 2008). Otherwise, chaos almost always results. That being the case, teachers need to create a workable structure within which students must operate. So what, exactly, do we mean by "a workable structure"? Quite simply, a clear and not overly long set of rules and procedures that tell students what they can and cannot do in the classroom. The first part of the structure, rules, are general guidelines for behavior. "Never do anything in the classroom that could injure you or a classmate" and "Always be polite and helpful" are two examples of rules. Procedures are a bit more specific and indicate how to carry out an activity. Two examples of procedures are "To participate in class discussions, raise your hand and wait to be recognized" and "Completed homework assignments are to be placed in the wire basket on my desk as you enter the classroom."

Effective teachers plan how to handle classroom routines.

Here are a few basic ideas taken from the research cited previously that should help you and your students get off on the right foot at the beginning of the school year:

1. Formulate your rules, procedures, and activities well before the school year begins. Not only will this increase the odds that things will go smoothly, but it will let students know that you are organized and in charge.

2. Everybody from children to adults likes to know what is expected of them. So at the beginning of the year, both describe and demonstrate the kinds of behaviors that your rules and procedures embody. Explain why these rules and procedures are necessary and what the consequences will be when they are violated. Give students a written copy of the rules and procedures.

3. Start slow. For the first several days, give relatively short and uncomplicated lessons and assignments that most students can easily follow and complete. This will not only allow students to become acclimated to you and your expectations but will give them confidence that they can meet those expectations.

4. Provide clear and complete written instructions about how to carry out in-class and at-home assignments. Include the standards you will use to evaluate the assignment.

5. Give timely, frequent, and specific feedback about assignments. This will let students know what they're doing right or wrong and how they can improve their work on future assignments. Make sure the feedback is constructive and not punitive.

Managing the Middle School, Junior High, and High School Classroom

Most of the classroom management techniques and suggestions we have discussed so far are sufficiently general that they can be used in a variety of classroom settings and with primary through secondary grade students. Nevertheless, teaching preadolescents and adolescents is sufficiently different from teaching younger students that the management of the middle school, junior high, and high school classroom requires a slightly different emphasis and a few unique practices.

Classroom management has to be approached somewhat differently in the secondary grades (and in those middle schools in which students change classes several times a day) because of the segmented nature of education for these grades. Instead of being in charge of the same 25 to 30 students all day, most junior high or high school teachers (and some middle school teachers) are responsible for as many as five different groups of 25 to 30 students for about 50 minutes each. This arrangement results in more individual differences, a greater likelihood that these teachers will see a wide range of behavior problems, and a greater concern with efficient use of class time. What kinds of behavior problems can you expect at this grade level? A survey of beginning middle school and high school teachers found persistent problems with students talking, being out of their seats without permission, using cell phones and electronic games, refusing to complete assignments, and being argumentative when confronted with violations of classroom and school rules (National Comprehensive Center for Teacher Quality & Public Agenda, 2008a).

{ **Manage behavior of adolescents by making and communicating clear rules and procedures.** }

Because of the special nature of adolescence, relatively short class times, and consecutive classes with different students, teachers at the middle school, junior high, and high school levels must concentrate their efforts on preventing misbehavior. Edmund Emmer and Carolyn Evertson, in *Classroom Management for Middle and High School Teachers* (2009), discussed how teachers can accomplish this goal by carefully organizing the classroom environment, establishing clear rules and procedures, and delivering effective instruction.

According to Emmer and Evertson, the physical features of the classroom should be arranged to optimize teaching and learning. They suggest an environment in which (1) the arrangement of the seating, materials, and equipment is consistent with the kinds of instructional activities the teacher favors; (2) high-traffic areas, such as the teacher's desk and the pencil sharpener, are kept free of congestion; (3) the teacher can easily see all students; (4) frequently used teaching materials and student supplies are readily available; and (5) students can easily see instructional presentations and displays.

Emmer and Evertson also suggested that classroom rules be specifically stated, discussed with

 ## Elementary Classroom Management: Basic Stratgies

Go to the Education CourseMate website and watch the video, study the artifacts in the case, and reflect upon the following questions:

1. Would you describe Ms. Moylan's classroom management style as authoritarian, permissive, or authoritative? Provide specific examples from the Video Case to support your answer.

2. What elements of the well-managed classroom do you see in this Video Case?

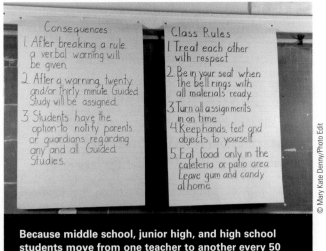

Because middle school, junior high, and high school students move from one teacher to another every 50 minutes or so, it is important to establish a common set of rules that govern various activities and procedures and to clearly communicate the reasons for those rules.

© Mary Kate Denny/Photo Edit

students on the first day of class, and—for seventh, eighth, and ninth grades—posted in a prominent place. Sophomores, juniors, and seniors should be given a handout on which the rules are listed. A set of five to eight basic rules should be sufficient.

The Suggestions for Teaching should help you put into practice the ideas presented in the first part of this chapter.

LO3 Techniques for Dealing With Behavior Problems

If you follow the procedures we have discussed, you should be able to establish a well-managed classroom.

Even if you do everything possible to prevent problems from developing, however, you are still likely to have to deal with the relatively minor disruptions of an individual student or two. This section discusses how to deal with violations of the classroom rules that you have established. More broad-based interventions that attempt to reduce the frequency of more serious problems, such as physical and verbal violence between students, and that involve entire classrooms or the entire school, are discussed in a later section.

Influence Techniques

In *Mental Hygiene in Teaching* (1959), Fritz Redl and William Wattenberg describe a list of behavior management interventions called *influence techniques*. Don't be put off by the fact that this book is now over 50 years old; its timeless value is illustrated by the fact that a recent book on classroom management (*Behavior Management: A Practical Approach for Educators*, 2007, by James Walker, Thomas Shea, and Anne Bauer) and a journal article (Kraft, 2010) recommend using some of the very same techniques.

Planned Ignoring As we pointed out in our discussion of operant conditioning (Chapter 7), you might be able to extinguish inappropriate attention-seeking behaviors by merely ignoring them. Such behaviors include finger snapping, body movements, book dropping, hand waving, and whistling. If you intend to use the planned-ignoring technique, make sure the student is aware that he is engaging in the inappropriate behavior. This technique should not be used if the behavior in question is interfering with other students' efforts.

 Secondary Classroom Management: Basic Strategies

TeachSource Video Case

Go to the Education CourseMate website and watch the video, study the artifacts in the case, and reflect upon the following questions:

1. How does Mr. Turner achieve successful classroom management with his high school students? What specific strategies from the textbook do you see in action?

2. Examine the arrangement of Mr. Turner's secondary-level classroom (e.g., arrangement of student desks, location of equipment, etc.). How do these factors influence his management of the classroom?

Suggestions for Teaching

Techniques of Classroom Management

1 Show you are confident and prepared the first day of class.

The first few minutes with any class are often crucial. Your students will be sizing you up, especially if they know you are a new teacher. If you act scared and unsure of yourself, some students may think they'll be able to engage in more off-task behavior than is the case in other teachers' classes. One way to demonstrate your confidence is to tell your students a little bit about yourself and your goals. You might, for example, explain why you chose teaching as a career, describe any teaching-related experiences you have had, note that your most successful experiences were ones in which you were able to establish a productive working relationship with that group of students, and then say that you expect this class to not only accomplish great things but to enjoy the process as well.

2 Know how you will handle the activities and routines that are a part of the everyday life of classrooms.

A large part of effective classroom management is preparation. Deciding before the school year begins how you will handle such details as taking attendance, assigning desks, handing out books and materials, permitting students to go to the restroom, and so forth has several benefits. For one, you are more likely to handle these tasks more efficiently than if you make decisions on the fly. This will help you accomplish everything you need to accomplish during those first few days. Another benefit is that your students will come to see you as someone who can be trusted and relied on.

3 Explain the reasons for your rules and procedures.

Many teachers, even veterans, fail to explain to their students why they make the decisions they do, and then wonder why students appear confused, frustrated, and lacking in motivation. We mentioned earlier, for example, that many teachers don't bother to explain why a new topic or skill is important for students to learn. Don't make that mistake with your rules and procedures. When students understand why you want things done in a certain way and that your decisions are not unreasonable, they will be more willing to follow them.

Examples

- "During class discussion, please don't speak out unless you raise your hand and are recognized. I want to be able to hear what each person has to say, and I won't be able to do that if more than one person is talking."

- "During work periods, I don't mind if you talk a bit to your neighbors. But if you do it too much and disturb others, I'll have to ask you to stop."

- "If you come in late, go to your desk by walking along the side and back of the room. It's disruptive—and not very polite—to walk between people who are interacting with each other."

4 Begin classwork the first day with an instructional activity that is clearly stated and can be completed quickly and successfully.

For the first day or two, use short lessons that students will easily be able to comprehend and short tasks they can complete successfully. Clearly specify what is to be done, and state the conditions and criteria for determining successful completion. In addition, mention an activity (such as examining the assigned text) that students should engage in after they have completed the assignment. In the elementary grades, you might give a short assignment that helps students review material covered in the preceding grade.

Examples

- "To help us get to know one another better, I would like you to write a one-page description of yourself that you will read to the class. Tell us your name, what kinds of things you like and don't like to do, what you're good at, and what you would like to be better at." (For primary grade students, oral presentations may be easier than writing.)

- "Last year in English you read the novel *Silas Marner*. One of the novels you will read this year is *Great Expectations*. Since both novels are set in England during the early part of the 1800s, I thought it would be helpful to have you recall what you learned about England from *Silas Marner*. Then we can compare that with your impressions of England from *Great Expectations*."

- "We will be doing a lot of writing in this class throughout the year. To give you some practice and to familiarize you with my grading standards, I will pass out a brief reading passage about recent developments in alternative energy. You will have a half hour to read the passage and write a brief summary of its main points. Since this is just for practice, the score will not count toward your final grade."

5 During the first week or so with a new group of students, have them spend most of their time engaging in whole-class activities under your direction.

Teachers who are good classroom managers know that you can't expect students to adjust to the routines of a new teacher and classroom in just a few days. Instructional tactics like group discussions, cooperative learning arrangements, and individual research projects usually work out more successfully when the participants have a degree of familiarity with one another and the material they will be studying. At first, stick to relatively simple whole-class activities like the examples in the previous suggestion.

6 Be professional but pleasant, and try to establish a businesslike but supportive classroom atmosphere.

Teachers who establish a businesslike and professional atmosphere, but do so in a pleasant and supportive way, have been referred to as warm demanders (Ross, Bondy, Gallingane, & Hambacher, 2008). Warm demanders insist that students meet their expectations, treat the teacher with respect, treat classmates with respect, put forth an honest effort to learn, and encourage their classmates to do the same. They do this by making sure their students understand and practice expected behaviors, providing both positive and negative examples of expected behavior, repeating a request until the student complies, reminding students of expected behaviors, reinforcing expected behaviors, and, when necessary, using negative consequences.

Examples

- "At the beginning of class you may speak quietly to your classmates, but when I start a lesson, all eyes are on me and all talking stops."

- "Jacob, please show everyone the proper way to line up to go out for recess."

- "When someone gives a wrong answer to a question, do we laugh at him or her? No! We remind ourselves that school is where we come to learn and that making mistakes is a normal part of learning."

- "Eduardo, thank you for helping Sonia finish the assignment on time. That is exactly what I mean when I say we should help one another do our best."

The following example illustrates this technique:

- Carl has recently gotten into the habit of tapping his pencil on his desk as he works on an assignment, as a way to engage you in a conversation that is unrelated to the work. The next several times Carl does this, do not look at him or comment on his behavior.

Signals In some cases, a subtle signal can put an end to budding misbehavior. The signal, if successful, will stimulate the student to control herself. (Note, however, that this technique should not be used too often and that it is effective only in the early stages of misbehavior.) Possible signals include:

- Clearing your throat.
- Staring at the offender.
- Stopping what you are saying in midsentence and staring.
- Shaking your head (to indicate no).
- Saying, "Someone is making it hard for the rest of us to concentrate" (or the equivalent).

Proximity and Touch Control Place yourself close to the misbehaving student. This makes a signal a bit more apparent, as in the following examples:

- Walk over and stand near the student.
- With an elementary grade student, it sometimes helps if you place a gentle hand on a shoulder or arm.

Interest Boosting If the student seems to be losing interest in a lesson or assignment, pay some additional attention to the student and the student's work. Some easy methods are:

- Ask the student a question, preferably related to what is being discussed. (Questions such as "Ariel, are you paying attention?" or "Don't you agree, Ariel?" invite wisecracks. *Genuine* questions are preferable.)
- Go over and examine some work the student is doing. It often helps if you point out something good about it and urge continued effort.

Humor Humor is an excellent all-around influence technique, especially in tense situations. However, remember that it should be *good*-humored humor—gentle and benign rather than derisive. Avoid irony and sarcasm. For instance:

- "Shawn, you've been to the pencil sharpener so often today I'm beginning to think that the two of you are best friends. But even best friends need a rest from one another."

Perhaps you have heard someone say, "We're not laughing at you; we're laughing *with* you." Before

Signals such as staring at a misbehaving student and putting a finger to your lips are examples of the influence techniques suggested by Redl and Wattenberg.

you say this to one of your students, you might take note that one second grader who was treated to that comment unhinged the teacher by replying, "I'm not laughing."

Helping Over Hurdles Some misbehavior undoubtedly occurs because students are confused about what they need to do or lack the ability to carry out an assignment. Try to remove the confusion for them:

- Make sure your directions are clear and complete.
- Arrange for students to have something to do at appropriate levels of difficulty.
- Let more advanced students help those who are having trouble.

Program Restructuring At the beginning of this book, we noted that teaching is partially an art because lessons do not always proceed as planned and must occasionally be changed in midstream. The essence of this program restructuring technique is to recognize when a lesson or activity is going poorly and to try something else:

- "Well, class, I can see that many of you are bored with this discussion of the pros and cons of congressional term limits. Let's turn it into a class debate instead, with the winning team getting 50 points toward its final grade."
- "I had hoped to complete this math unit before the Christmas break, but I can see that most of you are too excited to give it your best effort. Since today is the last day before the break, I'll postpone the lesson until school resumes in January. Let's do an art project instead."

Antiseptic Bouncing Sometimes a student will get carried away by restlessness, uncontrollable giggling, or the like. If you feel that this is nonmalicious behavior and due simply to lack of self-control, ask the student to leave the room. (You may have recognized that antiseptic bouncing is virtually identical to the *time-out* procedure described by behavior modification enthusiasts.) Be sure to let the student know what behavior change will allow her or him to rejoin the class:

- "Nancy, please move to the desk at the back of the room until you are ready to take part in our reading lesson. Raise you hand when you want to return to your own desk."
- "Randall, take your math book and report to Mr. Franklin's study room for at least the next 15 minutes. Then come back if you think you can control yourself."

> ## Give criticism privately, then offer encouragement.

Criticism and Encouragement Whenever you have to criticize a particular student, do so in private if possible. When public criticism is the only possibility, do your best to avoid ridiculing or humiliating the student. Such treatment may contribute to negative attitudes toward you and decreased motivation to learn. Because of the ripple effect, it may also have a negative impact on innocent students. One way to minimize the negative aftereffects of criticism is to tack on some encouragement in the form of a suggestion as to how the misbehavior can be replaced by more positive behavior:

- If a student doesn't take subtle hints (such as stares), you might say, "LeVar, you're disturbing the class. We all need to concentrate on this."
- Act completely flabbergasted, as though the misbehavior seems so inappropriate that you can't comprehend it. A kindergarten teacher used this technique to perfection. She would say, "Adam! Is that you?" (Adam just shoved Lucy away from the toy he was playing with.) "I can't believe my eyes. I wonder if you would help me over here." Obviously, this gambit can't be used too often, and the language and degree of exaggeration have to be altered a bit for older students. But indicating that you expect good behavior and providing an immediate opportunity for the misbehaving student to substitute an appropriate behavior can be a useful technique.

Defining Limits In learning about rules and regulations, children go through a process of testing the limits. Two-year-olds particularly, when they have learned how to walk and talk and manipulate things, feel the urge to assert their independence. In addition, they need to find out exactly what the house rules are. (Does Daddy *really* mean it when he says, "Don't take the pots out of the cupboard"? Does Mommy *really* mean it when she says, "Don't play with that hammer"?) Older children do the same thing, especially with new teachers and in new situations. The technique of defining limits includes not only establishing rules (as noted earlier) but also enforcing them:

- Establish class rules, with or without the assistance of students, and make sure the rules are understood.
- When someone tests the rules, show that they are genuine and that there *are* limits.

Postsituational Follow-Up Classroom discipline occasionally has to be applied in a tense, emotion-packed atmosphere. When this happens, it often helps to have a postsituational discussion—in private if an individual is involved, with the whole class if it was a group-wide situation, as the following examples show:

- In a private conference, you can say, "Leila, I'm sorry I had to ask you to leave the room, but you were getting kind of carried away."
- Addressing the group is similar: "Well, everybody, things got a bit wild during those group work sessions. I want you to enjoy yourselves, but we practically had a riot going, didn't we? And that's why I had to ask you to stop. Let's try to hold it down to a dull roar tomorrow."

Some practical suggestions for handling problem behavior appear in the Suggestions for Teaching on the next page.

Suggestions for Teaching

Handling Problem Behavior

1 Have a variety of influence techniques planned in advance.

Have you ever heard or read the phrase "forewarned is forearmed"? Applied to this chapter, it means if you know that classroom misbehavior occurs unexpectedly and often demands an immediate and effective solution, it's best to have some idea of how to respond. Instinctive reactions like getting overly angry and hurling insults may give you some satisfaction and produce short-term relief, but they are likely to be ineffective in the long run. We suggest that you make a list of the techniques mentioned in the preceding sections and think about how you might apply them when a particular problem arises.

2 Be prompt, consistent, and reasonable.

No attempt to control behavior will be effective if it is remote from the act that provokes it. If a student is to comprehend the relationship between his or her behavior and your response, one must quickly follow the other. Don't postpone dealing with misbehaving students or make vague threats to be put into effect sometime in the future (such as not permitting the students to attend an end-of-the-year event). By that time, most students will have forgotten what they did wrong.

Being consistent about classroom control can save a lot of time, energy, and misery. Strictness one day and leniency the next, or roughness on one student and gentleness with another, confuses students and prompts them to test you just to see whether this is a good day or a bad day, or whether they can get away with something more frequently than others do.

Overly harsh penalties for misbehavior do little more than generate fear and anxiety in students and undercut your ability to moti-

vate them to work productively. While beating them into submission, so to speak, may reduce the frequency of disruptive behavior, it usually comes at the cost of respect for you. Research shows that higher-level thinking and learning is much more likely to occur among students who trust their teacher to be accepting and fair (Mahwinney & Sagan, 2007).

3 Avoid empty threats.

If at all possible, avoid a showdown in front of the class. In a confrontation before the whole group, you are likely to get desperate. You may start out with a "Yes, you will"—"No, I won't" sort of duel and end up making a threat on the spur of the moment. Frequently, you will not be able to make good on the threat, and you will lose face. It's far safer and better for everyone to settle extreme differences in private.

4 Whenever you have to deal harshly with a student, make an effort to clear the air and reestablish a positive relationship.

In all likelihood, a student who has been severely reprimanded or punished will not come to you and apologize. You should take the lead and set up a confidential conference with the student as soon as possible. Otherwise, she could become your enemy for the rest of the year. Explain that the incident is in the past as far as you are concerned, but don't be surprised or disappointed if the student does not respond with signs or words of gratitude. It's hard for anybody, particularly students, to admit that they were wrong. One way to demonstrate that you have indeed put the incident in the past is to praise the student for some positive action shortly after the punishment.

© Ellen B. Senisi/The Image Works

Teachers who excel at classroom management have at their disposal a variety of influence techniques that they consistently and immediately apply to prevent or deal with misbehavior. In each case, they use a technique that is appropriate to the severity of the misbehavior.

5 Follow the advice of a master teacher.

Margaret Metzger is a veteran high school English teacher whose sensible and practical views on modeling and clearly communicating one's goals to students were mentioned in Chapter 9. She has also written, in the form of an open letter to new teachers, an insightful and compelling distillation of her experiences in learning the art of classroom management (Metzger, 2002). Metzger's recommendations for managing the behavior of adolescents also illustrate a point we have made in previous chapters: Successful teachers formulate practices that are consistent with, if not inspired by, research-based findings. Although we offer a summary of Metzger's recommendations, this is an article we urge you to read in its entirety and refer

---

LO4 Violence in American Schools

How Safe Are Our Schools?

You have probably read or heard reports about the frequency of crime in the United States, particularly among juveniles. According to figures compiled by the Office of Juvenile Justice and Delinquency Prevention (Puzzanchera, 2009), a little over 97,000 juveniles (any individual below the age of 18) were arrested in 2007

for committing violent crimes. While that figure seems large, it represents only about 16% of all juveniles. The good news about this figure is that it represents a 14% decline over the previous decade from the 1998 figure of 113,000.

Because the kinds of behaviors that occur in schools tend to reflect trends in society at large, it is natural that a certain amount of violent behavior occurs on school grounds and during school hours. However, schools are still relatively safe places (see M. J. Mayer

to repeatedly during your first few years of teaching.

Metzger (2002) divided her suggestions into two lists: "simple principles of survival," created during her early years of teaching, and "more complex principles," which grew out of her experiences during her middle teaching years. Here, in summary form, are both lists.

Simple Principles of Survival

1. *Use a light touch.* Don't immediately resort to a highly aversive technique to control students' behavior. Instead, try such simpler methods as whispering instead of yelling, using humorous statements, changing locations, talking to students privately, calling students by name, smiling a lot, and ignoring some infractions.
2. *Let students save face.* Instead of describing a student's misbehavior and issuing a reprimand, which takes time and interrupts the flow of a lesson, indicate that you've noticed the misbehavior and use such quick and somewhat humorous phrases as "It's a good thing I like you," "Here's the deal: I'll pretend I didn't see that, and you never do it again," "Consider yourself scolded," "Am I driving you over the edge?" and "That's inappropriate."
3. *Insist on the right to sanity.* To avoid becoming a burnout candidate, don't try to address all misbehaviors. Instead, make a list of possible classroom infractions and rank them. Decide which behaviors have to be addressed immediately, which can wait until some later time, and which can be ignored. Metzger, for example, decided to ignore when students came late to class. She was

often so busy trying to get the class under way (returning papers, talking with students about makeup work) that she wasn't in a position to notice who arrived late.
4. *Get help.* Learn who among the school staff (administrators, guidance counselors, truant officer, other teachers) are able and willing to help you solve certain discipline problems.
5. *Get out of the limelight.* This is Metzger's way of saying that you shouldn't feel as if you have to actively lead the class all period, every period. Learn to make appropriate use of student presentations, seatwork, movies, and group work.

More Complex Principles

1. *Ask questions.* Teachers often assume, incorrectly, that they have all the information they need to understand why one or more students misbehaved. Rather than make this assumption, take the time to ask students for an explanation. As Metzger said, "Sometimes you feel you have already spent too much time on the disruptive students. Frankly, you don't want to talk to them. Too bad. Do it" (2002, p. 80). Administrators, other teachers, and the students' parents can also be useful sources of information.
2. *Give adult feedback.* If students are engaging in behaviors that you find disruptive or that indicate a serious underlying problem, don't mince words. Tell them directly. Here are two examples offered by Metzger:
   - "Your posture, your mumbling under your breath, and your tardiness all show disrespect. If you hate this class, you should talk to me about it. If you like this class, you should

know that you are giving misleading signals." (p. 80)
   - "You have complained about everything we have done for the past two months. I now see you as a constant whiner. You probably don't want to give this impression, and it's getting on my nerves. So for the next two months, let's have a moratorium on complaining. You can start whining again in January. Does this seem fair?" (p. 80)
3. *Respect the rights of the whole class.* Try to remember that most of your students follow the rules and are just as deserving of your attention as those who do not.
4. *Ask students to do more.* This echoes a suggestion we have made several times in earlier chapters. Often the best-behaved classes are those in which the work is interesting, relevant to students' lives, and challenging.
5. *Bypass or solve perennial problems.* There will always be students who forget to bring a pencil or book to class. Rather than erupt every time this problem arises, take steps to eliminate it. For several dollars a year, you can buy a supply of pencils and allow students to borrow one for class. For students who forget to bring their books, you can keep a few extra copies on hand. To ensure that students return at the end of class what they have borrowed, you may need to require that they leave with you something that they will not leave the classroom without, such as a shoe or a watch.

Metzger ends her article with a copy of a 25-point memo that she gives to all students at the beginning of each semester and that reflects her philosophy of classroom management. Read it. You'll be glad you did.

> ## Incidents of crime and serious violence occur relatively infrequently in public schools and have been decreasing in recent years.

& Furlong, 2010, for an excellent discussion of school violence statistics and what they mean). One basis for

that claim is that the most common types of school-based conflicts fall into a few time-honored categories: verbal harassment (name calling, insulting, teasing), verbal arguments, and physical fights (hitting, kicking, scratching, and pushing). Most of the fights do not involve serious injury or violations of law (Dinkes, Kemp, Baum, & Snyder, 2009). Second, a recent government report found relatively low levels of school-based violence and crime (Dinkes, Kemp, Baum, & Snyder, 2009). Here are the main findings from that report:

- From July 1, 2005, through June 30, 2006, 14 school-age students (ages 5 through 19) were murdered at school. This translates to less than one homicide per million students for that 1-year period.

- In 2005, there were 136,500 serious violent crimes (rape, sexual assault, robbery, and aggravated assault) committed against students between the ages of 12 and 18. This figure translates to 5 serious violent crimes per 100,000 students. Ten years earlier the corresponding figures were considerably higher (222,500 serious crimes; 9 per 100,000 students).

- In 2005, 8% of high school students were threatened or injured with a weapon within a 12-month period.

- Six percent of students ages 12 through 18 reported avoiding school activities or one or more places at school because they feared for their own safety in 2005.

- The percentage of teachers threatened with injury by a student decreased from 12% during the 1993–1994 school year to 7% during the 2003–2004 school year. The percentage of teachers who were physically attacked decreased from 4% during 1993–1994 to 3% during 2003–2004. The percentage of elementary grade teachers who were attacked was twice as great as the percentage of secondary grade teachers (4% versus 2%, respectively).

These findings suggest that overall crime rates in schools are decreasing, students feel increasingly safe at school, and most teachers and students are likely to be physically safe in their own classrooms and school buildings. Nevertheless, school violence can occur in any school and at any time. One form of school violence that has gotten considerable attention, and for good reason, is bullying.

The Problem of Bullying

Although **bullying** has existed for as long as there have been schools, it is now recognized as a significant part of the school violence problem. Numerous studies have been conducted and scores of books have been written about various aspects of bullying. In this section, we will take a brief look at what bullying is and how often it occurs, what characterizes a bully, what effects bullying has on its victims, and how schools can reduce bullying and its negative effects.

What Bullying Is Bullying can be defined as "the repeated (not just once) harming of another through words or physical attack on the school grounds or on the way to or from school" (Devine & Cohen, 2007, p. 64). A similar definition calls it "the systematic abuse of power in interpersonal relationships" (Rigby, 2008, p. 22). In essence, bullying is a situation in which one person has more power than another and repeatedly abuses that power for his or her own benefit.

Some of the findings on bullying might surprise you. Although it occurs all too frequently, it is not the runaway problem that some might think, given the coverage it gets in the media. During the 2005–2006 school year, 28% of 12- to 18-year-olds reported having been bullied at least once. More girls than boys engage in bullying when you look at all of its forms. Girls are more likely than boys to use name calling and insults, start

Classroom Management: Best Practices

Go to the Education CourseMate website and watch the video, study the artifacts in the case, and reflect upon the following questions:

1. Can you give an example of "withitness" from this Video Case?

2. In this Video Case, several teachers provide their philosophies of and approaches to classroom management. Which statements align most closely with your own philosophies of classroom management? Are there any that you disagree with? Explain your answers.

and repeat rumors, and destroy property. The bullying behavior of boys, on the other hand, is more likely to take such physical forms as pushing, shoving, tripping, or spitting on someone else and trying to make someone else do things they do not want to do. Another aspect of bullying that surprises many people is that it occurs more frequently in middle school than in high school, and as students move from grade to grade a decrease in the rate of bullying usually occurs (Dinkes, Kemp, Baum, & Snyder, 2009).

Boys and girls favor different forms of bullying.

Although bullying often involves face-to-face encounters, it does not always take that form because of the prevalence of social networking websites. This form of bullying, in which one or more students post malicious statements about another student, is referred to as **cyberbullying**. Given the different styles of bullying behavior shown by boys and girls, it will probably not surprise you to learn that more than twice as many girls as boys engage in cyberbullying (5.3% versus 2.0% for the 2006–2007 school year) (Dinkes, Kemp, Baum, & Snyder, 2009).

There are some characteristics of cyberbullying that make it different from face-to-face bullying. First, it is anonymous. Those who use social networking websites such as Facebook and MySpace to bully others are known online only by their fictitious screen names. Second, because the Internet is designed to allow social exchanges among people anywhere in the world, the number of people who bully one or more others online, and the number of people who passively watch, can be quite large. It would not be unusual for virtually all students in a school to be aware of another student's embarrassing behavior and for many to tease the student about it. Third, the bullying can be constant. Threatening, insulting, or teasing e-mail messages can bombard a target student all day, every day. Unless taken down, website postings are constantly available for everyone to see (Shariff, 2008).

Characteristics of Bullies　How are students who bully different from other students? They're different in terms of internal characteristics, their relationships with teachers and classmates, and the quality of their home life.

- Students who engage in bullying behavior are more likely than their nonbullying peers to exhibit aggressive-impulsive behavior. They are often described by their teachers as being hyperactive, disruptive, likely to act without thinking of the consequences, and inclined to respond aggressively when provoked by peers (O'Brennan, Bradshaw, & Sawyer, 2008).

- Students who engage in bullying report getting less support from their classmates and teachers. That is, they are less likely than other students to feel there is someone at school, either a friend or a teacher, whom they can talk to about their problems (Flaspohler, Elfstrom, Vanderzee, & Sink, 2009).

- Children who engage in bullying are more likely to have witnessed domestic violence and are less likely to have a close relationship with their mother than their peers who do not bully others (Bowes et al., 2009).

How Bullying Affects Its Victims　Being a victim of bullying can produce any one or more of the following negative effects (Beran, 2009; Graham, 2010; O'Brennan, Bradshaw, & Sawyer, 2008; Rigby, 2008):

- Staying home from school.
- Avoiding certain places at school.
- Asking to transfer to another school.
- Lower grades due to difficulty concentrating on schoolwork (particularly if the victim believes he or she is not being supported by parents or teachers).
- Feelings of depression, anxiety, and insecurity that produce physical ailments.
- Social isolation.

> **cyberbullying**
> Bullying on social networks in which one or more students post malicious statements about another student.

© Beth Van Trees/Shutterstock Images

How Schools Can Address Bullying There are two ways that educators can deal with the problem of bullying. One is to implement school-wide programs to reduce its frequency. These can take many forms, such as teaching students who witness such incidents to immediately report them or to intervene; promoting rules that discourage discrimination; using videos, speakers, and discussions to make students aware of the feelings of bullies and their victims; and teaching those who bully more appropriate forms of social interaction (Flaspohler, Elfstrom, Vanderzee, & Sink, 2009; Hazler & Carney, 2006; C. T. Morrison, 2008). An obvious question to ask here is whether these programs work. The answer is that many do, but their effect—less reported bullying—is likely to be modest (Merrell, Gueldner, Ross, & Isava, 2008). Keep in mind that bullying is a complex phenomenon that is caused and supported by several variables. Changing this type of behavior requires persistent effort.

The other approach is for individual teachers to establish a classroom atmosphere that buffers bullying victims from its negative effects. Research (e.g., Flaspohler, Elfstrom, Vanderzee, & Sink, 2009; Meyer-Adams & Conner, 2008) has shown, for example, that students who feel valued and accepted by both their classmates and their teacher are less likely to demonstrate the negative effects of bullying than peers who do not believe they have that kind of social support.

{ **School violence is related to biological, cultural, academic, cognitive, and environmental factors.** }

Analyzing Reasons for Violence

School violence is a multifaceted phenomenon. That's a fancy way of saying that it has many possible causes. We say "possible causes" because proving that a given factor is a direct cause of violence is very difficult. Often the best that can be done is to state that a strong relationship exists between one or more factors and school violence. With that in mind, what follows are some of the major factors that are related to violent behavior and are thought to be at least a partial cause of its occurrence. Also, note that since boys commit most of the violence (Bloomquist & Schnell, 2002; Connor, 2002; Englander, 2007), the research findings are often broken down by gender.

- Boys have overactive behavioral activation systems, and underactive behavioral inhibition systems (both are located in the frontal lobes of the brain) (Bloomquist & Schnell, 2002; Connor, 2002).

- Aggressive boys have higher levels of testosterone and a higher tolerance for pain (Bloomquist & Schnell, 2002; Connor, 2002).

- Socialization patterns are different for boys and girls. Boys are encouraged to assert their independence and be aggressive; girls are encouraged to be dependent and cooperative (Englander, 2007; Lancey, 2002).

- Boys tend to become more frustrated with and hostile toward school because they experience academic failure more frequently than girls (Dinkes, Kemp, Baum, & Snyder, 2007).

- Aggressive individuals are more likely than others to misinterpret another person's actions or facial expressions as hostile and to respond in kind (Guerra & Leidy, 2008).

- Students who are deficient in the interpersonal problem-solving skills of *means–ends thinking* and *alternative–solution thinking* are more likely than others to show an inability to delay gratification, to have difficulty making friends, to have emotional blowups when frustrated, to show less sympathy to others in distress, and to exhibit verbal and physical aggression (Jimerson, Morrison, Pletcher, & Furlong, 2006; Shure, 1999).

- Higher levels of student violence have been associated with schools that are too large, impersonal, and competitive; that do not enforce rules fairly or consistently; that use punitive ways of resolving conflict; and that impose an unimaginative, non-meaningful curriculum on students (Bloomquist & Schnell, 2002; Guerra & Leidy, 2008; Lowry, Sleet, Duncan, Powell, & Kolbe, 1995).

Pause & Reflect *Do you agree with the argument that school violence can be caused by a non-meaningful, unimaginative curriculum and an impersonal school environment? If so, what can you do to make the subjects you teach lively, interesting, and useful? What ideas for making your school a more welcoming and pleasant place for students can you share with colleagues and administrators?*

Programs to reduce school violence and misbehavior abound. Some are designed to be used by individual teachers in their classrooms, and some are intended for school-wide implementation. By and large, these programs are quite effective. When the results from 99 studies were analyzed as a group, researchers found decreases in disruptive classroom behavior for 78% of the students (Stage & Quiroz, 1997). To give you a sense of what these programs are like, we describe one of each type in the following section.

LO5 Reducing School Violence, Bullying, and Misbehavior

Classroom Interventions

Because most teachers work with two dozen or more students, some of whom have disabilities, and typically have no assistance, classroom interventions that are designed to prevent misbehavior and keep small disruptions from escalating into serious problems need to be both effective and easy to implement. One such intervention, which has been shown to work with mainstreamed students with behavior disorders as well as with regular students, is called the Good Behavior Game. It is based on the idea that the behavior of a group determines whether positive reinforcement is given.

The reinforcement contingency used in the Good Behavior Game is called interdependent group contingency because it allows all students in a group or in the entire class to receive reinforcement as long as the group's performance meets or exceeds some specified level of performance, such as an average grade on a homework assignment or a maximum number of classroom rule violations. The advantage of this system is that all students must participate and make a contribution, but the group is not automatically denied reinforcement if a small number of students do not perform as well as the others. The Good Behavior Game was designed to prevent or reduce such highly disruptive behaviors as verbal and physical aggression, but it has also been used to moderate out-of-seat behavior, excessive talking, and low levels of classroom participation (Tingstrom, Sterling-Turner, & Wilczynski, 2006).

> **Classroom disruptions can be significantly reduced by an approach based on operant conditioning.**

There are, of course, many other effective classroom-wide approaches to managing student behavior that space limitations do not allow us to discuss. Aside from the Good Behavior Game, we suggest you also read about Judicious Discipline (Landau & Gathercoal, 2000), Classroom Check-Up (Reinke, Lewis-Palmer, & Merrell, 2008), and positive peer reporting (J. Q. Morrison & Jones, 2007). Note the emphasis on praising desired student behavior in most of these programs. This chapter's Case in Print describes a successful

Some experts on school violence argue that impersonal and punitively oriented schools produce higher-than-average levels of school violence.

© Richard Hutchings/Photo Edit

school-wide program that is also based on the idea of rewarding students for following school and classroom rules.

School-Wide Programs to Reduce Violence and Improve Discipline

Although classroom interventions such as the ones described in the previous section can make life less threatening and more enjoyable for individual teachers and their students, they do not address disruptive behavior elsewhere in a school, and they may conflict with other teachers' procedures. Consequently, some educators have designed violence-reduction programs that can be implemented throughout an entire school. This section describes a popular program called Resolving Conflict Creatively. Two other programs that are worth investigating are Unified Discipline and Smart and Good High Schools. An analysis of research on 74 school-based violence-reduction programs (Derzon, 2006) found that most produced reductions in criminal behavior, suspensions from school, and physical violence.

Resolving Conflict Creatively Program A somewhat different approach to decreasing physical violence, particularly between students, is the Resolving Conflict Creatively Program (RCCP), created by Linda Lantieri in 1985. The goal of the program is to teach students how to use nonviolent conflict resolution techniques in place of their more normal and more violent methods. Students are trained by teachers to monitor the school environment (such as the playground, the cafeteria, and the hallways) for imminent or actual physical

Catch 'Em Being Good

Although classroom interventions . . . can make life less threatening and more enjoyable for individual teachers and their students, they do not address disruptive behavior elsewhere in a school, and they may conflict with other teachers' procedures. Consequently, some educators have designed violence-reduction programs that can be implemented throughout an entire school. (p. 275)

To Teach Good Behavior, Schools Try More Carrots and Fewer Sticks

VALERIE SCHREMP HAHN

St. Louis Dispatch, 12/18/08

If you were a student at Halls Ferry Elementary School in Florissant, you'd know that when soft music comes on in the cafeteria, it's time to finish eating. If your teacher asked you to "slant," you'd know the acronym means to sit up straight and get ready to listen.

And if you were new here, and needed a primer on all the school's rules and procedures—and there are lots of them—you'd be invited to join the Newcomer's Club.

"I just think that's so good for kids, to come into an environment and know what is expected of them," said Lisa Hazel, principal of Halls Ferry, in the Ferguson-Florissant School District.

All schools have rules; just try keeping 500 children in line without them.

But schools like Halls Ferry have rules nailed down to a science. Administrators say they are using rules not just to keep order, but also to set kids up to succeed.

The schools practice PBS, or Positive Behavior Support. It's sometimes called PBIS, or Positive Behavioral Interventions and Supports.

Ask any of these schools to show you their rules and regulations binder, and you'll see procedures and lesson plans for everything.

Everything. How to line up in the cafeteria. How to use "nice hands and feet" on the bus. How to be kind to classmates.

But the program isn't about creating endless lists of rules and cracking down on violators. Instead, the focus is on setting expectations and catching students being good. In other words, schools are offering more carrots and fewer sticks.

Hazel said the approach makes her job easier—about half as many students were sent to her office last school year as the year before.

Positive Behavior Support is in schools in all 50 states. Halls Ferry was one of the first local schools to start it 10 years ago.

Hazelwood, University City, Clayton, Pattonville, Kirkwood, and Webster Groves are among area districts that have signed on more of their schools in the past few years.

The approach is not rigid; it evolves with the needs of a school. But there is consistency within individual schools.

"Everyone in the school uses the same words," says Thurma DeLoach, director of Kirkwood's special programs. "It's not like when I was in school, where in one classroom these were the expectations; in another classroom, you can get away with murder."

Teachers set up their own classroom rules and procedures, but they reflect the school's general philosophy and are similar to those in other classrooms in the same grade level.

The program is based on the theory that about three-fourths of students in the school don't have behavior issues. About a fourth of students might need some help, which could mean they get a mentor or an invitation to attend a school "social skills club." A small percentage of students have chronic issues and need more help; they're likely to be put on behavior plans.

When schools decide to adopt the program, they might start small with a problem that their school can work on, like cafeteria behavior. Teachers and staff members—from the recess aides to the janitors—agree on a way to address each issue.

At Eureka Elementary in the Rockwood district, cafeteria workers give tickets to students for every positive behavior they observe. Grade levels keep track of how many tickets they get and compete to win the week's "Golden Tray Award"—a spray-painted plastic cafeteria tray.

"It's unbelievable," Eureka Principal Brian Gentz said. "It has changed an entire lunch."

With the rules comes a common theme to make following them fun.

At Ritenour Middle School, Huskies get "paws for applause" for good behavior. At Ackerman School in Florissant, part of the Special School District, students' names are placed on a bee, which is taped next to a central beehive in a hallway. Halls Ferry students see handprints as a common theme, and they agree to follow the "high fives." There are six of them: Be safe, kind, cooperative, respectful, peaceful and responsible.

"When we do the high fives, you can earn good listening tickets and you can earn a lot of things, like lunch with a teacher," Halls Ferry second-grader Reggie Ross said.

The approach translates to good feelings all around, said Carol Fouse, principal of Hazelwood East Middle School in the Spanish Lake area. She recalled the story of a girl who visited her office at the end of last school year and asked, "Did you make up this school?"

"Yes, as far as coming up with the rules and everything," Fouse responded.

"Well, you did a good job," the girl said. "You know what? I haven't needed to fight this year. I got into fights all the time at elementary school, but I feel safe at this school."

"That," said Fouse, "was very cool."

Source: Valerie Schremp Hahn, "To teach good behavior, schools try more carrots and fewer sticks," from *St. Louis Post-Dispatch*, December 18, 2008. Reprinted by permission of *St. Louis Post-Dispatch*.

Questions and Activities

1. Are Positive Behavior Support (PBS) programs more consistent with Diana Baumrind's authoritarian or authoritative approaches? Why?
2. According to the article, schools that have a PBS program have rules and regulations for virtually every school setting and type of behavior. Despite their claimed success, do you think there are any drawbacks to having so many rules?
3. Find a nearby school that has a PBS program or something similar, observe for a day or two, and then talk to students, teachers, and administrators to see if they respond in the same way as those in the Halls Ferry Elementary School did to the author of this article.

Challenging Assumptions

Show Zero Tolerance for Zero Tolerance Policies

Zero tolerance policies mandate specific, nonnegotiable punishments, usually suspension from school, for specific offenses. These policies are typically aimed at curbing such serious offenses as fighting, sexual harassment, or bringing weapons or drugs to school. They are extremely popular, with as many as 75% of all schools having such policies. But, as we have pointed out many times in this book, popular ideas or practices are not always good ones. We believe that zero tolerance policies have more disadvantages than advantages and simply give the appearance that serious problems are being addressed. Here are several reasons why we believe educators should not support zero tolerance policies:

- The same punishment is handed out for violations that seem to be the same but involve very different behaviors and motives. Under the terms of a zero tolerance antidrug policy, do we really want to expel from school both the child who shares a zinc cough drop with a classmate and the child who brings marijuana to school? In the case of a zero tolerance for weapons policy, do we really want to suspend both the kindergarten student who brings a plastic knife to school to cut cookies with and the high school student who brings a large knife to school to threaten classmates?
- Zero tolerance policies do not teach students those behaviors that will produce positive reinforcement. This is why Skinner was adamantly opposed to the use of punishment as a means of modifying students' behavior.

- Zero tolerance policies result in more students being expelled from school than would otherwise be the case. For some students, being banished from an environment that they find aversive is positively reinforcing and encourages them to continue to exhibit those behaviors that produce suspension.
- Many research studies have failed to find a relationship between such policies and significant reductions in school violence.
- In some cases in which students were automatically expelled from school, extenuating circumstances should have led to a different decision.
- More often than not, courts will support an administrator's decision to suspend a student where the circumstances warrant, making zero tolerance policies redundant.

An analysis of the effectiveness of zero tolerance policies can be found in a report by the American Psychological Association's Zero Tolerance Task Force titled *Are Zero Tolerance Policies Effective in the Schools? An Evidentiary Review and Recommendations* (Skiba et al., 2006).

What Do You Think?

What are your views of zero tolerance policies? Have you seen them applied in your community? To explore this issue further, go to the "Challenging Assumptions" section of the textbook's Education CourseMate website.

---

confrontations between students. For example, picture two students who are arguing about a comment that struck one as an insult. As the accusations and counter-accusations escalate, one student threatens to hit the other. At that moment, one or two other students who are wearing T-shirts with the word *mediator* printed across the front and back intervene and ask if the two students would like help in resolving their problem. The mediating students may suggest that they all move to a quieter area where they can talk. The mediators then

{ **Students can play a role in helping others learn constructive ways to handle conflicts.** }

establish certain ground rules, such as that each student gets a turn to talk without being interrupted and that name calling is not allowed.

RCCP was designed as a primary prevention program. This means that all students, even those not prone to violence, are taught how to prevent disagreements from becoming violent confrontations. In schools in which the program has been implemented, teachers have noted less physical violence in their classrooms, fewer insults and verbal put-downs, and greater spontaneous use of conflict resolution skills (Lantieri, 1995).

Nevertheless, educators noticed that the program did not produce desirable results with all students. So during the 1997–1998 school year an intervention component was added for children who exhibited behaviors that are associated with violent behavior in later years. School counselors and RCCP-trained teachers, working

One approach to reducing school violence is to train students to mediate disputes between other students.

© Elizabeth Crews Photography

with groups of 15 to 20 children, engaged the students in activities that were designed to increase a sense of social responsibility (caring and cooperative behaviors, for example) and to develop such interpersonal skills as active listening.

The capstone of this 30-week program was the social action project. The group had to decide on and implement a community service project, such as fixing dinner for a family in need of assistance, making Easter baskets for the mentally disabled residents of a nearby center, or collecting books and art materials for a children's hospital. An evaluation of this new component reported improvements in listening skills, anger management skills, ability to share with others, relationships with teachers and students, self-esteem, and attitudes toward school (Lantieri, 1999). RCCP has been adopted by 400 schools in the United States and by schools in Brazil, England, and Puerto Rico (Roerden, 2001). An evaluation of RCCP conducted in more than 350 New York City classrooms reported gains in interpersonal negotiation strategies, prosocial behavior, and mathematics achievement, and decreases in aggressive behavior—but only in those classes in which teachers provided more instruction in RCCP techniques than the average teacher did (J. L. Brown, Roderick, Lantieri, & Aber, 2004).

Additional information about RCCP for the elementary and middle school grades can be found at http://esrnational.org by typing "RCCP" in the search box.

Pause & Reflect *If you were a primary or elementary grade teacher and had to choose between a program such as Positive Behavior Support (described in the Case in Print) and a peer mediation program such as the Resolving Conflict Creatively Program, which one would you choose? Why?*

Using Technology to Keep Students in School

As we pointed out previously, students who exhibit poor academic performance and believe that their teachers don't care about them are prone to engage in disruptive and violent behavior. They are also at risk for dropping out of school. In 2006, 9.3% of 16- to 24-year-olds were classified as dropouts (they were out of school and had not earned a diploma or alternative credential). The percentages for White, Black, and Latino youths were 5.8%, 10.7%, and 22.1%, respectively (Planty et al., 2009). Although these dropout rates have steadily fallen over the past 25 years, some believe that creative uses of technology can cause them to fall even faster. Here are a few examples of how some schools have used technology to reduce student absenteeism and the dropout rate:

- The Hueneme Elementary School District in Port Hueneme, California, created a "smart classroom" to help retain students who are at risk of dropping out. Students in this program were given experience in computerized robotics, computer-aided manufacturing, desktop publishing, and aeronautics and pneumatic technology. Average daily attendance for this program was close to 100% (Cardon & Christensen, 1998).

- The Azusa Unified School District in Azusa, California, made extensive use of an integrated learning system to encourage student attendance and retention. Students spent four class periods each day working at their computer terminals on English, reading, social studies, mathematics, and science. By the end of the program's second year, the average daily attendance was 96%, and 93% of students remained in the program from one year to the next (Cardon & Christensen, 1998).

- Virtual schools, a growing phenomenon that is also referred to as *distance education* or *distance learning*, are courses or entire programs (particularly at the high school level) that are available on the web and that may help students with high absentee rates—such as the children of migrant workers, students whose school districts don't offer desired courses, and students who are homeschooled—to take courses and complete their schooling (Roblyer, 2006). During the 2007–2008 school year, over one million public school students were enrolled in virtual classes (M. R. Davis, 2009), and almost all states offer some type of online education option (K. Ash, 2009). Although such programs are praised for the flexibility they offer, they are also criticized because low-income students may have limited Internet access, because computer failures result in lost time and assignments, and because the lack of face-to-face interaction makes learning more difficult for some students (Podoll & Randle, 2005; Roblyer, 2006). What little research exists suggests that, overall, students who take courses online learn about as much as students who take the same courses in actual classrooms. What is not known at this point is why some students succeed in a virtual school environment whereas others do not (Bernard et al., 2004; Rice, 2006).

WHAT ELSE? *RIP & REVIEW* **CARDS IN THE BACK**

13

APPROACHES TO INSTRUCTION

LEARNING OBJECTIVES

After studying this chapter, you will be able to . . .

LO1 Explain why you would use taxonomies in the cognitive, affective, and psychomotor domains to help you create lesson plans and classroom tests.

LO2 Compare and contrast the types of objectives recommended by Robert Mager and Norman Gronlund.

LO3 Describe the components that make up direct instruction.

LO4 Explain how the information-processing/social cognitive and constructivist approaches to instruction facilitate meaningful and self-regulated learning.

LO5 Describe the humanistic approach to teaching and defend its usefulness as an approach to instruction.

LO6 Note the elements that make up the social learning approach to teaching (also known as cooperative learning) and explain why it works.

This chapter is concerned with helping you answer two questions: What are my objectives? (or, What do I want students to know and be able to do after I complete a unit of instruction?) and How can I help students achieve those objectives? The ordering of these two questions is not arbitrary. Instructional planning should always begin with a description of what you want students to know and be able to do some weeks, or even months, after the beginning of an instructional unit. If you decide in advance what you want your students to achieve, you can prepare lessons that logically lead to a particular result and you can create assessments that are designed to determine what level of achievement has occurred.

Once you have a clear idea of what you are trying to accomplish with your students, you can consider how you are going to help get them there. Here is where you can use your knowledge of learning and motivation. After all, if the goal of teaching is to help students acquire and use a variety of knowledge and skills, what better way to do that than to use approaches and techniques that are consistent with what is known about how people learn and under which conditions they learn best?

The theories that underlie the approaches to instruction described in this chapter emphasize different aspects of the learning process, and each has been supported by research. Thus no one theory is sufficiently comprehensive and powerful that you can rely exclusively on it as a guide for designing classroom instruction. To work effectively with the diversity of students you will almost certainly encounter, you will need to use a variety of instructional approaches and techniques.

Lest you think that our recommendation to combine theories is an interesting but untested idea, this integrated approach has been put into practice by the staff of an alternative middle school in Rhode Island called the Urban Collaborative Accelerated Program (UCAP) (www.ucap.org/). The purpose of UCAP is to work with students who had been retained in a grade one or more times and were therefore at risk of dropping out of school. The most radical and striking characteristic of UCAP is the use of 50 criteria to determine whether students should be promoted to the next grade. This approach is quite consistent with the behavioral view that complex behaviors cannot be properly learned until more basic behaviors are mastered and that students must clearly and convincingly demonstrate those behaviors. It is also consistent with an approach to instruction and classroom assessment called mastery learning (which we discuss in Chapter 14). Other techniques that are used, and the approaches they represent, include having teachers play the role of coach instead of information provider through lectures (constructivist approach, humanistic approach); using problem- and project-based learning (constructivist approach); and using small-group learning and peer tutoring (social approach) (DeBlois, 2005). As of 2004, UCAP was meeting the achievement targets called for by No Child Left Behind and was classified by the state as a moderately performing and improving school.

LO1 Devising and Using Objectives

Contrasting Objectives With Educational Goals

One way to help you understand the nature of instructional objectives is to contrast them with something with which they are often confused: educational goals. Goals are relatively broad statements of what political and educational leaders would like to see schools accomplish. Consider, for example, the following two goal statements:

- Students will acquire the thinking skills that will allow them to become responsible citizens, independent learners, and productive workers.

- All adults will be sufficiently literate, knowledgeable, and skilled to compete in a global economy and behave as responsible citizens.

{ **Goals are broad, general statements of desired educational outcomes.** }

Although they are ambitious and laudable, statements of this sort do not provide very useful guidelines for teachers charged with the responsibility of achieving such goals. What exactly is meant by "thinking skills" or being "sufficiently literate, knowledgeable, and skilled"? And will these terms mean the same thing to every teacher? Thinking skills, for example, could be interpreted to mean everything from memorization to problem solving.

Instructional objectives, in contrast to these broad educational goals, specify the kinds of observable and measurable student behaviors that make it possible for the underlying goals to be achieved. To give teachers both a common vocabulary and a system for writing different kinds of objectives, psychologists have created organizational schemes called taxonomies.

Taxonomies of Objectives

Because goal statements are too vague to be of much use to teachers, a group of psychologists who specialized in testing identified different types of instructional objectives and organized them in a system called a taxonomy.

A **taxonomy** is a classification scheme with categories arranged in hierarchical order. Because goals of education are extremely diverse, there are taxonomies in three areas, or *domains*: cognitive, affective, and psychomotor. The **cognitive domain taxonomy** stresses knowledge and intellectual skills, the **affective domain taxonomy** concentrates on attitudes and values, and the **psychomotor domain taxonomy** focuses on physical abilities and skills.

> ## Instructional objectives specify observable, measurable student behaviors.

Taxonomy for the Cognitive Domain The first and most widely used taxonomy for the cognitive domain was prepared by Benjamin S. Bloom, Max D. Engelhart, Edward J. Furst, Walker H. Hill, and David R. Krathwohl (1956), and is commonly referred to as Bloom's taxonomy. It consists of six hierarchically ordered levels of instructional outcomes: knowledge, comprehension, application, analysis, synthesis, and evaluation. The taxonomy is described as a hierarchy because it was

Being familiar with the different taxonomies of objectives, such as the one for the cognitive domain, helps teachers plan lessons and create tests that require students to use different types of cognitive processes.

reasoned that comprehension relies on prior mastery of knowledge or facts, that application depends on comprehension of relevant ideas, and so on through the remaining levels.

Taxonomy of Educational Objectives: Cognitive Domain

1.0 *Knowledge.* Remembering previously learned information, such as facts, terms, procedures, and principles.

2.0 *Comprehension.* Grasping the meaning of information by putting it into one's own words, drawing conclusions, or stating implications.

3.0 *Application.* Applying knowledge to actual situations, as in taking principles learned in math and applying them to laying out a baseball diamond or applying principles of civil liberties to current events.

4.0 *Analysis.* Breaking down objects or ideas into simpler parts and seeing how the parts relate and are organized. For example, discussing how the public and the private sectors differ or detecting logical fallacies in an argument.

> { **Cognitive taxonomy: knowledge, comprehension, application, analysis, synthesis, evaluation** }

5.0 *Synthesis*. Rearranging component ideas into a new whole. For example, planning a panel discussion or writing a comprehensive term paper.

6.0 *Evaluation*. Making judgments based on internal evidence or external criteria. For example, evaluating a work of art, editing a term paper, or detecting inconsistencies in the speech of a politician.

The taxonomy of affective objectives stresses attitudes and values.

Taxonomy for the Affective Domain In addition to arranging instructional experiences to help students achieve cognitive objectives, virtually all teachers are interested in encouraging the development of attitudes and values.

To help teachers write objectives that target attitudes and values, a taxonomy for the affective domain was published several years after the cognitive domain taxonomy appeared (Krathwohl, Bloom, & Masia, 1964).

Taxonomy of Educational Objectives: Affective Domain

1.0 *Receiving (attending)*. Willingness to receive or attend.

2.0 *Responding*. Actively participating, indicating positive response or acceptance of an idea or policy.

3.0 *Valuing*. Expressing a belief or attitude about the value or worth of something.

4.0 *Organization*. Organizing various values into an internalized system.

5.0 *Characterization by a value or value complex*. The value system becomes a way of life.

Taxonomy for the Psychomotor Domain Cognitive and affective objectives are important at all grade levels, but so are psychomotor objectives. Regardless of the grade level or subject you teach, at some point you are likely to want to help your students acquire physical skills of various kinds. A few examples would be writing legibly, driving a car, playing a violin, adjusting a microscope, manipulating a computer keyboard, and operating a power saw. Recognition of the importance of physical skills prompted Elizabeth Simpson (1972) to prepare a taxonomy for the psychomotor domain.

Taxonomy of Educational Objectives: Psychomotor Domain

1.0 *Perception*. Using sense organs to obtain cues needed to guide motor activity.

2.0 *Set*. Being ready to perform a particular action.

3.0 *Guided response*. Performing under the guidance of a model.

4.0 *Mechanism*. Being able to perform a task habitually with some degree of confidence and proficiency. For example, demonstrating the ability to get the first serve in the service area 70% of the time.

5.0 *Complex or overt response*. Performing a task with a high degree of proficiency and skill. For example, typing all kinds of business letters and forms quickly with no errors.

6.0 *Adaptation*. Using previously learned skills to perform new but related tasks. For example, using skills developed while using a word processor to do desktop publishing.

7.0 *Origination*. Creating new performances after having developed skills. For example, creating a new form of modern dance.

{ The psychomotor taxonomy outlines steps that lead to skilled performance. }

Why Use Taxonomies? Using these taxonomies will help you avoid two common instructional failings: ignoring entire classes of outcomes (usually affective and psychomotor) and overemphasizing the lowest level of the cognitive domain (which requires little more on classroom tests than recognition or recall of verbatim or near-verbatim facts).

LO2 Two Ways to State Objectives

If you have had any experience in the work world, you know that managers sometimes give employees very specific directions about how to carry out a task but on other occasions may provide more general directions. Both approaches are valid, depending on the circumstances. It's the same with instructional objectives. You can follow the recommendation of Robert F. Mager (1962, 1997), and write **specific objectives**, as well as the recommendation of Norman E. Gronlund (2004), and write more **general objectives**. Which type you opt to use will depend on circumstances we'll mention shortly.

specific objective
An objective that specifies the behavior to be learned, the conditions under which it will be exhibited, and the criteria for acceptable performance.

general objective
An objective that uses the three taxonomies (cognitive, affective, and psychomotor) to describe types of behavior that would demonstrate a student's learning.

The type of objective favored by Mager has three components:

- A description of what the student should be able to do after instruction.

- A description of the conditions under which the behavior is to occur.

- A description of what constitutes an acceptable performance.

Here are a few examples of specific objectives:

- Correctly solve at least seven addition problems consisting of three 2-digit numbers within a period of 3 minutes.

- Given pictures of 10 trees, correctly identify at least eight as either deciduous or evergreen.

- Given a computer and word processing program, set it up to type a business letter (according to the specifications provided) within 2 minutes.

Gronlund argued that specific objectives are most useful when students have to learn factual knowledge and simple skills. But when more complex and

Mager recommended that teachers use objectives that identify the behavioral act that indicates achievement, define conditions under which the behavior is to occur, and state the criteria of acceptable performance.

advanced types of outcomes are desired, a more general approach to writing objectives is called for. This approach involves two steps:

1. Write general objectives that describe types of behavior students should exhibit to demonstrate what they have learned.

2. For each general instructional objective, list up to five *specific learning outcomes* that provide a representative sample of what students should be able to do when they have achieved the general objective. Each learning outcome should begin with an *action verb* (such as *explain* or *describe*) that names the particular action the student is expected to take.

Pause&Reflect *One criticism of objectives is that they limit the artistic side of teaching, locking teachers into a predetermined plan of instruction. Can you respond by recalling a teacher who provided objectives but was still enthusiastic, flexible, and inventive?*

To see how Gronlund's method differs from Mager's, imagine that you are teaching an educational psychology course and that you want to write objectives that reflect an understanding of the four stages of Piaget's theory of cognitive development. Figure 13.1 compares objectives you might develop using Gronlund's approach with objectives that follow Mager's method.

Aligning Assessment With Objectives and Instruction

Writing clear objectives in language that students understand is only the first step on the road to effective teaching. You also need to match your objectives with how you teach and what kinds of tests you give. Let's say that for a particular unit of instruction you want to focus on mastery of basic factual knowledge. One way to accomplish that goal is to use a teacher-centered approach to instruction and create multiple-choice, short-answer, and true–false tests. But for objectives that reflect the higher levels of the cognitive domain (such as comprehension, analysis, and synthesis), you may want to include some form of student-centered instruction (such as discussion groups and hands-on learning) and create tests that require solving problems and creating extended responses to essay questions.

Here's a small example of how things can go wrong if you don't align your tests with both your objectives and your instructional methods. If you tell students that you want them to organize information into logical structures, integrate ideas into broad themes, and make connections with knowledge learned elsewhere, and you teach them how to think along those lines, but you load your tests with short-answer and multiple-choice items that require rote memorization, don't be surprised when students simply memorize facts. From their perspective, the content and level of the test items are the real objectives.

One final comment about alignment. In the opening paragraph of this chapter, we referred to the assessments you *create* rather than the tests you *use*. These two terms imply a subtle but important distinction. The best way to ensure alignment of objectives, teaching approach, and assessment is for you to be the creator of the assessment. If you use a test that somebody else has designed, such as a standardized test, it is almost a certainty that some of the items will not match your objectives or instructional approach.

GRONLUND'S APPROACH

General objective

The student will understand the characteristics of Piaget's four stages of cognitive development.

Specific learning outcomes, stated with action verbs

Describe in his or her own words the type of thinking in which students at each stage can and cannot engage.

Predict behaviors of students of different ages.

Explain why certain teaching techniques would or would not be successful with students of different ages.

MAGER'S APPROACH

Specific objectives

Given a list of Piaget's four stages of cognitive development, the student, within twenty minutes, will describe in his or her own words two problems that students at each stage should and should not be able to solve.

Given a videotape of kindergarteners presented with a conservation-of-volume problem, the student will predict the response of 90 percent of the students.

Given a videotape of fifth-grade students presented with a class inclusion problem, the student will predict the response of 90 percent of the students.

Given eight descriptions of instructional lessons, two at each of Piaget's four stages, the student will be able to explain in each case why the lesson would or would not succeed.

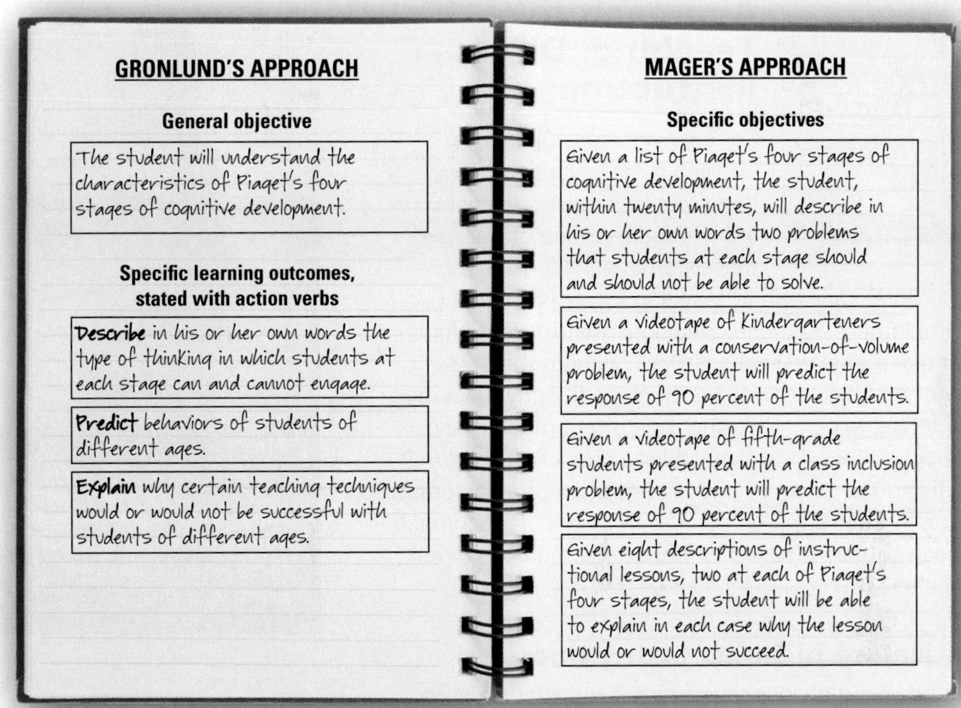

Photo: © Ohmega1982/Shutterstock Images

FIGURE 13.1 Types of Objectives: Gronlund's and Mager's Approaches Compared

The Effectiveness of Objectives

So far, we've pointed out that writing clear objectives will help you choose which instructional techniques to use and what types of tests to create. But what about your students? Do they learn more when their teachers provide them with clearly written objectives? The answer is yes, but only under certain conditions. Although most of the research on the effectiveness of objectives was conducted over 30 years ago (see, for example, Faw & Waller, 1976; Klauer, 1984; Melton, 1978), the major conclusions drawn from it are as valid today as they were then:

1. Objectives seem to work best when students are aware of them, treat them as directions to learn specific sections of material, and feel they will aid learning.

2. Objectives seem to work best when they are clearly written and the learning task is neither too difficult nor too easy.

3. Students of average ability seem to profit more from being given objectives than do students of higher or lower ability.

4. Objectives lead to an improvement in intentional learning (what is stressed as important) but a decline in incidental learning (not emphasized by the teacher). General objectives of the type that Gronlund recommended seem to lead to more incidental learning than do specific objectives of the type that Mager recommended.

Pause & Reflect *Based on this chapter and your own experience, do you agree that writing objectives and providing them to students are worthwhile uses of a teacher's time? If so, what steps will you take to make writing objectives a standard part of your professional behavior?*

As we mentioned at the beginning of the chapter, once you have decided what it is you want your students to learn, you need to decide which approaches you will use to help them achieve those objectives. Our use of the term *approaches* is deliberate. To repeat what we said at the beginning of the chapter, different approaches to instruction are based on different theories of learning and motivation, and given the complexity of the learning process and the diversity of learners in most classrooms, no one theory can be used for all instructional purposes and for all students. So as you read through the next several sections, try to imagine how you might use each approach over the course of a school year.

direct instruction
An approach to instruction that emphasizes the efficient acquisition of basic skills and subject matter through lectures and demonstrations, extensive practice, and corrective feedback.

LO3 The Behavioral Approach to Teaching: Direct Instruction

For behavioral psychologists, learning means acquiring new behaviors, and new behaviors are learned because of the role that external stimuli play. Thus a behavioral approach to teaching involves arranging and implementing those conditions that make it highly likely that a desired response will occur in the presence of a particular stimulus (such as fluently reading a sentence, accurately using the correct mathematical operations when faced with a long-division problem, and giving the correct English translation of a paragraph written in Spanish). Perhaps the most popular approach to teaching that is based on behavioral theory is direct instruction.

The Nature of Direct Instruction

The underlying philosophy of **direct instruction** (also called *explicit teaching*, *teacher-directed instruction*, and *teacher-led instruction*) is that if the student has not learned, the teacher has not effectively taught. The goal of direct instruction is to have students master basic skills and content before moving on to more advanced levels, through the design of effective lessons, corrective feedback, and opportunities for practice. Advocates of this method believe that students who mislearn information require substantially more time and effort to relearn concepts than would have been the case had they learned the concepts correctly in the first place.

Direct instruction is felt to be most useful for young learners and slow learners, and for all learners when the material is new and difficult to grasp at first. Although there are several variations of direct instruction, the following represents a synthesis of descriptions offered by Bruce Joyce and Marsha Weil (2009), Barak Rosenshine and Carla Meister (1994a), Bruce Larson and Timothy Keiper (2007), and Jennifer Goeke (2009).

The main characteristics of direct instruction are:

1. Focusing almost all classroom activity on learning basic academic knowledge and skills. Affective and social objectives, such as improved self-esteem and the ability to get along with others, are either de-emphasized or ignored.

2. Having the teacher make all instructional decisions, such as how much material will be covered at one time, whether students work individually or in groups, and whether students work on mathematics during the morning and social studies during the afternoon.

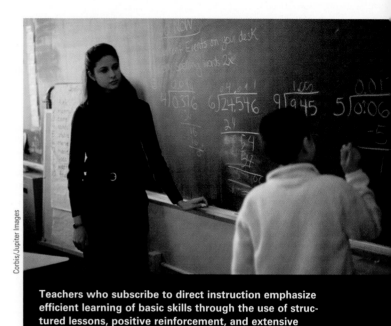

Teachers who subscribe to direct instruction emphasize efficient learning of basic skills through the use of structured lessons, positive reinforcement, and extensive practice.

Corbis/Jupiter Images

{ **Direct instruction: focus on learning basic skills, have teacher make all decisions, keep students on task, provide opportunities for practice, give feedback** }

3. Keeping students working productively toward learning new academic knowledge and skills (usually called being on task) as much as possible.

4. Designing all lessons to include demonstration, practice, and corrective feedback.

5. Maintaining a productive and pleasant classroom climate by emphasizing positive reinforcement and avoiding the use of aversive consequences.

The Components of Direct Instruction

Bruce Joyce and Marsha Weil (2009) identifed five general components, or phases, that make up direct instruction: orientation, presentation, structured practice, guided practice, and independent practice. These components are not derived just from theory; they reflect the techniques that effective teachers at all grade levels have been observed to use.

Orientation During the orientation phase, the teacher provides an overview of the lesson, explains why students need to learn the upcoming material, relates the new subject either to material learned during earlier lessons or to their life experience, and tells students what they will need to do to learn the material and what level of performance they will be expected to exhibit.

Presentation The presentation phase initially involves explaining, illustrating, and demonstrating the new material. As with all other forms of instruction based on operant conditioning, the lesson is broken down into small, easy-to-learn steps to ensure mastery of each step in the lesson sequence. Numerous examples of new concepts and skills are provided, and, consistent with social learning theory, the teacher demonstrates the kind of response students should strive for (such as a particular pronunciation of foreign vocabulary, a reading of a poem or story, the steps in mathematical operations, or an analysis of a novel for theme, character, or setting). At the first sign of difficulty, the teacher gives additional explanations.

The last step of the presentation phase is to evaluate students' understanding. This is typically done through a question-and-answer session in which the questions call for specific answers as well as explanations of how students formulated their answers. Some sort of system is used to ensure that all students receive an equal opportunity to respond to questions. Throughout the lesson, efforts are made to stay on task and avoid nonproductive digressions.

Structured, Guided, and Independent Practice The last three phases of the direct instruction model all focus on practice, although with successively lower levels of assistance.

Structured practice involves the greatest degree of teacher assistance. The teacher leads the entire class through each step in a problem or lesson so as to minimize incorrect responses. Visual displays, such as overhead transparencies, are commonly used during structured practice as a way to illustrate and help students recall the components of a lesson. As the students respond, the teacher reinforces correct responses and corrects errors.

During guided practice, students work at their own desks on problems of the type explained and demonstrated by the teacher. The teacher circulates among the students, checking for and correcting any errors.

When students can correctly solve at least 85% of the problems given to them during guided practice, they are deemed ready for independent practice. At this point, students are encouraged to practice on their own either in class or at home. Although the teacher continues to assess the accuracy of the students' work and provide feedback, it is done on a more delayed basis.

Getting the Most Out of Practice

Joyce and Weil (2009) offered the following suggestions to help make practice effective:

1. Shape student learning by systematically moving students from structured practice to guided practice to independent practice.

2. Schedule several relatively short but intense practice sessions, which typically produce more learning than fewer but longer sessions. For primary grade students, several 5- to 10-minute sessions scattered over the day are likely to produce better results than the one or two 30- to 40-minute sessions that middle school or high school students can tolerate.

3. Carefully monitor the accuracy of students' responses during structured practice to reinforce correct responses and correct unacceptable responses. The reason for this suggestion comes straight out of operant conditioning research. As you may recall from Chapter 7, Skinner found that new behaviors are learned most rapidly when correct responses are immediately reinforced and incorrect responses are eliminated. When a learner makes incorrect responses that are not corrected, they become part of the learner's behavioral repertoire and impede the progress of subsequent learning.

4. To ensure the high degree of success that results in mastery of basic skills, students should not engage in independent practice until they can respond correctly to at least 85% of the examples presented to them during structured and guided practice.

5. Practice sessions for any lesson should be spread over several months. The habit of some teachers of not reviewing a topic once that part of the curriculum has been covered usually leads to a lower quality of learning. Once again, distributed practice produces better learning than massed practice.

6. Space practice sessions close together during structured practice but further and further apart for guided practice and independent practice.

The Effectiveness of Direct Instruction

Studies of direct instruction that have been done in urban schools that enroll high percentages of minority and low-SES students have produced moderately positive results. For example, a version of direct instruction called the BIG Accommodation model (because instruction is organized around "big ideas") was implemented in a California middle school that served high-poverty neighborhoods. After 1 year, the percentage of seventh and eighth grade students who were reading at the fifth grade level or lower declined, whereas the percentage reading at

© 3dvin/Shutterstock Images

the sixth and seventh grade levels or higher increased. Similar results were obtained for math achievement scores. In percentage terms, the most dramatic increase occurred among English language learners. Before the program was implemented, only 10% scored at grade level (seventh grade or above) on reading and math tests. One year later that figure rose to about 36% (Grossen, 2002).

LO4 The Cognitive Approach to Teaching: Facilitating Meaningful and Self-Regulated Learning

The focus of cognitive learning theories is the mind and how it works. Hence, cognitive psychologists are primarily interested in studying those mental processes that expand our knowledge base and allow us to understand and respond to the world differently. In this section, we will lay out two approaches to instruction that are based on different forms of cognitive theory: information-processing/social cognitive instruction and constructivism. The information-processing/social cognitive approach to teaching involves implementing those conditions that help students effectively transfer information from the "outside" (a text or lecture, for example) to the "inside" (the mind), whereas the constructivist approach focuses on providing students opportunities to create their own meaningful view of reality.

The Nature and Elements of an Information-Processing/Social Cognitive Approach

Decades of research tell us that in order for information to be meaningfully learned, it must be attended to, its critical features must be noticed, it must be coded in an organized and meaningful way so as to make its retrieval more likely, and strategies must be devised that allow this process to occur for a variety of tasks and in a variety of circumstances (Joyce & Weil, 2009; Marx & Winne, 1987; Zimmerman, 2008).

The approach to teaching that flows from these theories has two main parts. First, design lessons and gear teaching behaviors to capitalize on what is known about the learning process. As you will see, this part of the information-processing/social cognitive approach has some elements in common with the behavioral approach that we just covered. Both approaches direct you to structure the classroom environment in a certain way (and to use some of the same tactics) to improve the effectiveness and efficiency of learning. Second—and this is what makes the information-processing/social cognitive approach unique—make students aware of how they learn and how they can use those processes to improve their classroom performance. Here

are some suggestions for helping students become more effective processors of classroom instruction.

Communicate Clear Goals and Objectives The first question that students ask themselves when they take a new course, encounter a new topic, or are asked to learn a new skill is "Why do I have to learn this?" We suspect you've asked yourself this question many times and not gotten a satisfactory answer. So, at the beginning of each lesson, tell students what you want them to accomplish, why you think it's important that they learn this knowledge or skill, and how you are going to assess their learning. If you intend to use paper-and-pencil tests, tell them what content areas will be covered, what kinds of questions you will include (in terms of whatever taxonomies you use to generate your objectives), and how many of each type of question will be on the test. Without this information, students will be unable to formulate a rational approach to learning and studying because they will be forced to guess about these features. They may, for example, take your general directive to "learn this material for the test" as a cue to memorize, when you expected them to be able to explain ideas in their own words. If you intend to use performance measures, tell students the conditions under which they will have to perform and what criteria you will use to judge their performance.

Use Attention-Getting Devices Information-processing/social cognitive theory holds that material not attended to is not processed, and material that is not processed is not stored in memory. Consequently, you should use (but not overuse) a variety of attention-

One implication of the information-processing/social cognitive approach to instruction is that attention-getting devices should be used, because information not attended to will not be learned.

getting devices. The suggestion we just made to explain what the purpose of a lesson is, what students will be held accountable for learning, and how student learning will be assessed will likely capture the attention of some students. But once you are into a lesson, you may need to gain and maintain students' attention repeatedly (see this chapter's Case in Print for an illustration of how one teacher accomplishes this goal). Here are a few additional ideas:

- Orally emphasize certain words or phrases by raising or lowering your voice.

- Use dramatic gestures.

- Underline key words and phrases that you write on a chalkboard or whiteboard.

- When discussing the work of important people, whether in science, math, social studies, or history, dress up to look like the person and speak as you think the person might have spoken.

One approach to teaching that gets students' attention by embedding lessons in unusual but meaningful contexts is worth examining; it is called *outrageous instruction* by its creator (Pogrow, 2008, 2009b).

Emphasize Organization and Meaningfulness
Students learn and recall more information when it is presented in an organized format and a meaningful context. Information is orga-

nized when the components that make it up are linked together in some rational way. If you teach high school physics, you can organize material according to major theories, basic principles, or key discoveries, depending on your purpose. For history, you can identify main ideas and their supporting details or describe events as a chain of causes and effects. Figure 13.2 illustrates how the same information can be organized in different ways. Just about any form of organization would be better than having students memorize names, dates, places, and other facts as isolated fragments of information.

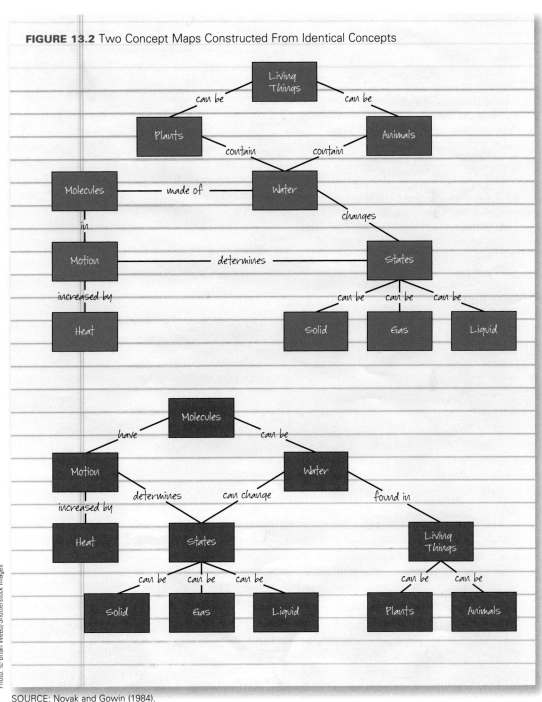

FIGURE 13.2 Two Concept Maps Constructed From Identical Concepts

Photo: © Brian Weed/Shutterstock Images

SOURCE: Novak and Gowin (1984).

Getting Their Attention! Solving the First Challenge of Teaching

Information-processing/social cognitive theory holds that material not attended to is not processed, and material that is not processed is not stored in memory. Consequently, you should use (but not overuse) a variety of attention-getting devices. (p. 289)

Geology Teacher Finds Creative Ways to Keep Students Engaged

CHRISTINE BYERS

St. Louis Post-Dispatch, 03/23/07

Stepping into Art Casey's earth science classroom is almost like visiting a mad scientist's laboratory, but the experiments conducted here have brought him closer to solving a mystery that teachers have struggled with for centuries: getting students to pay attention.

The black walls are covered by pictures of the estimated 8,700 students he has taught in 36 years at Fox High School—70 of whom have died, most in car accidents—along with various old inventions he has amassed in his lifetime as a self-proclaimed pack rat.

One wall has about 35 concrete blocks that enclose time vaults, which he began making with students in the 1971–1972 school year. The tradition started with students' enclosing notes to children of the future in jars to be opened in 1984 and another to be opened in 2001 to coincide with the novel *1984* and the movie "2001: A Space Odyssey."

The tradition has continued, with seniors making two vaults and opening two vaults each year. The vault opened this month came from a generation growing up 29 years ago with a fear of nuclear war. They wrote messages such as, "Civilization will be dead."

"It helps students get the concept of time," Casey said. "We talk about things in geological time, and this helps them get the feeling of the immensity of time."

Beyond the wall of vaults, a secret passage leads to the hallway, where a display case is filled with "treasure tiles," and clues on ways to find them. The tiles, which are signed by Casey's students, have been hidden in places all around the world, including the Swiss Alps and an arctic ice formation. Those who find them get cash rewards ranging from $25 to $100.

"They may think, 'I'm not going to go there,' but they're paying attention to subjects like oceanography and topography that are otherwise considered boring," he said.

Despite Casey's elaborately decorated classroom and creative traditions, students doze off in his class occasionally. But he's devised a way to combat the problem while offering a lesson at the same time: A spray bottle named Nimbus after the scientific term for rain cloud will rouse sleepy students, he said.

Beyond his unorthodox approach to teaching, Casey's oddities also have made him somewhat of a legend among parents and older siblings who relish telling incoming students about how his trademark white lab coats and black clip-on ties are stored behind a secret panel in his classroom and how administrators have approved schemes that students use to get him back at the end of the year for using "Nimbus."

"My older brother said he was crazy," said Kyle LaChance, 17, of Arnold. "He makes it interesting and everybody likes him."

He nearly foiled one attempt made by seniors equipped with water cannons by wearing an impenetrable hazardous-materials suit. Ultimately, though, one student pulled the suit away from his neck and dumped water down his back.

But perhaps one of Casey's greatest tactics for maintaining his students' attention has been keeping his personal life the ultimate secret. They listen every day in hopes he will reveal any clues as to his age, his family and where he lives.

It seems they just don't buy the Arnold water tower address and Jan. 22, 1899, birth date listed on his school identification card or the answer he gives when asked if he has children, "Yes, I have thousands of children. And they're all teenagers."

Source: Christine Byers, "Geology teacher finds creative ways to keep students engaged," from *St. Louis Post-Dispatch*, March 23, 2007. Reprinted by permission of *St. Louis Post-Dispatch*.

Questions and Activities

1. Teacher Art Casey uses various techniques to get students to attend to his earth science lessons. What evidence, if any, can you cite from this article that he was successful?
2. In what ways are this teacher's methods consistent with both the information-processing and constructivist approaches to teaching?
3. Would you use techniques as unorthodox as this teacher's to get your students' attention and make lessons more meaningful? Why? What, specifically, would you do?

Here are a few examples of how you can make your teaching more organized and meaningful:

- Using some form of overview or introduction that provides a meaningful context for new material.
- Using concrete examples and analogies to illustrate otherwise abstract ideas.
- Using visually based methods of representing information, such as maps, graphs, and three-dimensional models.
- Stressing practical applications and relationships to other subjects. (You may recall from Chapter 4 that this tactic is used to help adolescent girls remain interested in science.)

Present Information in Learnable Amounts and Over Realistic Time Periods Here's an experience most of us have had at one time or another: Someone gives you the 10-digit phone number of a business you want to call, but you have nothing with which to write down

{ Present organized and meaningful lessons. }

the number. It takes you about 15 seconds to get to a phone. You start to dial the number but realize about halfway through that you can't recall the rest of the sequence. Frustrating? Yes. Surprising? Not if you read and remember (and please say you do remember) what we pointed out in Chapter 8 about the limits imposed by short-term memory. OK, here's a quick reminder: We can only process a limited amount of information (about seven chunks) at any point in time. And the more unorganized and nonmeaningful the information (like a phone number), the smaller the size of the chunks.

While this example may strike you as trivial, it is relevant to what goes on in classrooms, since many tasks bump up against the limits of short-term memory. Learning to produce and recognize grammatically correct utterances ("The cat climbed up the tree" versus "Tree the climbed cat up the") is a task that places a high demand on working memory because the meaning of all the words must be considered simultaneously to determine if the sentence makes sense. For such tasks, minimizing the amount of information that students are required to learn is critically important because it leaves them with sufficient working memory to engage in schema construction (J. W. Montgomery, Magimairaj, & O'Malley, 2008; Savage, Lavers, & Pillay, 2007).

One instructional recommendation that flows from this analysis is the same as one of the recommendations for direct instruction: Break lessons into small, manageable parts and don't introduce new topics until you have evidence that students have learned the presented material. A second recommendation is to build into lessons opportunities for students to write about, discuss, and use the ideas they are learning. By monitoring the accuracy of their responses, you will also have the information you need to judge whether it is time to introduce new ideas.

Present new information in small chunks.

Facilitate Encoding of Information Into Long-Term Memory High-quality learning rarely occurs when students adopt a relatively passive orientation. Many students, for example, do little more than read assigned material and record ideas in verbatim form. They spend little time thinking about how ideas within topics and

between topics relate to one another or to concepts they have already learned. One reason is that they simply do not know what else to do with information. Another reason is that teachers do little to support the kind of encoding that results in more meaningful forms of learning. To help your students encode information for more effective storage in and retrieval from long-term memory, try the following techniques in your classroom instruction:

- Present information through such different media as pictures, video, audio, live models, and manipulation of physical objects.

- Use lots of examples and analogies (to foster elaboration).

- Prompt students to elaborate by asking them to put ideas in their own words, relate new ideas to personal experience, and create their own analogies.

Pause & Reflect *In Chapter 9 we noted that elementary grade teachers rarely give students instruction in how to process information effectively. One reason is that teacher education programs typically provide little or no coursework on this subject. Is this true of your program? What can you do when you teach to make full use of information-processing principles?*

The Nature and Elements of a Constructivist Approach

The essence of constructivist theory is that people learn best by creating their own understanding of reality. Using such characteristics as existing knowledge, attitudes, values, and experiences as filters, people interpret current experience in a way that seems to make sense to them at the time. As Figure 13.2 demonstrates by constructing two different concept maps from an identical set of concepts, knowledge can be organized in any number of ways, and the scheme one creates will reflect one's purpose or focal point. The goal of constructivist-oriented teaching, then, is to provide a set of conditions that will lead students to construct a view of reality that both makes sense to them and addresses the essence of your objectives (Delgarno, 2001).

A brief description of five of the more prominent elements that help define a constructivist-oriented classroom follows. Although two of these elements reflect a social constructivist orientation, bear in mind that the goal of both cognitive and social constructivism is the same: to help students become more effective thinkers and problem solvers by helping them construct richer and more meaningful schemes. A social constructivist orientation simply gives greater weight to the role of social interaction in this process.

Provide Scaffolded Instruction Within the Zone of Proximal Development The zone of proximal development is the difference between what a learner can accomplish without assistance and what he or she can accomplish with assistance, and the assistance that teachers give to students as they try to master new knowledge and skills is called scaffolding.

When you introduce students to new material, one of the most straightforward ways to provide scaffolded instruction is by the time-honored technique of providing explanations. An analysis of research (Wittwer & Renkl, 2008) suggested four guidelines for creating effective instructional explanations. First, make sure your explanations are within your students' zone of proximal development, so that you make learning neither too difficult nor too easy. This guideline implies that you will need to be aware of what students know and do not know, what misconceptions they have, and what kinds of cognitive skills they possess. Second, as we do in this textbook, make your explanations meaningful by emphasizing how concepts and principles are relevant to your students' everyday lives and to what they already know. Third, give students the opportunity to use the concepts and principles that are embedded in your explanations. Finally, using the factors mentioned in the first guideline, identify which students will learn best from very direct, detailed explanations and which will do best when left to figure things out for themselves.

The beneficial effect of scaffolding was demonstrated in a study (I. Hardy, Jonen, Möller, & Stern, 2006) in which third graders received either high or low levels of instructional support on a lesson about density and buoyancy (e.g., Why does a large iron ship float?). In the high-instructional-support condition, the teacher sequenced the material into consecutive units, decided when certain instructional materials and objects would be available, pointed out contradictory statements made by the students, and summarized their conclusions. In the low-instructional-support condition, students were given a variety of materials and objects and worked in small groups

to conduct experiments. The teacher's major role in the low-support condition was to provide support for the process of investigation. When tested on their understanding of the concepts of density and buoyancy, both groups significantly outscored an uninstructed control group. But 1 year later, the high-support group demonstrated a better grasp of these concepts than did the low-support group.

{ **Constructivist approach: help students construct meaningful knowledge schemes** }

Provide Opportunities for Learning by Discovery By its very nature, constructivism implies the need to let students discover things for themselves. But what things? Most constructivist theorists would agree on the following: understanding how ideas connect with one another, knowing how to analyze and frame problems, asking appropriate questions, recognizing when what we already know is relevant to what we are trying to learn, and evaluating the effectiveness of our strategies.

Foster Multiple Viewpoints Given the basic constructivist premise that all meaningful learning is constructed and that everyone uses a slightly different set of filters with which to build his or her view of reality, what we refer to as knowledge is actually a consensus of slightly different points of view. Thus another element of a constructivist approach to teaching is to help students understand that different views of the same phenomena exist and that they can often be reconciled to produce a broader understanding.

The technique of **cooperative learning** is an effective way to expose students to peers who may have different views about the "right" way to do something

© Tamara Murray/iStockphoto

or the "truth" of some matter and help them forge a broader understanding that is acceptable to all members of the group. In the last major section of this chapter, we describe cooperative learning in considerable detail.

Emphasize Relevant Problems and Tasks Can you recall completing a class assignment or reading a chapter out of a textbook that had no apparent relevance to anything that concerned you? Not very interesting or exciting, was it? Unfortunately, too many students perceive too much of schooling in that light. One constructivist remedy is to create interest and relevance by posing problems or assigning tasks that are both challenging and realistic (Delgarno, 2001; Jonassen, Howland, Marra, & Crismond, 2008). In a recent poll, parents also endorsed the goal of making schoolwork relevant with real-world examples (Bushaw & Lopez, 2010).

Problems can be challenging either because the correct answer is not immediately apparent or because there is no correct answer. The ill-structured problems and issues that we described in Chapter 10 are, by their nature, challenging and realistic and do not have solutions that everyone perceives as appropriate and useful. But if you assign students an ill-structured problem to investigate, pose it in such a way that they will see its relevance. For example, instead of asking high school students to debate the general pros and cons of laws that restrict personal freedoms, have them interview their community's mayor, chief of police, business owners, and peers about the pros and cons of laws that specify curfews for individuals under a certain age and that prohibit such activities as loitering and purchasing alcohol and tobacco. Because many adolescents consider themselves mature enough to regulate their own behavior, analyzing and debating laws that are intended to restrict certain adolescent behaviors is likely to produce a fair amount of disequilibrium.

Encourage Students to Become More Autonomous Learners According to constructivist and humanistic theory (which we discuss later in this chapter), students should, under the right circumstances, be able to work more independently of the teacher than they typically do. One important condition that paves the way for students' becoming more autonomous is the way in which teachers interact with them. Students in one study (Reeve & Jang, 2006) were more likely to feel as if they were in control of their own learning when teachers engaged in such behaviors as giving them time to work on a task in their own ways, giving them the opportunity to talk, encouraging them to complete tasks, listening to them, and being responsive to their questions. By contrast, student autonomy was more likely to be negatively related to such teacher behaviors as giving students the solutions to problems or the answers to questions, giving them commands and directions, telling them they should or should not do something, and asking them such controlling questions as "Can you do it the way I showed you?"

The technology section that follows presents some additional ideas for embedding learning in realistic settings.

Adopting a constructivist approach to teaching means arranging for students to work collaboratively in small groups on relevant problems and tasks, encouraging diverse points of view, and providing scaffolded instruction.

Using Technology to Support Cognitive Approaches to Instruction

As educators begin to understand and address cognitive learning theories, the focus of technology is shifting from remediating skill deficiencies in learners and rehearsing basic skills to finding ways to help learners build, extend, and amplify new knowledge (Cennamo, Ross, & Ertmer, 2010; Jonassen, Howland, Marra, & Crismond, 2008). Your willingness and readiness to use today's technology for constructivist and other cognitive approaches to instruction is likely to be partly a function of the extent to which you use computer technology to meet personal and professional goals. Fourth and eighth

exploratory environment
An electronic environment that provides students with materials and resources to discover interesting phenomena and construct new insights; for example, a computer simulation. Also called a *discovery environment*.

guided learning environment
A classroom or computer-based environment in which teachers, experts, or more knowledgeable peers support student inquiry by helping students set plans and goals, ask questions, discuss issues, solve problems, and reflect on strategies and solutions. Also called *guided discovery learning*.

problem-based learning An instructional method that requires learners to develop solutions to authentic and complex problems through problem analysis, hypothesis generation, collaboration, reflection, and extensive teacher coaching and facilitation.

grade teachers who reported higher levels of classroom technology use and personal computer use were more likely to use constructivist teaching practices than their peers who reported lower levels of technology use (Rakes, Fields, & Cox, 2006).

Exploratory Environments

Computers can be used for more than just transmitting or representing information to the learner; they also provide environments that allow for discoveries and insights. In such an **exploratory environment** (also called a *discovery environment*), students might explore ocean life or find the ideal ecosystem for a *Tyrannosaurus rex* dinosaur (see, for example, National Geographic Xpeditions at www.national geographic.com/xpeditions).

Exploratory tools for learning math include Logo, the Geometric Supposer, and the Geometer's Sketchpad, all of which have been shown to help students construct meaningful knowledge networks about geometric concepts and reduce the usual rote memorizing of rules and terms (D. H. Clements, Sarama, Yelland, & Glass, 2008; Funkhouser, 2002/2003).

Another exploratory tool, GenScope, was designed to help students better understand the principles of genetics. Two studies have illustrated the benefits to using this program. In the first, high school students in technical biology and general life science courses performed significantly better on a test of genetic reasoning than did students in classes without the program (Hickey, Kindfield, Horwitz, & Christie, 2003). In the second study, high school students in honors biology with little prior knowledge of the subject showed significant gains in conceptual understanding, whereas students who already knew something about genetics did not (Winters & Azevedo, 2005).

Guided Learning Although students can use modeling programs and simulations to plan experiments, take

measurements, analyze data, and graph findings, there is still a need for teacher scaffolding and guidance in support of the learning process (Delgarno, 2001). In these **guided learning environments**, teachers might help students set goals, ask questions, encourage discussions, and provide models of problem-solving processes. Such teachers provide a clear road map of the unit at the beginning, clear expectations and sequencing of activities, continued reinforcement and guidance, teacher modeling, opportunities for students to practice problem-solving steps, reflection on learning, and regular checking and sharing of student progress. (Note how this approach combines elements of the behavioral and social cognitive approaches.)

One guided learning environment, the Higher Order Thinking Skills program (HOTS), focuses on higher order thinking skills among at-risk youths in grades 4 through 8 (Pogrow, 1990, 1999, 2005, 2009a). HOTS was designed around active learning, Socratic questioning, and reflection activities in using computers. The goal of the program is to improve four key thinking processes: (1) metacognition, (2) inferential thinking, (3) transfer of learning, and (4) synthesis, or combining information from different sources into a coherent whole. Instead of the rote computer-based drills that these students would normally receive, they are prompted to reflect on their decision-making process while using computer tools. Teachers do not give away the answers but instead draw out key concepts by questioning students or telling them to go back and read the information on the computer screen. The developer of HOTS, Stanley Pogrow, calls this "controlled floundering," or leading students into frustration so that they have to reflect on the information on the screen to solve a problem.

Pogrow (2005) reported that students in the HOTS program recorded year-to-year gains that were twice those of the national average on standardized tests of reading and math and 3 times those of control groups on tests of reading comprehension. These gains were still noticeable when students were later given other math and reading tests as well as tests of writing, problem solving, and metacognition. Additional information on the HOTS program can be found at www.hots.org.

Problem-Based Learning Another way to implement constructivist trends in education is to use technology for **problem-based learning**, an instructional method that requires learners to develop solutions to real-life problems. Computer-based problem-solving programs typically provide students with story problems, laboratory problems, or investigation problems. Story problem programs are usually tutorials and are very much like the math story problems you probably encountered in school. Laboratory problems are typically simulations of laboratory science problems, as in chemistry or biology. Investigation problems are set in realistic environments (microworlds) and may involve such varied subject areas as astronomy, social studies, environmental science, and anthropology (Jonassen, Howland, Marra, & Crismond, 2008). When using problem-based learning with technology, students can plan and organize their own research while working collaboratively with others.

Although problem-based learning has its roots in medical and business school settings, it has been successfully adapted to the elementary, middle school, and high school grades. Problem-solving programs that are based on constructivist principles and are most likely to foster meaningful learning will do the following (Hung, 2002; Jonassen, Howland, Marra, & Crismond, 2008):

- Encourage students to be active learners, engaging in such behaviors as making observations, manipulating objects, and recording the results of their manipulations.

- Encourage students to reflect on their experiences and begin to construct mental models of the world.

- Provide students with complex tasks that are situated in real-world settings.

- Require students to state their learning goals, the decisions they make, the strategies they use, and the answers they formulate.

- Require students to work in cooperative groups in which there is a considerable amount of social interaction.

Situated Learning As you may recall from Chapter 10, situated learning (or situated cognition) is built on the concept that knowledge is closely linked to the environment in which it is acquired. The more true to life the task is, the more meaningful the learning will be. Technology can play a key role in providing access to a wide variety of real-world learning situations. For instance, computer-based instructional technology such as CSILE (www.knowledgeforum.com), WISE (http://wise.berkeley.edu), and the GLOBE program (www.globe.gov) can apprentice students into real-life learning and problem-solving settings by providing access to both authentic data and tools to manipulate the data (see, for example, Slotta & Linn, 2009, for a detailed description of the WISE science program).

One project that embodied the concept of situated learning was conducted with elementary grade students in two schools, one in Northern Ireland and one in the Republic of Ireland (L. Clarke & Heaney, 2003). In this Author-on-Line project, students in both schools read a book called *The Cinnamon Tree*, by Aubrey Flegg, and wrote a book report. The students then posted their reports on a portion of the website of the Northern Ireland Network for Education. As new reports appeared, they were read by all of the students and discussed. At this point, the author got involved by posting his reactions to each student's report. The students discussed his comments in class and, either individually or in small groups, composed a response. At one point the author adopted the persona of the book's main character, a 13-year-old girl, thereby giving the students the rather unique opportunity to interact with a fictional character.

> **humanistic approach**
> An approach to instruction that emphasizes the effect of student needs, values, motives, and self-perceptions on learning.

LO5 The Humanistic Approach to Teaching: Student-Centered Instruction

The **humanistic approach** pays particular attention to the role of noncognitive variables in learning, specifically students' needs, emotions, values, and self-perceptions. It assumes that students will be highly motivated to learn when the learning material is personally meaningful, when they understand the reasons for their own behavior, and when they believe that the classroom environment supports their efforts to learn, even if they struggle. Consequently, a humanistic approach to teaching strives to help students better understand themselves and to create a supportive classroom atmosphere that activates the inherent desire all human beings have to learn and fulfill their potential (Allender & Allender, 2008; Maslow, 1987; C. R. Rogers & Freiberg, 1994).

The relevance of a humanistic approach to teaching may not be immediately apparent to everyone, but it is easy to support. We've known for some time that learning is influenced as much by how students feel about themselves as by the cognitive skills they possess. When students conclude that the demands of a task are beyond their current level of knowledge and skill (what we referred to in a previous chapter as a low sense of self-efficacy), they are likely to experience such debilitating emotions as anxiety and fear. Once these negative self-perceptions and emotions are created, the student has to divert time and energy from the task at hand to figure out how to deal with the negative self-perceptions and emotions. And the solutions that students formulate are not always appropriate. Some may, for instance, decide to reduce their efforts and settle for whatever passing grade they can get. Others may give up entirely by cutting class, not completing homework assignments, and not studying for tests. A considerable amount of research from the health field has shown that people are more likely to use positive methods of coping with the stress of illness and disease when they perceive their environment to be *socially supportive*. The small amount of comparable research that exists on classroom learning suggests a similar outcome (Boekarts, 1993; A. M. Ryan & Patrick, 2001).

{ **The humanistic approach addresses needs, values, motives, and self-perceptions.** }

Pioneers of the Humanistic Approach

The humanistic approach to understanding human behavior blossomed during the 1960s principally because of the writings of three individuals: Abraham Maslow, Carl Rogers, and Arthur Combs. Although the primary focus of their careers was counseling, they also wrote about the relevance of humanistic principles to education in such books as *Toward a Psychology of Being* (Maslow, 1968), *Freedom to Learn* (Rogers & Freiberg, 1994), and *The Professional Education of Teachers* (Combs, 1965). We can sum up the essence of their ideas about learning and education as follows:

- People have an inherent desire to make the most of their capabilities, a characteristic that Maslow called *self-actualization*. Think of it as an inherent desire to learn and become competent.

- Self-actualization cannot occur until the more basic physiological, safety, belonging, and esteem needs have been satisfactorily met. Teachers can play a critical role in helping students meet these needs.

- The best way to understand a student's behavior is to understand how the student sees herself (what we referred to in earlier chapters as self-esteem and self-efficacy) and the situation she is in. Is she confident and comfortable, or self-doubting, anxious, and fearful?

- Learning is most meaningful when students understand how material and lessons relate to their own lives.

- Learning occurs best when the student is convinced that the teacher accepts the student for what he or she is and is there to help the student succeed.

Another way to summarize the humanistic approach to education is to say that teachers should strive to establish a caring atmosphere in their classrooms, a concept about which we will have more to say shortly.

Teaching From a Humanistic Orientation

Teachers who adopt a humanistic orientation seek to create a classroom atmosphere in which students believe that the teacher's primary goal is to understand their needs, values, motives, and self-perceptions and to help them learn. This atmosphere is established primarily by the teacher's expressing genuine interest in and acceptance of the student and valuing the contribution each student makes to the progress of the class. The teacher avoids giving the impression that he or she would like the student better if only the student dressed more appropriately, had a more positive attitude toward learning, associated with a different group of peers, and so on. In this kind of setting, students will be more inclined to discuss openly their feelings about and problems with learning and related issues. The teacher is then in a position to help students figure out better approaches to their schoolwork and relationships with others. The teacher does not tell students what to do but guides them to the correct action. Because the students' perceptions and decisions are the central focus, this approach is often referred to as either *student directed* or *nondirective* (Joyce & Weil, 2009; Tomlinson, 2002).

Pause & Reflect *Can you recall any teachers who practiced humanistic techniques? Did you like these teachers? Did you feel you learned as much from them as from other teachers? Would you model yourself after such teachers?*

To illustrate this approach, consider the case of a student who is unhappy about a poor grade on a test. The instinctive reaction of most teachers would be to explain how to study and prepare for the next test. The humanistically oriented teacher instead asks the student to describe his interest in the subject matter, how capable a learner he feels himself to be, how well he understands the subject, under what conditions he studies, whether he feels the teacher's instruction to be clear and well organized, and so on. To help students understand their feelings and the role they play in learning, the teacher may disclose some of his or her own feelings. For example, the teacher may tell this hypothetical student, "When I've had a bad day and feel as if I've let my students down, I sometimes question my ability as a teacher. Is that how you feel?" Once these self-perceptions have been raised and clarified, the teacher encourages the student to suggest a solution to the problem (Joyce & Weil, 2009).

The Humanistic Model

According to Joyce and Weil (2009), the nondirective model is made up of the following components:

1. *Defining the helping situation.* The topic that the student wants to discuss is identified, and the student is told that he or she is free to express any and all feelings that relate to the topic.

2. *Exploring the problem.* If the teacher has been able to establish the atmosphere of trust just described, it is assumed that students will be willing to describe the problem and any associated feelings. The teacher does not attempt to diagnose the student's problem but seeks to understand the situation as the student experiences it and then reflects this understanding back to the student. The teacher functions more as a resource, facilitator, and guide than as a director.

3. *Developing insight.* The student uses the information gained from exploring the problem to understand how various perceptions, emotions, beliefs, and behaviors cause various effects (such as a belief that one lacks ability, leading to incomplete homework assignments and lack of interest in the subject, or a need for affiliation that leads to more socializing than studying).

4. *Planning and decision making.* The teacher helps the student identify alternative behaviors and methods for carrying them out.

5. *Integration.* The student reports on actions taken, their effects, and plans for future actions.

This approach to instruction strongly implies that students who believe their teachers care about them as people and want to help them maximize their learning are likely to be highly motivated. Nel Noddings, an educational researcher who has written extensively about establishing a caring atmosphere in classrooms and whom we first mentioned in Chapter 2, described this approach (2003) as one that seeks to produce happy students. She argued that happiness should be, but rarely is, an explicit and high priority goal of educators and educational policy makers. (It already is for parents—they say so in overwhelming numbers in surveys of educational goals.) In her view, happy classrooms

* satisfy the physical needs of children;

* are clean and maintained, have reliable heating systems, are well lit, and are physically safe;

* are those in which learning is an exciting, meaningful, and pleasurable experience;

* are those in which children have an opportunity to learn through play;

* avoid the use of sarcasm, humiliation, and fear;

Adopting a humanistic approach to teaching means identifying and meeting students' physical, social, emotional, and intellectual needs, as well as helping students understand how their perceptions, emotions, and behaviors affect their achievement.

* capitalize on students' interests;

* foster intellectual growth in every student;

* foster the development of character; and

* foster interpersonal growth (learning how to get along with others).

Noddings is hardly alone in her view. Two longtime humanistic researchers, Jerome Allender and Donna Sclarow Allender (2008), noted that the curriculum should emphasize students' interests because "opportunities for following up on where one's curiosity leads are a sure bet for initial successful learning" (p. 86). Chrystal Johnson and Adrian Thomas (2009) argued that an ideal time to establish a caring environment is the primary grades because such an environment promotes a sense of community, safety, learning-oriented values, and positive interpersonal experiences that will lead to higher levels of motivation and learning in those and later grades. And Beverly Falk (2009), author of *Teaching the Way Children Learn*, commented that "children need to be in caring communities to develop the sense of self-worth necessary to take the risks that are involved in real learning" (p. 88).

Unfortunately, classrooms that provide this type of positive emotional support appear to be the exception rather than the rule. Observations in hundreds of primary and elementary grade classrooms (Pianta, Belsky, Houts, Morrison, & The National Institute of Child Health and Human Development Early Child Care Research Network, 2007) revealed that only 17% of students experienced a positive emotional climate as they went from one grade to the next. There are concrete steps, however, that you can take to create a supportive climate in your own classroom. To start, you might try to observe and emulate the practices of teachers who create productive personal relationships with students. Two former school principals (Mahwinney & Sagan, 2007) found that such teachers exhibit the following characteristics:

- They demonstrate respect, courtesy, and fairness. A veteran teacher that students rated year after year as being one of the best they ever had always said "please" and "thank you" when interacting with students, often gave students a last chance to improve their grade on a quiz or exam (we make the same recommendation in Chapter 14), insisted that students who were performing poorly see him for help, never raised his voice, and disciplined students privately.

- They demonstrate that they care about students' lives and try to put themselves in their shoes. As we note elsewhere in this and other chapters, students who believe that their teachers care about them are more likely to work harder and less likely to drop out of school.

- They use humor as a way to put students at ease and to defuse potentially disruptive situations. Margaret Metzger, the veteran high school teacher whose suggestions for managing classroom behavior we summarized in Chapter 12, also suggested using a light touch at times.

© ra2 studio/Shutterstock Images

> **Humanistic teachers show respect, courtesy, fairness, and a caring attitude.**

Does a Humanistic Approach to Education Work?

To the surprise of some, the humanistic approach is successful. Those who are surprised see the humanistic approach as "soft" in comparison to direct instruction and information-processing/social cognitive theory. It does not offer the highly structured approach to teaching basic knowledge and skills that direct instruction does, nor does it focus on the use of various cognitive skills as does information-processing/social cognitive theory. What these critics overlook, however, is that learning does not occur in a vacuum—it takes place in a social setting that involves all aspects of the learner. As you'll see shortly, the value of a humanistic approach has been demonstrated by different research methods and analyses.

As we noted previously, Maslow believed that children's academic and personal growth are enhanced when various needs are met. One of those needs, belonging, has been the subject of considerable research. Belonging, which is also referred to as *relatedness* and *sense of community*, means the desire to get support from and be accepted by teachers and classmates and to have opportunities to participate in classroom planning, goal setting, and decision making.

According to some motivational theorists (e.g., Bear, 2009), belonging is one of three basic psychological needs (autonomy and competence are the other two) essential to human growth and development. Yet the need to belong receives less attention from educators than autonomy or competence. One possible reason for this discrepancy is the belief that students' emotional needs are best met at home and in other out-of-school settings. This attitude does a disservice to students for two reasons: Teachers play an important role in helping to satisfy the need to belong, and research has uncovered positive relationships between satisfaction of the need to belong and the following school-related outcomes (L. H. Anderman & Leake, 2007; Osterman, 2000; Patrick, Ryan, & Kaplan, 2007):

- increased intrinsic motivation to learn;
- a strong sense of competence;
- a heightened sense of autonomy;
- a stronger sense of identity;

- the willingness to conform to classroom rules and norms;
- positive attitudes toward school, classwork, and teachers;
- higher expectations of success;
- lower levels of anxiety, depression, and frustration;
- supportiveness of others; and
- higher levels of achievement.

Feelings of rejection or exclusion from the group are associated with the following negative outcomes (L. H. Anderman & Leake, 2007; J. N. Hughes & Zhang, 2007; Osterman, 2000):

- higher levels of stress, anger, and health problems;
- behavior problems in school;
- lower interest in school;
- lower achievement; and
- dropping out of school.

Next we offer a trio of classroom-based studies that demonstrate the positive effect of a humanistic environment on a variety of student behaviors. The first piece of evidence comes from an unusual source: an analysis of why Japanese students outscore U.S. students after fourth grade on an internationally normed standardized test of mathematics and science. After observing 10 science lessons taught in five Japanese public schools, Marcia Linn, Catherine Lewis, Ineko Tsuchida, and Nancy Butler Songer (2000) attributed the difference in part to a classroom atmosphere that Abraham Maslow and Carl Rogers would have endorsed.

In addition to emphasizing cognitive development, elementary education in Japan places a high value on children's social and ethical development. This is done by such tactics as (1) giving children various classroom responsibilities so they feel a valued part of the school, (2) emphasizing such qualities as friendliness, responsibility, and persistence, and (3) communicating to students that teachers value their presence in the classroom and the contributions they make. By fourth grade, Japanese children have been steeped in a school culture that emphasizes responsibility to the group, collaboration, and kindness. In addition, Linn and her colleagues found that almost every lesson began with an activity that was designed to spark the students' interest in the topic by connecting it to either their personal experiences or previous lessons. The positive emotional attachment to school and the commitment to the values of hard work and cooperation that this approach produces are thought to play a strong role in how well students learn mathematics and science lessons.

Challenging Assumptions

The Perennial Relevance of Humanistic Theory

As you know from reading this section, humanistic approaches to learning and teaching were formulated during the 1960s and 1970s. What you probably don't know is that they were every bit as popular at that time as, say, constructivist theories are today. But humanistic theories gradually fell from favor and eventually almost disappeared from sight. By the late 1980s, many textbooks had either drastically cut back on or eliminated coverage of them, fewer papers on humanistic topics were delivered at major conferences, and fewer conceptual and research articles appeared in journals.

The reasons for the decline appeared to be threefold. First, information-processing theory, social cognitive theory, and constructivism ignited a torrent of research that promised, more than noncognitive conceptualizations, dramatic gains in achievement. Second, the humanistic theorists and researchers who came after Maslow, Rogers, and Combs were not of the same stature and did not have the same impact on the field. Third, concerns about students' emotions, needs, and values seemed to many people to be frivolous, if not irrelevant, at a time when American students appeared to be inferior to earlier generations of students, as well as to students from other countries, in terms of standardized test scores. Teachers and students were urged to get back to basics!

In recent years, however, humanistic theory has staged something of a comeback. Current conceptualizations of classroom instruction recognize that students' needs and self-perceptions are every bit as important to understanding and improving classroom learning as the quality of their thinking. The research we have described on the effects of belonging, teacher support, and social harmony among students exemplifies this trend. So if someone tries to convince you that humanistic theories are dead, tell them that humanistic approaches to education never die; they just hang around waiting to be acknowledged.

What Do You Think?

What are your thoughts about humanistic education? Will you use its principles in your classroom? Explore the debate about humanistic teaching at the "Challenging Assumptions" section of the textbook's Education CourseMate website.

The second of the three studies (A. M. Ryan & Patrick, 2001) examined eighth grade classroom environments. The atmosphere created by each teacher was described along four lines:

1. Teacher support (students' perceptions of how strongly teachers valued and established personal relationships with them)

2. Promoting interaction among classmates (e.g., allowing students to share ideas, work together in small groups, give help during individual seatwork)

3. Promoting mutual respect and social harmony among classmates

4. Promoting performance goals (emphasizing competition and relative ability comparisons among classmates)

Each of these classroom environment components was related to several outcome measures, including the four listed in Figure 13.3. The figure uses plus and minus signs to show the significant associations that the researchers reported. Notice that the first three environmental components—the ones that humanistic educators would favor—tended to increase desirable outcomes and decrease undesirable ones. The fourth, however—stressing competition and performance goals—raised students' off-task and disruptive behavior and decreased their confidence in being able to interact with the teacher.

Lastly, an extension of Ryan and Patrick's 2001 study (Patrick, Ryan, & Kaplan, 2007) found that teacher support, promoting interaction, promoting mutual respect, and student academic support (the perception that one's classmates want one to come to school every day and do well) contribute to the adoption of mastery goals and the strengthening of academic and social self-efficacy. These variables contributed, in turn, to task-related interactions (suggesting ideas, explaining one's reasoning, helping others), which affected self-regulation behaviors and achievement.

The findings from the three previous studies were supported by an analysis of 119 studies (Cornelius-White, 2007). Teachers who demonstrated empathy and warmth, encouraged thinking, and used a nondirective approach were more likely than other teachers to have students who scored significantly higher on tests of verbal skills, math skills, and critical and creative thinking skills. These students were also more likely to exhibit higher levels of class participation, score higher on measures of self-efficacy and satisfaction, and be less likely to drop out of school.

LO6 The Social Approach to Teaching: Teaching Students How to Learn From Each Other

Classroom tasks can be structured so that students are forced to compete with one another, to work individually, or to cooperate with one another to obtain the rewards that teachers make available for successfully completing these tasks. Traditionally, competitive arrangements have been assumed to be superior to the other two in increasing motivation and learning. But several analyses of the research literature (e.g., Gillies, 2003; Ginsburg-Block, Rohrbeck, Lavigne, & Fantuzzo, 2008; D. W. Johnson & Johnson, 2009a; Slavin, Lake, & Groff, 2009) found cooperative arrangements to be far superior in producing these benefits. In this section,

FIGURE 13.3 Results of the Ryan and Patrick Study of Eighth Grade Classrooms

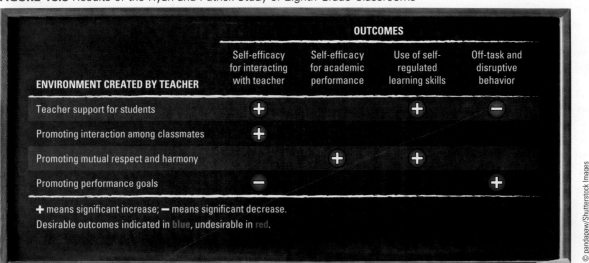

ENVIRONMENT CREATED BY TEACHER	Self-efficacy for interacting with teacher	Self-efficacy for academic performance	Use of self-regulated learning skills	Off-task and disruptive behavior
Teacher support for students	+		+	−
Promoting interaction among classmates	+			
Promoting mutual respect and harmony		+	+	
Promoting performance goals	−			+

+ means significant increase; **−** means significant decrease.
Desirable outcomes indicated in blue, undesirable in red.

Photo: © pandapaw/Shutterstock Images

SOURCE: Based on A. M. Ryan & Patrick (2001).

we will identify the elements that make up the major approaches to cooperative learning and examine the effect of cooperative learning on motivation, achievement, and interpersonal relationships.

Pause & Reflect *Have you ever experienced a competitive reward structure in school? Were your reactions positive or negative? Why? Would you use it in your own classroom? How and when? What about a cooperative reward structure?*

Elements of Cooperative Learning

Over the past 30 years, different approaches to cooperative learning have been proposed by different individuals. The three most popular are those of David and Roger Johnson (D. W. Johnson & Johnson, 2009a), Robert Slavin (1994, 1995), and Shlomo and Yael Sharan (S. Sharan, 1995; Y. Sharan & Sharan, 1999). To give you a general sense of what cooperative learning is like—and to avoid limiting you to any one individual's approach—the following discussion is a synthesis of the main features of each approach.

Group Heterogeneity The size of cooperative learning groups is relatively small, and groups should be as heterogeneous as circumstances allow. The recommended size is usually four or five students. At the very least, groups should contain both males and females and students of different ability levels. If possible, different ethnic backgrounds and social classes should be represented as well.

Group Goals and Positive Interdependence A specific goal, such as a grade or a certificate of recognition, is identified for the group to attain. Students are told that they will have to support one another because the group goal can be achieved only if each member learns the material being taught (in the case of a task that culminates in an exam) or makes a specific contribution to the group's effort (in the case of a task that culminates in a presentation or a project).

Promotive Interaction The existence of positive interdependence necessitates promotive interaction. Students are shown how to help one another overcome problems and complete whatever task has been assigned. This may involve episodes of peer tutoring, temporary assistance, exchanges of information and material, challenging of one another's reasoning, feedback, and encouragement to keep one another highly motivated. *Promotive* means simply that students promote each other's success.

Individual Accountability Each member of a group has to make a significant contribution to achieving the group's goal. This may be satisfied by requiring the group to achieve a minimum score on a test, having the group's test score be the sum or average of each student's quiz scores, or having each member be responsible for a particular part of a project (such as doing the research and writing for a particular part of a history report).

Interpersonal Skills Positive interdependence and promotive interaction are not likely to occur if students do not know how to make the most of their face-to-face interactions. And you can safely assume that the interpersonal skills most students possess are probably not highly developed. As a result, students have to be taught such basic skills as leadership, decision making, trust building, clear communication, and conflict management. The conflict that arises over differences of opinion, for example, can be constructive if it is used as a stimulus to search for more information or to rethink one's conclusions. But it can destroy group cohesion and productivity if it results in students' stubbornly clinging to a position or referring to one another as "stubborn," "dumb," or "nerdy."

Equal Opportunities for Success Because cooperative groups are heterogeneous with respect to ability and their success depends on positive interdependence, promotive interaction, and individual accountability, it is important that steps be taken to ensure that all students have an opportunity to contribute to their team. You can do this by awarding points for degree of improvement over previous test scores, by having students compete against comparable members of other teams in a game-like or tournament atmosphere, or by giving students learning assignments (such as math problems) that are geared to their current level of skill.

Team Competition Competition may seem to be an odd entry in a list of cooperative learning components, especially in the light of the comments we already made about the ineffectiveness of competition as a spur to motivation and learning. But we're not being contradictory. The main problem with competition is that it is rarely

© hanhanpeggy/iStockphoto

Cooperative learning has been shown to produce positive cognitive, social, and affective outcomes, provided that its basic elements are implemented.

used appropriately. When competition occurs between well-matched teams, in the absence of a norm-referenced grading system (grades are determined by how one compares to one's peers), and is not used too frequently, it can be an effective way to motivate students to cooperate with each other.

Does Cooperative Learning Work?

By now, you should be able to anticipate the answer to the question of effectiveness. We will simply not discuss any theory or concept that has not been at least partially supported by good-quality research. Cooperative learning more than meets that standard. In the vast majority of studies, forms of cooperative learning have been shown to be more effective than noncooperative reward structures at raising the levels of variables that contribute to motivation, raising achievement, and producing positive social outcomes.

Effect on Motivation An analysis of 15 studies (Ginsburg-Block, Rohrbeck, Lavigne, & Fantuzzo, 2008) that measured the effect of cooperative learning on the motivational levels of elementary grade students found moderate to strong effects in 11 of the studies. Those that had the strongest positive effects used interdependent rewards (each group member received a reward only if the group achieved its goal) and had additional motivational components (such as individualized curriculum materials). Motivational effects were larger for minority than for nonminority students and for urban students than for suburban or rural students.

Although most of the reported effects of cooperative learning have been positive, negative results have

occasionally appeared. Eleventh grade students whose chemistry classes used a form of cooperative learning experienced declines in motivation, whereas students in the whole-class instruction group reported slight increases (Shachar & Fischer, 2004). The researchers attributed this finding to students' being dissatisfied with the pace and amount of learning because of an upcoming high-stakes test. If this explanation is correct, the lesson to be taken from this finding is that the usefulness of any instructional approach or technique will depend on the context in which it occurs. Remember, nothing works for everybody in all circumstances!

Effect on Achievement The effect of cooperative learning on achievement has been extensively studied. Two recent analyses of research have added to the positive results that were reported during the 1970s and 1980s. The first analysis (Gillies, 2003) found that students in cooperative groups who worked on problem-solving activities that required them to use all six cognitive processes represented in Bloom's taxonomy (discussed in the first section of this chapter) scored significantly higher on a subsequent achievement test than did comparable peers who also worked in groups but received no training in group interaction. The second analysis (Slavin, Lake, & Groff, 2009) found that the math scores of middle school and high school students were considerably higher when teachers used cooperative learning programs than when they used either computer-based instruction or just a textbook (and it didn't matter which textbook they used).

Effect on Social Interaction An important part of cooperative learning programs is teaching students how to productively interact with one another, including how to ask relevant, leading questions and how to give group members cogent arguments and justifications for the explanations and help they offer. A team of researchers (Veenman, Denessen, van den Akker, & van der Rijt, 2005) examined whether pairs of students trained to interact in this way would use these skills more frequently to solve math problems than would student pairs not taught these skills. The study produced a somewhat unusual result: Although the students who received training made significantly more high level, or elaborative, responses when asking for and giving help on the math task than did the untrained students, they did so less frequently than they had before the training. Among the several explanations offered by the researchers, two appear to be particularly likely. First, the math problems that the students were given to solve were of the well-structured variety that we described in Chapter 10. This means that most students might have worked out a solution pretty much on their own, thereby reducing the need for elaborative discussions. A second possibility is that because the posttest problems were quite similar to the pretest problems, they required less effort to solve them. As one student put it: "The second time the problems were about the same as the first time; you still know how to solve them, and if you both know the answer, there is no need for an explanation" (p. 144). This finding highlights a point we have made in several previous chapters: All instructional practices and programs have their limits, and it pays to know what those limits are. The researchers also found that students who had prior experience with cooperative learning, whether or not they received specific, supplementary training in how to productively ask questions and provide assistance to a classmate, scored higher on the math task than students who had no prior exposure to cooperative learning.

Research has also shown that because average ability students are least likely to actively participate in group discussions (high ability students tend to take the lead), they are most in need of instruction in group interaction skills. Compared to average ability students in untrained groups, average ability students who were taught how to seek and give help engaged in more helping interactions and scored higher on achievement tests (Saleh, Lazonder, & De Jong, 2005).

Why Does Cooperative Learning Work?

When researchers attempt to explain the widespread positive effects that are typically found among studies of cooperative learning, they usually cite one or more of the following explanations (Slavin, 1995).

Motivational Effect The various features of cooperative learning, particularly positive interdependence, are highly motivating because they encourage such achieve- ment oriented behaviors as trying hard, attending class regularly, praising the efforts of others, and receiving help from one's group mates. Learning is seen as an obligation and a valued activity because the group's success is based on it and one's group mates will reward it (Ginsburg-Block, Rohrbeck, Lavigne, & Fantuzzo, 2008).

Cognitive Developmental Effect According to Lev Vygotsky, collaboration promotes cognitive growth because students model for each other more advanced ways of thinking than any would demonstrate individual- ly. According to Jean Piaget, collaboration among peers hastens the decline of egocentrism and allows the development of more advanced ways of understanding and dealing with the world. Research appears to sup- port both of these explanations, depending on how the group members interact, but that is not quite the end of the story. Recent research has suggested that con- tradictions or inconsistencies not resolved by the group stimulate later attempts by some participants to resolve the contradictions on their own (C. Howe, 2009).

Cognitive Elaboration Effect As we saw in the previ- ous discussion of information-processing theory, new information that is elaborated (restructured and related to existing knowledge) is more easily retrieved from memory than is information that is not elaborated. A particularly effective means of elaboration is explaining something to someone else (Ginsburg-Block, Rohrbeck, Lavigne, & Fantuzzo, 2008).

Now that you have read about the behavioral, cog- nitive, humanistic, and social approaches to instruction, take a few minutes to study Table 13.1. It summarizes the basic emphases of each approach and allows you to compare them for similarities and differences.

TABLE 13.1 Behavioral, Cognitive, Humanistic, and Social Approaches to Instruction

Behavioral (direct instruction)	Teacher presents information efficiently. Student accepts all information transmitted by teacher and text- book as accurate and potentially useful. Emphasis is on acquiring information in small units through clear presentations, practice, and corrective feedback, and gradually synthesizing the pieces into larger bodies of knowledge.
Cognitive (information-processing)	Teacher presents information and helps student to process it meaningfully. Student accepts all informa- tion transmitted by teacher and textbook as accurate and potentially useful. Emphasis is on understanding relationships among ideas and between ideas and prior knowledge, and on learning how to control one's cognitive processes effectively.
Cognitive (constructivist)	Teacher helps student to construct meaningful and adaptive knowledge structures by requiring student to engage in higher levels of thinking, such as classification, analysis, synthesis, and evaluation; providing scaffolded instruction within the zone of proximal development; embedding tasks in realistic contexts; pos- ing problems and tasks that cause uncertainty, doubt, and curiosity; exposing students to multiple points of view; and allowing students the time to formulate a consensus solution to a task or problem.
Humanistic	Teacher creates a classroom environment that addresses student's needs, helps student understand atti- tudes toward learning, promotes a positive self-concept in student, and communicates the belief that all students have value and can learn. Goal is to activate student's inherent desire to learn and grow.
Social	Teacher assigns students to small, heterogeneous groups and teaches them how to accomplish goals by working together. Each student is accountable for making a significant contribution to the achievement of the group goal. Because of its emphasis on peer collaboration, this approach is consistent with a social constructivist view of learning.

Using Technology to Support Social Approaches to Instruction

Social Constructivist Learning

Whereas the cognitive constructivist looks to find tools to help the child's mind actively construct relationships and ideas, the social constructivist looks as well for tools that help children negotiate ideas and findings in a community of peers. The social networking and media sharing websites that we mentioned in Chapter 3 (Twitter, Facebook, YouTube, and Flickr, for example), and that are collectively referred to as Web 2.0, may help teachers meet social constructivist goals. These sites allow teachers and students who share a common interest to work together on various school related projects. In addition, there are social networking sites that are specifically designed for educators. TeacherTube (www.teachertube.com), for example, contains video files, documents, audio files, photos, and blogs that teachers have posted and that other teachers can view, download, and comment on. Other sites that foster teacher collaboration are TeachAde (www.teachade .com), LearnCentral (www.learncentral.org), and We the Teachers (www.wetheteachers.com).

The claim that the quality and quantity of student learning increase when students are encouraged to be socially active, whether that be through social networking sites or some other form, is supported by a large number of studies. An analysis of the results from 122 studies (Lou, Abrami, & d'Apollonia, 2001) found that students whose computer-based instruction took place in the context of small group learning outscored students who worked alone at a computer by about 6 percentile ranks on individual tests of achievement. When the performance of the group as a whole was compared with that of students who worked alone, the difference increased to about 12 percentile ranks. In addition, students who worked on computer-based projects with other students exhibited more self-regulated learning behavior, greater persistence, and more positive attitudes toward group work and classmates as compared with students who worked on computers alone.

Cooperative and Collaborative Learning Cooperative learning is fairly well structured, with assigned roles, tasks, and procedures to help students learn material covered in a classroom setting; a related concept, **collaborative learning**, allows the students themselves to decide on their roles and use their individual areas of expertise to help investigate problems (Veermans & Cesareni, 2005). As noted throughout this book, with the emergence of the Internet and specifically Web 2.0 tools, there is no shortage of cooperative and collaborative learning opportunities. To cite just one example, consider the use of weblogs, or as they are more commonly known, blogs. A blog is basically a web-based version of a personal journal. What makes it different from the traditional journal is that it is intended to create an almost instantaneous dialogue with others who have an interest in the author's ideas. For example, students can post examples of their latest products, such as stories or research projects, or they can describe how new ideas have caused them to change the way they think about themselves and the world in which they live. A blog post may include

Cooperative Learning: High School History Lesson

TeachSource Video Case

Go to the Education CourseMate website and watch the video, study the artifacts in the case, and reflect upon the following questions:

1. How does this Video Case illustrate Vygotsky's theory of cognitive growth through collaboration?

2. Do you think the teacher's ad hoc learning groups are as effective as cooperative learning groups that are thoroughly planned in advance? Please explain your answer.

Using Blogs to Enhance Student Learning: An Interdisciplinary High School Unit

Go to the Education CourseMate website and watch the video, study the artifacts in the case, and reflect upon the following questions:

1. The blogs created by the students are graded for both content and grammatical structure. Do you agree with this approach or do you think it might inhibit students from writing creatively and about all their thoughts on the subject of genocide?

2. The history teacher in this video contends that the use of technology—doing online research and creating a blog—will cause the students to be more engaged in the topic. Using just your own experience, do you think the teacher is correct? Why? Could this goal be accomplished just as easily without the use of a blog?

drawings, photos, audio files, and video. Others (friends, teachers, parents, peers from halfway around the world) are then free to comment about the post as well as comment on the comments. In this fashion, all participants are exposed to different perspectives they may not have otherwise considered (Higdon & Topaz, 2009; D. Rosen & Nelson, 2008; Vogel, 2009).

Another way in which technology can be used to support cooperative and collaborative learning is through participation in virtual communities. Here are three of the many interesting opportunities that students and teachers have to enter into virtual communities with peers from other schools and countries and to share and discuss various data and ideas: ThinkQuest (www.thinkquest.org) is a website where

WHAT ELSE? *RIP & REVIEW* **CARDS IN THE BACK**

teachers and students can select curriculum-relevant projects, invite students from around the world to participate, and communicate with various message tools. The WEB Project (www.webproject.org) allows students to interact with and receive feedback from adult experts about works in progress. Art and music students, for example, get suggestions from artists, multimedia designers, musicians, and composers (Sherry & Billig, 2002). Last, the 4Directions project (www.4directions.org), which we mentioned in Chapter 5, allows Native American students in 10 states to interact with one another and with adult experts. They can, for example, discuss research ideas and career options with Native American professionals (Allen, Resta, & Christal, 2002).

14

ASSESSMENT OF CLASSROOM LEARNING

LEARNING OBJECTIVES

After studying this chapter, you will be able to . . .

LO1 Explain the various purposes of assessment and the kinds of evaluative judgments that derive from each purpose.

LO2 Provide examples of the different methods by which student learning can be assessed.

LO3 Explain the distinction between norm-referenced and criterion-referenced grading.

LO4 Provide examples of how technology can support assessment practices and evaluation practices, and how assessment information and evaluative judgments can be communicated effectively. ·

visit 4ltrpress.cengage.com

Earlier parts of this book discussed three major aspects of the teacher's role: understanding student differences and how to address them properly, understanding the learning process and how to use that knowledge to formulate effective approaches to instruction, and understanding motivation to learn and how to engage motivation to establish a positive learning environment. Now we turn to assessing performance, which is an equally significant aspect of the teacher's role. Virtually everyone connected with public schools, from students to teachers and administrators to state education officials to members of the U.S. Congress, is keenly interested in knowing how much and how well students have learned.

In this and the next chapter, we describe a twofold process for assessing student learning: using teacher-made measures to assess mastery of the teacher's specific objectives and using professionally prepared standardized tests to measure the extent of a student's general knowledge base and aptitudes. Although the items that make up teacher-made and standardized assessments can be very similar, if not identical, these two types of assessments differ significantly in their construction, the conditions under which they are administered, and the purposes for which they are used. In short, standardized tests are designed to highlight where students, classrooms, schools, and districts stand with respect to one another in terms of general levels of performance in various skills and subject areas. Period. Think of this as assessment *of* learning. Teacher-made assessments, by contrast, are designed to highlight students' strengths and weaknesses, to give students timely feedback about the effectiveness of their study habits, and to provide teachers with timely information that can help them make more effective instructional decisions. These assessments may or may not look like traditional tests. Think of them as assessment *for* learning (Stiggins, 2007).

LO1 The Role of Assessment in Teaching

The role of assessment is to enhance learning. Therefore, assessment is both integral and critical to effective teaching. To help a student learn, a teacher must know what the student knows and is able to do. To determine if a lesson worked, a teacher must know if learning objectives were met. We have examined a number of theories throughout this book to see how they apply to teaching. In order to apply those ideas, however, you will need to assess student learning. Consider, for a moment, the discussion in Chapter 2 of the Vygotskian zone of proximal development. Suppose, as a teacher, you decide that scaffolding—which research has shown to be an effective teaching strategy—should be employed to help your students learn. In order to scaffold a student's learning, you will first need to know the student's zone of proximal development; you will need to assess the student's knowledge and understanding in order to determine what the student knows and can do alone in order to determine the target of the necessary scaffolding. Assessment yields information about learning. Said another way, assessment informs learning. Because teaching is an effort to enhance learning, assessment also informs teaching.

Assessing student learning is a task that many teachers dislike and few do extremely well. One reason is that many lack in-depth knowledge of assessment principles (Guskey, 2003; Stiggins, 2002; Trevisan, 2002). Another reason is that the role of assessor is seen as being inconsistent with the role of teacher (or helper). A third reason is that many teachers think of assessment as merely grading rather than as instruction (a misconception we will address shortly). As a consequence, high quality assessment practices are too often not part of the culture of classrooms (Moss & Brookhart, 2009). This is unfortunate because, in fact, well-designed classroom assessment schemes contribute to student learning (Popham, 2006, 2011; Stiggins, 2002; Stiggins, Arter, Chappuis, & Chappuis, 2007).

A basic goal of this chapter is to help you understand how to use knowledge about assessment to enhance, rather than work against, your effectiveness as teacher. Toward that end, we will begin by defining what we mean by the term *assessment* and by two key elements of this process: *measurement* and *evaluation*.

What Is Assessment?

Broadly conceived, classroom assessment involves two major types of activities: first, collecting information about how much knowledge and skill students have learned (measurement); and then, making judgments about the adequacy or acceptability of each student's level of learning (evaluation). Some teachers, focusing heavily on the judgments they must make, tend to overlook the measurements that are used to make those judgments and how such information can help them teach more effectively. Those are the teachers that tend to think "grading" when they hear the word *assessment*. But as we will see, both aspects of classroom assessment are critical to understanding student learning, and understanding student learning is critical to enhancing student learning.

Both measurement and evaluation activities can be accomplished in a number of ways. The most common ways that teachers measure learning is to have students take quizzes or exams, respond to oral questions, do homework exercises, write papers, solve problems, create products, and make oral presentations. Teachers can then evaluate the scores (i.e., the measurements taken) from those activities by comparing them either with one another or with an absolute standard (such as an A equals 90% correct). In this chapter, we will explain and illustrate the various ways in which you can measure and evaluate student learning with assessments that you create and administer regularly in your classroom (Airasian & Russell, 2008; Nitko & Brookhart, 2011).

Measurement For educational purposes, **measurement** is defined as the assignment of either a number (such as the score from a test) or a rating (such as the designation "excellent" or "exceeds standards" from a performance assessment) to certain attributes of people according to a rule-governed system. For example, we can measure someone's level of keyboarding proficiency by counting the number of words the person accurately types per minute. For an oral presentation, we might measure the quality by using a guide called a scoring rubric (Arter & Chappuis, 2008). In a classroom or other group situation, the rules that are used to assign the numbers or provide the rating ordinarily create a ranking that reflects how much of the attribute different people possess (Airasian & Russell, 2008; Nitko & Brookhart, 2011).

© flyfloor/iStockphoto

Evaluation Although related to measurement, evaluation is a distinct process that makes use of measurements. **Evaluation** involves using a rule-governed system to make judgments about the value or worth of a set of measures (Airasian & Russell, 2008; Nitko & Brookhart, 2011). What does it mean, for example, to say that a student answered 80 out of 100 earth science questions correctly? Depending on the rules that are used, it could mean that the student has learned that body of knowledge exceedingly well and is ready to progress to the next unit of instruction or, conversely, that the student has significant knowledge gaps and requires additional instruction.

Why Should We Assess Students' Learning?

As implied earlier, the short answer to the question of why to assess student learning is: To enhance student learning. Although that simple answer frames assessment as crucial to student learning—and it is—it leads to other questions about how to use assessment to enhance learning. There are two general ways in which assessment data (measurements) can be used to make judgments (evaluations). Thus, there are two kinds of evaluative judgments: summative and formative.

The distinction between summative and formative evaluation originated in the work of Michael Scriven (1967). In the years since Scriven described how assessment serves different evaluative purposes, research on classroom assessment has evolved from an emphasis on the technical aspects of assessment (called psychometric theory) to research on how assessment practice contributes to a wide range of developmental, learning, and especially motivational outcomes for students. As a consequence of this shift, the terms *summative* and *formative evaluation* have been replaced by *summative* and *formative assessment* (Brookhart, 2009a).

After briefly describing summative and formative assessment, we will compare and contrast the two uses of assessment information in order to focus on assessment that can guide classroom teaching and learning day to day, hour to hour, or even minute to minute.

Summative Assessment (Assessment *of* Learning)

The first, and probably most obvious, reason for assessment is to provide to all interested parties a clear, meaningful, and useful summary or accounting of how well a student has met the teacher's objectives. When testing is done for the purpose of assigning a letter or numerical grade, it is often called **summative assessment** because its primary purpose is to provide an assessment *of* learning, to sum up how well a student has performed over time and at a variety of tasks.

Formative Assessment (Assessment *for* Learning)

A second reason for assessing students is to monitor their progress. The main things that teachers want to know from time to time are whether students are keeping up with the pace of instruction and are understanding all of the material that has been covered so far. For students whose pace of learning is either slower or faster than average, or whose understanding of certain ideas is faulty, instructional accommodations may be needed (recall the techniques discussed in Chapter 6). Because the purpose of such assessment is to facilitate, or form, learning and not to assign a grade, it is usually called **formative assessment**.

Assessment of *Learning Compared to Assessment* for *Learning*

A number of scholars have referred to assessment that leads to summative judgments as "assessment *of* learning" and assessment that is used to make formative judgments as "assessment *for* learning" (Moss & Brookhart, 2009; Stiggins, 2002, 2007; Tomlinson, 2007/2008). Two of these scholars, Connie Moss and Susan Brookhart, are with the Center for Advancing the Study of Teaching and Learning in the School of Education at Duquesne University. They have been conducting research for several years on how assessment practices advance teaching and learning. It is important to note that their research has been conducted *with* teachers, administrators and students in the Armstrong School District in Pennsylvania. Because they have worked closely with practicing educators, their conclusions are informed by practicing educators. Table 14.1 is based on Moss and Brookhart's work (2009): how they compare and contrast the characteristics of assessment *of* learning and assessment *for* learning.

The distinctions between summative assessment and formative assessment in Table 14.1 help us see that the process of assessment—first measuring and then evaluating—is tied closely to the underlying reason or purpose for assessing. As we will see later in this chapter (and in Chapter 15), summative assessment is not only legitimate, it is necessary. As a teacher, you will be required to assign grades to assignments, performances, quizzes, and tests. You will also be required to examine the grades that you have assigned to each assignment, each performance, each quiz, and each test and issue a summary judgment: a final grade for a course or a grading period—a summative assessment *of* learning.

Along the way to those summative assessments *of* learning, you will be engaged in helping students meet the learning goals and objectives that define successful learning in your classroom. That is where formative assessment comes into play. Formative assessments are conducted more or less continuously during an instructional unit, using both formal and informal assessment techniques. Periodic quizzes, homework assignments, in-class worksheets, oral readings, responses to teacher questions, and behavioral observations are all examples of formative assessments—if the results are used to generate timely feedback about what students have learned, what the source of any problems might be, and what might be done to prevent small problems from becoming major ones later in the year. Unlike summative assessment, which is a one-time event conducted only after instruction is finished, formative assessment has a more dynamic, ongoing, interactive relationship with teaching. The results of formative assessments affect instruction, which affects subsequent

summative assessment Testing done for the purpose of assigning a letter or numerical grade to sum up a student's performance at a variety of tasks over time.

formative assessment A type of assessment that monitors a student's progress in order to facilitate learning rather than to assign a grade. Also called *formative evaluation*.

TABLE 14.1 Characteristics That Distinguish Summative and Formative Assessment

Assessment *of* Learning (Summative Assessment)	Assessment *for* Learning (Formative Assessment)
Purpose is to summarize and audit learning	Purpose is to improve student learning
Conducted periodically to capture what learning has occurred	Conducted continuously while learning is in progress
Focus is on products of learning	Focus is on learning in process
Often perceived as an activity that occurs after the teaching–learning process has finished	Perceived as integral to the teaching–learning process
Teacher directed	Collaboration of teacher and student
Performance measures (e.g., scores on an exam) show where a student has arrived	Performance measures (e.g., scores on an exam) show a student's journey
Teachers use evidence to make a summary decision about success or failure (e.g., grades)	Teachers and students use evidence to make adjustments
Teachers take on the role of auditor; students are the audited	Teachers join with students as "intentional learners"

SOURCE: Adapted from Moss & Brookhart (2009).

Classroom assessments can provide both summative and formative information. The former—assessments *of* learning—can tell the teacher (and others) what knowledge and skills a student has acquired. The latter—assessments *for* learning—can tell the teacher and the student what adjustments need to be made in order to take the next steps for the student's learning.

performance, and so on. Think back to our discussion of response to intervention (RTI) in Chapter 6. The RTI approach is sometimes characterized as "teach–test–teach." The teacher instructs (or intervenes to help the student learn), student learning is measured and evaluated (to see if the intervention worked), and the teacher then modifies instruction based on the assessment. RTI can be thought of as a type of formative assessment.

Assessment as Learning Moss & Brookhart (2009) defined formative assessment as "an active and intentional learning process that partners the teacher and the students to continuously and systematically gather evidence of learning with the express goal of improving student achievement" (p. 6). In other words, they view assessment *for* learning as learning. Their claim is that unless both students and teachers are learning from the process, formative assessment is not occurring in the classroom. Whatever is happening might be something like formative assessment, but true formative assessment requires that the teacher and students are learning with the intention to improve student achievement. Their argument is that assessment *for* learning is successful only when teachers and students are becoming better and better because they are learning from their assessment activities in the classroom.

As we have indicated, learning about assessment is necessary to becoming an effective teacher. Mistilina

Sato, Ruth Chung Wei, and Linda Darling-Hammond (2008), for example, studied how the assessment practices of math and science teachers changed as a function of pursuing National Board Certification. Teachers who are candidates for certification by the National Board for Professional Teaching Standards go through an extensive assessment procedure and, at the end of the process, a summative judgment about whether they have or have not met the standards of the National Board. One becomes a National Board Certified Teacher or one does not. When teachers who sought National Board Certification were compared with those who did not, the authors found significant differences. National Board candidates exhibited substantial changes "in the variety of assessments used and the way assessment information was used to support student learning. National Board candidates attributed changes in practice to the National Board standards and assessment tasks" (Sato, Wei, & Darling-Hammond, p. 669). In being assessed themselves, the teachers learned how to improve their assessment practices with their own students. Thinking back to Moss and Brookhart's view of formative assessment, it is critical that assessment informs learning of both teachers and students.

In an essay entitled "Learning to Love Assessment," Carol Ann Tomlinson (2007/2008) reflected on her long teaching career and, in particular, what she learned about and from the practice of classroom assessment. She concluded her essay as follows:

Lorna Earl (2003) distinguishes between assessment of *learning, assessment* for *learning, and assessment* as *learning. In many ways, my growth as a teacher slowly and imperfectly followed that progression. I began by seeing assessment as judging performance, then as informing teaching, and finally as informing learning. In reality, all those perspectives play a role in effective teaching. The key is where we place the emphasis.*

Certainly a teacher and his or her students need to know who reaches (and exceeds) important learning targets, thus summative assessment, or assessment of *learning, has a place in teaching. Robust learning generally requires robust teaching, and both diagnostic and formative assessments, or assessments* for *learning, are catalysts for better teaching. In the end, however, when assessment is seen as learning for students as well as for teachers, it becomes most informative and generative for students and teachers alike. (p. 13)*

Having made the argument that assessment is integral to teaching and critical for learning, we turn first to ways of measuring student learning and then to ways of evaluating student learning.

LO2 Ways to Measure Student Learning

Just as measurement can play several roles in the class-room, teachers have several ways to measure what students have learned. Which type of measure you choose will depend, of course, on the objectives you have stated. For the purposes of this discussion, objectives can be classified in terms of two broad categories: knowing *about* something (for example, that knots are used to secure objects, that dance is a form of social expression, that microscopes are used to study things too small to be seen by the naked eye) and knowing *how to do* something (for example, tie a square knot, dance the waltz, operate a microscope). Measures that attempt to assess the range and accuracy of some-one's knowledge are usually called *written tests*. And measures that attempt to assess how well somebody can do something are often referred to as *performance assessments*. Keep in mind that both types have a legit-imate place in a teacher's assessment repertoire. Which type is used, and to what extent, will depend on the purpose or purposes you have for assessing students. In the next two sections, we will briefly examine the nature of both types.

Pause & Reflect *Over the past 10 to 12 years, you have taken probably hundreds of classroom tests. What types of tests best reflected what you learned? Why?*

Written Tests

As we indicated at the beginning of this chapter, teach-ers spend a substantial part of each day assessing stu-dent learning, and much of this assessment activity involves giving and scoring some type of written test. Most written tests are composed of one or more of the following categories and item types: *selected response* (multiple choice, true–false, and matching) and *con-structed response* (short answer and essay). In all likeli-hood, you have taken hundreds of these types of tests in your school career thus far.

{ **Written tests measure the degree of knowledge about a subject.** }

In the next couple of pages, we will briefly describe the main features, advantages, and disadvantages of each test. As you read, bear in mind that what we said about the usefulness of both written tests and perfor-mance assessments applies here as well. No one type

of written test will be equally useful for all purposes. You are more likely to draw correct inferences about students' capabilities by using a variety of selected and constructed-response items.

Selected-Response Tests Selected-response tests are so named because the student reads a relatively brief opening statement (called a stem) and selects one of the provided alternatives as the correct answer. Selected-response tests are typically made up of multiple-choice, true–false, or matching items. Quite often all three item types are used in a single test. Although guidelines exist for writing selected-response items (see, for example, the 31 guidelines for writing multiple-choice items discussed by Haladyna, Downing, & Rodriguez, 2002), many of these guidelines have not been validated by research. Hence, test-item writing is currently as much an art as a science.

> **Selected-response tests are objectively scored and efficient but usually measure lower levels of learning and do not reveal what students can do.**

Characteristics Selected-response tests are some-times called *objective* tests because they have a simple and set scoring system. If alternative B of a multiple-choice item is keyed as the correct response and the student chooses alternative D, the student's answer is marked wrong, and the teacher's desire for a correct response cannot change the result. Selected-response tests are typically used when the primary goal is to assess what might be called *foundational knowledge*. This knowledge comprises the basic factual informa-tion and cognitive skills that students need in order to do such high level tasks as solve problems and create products (Stiggins, 2007).

Advantages A major advantage of selected-response tests is efficiency: A teacher can ask many questions in a short period of time. Another advantage is ease and reliability of scoring. With the aid of a scoring template (such as a multiple-choice answer sheet that has holes punched out where the correct answer is located), many tests can be quickly and uniformly scored. Moreover, there is some evidence that selected-response tests, when well written, can measure higher level cognitive skills as effectively as constructed-response tests (Nitko & Brookhart, 2011; Stiggins, 2007).

Disadvantages Because items that reflect the lowest level of Bloom's taxonomy (verbatim knowledge) are the easiest to write, most teacher-made tests (and many standardized tests as well) are composed almost entirely of knowledge-level items (a point we made initially in Chapter 13). As a result, students focus on verbatim memorization rather than on meaningful learning. Another disadvantage is that, although we get some indication of what students know, such tests reveal nothing about what students can do with that knowledge. A third disadvantage is that heavy or exclusive use of selected-response tests leads students to believe that learning is merely the accumulation of universally agreed upon facts (Nitko & Brookhart, 2011; Martinez, 1999).

Short-Answer Tests As their name implies, short-answer tests require a brief written response from the student.

Characteristics Instead of *selecting* from one or more alternatives, the student is asked to *supply* from memory a brief answer consisting of a name, word, phrase, or symbol. Like selected-response tests, short-answer tests can be scored quickly, accurately, and consistently, thereby giving them an aura of objectivity. They are primarily used for measuring foundational knowledge.

Advantages Short-answer items are relatively easy to write, so a test, or part of one, can be constructed fairly quickly. They allow either broad or in-depth assessment of foundational knowledge because students can respond to many items within a short space of time. Because students have to supply an answer, they have to recall, rather than recognize, information.

> **Short-answer tests are easy to write but measure lower levels of learning.**

Disadvantages Short-answer tests have the same basic disadvantages as selected-response tests. Because short-answer items ask only for short verbatim answers, students are likely to limit their processing to that level; thus these items provide no information about how well students can use what they have learned. In addition, unexpected but plausible answers may be difficult to score.

Essay Tests Essay items require students to organize a set of ideas and write a somewhat lengthy response to a broad question.

Characteristics The student is given a somewhat general directive to discuss one or more related ideas according to certain criteria. An example of an essay question is, "Compare operant conditioning theory and information-processing theory in terms of basic assumptions, typical research findings, and classroom applications."

Advantages Essay tests reveal how well students can recall, organize, and clearly communicate previously learned information. When well written, essay tests call on such higher level abilities as analysis, synthesis, and evaluation. Because of these demands, students are more likely to try to meaningfully learn the material on which they are tested (Nitko & Brookhart, 2011; Stiggins, 2007).

Disadvantages Consistency of grading is likely to be a problem. Two students may have essentially similar responses yet receive different letter or numerical grades because of differences in vocabulary, grammar, and style. These test items are also very time consuming to grade. And because it takes time for students to formulate and write responses, only a few questions at most can be given (Nitko & Brookhart, 2011; Liu, 2010). But recent developments in essay scoring by computer programs may drastically reduce or even eliminate these disadvantages in the near future (Myers, 2003).

Constructing a Useful Test Understanding the characteristics, advantages, and disadvantages of different types of written test and knowing how to write such test items are necessary but not sufficient conditions for creating an instructionally useful test. James Popham (2006, 2011), a noted measurement scholar, maintains that a useful classroom test has the following five attributes:

- *Significance.* The test measures worthwhile skills (such as the last four levels of Bloom's taxonomy—application, analysis, synthesis, and evaluation) and substantial bodies of important knowledge.

- *Teachability.* Effective instruction can help students acquire the skills and knowledge measured by the test.

- *Describability.* The skills and knowledge measured by the test can be described with sufficient clarity that they make instructional planning easier.

- *Reportability.* The test produces results that allow a teacher to identify areas of instruction that were probably inadequate.

- *Nonintrusiveness.* The test does not take an excessive amount of time away from instruction.

Performance Assessments

In recent years, many teachers, learning theorists, and measurement experts have argued that the typical

Performance assessments provide students the opportunity to demonstrate what they can do with what they know.

David Young-Wolff/Getty Images

performance assessment An assessment device that attempts to gauge how well students can use basic knowledge and skill to perform complex tasks or solve problems under more or less realistic conditions. Also called *performance-based assessment* and *authentic assessment*.

portfolio A collection of one or more pieces of a person's work, some of which typically demonstrate different stages of completion.

of knowledge and skills over an extended period of time to complete a task or solve a problem under more or less realistic conditions. At the low end of the realism spectrum, students may be asked to construct a map, interpret a graph, or write an essay under highly standardized conditions. Everyone in the class completes the same task in the same amount of time and under the same conditions. At the high end of the realism spectrum, students may be asked to conduct a science experiment, produce a painting, or write an essay under conditions that are similar to those of real life. For example, students may be told to produce a compare-and-contrast essay on a particular topic by a certain date, but the resources they choose to use, the number of revisions they make, and the schedule on which they work on the essay are left unspecified. When performance assessment is conducted under such realistic conditions, it is also called *authentic assessment* (Nitko & Brookhart, 2011; Gronlund & Waugh, 2009; Janesick, 2001).

Perhaps the clearest way to distinguish between traditional paper-and-pencil tests (such as multiple-choice tests) and performance assessments is to say that the former measure how much students know, whereas the latter measure what students can do with what they know. In the sections that follow, we will define four different types of performance assessments and then look at their most important characteristics.

Types of Performance Assessments There are four ways in which the performance capabilities of students are typically assessed: direct writing assessments, portfolios, exhibitions, and demonstrations.

Direct Writing Assessments Students are asked to write about a specific topic ("Describe the person whom you admire the most, and explain why you admire that person") under a standard set of conditions. Each essay is then scored by two or more people according to a set of defined criteria.

Portfolios A **portfolio** contains one or more pieces of a student's work, some of which demonstrate different stages of completion. For example, a student's writing portfolio may contain business letters; pieces of fiction; poetry; and an outline, rough draft, and final draft of a research paper. Through the inclusion of various stages of a research paper, both the process and the end product can be assessed. Portfolios can also be constructed for

written test should be used far less often than it is because it reveals little or nothing of the depth of students' knowledge and the ways students use their knowledge to work through questions, problems, and tasks. These individuals argue that because we are living in a more complex and rapidly changing world than was the case a generation ago, schools can no longer be content to hold students accountable for just how well they can learn, store, and retrieve information in more or less verbatim form. Instead, we need to teach and assess students for such capabilities as framing problems, formulating and carrying out plans, generating hypotheses, finding information that is relevant to the solution to a problem, and working cooperatively with others, because those are the types of skills that are necessary to cope successfully with the demands of life after school in the twenty-first century (Calfee, 2009; Cunningham, 2001; Fredrick, 2009).

In addition, the learning standards of such professional groups as the National Council of Teachers of Mathematics (http://standards.nctm.org), the National Council for the Social Studies (www.socialstudies.org/standards), the National Council of Teachers of English (www.ncte.org/standards), and the National Research Council (www.nap.edu/catalog/10256.html) call for students to develop a sufficiently deep understanding of subject matter that they can demonstrate their knowledge in socially relevant ways. One way to address these concerns is to use performance assessments.

What Are Performance Assessments? **Performance assessments** require students to use a wide range

math and science, as well as for projects that combine two or more subject areas.

Either the student alone or the student in consultation with the teacher decides what is to be included in the portfolio. The portfolio is sometimes used as a showcase to illustrate exemplary pieces, but it also works well as a collection of pieces that represent a student's typical performances. In its best and truest sense, the portfolio functions not just as a housing for these performances but also as a means of self-expression, self-reflection, and self-analysis for an individual student (Chang, 2009; Lam & Lee, 2010).

Exhibitions Exhibitions involve just what the label suggests: a showing of such products as paintings, drawings, photographs, sculptures, videos, and models. As with direct writing assessments and portfolios, the products a student chooses to exhibit are evaluated according to a predetermined set of criteria.

Demonstrations In a demonstration, students are required to show how well they can use previously learned knowledge or skills to solve a somewhat unique problem (such as conducting a scientific inquiry to answer a question, interpreting a graph, or diagnosing the cause of a malfunctioning engine and describing the best procedure for fixing it) or to perform a task (such as reciting a poem, performing a dance, or playing a piece of music). Figure 14.1 shows a performance item for graph interpretation, the partially correct response of a student, and the corrective feedback offered by two classmates.

Characteristics of Performance Assessments

Performance assessments are different from traditional written tests in that they require the student to make an active response, are more like everyday tasks, contain problems that involve many variables, are closely related to earlier instructional activities, use scoring guides that clearly specify the criteria against which responses will be evaluated, emphasize formative assessment, and are probably more responsive to cultural diversity.

Emphasis on Active Responding As we pointed out previously, the goal of performance assessment is to gain some insight into how competently students can carry out various tasks. Consequently, such tests focus on processes (that is, the underlying skills that go into a performance), products (observable outcomes, such as a speech or a painting), or both. For example, an instrumental music teacher may want to know whether students can apply their knowledge of music technique and theory to use the correct fingering and dynamics when playing a woodwind or piano (R. E. Clark, 2002).

Degree of Realism Although performance assessments strive to approximate everyday tasks, not every test needs to be—or can be—done under the most realistic circumstances. How realistic the conditions should be depends on such factors as time, cost, availability of equipment, and the nature of the skill being measured. Imagine, for example, that you are a third grade teacher and that one of your objectives is that students will be able to determine how much change they should receive after making a purchase in a store. If this is a relatively minor objective or if you do not have a lot of props available, you might simply demonstrate the situation with actual money and ask the students to judge whether the amount of change received was correct. If, however, you consider this to be a major objective and

 Portfolio Assessment: Elementary Classroom

Go to the Education CourseMate website and watch the video, study the artifacts in the case, and reflect upon the following questions:

1. Portfolios can be time consuming for teachers to develop and grade. Based on this Video Case, do you think that using portfolios would be worth the extra time and effort? Explain your answer.

2. Based on this Video Case, why might some teachers find portfolios to be a more accurate representation of student abilities (as compared with other forms of assessment)?

TeachSource Video Case

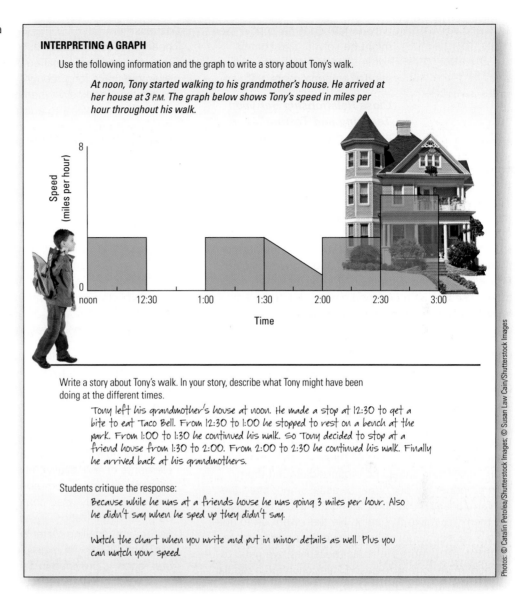

FIGURE 14.1 Example of a Performance Assessment: Interpreting a Graph

SOURCE: Parke & Lane (1997).

INTERPRETING A GRAPH

Use the following information and the graph to write a story about Tony's walk.

At noon, Tony started walking to his grandmother's house. He arrived at her house at 3 P.M. The graph below shows Tony's speed in miles per hour throughout his walk.

Write a story about Tony's walk. In your story, describe what Tony might have been doing at the different times.

> Tony left his grandmother's house at noon. He made a stop at 12:30 to get a bite to eat Taco Bell. From 12:30 to 1:00 he stopped to rest on a bench at the park. From 1:00 to 1:30 he continued his walk. So Tony decided to stop at a friend house from 1:30 to 2:00. From 2:00 to 2:30 he continued his walk. Finally he arrived back at his grandmothers.

Students critique the response:

> Because while he was at a friends house he was going 3 miles per hour. Also he didn't say when he sped up they didn't say.
>
> Watch the chart when you write and put in minor details as well. Plus you can watch your speed.

you have the props available, you might set up a mock store and have each student make a purchase using real money (Gronlund & Waugh, 2009).

An example of a task that is realistic in content and intellectual demands but not in its setting (it takes place in the classroom) is "Read All About It!" Playing the roles of newspaper staff writers and editorial board members, students put together a special series for their local newspaper that compares and contrasts the five major wars in which the United States was involved during the 1900s (World War I, World War II, Korean War, Vietnam War, and Persian Gulf War). Writing assignments include feature articles, opinion columns, and letters to the editor. Editorial responsibilities include story editor, photo editor, mock-up editor, layout editor, and copy editor (Moon, 2002).

Emphasis on Complex Problems To assess how well students can use foundational knowledge and skills in a productive way, the questions and problems they are given should be sufficiently open-ended and ill structured (Stiggins, 2007). The problems contained in the Quest Atlantis program that we described in earlier chapters are good examples of complex and somewhat ill-structured tasks. They have several interrelated parts,

> ## Performance tests may vary in degree of realism.

rubric A scoring guide used in performance assessment that helps define and clarify levels of student performance from poor to exemplary.

provide few cues as to how they might be solved, and contain some uncertainty about what constitutes an appropriate solution.

Close Relationship Between Teaching and Testing All too often students walk out of an exam in a state of high frustration (if not anger) because the content and format of the test seemed to have little in common with what was covered in class and how it was taught. It's the old story of teaching for one thing and testing for something else. Performance assessment strives for a closer match between teaching and testing. Often a performance assessment can be a variation or extension of a task used during instruction. For example, the mock store assessment mentioned earlier could follow an instructional activity in which students practiced making change.

This close relationship between assessment and instruction is not automatic, however; the teacher must deliberately establish it. For example, if in giving an oral book report a student is expected to speak loudly and clearly enough for everyone to hear, speak in complete sentences, stay on the topic, and use pictures or other materials to make the presentation interesting, the student needs to be informed of these criteria, and classroom instruction should be organized around them. One proponent of performance assessment cited the old farm adage "You don't fatten the cattle by weighing them" to make this point. He then went on to note, "If we expect students to improve their performance on these new, more authentic measures, we need to engage in 'performance-based instruction' on a regular basis" (McTighe, 1996/1997, p. 7).

By the same token, the assessment of students' performances should be limited to just the criteria emphasized during instruction (Nitko & Brookhart, 2011). One reason that proponents of performance

assessment push for this feature is that it has always been a standard part of successful programs in sports, the arts, and vocational education. Football coaches, for example, have long recognized that if they want their quarterback to know when during a game (the equivalent of a final exam) to attempt a pass and when not to, they must provide realistic opportunities for the quarterback to practice making this particular type of decision. Perhaps you recall our mentioning in Chapter 10 that realistic and varied practice are essential if students are to transfer what they learn in an instructional setting to an applied setting.

Pause&Reflect *Have you ever taken any kind of performance assessment as a student? Did you feel that it accurately reflected what you had learned? To what extent would you use performance measures for such academic subjects as writing, math, science, and social studies? Why?*

Use of Scoring Rubrics A **rubric** is a scoring guide that specifies the capabilities students should exhibit (also known as content standards), describes the qualitative levels or categories into which the responses will be sorted (also known as performance standards), and specifies how the responses will be scored (as separate elements or holistically). For writing tasks, which are probably the most common performance assessments, some commonly used content criteria are clarity of purpose, organization, voice, word choice, grammatical usage, and spelling (Arter & Chappuis, 2008; Arter & McTighe, 2001). An example of a scoring rubric for an oral report is provided in Table 14.2.

Creating and using scoring rubrics and providing them to students at the beginning of a task are highly desirable for at least three reasons:

1. They increase the objectivity, consistency, and efficiency of scoring.

TABLE 14.2 Scoring Rubric for a Group Oral Presentation

Level	Content	Audiovisual Components	Group Members	Audience Members
Excellent	Accurate, specific, research based, retold in own words	Are unique, add to presentation quality of materials used, are neat, present a clear message	All equally involved in presentation and well informed about the topic	Maintain eye contact with presenters, ask many questions
Good	Less detailed, lacking depth, using a limited number of sources	Support topic but do not enhance presentation, exhibit some attempts at originality, present a clear message	Most are active; most are informed about the topic	Some not attending; ask limited or off-topic questions
Minimal	Limited information, general, straying from topic, not presented in own words	Inappropriate, no originality, detract from presentation, present a confusing message	One or two dominate; some do not seem well prepared or well informed	Not attending; ask no questions or off-topic questions

SOURCE: K. Montgomery (2000).

Chapter 14: Assessment of Classroom Learning

2. They help teachers match their instructional activities to the demands of the performance measure, the goal we discussed in the previous section.

3. They provide students with verbal descriptions and examples of the desired performance or product, allowing teachers to clearly communicate to students the types of behaviors that represent the range from unacceptable to exceptional performance and help students better monitor their progress and make productive changes in the quality of their work (Arter & Chappuis, 2008; Whittaker, Salend, & Duhaney, 2001). Students with learning disabilities are likely to experience the greatest benefit from being given a scoring rubric and being shown how to use it (Heacox, 2009; A. W. Jackson & Larkin, 2002).

Bear in mind, however, that scoring rubrics have their limitations. Although the rubrics used by two teachers to score writing samples may have some of the same content standards (such as clarity of purpose, organization, and grammar), they may differ as well (for instance, in the presence or absence of idea development, use of detail, and figurative use of language), because there are different ways to define good writing. Thus any one rubric is not likely to represent the domain of writing fully and may provide few or no opportunities for scorers to reward certain desirable writing skills (Osborn Popp, Ryan, & Thompson, 2009).

Use of Formative Assessment As we pointed out earlier, and as we will see in this chapter's Case in Print, tests can be used as a source of feedback to help students improve the quality of their learning efforts. Because many real-life performances and products are the result of several feedback and revision cycles,

performance assessment often includes this feature as well. Anyone who has ever done any substantial amount of writing can tell you (and we are no exception): A satisfactory essay, story, or even personal letter is not produced in one attempt. Usually, there are critical comments from oneself and others and subsequent attempts at another draft. If we believe that the ability to write well, even among people who do it for a living, is partly defined by the ability to use feedback profitably, why should this be any different for students (Stiggins, 2001)? Some specific forms of formative assessment are dress rehearsals, reviews of writing drafts, and peer response groups (Gronlund & Waugh, 2009).

Responsiveness to Cultural Diversity Traditional written tests have been criticized over the years for being culturally biased. That is, they are thought to underestimate the capabilities of many ethnic minority students, as well as students of low socioeconomic status, because they rely on a narrow range of item types (mainly selected response) and on content that mostly reflects the experiences of the majority culture (C. C. Johnson & Fargo, 2010; Stobart, 2005; J. Wang, Spalding, Odell, Klecka, & Lin, 2010). This criticism is based in large part on the constructivist view of learning: that meaningful learning occurs within a cultural context with which one is familiar and comfortable. If this is so, say the critics, then tests should be more consistent with the cultural context in which learning occurs. Performance assessments have been promoted as a way to assess more fairly and accurately the knowledge and skills of all students, and particularly minority students, because of their realism (including group problem solving) and closer relationship between instruction and assessment (H. Hart, 2009; Santamaria, 2009).

 # Performance Assessment: Student Presentation

Go to the Education CourseMate website and watch the video, study the artifacts in the case, and reflect upon the following questions:

1. During each presentation in Ms. Mosman's class, students assess their peers' performance. How do the peer assessments contribute to the learning of both the presenters and the assessors?

2. In this Video Case, Ms. Mosman claims that performance assessment allows students to demonstrate their learning in ways that tests may not. How do such demonstrations affect student learning and motivation?

TeachSource Video Case

Challenging Assumptions

Practice Assessment for Learning

The classroom assessments that teachers devise are among the most powerful influences on the quality of students' learning, largely due to their effect on self-efficacy, interest, and the types of learning strategies that students construct. Whether these assessments have positive or negative effects on students depends on how they are constructed and what purpose they are primarily intended for.

As we have noted in this and other chapters, classroom assessments can be used both to sum up what students have learned (summative assessment) and to provide information about the effectiveness of instruction and students' specific strengths and weaknesses (formative assessment). All too often, unfortunately, the formative type of assessment tends to be overshadowed by the summative type.

Many teachers are more concerned with giving students grades than with using information gained from assessment to improve their instruction. Although both types of assessment are legitimate, we encourage you to emphasize formative assessment because of its potential to positively shape students' learning.

To ensure that assessments serve as a positive force for learning, we believe teachers should take the following steps:

- Make sure that you are knowledgeable about, understand, and use the basic measurement concepts and practices described in this chapter. Don't fall into the trap that so many teachers have fallen into of treating classroom assessment as a necessary evil.

- Recognize that the most accurate and useful assessments of learning are composed of multiple and varied measures. Use the full range of assessments (written tests, performance assessments, checklists, rating scales) available to you.

- Align the content of your assessments with your objectives, and fully inform students about the content and demands of your assessments.

- Finally, use the results to learn how to work even more productively with your students.

What Do You Think?

Have you been in classes in which formative assessment was downplayed in favor of summative assessment? If so, what effect did that have on your motivation to learn? If not, how did the emphasis on formative assessment affect you?

Some Concerns About Performance Assessments

There is no question that alternative assessment methods have excited educators and will be used with increasing frequency. But some of the same features that make these new assessment methods attractive also create problems. One problem concerns the increased emphasis on standardized tests. Standardized tests are typically used as summative assessments (assessments *of* learning). They are given at the end of the academic year and are used solely to rank and compare students, schools, and school districts. Performance-based classroom tests, on the other hand, lend themselves to formative assessment (assessment *for* leaning). They are given periodically to provide teachers, students, and parents with relevant information about the current level of student learning and to generate ideas about how performance might be improved. The challenge for the teachers is not to let the school district's preoccupation with high stakes tests (those on which poor performance has significant consequences for students, teachers, and administrators) crowd out their use of performance-based tests for formative evaluation purposes (Hargreaves, Earl, & Schmidt, 2002; Nichols & Berliner, 2007).

There are also questions about the reliability (how consistently the test performs) and validity (how accurately the test measures its target) of performance measures (Bachman, 2002). Susan Brookhart (2009b) described the "sort of" phenomenon that can occur with performance assessments: In such a case the performance "sort of taps a learning outcome but also requires extraneous skills or doesn't require all of the relevant skills" (p. 59). To illustrate, imagine a teacher who required her students to create and then perform a skit in order to demonstrate their understanding of a chapter in a novel the class was studying. Care would need to be taken to ensure that the assignment—and the assessment of the performance—focused on demonstrating understanding of the characters and the events in the chapter. In this situation, the teacher might be distracted by the dramatic performance and fail to assess the target of the performance.

LO3 Ways to Evaluate Student Learning

Once you have collected all the measures you intend to collect—for example, test scores, quiz scores, homework assignments, special projects, ratings of products and performances, and laboratory experiments—you will have to give the data some sort of value (the essence of evaluation). As you probably know, this is most often done by using an A-to-F grading scale. There are two general ways to approach this task. One approach is making comparisons among students. Such forms of evaluation are called *norm referenced* because students are identified as average (or normal), above average, or below average. An alternative approach is called *criterion referenced* because performance is interpreted in terms of defined criteria. Although both approaches can be used, we favor criterion-referenced grading for reasons we will mention shortly.

Norm-Referenced Grading

A **norm-referenced grading** system assumes that classroom achievement will naturally vary among a group of heterogeneous students because of differences in such characteristics as prior knowledge, learning skills, motivation, and aptitude (to be discussed in Chapter 15). Under ideal circumstances (hundreds of scores from a diverse group of students), this variation produces a bell-shaped, or "normal," distribution of scores that ranges from low to high, has few tied scores, and has only a very few low scores and only a very few high scores. For this reason, norm-referenced grading procedures are also referred to as "grading on a curve."

{ **Norm-referenced grading is based on the absence of external criteria.** }

The Nature of Norm-Referenced Grading Course grades, like standardized test scores, are determined through a comparison of each student's level of performance with the normal, or average, level of other, similar students in order to reflect the assumed differences in amount of learned material. The comparison may be with all other members of the student's class that year, or it may be with the average performance of several classes stretching back over several years. It is probably better for teachers to use a broad base of typical student performance, made up of several classes, as grounds for comparison than to rely on the current class of students. Doing so avoids two severe distorting effects: (1) When a single class

contains many weak students, those with more well-developed abilities will more easily obtain the highest grades; and (2) when the class has many capable students, the relatively weaker students are virtually predestined to receive low or failing grades (Brookhart, 2009b; Nitko & Brookhart, 2011; Gronlund & Waugh, 2009; Kubiszyn & Borich, 2010).

The basic procedure for assigning grades on a norm-referenced basis involves just a few steps:

1. Determine what percentage of students will receive which grades. If, for example, you intend to award the full range of grades, you may decide to give *A*s to the top 15%, *B*s to the next 25%, *C*s to the middle 35%, *D*s to the next 15%, and *F*s to the bottom 10%.

2. Arrange the scores from highest to lowest.

3. Calculate which scores fall in which category, and assign the grades accordingly.

Many other arrangements are also possible. How large or small you decide to make the percentages for each category will depend on such factors as the nature of the students in your class, the difficulty of your exams and assignments, and your own sense of what constitutes appropriate standards. Furthermore, a norm-referenced approach does not necessarily mean that each class will have a normal distribution of grades or that anyone will automatically fail. For example, it is possible for equal numbers of students to receive As, Bs, and Cs if you decide to limit your grading system to just those three categories and award equal numbers of each grade. A norm-referenced approach simply means that the grading symbols being used indicate one student's level of achievement relative to other students.

Proponents of norm-referenced grading typically point to the absence of acceptable external criteria for use as a standard in evaluating and grading student performance. In other words, there is no good way to determine externally how much learning is too little, just enough, or more than enough for some subject. And if there is no amount of knowledge or set of behaviors that all students must master, then grades may be awarded on the basis of relative performance among a group of students (Gronlund & Waugh, 2009).

norm-referenced grading A system of grading that assumes classroom achievement will vary among a group of heterogeneous students because of such differences as prior knowledge, learning skills, motivation, and aptitude, and so compares the score of each student to the scores of other students in order to determine grades.

How Am I Doing?

Formative assessments are conducted more or less continuously during an instructional unit, using both formal and informal assessment techniques. . . . Unlike summative assessment, which is a one-time event conducted only after instruction is finished, formative assessment has a more dynamic, ongoing, interactive relationship with teaching. The results of formative assessments affect instruction, which affects subsequent performance, and so on. (p. 309)

Remote Tracking: Teachers Click in Quickly on Students' Performance

AMY HETZNER

Milwaukee Journal Sentinel, 4/22/06

Hartland—When social studies teacher Maria Fricker wants to see how much her students remember about the Bosnian war or whether they know how many electoral votes are needed to elect a U.S. president, she has them take out their remote controls.

Forget asking questions and calling on the few students who raise their hands.

With a product called the Classroom Performance System, which allows students to interact with a computer program through infrared response pads, teachers such as Fricker at North Shore Middle School in Hartland can see with the press of a finger whether their students are following the lesson.

The instant feedback lets teachers know if they need to spend more time on a topic or if they're dwelling on something their students already understand and can move on.

"It shows not only the strengths and weaknesses of our kids," Fricker said, "but the strengths and weaknesses of me."

With the Classroom Performance System and other remote control-like products that have entered the educational market in recent years, technology has come to the call of schools and teachers clamoring for new ways to gauge what their students are learning.

North Shore library media specialist Sue Klopp first witnessed the Classroom Performance System at a Wisconsin Educational Media Association conference. She said she liked the instant feedback it provided and how it transfixed everyone who walked by.

Given that North Shore was looking for more ways to assess students, Klopp thought the system would be a good fit for the school's goals.

North Shore Principal Dale Fisher did, too. He authorized purchasing two systems, for about $2,000 each, for the current school year.

"The possibilities were quite endless for us to use it in the classroom," he said. "Traditional multiple-choice tests are given. The teacher can present the questions up on the board and then immediately get data on how their students understand the information. . . . You can differentiate your instruction better. It's better time management, as I see it."

The Classroom Performance System consists of a set of response pads and a software package.

Combined with a personal computer and a projector, it allows teachers to draft a set of questions that can be beamed onto a screen and then answered by students using the pads at their desks.

The pads, shaped and run like remote controls, have only eight buttons on them so the questions generally have to be crafted for multiple-choice or yes-no answers.

Because the computer program keeps track of how many students are keying in correct answers, as well as who is getting what wrong, teachers can get immediate feedback on how their entire class is doing.

Everyone Can See It

Not far from North Shore Middle School, Merton Intermediate School acquired a set of the Classroom Response System.

The hand-held responders, which look like the clunky cell phones of yore, contain a set of keys where students can answer multiple-choice questions, a calculating device and a small screen where teachers can transmit questions.

"What I really like is the potential for it to be real-time assessment—I'm talking to you and I ask questions as the lesson's going on. . . . I can see it, you can see it, we're getting the concept here," Merton Intermediate Principal Jon Wagner said.

A fourth-grade teacher is training herself on the system, which she plans to test with students next school year, Wagner said.

Help for Struggling Students

The Kettle Moraine School District recently purchased two sets of the responders for use with its special education students.

Strengths and Weaknesses of Norm-Referenced Grading There are at least two circumstances under which it may be appropriate to use norm-referenced measurement and evaluation procedures:

1. *Evaluating advanced levels of learning.* You might, for example, wish to formulate a two-stage instructional plan in which the first stage involves helping all students master a basic level of knowledge and skill in a particular subject. Performance at this stage would be measured and evaluated against a predetermined standard (such as 80% correct on an exam). Once this has been accomplished, you could supply advanced instruction and encourage students to learn as much of the additional material as possible. Because the amount of learning during the second stage is not tied to a predetermined standard and because it will likely vary due to differences in motivation and learning skills, a norm-referenced approach to grading can be used at this stage. This situation also fits certain guidelines for the use of competitive reward structures (discussed in Chapter 13) because everyone starts from the same level of basic knowledge.

Carol Smiley, who teaches cognitively disabled students at Kettle Moraine High School, said the devices are beneficial because they allow her to immediately direct her attention to struggling students.

But, while students like them, they haven't been trouble-free. Any assessment given on the responders has to be limited to a single class period, she said, and the technology doesn't allow for graphics that might be more helpful for certain students.

"It's nice because it does eliminate paper-pencil kind of things," Smiley said. "And also the anonymity—not everybody can look over your shoulder and see what you're doing."

The Merton and North Shore principals say the systems meet twin goals for their schools—incorporating technology into lessons and giving teachers data to help guide their instruction.

Recently in Fricker's class at North Shore, the teacher was able to see how well her students remembered their lessons about the workings of government by giving them a sample citizenship test used by the government.

While she controlled it through a computer set up in the middle of the classroom, the screen at the front of Fricker's room moved through a series of questions from who was Martin Luther King Jr. to how many branches of government there are at the federal level.

After students had keyed in their choices from the three she offered in response to each question, she clicked a button that placed a check next to the correct selection and showed how many students answered it right.

At the same time, a computer program recorded individual scores so Fricker could check back to see how students did individu-ally, which she promised to do on more than one question.

"Oh boy, I'm going to find out who thinks Jim Doyle is the vice president of the United States," Fricker said at one point during the quiz. "I'm going to look it up later, guys."

Lets Students Respond

In addition to giving her quick feedback on how her students are grasping the subject matter, Fricker said the anonymity of the Classroom Performance System also could come in handy in dealing with controversial areas where students otherwise might be afraid to speak their minds.

She said she could poll them on how they feel about subjects such as the death penalty and abortion, then pursue why students feel certain ways without embarrassing ones that might not want to share their beliefs.

Fricker's students are enthusiastic about the system. "I think it's better than writing, and you get to see the answers right away and whether you got it right or wrong," said Jocelyn Budzien, 13, a seventh-grader at the school.

Teachers use the systems often for pre-tests and have been creative about coming up with fun ways to use them, such as "Jeopardy!"-style quizzes, said Luke Zarling, 12.

"It's just a good way to remember certain things on the test, and it's funner," he said. "In a way, it's almost like a game. But you're learning while you play the game."

Questions and Activities

1. Formative evaluation means that teachers use assessments in order to make judgments about students' progress. It is also important that formative feedback be provided to students in a timely fashion. What advantages accrue to students who receive formative feedback immediately? What advantages accrue to teachers? To what extent do the advantages of the personal response system rest on a teacher's ability to formulate good questions?

2. The personal response system described in the article seems to provide useful information for students and helps teachers make instructional decisions, manage time, and maintain records of student performance. The system is also flexible in the sense that it allows teachers to tailor its use to specific lessons. But what are the disadvantages or limitations of the system described in the article? How might those disadvantages be minimized or overcome?

3. The students in the article report that using the response system is "better than writing" and "funner." Thinking back to our earlier study of motivation and social cognitive theory, how might the use of the system described in the article affect a student's sense of self-efficacy? Perhaps you or some of your friends have used a personal electronic response system in one or more of your classes. If so, reflect on your own reactions or ask your friends how they felt about their experiences with the system. To what extent did the system account for your reaction and to what extent did the questions used in the system account for your reaction?

---

2. *Selection for limited-enrollment programs.* Norm-referenced measurement and evaluation are also applicable in cases in which students with the best chances for success are selected for a limited-enrollment program from among a large pool of candidates. One example is the selection of students for honors programs who have the highest test scores and grade-point averages (Gronlund & Waugh, 2009).

The main weakness of the norm-referenced approach to grading is that there are few situations in

> There are few appropriate uses for norm-referenced grading in classrooms.

criterion-referenced grading A system in which grades are determined on the basis of whether each student has attained a defined standard of achievement or performance.

which the typical public school teacher can appropriately use it. Either the goal is not appropriate (as in mastery of certain material and skills by all students or diagnosis of an individual student's specific strengths and weaknesses) or the basic conditions cannot be met (classes are too small or homogeneous or both). When a norm-referenced approach is used in spite of these weaknesses, communication and motivation problems are often created.

Pause & Reflect *Have you ever taken a class that was graded on a curve? Did you feel that your grade accurately reflected how much you had learned? If not, why was the grade too low or too high?*

Consider the example of a group of high school sophomores having a great deal of difficulty mastering German vocabulary and grammar. The students may have been underprepared, the teacher may have done a poor job of organizing and explaining the material, or both factors may be at work. The top student averaged 48% correct on all of the exams, quizzes, and oral recitations administered during the term. That student and a few others with averages in the high 40s will receive the As. Although these fortunate few may realize their knowledge and skills are incomplete, others are likely to conclude falsely that these students learned quite a bit about the German language, as a grade of A is generally taken to mean superior performance.

At the other extreme, we have the example of a social studies class in which most of the students are doing well. Because the students were well prepared by previous teachers, used effective study skills, were exposed to high quality instruction, and were strongly motivated by the enthusiasm of their teacher, the final test averages ranged from 94% to 98% correct. And yet the teacher who uses a norm-referenced scheme would assign at least As, Bs, and Cs to this group. Not only does this practice seriously damage the motivation of students who worked hard and performed well, but it also miscommunicates to others the performance of students who received Bs and Cs (Airasian & Russell, 2008).

Criterion-Referenced Grading

A **criterion-referenced grading** system permits students to benefit from mistakes and improve their level of understanding and performance. Furthermore, it establishes an individual (and sometimes cooperative)

Norm-referenced grading systems should rarely, if ever, be used in classrooms because few circumstances warrant their use and they are likely to depress the motivation of all but the highest scoring students.

reward structure, which fosters a greater motivation to learn than other systems.

The Nature of Criterion-Referenced Grading Under a criterion-referenced system, grades are determined by the extent to which each student has attained a defined standard (or criterion) of achievement or performance. Whether the rest of the students in the class are successful or unsuccessful in meeting that criterion is irrelevant. Thus any distribution of grades is possible. Every student may get an A or an F, or no student may receive these grades. For reasons we will discuss shortly, very low or failing grades may occur less frequently under a criterion-referenced system.

A common version of criterion-referenced grading assigns letter grades on the basis of the percentage of test items answered correctly. For example, you may decide to award an A to anyone who correctly answers at least 85% of a set of test questions, a B to anyone who correctly answers 75% to 84%, and so on down to the lowest grade. To use this type of grading system fairly, which means specifying realistic criterion levels, you would need to have some prior knowledge of the levels at which students typically perform. You would thus be using normative information to establish absolute, or fixed, standards of performance. However, although both norm-referenced and criterion-referenced grading systems spring from a normative database (that is, from comparisons among students), only the former system uses those comparisons to directly determine grades.

{ **Criterion-referenced grades provide information about strengths and weaknesses.** }

Strengths and Weaknesses of Criterion-Referenced Grading Criterion-referenced grading systems (and criterion-referenced tests) have become increasingly popular in recent years, primarily because of the following advantages:

- Criterion-referenced tests and grading systems provide more specific and useful information about student strengths and weaknesses than do norm-referenced grading systems. Parents and teachers are more interested in knowing that a student received an A on an earth science test because she mastered 92% of the objectives for that unit than they are in knowing that she received an A on a test of the same material because she outscored 92% of her classmates.

- Criterion-referenced grading systems promote motivation to learn because they hold out the promise that all students who have sufficiently well-developed learning skills and receive good quality instruction can master most of a teacher's objectives (Gronlund & Waugh, 2009). The motivating effect of criterion-referenced grading systems is likely to be particularly noticeable among students who adopt mastery goals (which we discussed in Chapter 11) because they tend to use grades as feedback for further improvement (Moss & Brookhart, 2009; Stiggins, 2007).

One weakness of the criterion-referenced approach to grading is that the performance standards one specifies (such as a grade of A for 90% correct) are arbitrary and may be difficult to justify to parents and colleagues. (Why not 87% correct for an A? Or 92%?) A second weakness is that although a teacher's standards may appear to be stable from one test to another (90% correct for an A for all tests), they may in reality fluctuate as a result of unnoticed variation in the difficulty of each test and the quality of instruction (Gronlund & Waugh, 2009).

Finally, we would like to alert you to a characteristic of criterion-referenced evaluation that is not a weakness but is an unfortunate fact of educational life that you may have to address. In a variety of subtle and sometimes not so subtle ways, teachers are discouraged from using a criterion-referenced approach to grading because it tends to produce higher test scores and grades than a norm-referenced approach does. The reason for the higher scores is obvious and quite justified: When test items are based solely on the specific instructional objectives that teachers write and when

Assessment in the Middle Grades: Measurement of Student Learning

Go to the Education CourseMate website and watch the video, study the artifacts in the case, and reflect upon the following questions:

1. Evaluate the assessment practices used by Mr. Somers in this Video Case. Which ones did you find particularly effective? Support your answers using information from the textbook about effective assessment practices.

2. In this Video Case, Mr. Somers uses a written test to evaluate student understanding of course material. What are some other forms of assessment that could be used to gauge student understanding of a math unit?

those objectives are clear and provided to students, students know what they need to learn and what they need to do to meet the teacher's objectives. Also, because students' grades depend only on how well they perform, not how well their classmates perform, motivation for learning tends to be higher. The result is that students tend to learn more and score higher on classroom tests. So why should this happy outcome be a cause for concern? Because individuals who are not well versed in classroom measurement and evaluation may believe that the only reason large numbers of students achieve high grades is that the teacher has lower standards than other teachers. Consequently, you may find yourself in a position of having to defend the criteria you use to assign grades. Tom Kubiszyn and Gary Borich pointed out that although there is a great call for excellence in education, most people are hesitant to embrace marking systems that place excellence within every student's reach (2010).

Be aware of and avoid faulty measurement and grading practices.

A Mastery Approach   A particular criterion-referenced approach to grading is often referred to as a mastery approach because it allows students multiple opportunities to learn and demonstrate their mastery of instructional objectives. This approach stems in large part from the work of John Carroll (1963) and Benjamin Bloom (1968, 1976) on the concept of *mastery learning*. The basic idea behind mastery learning is that most students can master most objectives if they are given good quality instruction and sufficient time to learn and are motivated to continue learning (Lalley & Gentile, 2008).

In a mastery approach, tests are used for formative as well as summative evaluation purposes. Thus students whose scores indicate deficiencies in learning are given additional instruction and a second chance to show what they have learned. Although pedagogically sound, this approach is often criticized on the grounds that life outside of school often does not give people a second chance. Surgeons and pilots, for example, are expected to do their jobs without error each and every time (Anders Ericsson, 2009; Guskey, 2003). In our view, this criticism is flawed because it is shortsighted and involves an apples and oranges comparison. First, even surgeons and pilots made mistakes that they were allowed to correct. Surgeons made their mistakes on cadavers and pilots on flight simulators. Second, schooling is about helping students acquire the knowledge

and skills they need to move from novices to experts and become self-directed learners.

Using a mastery approach in your classroom means focusing on formative assessment: the ideas surrounding assessment *for* learning discussed earlier in this chapter. In addition to thinking about the characteristics of formative assessment (seen in Table 14.1), the mastery approach to assessment is closely aligned with the practices of response to intervention (RTI) discussed earlier in this chapter and in Chapter 6. Like the mastery approach, RTI is focused on helping students master the material, not necessarily on getting it right the first time. In both the mastery approach and RTI, there is a continuous cycle of teaching followed by testing followed by more teaching, but now the teaching is informed by the results of the testing. Figure 14.2 is an example of a mastery-oriented, criterion-referenced approach to grading. Note that students are given more than one opportunity to demonstrate their mastery on each of the three exams.

Improving Your Grading Methods: Assessment Practices to Avoid

Earlier in this chapter, we noted that the typical teacher has little systematic knowledge of assessment principles and as a result may engage in a variety of inappropriate testing and grading practices. We hope that the information in this chapter will help you become more proficient at these tasks. (In addition, we strongly encourage you to take a course in classroom assessment if you have not already done so.) To reinforce what you have learned here, we will describe some of the more common inappropriate testing and grading practices that teachers commit. The following list is based largely on the observations of Susan Brookhart and Anthony Nitko (2008), Thomas Haladyna (1999), and Thomas Guskey (2002).

1. *Worshiping averages.* Some teachers mechanically average all scores and automatically assign the corresponding grade, even when they know an unusually low score was due to an extenuating circumstance. Allowances can be made for physical illness, emotional upset, and the like; a student's lowest grade can be dropped, or he can repeat the test on which he performed most poorly. Although objectivity in grading is a laudable goal, it should not be practiced to the extent that it prevents you from altering your normal procedures when your professional judgment indicates an exception is warranted.

    Another shortcoming of this practice is that it ignores measurement error. No one can construct

	1st Exam		2nd Exam		3rd Exam		Exam	Projects			Extra Project	Grade
	1st Try	2nd Try	1st Try	2nd Try	1st Try	2nd Try	Total Points	1	2	3		
Adams, Ann	16	18	17	18	18			P	P	P		
Baker, Charles	13	14	14		10	14		P				
Cohen, Matthew	14	16	15	16	17			P	P			
Davis, Rebecca	19		19		20			P	P	P		
Evans, Deborah	16	18	17	18	16	18		P	P	P		
Ford, Harold	15	16	17		15			P	P			
Grayson, Lee	10	13	12	14	12	15		P				
Hood, Barbara	16		17		15			P	P			
Ingalls, Robert	16	18	16		15			P	P			
Jones, Thomas	11	14	12	16	15			P				
Kim, David	18		19		19			P	P	P		
Lapine, Craig	14	16	18		16			P	P			
Moore, James	17		17		17			P	P			
Nguyen, Tuan	17	18	19		16	17		P	P	P		
Orton, John	10	10	11		9							
Peck, Nancy	14		15		14			P				
Quist, Ann	16	18	17	18	18			P	P	P		
Richards, Mary	16		17		15			P	P			
Santos, Maria	13		15		14			P				
Thomas, Eric	15	16	15	17	15			P	P			
Wong, Yuen	14		15		16			P				
Vernon, Joan	11	14	13	14	12	14		P				
Zacharias, Saul	16	18	17		16	19		P	P	P		

INSTRUCTIONS FOR DETERMINING YOUR GRADE IN SOCIAL STUDIES

Your grade in social studies this report period will be based on three exams (worth 20 points each) and satisfactory completion of up to three projects.

Here are the standards for different grades:

A—Average of 18 or more on three exams, plus three projects at Pass level
B—Average of 16 or 17 on three exams, plus two projects at Pass level
C—Average of 14 or 15 on three exams, plus one project at Pass level
D—Average of 10 to 13 on three exams
F—Average of 9 or less on three exams

Another way to figure your grade is to add together points as you take exams. This may be the best procedure to follow as we get close to the end of the report period. Use this description of standards as a guide:

A—At least 54 points, plus three projects at Pass level
B—48 to 53 points, plus two projects at Pass level
C—42 to 47 points, plus one project at Pass level
D—30 to 41 points
F—29 points or less

If you are not satisfied with the score you earn on any exam, you may take a different exam on the same material in an effort to improve your score. (Some of the questions on the alternate exam will be the same as those on the original exam; some will be different.) Projects will be graded P (Pass) or DO (Do Over). If you receive a DO on a project, you may work to improve it and hand it in again. You may also submit an *extra* project, which may earn up to 3 points of bonus credit (and can help if your exam scores fall just below a cutoff point). As you take each exam and receive a Pass for each project, record your progress on this chart.

First Exam		Second Exam		Third Exam		Project			Extra Project	Grade
1st Try	2nd Try	1st Try	2nd Try	1st Try	2nd Try	1	2	3		

the perfect test, and no person's score is a true indicator of knowledge and skill. Test scores represent estimates of these characteristics. Accordingly, giving a student with an average of 74.67 a grade of D when 75 is the minimum needed for a C pretends that the test is more accurate than it really is. This is why it is so important to conduct an item analysis of your tests. If you discover several items that are unusually difficult, you may want to make allowances for students who are a point or two from the next highest grade (and modify the items if you intend to use them again).

2. *Using zeros indiscriminately.* The sole purpose of grades is to communicate to others how much of the curriculum a student has mastered. When teachers also use grades to reflect their appraisal of a student's work habits or character, the validity of the grades is lessened. This occurs most dramatically when students receive zeros for assignments that are late (but are otherwise of good quality), incomplete, or not completed according to directions, or for exams on which they are suspected of cheating. This is a flawed practice for two reasons:

• First, and to repeat what we said in point 1, there may be good reasons why projects and homework assignments are late, incomplete, or different from what was expected. You should try to uncover such circumstances and take them into account.

- Second, zeros cause communication problems. If a student who earns grades in the low 90s for most of the grading period is given two zeros for one or more of the reasons just mentioned, that student could easily receive a D or an F. Such a grade is not an accurate reflection of what was learned.

  If penalties are to be given for work that is late, incomplete, or not done according to directions, and for which there are no extenuating circumstances, they should be clearly spelled out far in advance of the due date and should not seriously distort the meaning of the grade. For students suspected of cheating, for example, a different form of the exam can be given.

Pause & Reflect *Because students in American schools feel considerable pressure to obtain high grades, a significant number of them feel driven to cheat. What might you do to reduce your students' tendency to cheat?*

3. *Providing insufficient instruction before testing.* For a variety of reasons, teachers occasionally spend more time than they had planned on certain topics. In an effort to "cover the curriculum" prior to a scheduled exam, they may significantly increase the pace of instruction or simply tell students to read the remaining material on their own. The low grades that typically result from this practice will unfortunately be read by outsiders (and this includes parents) as a deficiency in students' learning ability, when in fact they more accurately indicate a deficiency in instructional quality.

4. *Teaching for one thing but testing for another.* This practice takes several forms. For instance, teachers may provide considerable supplementary material in class through lecture—thereby encouraging students to take notes and study them extensively—but base test questions almost entirely on text material. Or if teachers emphasize the text material during class discussion, they may take a significant number of questions from footnotes and less important parts of the text. A third form of this flawed practice is providing students with simple problems or practice questions in class that reflect the knowledge level of Bloom's taxonomy but then giving complex problems and higher level questions on a test. Remember what we said earlier in this book: If you want transfer, then teach for transfer.

5. *Using pop quizzes to motivate students.* If you recall our discussion of reinforcement schedules, you will recognize that surprise tests represent a variable interval schedule and that such schedules

produce a consistent pattern of behavior in humans under certain circumstances. Being a student in a classroom is not one of those circumstances. Surprise tests produce an undesirable level of anxiety in many students and cause others to simply give up. If you sense that students are not sufficiently motivated to read and study more consistently, consult Chapter 11 for better ideas on how to accomplish this goal.

6. *Keeping the nature and content of the test a secret.* Many teachers scrupulously avoid giving students any meaningful information about the type of questions that will be on a test or the material that test items will cover. The assumption that underlies this practice is that if students have been paying attention in class, diligently doing their homework, and studying at regular intervals, they will do just fine on a test. But they usually don't—and the main reason can be seen in our description of learning strategies (see Chapter 9). A good learning strategist first analyzes all of the available information that bears on attaining a goal. But if certain critical information about the goal is not available, the rest of the strategy (planning, implementing, monitoring, and modifying) will suffer.

7. *Keeping the criteria for assignments a secret.* This practice is closely related to the previous one. Students may be told, for example, to write an essay on what the world would be like if all diseases were eliminated, and to give their imagination free rein in order to come up with many original ideas. But when the papers are graded, equal weight is given to spelling, punctuation, and grammatical usage. If these aspects of writing are also important to you and you intend to hold students accountable for them, make sure you clearly communicate that fact.

8. *Shifting criteria.* Teachers are sometimes disappointed in the quality of students' tests and assignments and decide to change the grading criteria as a way to shock students into more appropriate learning behaviors. For example, a teacher may have told students that mechanics will count for one third of the grade on a writing assignment. But when the teacher discovers that most of the papers contain numerous spelling, punctuation, and grammatical errors, she may decide to let mechanics determine half of the grade. As we indicated before, grades should not be used as a motivational device or as a way to make up for instructional oversights. There are far better ways to accomplish these goals.

9. *Combining apples and oranges.* Students' grades are supposed to indicate how much they have learned in different subject matter areas. When

factors such as effort and ability are combined with test scores, the meaning of a grade becomes unclear. Consequently, measurement experts routinely recommend that teachers base students' grades solely on how well they have performed on written tests and performance assessments. Assessments of effort and ability should be reported separately (Gronlund & Waugh, 2009). Nevertheless, many teachers do not follow this recommendation. A survey (McMillan, Myran, & Workman, 2002) of just over 900 third through fifth grade teachers revealed that 36% factored a student's level of effort into a grade either quite a bit, extensively, or completely and that 47% used a student's ability level to help determine a grade either quite a bit, extensively, or completely. Many high school teachers engage in this practice as well.

A number of technological formats and products have been developed to make the task of classroom assessment easier, more informative, and less prone to error. The next section describes several of these formats and products.

LO4 Technology for Classroom Assessment

Assessment activities can account for about one third of a teacher's time. This large investment in time is partly due to the importance of assessment in both teaching and learning, but it is also related to the fact that many assessment activities involve time-consuming methods of creating, administering, and scoring tests and analyzing and recording scores. Fortunately, computer-based technology supports many of the assessment functions teachers must execute (Beatty & Gerace, 2009; Cardwell, 2000). As the technological tools for learning and assessment have grown, so have the expectations that aspiring teachers will demonstrate their capacity to use the technology (Yao, 2006).

Electronic Grade Books and Grading Programs

Electronic grade books can store records of student test performance, compute test averages and cumulative averages, weight scores, note students with particular scores or characteristics, and print grade reports with standard as well as specific student comments. Combining digital grade books with grading software allows teachers be consistent with the point-based grading systems that are used by most middle and high school teachers. These programs can scan and mark students' choices to selected-response test items (true–false, matching, multiple choice) and allow teachers to track, summarize, and present student performance in a variety of ways. But the efficiency and seeming objectivity of such programs mask a serious potential drawback: They can lead to unfair assignment of grades when used uncritically. The challenge of accurately assigning grades usually involves more than just mathematical precision.

To demonstrate the complex nature of grading and the need for professional judgment to supplement the use of computerized grading programs, consider the example offered by Thomas Guskey (2002) in Table 14.3.

The table represents a group of seven students, each of whom has been graded using three methods: calculating the simple average of all scores, calculating the median or middle score, and calculating the average with the lowest score deleted. Using the simple arithmetic average produces a grade of C for all students despite the differences in their grade patterns. Student 1, for example, started slowly but gradually improved. Student 2 exhibited the opposite pattern. Student 3's performance was consistently around the average. Student 4 failed the first two unit tests but scored near or at the top for the last three. Student 5 exhibited the opposite pattern from student 4. Student 6 had an unexcused absence for the first test and was given a

TABLE 14.3 Summary Grades Tallied by Three Different Methods

Student	Unit 1	Unit 2	Unit 3	Unit 4	Unit 5	Avg Score	Grade	Median Score	Grade	Avg With Lowest Deleted	Grade
1	59	69	79	89	99	79	C	79	C	84	B
2	99	89	79	69	59	79	C	79	C	84	B
3	77	80	80	78	80	79	C	80	B	79.5	B
4	49	49	98	99	100	79	C	98	A	86.5	B
5	100	99	98	49	49	79	C	98	A	86.5	B
6	0	98	98	99	100	79	C	98	A	98.8	A
7	100	99	98	98	0	79	C	98	A	98.8	A

Grading Scale: 90–100% = A; 80–89% = B; 70–79% = C; 60–69% = D; 59% or lower = F.
SOURCE: Guskey (2002).

score of 0 but scored near or at the top for the last four tests. Student 7 had virtually perfect scores for the first four tests but was caught cheating on the last one and received a score of 0. If giving all seven students the same grade strikes you as inappropriate, note that using the median score or the average with the lowest score deleted produces grades that range from A through C, and that students 4 and 5 could receive an A, B, or C, depending on which method is used.

Our purpose here is not to tell you which of these methods to use, as that will depend on other information that teachers typically have about student capabilities and their own beliefs about the appropriateness of different grading methods, but to remind you that computerized grading books should not be allowed to substitute for your professional judgment in awarding grades.

Technology-Based Performance Assessment

As you may recall from our earlier discussion, performance assessments give students the opportunity to demonstrate how well they can use the knowledge and skills that were the focus of an instructional unit to carry out realistic and meaningful tasks. Computer-based technology is an excellent vehicle for this purpose. For example, simulations are likely to be more effective than traditional paper-and-pencil tests for determining how well students understand and can carry out the process of scientific inquiry (planning an investigation, collecting data, organizing and analyzing the data, forming conclusions, and communicating findings). Recent research on the development of performance assessment procedures in complex task domains such as engineering design and medical diagnosis promises even greater effectiveness of technology-based performances in the future (Spector, 2006). A web-based simulation that lends itself to the assessment of scientific inquiry is the GLOBE environmental science education program

(www.globe.gov). Students who participate in GLOBE collect environmental data at a local site and submit it to a scientific database on the web. About 4,000 schools from countries around the world participate in this program. Teachers could use the GLOBE database to assess how well students analyze and interpret climate data by having them use a set of climate-related criteria (such as temperature at different altitudes, amount of sunshine, and amount of snow) to determine in which of several cities the next Winter Olympics should be held (Means & Haertel, 2002). Multimedia tools with text, audio, video, and graphics, such as the Quest Atlantis program mentioned in other chapters, also offer opportunities for students to demonstrate their ability to solve real-world problems in a number of content areas.

Digital Portfolios

What Is a Digital Portfolio? Digital portfolios (also called *electronic portfolios*) are similar in purpose to the more traditional portfolios, but they extend beyond paper versions because they can include sound effects, audio and video testimonials, voice-over explanations of a student's thinking process as a project is worked on, and photographs of such products as drawings, paintings, and musical compositions (Siegle, 2002).

The Components and Contents of Digital Portfolios Because the purposes for having students construct a digital portfolio (such as to assign grades, assess students' strengths and weaknesses, evaluate a program or curriculum) are not always the same, the portfolio structure will vary somewhat across teachers and school districts. But some components, such as those in the list that follows, are frequently recommended (for instance, Beatty & Gerace, 2009; Goldsby & Fazal, 2001; Janesick, 2001) and should always be seriously considered for inclusion:

- The goals the student was attempting to achieve
- The guidelines that were used to select the included material
  - Work samples
  - Teacher feedback
  - Student self-reflection
  - The criteria that were used to evaluate each entry
  - Examples of good quality work

© basketman23/Shutterstock Images

Just as the general components of a digital portfolio may vary, so may the particular media that are used. Following are some specific examples of the types of media a student may use and information that would be represented by each medium (Barrett, 2000; Gatlin & Jacob, 2002; Janesick, 2001; O'Lone, 1997; Siegle, 2002):

- *Digitized pictures and scanned images*: Photos of the student or objects the student has has created, artwork, models, science experiments over time, fax exchanges with scientists, spelling tests, math work, self-assessment checklists.

- *Documents*: Electronic copies of student writing, reflection journals, publications, copies of web pages created, teacher notes and observations.

- *Audio recordings*: Persuasive speeches, poetry readings, rehearsals of foreign language vocabulary, readings of select passages, self-evaluations, interviews or voice notes regarding the rationale for work included.

- *Video clips*: Short videos showing the student or teams of students engaged in science experiments and explaining their steps, showing student performances in physical education or the performing arts, or students generating and/or presenting interdisciplinary projects.

Rubrics for Digital Portfolios and Presentations With all the information a digital portfolio might contain, how can a classroom teacher fairly and efficiently assess student learning? First, electronic writing, just like paper-based compositions, can be assessed holistically in a general impression rating. It can also be analyzed with specific criteria such as whether the work is insightful, well organized, clear, focused, relevant, sequentially flowing, persuasive, inspirational, and original (see Arter & Chappuis, 2008). There are also rubrics for analyzing the quality of a portfolio that has been posted to a website. One uses a 4-point scale (exceeds requirements, meets requirements, close to meeting standards, clearly

does not meet standards) to assess the design and aesthetics of the website, its usability, and the presence and clarity of the portfolio's contents (Goldsby & Fazal, 2001). The website 4teachers (www.4teachers.org) contains, among other things related to technology, a tool called RubiStar that provides templates for creating rubrics for several types of digital products.

Performance and Portfolio Assessment Problems

We would be remiss not to point out the problems often associated with technology-based performance and portfolio assessment. High quality performance assessments require multiple assessments (for both formative and summative purposes), extensive time, electronic equipment, careful planning, and continued modification (McGrath, 2003). Electronic portfolios can become large, complex, and time consuming to grade fairly and thus can overload teachers with work (A. Goodman, 2008; Pope, Hare, & Howard, 2002).

Staff development and teacher training are additional barriers to effective use of performance assessment and digital portfolios. But with proper training, teachers may begin to find ways in which technology-based school and classroom assessment plans are practical, cost effective, and qualitatively better than traditional assessments.

The Suggestions for Teaching that follow should help you properly implement the assessment concepts and research findings presented in this chapter.

© vgstudio/Shutterstock Images

Suggestions for Teaching

Communicating Assessment and Evaluative Judgments

Teaching is a profession; its practitioners are professionals. As professionals, teachers are called on to make decisions, take actions based on those decisions, and justify both their decisions and their actions. Another way of saying it is that teachers, because they are professionals, are accountable. High on the list of decisions and actions for which they must account are assessment and evaluation.

In the first chapter of this book, we mentioned the National Board for Professional Teaching Standards, and we will see the five key propositions underlying those standards in the last chapter. To become a National Board Certified Teacher, one must account—clearly and convincingly—for her or his teaching practice, including the proposition that "teachers are responsible for managing and monitoring student learning."

Lee S. Shulman, who was instrumental in creating the National Board for Professional Teaching Standards, is president emeritus of the Carnegie Foundation for the Advancement of Teaching. In 2007, Dr. Shulman published an essay entitled "Counting and Recounting: Assessment and the Quest for Accountability." He opened that essay by describing how his daughter had just returned from her first MBA class in managerial accounting and he had asked her how the first class went. He described his reaction as follows:

> Imagine my surprise when [my daughter] responded that accounting was unexpectedly interesting because, she now realized, it should be understood as a form of narrative, a kind of drama. Within the ethical and technical rules of the field, the task of the accountant is to figure out . . . the stories [that] should be told. Accounting is basically about creating the plot, characters, and setting of the story. As the instructor explained to the class, "Your task is to render an account: to tell the facts of the case, the story . . ., in an accurate and yet ultimately persuasive way." (p. 20)

Telling a story, rendering an account, requires the author of the story to communicate clearly in order to be persuasive. As a teacher, engaged in the practice of assessment and evaluation, you will author many stories of learning. Here are some sugges-

tions that may help you render informative, useful, and convincing accounts of student learning. (The suggestions are adapted from a section in Shulman's essay headed "Seven Pillars of Assessment and Accountability.")

1 **Be clear about the learning story you need to tell and why it needs to be told.**
Chapter 13 began by examining learning goals, instructional objectives, and taxonomies of learning outcomes. The idea in planning instruction is to *begin with the end in mind*, to determine what your students need to learn and why.

a. Use taxonomies.
What are the learning goals for your students? What learning standards are they supposed to meet? What are your goals for them? Use the taxonomies discussed in Chapter 13 to think about the standards that your district and state will expect your students to meet. The taxonomies can help you move from general education standards to more specific learning goals—and help you justify why those learning goals are important for your students to meet. Once you have identified the kinds of cognitive, affective, and psychomotor outcomes your students should demonstrate, you can move to generating the specific instructional objectives that your students need to attain and that will guide the learning activities you employ in your classroom.

b. Write clear objectives.
Use either Mager's or Gronlund's approach (see Chapter 13) to specify the objectives your students need to meet. Either approach—correctly applied—yields clear, specific statements of what your students should know and be able to do.

Specifying objectives will not tell you how your story ends—that comes later—but with clear, specific instructional objectives in place, you will know how a successful story of learning *should* end.

2 **Be clear about what you are assessing and what you are not assessing.**
With your objectives for a unit of study specified, you are now ready to start building the assessments that will help you tell the learning story of each student. To make sure that your story is true and honest, you need to be clear about what you are and are not assessing.

For students to plan effectively how they will master your objectives, they need to know as early as possible how many test they will have to take, when the tests will occur, what types of items each test will contain, and what content they will be tested on.

One tool that can be very helpful in this regard is a *table of specifications*. Such a table specifies what objectives are being assessed and how those objectives contribute to the various taxonomic outcomes you are seeking for your students.

Take a look at the example in Figure 14.3. It identifies the major topics of this chapter and the taxonomic outcomes in the cognitive domain. The objectives can be organized by the major topics of the unit of study and the types of cognitive capabilities that students might demonstrate.

This practice forces you to think about both the number and the relative importance of your objectives before you start teaching or writing test items. Thus, if some objectives are more important to you than others, you will have a way of ensuring that these are tested more thoroughly. If, however, a test is going to be brief and emphasize all objectives more or less equally, you may wish to put a check mark in each box as you write

FIGURE 14.3 Example of a Table of Specifications for Material Covered in This Chapter

TOPIC	OBJECTIVES					
	Knows	Comprehends	Applies	Analyzes	Synthesizes	Evaluates
Nature of measurement and evaluation						
Purposes of measurement and evaluation						
Types of written tests						
Nature of performance tests						

questions. The important point is that by taking steps to ensure that your tests cover what you want your students to know, you will be increasing the tests' validity.

In preparing assessments for your own students, you may choose to use outcomes from the affective or psychomotor domains or you may choose not to list all of the categories in the taxonomy for all subjects or at all grade levels.

3 **Use multiple assessments to tell the story of student learning.**

Suppose you asked one multiple-choice question on one test to determine if your students had attained a particular objective. Suppose further that some of your students got that question correct and some did not. In telling the story of a student who got the item correct, how confident would you be in claiming that the student had learned? What about the story of one who missed the item?

Our suggestion here is that you assess the objectives you have specified a number of times, using a variety of the methods of assessment. If you found that students do well on several multiple-choice items, on

several short-answer items, on an extended essay, and on a presentation—all assessing a single objective—you would be able to make a more convincing case that those students had sufficiently demonstrated the learning required to meet the objective. The stories of learning—whether they are stories of success or of postponed completion—must be convincing if they are to be used.

4 **Synthesize the information from across multiple measures.**

For the same reason that it is important to use multiple assessments to collect information about what students know and are able to do, it is important that the story of each student's learning be based on the evidence of learning and that the assessments and evidence be synthesized. Simply listing test results, scores on homework, and grades on term papers provides the raw data gathered across assessments, but a list of scores does not qualify as evidence. Evidence is what is used to support a claim that a student has or has not learned. Remember that justifying your assessment and evaluation practices requires you to render an account. The

accountant for a large company does not simply list assets and liabilities; an account based on the available information is rendered. Following this advice becomes very important when communicating with parents.

5 **Avoid creating "high stakes" assessment when possible.**

In our current era of accountability in education, testing—especially standardized testing of the type discussed in the next chapter—has created an environment of high stakes. Think back to the emphasis placed on doing well on the state tests of achievement when you were in high school. Reflect also on what we know about academic cheating behavior: If the stakes are high enough, cheating will occur. This can happen in classrooms as well. Imagine that you took a class that had only one final exam, that your entire grade for the course rested on your performance at a particular time, on a particular day, in a particular place.

In order to gather accurate information about your students' learning, so that you can make sound evaluative judgments, do not create assessments that have high stakes.

continued

Suggestions for Teaching—*continued*

Rather than give one unit exam, give several or—following the mastery approach to assessment—provide multiple opportunities for students to demonstrate on each assessment what they know and are able to do. The next suggestion can also help avoid creating high stakes environments.

6 Make sure assessment is embedded in instruction.

In order to provide a useful and compelling account of a student's learning, you need to know not just where the student ended up but how the student got there. The story comes from the journey. We offer this suggestion not only because it will help you communicate effectively and help you justify your assessment and evaluation decisions, but because it will help you teach more effectively and will increase the probability that your students' story of learning will end where it should.

This suggestion boils down to following the guidelines for formative assessment (see Table 14.1). By assessing consistently and persistently, you align instruction with your objectives and with data about those objectives, you generate multiple measures, you provide more sources of information to help you synthesize across those measures, and you minimize high stakes environments. Embedding assessment in instruction will facilitate following the five previous suggestions.

7 Actively share and collaborate on the design and development of assessment and evaluation strategies.

Assessment and evaluation are integral to teaching; they are critical teaching functions. As promulgated by the National Board for Professional Teaching Standards, assessment and evaluation must not be treated as afterthoughts in teaching.

One way to develop your professional practice on a trajectory toward teaching expertise is to share and work with others on designing, using, and improving classroom assessments and evaluative strategies. If you develop a quiz that you intend to use formatively, share it with a colleague who teaches the same class, invite her or his critique, and offer to compare results (while maintaining appropriate confidentiality). Sharing your assessment and evaluation practices and experiences is one way to develop your professional knowledge and your skills as an author of leaning accounts. Highly qualified professionals are seen as authorities on their practice. Developing your skills as an author of assessments will help establish your authority.

Having considered the Suggestions for Teaching, we close this chapter with one last thought and one last suggestion.

Aspiring teachers are, understandably, excited and eager to present what they know to their students. Aspiring teachers are enthused to find and implement classroom activities that capture students' attention, that engage students deeply, that motivate them, and that leave them thinking. But it is important to remember that teaching is more than presenting what one knows to others. As we have learned in this chapter, assessment is not something that is done after one has taught. Rather, assessment

WHAT ELSE? *RIP & REVIEW* **CARDS IN THE BACK**

is integral to teaching and to learning: Recall our discussions of assessment *of* learning, assessment *for* learning, and assessment *as* learning.

Our suggestion is that including your students in the assessment of their own learning captures their attention, engages them deeply in what and how they are learning, increases motivation, and helps them think and view themselves as capable of exerting influence on their own learning. Our point is this: Of all the outcomes of learning that can be assessed, the one that might have the greatest long-term impact on your students is that they are capable of assessing and influencing their own learning.

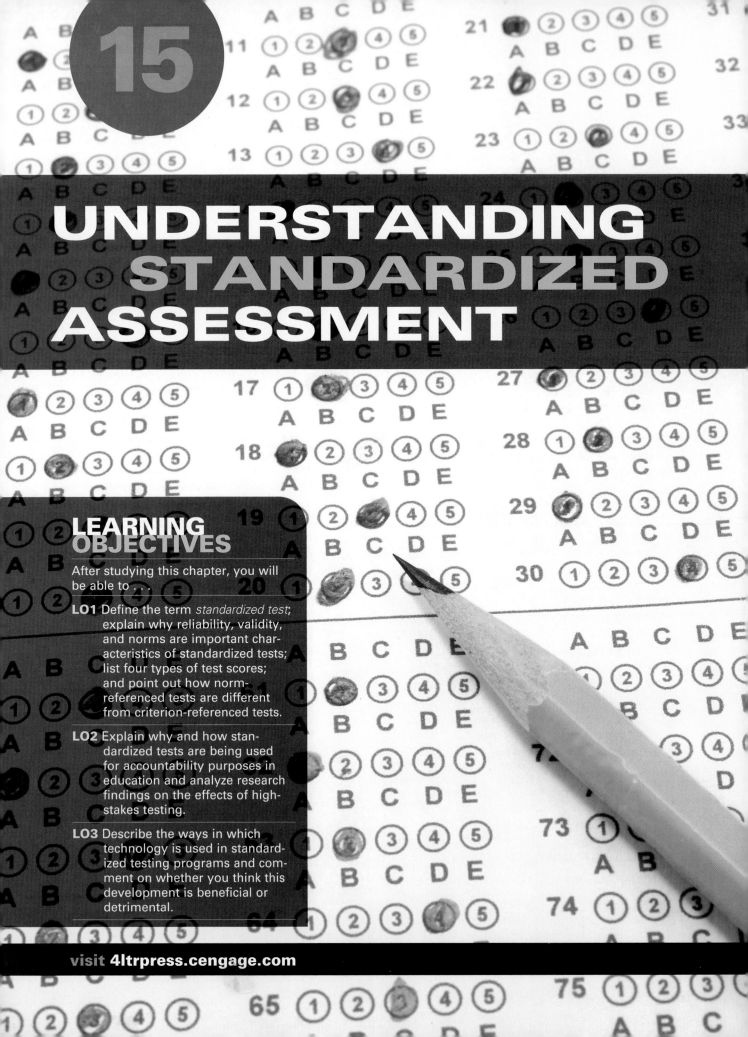

15

UNDERSTANDING STANDARDIZED ASSESSMENT

LEARNING OBJECTIVES

After studying this chapter, you will be able to . . .

LO1 Define the term *standardized test*; explain why reliability, validity, and norms are important characteristics of standardized tests; list four types of test scores; and point out how norm-referenced tests are different from criterion-referenced tests.

LO2 Explain why and how standardized tests are being used for accountability purposes in education and analyze research findings on the effects of high-stakes testing.

LO3 Describe the ways in which technology is used in standardized testing programs and comment on whether you think this development is beneficial or detrimental.

Because standardized assessment of scholastic aptitude and achievement is such a popular practice in the United States (as well as in many other countries), this chapter will focus on the nature of standardized tests, how they are used to assess student variability, how, as part of the No Child Left Behind law, test results are used to draw conclusions about the effectiveness of a school's instruction, and whether No Child Left Behind has been beneficial or detrimental to students and educators.

> ## Standardized tests: items presented and scored in standard fashion; results reported with reference to standards

LO1 Standardized Tests

The Nature of Standardized Tests

The kinds of assessment instruments described in this chapter are typically referred to as **standardized tests**, although the term *published tests* is sometimes used (because they are prepared, distributed, and scored by publishing companies or independent test services). Some of the more commonly used types are achievement tests, diagnostic tests, and intelligence tests. You have almost certainly taken several of these tests during your academic career, and so you are probably familiar with their appearance and general characteristics. They are called standardized tests for the following reasons:

- They are designed by people with specialized knowledge and training in test construction.

- Every person who takes the test responds to the same items under the same conditions.

- The answers are evaluated according to the same scoring standards.

- The scores are interpreted through comparison with the scores obtained from a group (called a *norm group*) that took the same test under the same conditions or (in the case of some achievement tests) through comparison with a predetermined standard.

The basic purpose of giving a standardized test is to obtain a *representative sample* of how much of some characteristic a person possesses (such as knowledge of a particular set of mathematical concepts and operations) that is both reliable and accurate (the reasons are mentioned in the next section). If you're not sure exactly what is meant by the terms *representative sample*, *reliable*, and *accurate*, fret not. We will define those for you shortly.

Uses of Standardized Tests

Historically, educators have used scores on standardized tests, particularly achievement tests, for a variety of instructionally related purposes. Teachers, guidance counselors, and principals have used test data to identify general strengths and weaknesses in student achievement, to inform parents of their child's general level of achievement, to plan instructional lessons, to group students for instruction, and to recommend students for placement in special programs. To cite just one example, when a child moves to a different school, it is highly desirable for those in the new school to have some idea of what the child knows about basic subjects. Standardized achievement tests do an effective job of providing information about the mastery of general subject matter and skills and thus can be used for planning, grouping, placement, and instructional purposes.

> The basic purpose of a standardized test is to obtain an accurate, representative sample of some aspect of a person.

Pause & Reflect *If you are like most people, you took a variety of standardized tests throughout your elementary and high school years. Do you think that those tests adequately reflected what you had learned and were capable of learning, and therefore were always used in your best interest? What can you do to increase the chances that you will use test scores to help your students fulfill their potential?*

Criteria for Evaluating Standardized Tests

Like most other things, standardized tests vary in quality. To use test scores wisely, you need to be an informed consumer—to know what characteristics distinguish well-constructed from poorly constructed tests. Three criteria are widely used to evaluate standardized tests: reliability, validity, and norms.

Reliability A basic assumption that psychologists make about human characteristics (such as intelligence and achievement) is that they are relatively stable, at least over short periods of time. For most people, this assumption seems to be true. Thus you should be able to count on a test's results being consistent, just as you might count on a reliable worker to do a consistent job time after time. This stability in test performance is known as **reliability**. You can think of reliability as the extent to which test scores are free of measurement errors that arise from such factors as test anxiety, motivation, correct guesses, and vaguely worded items, thereby producing a consistent performance over the course of a test or over repeated assessments of the same characteristic (Koretz, 2008). It is one of the most important characteristics of standardized tests.

{ **Reliability: similarity between two rankings of test scores obtained from the same individual** }

To illustrate the importance of reliability, imagine that you wish to form cooperative learning groups for mathematics. Because these types of groups should be composed of five or six students who differ on a number of characteristics, including achievement, you use the students' most recent scores from a standardized mathematics test to assign two high, two medium, and two low achievers to each group. One month later the children are retested, and you now find that many of those who scored at the top initially (and whom you thought were very knowledgeable about mathematics) now score in the middle or at the bottom. Conversely, many students who initially scored low now have average or above-average scores. What does that do to your confidence in being able to form heterogeneous groups based on scores from this test? If you want to be able to differentiate among individuals consistently, you need to use an instrument that performs consistently.

© Ilene MacDonald/Alamy

When properly used, standardized test scores can keep parents, students, and educators aware of a student's general level of achievement, and they can help teachers and administrators make decisions about placing students in special programs.

Psychologists who specialize in constructing standardized tests assess reliability in a variety of ways:

- *Split-half reliability.* Psychologists administer a single test to a group of students, create two scores by dividing the test in half, and measure the extent to which the rankings change from one half to the other. This method gauges the internal consistency of the test.

- *Test–retest reliability.* Psychologists administer the same test to the same people on two occasions and measure the extent to which the rankings change over time.

- *Alternate-form reliability.* Psychologists administer two equivalent forms of a test to the same group of students at the same time and compare the results.

Regardless of which method is used to assess reliability, the goal is to create two rankings of scores and see how similar the rankings are. This degree of consistency is expressed as a correlation coefficient (abbreviated with a lowercase r) that ranges from 0 to 1. Well-constructed standardized tests should have correlation coefficients of about .95 for split-half reliability, .90 for test–retest reliability, and .85 for alternate-form reliability (Kubiszyn & Borich, 2010).

The importance of high reliability is easily seen when readiness tests are used for deciding if a child should be admitted to kindergarten early or be required to repeat kindergarten or first grade. Young children change physically, socially, emotionally, and intellectually so rapidly that many of them score very differently when retested 6 months later (Bjorklund, 2005). As a result, these decisions should *never* be made solely on the basis of a standardized test score.

Validity: how accurately a test measures what it claims to measure

Validity A second important characteristic of a test is that it accurately measures what its designers intended it to measure and what its users expect it to measure. Whenever we speak of a test's accuracy in this sense, we are referring to its **validity**. Here's an example of what we mean: In the spring of the school year, all students in your school district are required to take your state's standardized exam, including students who have recently immigrated from Spanish-speaking countries and are still learning the language. Do you give these students a Spanish language version of the test or the English language version that all other students will take? That's a no-brainer if what you want to know is how much of the test's content the students have learned. Research has clearly shown that Spanish-speaking ELLs score higher on math tests when the test is written in Spanish than when it is written in English (Robinson, 2010).

Because most of the characteristics we are interested in knowing something about (such as arithmetic skills, spatial aptitude, intelligence, and knowledge of the American Civil War) are internal and hence not directly observable, tests are indirect measures of those attributes. Therefore, any test-based conclusions we may draw about how much of a characteristic a person possesses, or any predictions we may make about how well a person will perform in the future (on other types of tests, in a job, or in a specialized academic program, for example), are properly referred to as *inferences*. So when we inquire about the validity of a test by asking, "Does this test measure what it claims to measure?" we are really asking, "How accurate are the inferences that I wish to draw about the test taker?" (Koretz, 2008).

The degree to which these inferences can be judged accurate, or valid, depends on the type and quality of the supporting evidence that we can muster. Three kinds of evidence that underlie test-based inferences are content validity evidence, predictive validity evidence, and construct validity evidence.

Content Validity Evidence The basis of content validity evidence is a set of judgments about how well a test's items reflect the particular body of knowledge and skill (called a *domain* by measurement specialists) about which we want to draw inferences. If a test on the American Civil War, for example, contained no items on the war's causes, its great battles, or the years it encompassed, some users might be hesitant to call someone who had achieved a high score knowledgeable about the topic. Then again, other users might not be nearly so disturbed by these omissions (and the inference that would be drawn from the test score) if they considered such information to be relatively unimportant. Regardless of how a domain is ultimately defined, it has to be a *representative sample* of the characteristic that is being assessed. A comprehensive measure would simply be too expensive, time consuming, and cumbersome to be of much use (Deneen & Deneen, 2008; Koretz, 2008).

validity The extent to which a test measures what it claims to measure.

{ Content validity: how well test items cover a body of knowledge and skill }

Predictive Validity Evidence Evidence of predictive validity allows us to make probabilistic statements about how well students will behave in the future ("Based on his test scores, there is a strong likelihood that Yusef will do well in the creative writing program next year"). Many colleges, for example, require students to take the ACT Test or the SAT and then use the results (along with other information) to predict each prospective student's grade-point average at the end of the first year. All other things being equal, students with higher test scores are expected to have higher grade-point averages than students with lower test scores, and thus stand a better chance of being admitted.

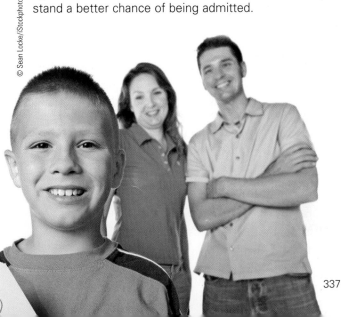

© Sean Locke/iStockphoto

norm group
A sample of individuals carefully chosen to reflect the larger population of students for whom a test is intended.

Construct Validity Evidence

Evidence relating to construct validity indicates how accurately a test measures a theoretical description of some internal attribute of a person. Such attributes—for example, intelligence, creativity, motivation, and anxiety—are called *constructs* by psychologists.

To illustrate the nature of construct validity, we will use a hypothetical theory of intelligence called the Perfectly Valid theory. This theory holds that highly intelligent individuals should have higher-than-average school grades now and in the future, demonstrate superior performance on tasks that involve abstract reasoning, and be able to distinguish worthwhile from non-worthwhile goals. They may or may not, however, be popular among their peers. If the Perfectly Valid theory is accurate and if someone has done a good job of constructing an intelligence test based on this theory (the Smart Intelligence Test), people's scores on the Smart Intelligence Test should vary in accordance with predictions derived from the Perfectly Valid theory. We should see, for example, a strong positive relationship, or correlation, between IQ scores and grade-point average but no relationship between IQ scores and measures of popularity. As more and more of this type of evidence is supplied, we can feel increasingly confident in drawing the inference that the Smart Intelligence Test is an accurate measure of the Perfectly Valid theory of intelligence.

Norms For a test score to have any meaning, it has to be compared with some yardstick, or measure of performance. Most standardized tests use the performance of a norm group as the measure against which all other scores are compared. A **norm group** is a sample of individuals carefully chosen so as to reflect the larger population of students for whom the test is intended. In many cases, the larger population consists of all elementary school children, all middle school children, or all high school children in the United States.

> **Predictive validity: how well a test score predicts later performance**

The norm group must closely match the larger population it represents on such major demographic variables as age, sex, race, ethnic group, region of country, family income, and occupation of head of household. These variables are considered major because they are strongly associated with differences in school performance. If, for example, the U.S. Census Bureau reports that 38% of all Latino males between the ages of 6 and 13 live in the Southwestern region of the country, a good test constructor testing in the Southwest will try

TeachSource Video Case

▶❚❚

Assessment in Elementary Grades: Formal and Informal Literacy Assessment

Go to the Education CourseMate website and watch the video, study the artifacts in the case, and reflect upon the following questions:

1. In your own words, how will the standardized test in the Video Case benefit Myto and allow teachers to plan his instruction more effectively?

2. What factors might influence the reliability and validity of this standardized test?

Standardized achievement tests are given to assess how much of a particular subject students have learned, and aptitude tests are given to assess the level of a student's capabilities in a particular area.

© Spencer Grant/Photo Edit

to put together a norm group that contains the same percentage of 6- to 13-year-old Latino males.

Two Approaches to Interpreting Standardized Test Scores: Norm Referenced and Criterion Referenced

For standardized test scores to have any meaning, they have to be compared to some kind of standard. Essentially all standardized tests allow score interpretations that are either norm-referenced or criterion-referenced (although some tests offer both options).

{ **The meaningfulness of standardized test scores depends on the representativeness of norm group** }

Norm-Referenced Tests Most achievement and aptitude tests are referred to as **norm-referenced tests** because performance is evaluated with reference to norms—the performance of others—established when the final form of the test was administered to the sample of students who made up the norm group. Achievement tests, by the way, measure how much has been learned from a particular subject area whereas aptitude tests measure an underlying predisposition to respond to a task in a particular way, as in tests of

mechanical or musical aptitude. As you might suspect, problems of score interpretation arise when the major demographic characteristics of individuals who take the test are not reflected in the norm group. Suppose you were trying to interpret the score of a 14-year-old Black male on the EZ Test of Academic Achievement. If the oldest students in the norm group were 12 and if Black children were not part of the norm group, you would have no way of knowing whether your student's score was below average, average, or above average, compared with the norm. Tests that are constructed according to norm-referenced criteria tend to cover a broad range of knowledge and skill but have relatively few items for each topic or skill tested.

Norm-referenced tests compare one student with others.

Criterion-Referenced Tests A different approach to reporting achievement test scores is used by **criterion-referenced tests**. When a test is scored in this manner, an individual's performance is not compared with the performance of others. Instead, students are evaluated according to how well they have mastered specific objectives in various well-defined skill areas. Because of this feature, you may find criterion-referenced tests more useful than norm-referenced tests in determining who needs how much additional instruction in what areas (provided, of course, that the test's objectives closely match your own).

Tests that have criterion-referenced scoring systems tend to cover less ground than norm-referenced tests but contain more items for the objectives they do assess.

Pause & Reflect *Do you prefer norm-referenced or criterion-referenced tests? Why? Can you describe circumstances in which a norm-referenced test would be clearly preferable to a criterion-referenced test, and vice versa?*

Types of Standardized Test Scores

Scores on the most widely used standardized tests are typically reported on student profile forms that summarize and explain the results. Although most profiles contain sufficient information to make it possible to interpret scores without additional background, you should know in advance about the kinds of scores you may encounter, particularly because you may be asked to explain scores to students as well as to their parents.

Grade Equivalent Scores The **grade equivalent score** interprets test performance in terms of grade levels. A third grade student who earns a grade equivalent score of 5.2 on a math achievement test, for example, got the same number of items right on this test as the average fifth grader in the norm group who was 2 months into the school year.

Because grade equivalent scores are easily misinterpreted by students and parents, what they do and do not mean needs to be clearly understood and communicated by teachers. The fact that our third grader earned the same score as the average fifth grader who was tested in October (the second month of the school year) *does not* mean that she should be in the fifth grade or even that she should be doing fifth grade math. She may well be missing certain fourth grade math concepts that are necessary to understand fifth grade math concepts. Decisions about accelerated instruction and skipping grades require additional and different types of data.

{ Percentile rank: percentage of scores at or below a given point }

Percentile Ranks Probably the most widely used score for standardized tests is the **percentile rank**. This score indicates the percentage of students who are at and below a given student's score. It provides specific information about relative position.

Students earning a percentile rank of 87 did as well as or better than 87% of the students in the particular norm group being used (which can be national, state, or local). They did not get 87% of the questions right—unless by coincidence—and this is the point parents are most likely to misunderstand if they think of

standardized test scores the same way they think of traditional classroom grading (90 or above is A, 80 to 89 is B, and so on down the line). If you report that a son or daughter has a percentile rank of 50, some parents are horror-struck or outraged, not understanding that the child's score on this test is average, not a failure. One way to explain a percentile rank is in terms of a hypothetical group of 100; for example, a child with a percentile rank of 78 did as well as or better than 78 out of every 100 students who took the test.

Although the percentile rank gives simple and direct information on relative position, it has a major disadvantage: The difference in achievement among students clustered around the middle of the distribution is often considerably less than the difference among those at the extremes. The reason is that *most* scores are clustered around the middle of most distributions of large groups of students. The difference in raw score (number of items answered correctly) between students at percentile ranks 50 and 51 may be 1 point. But the difference in raw score between students ranked 98 and ranked 97 may be 10 or 15 points, because the best (and worst) students scatter toward the extremes. This quality of percentile ranks means that ranks on different tests cannot be averaged. To get around that difficulty, standard scores are often used.

Standard deviation: degree to which scores deviate from the mean of a distribution

Standard Scores Standard scores are expressed in terms of a common unit: the **standard deviation**. This statistic indicates the degree to which a test score differs from the average or mean of a group (a distribution) of scores. Figure 15.1 shows a normal probability curve—or **normal curve**, as it is usually known—indicating the percentage of cases to be found within three standard deviations above and below the mean. The horizontal axis indicates the score, ranging from low on the left to high on the right; the vertical axis represents the number of cases corresponding to each score. Notice, for example, that more than 68% of the cases fall between +1 SD (one standard deviation above the mean) and −1 SD (one standard deviation below the mean).

Most of the standardized tests that you're likely to encounter will probably report scores in terms of percentile ranks as well as one of two types of standard

FIGURE 15.1 Normal Probability Curve

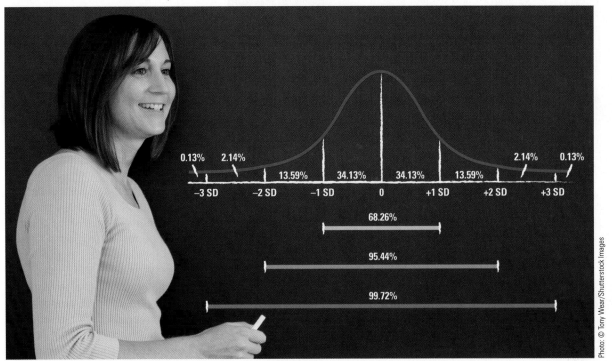

Figures do not add up to 100% because of rounding.

scores (both of which are based on standard deviations). One, called a **z score**, tells how far a given raw score is from the mean in standard deviation units. A z score of >1.5, for example, would mean that the student was 1.5 standard deviation units below the mean. Because some z scores (such as the one in the example just given) are negative and involve decimals, **T scores** are often used instead. T scores range from 0 to 100 and use a preselected mean of 50 to get away from negative values.

To grasp the relationship among z scores, T scores, and percentile ranks, examine Figure 15.2. The diagram shows each scale marked off below a normal curve. It supplies information about the interrelationships of these various scores, provided that the distribution you are working with is essentially normal. In a normal distribution, for example, a z score of +1 is the same as a T score of 60 or a percentile rank of 84; a z score of >2 is the same as a T score of 30 or a percentile rank of about 2. (In addition, notice that the distance between the percentile ranks clustered around the middle is only a small fraction of the distance between the percentile ranks at the ends of the distribution.)

Stanine Scores The **stanine score** (an abbreviation of "standard 9-point scale") is a type of standard score that divides a population into nine groups. Each stanine is one half of a standard deviation unit, as indicated in Figure 15.3. They are easier to understand than z scores or T scores, as any child or parent can understand that

stanines represent a 9-point scale with 1 as the lowest, 5 as the average, and 9 as the highest. Furthermore, unlike percentile ranks, stanine scores can be averaged. When it is desirable to have more precise information about relative standing, however, percentile ranks may be more useful, even though they cannot be averaged.

Pause& Reflect If you had to tell parents about the results of a standardized test, which type of score could you explain most clearly: raw score, percentile rank, z score, T score, or stanine score? Which do you think would be most informative for parents? For you? If you do not understand these tests completely, what can you do about this situation?

Misconceptions About the Nature and Use of Standardized Tests

Although the concept of psychological and educational assessment is not a particularly difficult one to grasp, many members of the general public, including

z score A standardized test score that tells how far a given raw score differs from the mean in standard deviation units.

T score A standardized test score that ranges from 0 to 100 and uses a preselected mean of 50 to avoid negative values.

stanine score A statistic reflecting a division of a score distribution into nine groups, with each stanine being one half of a standard deviation unit.

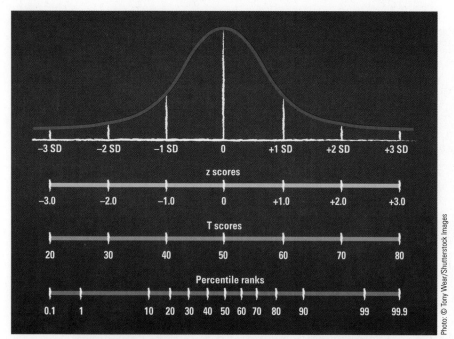

FIGURE 15.2 Relationship Among z Scores, T Scores, and Percentile Ranks

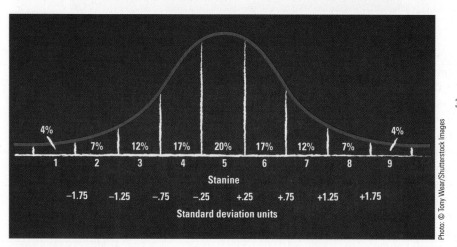

FIGURE 15.3 Percentage of Cases in Each Stanine (With Standard Deviation Units Indicated)

Photo: © Tony Wear/Shutterstock Images

person who constructed the test defined that attribute. Consequently, one person's intelligence test may assess certain characteristics that another person's intelligence test chooses to ignore. A common result of holding this naïve belief is that people draw inferences from test scores that are not supported by the validity evidence for that test.

2. *All tests with the same title are the same.* Even though two tests are called seventh grade science tests, this doesn't mean that they are interchangeable. Even if they have the same format (multiple-choice questions, for example), one may emphasize recall of factual material while the other may emphasize conceptual understanding or problem solving. The goal in assessment is to match a school district's objectives and standards with what a test measures.

3. *A test score accurately reflects what people know and can do.* No test provides a "true" score of an individual's knowledge and capabilities because all tests have built-in measurement error. Consequently, when people retake the same or an equivalent test, their scores vary. The best we can do is to say that a person's so-called true score probably lies between a lower and an upper boundary.

educators, draw incorrect inferences about what test scores mean because, for one reason or another, they have one or more of the following misconceptions (Braun & Mislevy, 2005):

1. *A test measures what its name implies.* This misconception can take a couple of forms. First, many people do not realize that a test measures a lot of things, some of which have nothing to do with its title. All test performances are influenced by, for example, familiarity with the testing situation, the type of test used, the way the test is administered, and the way the test is scored. Second, a test measures a particular attribute according to how the

4. *Two tests that claim to measure the same thing can be made interchangeable.* For the reasons mentioned in point 1, this is the exception rather than the rule. The noninterchangeability of tests explains why students in some school districts score well on the reading and math tests of the National Assessment of Educational Progress (NAEP) but not as well on their state's tests of the same skills.

5. *Tests are scored by adding up the number of items people answer correctly.* Whereas this is true for unidimensional tests, or tests in which all items measure the same thing, it is not true for tests that measure different skills in different ways. A lan-

guage test that measures knowledge of vocabulary and grammar as well as reading comprehension and conversational fluency should report separate scores for each capability.

6. *Scores of 70% correct, 80% correct, and 90% correct are equivalent to grades of C, B, and A, respectively.* This belief comes from the assumption that all tests are basically the same. But because test items can be written at different levels of difficulty, two tests that measure the same knowledge base are likely to produce different scores when taken by the same students.

7. *Multiple-choice questions are useful only for measuring how well students can recognize and recall factual knowledge.* This belief undoubtedly stems from the fact that the vast majority of multiple-choice items that appear on tests are written at the knowledge level of Bloom's taxonomy (first discussed in Chapter 13). But it is possible to write multiple-choice items that reflect the rest of the taxonomy.

8. *One can tell if an item is good just by looking at it.* As with most things, the mere appearance of an item can be deceiving. Whether or not a test item is good, which is to say useful, depends largely on how well the form and cognitive demands of an item match both the instruction received by the student and the stated purpose of the test. An item for which students have not been adequately prepared or which measures factual knowledge when a test is advertised as measuring ability to apply knowledge is not a good item, at least for that particular test.

The Suggestions for Teaching on the next page will help you and your students appropriately use standardized tests and interpret the scores from them.

Historically, standardized tests have been used to assess the knowledge and skills students have learned and how well they are likely to do in school in the near future. In recent years, however, test scores have also been used to judge how well educators are carrying out their main task—helping students learn the content and skills that are reflected in their state's standards. Is this an appropriate use of standardized tests? And does it work? The next section will try to answer both of those questions.

Pause&Reflect *We learned in school that standardized tests are critically important to our futures. Indeed, you will likely have to pass a standardized test to earn your license to teach, even after you have earned your degree. The No Child Left Behind Act requires the use of testing as a way to hold schools and school districts accountable for student progress. Because much attention is given to standardized test scores, it is commonly assumed that standardized tests are the best measures we have. But what precisely do they measure? Are there other, perhaps better, ways to accomplish the goals of schooling?*

© Yuriy Kirsanov/iStockphoto

LO2 Using Standardized Tests for Accountability Purposes: High-Stakes Testing

The Push for Accountability in Education

What does it mean to be held accountable for your actions? Generally, that you must explain and justify your actions to one or more people who have a stake in what you do, and, depending on how your actions are judged, you may be either rewarded or punished. Company employees, for example, are accountable to their supervisors or managers for the decisions they make and the quality of the products they produce. Likewise, students are accountable to both their teachers and parents for the quality of their learning. What about teachers, school administrators, and entire school districts? To whom are they accountable? Historically, they have operated under a looser and less well defined accountability system. Except in cases of blatant incompetence and illegal or immoral behavior, teachers and administrators were not likely to be either rewarded or punished for their efforts. That situation changed in 2001, and the reasons for the change can be traced to a growing discontent with the perceived quality of American education during the last two decades of the twentieth century.

In 1983, the National Commission on Excellence in Education published a report titled *A Nation at Risk: The Imperative for Educational Reform*. The report painted a bleak picture of the quality of education in the United States. It noted, for example, that about 13% of all 17-year-olds were judged to be functionally illiterate, that standardized test scores had generally fallen below levels achieved 25 years earlier, and that many

Suggestions for Teaching

Using Standardized Tests

1 Before you give a standardized test, emphasize that students should do their best.

For maximum usefulness, scores on standardized tests should be as accurate a representation as possible of what they intend to measure. Accordingly, the day before a standardized test is scheduled, tell your students that they should do their best. Emphasize that the scores will be used to help them improve their school performance and will provide useful feedback to you about the quality of your instruction. If you're thinking about ignoring this suggestion because you don't believe that students will score significantly higher on a standardized test in response to a simple pep talk, you might want to reconsider. Research has shown that students who have a positive attitude toward learning and test taking score higher on tests than do students whose attitudes are less positive or are negative (S. M. Brown & Walberg, 1993; Gulek, 2003).

2 Help your students improve their test-taking skills.

As we just mentioned, students' low motivation to do their best on a standardized test can negatively affect the usefulness of the inferences we draw from their scores. Is a low score due to insufficient knowledge, low motivation, or both factors? The same is true of students' test-taking skill. To maximize students' scores, testing experts (Linn & Miller, 2005, pp. 450–451) have recommended that teachers provide the following tips just before a test is scheduled:

1. Listen to or read directions carefully.
2. Listen to or read test items carefully.
3. Set a pace that will allow time to complete the test.
4. Bypass difficult items and return to them later.
5. Make informed guesses rather than omit items.
6. Eliminate as many alternatives as possible on multiple-choice items before guessing.

7. Follow directions carefully when marking the answer sheet (for example, be sure to darken the entire space).
8. Check to be sure the item number and answer number match when marking an answer.
9. Check to be sure the appropriate response is marked on the answer sheet.
10. Go back and check the answers if time permits.

3 Examine the test booklet and answer sheet in advance so that you are familiar with the test.

Ideally you might take an earlier released version of the test or a publicly available practice test yourself, so that you become thoroughly familiar with what your students will be doing. If there are any aspects of recording answers that are especially tricky, or if the test contains unfamiliar terminology, you might mention these when you give your test-taking skills presentation or when you hand out examination booklets and answer sheets. Knowledge of test vocabulary and terminology has been found to have a significant effect on students' performance on high-stakes tests (Gulek, 2003).

4 Be cautious when interpreting scores, and do what you can to avoid negative expectations.

The profiles or reports you will receive several weeks after a test has been administered will contain information that is potentially beneficial to you and your students, but only if it is interpreted and used properly. For example, if a student's test scores are lower than you expected them to be, don't automatically write the student off as a lost cause. Instead, examine the report to discover areas of weakness that you might attack with different instructional tactics and motivational incentives. If the student's performance in class is consistently better than his or her test performance, and if you are confident that your standards and assessment procedures are challenging, assume that how the student performs in class is a more accurate estimate of general capability.

5 Be prepared to offer parents clear and accurate information about their children's test scores.

For a variety of reasons, misconceptions about the nature of standardized tests are common. As a result, many parents do not fully understand what their children's scores mean. Parent–teacher conferences are probably the best time to correct misconceptions and provide some basic information about the meaning of standardized test scores.

The primary point you want to make is that test scores should be treated as *estimates* of whatever was measured because (a) tests do not (indeed, they cannot) assess everything that students know or that makes up a particular capability and (b) all tests contain some degree of error because of such factors as vaguely worded items, confusing directions, and low motivation on the day the test is administered. A student may have strengths and weaknesses not measured by a particular test, and because of changes in such characteristics as interests, motives, and cognitive skills, test scores can change, sometimes dramatically. The younger the student is and the longer the interval is between testings (on the same test), the greater the likelihood is that a test score will change significantly.

The instructional decisions you make in the classroom will be *guided* but not dictated by the test scores. Many parents fear that if their child obtains a low score on a test, she will be labeled a slow learner by the teacher and receive less attention than higher scoring students do. This is a good opportunity to lay such a fear to rest in two ways. First, note that test scores are but *one* source of information about students. You will also take into account how well they perform on classroom tests, homework assignments, and special projects, as well as in classroom discussions. Second, emphasize that you are committed to using test scores not to classify students but to help them learn.

17-year-olds were judged to be deficient in such higher order thinking skills as drawing inferences from written material and writing a persuasive essay. To justify the amount of money being spent on education and to improve student outcomes, the report called for standardized tests to be used as a way of documenting students' achievement and spurring educators to focus on raising achievement in such basic areas as reading, math, and science.

Subsequent reports of students' performance on standardized tests continued to paint a bleak picture (but see Bracey, 2008a, 2008b, for alternative interpretations). Discontent with the performance of American students and the desire to improve matters resulted in a piece of landmark federal legislation in the early part of this century.

{ **High-stakes testing: using test results to hold students and educators accountable for achievement** }

To hold students accountable for learning certain subjects and skills at acceptable levels and to improve the quality of education, all states annually administer standardized achievement tests in several subject areas. These tests are linked to state learning standards.

No Child Left Behind (NCLB)

In December 2001, the U.S. Congress passed legislation proposed by President George W. Bush to implement testing of students in reading and mathematics in all public schools that receive federal funds (which means virtually all schools). Testing students on their knowledge of science was added in 2007. This legislation, a reauthorization of the Elementary and Secondary Education Act, is commonly known as the No Child Left Behind Act (NCLB). Because the scores from these tests, either by themselves or in conjunction with other data, are used to determine such rewards and punishments as whether students get promoted to the next grade or are denied graduation from high school, whether teachers and administrators receive financial rewards or demotions, and whether school districts receive additional state funds or lose their accreditation, this practice is commonly referred to as high-stakes testing. You can read and download a copy of NCLB at the Department of Education's website (www.ed.gov).

TeachSource Video Case

Teaching Accountability: A Student Teacher's Perspective

Go to the Education CourseMate website and watch the video, study the artifacts in the case, and reflect upon the following questions:

1. A major concern of Caitlin Hollister, the student teacher in this video, is how to deal with students' poor performance on the state exam. On the one hand, she asks, how do you not get discouraged? On the other hand, she asks, how do you help students learn what they did not learn initially? What advice would you offer her?

2. The principal and veteran teachers in this video all put accountability in a positive light. In what ways do they do so?

Requirements of NCLB The No Child Left Behind Act (2001) contains several requirements that states must meet:

- *Standards.* States must establish what the law calls challenging content and achievement standards in mathematics, reading or language arts, and science, but the legislation leaves it to each state to decide for itself the meaning of the word *challenging*.

- *Testing.* Annual testing of all students in grades 3 through 8 in math and reading or language arts and at least one assessment of students in grades 9 through 12 in the same two subjects. In 2007, states were required to also administer a science assessment at least once to students in grades 3 through 5, 6 through 9, and 10 through 12. Decisions about test format, length, and item type have been left to each state. Vermont's assessment program, for example, includes mathematics problem-solving items, writing samples, and science performance tasks, in addition to the more familiar selected-response items (Vermont Department of Education, 2009). Kentucky's program also includes writing samples, as well as open-ended questions that require students to explain the reasoning behind their answers in reading, science, social studies, mathematics, and the humanities (Kentucky Department of Education, 2009).

- *Adequate yearly progress (AYP).* By 2014, all students must score at least at the "proficient" level (as defined by each state) of their state assessment in reading or language arts and math. To ensure that this goal is met, states must demonstrate each year that a certain additional percentage of all students have met that goal. This feature is referred to as adequate yearly progress, or AYP. Adequate yearly progress must be demonstrated by all groups of students, including racial and ethnic minorities, students of low socioeconomic status (SES), English language learners, and students with disabilities. Schools that fail to meet the AYP requirement not only must use different instructional approaches and programs but also must choose approaches and programs that have been shown to be effective by scientific research.

- *Reporting.* States and school districts must issue report cards to parents and the general public that describe how every group of students has performed on the annual assessment.

- *Accountability system.* School districts that fail to demonstrate AYP for 2 or more consecutive years are subject to a series of increasingly severe sanctions that may eventually result in replacement of all or most of the school staff, state takeover of school operations, or conversion to a charter school. Schools that meet or exceed AYP for 2 or more consecutive years and that have made the greatest gains are designated "distinguished schools" and may make financial awards to teachers.

Although NCLB mandates that students be tested in the areas of reading or language arts, math, and science and that they perform at a particular level, it has been left up to the states to decide which aspects of those subjects will be tested and how different levels of performance will be defined. This does not mean that states have free rein to do whatever they please; each state has an accountability plan for meeting the requirements of NCLB that has been approved by the federal government. States are free to amend these plans in the future, but changes have to be approved by the U.S. Department of Education.

Problems With Implementing NCLB The No Child Left Behind law is complex and has high stakes attached to it. Consequently, problems with its implementation, both potential and actual, have been noted. Here are a few of them:

- When NCLB was enacted in 2002, states were allowed to specify different schedules for meeting the goal of 100% proficiency in math and reading or language arts by 2014. Twenty-three states opted for smaller achievement gains in the early years and larger gains as the deadline of 2014 drew closer, a schedule that is referred to as backloading. California's goal, for example, was that 13.6% of students would score proficient or above in language arts for each of the first 3 years. The percentage of students scoring proficient or above would rise to 24.4% for each of the next 3 years. But for each year from 2007–2008 through 2013–2014,

---

NCLB requires standards; annual testing in math, reading, and science; annual progress for all students; public reports; and an accountability system.

the schedule called for increases of 11 percentage points. Because achievement gains have been harder to achieve than was anticipated, California and other states that have backloaded schedules are unlikely to meet NCLB's goal of 100% proficiency (Chudowsky & Chudowsky, 2008).

- Setting the cut score that determines whether or not a student has reached the proficiency level is based on the judgment of educators and carries significant consequences. If the score is set too low, a state's accountability plan may not pass federal muster. If it is set too high, the school may have a difficult time demonstrating AYP. This difference in defining the standard for proficiency probably accounts for a good part of the difference between low scoring and high scoring states (Ho, 2008).

- NCLB classifies students as belonging to particular subgroups (e.g., English language learners, students with disabilities, members of minorities) and requires that all be held to the same proficiency standard, except if there are too few students in any subgroup. The performance of these students is then ignored in determining whether a school district has met its AYP requirement. Some states, however, have negotiated with the U.S. Department of Education for a larger minimum subgroup size than the law specifies, thereby increasing the likelihood that more of their school districts will be satisfy their AYP requirement (Goldberg, 2005; Popham, 2005; Sunderman, 2006). The result of these changes is a lack of common accountability standards.

- The law fails to acknowledge that many minority students, students with disabilities, and English language learners have long-standing and deep-seated learning problems that make it difficult to accurately assess what they have learned (Abedi & Dietel, 2004; J. Thomas, 2005). For example, in some states English language learners are placed in 1-year immersion programs and are then required to take a test in English. Another problem is that because many state tests either omitted or under-represented English language learners during the norming process, their tests may well be inaccurate measures of what these students have learned (Solórzano, 2008). Although English language learners can take state tests in their native languages, such tests are often not available (Center on Education Policy, 2005; Solórzano, 2008).

- Students who qualify for special education must, according to the Individuals With Disabilities Education Act, have goals and objectives that match their learning levels incorporated into their individualized education programs. But NCLB requires that these students meet the same standards as students without disabilities (Houston, 2005).

Modifications of NCLB

Because of the structural problems inherent in NCLB and the research findings that we note a bit later in this chapter, the federal government has begun to make some changes in the law's accountability system. In March of 2008 the secretary of education announced that schools in which most students are meeting the AYP requirement, except for one subgroup, will not have to be labeled as needing improvement. The financial and other resources that ordinarily would have been

Foundations: Aligning Instructions With Federal Legislation

Go to the Education CourseMate website and watch the video, study the artifacts in the case, and reflect upon the following questions:

1. In this Video Case, various school professionals discuss the challenges of complying with NCLB. As a prospective teacher, what aspects of NCLB do you find most daunting?

2. In your opinion, has federal legislation such as NCLB improved the quality of public education? Use the material in this chapter to find information that will support your argument.

Pep Rallies for High-Stakes Tests: Does Hype Help?

Concern with rankings and the rewards and punishments attached to state assessment programs leads many teachers to provide students with intensive test preparation. Although this practice may raise scores, it often comes at the expense of meaningful learning. (p. 352)

Incentives Are All Over the MAP

VALERIE SCHREMP HAHN
AND CORINNE LESTCH
St. Louis Post-Dispatch, 4/8/09

It's that time of year when principals reward kids with Dilly Bars, pep rallies and parties, and when teachers tend to their students' needs by scrambling eggs at breakfast or assembling s'mores around a campfire.

Welcome to the season of state standardized exams.

In an era when state and federal governments are applying ever increasing pressure for all students to excel on tests, many schools in the St. Louis region are pursuing all avenues to coax better brain performance out of kids.

Tactics range from simple incentives and rewards, to elaborate themed events designed to make the drudgery of filling out test sheet bubbles seem as fun as recess.

And while critics caution about going overboard, the stakes for schools are high.

Under the federal No Child Left Behind Act, all students have to be "proficient" or better on state exams by 2014 or schools face consequences as serious as a state takeover.

This year, the window for taking the Missouri standardized test, or the Missouri Assessment Program, started March 30 and ends April 24. Illinois' two weeks of testing was last month.

Iveland Elementary School in the Ritenour district has converted classrooms into "cabins" so students equate taking a test to going to camp. They also hosted a night of activities with students, parents and teachers that included a campfire and s'mores and special camp T-shirts.

"It relieves some of the stress," said Danielle Sever, a fifth-grade teacher who spearheaded the idea of "Kamp MAP" with other faculty. "They're not taking a test, they're going to camp, and it's amazing how well my students tested this morning."

Some schools keep it low key, simply reminding parents to make sure their children get a good night's sleep and eat a good breakfast during test time.

Other schools base their test motivators on scientific research. At Hanna Woods

Elementary in the Parkway district, for example, students taking the test will get goody bags from younger students that include No. 2 pencils and mints. Peppermint, according to research from the University of Cincinnati, can help increase concentration.

At Kennerly Elementary in the Lindbergh School District, the parent association encouraged parents to donate bananas, which are rich in mind-boosting potassium.

In Missouri, students in grades three to eight will be tested in math and communication arts, with students in grades five and eight also being tested in science. High school exams, meanwhile, now have a built-in incentive for students. Under a new system, schools are urged by the state to include standardized exams scores toward a student's final grade in select courses.

Keysor Elementary in Kirkwood calls the standardized testing window a "Big Show," giving students a chance to show off their intelligence.

In Pattonville, Rose Acres Elementary teachers roll out the "red carpet" (a roll of red paper) for students to walk on in the morning on their way to test.

In Brentwood, all elementary students get breakfast in the morning, not just students from low-income families. The middle school teachers even raid the school kitchen to prepare breakfast for their students, who get to carry around special MAP-testing water bottles to ensure they stay hydrated for the test.

---

spent on that school instead can be used to improve the test scores of the lowest performing schools (U.S. Department of Education, 2008a).

Research on the Effects of High-Stakes Testing

Once NCLB was signed into law, its supporters and critics wasted no time in mounting passionate arguments about the beneficial and detrimental effects it would produce. Supporters, for example, maintained that the quality of teaching would improve because teachers could gear their instruction to their state's standards; that the achievement of racial and ethnic minorities, students with disabilities, and English language learners would improve because of closer monitoring of

their progress; and that students would be more highly motivated to learn. Critics, on the other hand, claimed among other things that the goal of NCLB (all students proficient in reading and math by 2014) was unrealistic and could not be reached; that NCLB would negatively change what and how teachers taught; that NCLB's emphasis on math and reading would produce a narrowing of the curriculum; that test preparation activities would be substituted for curriculum enrichment activities; and that states would lower their standards to avoid the penalties of not meeting the AYP requirement.

The first bits of evidence to appear were largely anecdotal: stories about how NCLB affected a teacher, one or more students, or a particular school district. But as a wise person once said, "the plural of anecdote is not data." What were needed were studies based on

"We encourage them, but we don't want to get them stressed out about it," said Assistant Superintendent David Faulkner.

Last week, Rapper Joka, also known as Robert McKee, visited a pep rally at Livingston Elementary in St. Louis, and performed the "MAP Rap." It says, in part: "I can be successful, I can be successful, watch me be successful, 'cause I can zap the MAP!"

Other school districts take a more temperate view on the rallies and incentives. Ladue and Clayton, for example, don't do anything particularly special to motivate students.

"While there may be snacks from parent associations during the breaks, I think the main focus is on encouraging the students to show what they know," said Kathy Reznikov, spokeswoman for Ladue schools.

Consciously or not, teachers don't want to send the message that they "teach to the test" or that the future of students relies solely within a certain testing window.

Robert Schaeffer, public education director for FairTest, a group that promotes a rethinking of standardized exams, says teachers and principals are caught between their obligation to students and policymakers who put an emphasis on standardized testing.

"Providing a good breakfast—you can't argue with that," said Schaeffer. "But some of the gimmicks, like car lotteries, go way too far. The amount of effort and money spent on getting kids ready for tests show how important a test has become. You don't do that sort of stuff for the debate society or the math team or the science fair."

David Figlio, an education and social policy professor at Northwestern University, said pretending that students are going to camp and bringing in a rapper is a way for educators to make sure students know they're responsible for their performance.

As for doling out breakfast foods and mints, Figlio said it works—but schools have to be careful of the short-term effects.

"If you carbo-load kids to do really well in March 2009, now if you're trying to make gains from there and have scores artificially inflated, what happens in 2010?" he said. "It has to be inflated even more, and you can see it kind of gets absurd."

Still, many teachers say their motivation strategies are producing surprising results.

Third-graders at Green Pines Elementary in Rockwood have capped off each morning of testing with daily rewards such as an extra recess, board game time and snacks. Teacher Kristin Kemp said one of her students missed testing time because of the flu. The girl's mother e-mailed to say how disappointed her daughter was to miss testing and class celebrations.

"I'm like, 'Excuse me?'" said Kemp, pleasantly surprised by the response.

And at Hanna Woods, Assistant Principal Nicole Evans says even the younger students who don't have to take the test get into the spirit. "We've heard them say, 'Ooh, I can't wait to take the test,'" she said.

Source: Valerie Schremp Hahn and Corinne Lestch, "Incentives are all over the MAP," from *St. Louis Post-Dispatch,* April 8, 2009. Reprinted by permission of *St. Louis Post-Dispatch.*

Questions and Activities

1. The schools mentioned in this article used a variety of methods to motivate students to do well on their state's standardized test. These methods ranged from reminding parents to make sure their children get a good night's sleep and eat a balanced breakfast the morning of the test to simulating a nighttime camp experience. Which, if any, of these activities would you endorse as a teacher? Why?

2. Robert Schaeffer, the public education director of FairTest, argued against the use of extreme incentives for testing programs, partly on the grounds that schools do not do the same thing for debate societies, math teams, or science fairs. What do you think would be the first rebuttal teachers and administrators would probably make to Mr. Schaeffer's criticism?

3. High schools in Missouri are being encouraged to use students' test scores as a factor in calculating their final grade. Based on what you read in this chapter about test validity, does this strike you as a reasonable practice?

---

hundreds and thousands of students and teachers. Those studies were eventually conducted; what follows is a summary of NCLB's effects on students' achievement, students' motivation, teachers' classroom behavior, classroom instruction, the dropout rate, state standards and test quality, and the use of supplemental education services. When we use the term *high-stakes testing*, we're referring mostly to the annual standardized tests that are given to satisfy NCLB's requirements, but it also pertains to exams that are given to determine eligibility for high school graduation (high school exit exams).

{ **High-stakes testing has so far failed to live up to its promise.** }

Effect on Achievement A major assumption underlying NCLB is that the consequences of failing to meet its accountability standards will drive states and school districts to improve the quality of classroom instruction and the level of student achievement. This hypothesis was tested by a group of researchers (Nichols, 2007; Nichols, Glass, & Berliner, 2006), who classified 25 states in terms of how much pressure their testing programs placed on teachers and students and then examined the relationship between these various programs and performance by fourth and eighth grade students on the math and reading scores of the National Assessment of Educational Progress (NAEP) tests. The researchers found no relationship between earlier pressure from high-stakes tests and later achievement. Additionally, in a different study, high school exit exams

A possible negative effect of high-stakes testing programs is that teachers may spend more time preparing students for the test and less time on topics and subjects that are not covered by the test.

appeared to have no noticeable effect on student achievement (Holme, Richards, Jimerson, & Cohen, 2010).

Other analyses have reported positive but small effects. Jaekyung Lee (2008) analyzed 14 studies and concluded that the effect of high-stakes testing on NAEP reading and math scores was so modest that NCLB's goal of achieving 100% proficiency for all students by 2014 would not likely be attained. The Center on Education Policy (2008a, 2009) found that between 2002 and 2008, more states reported gains in both average test scores and percentage of students scoring at the proficient level than reported declines. Gains in math were stronger than gains in reading.

Because the express purpose of NCLB is to raise the achievement of *all* students, we also need to examine the evidence pertaining to gains for minority students, low-SES students, students with disabilities, and English language learners. As we noted in Chapter 5, there is a long-standing achievement gap between White students and Black and Hispanic students. The evidence to date suggests that NCLB has had, at best, a small effect on narrowing that gap. The gaps between White and Black and between White and Hispanic students on NAEP reading and math scores from 2004 through 2008 have not changed (U.S. Department of Education, 2008b). On state tests, gaps between White and minority students have narrowed somewhat but still remain as large as 20 percentage points in many instances (Center on Education Policy, 2009). Similar conclusions can be drawn about the performance of low-SES students, students with learning disabili-

ties, and English language learners (Holme, Richards, Jimerson, & Cohen, 2010; Jones, 2007; J. Lee, 2008).

Before concluding that NCLB has or has not improved students' achievement, a few important caveats need to be kept in mind. First, the gains reported by some states may be due to intensive teaching to the test, changes in the cut scores that define proficiency, and school reform programs begun by some states prior to the implementation of NCLB. Second, comparing state test scores with NAEP scores should be done cautiously because NAEP tests are not as closely aligned with state standards and local curricula as are state tests (see, for example, Fuller, Gesicki, Kang, & Wright, 2006). Third, as the Center on Education Policy (2008a) pointed out, and as we have pointed out in earlier chapters, test scores are not the same thing as achievement because they measure learning imperfectly and incompletely.

Effect on Motivation Some evidence suggests that the presence of high stakes motivates some students to work harder. Among Massachusetts high school students who failed that state's high-stakes test the first time they took it, about two thirds said they were now working harder and paying more attention in class, and almost 75% said that missing too much school was a major reason for failing the test (Cizek, 2003). On the other hand, the prospect of having to take an exit exam in either in the 10th or 11th grade, or having just failed to pass one, does not appear to affect student motivation one way or the other (Holme, Richards, Jimerson, & Cohen, 2010).

A study of 20 elementary and middle schools in three states (A. B. Brown & Clift, 2010) clearly demonstrated that NCLB does affect the motivation of administrators, teachers, and students, but not always in a positive way. It depends on where a school stands with respect to the AYP requirement. Schools that have either just passed or just failed the AYP requirement, for example, tend to be more hopeful about improving and so take active steps to either stay ahead of the curve or catch up. Those steps, of course, may or may not please everyone. Such actions as de-emphasizing tests that encourage higher level thinking in favor of multiple-choice questions, devoting more time to test preparation, making more time available for professional development, and reinforcing math and English lessons during teaching of other subjects may be viewed positively or negatively, depending on one's educational philosophy. But there's no denying that these schools are motivated.

Schools that are so far behind that they have no hope of ever satisfying AYP tend to behave quite differently. Even if these schools achieve positive results with new curricula, teaching methods, and other initiatives, they know they will receive no credit or rewards

© 2010 Creatas/Jupiterimages Corporation

if they still fall short of meeting AYP. As a result, motivation levels decline, curriculum changes are more superficial, and tactics like trying to attract high scoring students from private or magnet schools are used more often. Behavior problems often increase. As one teacher said, "The kids don't have the academics and it's gotten to the point where they'd rather be the bad apple than the stupid one" (A. B. Brown & Clift, 2010, pp. 788–789).

In the last group are those schools that exceed the AYP standard by a comfortable margin every year. As might be expected, NCLB has little or no impact on motivation. There are few changes to the curriculum or how teachers teach. Their main concern is that they cover all the standards mandated by their state. One noticeable effect was a sort of "circle the wagons" mind-set by a number of parents and teachers. Several worried about what would happen if large numbers of students from failing schools in their district enrolled in their child's school by invoking the choice provision of NCLB.

A similar differential effect on motivation was noticed in a study of low achieving Chicago public school students (Roderick & Engel, 2001). In order to be promoted to the next grade, students had to earn a passing score on a standardized test. During the school year leading up to the test, students could receive extra help both before school and through an after-school program. Students who failed the test were required to attend a summer program before they could retake the test and be promoted for the fall semester. Those who failed the second test were retained.

Of those students who were judged to have put in a substantial amount of work either in or out of school because of the stakes involved, 57% passed the test in June and an additional 23% passed in August. Those students who demonstrated no effort to improve their score did not fare so well. About 11% passed in June and an additional 25% in August. A third group was considered to have substantial home or learning skill problems. About 12% of these students passed in June and an additional 47% passed in August.

The findings from these two studies clearly show, as have other interventions mentioned in previous chapters, that no single policy or approach will work for all students because classroom learning is an extremely complex phenomenon that is only partly under the teacher's control. Although the threat of retention was sufficient to motivate some of the Chicago students to work harder and take advantage of the additional resources that were provided, it had a much smaller effect on students with serious learning skill deficits or problems at home and on students who simply declined to put forth more effort. Retaining students who fall into these latter two groups is likely to cause them to become even more disengaged and eventually drop out of school. Obviously, an alternative to retention is required to motivate these students and raise their achievement levels.

NCLB changes how teachers teach.

Effect on Teachers and Teaching Numerous studies have documented that high-stakes testing programs affect how teachers teach and their motivation for teaching. The effects have been mostly negative, although positive effects are occasionally noted.

A review of research on the effects of NCLB (Au, 2007) found that teachers were focusing on small, isolated, test-size pieces of information at the expense of relating new content to other subject matter and were emphasizing lecture rather than more student-centered instructional techniques. But a few studies reported an increase in lessons that emphasized knowledge integration and the use of student-centered instruction (such as cooperative learning).

School districts have shown an increasing tendency to focus additional instructional time and resources on so-called bubble kids. These are students who are "on the bubble," meaning they narrowly missed the proficiency cut score. If their scores can be raised by a relatively small amount the next time the test is given, they offer schools an easy and inexpensive way to meet

© Christopher Futcher/iStockphoto

their AYP requirement—but often at the expense of those who score even lower (A. B. Brown & Clift, 2010; Ho, 2008; Houston, 2007).

A 2-year study of 10 low performing Chicago elementary schools (Finnigan & Gross, 2007) found that in response to their schools being placed on probation, a majority of teachers reported that they tried new instructional methods, increased the amount of time devoted to test preparation, grouped students by skill level, spent more time preparing lesson plans, and spent more time working with students who had failed to pass the test by a small amount (the so-called bubble kids referred to before). But these efforts were not sustained for the most part because students' subsequent test scores did not increase and administrators did not support teachers' efforts (many teachers complained, for example, about a lack of professional development workshops). As a result, teacher morale decreased.

Observations of and interviews with teachers in other states have reported similar findings. In response to the pressures produced by NCLB, teachers devote more time to test preparation (3 to 5 weeks, by some accounts), gear lessons to the content of the test, use more teacher-directed forms of instruction (such as lecture, assigned seatwork, and asking questions that have only one brief answer), increase the pace of instruction to ensure that the prescribed content for each day's lesson is covered, and spend less time devising instructional strategies aimed at helping all students understand lesson content and more time grouping and regrouping students. The only instructional benefit mentioned by teachers was that test result data could be used to identify students' weaknesses (Anderson, 2009; Center on Education Policy, 2008b; Jennings & Rentner, 2006; Thomas B. Fordham Institute, 2008; Valli & Buese, 2007).

Concern with rankings and the rewards and punishments attached to state assessment programs leads many teachers to provide students with intensive test preparation. Although this practice may raise scores, it often comes at the expense of meaningful learning (Center on Education Policy, 2005; Goldberg, 2004; Houston, 2007; Nichols & Berliner, 2005).

Consequently, there is often little transfer to other tests that purport to measure the same knowledge and skills (R. L. Linn, 2009; McGill-Franzen & Allington, 2006).

For example, in one study 83% of students in a Pittsburgh elementary school scored above the national norm on the reading test of the Iowa Tests of Basic Skills (a standardized achievement test). But on the reading test of the Pennsylvania state assessment, only 26% scored within the top two proficiency levels (Yau, 2002). The phenomenon this study highlights is sometimes referred to as WYTIWYG: what you test is what you get. In other words, high-stakes assessments lead teachers to focus on preparing students for a particular type of test, and as a result, there is little carryover to other tests that measure the same or similar skills.

Effect on the Curriculum NCLB and high school exit exams have affected school curricula in two ways, one of which tends to be perceived positively and the other almost always negatively. On the positive side, many school districts have done a better job of aligning state standards with what is taught in class and what is tested (Holme, Richards, Jimerson, & Cohen, 2010). The negative effect has to do with the widespread practice of curriculum narrowing (Au, 2007; Center on Education Policy, 2008b; Jennings & Rentner, 2006; Jones, 2007; McMurrer, 2007). A survey of 349 school districts conducted by the Center on Education Policy (McMurrer, 2007) found that between 2001–2002 and 2006–2007, almost two thirds of these districts increased instructional time for reading and language arts by an average of 46% and increased math instruction by an average of 37%. In addition, the specific aspects of reading or language arts and math that were emphasized were those covered by the appropriate state test. Because school days are rarely lengthened, this increase had to come at the expense of other subjects and activities. As expected, almost half of the surveyed districts reported that they decreased instructional time for social studies (ironic, when you think about the criticism that schools receive when students are unable to locate various countries on a map), science, art, music, physical education, lunch, and recess (recall our discussion in Chapter 3 about the value of recess). A school district in Missouri did just that when it eliminated a semester-long course on world geography to create a yearlong course on U.S. government. This change was made, despite protests from parents and some students, to align the district's curriculum with the state's standards and assessment program (Bock, 2008).

Effect on the Dropout Rate The question of whether high-stakes exams, particularly high school exit exams, increase the dropout rate (currently about 5% of all high school students) is a difficult one to answer definitively.

Chapter 15: Understanding Standardized Assessment

Not only is the research limited, it is also inconclusive because states define and count dropouts differently, and it is difficult for researchers to isolate the effect of a high-stakes test from other factors that may also play a role (Kober et al., 2006). Nevertheless, a report from the Center on Education Policy concluded that exit exams cause more students to drop out of school than would otherwise be the case, with the greatest impact occurring among minority students, students from low-income families, and English language learners (Y. Zhang, 2009). Other researchers (e.g., Holme, Richards, Jimerson, & Cohen, 2010; McNeil, Coppola, Radigan, & Vazquez Heilig, 2008) have reported similar findings, so the phenomenon seems to be real. To eliminate the arguments about calculating dropout rates that arose from different definitions and formulas, the U.S. Secretary of Education in April of 2008 announced that all states would use the same federal formula to calculate graduation and dropout rates (U.S. Department of Education, 2008a).

{ **No common meaning of proficiency exists among the states.** }

Effect on State Standards and Test Quality Critics of NCLB warned that some states would be tempted to formulate weaker standards and establish lower cut scores for judging students proficient, so as to avoid the penalties of not meeting AYP requirements. Recent research indicates that this has indeed happened. A study of 26 states by the Thomas B. Fordham Institute and the Northwest Evaluation Association (Cronin, Dahlin, Adkins, & Kingsbury, 2007) found that state tests differed significantly in their difficulty, states with the highest standards (meaning higher cut scores) were more likely to lower their cut scores than other states, some state tests replaced more difficult items with easier items, and tests given to eighth graders were consistently more difficult for the students than tests given to third graders (tests for each grade level should be equally difficult for students in those grades). Because of these inconsistencies, the authors of this report noted, "five years into implementation of the No Child Left Behind Act, there is no common understanding of what 'proficiency' means" (p. 7). Furthermore, states that have the lowest standards for attaining proficiency also have larger concentrations of low-SES students and students of color. In other words, ethnic and racial minority students and students from poor homes are often held to lower standards—just the sort of discrepancy that NCLB was supposed to eliminate (D. S. Reed, 2009).

A major test quality issue is the breadth of testing that is done to satisfy state and federal requirements.

As we noted earlier, the inferences that are drawn from test scores about what students have learned are likely to be more accurate as more and different types of tests are used. Critics of NCLB feared that states would either adopt a single commercially published standardized test whose correspondence to state standards was less than desirable or would create relatively simple constructed-response tests for the sake of efficiency and cost. Although many states chose one of these two solutions, some have opted for a broad range of assessment instruments that are likely to give teachers more diagnostically useful information. In New York, for example, a group of 28 high schools called the New York Performance Standards Consortium practices and promotes the use of alternative assessments (New York Performance Standards Consortium, 2007). These schools, which are not unlike most high schools in New York, use inquiry-based methods of learning that emphasize classroom discussion, project-based assignments, and student choice. Their assessments are performance based, and to graduate, all students must receive a passing grade on an analytic literary essay, a social studies research paper, an original science experiment, and an application of higher level mathematics. At least one study found that 77% of students from these schools attended a 4-year college and earned, on average, a grade-point average of 2.7 (on a 1–4 scale) (Foote, 2007).

Effect on the Use of Supplemental Education Services Although NCLB requires schools that fail to meet AYP for 3 or more consecutive years to provide free tutoring to students, only 17% of eligible students received this service during the 2005–2006 school year (Vernez, et al., 2009). Students in small and rural school systems were less likely to receive tutoring than those in urban districts because of the lack of providers in those areas, the lack of transportation to a tutoring provider, or the lack of computers to access Internet-provided services (Goldberg, 2005; Richard, 2005). Although school districts that have failed to meet AYP goals are prohibited from providing their own tutoring services, the Department of Education in 2005 allowed the city of Chicago to do so to encourage more students to take advantage of the service. Several other large urban districts were said to be readying their own proposals for a similar exemption (Gewertz, 2005).

Recommendations for Improving High-Stakes Testing

If NCLB and state-mandated assessment programs are to fulfill their goals of improving the quality of instruction and raising achievement levels, they will have to be implemented in such a way that all stakeholders believe they are being treated fairly. On this score, NCLB

Challenging Assumptions

Healing the Patient: Using the Medical Model to Guide Educational Accountability

Almost everybody, including educators, accepts the contention that educators should be held accountable for their efforts. Indeed, every person should be accountable to others in some fashion. What is, and should be, vigorously debated is the way in which accountability is defined and practiced. We believe that the accountability systems of many states are less effective than they could be because their primary focus is on identifying and punishing substandard performance rather than identifying and remediating the causes of those weaknesses.

We agree with measurement expert Gregory Cizek, who argues that if high-stakes programs are to be more widely embraced by educators, students, and parents, they should mimic the assessment approach that physicians use in their practices. Medical tests tend to be diagnostic in nature because of the detailed level at which they report results. A typical analysis of a blood sample, for example, provides information on the levels of more than 20 elements (e.g., blood sugar, sodium, potassium, calcium, protein, HDL cholesterol, LDL cholesterol, and triglycerides). Abnormal results are then followed by

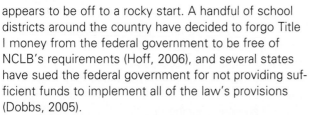

specific recommendations for treatment. The patient isn't accused of being inferior and charged twice the doctor's normal fee as a penalty for having "failing" test scores.

Consequently, a reasonable stand for teachers to take regarding high-stakes testing programs is that they should be constructed to provide detailed information about students' strengths and weaknesses; these results should then serve as a basis for additional instruction. In addition, professional development workshops and seminars should be provided, focusing on how teachers can help students learn the knowledge and skills that are assessed.

What Do You Think?

Do you agree with using a medical model for high-stakes testing? What can you do in your own school to promote this view of testing? To explore this issue further, see the "Challenging Assumptions" section of the textbook's Education CourseMate website.

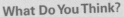

---

appears to be off to a rocky start. A handful of school districts around the country have decided to forgo Title I money from the federal government to be free of NCLB's requirements (Hoff, 2006), and several states have sued the federal government for not providing sufficient funds to implement all of the law's provisions (Dobbs, 2005).

While political leaders complain about funding, educators argue that the goal of having all students be proficient in math and reading or language arts by 2014 is unrealistic and will bring about the demise of fundamentally sound schools (Mabry, 2008; Nichols & Berliner, 2005; Popham, 2009; J. Thomas, 2005). Still others (for example, Darling-Hammond, 2009; D. Sadker & Zittleman, 2004) argue that most accountability programs have adopted the wrong focus. A more useful accountability system is one that holds policy makers accountable for the effects of their high-stakes accountability systems. In this view, an accountability system that focuses exclusively on the test scores of students, classes, schools, and districts—ignoring wide disparities in educational opportunity because of differences in funding and facilities—is an irresponsible system.

Pause & Reflect *Critics of high-stakes testing suggest that teachers try to persuade policy makers to change the worst aspects of such programs. They recommend steps such as these: speak out at school board meetings; organize a letter-writing campaign to the school board and legislators; assemble a delegation to visit legislators; write letters to the local newspaper; set up a workshop on the abuses of high-stakes testing. How many of these activities are you willing to engage in? Why?*

In response to the many criticisms of high-stakes testing programs, several professional and nonprofit organizations (see, for example, Center on Education Policy, 2007; Commission on Instructionally Supportive Assessment, 2002) have made numerous recommendations for improving NCLB, including the following:

1. Each state should adopt only those content standards that represent the most important knowledge and skills that students need to learn. This will help states avoid having more standards than teachers can cover, students can master, and test makers can

assess. Having a more modest set of standards also allows educators, students, and parents to get feedback about performance for each standard instead of a single score summed over hundreds of standards.

2. A state's content standards should clearly describe exactly what is being assessed, so teachers can create lessons that directly address those standards. Phrases such as "express and interpret information and ideas," for example, should be translated into more precise language.

3. Scores on a state assessment should be reported on a standard-by-standard basis for each student, school, and district.

4. States should provide school districts with additional assessment procedures to assess those standards that the required assessment does not cover.

5. States should monitor the curricula of school districts to ensure that instruction addresses all content standards and subjects, not just those assessed by the required state test.

6. State assessments should be designed so that all students have an equal opportunity to demonstrate which of the state's standards they have mastered. This includes providing accommodations and alternative assessments for students with disabilities and those who are limited in their English proficiency. The IEPs of students with disabilities should be used to determine how they should be tested and to what standards they should be held accountable.

7. All tests should satisfy the Standards for Educational and Psychological Testing that were jointly developed by the American Educational Research Association, The American Psychological Association, and the National Council on Measurement in Education and similar test-quality guidelines.

8. Teachers and principals should receive professional development training that helps them use test results to optimize children's learning.

9. At least once every 3 years, states should be required to have their standards and assessments independently reviewed.

10. To satisfy the AYP requirement, states should have the option of substituting improvement of test scores of individual students rather than the current requirement of measuring an entire group's progress.

LO3 Standardized Testing and Technology

Given the prevalence of standardized testing and the large amount of money that schools spend on testing programs, it is not too surprising that technology tools exist for a wide range of assessment formats, including the standard true–false, multiple-choice, and fill-in-the-blank questions, as well as alternative assessments such as essays, debate forums, simulations, and electronic exhibitions of student work. As we discuss in this section, technology can be used in all phases of testing, including preparing students for standardized tests, assessing mastery of state standards, and helping more students meet state standards.

Using Technology to Prepare Students for Assessments

To perform well on standardized tests, students need to have a clear understanding of the standards for which they will be held accountable and the types of items that will be used to assess those standards. Toward that end, many states provide web-based resources to help students become familiar with and prepare for state assessments. On the websites of state departments of education, students, teachers, and parents can read or download copies of their state's content and performance standards, study examples of the types of items that will appear on the test, and, in some cases, take practice tests. The University of Texas, for example, provides online tutorials and practice tests to that state's high school students to help them prepare for the required graduation exam (Carnevale, 2004). During the 2006–2007 school year, 112 Tennessee schools participated in the Tennessee Formative Assessment Program. Students in grades 3 through 8 took online formative assessments that were aligned with state standards to help teachers monitor which students

Websites of state departments of education and private companies provide services that help prepare students for state assessments.

In coming years, it is likely that increasing numbers of students will take high-stakes and other standardized tests on a computer.

were and were not on track to pass the end-of-year state assessment (Tennessee Department of Education, 2006).

Some states and school districts also make available the online test preparation services of private, for-profit companies. The Princeton Review, for example, has a 130,000-question test bank that school districts can use to create online practice tests that are aligned with their state's standards for grades 3 through 12. A company called Smarthinking (www.smarthinking.com) provides tutoring through online instructors (called "e-structors") and digital whiteboards. Students can correspond with tutors in real time or submit questions and assignments and get a response within 24 hours. The digital whiteboard is used by students to demonstrate their understanding of concepts and skills (such as English grammar or mathematical problem solving), and also by the tutor, who adds comments and corrections.

On the website of TestGEAR (www.testu.com), students take a diagnostic pretest and are then provided with individualized courses in various aspects of math and language arts. Teachers receive diagnostic reports that analyze students' responses to test questions. A teacher in an Orlando,

Florida, school who used the TestGEAR service was convinced that it helped his students improve their scores on that state's high-stakes test, the Florida Comprehensive Assessment Test (Borja, 2003).

Using Technology to Assess Mastery of Standards

Standardized tests administered via computer (called computer-based testing, or CBT) are something you are likely to see more often in the coming years. One reason is that the National Assessment of Educational Progress is moving in that direction. The 2009 science assessment, which includes simulations, is given on computer, and the 2011 writing assessment is scheduled to be given that way as well (M. Schneider, 2006). Another factor that may push schools in the direction of CBT is that students who take the same test either on a computer or on paper earn the same scores. This should eliminate the concern that factors like computer familiarity and anxiety will adversely affect students' scores (S. Wang, Jiao, Young, Brooks, & Olson, 2008). Nevertheless, you should still be aware of CBT's advantages and disadvantages. On the plus side:

- You can get scores and detailed reports at any time, from immediately after a test is completed to a few days later, and can therefore provide students with timely feedback (Chaney & Gilman, 2005; A. Olson, 2002; Russo, 2002).

- CBT reduces the chances of cheating by allowing you to create as many random sequences of test items as there are students taking the test (Chaney & Gilman, 2005).

- It is easier to use novel items to assess certain skills. For example, a computer screen could display the periodic table of elements with a question mark in five of the cells and the five elements that belong in those cells above the table. The student would have to drag each element to its correct location and then drop it (release the mouse button) (Zinesky & Sireci, 2002).

On the negative side:

- It is costly to buy and maintain enough computers to test large groups of students. One high school in Indiana, for example, had to close four computer labs for a month to test every student.

Chapter 15: Understanding Standardized Assessment

- Schools need to have a plan for dealing with interruptions due to a faulty computer or a power loss (L. Olson, 2003).

Using Technology to Promote Mastery of Standards

Given the high stakes involved in meeting the AYP requirement of NCLB, you can expect to see school districts doing everything they can to raise test scores, including using technology. A case in point is a Massachusetts high school that used computer-based instruction (CBI) to significantly increase the math scores of students who were at risk of failing that part of the state's standardized test, the Massachusetts Comprehensive Assessment System (MCAS) (Hannafin & Foshay, 2008). Sophomores whose eighth grade MCAS scores were less than acceptable were required to take a daily 45-minute CBI course whose content was aligned with the math standards assessed by the MCAS. The program adopted by the school district was based on the mastery approach that we outlined in Chapter 14. Students worked independently at their own pace on relatively brief segments of material called modules. Before being allowed to progress to the next module, students had to score at least 80% correct on the end-of-module exam. The effect on their 10th grade math MCAS scores was quite noticeable. Although the average scale score (a type of standardized score) of students not required to take the CBI course was higher than the average score of those who were in the CBI program (245 vs. 236, respectively), the eighth grade scores of the CBI students (who were considered to be at-risk) were considerably lower (215 vs. 234, respectively). Thus, the CBI students experienced a greater gain from eighth grade to 10th grade than did the non-CBI students. The gap between these two groups in the eighth grade was 19 points.

WHAT ELSE? *RIP & REVIEW* **CARDS IN THE BACK**

16

BECOMING A BETTER TEACHER BY BECOMING A REFLECTIVE TEACHER

LEARNING OBJECTIVES

After studying this chapter, you will be able to . . .

LO1 Explain how you can improve your reflection skills by using specific tools to collect information from students, peers, and yourself about how effectively you teach.

LO2 Describe how such technology tools as digital portfolios can be used to improve your reflection skills.

What makes a great teacher? It is a question that every aspiring and practicing teacher *should* ask and—we believe—it is a question that every aspiring and practicing teacher who seeks to improve in her or his profession *does* ask. Amanda Ripley (2010) used this question as the title of her story in *The Atlantic* magazine.[1] Her story opens as follows:

> On August 25, 2008, two little boys walked into public elementary schools in Southeast Washington, D.C. Both were African American fifth graders. The previous spring, both had tested below grade level in math.
>
> One walked into Kimball Elementary School and climbed the stairs to Mr. William Taylor's math classroom, a tidy, powder-blue space in which neither the clocks nor most of the electrical outlets worked.
>
> The other walked into a very similar classroom a mile away at Plummer Elementary School. In both schools, more than 80 percent of the children received free or reduced-price lunches. At night, all the children went home to the same urban eco-system, a ZIP code in which almost a quarter of the families lived below the poverty line and a police district in which somebody was murdered every week or so.
>
> At the end of the school year, both little boys took the same standardized test given at all D.C. public schools—not a perfect test of their learning, to be sure, but a relatively objective one (and, it's worth noting, not a very hard one).
>
> After a year in Mr. Taylor's class, the first little boy's scores went up—way up. He had started below grade level and finished above. On average, his classmates' scores rose about 13 points—which is almost 10 points more than fifth-graders with similar incoming test scores achieved in other low-income D.C. schools that year. On that first day of school, only 40 percent of Mr. Taylor's students were doing math at grade level. By the end of the year, 90 percent were at or above grade level.
>
> As for the other boy? Well, he ended the year the same way he'd started it—below grade level. In fact, only a quarter of the fifth-graders at Plummer finished the year at grade level in math—despite having started off at about the same level as Mr. Taylor's class down the road.
>
> This tale of two boys, and of the millions of kids just like them, embodies the most stunning finding to come out of education research in the past decade: more than any other variable in education—more than schools or curriculum—teachers matter. Put concretely, if Mr. Taylor's student continued to learn at the same level for a few more years, his test scores would be no different from those of his more affluent peers in Northwest D.C. And if these two boys were to keep their respective teachers for three years, their lives would likely diverge forever. By high school, the compounded effects of the strong teacher—or the weak one—would become too great.

Teachers matter. We know this to be true not only because of a story of two students, but from our own experience. Reflect for a moment on as many teachers as you can remember. How many of them were really outstanding in the sense that they established a vital, engaging learning environment, were sensitive to the needs of students, and—when you encountered difficulty—found techniques to help you learn? How many of them did an adequate job but left you bored or indifferent most of the time? How many of them made you dread entering their classrooms because they were either ineffective or insensitive or even cruel in dealing with you and your classmates? Of those ineffective or vindictive teachers, how many were dissatisfied with themselves and with their jobs? How many lousy teachers are unhappy people?

Teachers matter. And what matters most about teachers is whether they are learners. As Linda Darling-Hammond and her colleagues (2009) put it, students need "teachers who can learn *from* teaching, as well as learning *for* teaching" (p. 11, emphasis in original).

Teacher learning matters. It matters to students and it matters to the teachers themselves. To become a better teacher you must learn *from* teaching. The best way to learn from your teaching is to become a reflective teacher. This chapter offers some suggestions.

[1] Source: Ripley, Amanda. "What Makes a Great Teacher?" from *Atlantic Magazine*, Jan/Feb 2010. Copyright 2010, The Atlantic Media Co. as published in *The Atlantic*. Distributed by Tribune Media Services.

LO1 Improving Your Reflection Skills to Improve Your Teaching

Scholars who study instructional processes (e.g., Freiberg, 2002; Yilmaz-Tuzun, 2008) often note that effective teachers know how to coordinate a diverse array of instructional elements (such as planning, lesson design, time management, classroom management, instructional methods, student motivation, and assessment techniques) and adapt them to differences in student needs, materials, and purposes. Their insights highlight the point that to be consistently effective, you will need to observe and analyze what you do in the classroom. In essence, you will be conducting formative assessment: observing and analyzing your own action with the intent to improve student outcomes. Connie Moss and Susan Brookhart (2009) stated:

> Formative assessment can have a transformational effect on teachers and teaching. In a very real way, it flips a switch, shining a bright light on individual teaching decisions so that teachers can see clearly . . . the difference between the **intent** and the **effect** of their actions. (p. 10, emphasis in original)

Thus, being reflective does not simply mean sitting back and thinking about teaching and learning; it is more active than that. Being reflective means bringing a scholarly mind-set to your work: using techniques that provide you with the information you need to inquire critically into your decisions and actions as a teacher. In the sections that follow, we will explore several such techniques.

Student Feedback

One useful source of information about the effectiveness of your actions is always right in front of you: your own students. Unlike your colleagues and other visitors, they are there every day. After several months of watching and interacting with you, you can be assured that they have some well-formed opinions on what they like and don't like about your methods and behaviors. You may not agree with their opinions or their reasons for them, but it is worth collecting and reflecting on this type of feedback.

The easiest and least intrusive way to collect this information is to just watch how students behave over the course of several lessons. If they're chatting with one another, surfing the web on their cell phones, looking bored, or looking confused and anxious more often than they appear to be engaged in the task at hand, that's a clear signal that something is wrong and needs to be fixed as quickly as possible.

You can also solicit student feedback in more formal ways. You can, for example, ask a sample of students (or the entire class, if it's small enough) to tell you what they liked about a lesson, what they didn't like, and why. With older students, you can also ask them to fill out a 5-point rating scale that covers various aspects of your teaching methods and the general classroom atmosphere. If you do use a rating scale, bear in mind that many students tend to ignore the extreme ends of the scale, even when such a response is warranted.

For teachers who adopt a constructivist approach and value students' perceptions of how well constructivist learning principles are implemented in the classroom, Peter Taylor and his colleagues (Taylor & Fraser, 1998; Taylor, Fraser, & Fisher, 1997) developed the Constructivist Learning Environment Survey, which is also available on the textbook's Education CourseMate website.

Peer and Self-Assessment Techniques

Classroom Observation Schedules In addition to student evaluations, you will probably find feedback from fellow teachers and supervisors to be a particularly valuable resource, since they have the background and pedagogical knowledge to help you understand why some things worked well and other things did not (although it may be a bit disconcerting, the first time or two, to be judged by your peers).

One of the simplest classroom observation instruments to create and use is the checklist. Figure 16.1 contains a set of six relatively brief checklists that reflect many of the topics discussed in this book. You can adopt this instrument as is or modify it to suit your circumstances (such as your grade level and your state's learning standards) to help you evaluate your effectiveness in several important areas.

Another useful observation instrument was developed by Donna Sobel, Sheryl Taylor, and Ruth Anderson (2003). Called the Diversity-Responsive Teaching Observation Tool, it was created for a Colorado school district with a broad diversity of students. The instrument contains three sections and focuses on how well teachers address diversity as well as exhibit appropriate classroom instruction and classroom management behaviors. Because the form is too lengthy to reproduce here, we encourage you to consult the article in which it appears if you think you might want to have a colleague use it to evaluate your teaching.

© Don Bayley/iStockphoto

FIGURE 16.1 Examples of Classroom Observation Checklists

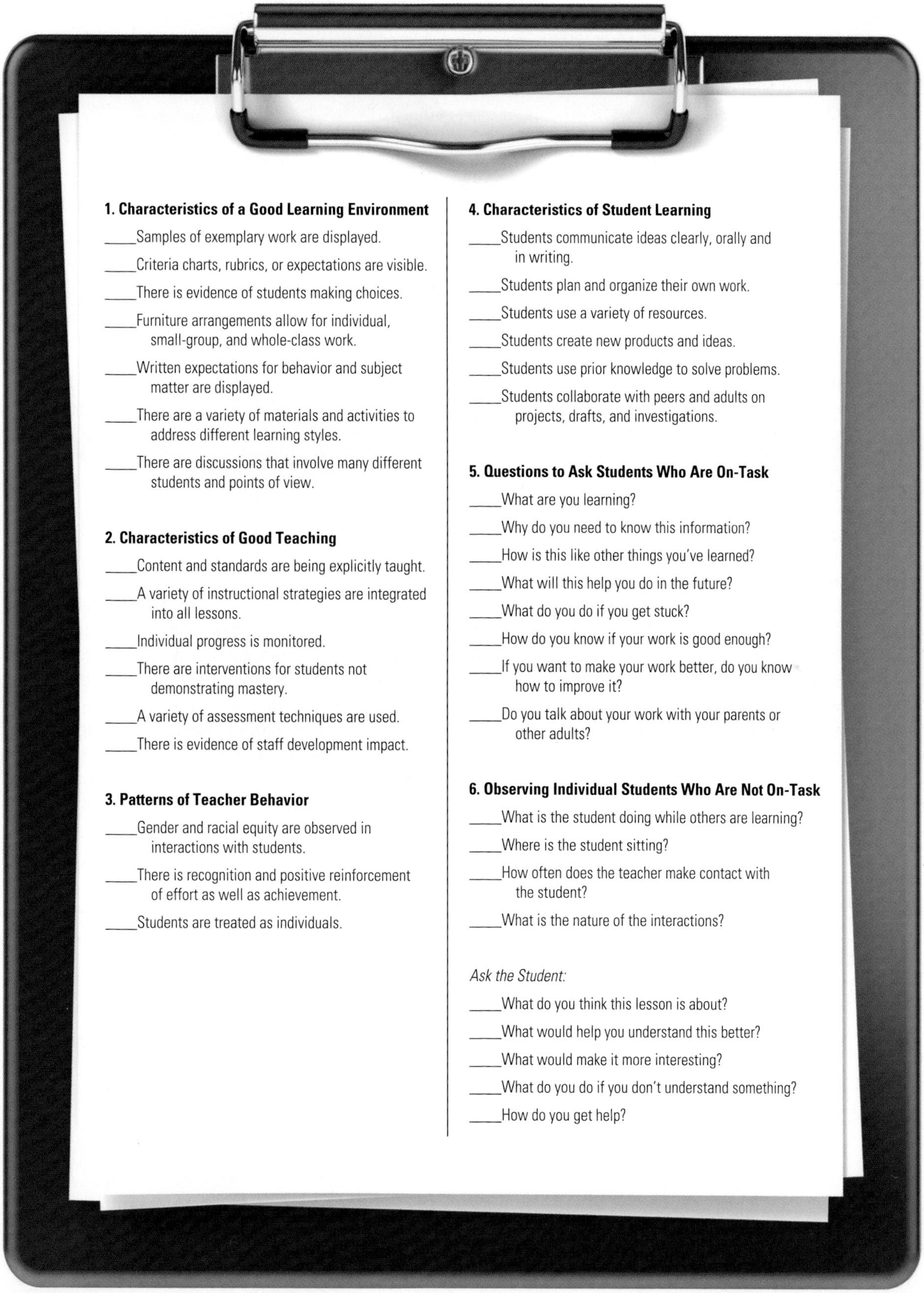

1. Characteristics of a Good Learning Environment

____Samples of exemplary work are displayed.

____Criteria charts, rubrics, or expectations are visible.

____There is evidence of students making choices.

____Furniture arrangements allow for individual, small-group, and whole-class work.

____Written expectations for behavior and subject matter are displayed.

____There are a variety of materials and activities to address different learning styles.

____There are discussions that involve many different students and points of view.

2. Characteristics of Good Teaching

____Content and standards are being explicitly taught.

____A variety of instructional strategies are integrated into all lessons.

____Individual progress is monitored.

____There are interventions for students not demonstrating mastery.

____A variety of assessment techniques are used.

____There is evidence of staff development impact.

3. Patterns of Teacher Behavior

____Gender and racial equity are observed in interactions with students.

____There is recognition and positive reinforcement of effort as well as achievement.

____Students are treated as individuals.

4. Characteristics of Student Learning

____Students communicate ideas clearly, orally and in writing.

____Students plan and organize their own work.

____Students use a variety of resources.

____Students create new products and ideas.

____Students use prior knowledge to solve problems.

____Students collaborate with peers and adults on projects, drafts, and investigations.

5. Questions to Ask Students Who Are On-Task

____What are you learning?

____Why do you need to know this information?

____How is this like other things you've learned?

____What will this help you do in the future?

____What do you do if you get stuck?

____How do you know if your work is good enough?

____If you want to make your work better, do you know how to improve it?

____Do you talk about your work with your parents or other adults?

6. Observing Individual Students Who Are Not On-Task

____What is the student doing while others are learning?

____Where is the student sitting?

____How often does the teacher make contact with the student?

____What is the nature of the interactions?

Ask the Student:

____What do you think this lesson is about?

____What would help you understand this better?

____What would make it more interesting?

____What do you do if you don't understand something?

____How do you get help?

SOURCE: Examples of Classroom Observation checklist from L. Schmidt, "Getting smarter about supervising instruction" in PRINCIPAL, 82(4), 2003, pp. 24–28. Reprinted with permission. Copyright 2003 National Association of Elementary School Principals. All Rights Reserved.

Photo: © Sashkin/Shutterstock Images

Lesson Study According to Catherine Lewis, Rebecca Perry, and Shelley Friedkin (2009), "Lesson study is *a system for building and sharing practitioner knowledge* that involves teachers in learning from colleagues as they research, plan, teach, observe, and discuss a classroom lesson" (p. 142, emphasis in original). Lesson study is focused by a cycle of inquiry conducted by a research team of, typically, three to as many as eight teachers. The team concept is critical; the cycle represented in Figure 16.2 is undertaken by a team of teacher-researchers rather than by an individual teacher.

A cycle of lesson study begins with the *study phase.* The research team studies the curriculum and formulates learning goals. In doing so, the team considers long-term learning goals for students and the professional standards that apply to the content being learned, and selects a topic that will be the focus for planning the lesson to be researched.

The *planning phase* of the cycle includes selecting or revising a lesson plan that focuses on the learning outcomes identified in the study phase. In some cases, a new lesson plan might be created. The lesson plan that emerges from the planning phase includes anticipating student thinking, planning data collection on student learning (for formative purposes), and providing a rationale for the activities and assessments that will be part of the lesson.

The *teaching phase* occurs when one member of the research team conducts the lesson (called the "research lesson" or the "study lesson"). Other members of the research team observe the lesson being studied and collect data.

The *reflection phase* is again a team effort. Those who observed the research lesson share the data they

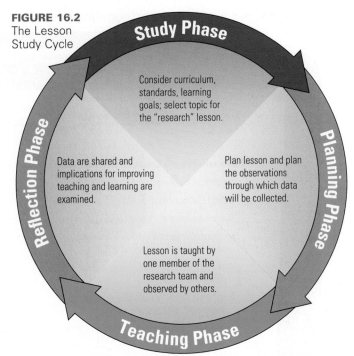

FIGURE 16.2
The Lesson Study Cycle

Study Phase
Consider curriculum, standards, learning goals; select topic for the "research" lesson.

Planning Phase
Plan lesson and plan the observations through which data will be collected.

Teaching Phase
Lesson is taught by one member of the research team and observed by others.

Reflection Phase
Data are shared and implications for improving teaching and learning are examined.

SOURCES: Adapted from C. Lewis, Perry, & Friedkin (2009) and Mark, Gorman, & Nikula (2009).

collected in an effort to focus on student learning and how the teacher influenced that learning. The implications of the data collected during the lesson are also addressed for broader issues of content coverage, student engagement, and lesson and unit design.

Joanne Lieberman (2009) argued that lesson study can change the "norms of individualism" that keep many American teachers from learning with and from one another. In her case study of a math department

Teaching as a Profession: Collaboration With Colleagues

Go to the Education CourseMate website and watch the video, study the artifacts in the case, and reflect upon the following questions:

1. The text and this Video Case both show how colleagues play a role in improving the teaching practice of others. Which examples of peer assessment and collaboration do you think would be most helpful to you? Explain your answers.

2. In the Video Case, we see several teachers collaborating on an important issue related to their students. Briefly, what are they trying to achieve? Do you think their collaborative process is successful?

that employed lesson study, she found that teachers became more willing to accept the uncertainty of teaching a research lesson because they wanted to discover what would happen. The norms of the teacher-researchers evolved to focus on student learning more directly and to willingly design innovations that could be tested, improved, and tested again.

Lesson study, which has a long history in Japan, has only recently begun to have an impact on American teachers' efforts to learn *from* teaching (C. Lewis, 2009; C. Lewis, Perry, & Friedkin, 2009; Mark, Gorman, & Nikula, 2009). But lesson study is a very promising practice, especially when considered in light of the reform effort represented by the National Board for Professional Teaching Standards. We will see more about that effort in this chapter's Case in Print; for now we examine other ideas that you might use to help you learn from teaching.

Self-Recorded Lessons If it is not possible for you to team with colleagues—or even in addition to working with a team—you might consider examining your own teaching through self-recorded lessons. Employing audio only or audio and image recording is becoming increasingly convenient with portable digital devices. Once you have decided to document your teaching for further study, your first step should be to decide which classes or parts of classes you want to record, for how long, and on what day of the week. The goal should be to create a representative sample of the circumstances under which you teach. Then you should inform your students that you intend to record a sample of your lessons over a period of several weeks to study and improve your instructional methods and that you will protect their confidentiality by not allowing anyone else but you to listen to the recordings.

One first-year high school teacher decided after analyzing an audio recording of one of her lessons that she needed to wait longer for students to respond to high level questions, give students more opportunities to ask questions, give students more feedback, use specific praise, review and integrate previous concepts with new lessons, and stop saying "OK" and "all right." Impressed with these insights, she continued to record and analyze her lessons, and at the end of the year was nominated for an award as the district's best new teacher (Freiberg, 2002).

Guided Reflection Protocol Analyzing self-recorded lessons, even a set of "day notes" or other written comments about the events of a lesson, can be a useful way to reflect on lessons to learn from your teaching. One analytic technique is the guided reflection protocol (McEntee et al., 2003). After choosing one or more teaching episodes that you would like to examine, try

Soliciting comments about the effectiveness of one's teaching methods from students and colleagues and reflecting on these comments is an excellent way to become a better teacher.

to answer as honestly as possible the following four questions:

1. *What happened?* The main requirement of this step is simply to describe the incident as fully as possible. Note, for instance, when and where the incident occurred, who was involved, and what occurred just prior to, during, and immediately after the incident. Avoid analysis and interpretation.

2. *Why did it happen?* If you've provided enough context in answering the first question, you should be able to identify the events that produced the incident.

3. *What might it mean?* Note the conditional wording of this question. Using the word *might* instead of *does* is intended to help you realize that there are usually several possible interpretations of the meaning of an incident. A teacher who reprimands a class for not finishing an assignment on time may, for example, need to examine the clarity of her objectives, the amount of time she budgets for the completion of assignments, the ability of students to use their time productively, or her ability to cope with administrative pressure to cover the curriculum in time for an upcoming high stakes test.

4. *What are the implications for my practice?* Consider what you might do differently in a similar situation, in light of how you answered the first three questions.

Reflective Journal Seymour Sarason (1993, 2005; Glazek & Sarason, 2006), who has written extensively about schooling and school reform, has pointed out what may seem obvious but is often missed in practice: Every teacher should be an expert in both subject matter and how children learn in classrooms. The goal, and the challenge, is to figure out how to present the subject matter so that students understand it, remember it, and use it. To do that, you must constantly prepare, observe, and reflect on how closely your instructional practices relate to theory and research and produce the desired outcome (Heath, 2002). A reflective journal will help you begin that process in a systematic way. What follows are some detailed suggestions for keeping such a journal.

We recommend that you develop a reflective journal for two basic purposes: (1) to serve as a repository of instructional ideas and techniques that you have either created from your own experiences or gleaned from other sources, and (2) to give yourself a format for recording your observations and reflections on teaching (Lyons & Kubler LaBoskey, 2002). These two purposes can be separate from each other or, if you choose, related to each other in a cycle of reflectivity that we will describe. As you read this section, refer to Figure 16.3 for an illustration of how a journal page might look.

The form your reflective journal takes will probably change over the years to reflect your experiences and changing needs. But to begin, we suggest that you organize your first journal around the Suggestions for Teaching in Chapters 2, 4–12, 14, and 15. For Chapter 3, you can use those numbered points that best correspond to the grade level you expect to teach. Use the numbered suggestions as page headings in your reflective journal. To allow room for both the expansion of your teaching ideas and the inclusion of your ongoing reflections, you might purchase a three-ring binder so that you can add and drop pages. Alternatively, you might want to create your reflective journal as computer files, which would give you unlimited capacity for interaction and expansion.

Under each heading, you can develop a two-part page or multipage entry. As illustrated in the top half of Figure 16.3, the first part should contain your own teaching ideas, customtailored from the Suggestions for Teaching in the chapters of this book and from personal experience and other sources to fit the grade level and subjects you expect to teach.

To illustrate, let's use the second Suggestion for Teaching from Chapter 9—"Teach students how to use both memory-directed and comprehension-directed tactics":

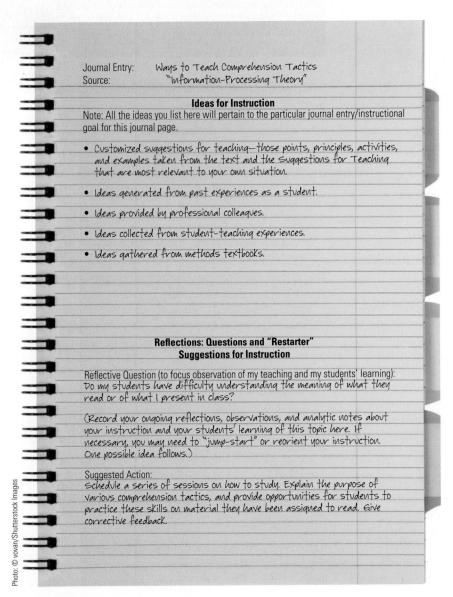

Journal Entry: Ways to Teach Comprehension Tactics
Source: "Information-Processing Theory"

Ideas for Instruction

Note: All the ideas you list here will pertain to the particular journal entry/instructional goal for this journal page.

- Customized suggestions for teaching—those points, principles, activities, and examples taken from the text and the Suggestions for Teaching that are most relevant to your own situation.

- Ideas generated from past experiences as a student.

- Ideas provided by professional colleagues.

- Ideas collected from student-teaching experiences.

- Ideas gathered from methods textbooks.

Reflections: Questions and "Restarter" Suggestions for Instruction

Reflective Question (to focus observation of my teaching and my students' learning):
Do my students have difficulty understanding the meaning of what they read or of what I present in class?

(Record your ongoing reflections, observations, and analytic notes about your instruction and your students' learning of this topic here. If necessary, you may need to "jump-start" or reorient your instruction. One possible idea follows.)

Suggested Action:
Schedule a series of sessions on how to study. Explain the purpose of various comprehension tactics, and provide opportunities for students to practice these skills on material they have been assigned to read. Give corrective feedback.

FIGURE 16.3 Sample Page for Your Reflective Journal

- Search your memory for techniques that your past teachers used. Did your fifth grade teacher, for instance, have a clever way of relating new information to ideas that you had learned earlier to make the new information easier to understand? Describe the technique so you will remember to try it yourself. Did a high school teacher have an ingenious way of displaying the similarities and differences among a set of ideas? Exactly how did she or he do it?

- After you exhaust your own recollections, ask roommates or classmates if they can remember any successful ways that their teachers made understanding easier.

- Examine the examples given in Chapter 9's Suggestions for Teaching. Which ones seem most appropriate for the grade level and subject you will be teaching? Jot them down. Do any of the examples suggest variations you can think of on your own? Write them down before you forget them.

- Add ideas that you pick up in methods classes or during your student-teaching experience. If you see a film in a methods class that shows how a teacher helps students understand a particular point, describe it in your journal. If your master teacher uses a successful technique to clarify difficult-to-understand material, record it.

If you follow some or all of these suggestions, you will have a rich source of ideas to turn to when you discover that your students seem confused and anxious because of poor comprehension and you find yourself wondering if there is anything you can do about it.

With this part of the journal under way, you should feel reasonably well prepared when you first take charge of a class. But given the complexity of classroom teaching, lessons or techniques that looked good on paper do not always produce the intended effect. This is the point at which you need to reflect on and analyze what you are doing and how you might bring about improvements. On the bottom half of your journal page, or on a new page, write in question form what the nature of the problem seems to be. Then try to identify the cause (or causes) of the problem and at least one possible solution. You can use this suggestion to get restarted or headed in a new direction with your teaching. If, for example, some of your students still have difficulty comprehending what they read despite the comprehension-enhancing techniques that you embedded into your lessons, you might reread Chapter 8, as well as other articles and books on information processing, and decide that your students really need systematic instruction in how to use various comprehension-directed learning tactics.

© 2010 Tetra Images/Jupiterimages Corporation

Research has shown that keeping a personal journal about one's teaching activities and outcomes helps teachers improve their effectiveness because it forces them to focus on what they do, why they do it, and what kinds of results they typically obtain.

Portfolio Middle school teacher Linda Van Wagenen used a personal portfolio along with a reflective journal to analyze and improve the quality of her instruction (Van Wagenen & Hibbard, 1998). She compiled a portfolio of her efforts to achieve certain teaching goals and used that to examine her effectiveness. She judged her first two efforts at analysis to be unsatisfactory because they were largely descriptive; they emphasized what she had done and ignored what effects those efforts had on her students (self-assessment), what she thought about the quality of her own instruction (self-evaluation), and what she planned to do next (self-regulation). Her third attempt focused on ways to motivate students to improve their performance in persuasive and expository writing. She identified a set of steps that would help her understand the problem and produce improvements. Evidence of her successes and failures made up the portfolio. In addition, she kept a reflective journal because she felt it would help her stay focused on finding a solution to the problem and would stimulate attempts at self-evaluation and self-regulation. The result of this third attempt was judged to be much more useful than either of her first two efforts. In addition to addressing the question "What did I do?" she also addressed the questions "What did I learn?" and "Now what will I do?" Essentially, she engaged in "an intentional reflective process" (Lyons & Kubler LaBoskey, 2002, p. 2), which told the story of her teaching and her students' learning. Narrative accounts (i.e., telling the stories of your teaching) have been shown to be an effective form

Case in Print

Highly Qualified Teachers Are Those Who Learn From Teaching

Bill Ferriter, in his 2009 article in Educational Leadership, suggested that two important changes have occurred and that those changes have resulted in more portals for learning about teaching and learning from teaching.

One of those changes is the increased emphasis on professional collaboration among teachers. Lesson study—a way to research and thus improve teaching practice (discussed earlier in this chapter)—is one example of this emphasis on collaboration. This emerging emphasis is also exemplified in one of the core propositions from the National Board for Professional Teaching Standards ("Teachers Are Members of Learning Communities"). (p. 368)

2009 Class of National Board Certified Teachers Advances Nation's School Reform Movement

NATIONAL BOARD FOR PROFESSIONAL TEACHING STANDARDS

Arlington, VA (December 16, 2009)—The National Board for Professional Teaching Standards (NBPTS) continues its progress in advancing the National Board Certification education reform movement with *the announcement of nearly 8,900 new National Board Certified Teachers* (NBCTs). Today's announcement brings the total number of accomplished teachers and school counselors certified by NBPTS to more than 82,000.

An "extraordinary group," is how U.S. Secretary of Education Arne Duncan referred to this year's class of National Board Certified Teachers in a September interview with NBPTS. He said teachers who achieved National Board Certification have "demonstrated a commitment to taking their teaching practice and the teaching profession to a different level."

"The leadership and example they're setting for the system is phenomenal," said Duncan, former CEO of Chicago Public Schools (CPS). With more than 300 new NBCTs, CPS had more teachers achieving National Board Certification this year than any other school district in the nation.

"What if every child had a chance to be taught by a National Board Certified Teacher? I think the difference it would make in students' lives would be extraordinary," said Duncan. "As we move forward on this turnaround agenda nationally, I would love for National Board Certified Teachers to be at the forefront of that movement."

"In Chicago Public Schools we also imagined teams of National Board Certified Teachers alongside effective principals in schools that need them most," said Janet Knupp, founding president and chief executive officer, The Chicago Public Education Fund. "With our new class, we now have more than 60 Chicago public schools—traditional and charter—with 15 percent or more of their faculties National Board certified. These teachers are building cultures of excellence for everyone in their buildings, where adults as much as children aspire to the highest standards."

In many schools, districts and states across the nation, National Board Certified Teachers are assuming leadership roles—serving as mentors, facilitating professional development and leading education reform efforts in their districts and states. Several states are capitalizing on the expertise of these outstanding teacher leaders in their "Race to the Top" proposals. They are using accomplished teachers to increase effectiveness and improve school conditions to better meet the academic learning needs of students in targeted high-need schools.

"Our focus is expanding from individuals achieving National Board Certification to a systemic movement that changes the culture of classrooms, schools and districts by leveraging National Board Certified Teachers to build human capital, especially in high-need schools," said Joseph A. Aguerrebere, president and chief executive officer, NBPTS. "This announcement symbolizes what we're all about—improving the capacity of professionals in working with all students."

The latest numbers providing further evidence that the teaching quality movement is growing include:

- The number of NBCTs has more than doubled in the past five years (from more than 40,000 in 2004 to more than 82,000 in 2009).
- States with the highest number of teachers achieving National Board Certification in 2009 were: North Carolina (1,509), Washington (1,248), South Carolina (798), Illinois (732) and Florida (651).
- School districts with the highest number of teachers achieving National Board

---

of self-study to improve teaching (Anderson-Patton & Bass, 2002). By asking and answering questions, as Van Wagenen did on her third attempt, you can build a narrative account in your reflective journal.

In thinking about the contents of your own portfolio, you might want to start with the following list of items (Drake & McBride, 2000; R. S. Johnson, Mims-Cox, & Doyle-Nichols, 2010):

1. A title page
2. A table of contents
3. A statement of your educational philosophy, which may include the reasons that you chose teaching as a career
4. A résumé
5. A statement of your teaching goals
6. Example(s) of a lesson plan, keyed to state standards
7. Examples of learning activities (especially those that contain innovative ideas)
8. Samples of students' work
9. Photographs and videos
10. Letters of recommendation
11. Teaching evaluations
12. Samples of college work

Certification in 2009 were: Chicago Public Schools, Charlotte-Mecklenburg Schools, Wake County Schools, the Los Angeles Unified School District and Miami-Dade County Public Schools.

- Fifteen states had at least a 20 percent increase in the number of 2009 NBCTs over the number of teachers who achieved certification in 2008.
- Nearly 1,700 NBCTs successfully met the standards for the "Profile of Professional Growth" to renew National Board Certification.

More than half of all NBCTs teach in Title I eligible schools as reported by the National Center for Education Statistics.

"Growing groups of National Board Certified Teachers and leveraging them to build school-based learning communities are critical components many states and districts are already using to turn around low-performing schools," said Gov. Bob Wise, chair of the NBPTS Board of Directors and former governor of West Virginia. "This whole school reform movement is creating a culture of learning we're all looking for—one that advances student engagement and achievement, retains the best teachers and improves teacher and school performance."

In a congressionally mandated report, the National Research Council (NRC) confirmed that National Board Certified Teachers advance student achievement and learning, stay in the classroom longer, support new and struggling teachers, and assume other school-based leadership roles. The NRC acknowledged that students taught by National Board Certified Teachers make higher gains on achievement tests than students taught by non-board-certified teachers. National Board Certification is recognized as a model of pay-for-performance and is supported by teachers and administrators nationwide. Many states and local school districts provide salary incentives and cover the cost for teachers who pursue and achieve this advanced teaching credential. A voluntary assessment program designed to develop, recognize and retain accomplished teachers, National Board Certification is achieved through a performance-based assessment that typically takes one to three years to complete. While state licensing systems set basic requirements to teach in each state, NBCTs have successfully demonstrated advanced teaching knowledge, skills and practices.

National Board Certification for Educational Leaders/Principals

Last week, NBPTS launched the development of National Board Certification for Principals, the first phase of an expanded program, National Board Certification for Educational Leaders, which will also lay the groundwork for a new teacher leader certification. Investments from the nation's major public, private and philanthropic sectors have contributed to the development of National Board Certification for Educational Leaders. For more information about this initiative, including the Core Propositions, visit www.nbpts.org/principals.

For more information about NBPTS and National Board Certification, visit www.nbpts.org.

Source: 2009 Class of National Board Certified Teachers Advances Nation's School Reform Movement, National Board for Professional Teaching Standards, Arlington, VA, December 16, 2009. Reprinted with permission from the National Board for Professional Teaching Standards, www.nbpts.org. All rights reserved.

Questions and Activities

1. The article describes how the education profession is changing and how the effort to certify teachers at a national level is making a difference. How do you see National Board Certification of teachers as contributing to learning *from* teaching? What kinds of assessments do you think should be used to determine if someone is a highly qualified teacher?

2. If you had the opportunity to observe National Board Certified Teachers in their classrooms, what do you think you might see? How do you think the students in those classrooms might engage with the material they are learning? With each other? With the teacher?

---

13. An autobiography
14. Reflections about how teaching (or student teaching) has contributed to your growth as a person and a teacher
15. Official documents (transcripts, teaching certificates, test scores)

LO2 Using Technology for Reflective Inquiry

Throughout this book, we have described how you can use various technology tools to help your students become more effective learners. Now it's time to consider how you can use such technologies to reflect in ways that will help you learn from your teaching.

Digital Portals for Professional Development

Richard Elmore, in a report for the Albert Shanker Institute published in 2002, complained that schools—with increased emphasis on testing and accountability—offer "few portals" for new ideas about teaching and learning to enter into educational practice. Bill Ferriter, in his 2009 article in *Educational Leadership*, suggested that two important changes have occurred and that those changes have resulted

Teaching as a Profession: What Defines Effective Teaching?

Go to the Education CourseMate website and watch the video, study the artifacts in the case, and reflect upon the following questions:

1. In this Video Case, different school professionals share their thoughts on what defines an effective teacher. Of the various teacher attributes that they describe (e.g., knowledge of child development, command of subject matter, being organized, knowing your students, etc.), which ones do you think are most critical?

2. Based on this Video Case and the content in this text, think about the concept of teacher self-reflection. In your opinion, what are some effective ways for teachers to reflect on their own practice? Which self-reflection techniques make the most sense to you?

in more portals for learning *about* teaching and learning *from* teaching.

One of those changes is the increased emphasis on professional collaboration among teachers. Lesson study—a way to research and thus improve teaching practice (discussed earlier in this chapter)—is one example of this emphasis on collaboration. This emerging emphasis is also exemplified in one of the core propositions from the National Board for Professional Teaching Standards ("Teachers Are Members of Learning Communities"). According to the National Board, highly qualified teachers are collaborative in their practice. This chapter's Case in Print documents the growing number of practicing teachers who are pursuing National Board Certification.

The second change that is allowing teachers more opportunities for learning *about* teaching and learning *from* teaching, according to Ferriter (2009), is that digital tools now provide the portals that Elmore saw as lacking. In particular, Ferriter advocates for reading and writing blogs and wikis (see also S.-H. Yang, 2009). A wiki, if you're not familiar with the term, is a website that is created by one or more people and can be edited by anyone who has access to the site. With regard to reading blogs, Ferriter stated: "Some [blogs] leave me challenged. Some leave me angry. Some leave me jazzed. All leave me energized and ready to learn more" (2009, p. 36). As to using digital tools as a forum for sharing questions and ideas in writing, he remarked: "Blogs become

a forum for public articulation—and public articulation is essential for educators interested in refining and revising their thinking about teaching and learning" (p. 37). Ferriter recommended several blogging sites; among them is Edublogs (www.edublogs.org), a free blogging service dedicated entirely to educators.

There are numerous other websites that have been designed for K–12 teachers and contain discussion forums, chat rooms, blogs, or wikis. Here are five you might consider using:

- The Connect page of Active Learning Practice for Schools, Harvard Graduate School of Education (learnweb.harvard.edu/alps/bigideas/q5.cfm)

- The New Teachers Online page of Teachers Network (www.teachersnetwork.org/ntol)

- The Interactive Forums page of the International Education and Resource Network (www.iearn.org)

- The Teacher-2-Teacher page of Teachnet .com (www.teachnet.com/t2t)

- The Chat Center page at Teachers.net (http://teachers.net/chat)

Technological tools for reflection can be very helpful to teachers at any stage of their professional development. If your intention is to learn *from* teaching, the digital portals that provide access to information and the thoughts and experiences of fellow educators can help you do just that.

WHAT ELSE? *RIP & REVIEW* **CARDS IN THE BACK**

Abedi, J., & Dietel, R. (2004). Challenges in the No Child Left Behind Act for English-language learners. *Phi Delta Kappan, 85*(10), 782–785.

Abrami, P. C., Lou, Y., Chambers, B., Poulsen, C., & Spence, J. C. (2000). Why should we group students within-class for learning? *Educational Research and Evaluation, 6*(2), 158–179.

Adelson, J. (1972). The political imagination of the young adolescent. In J. Kagan & R. Coles (Eds.), *Twelve to sixteen: Early adolescence.* New York: Norton.

Adelson, J. (1986). *Inventing adolescence: The political psychology of everyday schooling.* New Brunswick, NJ: Transaction Books.

Adey, P. S., Shayer, M., & Yates, C. (2001). *Thinking science* (3rd ed.). London: Nelson Thornes.

Ainley, M., Hidi, S., & Berndorff, D. (2002). Interest, learning, and the psychological processes that mediate their relationship. *Journal of Educational Psychology, 94*(3), 545–561.

Airasian, P., & Russell, M. (2008). *Classroom assessment: Concepts and applications* (6th ed.). Boston: McGraw-Hill.

Akin-Little, K. A., Eckert, T. L., Lovett, B. J., & Little, S. G. (2004). Extrinsic reinforcement in the classroom: Bribery or best practices. *School Psychology Review, 33*(3), 344–362.

Alavi, M., & Leidner, D. E. (2001). Technology-mediated learning: A call for greater depth and breadth of research. *Information Systems Research, 12*(1), 1–10.

Alberto, P. A., & Troutman, A. C. (2009). *Applied behavior analysis for teachers* (8th ed.). Upper Saddle River, NJ: Pearson/Merrill.

Alexander, B., & Levine, A. (2008). Storytelling: Emergence of a new genre. *EDUCAUSE Review, 43*(6), 41–56.

Alexander, P. A., Graham, S., & Harris, K. R. (1998). A perspective on strategy research: Progress and prospects. *Educational Psychology Review, 10*(2), 129–154.

Alfassi, M. (1998). Reading for meaning: The efficacy of reciprocal teaching in fostering reading comprehension in high school students in remedial reading classes. *American Educational Research Journal, 35*(2), 309–332.

Allegretto, S. A., Corcoran, S. P., & Mishel, L. (2004). How does teacher pay compare? Washington, DC: Economic Policy Institute.

Allen, N., Christal, M., Perrot, D., Wilson, C., Grote, B., & Earley, M. A. (1999). Native American schools move into the new millennium. *Educational Leadership, 56*(7), 71–74.

Allen, N., Resta, P. E., & Christal, M. (2002). Technology and tradition: The role of technology in Native American schools. *TechTrends, 46*(2), 50–55.

Allender, J. S., & Allender, D. S. (2008). *The humanistic teacher: First the child, then curriculum.* Boulder, CO: Paradigm.

Allison, B. N., & Schultz, J. B. (2001). Interpersonal identity formation during early adolescence. *Adolescence, 36*(143), 509–523.

American Association of University Women. (1999). *Gender gaps: Where schools still fail our children.* New York: Marlowe & Company.

American Association on Intellectual and Developmental Disabilities. (2009). *Definition of mental retardation.* AAIDD website. Retrieved October 31, 2009, from http://www.aaidd.org/content_100.cfm?navID521.

American Educational Research Association. (2004). Teachers matter: Evidence from value-added assessments. *Research Points, 2*(2), 1–4.

American Psychiatric Association. (2000). *Diagnostic and Statistical Manual of Mental Disorders* (4th ed., Text Revision). Washington, DC: Author.

Anderman, E. M., & Maehr, M. L. (1994). Motivation and schooling in the middle grades. *Review of Educational Research, 64*(2), 287–309.

Anderman, E. M., & Midgley, C. (2004). Changes in self-reported academic cheating across the transition from middle school to high school. *Contemporary Educational Psychology, 29*(4), 499–517.

Anderman, E. M., & Murdock, T. B. (Eds.). (2007). *Psychology of academic cheating.* Boston: Elsevier Academic Press.

Anderman, L. H., & Leake, V. S. (2007). The interface of school and family in meeting the belonging needs of young adolescents. In S. B. Mertens, V. A. Anfara, Jr., & M. M. Caskey (Eds.), *The young adolescent and the middle school* (pp. 163–182.). Charlotte, NC: Information Age Publishing.

Anders Ericsson, K. (Ed.). (2009). *Development of professional expertise: Toward measurement of expert performance and design of optimal learning environments.* New York: Cambridge University Press.

Anderson, L. W. (2009). Upper elementary grades bear the brunt of accountability. *Phi Delta Kappan, 90*(6), 413–418.

Anderson-Patton, V., & Bass, E. (2002). Using narrative teaching portfolios for self-study. In N. P. Lyons & V. Kubler LaBoskey (Eds.), *Narrative inquiry in practice: Advancing the knowledge of teaching.* New York: Teachers College Press.

Applebee, A. N., Langer, J. A., Nystrand, M., & Gamoran, A. (2003). Discussion-based approaches to developing understanding: Classroom instruction and student performance in middle and high school English. *American Educational Research Journal, 40*(3), 685–730.

Appleton, N. (1983). *Cultural pluralism in education.* New York: Longman.

Armstrong, T. (1994). *Multiple intelligences in the classroom.* Alexandria, VA: Association for Supervision and Curriculum Development.

Armstrong, T. (2009). *Multiple intelligences in the classroom* (3rd ed.). Alexandria, VA: Association for Supervision and Curriculum Development.

Arnold, M. L. (2000). Stage, sequence, and sequels: Changing conceptions of morality, post-Kohlberg. *Educational Psychology Review, 12*(4), 365–383.

Arter, J., & Chappuis, J. (2008). *Creating and recognizing quality rubrics.* Upper Saddle River, NJ: Allyn & Bacon/Pearson.

Arter, J., & McTighe, J. (2001). *Scoring rubrics in the classroom.* Thousand Oaks, CA: Corwin Press.

Artiles, A. J., Klingner, J. K., & Tate, W. F. (2006). Representation of minority students in special education: Complicating traditional explanations. *Educational Researcher, 35*(6), 3–5.

Ash, C. (2000). *Voices of a new century: Students' perspectives on the achievement gap.* Chicago: North Central Regional Educational Laboratory. Retrieved from http://msan.wceruw.org/publications/Student%20Voices%202000.pdf.

Ash, K. (2009). Virtual approaches vary. *Education Week, 28*(26), 26–27.

Ashcraft, M. H., & Radvansky, G. A. (2010). *Cognition* (5th ed.). Boston: Prentice Hall.

Assouline, S., Nicpon, M. F., & Doobay, A. (2009). Profoundly gifted girls and autism spectrum disorder: A psychometric case study comparison. *Gifted Child Quarterly, 53*(2), 89–105.

Astington, J. W. (1998). Theory of mind goes to school. *Educational Leadership, 56*(3), 46–48.

Atkinson, R. C. (1975). Mnemotechnics in second language learning. *American Psychologist, 30*(2), 821–828.

Atkinson, R. C., & Raugh, M. R. (1975). An application of the mnemonic keyword method to the acquisition of a Russian vocabulary. *Journal of Experimental Psychology: Human Learning and Memory, 104*(2), 126–133.

Atkinson, R. C., & Shiffrin, R. M. (1968). Human memory: A proposed system and its control processes. In K. W. Spence & J. T. Spence (Eds.), *The psychology of learning and motivation* (Vol. 2). New York: Academic Press.

Atkinson, R. K., Derry, S. J., Renkl, A., & Wortham, D. (2000). Learning from examples: Instructional principles from the worked examples research. *Review of Educational Research, 70*(2), 181–214.

Atkinson, R. K., Renkl, A., & Merrill, M. M. (2003). Transitioning from studying examples to solving problems: Effects of self-explanation prompts and fading worked-out steps. *Journal of Educational Psychology, 95*(4), 774–783.

Au, W. (2007). High-stakes testing and curricular control: A qualitative metasynthesis. *Educational Researcher, 36*(5), 258–267.

Ausubel, D. P., Novak, J. D., & Hanesian, H. (1978). *Educational psychology: A cognitive view* (2nd ed.). New York: Holt, Rinehart & Winston.

Azevedo, R. (2009). Theoretical, conceptual, methodological, and instructional issues in research on metacognition and self-regulated learning: A discussion. *Metacognition and Learning, 4*(1), 1556–1623.

Bachman, L. F. (2002). Alternative interpretations of alternative assessments: Some validity issues in educational performance assessments. *Educational Measurement: Issues and Practice, 21*(5), 5–18.

Bae, Y., Choy, S., Geddes, C., Sable, J., & Snyder, T. (2000). *Trends in educational equity of girls and women.* Washington, DC: National Center for Educational Statistics. Retrieved January 2, 2002, from http://nces.ed.gov/pubs2000/2000030.pdf.

Bailey, S. M. (1996). Shortchanging girls and boys. *Educational Leadership, 53*(8), 75–79.

Bandura, A. (1986). *Social foundations of thought and action: A social cognitive theory.* Englewood Cliffs, NJ: Prentice Hall.

Bandura, A. (1997). *Self-efficacy: The exercise of control.* New York: W. H. Freeman.

Bandura, A. (2001). Social cognitive theory: An agentic perspective. In S. T. Fiske, D. L. Schacter, & C. Zahn-Waxler (Eds.), *Annual Review of Psychology, 52*, 1–26.

Bandura, A. (2002). Social cognitive theory in cultural context. *Applied Psychology, 51*(2), 269–290.

Bangert-Drowns, R. L., Kulik, C.-L., Kulik, J. A., & Morgan, M. (1991). The instructional effect of feedback in test-like events. *Review of Educational Research, 61*(2), 213–238.

Banks, J. A. (2008). Diversity, group identity, and citizenship education in a global age. *Educational Researcher, 37*(3), 129–139.

Banks, J. A. (2009). *Teaching strategies for ethnic studies* (8th ed.). Boston: Pearson/Allyn & Bacon.

Barab, S. & Dede, C. (2007). Games and immersive participatory simulations for science education: An emerging type of curricula. *Journal of Science Education and Technology, 16*(1), 1–3.

Barab, S., Dodge, T., Thomas, M., Jackson, C., & Tuzun, H. (2007). Our designs and the social agendas they carry. *Journal of the Learning Sciences, 16*(2), 263–305.

Barab, S., Gresalfi, M., Ingram-Noble, A., Jameson, E., Hickey, D., Akram, S., & Kizer, S. (2009). Transformational play and virtual worlds: Worked examples from the Quest Atlantis project.

International Journal of Learning and Media, 1(2). Retrieved from http://www.mitpressjournals.org.

Barab, S., & Luehmann, A. (2003). Building sustainable science curriculum: Acknowledging and accommodating local adaptation. *Science Education, 87*(4), 454–467.

Barab, S., Scott, B., Siyahhan, S., Goldstone, S., Ingram-Goble, A., Zuiker, S., & Warren, S. (2009). Transformational play as a curricular scaffold: Using videogames to support science education. *Journal of Science Education and Technology, 18*(4), 305–320.

Barnett, S. M., & Ceci, S. J. (2002). When and where do we apply what we learn?: A taxonomy for far transfer. *Psychological Bulletin, 128*(4), 612–637.

Barrett, H. C. (2000). Create your own electronic portfolio. *Learning and Leading with Technology, 27*(7), 14–21.

Barros, R. M., Silver, E. J., & Stein, R. E. K. (2009). School recess and group classroom behavior. *Pediatrics, 123*(2), 431–436.

Bartlett, F. C. (1932). *Remembering.* London: Cambridge University Press.

Barton, P. E., & Coley, R. J. (2007). *The family: America's smallest school.* Princeton, NJ: Policy Evaluation and Research Center, Educational Testing Service. Retrieved from http://www.ets.org/Media/Education_Topics/pdf/5678_PERCReport_school.pdf.

Baumert, J., Kunter, M., Blum, W., Brunner, M., Voss, T., Jordan, A., et al. (2010). Teachers' mathematical knowledge, cognitive activation in the classroom, and student progress. *American Educational Research Journal, 47*(1), 133–180.

Baumrind, D. (1971). Current patterns of parental authority. *Developmental Psychology Monographs, 4*(1, Pt. 2), 1–103.

Baumrind, D. (1991). Parenting styles and adolescent development. In R. M. Lerner, A. C. Peterson, & J. Brooks-Gunn (Eds.), *Encyclopedia of adolescence.* New York: Garland.

Baumrind, D., Larzelere, R. E., & Cowan, P. A. (2002). Ordinary physical punishment: Is it harmful? Comment on Gershoff (2002). *Psychological Bulletin, 128*(4), 580–589.

Bear, G. G. (2009). The positive in positive models of discipline. In R. Gilman, E. S. Huebner, & M. J. Furlong (Eds.), *Handbook of positive psychology in schools* (pp. 305–321). New York: Routledge.

Beatty, I., & Gerace, W. (2009). Technology-enhanced formative assessment: A research-based pedagogy for teaching science with classroom response technology. *Journal of Science Education and Technology, 18*(2), 146–162.

Beiser, M., Erickson, D., Fleming, J. A. E., & Iacono, W. G. (1993). Establishing the onset of psychotic illness. *American Journal of Psychiatry, 150*(9), 1349–1354.

Beishuizen, J. J., & Stoutjesdijk, E. T. (1999). Study strategies in a computer assisted study environment. *Learning and Instruction, 9*(3), 281–301.

Bellezza, F. S. (1981). Mnemonic devices: Classification, characteristics, and criteria. *Review of Educational Research, 51*(2), 247–275.

Ben-Hur, M. (1998). Mediation of cognitive competencies for students in need. *Phi Delta Kappan, 79*(9), 661–666.

Benjamin, A. (2005). *Differentiated instruction using technology: A guide for middle and high school teachers.* Larchmont, NY: Eye on Education.

Benner, A. D., & Mistry, R. S. (2007). Congruence of mother and teacher educational expectations and low-income youth's academic competence. *Journal of Educational Psychology, 99*(1), 140–153.

Bennett, C. I. (2007). *Comprehensive multicultural education: Theory and practice* (6th ed.). Boston: Pearson/Allyn & Bacon.

Bennett, N., Desforges, C., Cockburn, A., & Wilkinson, B. (1984). *The quality of pupil learning experiences.* Hillsdale, NJ: Erlbaum.

Beran, T. (2009). Correlates of peer victimization and achievement: An exploratory model. *Psychology in the Schools, 46*(4), 348–361.

Bereiter, C. (1997). Situated cognition and how to overcome it. In D. Kirshner & J. A. Whitson (Eds.), *Situated cognition: Social, semiotic, and psychological perspectives* (pp. 281–300). Mahwah, NJ: Erlbaum.

Bergen, D., & Fromberg, D. P. (2009). Play and social interaction in middle childhood. *Phi Delta Kappan, 90*(6), 426–430.

Berk, L. E. (2009). *Child development* (8th ed.). Boston: Pearson/Allyn & Bacon.

Berliner, D. C. (2002). Educational research: The hardest science of all. *Educational Researcher, 31*(8), 18–20.

Berliner, D. C. (2006). Educational psychology: Searching for essence throughout a century of influence. In P. A. Alexander & P. H. Winne (Eds.), *Handbook of educational psychology* (2nd ed., pp. 3–27). Mahwah, NJ: Erlbaum.

Berliner, D. C., & Casanova, U. (1996). *Putting research to work in your school.* Arlington Heights, IL: IRI/Skylight Training and Publishing.

Bernard, R. M., Abrami, P. C., Lou, Y., Borokhovski, E., Wade, A., Wozney, L., Wallet, P. A., Fiset, M., & Huang, B. (2004). How does distance education compare with classroom instruction? A meta-analysis of the empirical literature. *Review of Educational Research, 74*(3), 379–439.

Berry, B., Hoke, M., & Hirsch, E. (2004). The search for highly qualified teachers. *Phi Delta Kappan, 85*(9), 684–689.

Berson, I. R. (2009). Here's what we have to say! Podcasting in the early childhood classroom. *Social Studies and the Young Learner, 21*(4), 8–11.

Bielefeldt, T. (2005). Computers and student learning: Interpreting the multivariate analysis of PISA 2000. *Journal of Research on Technology in Education, 37*(4), 339–347.

Billig, S. H. (2000). Research on K–12 school-based service-learning: The evidence builds. *Phi Delta Kappan, 81*(9), 658–664.

Bjorklund, D. F. (2005). *Children's thinking: Cognitive development and individual differences* (4th ed.). Belmont, CA: Thomson/Wadsworth.

Blachowicz, C., Bates, A., Berne, J., Bridgman, T., Chaney, J., & Perney, J. (2009). Technology and at-risk young readers and their classrooms. *Reading Psychology, 30*(5), 387–411.

Black, A. C., & McCoach, D. B. (2008). Validity study of the thinking styles inventory. *Journal for the Education of the Gifted, 32*(2), 180–210.

Blanchett, W. (2006). Disproportionate representation of African American students in special education: Acknowledging the role of White privilege and racism. *Educational Researcher, 35*(6), 24–28.

Blanchett, W., Klingner, J., & Harry, B. (2009). The intersection of race, culture, language, and disability. *Urban Education, 44*(4), 389–409.

Block, J. H., Efthim, H. E., & Burns, R. B. (1989). *Building effective mastery learning schools.* New York: Longman.

Blok, H., Oostdam, R., Otter, M. E., & Overmaat, M. (2002). Computer-assisted instruction in support of beginning reading instruction: A review. *Review of Educational Research, 72*(1), 101–130.

Bloom, B. S. (1968). Learning for mastery. *Evaluation Comment, 1*(2), 1–12.

Bloom, B. S. (1976). *Human characteristics and school learning.* New York: McGraw-Hill.

Bloom, B. S., Engelhart, M. B., Furst, E. J., Hill, W. H., & Krathwohl, D. R. (Eds.). (1956). *Taxonomy of educational objectives: The classification of educational goals. Handbook I: Cognitive domain.* New York: McKay.

Bloomquist, M. L., & Schnell, S. V. (2002). *Helping children with aggression and conduct problems: Best practices for intervention.* New York: Guilford Press.

Bocala, C., Mello, D., Reedy, K., & Lacireno-Paquet, N. (2009). *Features of state response to intervention initiatives in North-east and Islands Region states* (Issues & Answers Report, REL 2009–No. 083). Washington, DC: U.S. Department of Education, Institute of Education Sciences, National Center for Education Evaluation and Regional Assistance, Regional Educational Laboratory Northeast and Islands. Retrieved from http://ies.ed.gov/ncee/edlabs/regions/northeast/pdf/REL_2009083.pdf.

Bock, J. (2008, April 14). A geography class for freshmen in the Fort Zumwalt School District could soon fall off the map. *St. Louis Post-Dispatch*, pp. C1, C8.

Boekaerts, M. (1993). Being concerned with well-being and with learning. *Educational Psychologist, 28*(2), 149–167.

Bohman, J. (2009). Critical theory. *The Stanford Encyclopedia of Philosophy* (Fall 2009 ed.), E. N. Zalta (Ed.). Retrieved from http://plato.stanford.edu/archives/fall2009/entries/critical-theory.

Bond, C. L., Miller, M. J., & Kennon, R. W. (1987). Study skills: Who is taking the responsibility for teaching? *Performance & Instruction, 26*(7), 27–29.

Bong, M., & Skaalvik, E. (2003). Academic self-concept and self-efficacy: How different are they really? *Educational Psychology Review, 15*(1), 1–40.

Boniecki, K. A., & Moore, S. (2003). Breaking the silence: Using a token economy to reinforce classroom participation. *Teaching of Psychology, 30*(3), 224–227.

Bonk, C. J., & Reynolds, T. H. (1992). Early adolescent composing within a generative-evaluative computerized prompting framework. *Computers in Human Behavior, 8*(1), 39–62.

Borja, R. R. (2003). Prepping for the big test. *Education Week, 22*(35), 22–24, 26.

Borthick, A. F., Jones, D. R., & Wakai, S. (2003). Designing learning experiences within learners' zones of proximal development: Enabling collaborative learning on-site and on-line. *Journal of Information Systems, 17*(1), 107–134.

Bower, G. H., Clark, M. C., Lesgold, A. M., & Winzenz, D. (1969). Hierarchical retrieval schemes in recall of categorized word lists. *Journal of Verbal Learning and Verbal Behavior, 8*(3), 323–343.

Bowes, L., Arsenault, L., Maughan, B., Taylor, A., Caspi, A., & Moffitt, T. E. (2009). School, neighborhood, and family factors are associated with children's bullying involvement: A nationally representative longitudinal study. *Journal of the American Academy of Child and Adolescent Psychiatry, 48*(5), 545–553.

Bowman, D. H. (2002). National survey puts ADHD incidence near 7 percent. *Education Week, 21*(38), 3.

Boyer, E. L. (1983). *High school.* New York: Harper & Row.

Braaksma, M. A. H., Rijlaarsdam, G., & van den Bergh, H. (2002). Observational learning and the effects of model-observer similarity. *Journal of Educational Psychology, 94*(2), 405–415.

Bracey, G. W. (2008a). The 18th Bracey report on the condition of public education: Schools-are-awful bloc still busy in 2008. *Phi Delta Kappan, 90*(2), 103–114.

Bracey, G. W. (2008b). International comparisons: Worth the cost? In S. Mathison & E. W. Ross (Eds.), *The nature and limits of standards-based reform and assessment* (pp. 35–47). New York: Teachers College Press.

Branch, C. W., & Boothe, B. (2002). The identity status of African Americans in middle adolescence: A replication and extension of Forbes and Ashton (1998). *Adolescence, 37*(148), 815–821.

Bransford, J. D., Sherwood, R., Vye, N., & Rieser, J. (1986). Teaching thinking and problem solving: Research foundations. *American Psychologist, 41*(10), 1078–1089.

Bransford, J. D., & Stein, B. S. (1993). *The ideal problem solver* (2nd ed.). New York: W. H. Freeman.

Braun, H. I., & Mislevy, R. (2005). Intuitive test theory. *Phi Delta Kappan, 86*(7), 489–497.

Brendgen, M., Wanner, B., Vitaro, F., Bukowski, W. M., & Tremblay, R. E. (2007). Verbal abuse by the teacher during childhood and academic, behavioral, and emotional adjustment in young adulthood. *Journal of Educational Psychology, 99*(1), 26–38.

Brinthaupt, T. M., Lipka, R. P., & Wallace, M. (2007). Aligning student self and identity concerns with middle school practices. In S. B. Mertens, V. A. Anfara, Jr., & M. M. Caskey (Eds.), *The young adolescent and the middle school* (pp. 201–218). Charlotte, NC: Information Age.

Britner, S. L., & Pajares, F. (2006). Sources of science self-efficacy beliefs of middle school students. *Journal of Research in Science Teaching, 43,* 485–499.

Broekkamp, H., & van Hout-Wolters, B. H. A. M. (2007). Students' adaptation of study strategies when preparing for classroom tests. *Educational Psychology Review, 19*(4), 401–428.

Broekkamp, H., van Hout-Wolters, B. H. A. M., Rijlaarsdam, G., & van den Bergh, H. (2002). Importance in instructional text: Teachers' and students' perceptions of task demands. *Journal of Educational Psychology, 94*(2), 260–271.

Brookhart, S. (2009a). Editorial. *Educational Measurement: Issues and Practice, 28*(1), 1–2.

Brookhart, S. (2009b). *Grading* (2nd ed.). Upper Saddle River, NJ: Merrill/Pearson Education.

Brookhart, S., & Nitko, A. (2008). *Assessment and grading in classrooms.* Upper Saddle River, NJ: Allyn & Bacon/Pearson.

Brooks, J. G., & Brooks, M. G. (2001). *In search of understanding: The case for constructivist classrooms.* Upper Saddle River, NJ: Merrill Prentice Hall.

Brophy, J. E. (1981). Teacher praise: A functional analysis. *Review of Educational Research, 51*(1), 5–32.

Brouwer, N., & Korthagen, F. (2005). Can teacher education make a difference? *American Educational Research Journal, 42*(1), 153–224.

Brown, A. B., & Clift, J. W. (2010). The unequal effect of adequate yearly progress: Evidence from school visits. *American Educational Research Journal, 47*(4), 774–798.

Brown, J. L., Roderick, T., Lantieri, L., & Aber, J. L. (2004). The Resolving Conflict Creatively Program: A school-based social and emotional learning program. In J. E. Zins, R. P. Weissberg, M. C. Wang, & H. J. Walberg (Eds.), *Building academic success on social and emotional learning: What does the research say?* New York: Teachers College Press.

Brown, S. M., & Walberg, H. J. (1993). Motivational effects on test scores of elementary students. *Journal of Educational Research, 86*(3), 133–136.

Bruner, J. S. (1983). *In search of mind: Essays in autobiography.* New York: Harper & Row.

Bruning, R. H., Schraw, G. J., Norby, M. M., & Ronning, R. R. (2004). *Cognitive psychology and instruction* (4th ed.). Upper Saddle River, NJ: Merrill Prentice Hall.

Brush, T., & Saye, J. (2001). The use of embedded scaffolds with hypermedia-supported student-centered learning. *Journal of Educational Multimedia and Hypermedia, 10*(4), 333–356.

Bryant, D. P., Vaughn, S., Linan-Thompson, S., Ugel, N., Hamff, A., & Hougen, M. (2000). Reading outcomes for students with and without reading disabilities in general education middle-school content area classes. *Learning Disability Quarterly, 23*(4), 238–252.

Bukatko, D. (2008). *Child and adolescent development: A chronological approach.* Boston: Houghton Mifflin.

Bull, G., Hammond, T., & Ferster, B. (2008). Developing Web 2.0 tools for support of historical inquiry in social studies. *Computers in the Schools, 25*(3–4), 275–287.

Bunz, U. (2009). A generational comparison of gender, computer anxiety, and computer-email-web fluency. *Studies in Media & Information Literacy Education, 9*(2), 54–69.

Burchinal, M. R., Peisner-Feinberg, E., Pianta, R., & Howes, C. (2002). The development of academic skills from preschool through second grade: Family and classroom predictors of developmental trajectories. *Journal of School Psychology, 40*(5), 415–436.

Burris, C. C., & Welner, K. G. (2005). Closing the achievement gap by detracking. *Phi Delta Kappan, 86*(8), 594–598.

Burris, C. C., Wiley, E., Welner, K., & Murphy, J. (2008). Accountability, rigor and detracking: Achievement effects of embracing a challenging curriculum as a universal good for all students. *Teachers College Record, 110*(3), 571–608.

Burton, D., Lee, K., & Younie, S. (2009). Understanding learning theories and strategies. In S. Younie, S. Capel, & M. Leask (Eds.), *Supporting teaching and learning in schools* (pp. 82–90). New York: Routledge.

Bushaw, W. J., & Lopez, S. J. (2010). A time for change: The 42nd annual *Phi Delta Kappan*/Gallup poll of the public's attitudes toward the public schools. *Phi Delta Kappan, 92*(1), 9–26.

Bushrod, G., Williams, R. L., & McLaughlin, T. F. (1995). An evaluation of a simplified daily report system with two kindergarten pupils. *B.C. Journal of Special Education, 19*(1), 35–43.

Butler, R. (2005). Competence assessment, competence, and motivation between early and middle childhood. In A. J. Elliot & C. S. Dweck (Eds.), *Handbook of competence and motivation* (pp. 202–221). New York: Guilford Press.

Caine, G., Caine, R. N., & McClintic, C. (2002). Guiding the innate constructivist. *Educational Leadership, 60*(1), 70–73.

Calderón, M. E., & Minaya-Rowe, L. (2003). *Designing and implementing two-way bilingual programs.* Thousand Oaks, CA: Corwin Press.

Calfee, R. (2009). Teacher-based assessment in the elementary and middle grades. *Perspectives on Language Learning and Education, 16*(1), 21–27.

Callahan, R. M. (2005). Tracking and high school English learners: Limiting opportunity to learn. *American Educational Research Journal, 42*(2), 305–328.

Callender, A. A., & McDaniel, M. A. (2009). The limited benefits of rereading educational texts. *Contemporary Educational Psychology, 34*(1), 30–41.

Cameron, J. (2001). Negative effects of reward on intrinsic motivation—A limited phenomenon: Comment on Deci, Koestner, & Ryan (2001). *Review of Educational Research, 71*(1), 29–42.

Cameron, J., Banko, K. M., & Pierce, W. D. (2001). Pervasive negative effects of rewards on intrinsic motivation: The myth continues. *Behavior Analyst, 24*(1), 1–44.

Camnalbur, M., & Erdogan, Y. (2008). A meta-analysis on the effectiveness of computer-assisted instruction: Turkey sample. *Educational Sciences: Theory and Practice, 8*(2), 497–505.

Camp, C., & Stark, W. (2006). *More than words on the screen* [Electronic version]. Paper presented at the 2006 PEPNet conference Roots & Wings. (Proceedings available from the University of Tennessee, Postsecondary Education Consortium Web site: http://sunsite.utk.edu/cod/pec/products.html).

Campbell, L. (1997). How teachers interpret MI theory. *Educational Leadership, 55*(1), 14–19.

Canivez, G. L. (2008). Orthogonal higher order factor structure of the Stanford-Binet Intelligence Scales—Fifth Edition for children and adolescents. *School Psychology Quarterly, 23*(4), 533–541.

Cardon, P. L., & Christensen, K. W. (1998). Technology-based programs for drop-out prevention. *Journal of Technology Studies, 24*(1), 50–54.

Cardwell, K. (2000). Electronic assessment. *Learning and Leading with Technology, 27*(7), 22–26.

Carnevale, D. (2004). Online study tools help Texas students prepare for graduation exam. *Chronicle of Higher Education, 50*(38), p. A31.

Carney, R. N., & Levin, J. R. (2002). Pictorial illustrations still improve students' learning from text. *Educational Psychology Review, 14*(1), 5–26.

Carney, R. N., Levin, J. R., & Levin, M. E. (1994). Enhancing the psychology of memory by enhancing memory of psychology. *Teaching of Psychology, 21*(3), 171–174.

Carr, N. (2010). The juggler's brain. *Phi Delta Kappan, 92*(4), 8–14.

Carroll, J. B. (1963). A model of school learning. *Teachers College Record, 64*(8), 723–733.

Carter, C. J. (1997). Why reciprocal teaching? *Educational Leadership, 54*(6), 64–68.

Carter, D. B. (1987). The role of peers in sex role socialization. In D. B. Carter (Ed.), *Current conceptions of sex roles and sex typing.* New York: Praeger.

Case, R. (1975). Gearing the demands of instruction to the developmental capacities of the learner. *Review of Educational Research, 45*(1), 59–88.

Case, R. (1999). Conceptual development in the child and in the field: A personal view of the Piagetian legacy. In E. K. Scholnick, K. Nelson, S. A. Gelman, & P. H. Miller (Eds.), *Conceptual development: Piaget's legacy.* Mahwah, NJ: Erlbaum.

Castagno, A. E., & Brayboy, B. M. J. (2008). Culturally indigenous youth: A review of the literature. *Review of Educational Research, 78*(4), 941–993.

Cennamo, K., Ross, J., & Ertmer, P. (2010). Technology integration for meaningful classroom use: A standards-based approach. Belmont, CA: Wadsworth/Cengage Learning.

Center for Applied Linguistics. (2009). *Directory of two-way bilingual immersion programs in the U.S.* Retrieved from http://www.cal.org/twi/directory.

Center for Applied Special Technology. (2008). *Universal design for learning guidelines version 1.0.* Wakefield, MA: Author. Retrieved March 11, 2009, from http://www.cast.org/publications/UDLguidelines/UDL_Guidelines_v1.0.doc.

Center on Education Policy. (2005, March). *From the capital to the classroom: Year 3 of the No Child Left Behind Act.* Washington, DC: Author. Retrieved from http://www.cep-dc.org/cfcontent_file.cfm?Attachment=FullReport_NCLB3_030105.pdf.

Center on Education Policy. (2007, August). *Reauthorizing the Elementary and Secondary Education Act of 1965: Recommendations from the Center on Educational Policy.* Retrieved from http://www.cep-dc.org/cfcontent_file.cfm?Attachment=CEP_ESEARecommendations_082807.pdf.

Center on Education Policy. (2008a, June). *Has student achievement increased since 2002? State test score trends through 2006–07.* Retrieved from http://www.cep-dc.org/cfcontent_file.cfm?Attachment=KoberChudowsky2_StudentAchievement_061708.pdf.

Center on Education Policy. (2008b, November). *Lessons from the classroom level: Federal and state accountability in Rhode Island.* Retrieved from http://www.cep-dc.org/cfcontent_file.cfm?Attachment=SrikantaiahZhangSwayhoover_FSA-RI_112508.pdf.

Center on Education Policy. (2009, October). *Are achievement gaps closing and is achievement rising for all?* Retrieved from http://www.cep-dc.org/cfcontent_file.cfm?Attachment=Chudowsky2Kober_STST07-08_P3-GapandAchievementForAll_100109.pdf.

Centers for Disease Control and Prevention. (2008). Youth risk behavior surveillance—United States, 2007. *Morbidity and Mortality Weekly Report, 57*(SS–4), 1–131.

Centers for Disease Control and Prevention. (2009). Sexual and reproductive health of persons aged 10–24 years—United States, 2002–2007. *Surveillance Summaries. Morbidity and Mortality Weekly Report, 58*(SS–6), 1–60.

Cepeda, N., Coburn, N., Rohrer, D., Wixted, J., Mozer, M., & Pashler, H. (2009). Optimizing distributed practice theoretical analysis and practical implications. *Experimental Psychology, 56*(4), 236–246.

Chabris, C., & Simons, D. (2010). *The invisible gorilla: And other ways our intuitions deceive us.* New York: Crown.

Chan, C. K. K., & Pang, M. F. (2006). Teacher collaboration in learning communities. *Teaching Education, 17*(1), 1–5.

Chance, P. (1992). The rewards of learning. *Phi Delta Kappan, 74*(3), 200–207.

Chance, P. (1993). Sticking up for rewards. *Phi Delta Kappan, 74*(10), 787–790.

Chaney, E., & Gilman, D. A. (2005). Filling in the blanks: Using computers to test and teach. *Computers in the Schools, 22*(1/2), 157–168.

Chang, C.-C. (2009). Self-evaluated effects of web-based portfolio assessment system for various student motivation levels. *Journal of Educational Computing Research. 41*(4), 391–405.

Chen, J. A., & Pajares, F. (2010). Implicit theories of ability of grade 6 science students: Relation to epistemological beliefs and academic motivation and achievement in science. *Contemporary Educational Psychology, 35*(1), 75–87.

Chen, J.-Q., Moran, S., & Gardner, H. (Eds.). (2009). *Multiple intelligences around the world.* San Francisco: John Wiley & Sons.

Chen, M., & Bargh, J. A. (1997). Nonconscious behavioral confirmation processes: The self-fulfilling consequences of automatic stereotype activation. *Journal of Experimental Social Psychology, 33*(5), 541–560.

Chetty, R., Friedman, J. N., Hilger, N., Saez, E., Schanzenbach, D. W., & Yagan, D. (2010). $320,000 kindergarten teachers. *Phi Delta Kappan, 92*(3), 22–25.

Choi, I., & Lee, K. (2009). Designing and implementing a case-based learning environment for enhancing ill-structured problem solving: Classroom management problems for prospective teachers. *Educational Technology Research and Development, 57*(1), 99–129.

Chudowsky, N., & Chudowsky, V. (2008, May). *Many states have taken a "backloaded" approach to No Child Left Behind goal of all students scoring "proficient."* Retrieved from http://www.cep-dc.org/cfcontent_file.cfm?Attachment=Chudowsky2_NCLBStatesBackloaded_051908.pdf.

Cicchetti, D., & Toth, S. L. (1998). The development of depression in children and adolescents. *American Psychologist, 53*(2), 221–241.

Cizek, G. J. (2003). Rejoinder. *Educational Measurement: Issues and Practice, 22*(1), 40–44.

Clark, J. M., & Paivio, A. (1991). Dual coding theory and education. *Educational Psychology Review, 3*(3), 149–210.

Clark, R. E. (2002). Performance assessment in the arts. *Kappa Delta Pi Record, 39*(1), 29–32.

Clarke, L., & Heaney, P. (2003). Author On-Line: Using asynchronous computer conferencing to support literacy. *British Journal of Educational Psychology, 34*(1), 57–66.

Clawson, M. A., & Robila, M. (2001). Relations between parenting style and children's play behavior: Issues in education. *Journal of Early Education and Family Review, 8*(3), 13–19.

Clements, D. H., Sarama, J., Yelland, N. J., & Glass, B. (2008). Learning and teaching geometry with computers in the elementary and middle school. In M. K. Heid & G. W. Blume (Eds.), *Research on technology and the teaching and learning of mathematics: Volume 1. Research syntheses* (pp. 109–154). Charlotte, NC: Information Age Publishing.

Cochran-Smith, M. (2003). The unforgiving complexity of teaching: Avoiding simplicity in the age of accountability. *Journal of Teacher Education, 54*(1), 3–5.

Colangelo, N., & Davis, G. A. (2003). Introduction and overview. In N. Colangelo & G. A. Davis (Eds.), *Handbook of gifted education* (3rd ed., pp. 3–10). Boston: Allyn & Bacon.

Cole, J., Bergin, D., & Whittaker, T. (2008). Predicting student achievement for low stakes tests with effort and task value. *Contemporary Educational Psychology, 33*(4), 609–624.

Cole, J. M., & Hilliard, V. R. (2006). The effects of web-based reading curriculum on children's reading performance and motivation. *Journal of Educational Computing Research, 34*(4), 353–380.

Cole, M. (1996). *Cultural psychology: A once and future discipline.* Cambridge, MA: Harvard University Press.

Cole, M. (2005). Putting culture in the middle. In H. Daniels (Ed.), *An introduction to Vygotsky* (2nd ed.). New York: Routledge.

Cole, M., & Gajdamaschko, N. (2007). Vygotsky and culture. In H. Daniels, M. Cole, & J. Wertsch (Eds.), *The Cambridge companion to Vygotsky* (pp. 193–211). New York: Cambridge University Press.

Combs, A. W. (1965). *The professional education of teachers.* Boston: Allyn & Bacon.

Commission on Instructionally Supportive Assessment. (2002, March). *Implementing ESEA's testing provisions.* Retrieved from http://www.nea.org/accountability/images/02eseatesting.pdf.

Compton, M., Tucker, D., & Flynn, P. (2009). Preparation and perceptions of speech-language pathologists working with children with cochlear implants. *Communication Disorders Quarterly, 30*(3), 142–154.

Compton-Lilly, C. (2009). Introduction. In C. Compton-Lilly (Ed.), *Breaking the silence: Recognizing social and cultural resources students bring to the classroom* (pp. 1–12). Newark, DE: International Reading Association.

Conger, J. J., & Galambos, N. L. (1997). *Adolescence and youth* (5th ed.). New York: Longman.

Connor, D. F. (2002). *Aggression and antisocial behavior in children and adolescents.* New York: Guilford Press.

Cooke-Simpson, A., & Voyer, D. (2007). Confidence and gender differences on the mental rotations test. *Learning and Individual Differences, 17*(2), 181–186.

Cooper, H. (2001). Homework for all—in moderation. *Educational Leadership, 58*(7), 34–38.

Cooper, H., & Dorr, N. (1995). Race comparisons on need for achievement: A meta-analytic alternative to Graham's narrative review. *Review of Educational Research, 65*(4), 438–508.

Cooper, H., Robinson, J. C., & Patall, E. A. (2006). Does homework improve academic achievement? A synthesis of research, 1987–2003. *Review of Educational Research, 76*(1), 1–62.

Corbett, C., Hill, C., & St. Rose, A. (2008). *Where the girls are: The facts about gender equity in education.* Washington, DC: American Association of University Women.

Corbett, D., & Wilson, B. (2002). What urban students say about good teaching. *Educational Leadership, 60*(1), 18–22.

Cornelius-White, J. (2007). Learner-centered teacher–student relationships are effective: A meta-analysis. *Review of Educational Research, 77*(1), 113–143.

Cornoldi, C. (2010). Metacognition, intelligence, and academic performance. In H. Salatas Waters & W. Schneider (Eds.), *Metacognition, strategy use, and instruction* (pp. 257–280). New York: Guilford Press.

Cothran, J. C. (2006). *A search of African-American life, achievement and culture.* Carrolltown, TX: Stardate.

Cotterall, S., & Cohen, R. (2003). Scaffolding for second language writers: Producing an academic essay. *ELT Journal, 57*(2), 158–166.

Covington, M. V. (2009). Self-worth theory: Retrospection and prospects. In K. Wentzel & A. Wigfield (Eds.), *Handbook of motivation at school* (pp. 141–170). New York: Routledge.

Cowan, N. (2005). *Working memory capacity.* New York: Psychology Press.

Cox, B. D. (1997). The rediscovery of the active learner in adaptive contexts: A developmental-historical analysis of transfer of training. *Educational Psychologist, 32*(1), 41–55.

Craig, S., Chi, M., & VanLehn, K. (2009). Improving classroom learning by collaboratively observing human tutoring videos while problem solving. *Journal of Educational Psychology, 101*(4), 779–789.

Crain, W. (2005). *Theories of development: Concepts and applications* (5th ed.). Upper Saddle River, NJ: Pearson/Prentice Hall.

Cronin, J., Dahlin, M., Adkins, D., & Kingsbury, G. G. (2007, October). *The proficiency illusion.* Retrieved from http://www.edexcellence media.net/publications/2007/200710_theproficiencyillusion/Proficiency_Illusion_092707.pdf.

Csikszentmihalyi, M. (1975). *Beyond boredom and anxiety.* San Francisco: Jossey-Bass.

Csikszentmihalyi, M. (1996). *Creativity.* New York: Harper/Perennial.

Csikszentmihalyi, M. (2000). *Finding flow: The psychology of engagement with everyday life.* New York: Basic Books.

Csikszentmihalyi, M. (2002). *Flow: The classic work on how to achieve happiness.* London: Rider.

Cuban, L. (1990). What I learned from what I had forgotten about teaching: Notes from a professor. *Phi Delta Kappan, 71*(6), 479–482.

Cummins, J. (1999). Alternative paradigms in bilingual education research. *Educational Researcher, 28*(7), 26–32, 41.

Cunningham, D. J. (1992). Beyond educational psychology: Steps toward an educational semiotic. *Educational Psychology Review, 4*(2), 165–194.

Cunningham, D. J. (2001, April). *Fear and loathing in the information age.* Paper presented at the annual meeting of the American Education Research Association, Seattle, WA.

Curtis, D. (2002). The power of projects. *Educational Leadership, 60*(1), 50–53.

Cury, F., Da Fonseca, D., Zahn, I., & Elliot, A. (2008). Implicit theories and IQ test performance: A sequential mediational analysis. *Journal of Experimental Social Psychology, 44*(3), 783–791.

D'Agostino, J. V., & Powers, S. J. (2009). Predicting teacher performance with test scores and grade point average: A meta-analysis. *American Educational Research Journal, 46*(1), 146–182.

Daiute, C. (1985). Issues in using computers to socialize the writing process. *Educational Communication and Technology, 33*(1), 41–50.

Daly, E. (III), Martens, B., Barnett, D., Witt, J., & Olson, S. (2007). Varying intervention delivery in response to intervention: Confronting and resolving challenges with measurement, instruction, and intensity. *School Psychology Review, 36*(4), 562–581.

Daniel, D. B., & Poole, D. A. (2009). Learning for life: An ecological approach to pedagogical research. *Perspectives on Psychological Science, 4*(1), 91–96.

Dardig, J. C. (2005). The McClurg monthly magazine and 14 more practical ways to involve parents. *Teaching Exceptional Children 38*(2), 46–51.

Darling-Hammond, L. (2009). America's commitment to equity will determine our future. *Phi Delta Kappan, 91*(4), 8–14.

Darling-Hammond, L. (with Fickel, L., Koppich, J., Macdonald, M., Merseth, K., Miller, L., Ruscoe, G., Silvernail, D., Snyder, J., Whitford, B., & Zeichner, K.). (2009). *Powerful teacher education: Lessons from exemplary programs.* San Francisco: Jossey-Bass.

Darling-Hammond, L., & Falk, B. (1997). Using standards and assessments to support student learning. *Phi Delta Kappan, 79*(3), 190–199.

Darling-Hammond, L., Holtzman, D. J., Gatlin, S. J., & Heilig, J. V. (2005). Does teacher preparation matter? Evidence about teacher certification, Teach for America, and teacher effectiveness. *Education Policy Analysis Archives, 13*(42), 1–51. Retrieved from http://epaa.asu.edu/ojs/article/view/147.

Darling-Hammond, L., & Youngs, P. (2002). Defining "highly qualified teachers": What does "scientifically-based research" actually tell us? *Educational Researcher, 31*(9), 13–25.

Dasen, P., & Heron, A. (1981). Cross-cultural tests of Piaget's theory. In H. C. Triandis & A. Heron (Eds.), *Handbook of cross-cultural psychology, developmental psychology* (Vol. 4). Boston: Allyn & Bacon.

Davis, M. R. (2009). Breaking away from tradition. *Education Week, 28*(26), 8–9.

Davis, S. H. (2007). Bridging the gap between research and practice: What's good, what's bad, and how can one be sure? *Phi Delta Kappan, 88*(8), 568–578.

DeBell, M., & Chapman, C. (2003). *Computer and Internet use by children and adolescents in 2001.* Washington, DC: National Center for Educational Statistics. Retrieved January 5, 2004, from http://nces.ed.gov/pubs2004/2004014.pdf.

DeBlois, R. (2005). When to promote students. *Phi Delta Kappan, 87*(4), 306–310.

Deci, E. L., Koestner, R., & Ryan, R. M. (1999). A meta-analytic review of experiments examining the effects of extrinsic rewards on intrinsic motivation. *Psychological Bulletin, 125*(6), 627–668.

Deci, E. L., Koestner, R., & Ryan, R. M. (2001). Extrinsic rewards and intrinsic motivation in education: Reconsidered once again. *Review of Educational Research, 71*(1), 1–27.

De Corte, E. (2003). Transfer as the productive use of acquired knowledge, skills, and motivations. *Current Directions in Psychological Science, 12*(4), 142–146.

Dehn, M. J. (2008). *Working memory and academic learning: Assessment and intervention.* Hoboken, NJ: John Wiley & Sons.

Delgarno, B. (2001). Interpretations of constructivism and consequences for computer assisted learning. *British Journal of Educational Technology, 32*(2), 183–194.

De Lisi, R. (2006). A developmental perspective on virtual scaffolding for learning in home and school contexts. In A. O'Donnell, C. E. Hmelo-Silver, & G. Erkens (Eds.), *Collaborative learning, reasoning, and technology.* Mahwah, NJ: Erlbaum.

Dempster, F. N. (1988). The spacing effect: A case study in the failure to apply the results of psychological research. *American Psychologist, 43*(8), 627–634.

DeNavas-Walt, C., Proctor, B. D., & Smith, J. C. (2009, September). *Income, poverty, and health insurance coverage in the United States: 2008. Current Population Reports, P60-236.* Washington, DC: U.S. Government Printing Office. Retrieved from http://www.census.gov/prod/2009pubs/p60-236.pdf.

Denbo, S. J. (2002). Institutional practices that support African American student achievement. In S. J. Denbo & L. M. Beaulieu (Eds.), *Improving schools for African American students* (pp. 55–71). Springfield, IL: Charles C. Thomas.

Deneen, C., & Deneen, J. (2008). *Assessing student achievement: A guide for teachers and administrators.* Lanham, MD: Rowman & Littlefield Education.

DeRose, L. M., & Brooks-Gunn, J. (2009). Pubertal development in early adolescence: Implications for affective processes. In N. B. Allen & L. B. Sheeber (Eds.), *Adolescent emotional development and the emergence of depressive disorders* (pp. 56–73). Cambridge, England: Cambridge University Press.

Derry, S. J. (1996). Cognitive schema theory in the constructivist debate. *Educational Researcher, 31*(3/4), 163–174.

Derry, S. J., Hmelo-Silver, C. E., Nagarajan, A., Chernobilsky, E., Feltovich, J., & Halfpap, B. (2005). Making a mesh of it: A STELLAR approach to teacher professional development. In T. Koschmann, D. D. Suthers, & T.-W. Chan (Eds.), *Proceedings of Computer Support for Collaborative Learning (CSCL) 2005, Taipei, Taiwan.* Mahwah, NJ: Erlbaum.

Derzon, J. (2006). How effective are school-based violence prevention programs in preventing and reducing violence and other antisocial behaviors? A meta-analysis. In S. R. Jimerson & M. J. Furlong (Eds.), *The handbook of school violence and school safety* (pp. 429–441). Mahwah, NJ: Erlbaum.

Devine, J., & Cohen, J. (2007). *Making your school safe: Strategies to protect children and promote learning.* New York: Teachers College Press.

De Vries, B., Van der Meij, H., Boersma, K., & Pieters, J. M. (2005). Embedding e-mail in primary schools: Developing a tool for collective reflection. *Journal of Educational Computing Research, 32*(2), 167–183.

DeVries, R. (1997). Piaget's social theory. *Educational Researcher, 26*(2), 4–17.

Dill, E. M., & Boykin, A. W. (2000). The comparative influence of individual, peer tutoring, and communal learning contexts of the text recall of African American children. *Journal of Black Psychology, 26*(1), 65–78.

Dinkes, R., Kemp, J., Baum, K., & Snyder, T. D. (2009). *Indicators of school crime and safety: 2008* (NCES 2009-022/NCJ 226343). Washington, DC: U.S. Department of Education and U.S. Department of Justice. Retrieved from http://nces.ed.gov/programs/crimeindicators/crimeindicators2008.

Dobbs, M. (2005, April 21). NEA, states challenge "No Child" program. *Washington Post*, p. A21.

Donovan, C. A., & Smolkin, L. B. (2002). Children's genre knowledge: An examination of K–5 students' performance on multiple tasks providing differing levels of scaffolding. *Reading Research Quarterly, 37*(4), 428–465.

Doppelt, Y. (2009). Assessing creative thinking in design-based learning. *International Journal of Technology and Design Education, 19*(1), 55–65.

Doppelt, Y., & Barak, M. (2002). Pupils identify key aspects and outcomes of a technological learning environment. *Journal of Technology Studies, 28*(1), 22–28.

Dornbusch, S. M., & Kaufman, J. G. (2001). The social structure of the American high school. In T. Urdan & F. Pajares (Eds.), *Adolescence and education* (Vol. 1, pp. 61–91). Greenwich, CT: Information Age.

Doty, D. E., Popplewell, S. R., & Byers, G. O. (2001). Interactive CD-ROM storybooks and young readers' reading comprehension. *Journal of Research on Computing in Education, 33*(4), 374–384.

Doyle, W. (1983). Academic work. *Review of Educational Research, 53*(2), 159–200.

Drake, F. D., & McBride, L. W. (2000). The summative teaching portfolio and the reflective practitioner of history. *History Teacher, 34*(1), 41–60.

Drier, H. S. (2001). Conceptualization and design of Probability Explorer. *TechTrends, 45*(2), 2–24.

Driscoll, M. P. (2005). *Psychology of learning for instruction* (3rd ed.). Boston: Allyn & Bacon.

Duckworth, A. L., & Seligman, M. E. P. (2006). Self-discipline gives girls the edge: Gender in self-discipline, grades, and achievement test scores. *Journal of Educational Psychology, 98*(1), 198–208.

Duell, O. K. (1986). Metacognitive skills. In G. D. Phye & T. Andre (Eds.), *Cognitive classroom learning.* Orlando, FL: Academic Press.

Duff, C. (2000). Online mentoring. *Educational Leadership, 58*(2), 49–52.

Duffrin, E. (2004a, May). What we know about efforts to end "social promotion." *Catalyst Chicago*, 8–10.

Duffrin, E. (2004b, May). Popular despite the research. *Catalyst Chicago*, 6–7.

Duffy, T. M., & Cunningham, D. J. (1996). Constructivism: Implications for the design and delivery of instruction. In D. Jonassen (Ed.), *Handbook of research for educational communications and technology* (pp. 170–198). New York: Macmillan Library Reference.

Duhaney, L. M., & Duhaney, D. C. (2000). Assistive technology: Meeting the needs of learners with disabilities. *International Journal of Instructional Media, 27*(4), 393–401.

Dunlosky, J., & Bjork, R. (2008a). The integrated nature of metamemory and memory. In J. Dunlosky & R. Bjork (Eds.), *Handbook of metamemory and memory* (pp. 11–28). New York: Taylor & Francis.

Dunlosky, J., & Bjork, R. (Eds.). (2008b). *Handbook of metamemory and memory.* New York: Taylor & Francis.

Dupper, D. R., & Dingus, A. E. M. (2008). Corporal punishment in U.S. public schools: A continuing challenge for school social workers. *Children & Schools, 30*(4), 243–250.

Dweck, C. S. (2002a). The development of ability conceptions. In A. Wigfield & J. S. Eccles (Eds.), *Development of achievement motivation* (pp. 57–88). San Diego, CA: Academic Press.

Dweck, C. S. (2002b). Messages that motivate: How praise molds students' beliefs, motivation, and performance (in surprising ways). In J. Aronson (Ed.), *Improving academic achievement* (pp. 37–59). San Diego, CA: Academic Press.

Dweck, C., & Master, A. (2009). Self-theories and motivation: Students' beliefs about intelligence. In K. Wentzel & A. Wigfield (Eds.), *Handbook of motivation at school* (pp. 55–76). New York: Routledge.

Earl, L. (2003). *Assessment as learning: Using classroom assessment to maximize student learning.* Thousand Oaks, CA: Corwin.

Eberstadt, M. (2003). The child-fat problem. *Policy Review, 117,* 3–19.

Eby, J. W., Herrell, A., & Hicks, J. L. (2002). *Reflective planning, teaching, and evaluation: K–12.* Upper Saddle River, NJ: Merrill Prentice Hall.

Eby, J. W., Herrell, A. L., & Jordan, M. (2006). *Teaching in K–12 schools: A reflective action approach.* Upper Saddle River, NJ: Pearson Merrill Prentice Hall.

Eccles, J. (2009). Who am I and what am I doing with my life? Personal and collective identities as motivators of action. *Educational Psychologist, 44*(2), 78–89.

Economics and Statistics Administration & National Telecommunications and Information Administration. (2010, November). *Exploring the digital nation: Home broadband and Internet adoption in the United States.* Washington, DC: U.S. Department of Commerce. Retrieved from http://www.ntia.doc.gov/files/ntia/publications/esa_ntia_us_broadband_adoption_report_11082010_1.pdf.

Eisner, E. W. (2002). What can education learn from the arts about the practice of education? *Journal of Curriculum and Supervision, 18*(1), 4–16.

Elkind, D. (1968). Cognitive development in adolescence. In J. F. Adams (Ed.), *Understanding adolescence.* Boston: Allyn & Bacon.

Elkind, D. (1989). Developmentally appropriate practice: Philosophical and practical implications. *Phi Delta Kappan, 71*(2), 113–117.

Elkind, D. (2005). Response to objectivism and education. *Educational Forum, 69*(4), 328–334.

Elliott, T., Welsh, M., Nettelbeck, T., & Mills, V. (2007). Investigating naturalistic decision making in a simulated microworld: What questions should we ask? *Behavior Research Methods, 39*(4), 901–910.

Ellis, A. K. (2001). *Teaching, learning, and assessment together: The reflective classroom.* Larchmont, NY: Eye on Education.

Elmore, R. F. (2002). *Bridging the gap between standards and achievement: The imperative for professional development in education.* Washington, DC: Albert Shanker Institute.

Emmer, E. T., & Evertson, C. M. (2009). *Classroom management for middle and high school teachers* (8th ed.). Boston: Pearson/Allyn & Bacon.

Emmer, E. T., & Stough, L. M. (2001). Classroom management: A critical part of educational psychology, with implications for teacher education. *Educational Psychologist, 36*(2), 103–112.

Engeström, Y. (1999). Activity theory and individual and social transformation. In Y. Engeström, R. Miettinen, & R.-L. Punamaki (Eds.), *Perspectives on activity theory* (pp. 19–38). New York: Cambridge University Press.

Englander, E. K. (2007). *Understanding violence* (3rd ed.). Mahwah, NJ: Erlbaum.

Ericsson, K. A., Chase, W. G., & Faloon, S. (1980). Acquisition of a memory skill. *Science, 208*(4448), 1181–1182.

Erikson, E. H. (1963). *Childhood and society* (2nd ed.). New York: Norton.

Evans, R. (2005). Reframing the achievement gap. *Phi Delta Kappan, 86*(8), 582–589.

Evertson, C. M., & Emmer, E. T. (2009). *Classroom management for elementary teachers* (8th ed.). Boston: Pearson/Allyn & Bacon.

Fabes, R. A., Martin, C. L., & Hanish, L. D. (2003). Young children's play qualities in same-, other-, and mixed-sex peer groups. *Child Development, 74*(3), 921–932.

Fadjukoff, P., Pulkkinen, L., & Kokko, K. (2005). Identity processes in adulthood: Diverging domains. *Identity, 5*(1), 1–20.

Falk, B. (2009). *Teaching the way children learn.* New York: Teachers College Press.

Faw, H. W., & Waller, T. G. (1976). Mathemagenic behaviors and efficiency in learning from prose materials. *Review of Educational Research, 46*(4), 691–720.

Feigenbaum, P. (2002). Private speech: Cornerstone of Vygotsky's theory of the development of higher psychological processes. In D. Robbins & A. Stetsenko (Eds.), *Voices within Vygotsky's non-classical psychology: Past, present, and future* (pp. 161–174). New York: Nova Science.

Feiman-Nemser, S. (2003). What new teachers need to learn. *Educational Leadership, 60*(8), 25–29.

Feist, J., & Feist, G. J. (2001). *Theories of personality* (5th ed.). Dubuque, IA: McGraw-Hill.

Ferriter, B. (2009). Learning with blogs and wikis. *Educational Leadership, 66*(5), 34–38.

Feynman, R. P. (1985). *"Surely you're joking, Mr. Feynman."* New York: Norton.

Feyten, C. M., Macy, M. D., Ducher, J., Yoshii, M., Park, E., Calandra, B., & Meros, J. (2002). *Teaching ESL/EFL with the Internet.* Upper Saddle River, NJ: Merrill Prentice Hall.

Finarelli, M. G. (1998). GLOBE: A worldwide environmental science and education partnership. *Journal of Science Education and Technology, 7*(1), 77–84.

Finnigan, K. S., & Gross, B. (2007). Do accountability policy sanctions influence teacher motivation? Lessons from Chicago's low-performing school. *American Educational Research Journal, 44*(3), 594–629.

Flaspohler, P. D., Elfstrom, J. L., Vanderzee, K. L., & Sink, H. E. (2009). Stand by me: The effects of peer and teacher support in mitigating the impact of bullying on quality of life. *Psychology in the Schools, 46*(7), 636–649.

Flavell, J. H. (1976). Metacognitive aspects of problem solving. In L. B. Resnick (Ed.), *The nature of intelligence.* Hillsdale, NJ: Erlbaum.

Fletcher, J., & Vaughn, S. (2009). Response to intervention: Preventing and remediating academic difficulties. *Child Development Perspectives, 3*(1), 30–37.

Flieller, A. (1999). Comparison of the development of formal thought in adolescent cohorts aged 10 to 15 years (1967–1996 and 1972–1993). *Developmental Psychology, 35*(4), 1048–1058.

Flinders, D. J. (1989). Does the "art of teaching" have a future? *Educational Leadership, 46*(8), 16–20.

Flora, S. R. (2004). *The power of reinforcement.* Albany, NY: State University of New York Press.

Fok, A., & Watkins, D. (2009). Does a critical constructivist learning environment encourage a deeper approach to learning? *Asia-Pacific Education Researcher, 16*(1), 1–10.

Foote, M. (2007). Keeping accountability systems accountable. *Phi Delta Kappan, 88*(5), 359–363.

Forbes, S., & Ashton, P. (1998). The identity status of African Americans in middle adolescence: A replication and extension of Watson & Protinsky (1991). *Adolescence, 33*(132), 845–849.

Fosnot, C. T., & Perry, R. S. (2005). Constructivism: A psychological theory of learning. In C. T. Fosnot (Ed.), *Constructivism: Theory, perspective and practice* (2nd ed., pp. 8–38). New York: Teachers College Press.

Franzke, M., Kintsch, E., Caccamise, D., Johnson, N., & Dooley, S. (2005). Summary Street: Computer support for comprehension and writing. *Journal of Educational Computing Research, 33*(1), 53–80.

Fredrick, T. (2009). Looking in the mirror: Helping adolescents talk more reflectively during portfolio presentations. *Teachers College Record, 111*(8), 1916–1929.

Freeman, C. E. (2004). *Trends in educational equity of girls & women: 2004* (NCES 2005-016). U.S. Department of Education, National Center for Education Statistics. Washington, DC: U.S. Government Printing Office. Retrieved from http://nces.ed.gov/pubs2005/2005016.pdf.

Freiberg, H. J. (2002). Essential skills for new teachers. *Educational Leadership, 59*(6), 56–60.

French, S. E., Seidman, E., Allen, L., & Aber, J. L. (2006). The development of ethnic identity during adolescence. *Developmental Psychology, 42*(1), 1–10.

Friedlaender, D. (2009). *Oakland Unified School District case study: ASCEND.* Stanford, CA: School Redesign Network at Stanford University. Retrieved November 12, 2009, from http://www.srnleads.org/resources/publications/ousd/cases/ascend.pdf.

Fryer, R. G., Jr., & Torelli, P. (2005, May). *An empirical analysis of "acting white"* (Working Paper 11334). Cambridge, MA: National Bureau of Economic Research. Retrieved from http://www.nber.org/papers/w11334.

Fuchs, D., & Fuchs, L. (2006). Introduction to response to intervention: What, why, and how valid is it? *Reading Research Quarterly, 41*(1), 93–99.

Fuchs, D., & Fuchs, L.S. (2009, November). Responsiveness to intervention: Multilevel assessment and instruction as early intervention and disability identification. *Reading Teacher, 63*(3), 250–252.

Fuchs, D., Fuchs, L., Compton, D., Bouton, B., Caffrey, E., & Hill, L. (2007). Dynamic assessment as responsiveness to intervention: A scripted protocol to identify at-risk readers. *Teaching Exceptional Children, 39*(5), 58–63.

Fuchs, D., Fuchs, L. S., Mathes, P. G., & Simmons, D. C. (1997). Peer-assisted learning strategies: Making classrooms more responsive to diversity. *American Educational Research Journal, 34*(1), 174–206.

Fuller, B., Gesicki, K., Kang, E., & Wright, J. (2006). *Is the No Child Left Behind Act working?* (Working Paper 06-1). Berkeley, CA: University of California, Berkeley, Policy Analysis for California Education.

Fulmer, S., & Frijters, J. (2009). A review of self-report and alternative approaches in the measurement of student motivation. *Educational Psychology Review, 21*(3), 219–246.

Funkhouser, C. (2002/2003). The effects of computer-augmented geometry instruction on student performance and attitudes. *Journal of Research on Technology in Education, 35*(2), 163–175.

Furnham, A., Monsen, J., & Ahmetoglu, G. (2009). Typical intellectual engagement, big five personality traits, approaches to learning and cognitive ability predictors of academic performance. *British Journal of Educational Psychology, 79*(4), 769–782.

Gagné, E. D., Yekovich, C. W., & Yekovich, F. R. (1993). *The cognitive psychology of school learning* (2nd ed.). New York: HarperCollins.

Gallagher, J. J. (2003). Issues and challenges in the education of gifted students. In N. Colangelo & G. A. Davis (Eds.), *Handbook of gifted education* (3rd ed., pp. 11–23). Boston: Allyn & Bacon.

Gallimore, R., & Tharp, R. (1990). Teaching mind in society: Teaching, schooling, and literate discourse. In L. C. Moll (Ed.), *Vygotsky and education: Instructional implications and applications of sociohistorical psychology.* Cambridge, England: Cambridge University Press.

Gantner, M. W. (1997). Lessons learned from my students in the barrio. *Educational Leadership, 54*(7), 44–45.

García, E. (2002). *Student cultural diversity: Understanding and meeting the challenge* (3rd ed.). Boston: Houghton Mifflin.

Gardner, D. (2007). Confronting the achievement gap. *Phi Delta Kappan, 88*(7), 542–546.

Gardner, H. (1999). *Intelligence reframed: Multiple intelligences for the 21st century.* New York: Basic Books.

Gatlin, L., & Jacob, S. (2002). Standards-based digital portfolios: A component of authentic assessment for preservice teachers. *Action in Teacher Education, 23*(4), 35–41.

Gee, J. P. (2007). *Good video games and good learning: Collected essays on video games, learning, and literacy.* New York: Peter Lang.

Gentile, J. R., & Lalley, J. P. (2003). *Standards and mastery learning.* Thousand Oaks, CA: Corwin Press.

Gentner, D., Loewenstein, J., Thompson, L., & Forbus, K. (2009). Reviving inert knowledge: Analogical abstraction supports relational retrieval of past events. *Cognitive Science, 33*(8), 1343–1382.

Gentry, M., Gable, R. K., & Rizza, M. G. (2002). Students' perceptions of classroom activities: Are there grade-level and gender differences? *Journal of Educational Psychology, 94*(3), 539–544.

Gershoff, E. T. (2002). Corporal punishment by parents and associated child behaviors and experiences: A meta-analytic and theoretical review. *Psychological Bulletin, 128*(4), 539–579.

Gersten, R. (1999). The changing face of bilingual education. *Educational Leadership, 56*(7), 41–45.

Gersten, R., Fuchs, L. S., Williams, J. P., & Baker, S. (2001). Teaching reading comprehension strategies to students with learning disabilities: A review of research. *Review of Educational Research, 71*(2), 279–320.

Gettinger, M., & Stoiber, K. C. (2006). Functional assessment, collaboration, and evidence-based treatment: Analysis of a team approach for addressing challenging behaviors in young children. *Journal of School Psychology, 44*(3), 231–252.

Gewertz, C. (2005). Ed. dept. allows Chicago to provide NCLB tutoring. *Education Week, 25*(2), 3, 18.

Ghosh, R., Michelson, R. A., & Anyon, J. (2007). Introduction to the special issue on new perspectives on youth development and social identity in the 21st century. *Teachers College Record, 109*(2), 275–284.

Giaccardi, E. (2005). Metadesign as an emergent design culture. *Leonardo, 38*(4), 342–349.

Gick, M. L. (1986). Problem-solving strategies. *Educational Psychologist, 21*(1–2), 99–120.

Gijbels, D., van de Watering, G., Dochy, F., & van den Bossche, P. (2006). New learning environments and constructivism: The students' perspective. *Instructional Science, 34*(3), 213–226.

Gilberg, C. (2001). Epidemiology of early onset schizophrenia. In H. Remschmidt (Ed.), *Schizophrenia in children and adolescents* (pp. 43–59). New York: Cambridge University Press.

Gillespie, C. W., & Beisser, S. (2001). Developmentally appropriate LOGO computer programming with young children. *Information Technology in Childhood Education Annual*, 229–245.

Gillies, R. M. (2003). Structuring cooperative group work in classrooms. *International Journal of Educational Research, 39*(1–2), 35–49.

Gilligan, C. (1979). Women's place in man's life cycle. *Harvard Educational Review, 49*(4), 431–446.

Gilligan, C. (1982). *In a different voice: Psychological theory and women's development.* Cambridge, MA: Harvard University Press.

Gilligan, C. (1988). Exit-voice dilemmas in adolescent development. In C. Gilligan, J. Ward, J. Taylor, & B. Bardige (Eds.), *Mapping the moral domain: A contribution of women's thinking to psychological theory and education.* Cambridge, MA: Harvard University Press.

Gilness, J. (2003). How to integrate character education into the curriculum. *Phi Delta Kappan, 85*(3), 243–245.

Ginsburg, H. P., & Opper, S. (1988). *Piaget's theory of intellectual development* (3rd ed.). Englewood Cliffs, NJ: Prentice Hall.

Ginsburg-Block, M., Rohrbeck, C. A., & Fantuzzo, J. W. (2006). A meta-analytic review of social, self-concept, and behavioral outcomes of peer-assisted learning. *Journal of Educational Psychology, 98*(4), 732–749.

Ginsburg-Block, M., Rohrbeck, C. A., Lavigne, N., & Fantuzzo, J. W. (2008). Peer-assisted learning: An academic strategy for enhancing motivation among diverse students. In C. Hudley & A. E. Gottfried (Eds.), *Academic motivation and the culture of school in childhood and adolescence* (pp. 247–273). Oxford, England: Oxford University Press.

Glaser, C., & Brunstein, J. C. (2007). Improving fourth-grade students' composition skills: Effects of strategy instruction and self-regulation procedures. *Journal of Educational Psychology, 99*(2), 297–310.

Glazek, S. D., & Sarason, S. B. (2006). *Productive learning: Science, art, and Einstein's relativity in educational reform.* Thousand Oaks, CA: Corwin Press.

Goeke, J. L. (2009). *Explicit instruction: A framework for meaningful direct teaching.* Upper Saddle River, NJ: Pearson Merrill.

Gold, M., & Lowe, C. (2009). The integration of assistive technology into standard classroom practices: A guide for K–12 general educators. In I. Gibson et al. (Eds.), *Proceedings of Society for Information Technology & Teacher Education International Conference 2009* (pp. 3964–3968). Chesapeake, VA: Association for the Advancement of Computing in Education. Retrieved from http://www.editlib.org/p/31275.

Goldberg, M. (2004). The test mess. *Phi Delta Kappan, 85*(5), 361–366.

Goldberg, M. (2005). Test mess 2: Are we doing better a year later? *Phi Delta Kappan, 86*(5), 389–395.

Goldsby, D., & Fazal, M. (2001). Now that your students have created web-based digital portfolios, how do you evaluate them? *Journal of Technology and Teacher Education, 9*(4), 607–616.

Gollnick, D. A., & Chinn, P. C. (2009). *Multicultural education in a pluralistic society* (8th ed.). Upper Saddle River, NJ: Pearson Merrill.

Good, T. L., & Brophy, J. (1995). *Contemporary educational psychology* (5th ed.). New York: Longman.

Good, T. L., & Nicholls, S. L. (2001). Expectancy effects in the classroom: A special focus on improving the reading performance of minority students in first-grade classrooms. *Educational Psychologist, 36*(2), 113–126.

Goodlad, J. I. (1984). *A place called school.* New York: McGraw-Hill.

Goodman, A. (2008). Student-led, teacher-supported conferences: Improving communication across an urban district. *Middle School Journal, 39*(3), 48–54.

Goodman, G. (Ed.). (2008). *Educational psychology: An application of critical constructivism.* New York: Peter Lang.

Gould, S. J. (1981). *The mismeasure of man.* New York: Norton.

Grabe, M., & Grabe, C. (2007). *Integrating technology for meaningful learning* (5th ed.). Boston: Houghton Mifflin.

Grabinger, R. S., Aplin, C., & Ponnappa-Brenner, G. (2008). Supporting learners with cognitive impairments in online environments. *TechTrends, 52*(1), 63–69.

Graham, S. (2010). What educators need to know about bullying behaviors. *Phi Delta Kappan, 92*(1), 66–69.

Graham, S., & Hudley, C. (2005). Race and ethnicity in the study of motivation and competence. In A. J. Elliot & C. S. Dweck (Eds.), *Handbook of competence and motivation* (pp. 392–413). New York: Guilford Press.

Graham, S., & Perin, D. (2007). A meta-analysis of writing instruction for adolescent students. *Journal of Educational Psychology, 99*(3), 445–476.

Graham, S., & Williams, C. (2009). An attributional approach to motivation in school. In K. Wentzel & A. Wigfield (Eds.), *Handbook of motivation at school* (pp. 11–34). New York: Routledge.

Graue, M. E., & DiPerna, J. (2000). Redshirting and early retention: Who gets the "gift of time" and what are its outcomes? *American Educational Research Journal, 37*(2), 509–534.

Gredler, M., & Shields, C. (2004). Does no one read Vygotsky's words? Commentary on Glassman. *Educational Researcher, 33*(2), 21–25.

Green, E. (2010, March 7). Building a better teacher. *New York Times.* Retrieved from http://www.nytimes.com.

Greenberg, E. R., Canzoneri, C., & Joe, A. (2000). *2000 AMA survey on workplace testing: Basic skills, job skills, psychological measurement.* Retrieved January 2, 2002, from www.amanet.org/research/pdfs/psych.pdf.

Greene, J. A., & Azevedo, R. (2007). A theoretical review of Winne and Hadwin's model of self-regulated learning: New perspectives and directions. *Review of Educational Research, 77*(3), 334–372.

Greene, J. A., & Azevedo, R. (2009). A macro-level analysis of SRL processes and their relations to the acquisition of a sophisticated mental model of a complex system. *Contemporary Educational Psychology, 34*(1), 18–29.

Greenfield, P. M. (2009). Technology and informal education: What is taught, what is learned. *Science, 323*(5910), 69–71.

Greenhow, C., Robelia, B., & Hughes, J. E. (2010). Web 2.0 and classroom research: What path should we take now? *Educational Researcher, 38*(4), 246–259.

Gregory, G. H. (2003). *Differentiated instructional strategies in practice.* Thousand Oaks, CA: Corwin Press.

Gregory, G. H., & Kuzmich, L. (2005). *Differentiated literacy strategies for student growth and achievement in grades 7–12.* Thousand Oaks, CA: Corwin Press.

Gresalfi, M., Barab, S., Siyahhan, S., & Christensen, T. (2009). Virtual worlds, conceptual understanding, and me: Designing for consequential engagement. *On the Horizon, 17*(1), 21–34.

Gresham, F. M., & MacMillan, D. L. (1997). Social competence and affective characteristics of students with mild disabilities. *Review of Educational Research, 67*(4), 377–415.

Griffin, H. C., Williams, S. C., Davis, M. L., & Engleman, M. (2002). Using technology to enhance cues for children with low vision. *Teaching Exceptional Children, 35*(2), 36–42.

Griffiths, A.-J., VanDerHeyden, A., Skokut, M., & Lilles, E. (2009). Progress monitoring in oral reading fluency within the context of RTI. *School Psychology Quarterly, 24*(1), 13–23.

Griffiths, T. L., Steyvers, M., & Tenenbaum, J. B. (2007). Topics in semantic association. *Psychological Review, 114*(2), 211–244.

Grigorenko, E. L., Jarvin, L., & Sternberg, R. J. (2002). School-based tests of the triarchic theory of intelligence: Three settings, three samples, three syllabi. *Contemporary Educational Psychology, 27*(2), 167–208.

Gronlund, N. E. (2004). *Writing instructional objectives for teaching and assessment* (7th ed.). Upper Saddle River, NJ: Merrill Prentice Hall.

Gronlund, N., & Waugh, C. (2009). *Assessment of student achievement* (9th ed.). Boston: Allyn & Bacon.

Grossen, B. J. (2002). The BIG Accommodation model: The direct instruction model for secondary schools. *Journal of Education for Students Placed At Risk, 7*(2), 241–263.

Guay, F., Marsh, H. W., & Boivin, M. (2003). Academic self-concept and academic achievement: Developmental perspectives on their causal ordering. *Journal of Educational Psychology, 95*(1), 124–136.

Guccione, L. M. (2011). In a world of mandates, making space for inquiry. *Reading Teacher, 64*(7), 515–519.

Guerra, N. G., & Leidy, M. S. (2008). Lessons learned: Recent advances in understanding and preventing childhood aggression. In R. V. Kail (Ed.), *Advances in child development and behavior* (pp. 287–330). San Diego, CA: Academic Press.

Gulek, C. (2003). Preparing for high-stakes testing. *Theory Into Practice, 42*(1), 42–50.

Guskey, T. R. (2002). Computerized gradebooks and the myth of objectivity. *Phi Delta Kappan, 83*(10), 775–780.

Guskey, T. R. (2003). How classroom assessments improve learning. *Educational Leadership, 60*(5), 6–11.

Gutek, G. L. (1992). *Education and schooling in America* (3rd ed.). Boston: Allyn & Bacon.

Gutiérrez, K. D., & Rogoff, B. (2003). Cultural ways of learning: Individual traits or repertoires of practice. *Educational Researcher, 32*(5), 19–25.

Hadwin, A. F., Winne, P. H., Stockley, D. B., Nesbit, J. C., & Woszczyna, C. (2001). Context moderates students' self-reports about how they study. *Journal of Educational Psychology, 93*(3), 477–487.

Haladyna, T. (1999). *A complete guide to student grading.* Boston: Allyn & Bacon.

Haladyna, T. M., Downing, S. M., & Rodriguez, M. C. (2002). A review of multiple-choice item-writing guidelines for classroom assessment. *Applied Measurement in Education, 15*(3), 309–334.

Halpern, D. F., & LaMay, M. L. (2000). The smarter sex: A critical review of sex differences in intelligence. *Educational Psychology Review, 12*(2), 229–246.

Halpern, D. F., Wai, J., & Saw, A. (2005). A psychobiosocial model: Why females are sometimes greater than and sometimes less than males in math achievement. In A. M. Gallagher & J. C. Kaufman (Eds.), *Gender differences in mathematics* (pp. 48–72). New York: Cambridge University Press.

Hamman, D., Berthelot, J., Saia, J., & Crowley, E. (2000). Teachers' coaching of learning and its relation to students' strategic learning. *Journal of Educational Psychology, 92*(2), 342–348.

Hamre, B. K., & Pianta, R. C. (2005). Can instructional and emotional support in the first-grade classroom make a difference for children at risk of school failure? *Child Development, 76*(5), 949–967.

Haney, J. J., & McArthur, J. (2002). Four case studies of prospective science teachers' beliefs concerning constructivist teaching practices. *Science Education, 86*(6), 783–802.

Hannafin, R. D., & Foshay, W. R. (2008). Computer-based instruction's (CBI) rediscovered role in K–12: An evaluation case study of one high school's use of CBI to improve pass rates on high-stakes tests. *Education Technology Research & Development, 56*(2), 147–160.

Hansen, J. (2010). Teaching without talking. *Phi Delta Kappan, 92*(1), 35–40.

Hansgen, R. D. (1991). Can education become a science? *Phi Delta Kappan, 72*(9), 689–694.

Hardman, M., Drew, C., & Egan, M. (2011). *Human exceptionality: School, community, and family* (10th ed.). Belmont, CA: Wadsworth/Cengage Learning.

Hardy, C. L., Bukowski, W. M., & Sippola, L. K. (2002). Stability and change in peer relationships during the transition to middle-level school. *Journal of Early Adolescence, 22*(2), 117–142.

Hardy, I., Jonen, A., Möller, K., & Stern, E. (2006). Effects of instructional support within constructivist learning environments for elementary school students' understanding of "floating and sinking." *Journal of Educational Psychology, 98*(2), 307–326.

Hargreaves, A., Earl, L., & Schmidt, M. (2002). Perspectives on alternative assessment reform. *American Educational Research Journal, 39*(1), 69–95.

Harold, R. D., Colarossi, L. G., & Mercier, L. R. (2007). *Smooth sailing or stormy waters? Family transitions through adolescence and their implications for practice and policy.* Mahwah, NJ: Erlbaum.

Harrington, R., & Enochs, L. (2009). Accounting for preservice teachers' constructivist learning environment experiences. *Learning Environments Research, 12*(1), 45–65.

Harris, B., Plucker, J., Rapp, K., & Martínez, R. (2009). Identifying gifted and talented English language learners: A case study. *Journal for the Education of the Gifted, 32*(3), 368–393.

Harris, K. R., Alexander, P., & Graham, S. (2008). Michael Pressley's contributions to the history and future of strategies research. *Educational Psychologist, 43*(2), 89–96.

Harris, K. R., Graham, S., & Mason, L. H. (2006). Improving the writing, knowledge, and motivation of struggling young writers: Effects of self-regulated strategy development with and without peer support. *American Educational Research Journal, 43*(2), 295–340.

Harry, B., & Klingner, J. K. (2006). *Why are so many minority students in special education? Understanding race and disability in schools.* New York: Teachers College Press.

Hart, B., & Risley, T. R. (1995). *Meaningful differences in the everyday experience of young American children.* Baltimore, MD: Paul H. Brookes.

Hart, H. (2009). Strategies for culturally and linguistically diverse students with special needs. *Preventing School Failure, 53*(3), 197–208.

Harter, S. (1999). *The construction of the self: A developmental perspective.* New York: Guilford Press.

Harter, S., Waters, P. L., & Whitesell, N. R. (1997). Lack of voice as a manifestation of false self-behavior among adolescents: The school setting as a stage upon which the drama of authenticity is enacted. *Educational Psychologist, 32*(3), 153–174.

Hartshorne, H., & May, M. A. (1929). *Studies in service and self-control.* New York: Macmillan.

Hartshorne, H., & May, M. A. (1930a). *Studies in deceit.* New York: Macmillan.

Hartshorne, H., & May, M. A. (1930b). *Studies in the organization of character.* New York: Macmillan.

Hartup, W. W. (1989). Social relationships and their developmental significance. *American Psychologist, 44*(2), 120–126.

Hatch, T. (1997). Getting specific about multiple intelligences. *Educational Leadership, 54*(6), 26–29.

Hattie, J. A. C. (2009). *Visible learning: A synthesis of over 800 meta-analyses relating to achievement.* New York: Routledge.

Hattie, J., & Timperley, H. (2007). The power of feedback. *Review of Educational Research, 77*(1), 81–112.

Hazler, R. J., & Carney, J. V. (2006). Critical characteristics of effective bullying prevention programs. In S. R. Jimerson & M. J. Furlong (Eds.), *The handbook of school violence and school safety.* Mahwah, NJ: Erlbaum.

Heacox, D. (2009). *Making differentiation a habit: How to ensure success in academically diverse classrooms.* Minneapolis, MN: Free Spirit.

Healy, L., & Hoyles, C. (2001). Software tools for geometrical problem solving: Potentials and pitfalls. *International Journal of Computers for Mathematical Learning, 6*(3), 235–256.

Heath, M. (2002). Electronic portfolios for reflective self-assessment. *Teacher Librarian, 30*(1), 19–23.

Henderson, J. G. (Ed.). (2001). *Reflective teaching: Professional artistry through inquiry.* Upper Saddle River, NJ: Merrill Prentice Hall.

Hersh, R. H., Paolitto, D. P., & Reimer, J. (1979). *Promoting moral growth: From Piaget to Kohlberg.* New York: Longman.

Hester, P., Hendrickson, J., & Gable, J. (2009). Forty years later—The value of praise, ignoring, and rules for preschoolers at risk for behavior disorders. *Education and Treatment of Children, 32*(4), 513–535.

Hetherington, E. M., & Parke, R. D. (1993). *Child psychology: A contemporary viewpoint* (4th ed.). New York: McGraw-Hill.

Heward, W. L. (2009). *Exceptional children: An introduction to special education* (9th ed.). Englewood Cliffs, NJ: Prentice Hall.

Hewitt, J. (2002). From a focus on tasks to a focus on understanding: The cultural transformation of a Toronto classroom. In T. Koschmann, R. Hall, & N. Miyake (Eds.), *CSCL2: Carrying forward the conversation* (pp. 11–41). Mahwah, NJ: Erlbaum.

Hickey, D. T., Kindfield, A. C. H., Horwitz, P., & Christie, M. T. (2003). Integrating curriculum, instruction, assessment, and evaluation in a technology-supported genetics learning environment. *American Educational Research Journal, 40*(2), 495–538.

Hidi, S. (2001). Interest, reading, and learning: Theoretical and practical considerations. *Educational Psychology Review, 13*(3), 191–209.

Hiebert, J., Gallimore, R., & Stigler, J. W. (2002). A knowledge base for the teaching profession: What would it look like and how can we get one? *Educational Researcher, 31*(5), 3–15.

Higdon, J., & Topaz, C. (2009). Blogs and wikis as instructional tools: A social software adaptation of just-in-time teaching. *College Teaching, 57*(2), 105–109.

Higgins, J. W., Williams, R. L., & McLaughlin, T. F. (2001). The effects of a token economy employing instructional consequences for a third-grade student with learning disabilities: A case study. *Education and Treatment of Children, 24*(1), 99–106.

Hilbert, T., & Renkl, A. (2009). Learning how to use a computer-based concept-mapping tool: Self-explaining examples help. *Computers in Human Behavior, 25*(2), 267–274.

Hill, J. P. (1987). Research on adolescents and their families: Past and prospect. In C. E. Irwin, Jr. (Ed.), *Adolescent social behavior and health.* San Francisco: Jossey-Bass.

Hitchcock, C., & Stahl, S. (2003). Assistive technology, universal design, universal design for learning: Improved learning outcomes. *Journal of Special Education Technology, 18*(4), 45–52.

Ho, A. D. (2008). The problem with "proficiency": Limitations of statistics and policy under No Child Left Behind. *Educational Researcher, 37*(6), 351–360.

Hoegh, D. G., & Bourgeois, M. J. (2002). Prelude and postlude to the self: Correlates of achieved identity. *Youth & Society, 33*(4), 573–594.

Hoff, D. J. (2006). Colo. town raises taxes to finance NCLB withdrawal. *Education Week, 25*(16), 3, 9.

Hoffman, B., & Schraw, G. (2009). The influence of self-efficacy and working memory capacity on problem-solving efficiency. *Learning and Individual Differences, 19*(1), 91–100.

Hoffman, M. L. (1980). Moral development in adolescence. In J. Adelson (Ed.), *Handbook of adolescent psychology.* New York: Wiley.

Hoge, R. D., & Renzulli, J. S. (1993). Exploring the link between giftedness and self-concept. *Review of Educational Research, 63*(4), 449–465.

Holme, J. J., Richards, M. P., Jimerson, J. B., & Cohen, R. W. (2010). Assessing the effects of high school exit examinations. *Review of Educational Research, 80*(4), 476–526.

Holzman, L. (2009). *Vygotsky at work and play.* New York: Routledge.

Home, J. (2007). Gender differences in computerized and conventional educational tests. *Journal of Computer Assisted Learning, 23*(1), 47–55.

Hong, G., & Hong, Y. (2009). Reading instruction time and homogeneous grouping in kindergarten: An application of marginal mean weighting through stratification. *Educational Evaluation and Policy Analysis, 31*(1), 54–81.

Hong, G., & Raudenbush, S. W. (2005). Effects of kindergarten retention policy on children's cognitive growth in reading and mathematics. *Educational Evaluation and Policy Analysis, 27*(3), 205–224.

Hong, H.-Y., & Sullivan, F. (2009). Towards an idea-centered, principle-based design approach to support learning as knowledge creation. *Educational Technology Research and Development, 57*(5), 613–627.

Houston, P. D. (2005). NCLB: Dreams and nightmares. *Phi Delta Kappan, 86*(6), 469–470.

Houston, P. D. (2007). The seven deadly sins of No Child Left Behind. *Phi Delta Kappan, 88*(10), 744–748.

Howard, B. C., McGee, S., Shin, N., & Shia, R. (2001). The triarchic theory of intelligence and computer-based inquiry learning. *Educational Technology Research and Development, 49*(4), 49–69.

Howe, C. (2009). Collaborative group work in middle childhood. *Human Development, 52*(4), 215–239.

Howe, N., Rinaldi, C. M., Jennings, M., & Petrakos, H. (2002). "No! the lambs can stay out because they got cozies": Constructive and destructive sibling conflict, pretend play, and social understanding. *Child Development, 73*(5), 1460–1473.

Hughes, F. P., & Noppe, L. D. (1991). *Human development across the life span.* New York: Macmillan.

Hughes, J. N., & Zhang, D. (2007). Effects of the structure of classmates' perceptions of peers' academic abilities on children's perceived cognitive competence, peer acceptance, and engagement. *Contemporary Educational Psychology, 32*(3), 400–419.

Hung, D. (2002). Situated cognition and problem-based learning: Implications for learning and instruction with technology. *Journal of Interactive Learning Research, 13*(4), 393–414.

Hunt, N., & Marshall, K. (2006). *Exceptional children and youth* (4th ed.). Boston: Houghton Mifflin.

Hyde, J. S. (2005). The gender similarities hypothesis. *American Psychologist, 60*(6), 581–592.

Hyde, J. S., Lindberg, S. M., Linn, M. C., Ellis, A. B., & Williams, C. C. (2008). Gender similarities characterize math performance. *Science, 321*(5888), 494–495.

Inal, Y., & Cagiltay, K. (2007). Flow experiences of children in an interactive social game environment. *British Journal of Educational Technology, 38*(3), 455–464.

Individuals with Disabilities Education Act Amendments of 1997. (1997, June). Retrieved September 15, 2003, from http://frwebgate.access.gpo.gov/cgi-bin/useftp .cgi?IPaddress5162.140.64.21&file-name 5publ17.105& directory5/diskc/wais/data/105_cong_public_laws.

Ireson, J., & Hallam, S. (2009). Academic self-concepts in adolescence: Relations with achievement and ability grouping in schools. *Learning and Instruction, 19*(3), 201–213.

Jackson, A. W., & Davis, G. A. (2000). *Turning points 2000: Educating adolescents in the 21st century.* New York: Teachers College Press.

Jackson, A. W., & Larkin, M. J. (2002). Rubric: Teaching students to use grading rubrics. *Teaching Exceptional Children, 35*(1), 40–45.

Jackson, B. (2007). Homework inoculation and the limits of research. *Phi Delta Kappan, 89*(1), 55–59.

Jackson, D. B. (2003). Education reform as if student agency mattered: Academic microcultures and student identity. *Phi Delta Kappan, 84*(8), 579–585.

Jackson, S., Pretti-Frontczak, K., Harjusola-Webb, S., Grisham-Brown, J., & Romani, J. (2009). Response to intervention: Implications for early childhood professionals. *Language, Speech, and Hearing Services in Schools, 40*(4), 424–434.

Jaffee, S., Hyde, J. S., & Shibley, J. (2000). Gender differences in moral orientation: A meta-analysis. *Psychological Bulletin, 126*(5), 703–726.

James, W. (1899). *Talks to teachers on psychology: And to students on some of life's ideals.* New York: Holt.

Janesick, V. J. (2001). *The assessment debate: A reference handbook.* Santa Barbara, CA: ABC-CLIO.

Jean-Marie, G., Normore, A., & Brooks, J. (2009). Leadership for social justice: Preparing 21st century school leaders for a new social order. *Journal of Research on Leadership Education, 4*(1), 1–31.

Jennings, J., & Rentner, D. S. (2006). Ten big effects of the No Child Left Behind Act on public schools. *Phi Delta Kappan, 88*(2), 110–113.

Jensen, E. P. (2008). A fresh look at brain-based education. *Phi Delta Kappan, 89*(6), 409–417.

Jensen, L. A., Arnett, J. J., Feldman, S. S., & Cauffman, E. (2002). It's wrong, but everybody does it: Academic dishonesty among high school and college students. *Contemporary Educational Psychology, 27*(2), 209–228.

Jensen, L. A., Arnett, J. J., Feldman, S., & Cauffman, E. (2004). The right to do wrong: Lying to parents among adolescents and emerging adults. *Journal of Youth and Adolescence, 33*(2), 101–112.

Jeong, H., & Hmelo-Silver, C. (2010). Productive use of learning resources in an online problem-based learning environment. *Computers in Human Behavior, 26*(1), 84–99.

Jimerson, S. R. (2001). Meta-analysis of grade retention research: Implications for practice in the 21st century. *School Psychology Review, 30*(3), 420–437.

Jimerson, S. R., Anderson, G. E., & Whipple, A. D. (2002). Winning the battle and losing the war: Examining the relation between grade retention and dropping out of high school. *Psychology in the Schools, 39*(4), 441–457.

Jimerson, S. R., & Kaufman, A. M. (2003). Reading, writing, and retention: A primer on grade retention research. *Reading Teacher, 56*(7), 622–635.

Jimerson, S. R., Morrison, G. M., Pletcher, S. W., & Furlong, M. J. (2006). Youth engaged in antisocial and aggressive behaviors: Who are they? In S. R. Jimerson & M. J. Furlong (Eds.), *The handbook of school violence and school safety* (pp. 3–19). Mahwah, NJ: Erlbaum.

Jobe, D. A. (2002/2003). Helping girls succeed. *Educational Leadership, 60*(4), 64–66.

Johnson, C. C., & Fargo, J. D. (2010). Urban school reform enabled by transformative professional development: Impact on teacher change and student learning of science. *Urban Education, 45*(1), 4–29.

Johnson, C. S., & Thomas, A. T. (2009). Caring as classroom practice. *Social Studies and the Young Learner, 22*(1), 8–11.

Johnson, D. W., & Johnson, R. T. (1998). Cultural diversity and cooperative learning. In J. W. Putnam (Ed.), *Cooperative learning and strategies for inclusion* (2nd ed.). Baltimore, MD: Brookes.

Johnson, D. W., & Johnson, R. T. (2009a). Energizing learning: The instructional power of conflict. *Educational Researcher, 38*(1), 37–51.

Johnson, D. W., & Johnson, R. T. (2009b). An educational success story: Social interdependence theory and cooperative learning. *Educational Researcher, 38*(5), 365–379.

Johnson, J., Farkas, S., & Bers, A. (1997). *What American teenagers really think about their schools: A report from Public Agenda.* New York: Public Agenda.

Johnson, R. E. (1975). Meaning in complex learning. *Review of Educational Research, 45*(3), 425–460.

Johnson, R. S., Mims-Cox, J., & Doyle-Nichols, A. (2010). *Developing portfolios in education: A guide to reflection, inquiry, and assessment* (2nd ed.). Thousand Oaks, CA: Sage.

Johnson, S. (2006). *Everything bad is good for you.* New York: Riverhead Books (Penguin Group).

Johnson, S. P. (Ed.). (2010). *Neoconstructivism: The new science of cognitive development.* New York: Oxford University Press.

Jonassen, D. H., Howland, J., Marra, R. M., & Crismond, D. (2008). *Meaningful learning with technology* (3rd ed.). Upper Saddle River, NJ: Pearson/Merrill Prentice Hall.

Jones, B. D. (2007). The unintended outcomes of high-stakes testing. *Journal of Applied School Psychology, 23*(2), 65–86.

Jovanovic, J., & King, S. S. (1998). Boys and girls in the performance-based science classroom: Who's doing the performing? *American Educational Research Journal, 35*(3), 477–496.

Joyce, B., & Weil, M. (2009). *Models of teaching* (8th ed.). Boston: Pearson/Allyn & Bacon.

Jussim, L., Eccles, J., & Madon, S. (1996). Social perception, social stereotypes, and teacher expectations: Accuracy and the quest for the powerful self-fulfilling prophesy. In M. Zanna (Ed.), *Advances in experimental social psychology, Vol. 28.* (pp. 281–383). San Diego, CA: Academic Press.

Juvonen, J. (2000). The social functions of attributional face-saving tactics among early adolescents. *Educational Psychology Review, 12*(1), 15–32.

Juvonen, J. (2007). Reforming middle schools: Focus on continuity, social connectedness, and engagement. *Educational Psychologist, 42*(4), 197–208.

Kagan, J. (1964a). *Developmental studies of reflection and analysis.* Cambridge, MA: Harvard University Press.

Kagan, J. (1964b). Impulsive and reflective children. In J. D. Krumbolz (Ed.), *Learning and the educational process.* Chicago: Rand McNally.

Kail, R. V. (2010). *Children and their development* (5th ed.). Upper Saddle River, NJ: Pearson Prentice Hall.

Kail, R. V., & Cavanaugh, J. C. (2010). *Human development: A life-span view* (5th ed.). Belmont, CA: Wadsworth/Cengage Learning.

Kalbaugh, P., & Haviland, J. M. (1991). Formal operational thinking and identity. In R. M. Lerner, A. C. Peterson, & J. Brooks-Gunn (Eds.), *Encyclopedia of adolescence.* New York: Garland.

Kalyuga, S. (2009). Knowledge elaboration: A cognitive load perspective. *Learning and Instruction, 19*(5), 402–410.

Kamii, C. (2000). *Young children reinvent arithmetic: Implications of Piaget's theory* (2nd ed.). New York: Teachers College Press.

Kaplan, A., & Flum, H. (2009). Motivation and identity: The relations of actions and development in educational contexts—An introduction to the special issue. *Educational Psychologist, 44*(2), 73–77.

Kapur, M., & Kinzer, C. (2007). The effect of problem type on collaborative problem solving in a synchronous computer-mediated environment. *Educational Technology Research and Development, 55*(5), 439–459.

Kapur, M., & Kinzer, C. (2009). Productive failure in CSCL groups. *International Journal of Computer-Supported Collaborative Learning, 4*(1), 21–46.

Karchmer, R. A. (2001). The journey ahead: Thirteen teachers report how the Internet influences literacy and literacy instruction in their K–12 classrooms. *Reading Research Quarterly, 36*(4), 442–466.

Karpicke, J. D., & Blunt, J. R. (2011). Retrieval practice produces more learning than elaborative studying with concept mapping. *Science,* in press.

Karpicke, J. D., Butler, A. C., & Roediger, H. L., III (2009). Metacognitive strategies in student learning: Do students practice retrieval when they study on their own? *Memory, 17*(4), 471–479.

Karpov, Y. V., & Bransford, J. D. (1995). L. S. Vygotsky and the doctrine of empirical and theoretical learning. *Educational Psychologist, 30*(2), 61–66.

Kaufman, J., & Beghetto, R. (2009). Beyond big and little: The Four C Model of Creativity. *Review of General Psychology, 13*(1), 1–12.

Kavale, K. A. (2002). Mainstreaming to full inclusion: From orthogenesis to pathogenesis of an idea. *International Journal of Disability, Development and Education, 49*(2), 201–214.

Keengwe, J., Onchwari, G., & Wachira, P. (2008). The use of computer tools to support meaningful learning. *AACE Journal, 16*(1), 77–92.

Kehle, T. J., Bray, M. A., Theodore, L. A., Jenson, W. R., & Clark, E. (2000). A multi-component intervention designed to reduce disruptive classroom behavior. *Psychology in the Schools, 37*(5), 475–481.

Kelly, M., & Moag-Stahlberg, A. (2002). Battling the obesity epidemic. *Principal, 81*(5), 26–29.

Kennedy, M. M. (2010). Attribution error and the quest for teacher quality. *Educational Researcher, 39*(8), 591–598.

Kentucky Department of Education. (2009). *2007 Kentucky Core Content Test (KCCT) released items.* Retrieved from http://www.education.ky.gov/KDE/Administrative+Resources/Testing+and+Reporting+/District+Support/Link+to+Released+Items/2007+Kentucky+Core+Content+Test+(KCCT)+Released+Items.htm.

Kerr, M. M., & Nelson, C. M. (2010). *Strategies for addressing behavior problems in the classroom* (6th ed.). Columbus, OH: Merrill/Prentice Hall.

Kim, Y., Baylor, A. L., & PALS Group. (2006). Pedagogical agents as learning companions: The role of agent competency and type of interaction. *Educational Technology Research and Development, 54*(3), 223–243.

King, A. (1992). Facilitating elaborative learning through guided student-generated questioning. *Educational Psychologist, 27*(1), 111–126.

King, A. (1994). Guiding knowledge construction in the classroom: Effects of teaching children how to question and how to explain. *American Educational Research Journal, 31*(2), 338–368.

King, A. (1998). Transactive peer tutoring: Distributing cognition and metacognition. *Educational Psychology Review, 10*(1), 57–74.

King, D., Bellocchi, A., & Ritchie, S. (2008) Making connections: Learning and teaching chemistry in context. *Research in Science Education, 38*(3), 365–384.

Kirk, S. A., Gallagher, J. J., Coleman, M. R., & Anastasiow, N. J. (2009). *Educating exceptional children* (12th ed.). Belmont, CA: Wadsworth/Cengage Learning.

Kirschner, P. A., Sweller, J., & Clark, R. E. (2006). Why minimal guidance during instruction does not work: An analysis of the failure of constructivist, discovery, problem-based, experiential, and inquiry-based teaching. *Educational Psychologist, 41*(2), 75–86.

Klauer, K. (1984). Intentional and incidental learning with instructional texts: A meta-analysis for 1970–1980. *American Educational Research Journal, 21*(2), 323–339.

Kleinert, H., Browder, D., & Towles-Reeves, E. (2009). Models of cognition for students with significant cognitive disabilities: Implications for assessment. *Review of Educational Research, 79*(1), 301–326

Klingberg, T. (2009). *The overflowing brain: Information overload and the limits of working memory* (N. Betteridge, Trans.). New York: Oxford University Press.

Knapp, M. S., Shields, P. M., & Turnbull, B. J. (1995). Academic challenge in high-poverty classrooms. *Phi Delta Kappan, 76*(10), 770–776.

Kober, N., Zabala, D., Chudowsky, N., Chudowsky, V., Gayler, K., & McMurrer, J. (2006, August). *State high school exit exams: A challenging year.* Washington, DC: Center on Education Policy. Retrieved from http://www.cep-dc.org/cfcontent_file .cfm?Attachment=CEP_HSEE06Report_080106.pdf.

Kohlberg, L. (1963). The development of children's orientations toward a moral order: 1. Sequence in the development of moral thought. *Vita Humana, 6*(1–2), 11–33.

Kohlberg, L. (1969). Stage and sequence: The cognitive-developmental approach to socialization. In D. A. Goslin (Ed.), *Handbook of socialization theory and research.* Chicago: Rand McNally.

Kohn, A. (1993). Rewards versus learning: A response to Paul Chance. *Phi Delta Kappan, 74*(10), 783–787.

Kohn, A. (1999). *Punished by rewards: The trouble with gold stars, incentive plans, A's, praise, and other bribes.* Boston: Houghton Mifflin.

Kohn, A. (2006). *The homework myth: Why our kids get too much of a bad thing.* Philadelphia: Perseus Books.

Kontos, G., & Mizell, A. P. (1997). Global village classroom: The changing roles of teachers and students through technology. *TechTrends, 42*(5), 17–22.

Koohang, A., Riley, L., Smith, T., & Schreurs, J. (2009). E-learning and constructivism: From theory to application. *Interdisciplinary Journal of E-Learning and Learning Objects, 5,* 91–109.

Kordaki, M. (2009). "MULTIPLES": A challenging learning framework for the generation of multiple perspectives within e-collaboration settings. In T. Daradoumis, S. Caballé, J. Marquès, & F. Xhafa (Eds.), *Intelligent collaborative e-learning systems and applications* (pp. 37–52). Berlin: Springer-Verlag.

Kordaki, M., & Potari, D. (2002). The effect of area measurement tools on student strategies: The role of a computer microworld. *International Journal of Computers for Mathematical Learning, 7*(1), 65–100.

Koretz, D. (2008). *Measuring up: What educational testing really tells us.* Cambridge, MA: Harvard University Press.

Kornell, N., & Bjork, R. A. (2007). The promise and perils of self-regulated study. *Psychonomic Bulletin and Review, 14*(2), 219–224.

Kosunen, T., & Mikkola, A. (2002). Building a science of teaching: How objectives and reality meet in Finnish teacher education. *European Journal of Teacher Education, 25*(2/3), 135–150.

Kounin, J. S. (1970). *Discipline and group management in classrooms.* New York: Holt, Rinehart & Winston.

Kozol, J. (2007). *Letters to a young teacher.* New York: Crown.

Kraft, M. A. (2010). From ringmaster to conductor: 10 simple techniques can turn an unruly class into a productive one. *Phi Delta Kappan, 91*(7), 44–47.

Kramarski, B., & Zeichner, O. (2001). Using technology to enhance mathematical reasoning: Effects of feedback and self-regulation learning. *Educational Media International, 38*(2/3), 77–82.

Krathwohl, D. R., Bloom, B. S., & Masia, B. B. (1964). *Taxonomy of educational objectives. Handbook II: Affective domain.* New York: McKay.

Krätzig, G. P., & Arbuthnot, K. D. (2006). Perceptual learning style and learning proficiency. *Journal of Educational Psychology, 98*(1), 238–246.

Kruse, S. (2009). *Working smart: Problem-solving strategies for school leaders.* Lanham, MD: Rowman & Littlefield Education.

Kubiszyn, T., & Borich, G. (2010). *Educational testing and measurement: Classroom application and practice* (9th ed.). New York: Wiley.

Kuhn, D. (1999). A developmental model of critical thinking. *Educational Researcher, 28*(2), 16–26, 46.

Kuhn, D. (2002). What is scientific thinking and how does it develop? In U. Goswami (Ed.), *Blackwell handbook of childhood cognitive development* (pp. 371–393). Malden, MA: Blackwell.

Kulik, C.-L., Kulik, J. A., & Bangert-Drowns, R. L. (1990). Effectiveness of mastery learning programs. *Review of Educational Research, 60*(2), 265–299.

Kulik, J. A. (2003a, May). *Effects of using instructional technology in elementary and secondary schools: What controlled evaluation studies say.* Arlington, VA: SRI International. Retrieved from http://www.sri.com/policy/csted/reports/sandt/it/Kulik_ ITinK-12_Main_Report.pdf.

Kulik, J. A. (2003b). Grouping and tracking. In N. Colangelo & G. A. Davis (Eds.), *Handbook of gifted education* (3rd ed., pp. 268–281). Boston: Allyn & Bacon.

Kulik, J. A., & Kulik, C.-L. (1991). Ability grouping and gifted students. In N. Colangelo & G. A. Davis (Eds.), *Handbook of gifted education.* Boston: Allyn & Bacon.

Kusku, F., Ozbilgin, M., & Ozkale, L. (2007). Against the tide: Gendered prejudice and disadvantage in engineering. *Gender Work and Organization, 14*(2), 109–129.

Lach, C., Little, E., & Nazzaro, D. (2003). From all sides now: Weaving technology and multiple intelligences into science and art. *Learning and Leading with Technology, 30*(6), 32–35, 59.

Lacina, J. (2004/2005). Promoting language acquisitions: Technology and English language learners. *Childhood Education, 81*(2), 113–115.

Laczko-Kerr, I., & Berliner, D. C. (2003). In harm's way: How under-certified teachers hurt their students. *Educational Leadership, 60*(8), 34–39.

Ladson-Billings, G. (2002). But that's just good teaching! The case for culturally relevant pedagogy. In S. J. Denbo & L. M. Beaulieu (Eds.), *Improving schools for African American students* (pp. 95–102). Springfield, IL: Charles C. Thomas.

Lai, S.-L., Chang, T.-S., & Ye, R. (2006). Computer usage and reading in elementary schools: A cross-cultural study. *Journal of Educational Computing Research, 34*(1), 47–66.

Lalley, J., & Gentile, J. (2008). Classroom assessment and grading to assure mastery. *Theory Into Practice, 48*(1), 28–35.

Lam, R., & Lee, I. (2010). Balancing the dual functions of portfolio assessment. *ELT Journal, 64*(1), 54–64.

Lampinen, J. M., & Odegard, T. N. (2006). Memory editing mechanisms. *Memory, 14*(6), 649–654.

Lancey, D. F. (2002). Cultural constraints on children's play. In J. L. Roopnarine (Ed.), *Conceptual, social-cognitive, and contextual issues in the fields of play* (pp. 53–60). Westport, CT: Ablex.

Landau, B. M., & Gathercoal, P. (2000). Creating peaceful classrooms: Judicious Discipline and class meetings. *Phi Delta Kappan, 81*(6), 450–452, 454.

Lantieri, L. (1995). Waging peace in our schools: Beginning with the children. *Phi Delta Kappan, 76*(5), 386–388.

Lantieri, L. (1999). Hooked on altruism: Developing social responsibility in at-risk youth. *Reclaiming Children and Youth, 8*(2), 83–87.

Larkin, S. (2010). *Metacognition in young children.* New York: Routledge.

Larson, B. E., & Keiper, T. A. (2007). *Instructional strategies for middle and high school.* New York: Routledge.

Larson, R. W., & Sheeber, L. B. (2009). The daily emotional experience of adolescents: Are adolescents more emotional, why, and how is that related to depression? In N. B. Allen & L. B. Sheeber (Eds.), *Adolescent emotional development and the emergence of depressive disorders* (pp. 11–32). Cambridge, England: Cambridge University Press.

Lazear, D. G. (2003). *Eight ways of teaching: The artistry of teaching with multiple intelligences.* Thousand Oaks, CA: Sage.

Leacock, T. L., & Nesbit, J. C. (2007). A framework for evaluating the quality of multimedia learning resources. *Educational Technology & Society, 10*(2), 44–59.

Leadbeater, B. (1991). Relativistic thinking in adolescence. In R. M. Lerner, A. C. Peterson, & J. Brooks-Gunn (Eds.), *Encyclopedia of adolescence.* New York: Garland.

Lee, J. (2008). Is test-driven external accountability effective? Synthesizing the evidence from cross-state causal-comparative and correlational studies. *Review of Educational Research, 78*(3), 608–644.

Lee, J.-S., & Bowen, N. K. (2006). Parent involvement, cultural capital, and the achievement gap among elementary school children. *American Educational Research Journal, 43*(2), 193–218.

Leming, J. S. (1993). In search of effective character education. *Educational Leadership, 51*(3), 63–71.

Leming, J. S. (2008). Research and practice in moral and character education: Loosely coupled phenomena. In L. P. Nucci & D. Narvaez (Eds.), *Handbook of moral and character education* (pp. 134–157). New York: Routledge.

Lepper, M. R., Corpus, J. H., & Iyengar, S. S. (2005). Intrinsic and extrinsic motivational orientations in the classroom: Age differences and academic correlates. *Journal of Educational Psychology, 97*(2), 184–196.

Lerner, J. (2003). *Learning disabilities: Theories, diagnosis, and teaching strategies* (9th ed.). Boston: Houghton Mifflin.

Lerner, J., and Johns, B. (2009). *Learning disabilities and related mild disabilities: Characteristics, teaching strategies and new directions.* Boston: Houghton Mifflin.

Levin, J. R. (1982). Pictures as prose-learning devices. In A. Flammer & W. Kintsch (Eds.), *Advances in psychology, Vol. 8. Discourse processing.* Amsterdam: North-Holland.

Levin, J. R. (1993). Mnemonic strategies and classroom learning: A 20-year report card. *Elementary School Journal, 94*(2), 235–244.

Lewandowsky, S., & Thomas, J. (2009). Expertise: Acquisition, limitations, and control. In F. Durso (Ed.), *Reviews of human factors and ergonomics* (Vol. 5, pp. 140–165). Santa Monica, CA: Human Factors and Ergonomics Society.

Lewis, C. (2009). What is the nature of knowledge development in lesson study? *Educational Action Research, 17*(1), 95–110.

Lewis, C., Perry, R., & Friedkin, S. (2009). Lesson study as action research. In S. Noffke & B. Somekh (Eds.), *The Sage handbook of educational action research* (pp. 142–154). Thousand Oaks, CA: Sage.

Lewis, T. (2005). Creativity: A framework for the design/problem solving discourse in technology education. *Journal of Technology Education, 17*(1). Retrieved September 16, 2006, from http://scholar.lib.vt.edu/ejournals/JTE/v17n1/lewis.html.

Lewis-Moreno, B. (2007). Shared responsibility: Achieving success with English-language learners. *Phi Delta Kappan, 88*(10), 772–775.

Ley, K., & Young, D. B. (2001). Instructional principles for self-regulation. *Educational Technology Research and Development, 49*(2), 93–103.

Li, J. (2002). Learning models in different cultures. In J. Bempechat & J. G. Elliott (Eds.), *Learning in culture and context, Vol. 96. New directions for child and adolescent development* (pp. 45–63). San Francisco: Jossey-Bass.

Liao, Y.-K. C. (2007). Effects of computer-assisted instruction on students' achievement in Taiwan: A meta-analysis. *Computers & Education, 48*(2), 216–233.

Liben, L. S., Bigler, R. S., & Krogh, H. R. (2002). Language at work: Children's gendered interpretations of occupational titles. *Child Development, 73*(3), 810–828.

Lickona, T. (1976). Research on Piaget's theory of moral development. In T. Lickona (Ed.), *Moral development and behavior: Theory, research, and social issues.* New York: Holt, Rinehart & Winston.

Lieberman, J. (2009). Reinventing teacher professional norms and identities: The role of lesson study and learning communities. *Professional Development in Education, 35*(1), 83–99.

Light, P., & Littleton, K. (1999). *Social processes in children's learning.* Cambridge, England: Cambridge University Press.

Lim, J., Reiser, R., & Olina, Z. (2009). The effects of part-task and whole-task instructional approaches on acquisition and transfer of a complex cognitive skill. *Educational Technology Research and Development, 57*(1), 61–77.

Linell, P. (2007). Dialogicality in languages, minds and brains: Is there a convergence between dialogism and neurobiology? *Language Sciences, 29*(5), 605–620.

Linn, M. C. (1992). Science education reform: Building on the research base. *Journal of Research in Science Teaching, 29*(8), 821–840.

Linn, M. C., Lewis, C., Tsuchida, I., & Songer, N. B. (2000). Beyond fourth-grade science: Why do U.S. and Japanese students diverge? *Educational Researcher, 29*(3), 4–14.

Linn, M. C., & Slotta, J. D. (2000). WISE science. *Educational Leadership, 58*(2), 29–32.

Linn, R. L. (2009). Improving the accountability provisions of NCLB. In M. A. Rebell & J. R. Wolf (Eds.), *NCLB at the crossroads: Reexamining the federal effort to close the achievement gap* (pp. 163–184). New York: Teachers College Press.

Linn, R. L., & Miller, M. D. (2005). *Measurement and assessment in teaching* (9th ed.). Upper Saddle River, NJ: Pearson Prentice Hall.

Liu, X. (2010). *Essentials of science classroom assessment.* Thousand Oaks, CA: Sage.

Llabo, L. D. (2002). Computers, kids, and comprehension: Instructional practices that make a difference. In C. C. Block, L. B. Gambrell, & M. Pressley (Eds.), *Improving comprehension instruction: Rethinking research, theory, and classroom practice* (pp. 275–289). San Francisco: Jossey-Bass.

Lleras, C., & Rangel, C. (2009). Ability grouping practices in elementary school and African American/Hispanic achievement. *American Journal of Education, 115*(Feb), 279–304.

Lodewyk, K. R. (2007). Relations among epistemological beliefs, academic achievement, and task performance in secondary school students. *Educational Psychology, 27*(3), 307–327.

Lodewyk, K. R., & Winne, P. H. (2005). Relations among the structure of learning tasks, achievement, and changes in self-efficacy in secondary students. *Journal of Educational Psychology, 97*(1), 3–12.

Lou, Y., Abrami, P. C., & d'Apollonia, S. (2001). Small group learning and individual learning with technology: A meta-analysis. *Review of Educational Research, 71*(3), 499–521.

Lou, Y., Abrami, P. C., & Spence, J. C. (2000). Effects of within-class grouping on student achievement: An exploratory model. *Journal of Educational Research, 94*(2), 101–112.

Lowry, R., Sleet, D., Duncan, C., Powell, K, & Kolbe, L. (1995). Adolescents at risk for violence. *Educational Psychology Review, 7*(1), 7–39.

Loyens, S., & Gijbels, D. (2008). Understanding the effects of constructivist learning environments: Introducing a multi-directional approach. *Instructional Science, 36*(5–6), 351–357.

Loyens, S. M. M., & Rikers, M. J. P. (2011). Instruction based on inquiry. In R. E. Mayer & P. A. Alexander (Eds.), *Handbook of research on learning and instruction* (pp. 361–381). New York: Routledge.

Loyens, S., Rikers, R., & Schmidt, H. (2007). Students' conceptions of distinct constructivist assumptions. *European Journal of Psychology of Education, 12*(2), 179–199.

Loyens, S., Rikers, R., & Schmidt, H. (2008). Relationships between students' conceptions of constructivist learning and their regulation and processing strategies. *Instructional Science, 36*(5–6), 445–462.

Lu, Y., Zhou, T., & Wang, B. (2008). Exploring Chinese users' acceptance of instant messaging using the theory of planned behavior, the technology acceptance model, and the flow theory. *Computers in Human Behavior, 25*(1), 29–39.

Lyons, N. P., & Kubler LaBoskey, V. (2002). Introduction. In N. P. Lyons & V. Kubler LaBoskey (Eds.), *Narrative inquiry in practice: Advancing the knowledge of teaching.* New York: Teachers College Press.

Maag, J. W. (2001). Rewarded by punishment: Reflections on the disuse of positive reinforcement in schools. *Exceptional Children, 67*(2), 173–186.

Maanum, J. L. (2009). *The general educator's guide to special education* (3rd ed.). Thousand Oaks, CA: Corwin Press.

Mabry, L. (2008). Assessment, accountability, and the impossible dream. In S. Mathison & E. W. Ross (Eds.), *The nature and limits of standards-based reform and assessment* (pp. 49–56). New York: Teachers College Press.

Mager, R. F. (1962). *Preparing instructional objectives.* Palo Alto, CA: Fearon.

Mager, R. F. (1997). *Preparing instructional objectives* (3d ed.). Atlanta, GA: The Center for Effective Performance.

Mahwinney, T. S., & Sagan, L. L. (2007). The power of personal relationships. *Phi Delta Kappan, 88*(6), 460–464.

Maloch, B., Fine, J., & Flint, A. S. (2002/2003). Trends in teacher certification and literacy. *Reading Teacher, 56*(4), 348–350.

Marcia, J. E. (1966). Development and validation of ego identity status. *Journal of Personality and Social Psychology, 3*(5), 551–558.

Marcia, J. E. (1967). Ego identity status: Relationship to change in self-esteem, "general adjustment," and authoritarianism. *Journal of Personality, 35*(1), 119–133.

Marcia, J. E. (1980). Identity in adolescence. In J. Adelson (Ed.), *Handbook of adolescent psychology.* New York: Wiley.

Marcia, J. E. (1999). Representational thought in ego identity, psychotherapy, and psychosocial developmental theory. In I. E. Sigel (Ed.), *Development of mental representation: Theories and application* (pp. 391–414). Mahwah, NJ: Erlbaum.

Marcia, J. E. (2001). A commentary on Seth Schwartz's review of identity theory and research. *Identity, 1*(1), 59–65.

Marcia, J. E. (2002). Identity and psychosocial development in adulthood. *Identity, 2*(1), 7–28.

Marcia, J. E. (2007). Theory and measure: The identity status interview. In M. Watzlawik & A. Born (Eds.), *Capturing identity: Quantitative and qualitative methods.* Lanham, MD: University Press of America.

Marcovitch, S., Boseovski, J. J., Knapp, R. J., & Kane, M. J. (2010). Goal neglect and working memory capacity in 4- to 6-year-old children. *Child Development, 81*(6), 1687–1695.

Marinak, B., & Gambrell, L. (2008). Intrinsic motivation and rewards: What sustains young children's engagement with text? *Literacy Research and Instruction, 47*(1), 9–26.

Mark, J., Gorman, J., & Nikula, J. (2009). Keeping teacher learning of mathematics central in lesson study. *NCSM Journal of Mathematics Education Leadership, 11*(1), 3–11.

Marley, S. C., & Levin, J. R. (2006). Pictorial illustrations, visual imagery, and motor activity: Their instructional implications for Native American children with learning disabilities. In R. J. Morris (Ed.), *Disability research and policy: Current perspectives* (pp. 102–123). Mahwah, NJ: Erlbaum.

Marley, S. C., Levin, J. R., & Glenberg, A. M. (2007). Improving Native American children's listening comprehension through concrete representations. *Contemporary Educational Psychology, 32*(3), 537–550.

Marquis, J. G., Horner, R. H., Carr, E. G., Turnbull, A. P., Thompson, M., Behrens, G. A., Magito-McLaughlin, D., McAtee, M. L., Smith, C. E., Ryan, K. A., & Doolabh, A. (2000). A meta-analysis of positive behavior support. In R. Gersten, E. P. Schiller, & S. R. Vaughn, (Eds.), *Contemporary special education research* (pp. 137–178). Mahwah, NJ: Erlbaum.

Marr, P. M. (2000). Grouping students at the computer to enhance the study of British literature. *English Journal, 90*(2), 120–125.

Marsh, H. W., Martin, A., & Cheng, J. (2008). A multilevel perspective on gender in classroom motivation and climate: Potential benefits of male teachers for boys? *Journal of Educational Psychology, 100*(1), 78–95.

Martin, A., & Dowson, M. (2009). Interpersonal relationships, motivation, engagement, and achievement: Yields for theory, current issues, and educational practice. *Review of Educational Research, 79*(1), 327–365.

Martin, J. (2004). Self-regulated learning, social cognitive theory, and agency. *Educational Psychologist, 39*(2), 135–145.

Martinez, M. E. (1998). What is problem solving? *Phi Delta Kappan, 79*(8), 605–609.

Martinez, M. E. (1999). Cognition and the question of test item format. *Educational Psychologist, 34*(1), 207–218.

Martinez, M. E. (2010). Human memory: The basics. *Phi Delta Kappan, 91*(8), 62–65.

Marx, R. W., & Winne, P. H. (1987). The best tool teachers have—their students' thinking. In D. C. Berliner & B. V. Rosenshine (Eds.), *Talks to teachers.* New York: Random House.

Marzano, R. J., & Pickering, D. J. (2007). Errors and allegations about research on homework. *Phi Delta Kappan, 88*(7), 507–513.

Marzano, R. J., Pickering, D. J., & Pollock, J. E. (2005). *Classroom instruction that works: Research-based strategies for increasing student achievement.* Upper Saddle River, NJ: Pearson/Prentice Hall.

Maslow, A. H. (1943). A theory of human motivation. *Psychological Review, 50*(4), 370–396.

Maslow, A. H. (1968). *Toward a psychology of being* (2nd ed.). Princeton, NJ: Van Nostrand.

Maslow, A. H. (1987). *Motivation and personality* (3rd ed.). New York: Harper & Row.

Mathes, L. (2002). Theme and variation: The crosshatch portrait. *Arts and Activities, 131*(2), 32–33, 70, 74.

Mathis, W. J. (2005). Bridging the achievement gap: A bridge too far? *Phi Delta Kappan, 86*(8), 590–593.

Matos, L., Lens, W., & Vansteenkiste, M. (2009). School culture matters for teachers' and students' achievement goals. In A. Kaplan, S. Karabenick, & E. De Groot (Eds.), *Culture, self, and, motivation: Essays in honor of Martin L. Maehr* (pp.161–181). Charlotte, NC: Information Age.

Matthew, C., & Sternberg, R. (2009). Developing experience-based (tacit) knowledge through reflection. *Learning and Individual Differences, 19*(4), 530–540.

Matthew, K. I. (1996). The impact of CD-ROM storybooks on children's reading comprehension and reading attitude. *Journal of Educational Multimedia and Hypermedia, 5*(3/4), 379–394.

Matthews, J. S., Ponitz, C. C., & Morrison, F. J. (2009). Early gender differences in self-regulation and academic achievement. *Journal of Educational Psychology, 101*(3), 689–704.

Mau, W.-C., & Lynn, R. (2001). Gender differences on the Scholastic Aptitude Test, the American College Test, and college grades. *Educational Psychology, 21*(2), 133–136.

Mayer, M. J., & Furlong, M. J. (2010). How safe are our schools? *Educational Researcher, 39*(1), 16–26.

Mayer, R. E. (1987). Learnable aspects of problem solving: Some examples. In D. E. Berger, K. Pezdek, & W. P. Banks (Eds.), *Applications of cognitive psychology: Problem solving, education, and computing.* Hillsdale, NJ: Erlbaum.

Mayer, R. E. (2004). Should there be a three-strike rule against pure discovery learning? The case for guided methods of instruction. *American Psychologist, 59*(1), 14–19.

Mayer, R. E. (2008). *Learning and instruction* (2nd ed.). Upper Saddle River, NJ: Merrill Prentice Hall.

Mayer, R. E. (2009). Constructivism as a theory of learning versus constructivism as a prescription for instruction. In S. Tobias & T. Duffy (Eds.), *Constructivist instruction: Success or failure?* (pp. 184–200). New York: Routledge.

Mayer, R. E., & Moreno, R. (2002). Animation as an aid to multimedia learning. *Educational Psychology Review, 14*(1), 87–99.

Mayer, R. E., & Moreno, R. (2003). Nine ways to reduce cognitive load in multimedia learning. *Educational Psychologist, 38*(1), 43–52.

Maynard, A. E. (2008). What we thought we knew and how we came to know it: Four decades of cross-cultural research from a Piagetian point of view. *Human Development*, 51(1), 56–65.

McCrea, S. (2008). Self-handicapping, excuse making, and counterfactual thinking: Consequences for self-esteem and future motivation. *Journal of Personality and Social Psychology, 95*(2), 274–292.

McDaniel, M. A., Howard, D. C., & Einstein, G. O. (2009). The read-recite-review study strategy. *Psychological Science, 20*(4), 516–522.

McDevitt, T. M., & Ormrod, J. E. (2010). *Child development and education* (4th ed.). Upper Saddle River, NJ: Merrill.

McEntee, G. H., Appleby, J., Dowd, J., Grant, J., Hole, S., & Silva, P. (2003). *At the heart of teaching: A guide to reflective practice.* New York: Teachers College Press.

McGill-Franzen, A., & Allington, R. (2006). Contamination of current accountability systems. *Phi Delta Kappan, 87*(10), 762–766.

McGrath, D. (2003). Rubrics, portfolios, and tests, oh my! *Learning and Leading with Technology, 30*(8), 42–45.

McInerney, D. M. (2005). Educational psychology—Theory, research, and teaching: A 25-year retrospective. *Educational Psychology, 25*(6), 585–599.

McKenna, M. C., Cowart, E., & Watkins, J. (1997, December). *Effects of talking books on the growth of struggling readers in second grade.* Paper presented at the meeting of the National Reading Conference, Scottsdale, AZ.

McKenzie, W. (2002). *Multiple intelligences and instructional technology: A manual for every mind.* Eugene, OR: International Society for Technology in Education.

McLoyd, V. C. (1998). Socioeconomic disadvantage and child development. *American Psychologist, 53*(2), 185–204.

McMillan, J. H., Myran, S., & Workman, D. (2002). Elementary teachers' classroom assessment and grading practices. *Journal of Educational Research, 95*(4), 203–213.

McMurrer, J. (2007, July). *Choices, changes, and challenges: Curriculum and instruction in the NCLB era.* Retrieved from http://www.cep-dc.org/cfcontent_file.cfm?Attachment=McMurrer_FullReport_CurricAndInstruction_072407.pdf.

McNeil, L. M., Coppola, E., Radigan, J., & Vasquez Heilig, J. (2008). Avoidable losses: High-stakes accountability and the dropout crisis. *Education Policy Analysis Archives, 16*(3). Retrieved from http://epaa.asu.edu/ojs/article/view/28.

McTighe, J. (1996/1997). What happens between assessments? *Educational Leadership, 54*(4), 6–12.

Means, B., & Haertel, G. (2002). Technology supports for assessing science inquiry. In National Research Council (Ed.), *Technology and assessment: Thinking ahead* (pp. 12–25). Washington, DC: National Academy Press.

Meilinger, T., Knauff, M., Bülthoff, H. (2008). Working memory in wayfinding—A dual task experiment in a virtual city. *Cognitive Science, 32*(4), 755–770.

Melton, R. F. (1978). Resolution of conflicting claims concerning the effect of behavioral objectives on student learning. *Review of Educational Research, 48*(2), 291–302.

Mendoza, J. I. (1994). On being a Mexican American. *Phi Delta Kappan, 76*(4), 293–295.

Menzer, J. D., & Hampel, R. L. (2009). Lost at the last minute. *Phi Delta Kappan, 90*(9), 660–664.

Meo, G. (2008). Curriculum planning for all learners: Applying universal design for learning (UDL) to a high school reading comprehension program. *Preventing School Failure, 52*(2), 21–30.

Merrell, K. W., Gueldner, B. A., Ross, S. W., & Isava, D. M. (2008). How effective are school bullying intervention programs? A meta-analysis of intervention research. *School Psychology Quarterly, 23*(1), 26-42.

Metzger, M. (1998). Teaching reading: Beyond the plot. *Phi Delta Kappan, 80*(3), 240–246, 256.

Metzger, M. (2002). Learning to discipline. *Phi Delta Kappan, 84*(1), 77–84.

Meyer, M. S. (2000). The ability-achievement discrepancy: Does it contribute to our understanding of learning difficulties? *Educational Psychology Review, 12*(3), 315–337.

Meyer-Adams, N., & Conner, B. T. (2008). School violence: Bullying behaviors and the psychosocial school environment in middle schools. *Children & Schools, 30*(4), 211–221.

Midgley, C. (2001). A goal theory perspective on the current status of middle level schools. In T. Urdan & F. Pajares (Eds.), *Adolescence and education, Vol. 1. General issues in the education of adolescents* (pp. 33–59). Greenwich, CT: Information Age.

Midgley, C., Middleton, M. J., Gheen, M. H., & Kumar, R. (2002). Stage-environment fit revisited: A goal theory approach to examining school transitions. In C. Midgley (Ed.), *Goals, goal structures, and patterns of adaptive learning* (pp. 109–142). Mahwah, NJ: Erlbaum.

Miller, P., Fagley, N., & Casella, N. (2009). Effects of problem frame and gender on principals' decision making. *Social Psychology of Education, 12*(3), 397–413.

Miller, P. C., & Endo, H. (2004). Understanding and meeting the needs of ESL students. *Phi Delta Kappan, 85*(10), 786–791.

Miller, R., & Brickman, S. (2004). A model of future-oriented motivation and self-regulation. *Educational Psychology Review, 16*(1), 9–33.

Miller, S. R., Drill, K., & Behrstock, E. (2010). Meeting teachers half way: Making educational research relevant to teachers. *Phi Delta Kappan, 91*(7), 31–34.

Miltenberger, R. G. (2008). *Behavior modification: Principles and procedures* (4th ed.). Belmont, CA: Thomson Wadsworth.

Mishel, L., & Roy, J. (2006). Accurately assessing high school graduation rates. *Phi Delta Kappan, 88*(4), 287–292.

Mistler-Jackson, M., & Songer, N. B. (2000). Student motivation and Internet technology: Are students empowered to learn science? *Journal of Research in Science Teaching, 37*(5), 459–479.

Mock, D. R., & Kauffman, J. M. (2002). Preparing teachers for full inclusion: Is it possible? *Teacher Educator, 37*(3), 202–215.

Moely, B. E., Hart, S. S., Leal, L., Santulli, K. A., Rao, N., Johnson, T., & Hamilton, L. B. (1992). The teacher's role in facilitating memory and study strategy development in the elementary school classroom. *Child Development, 63*(3), 653–672.

Montalvo, G., Mansfield, E., & Miller, R. (2007). Liking or disliking the teacher: Student motivation, engagement and achievement. *Evaluation and Research in Education, 20*(3), 144–158.

Montgomery, J. W., Magimairaj, B. M., & O'Malley, M. H. (2008). Role of working memory in typically developing children's complex sentence comprehension. *Journal of Psycholinguistics Research, 37*(5), 331–354.

Montgomery, K. (2000). Classroom rubrics: Systematizing what teachers do naturally. *Clearing House, 73*(6), 324–328.

Moon, T. R. (2002). Using performance assessment in the social studies classroom. *Gifted Child Today, 25*(3), 53–59.

Moos, D. C., & Azevedo, R. (2009). Learning with computer-based learning environments: A literature review of computer self-efficacy. *Review of Educational Research, 79*(2), 576–600.

Mora, J. K., Wink, J., & Wink, D. (2001). Dueling models of dual language instruction: A critical review of the literature and program implementation guide. *Bilingual Research Journal, 25*(4), 435–460.

Moreno, R. (2006). Learning in high-tech and multimedia environments. *Current Directions in Psychological Science, 15*(2), 63–67.

Moreno, R., & Mayer, R. E. (2002). Learning science in virtual reality multimedia environments: Role of methods and media. *Journal of Educational Psychology, 94*(3), 598–610.

Moreno, R., & Mayer, R. E. (2005). Role of guidance, reflection, and interactivity in an agent-based multimedia game. *Journal of Educational Psychology, 97*(1), 117–128.

Morgan, H. (1997). *Cognitive styles and classroom learning.* Westport, CT: Praeger.

Morisi, T. L. (2008). Youth enrollment and employment during the school year. *Monthly Labor Review, 131*(2). Retrieved from http://www.bls.gov/opub/mlr/2008/02/art3full.pdf.

Morra, S., Gobbo, C., Marini, Z., & Sheese, R. (2008). *Cognitive development: Neo-Piagetian perspectives.* Mahwah, NJ: Erlbaum.

Morris, P. (1977). Practical strategies for human learning and remembering. In M. J. A. Howe (Ed.), *Adult learning.* New York: Wiley.

Morrison, C. T. (2008). "What would you do, what if it's you?" Strategies to deal with a bully. *Journal of School Health, 79*(4), 201–204.

Morrison, J. Q., & Jones, K. M. (2007). The effects of positive peer reporting as a class-wide positive behavior support. *Journal of Behavioral Education, 16*(2), 111–124.

Morrison, K. (2009). Lessons of diversity learned the hard way. *Phi Delta Kappan, 90*(5), 360–362.

Moskvina, V., & Kozhevnikov, M. (2011). Determining cognitive styles: Historical perspective and directions for future research. In S. Rayner & E. Cools (Eds.), *Style differences in cognition, learning, and management* (pp. 19–31). New York: Routledge.

Moss, C. M., & Brookhart, S. (2009). *Advancing formative assessment in every classroom: A guide for instructional leaders.* Alexandria, VA: ASCD.

Mueller, M. (2009). The co-construction of arguments by middle school students. *Journal of Mathematical Behavior, 28*(2–3), 138–149.

Muhlenbruck, L., Cooper, H., Nye, B., & Lindsay, J. J. (2000). Homework and achievement: Explaining the different strengths at the elementary and secondary levels. *Social Psychology in Education, 3*(4), 295–317.

Muis, K. R. (2007). The role of epistemic beliefs in self-regulated learning. *Educational Psychologist, 42*(3), 173–190.

Murayama, K., & Elliot, A. (2009). The joint influence of personal achievement goals and classroom goal structures on achievement-relevant outcomes. *Journal of Educational Psychology, 101*(2), 432–447.

Murdock, T. B., Miller, A., & Kohlhardt, J. (2004). Effects of classroom context variables on high school students' judgments of the acceptability and likelihood of cheating. *Journal of Educational Psychology, 96*(4), 765–777.

Murphy, B. C., & Eisenberg, N. (2002). An integrative examination of peer conflict: Children's reported goals, emotions, and behavior. *Social Development, 11*(4), 534–557.

Murray, S. (2009). Telementoring: Pre-service teachers and teachers partner for technology integration. In I. Gibson et al. (Eds.), *Proceedings of Society for Information Technology & Teacher Education International Conference 2009* (pp. 3493–3496). Chesapeake, VA: Association for the Advancement of Computing in Education.

Myers, M. (2003). What can computers contribute to a K–12 writing program? In M. D. Shermis & J. C. Burstein (Eds.), *Automated essay scoring* (pp. 3–20). Mahwah, NJ: Erlbaum.

Nagaoka, J., & Roderick, M. (2004, March). *Ending social promotion: The effects of retention.* Chicago, IL: Consortium on Chicago School Research. Retrieved from http://ccsr.uchicago.edu/publications/p70.pdf.

Nagy, P., & Griffiths, A. K. (1982). Limitations of recent research relating Piaget's theory to adolescent thought. *Review of Educational Research, 52*(4), 513–556.

Nakamura, J., & Csikszentmihalyi, M. (2009). Flow theory and research. In C. Snyder & S. Lopez (Eds.), *Oxford handbook of positive psychology* (2nd ed., pp. 195–206). New York: Oxford University Press.

Narvaez, D. (2002). Does reading moral stories build character? *Educational Psychology Review, 14*(2), 155–172.

Nasir, N. S. (2008). Everyday pedagogy: Lessons from basketball, track, and dominoes. *Phi Delta Kappan, 89*(7), 529–532.

National Center for Education Statistics. (2009). *The nation's report card: Mathematics 2009. National assessment of educational progress at grades 4 and 8* (NCES 2010-451). Washington, DC: U.S. Department of Education. Retrieved from http://nces.ed.gov/nationsreportcard/pdf/main2009/2010451.pdf.

National Center for Education Statistics. (2010a). *The nation's report card: Reading 2009. National assessment of educational progress at grades 4 and 8* (NCES 2010-458). Washington, DC: U.S. Department of Education. Retrieved from http://nces.ed.gov/nationsreportcard/pdf/main2009/2010458.pdf.

National Center for Education Statistics. (2010b). *The nation's report card: Grade 12 reading and mathematics 2009 national and pilot state results* (NCES 2011-455). Washington, DC: U.S. Department of Education. Retrieved from http://nces.ed.gov/nationsreportcard/pdf/main2009/2011455.pdf.

National Center for Health Statistics. (2007). *Health, United States, 2007 with chartbook on trends in the health of Americans.* Hyattsville, MD: U.S. Department of Health and Human Services.

National Commission on Excellence in Education. (1983). *A nation at risk: The imperative for educational reform.* Washington, DC: U.S. Department of Education.

National Comprehensive Center for Teacher Quality & Public Agenda. (2008a). *Lessons learned: New teachers talk about their jobs, challenges and long-range plans. Issue No. 1. They're not little kids anymore: The special challenges of new teachers in high schools and middle schools.* Retrieved from http://www.publicagenda.org/files/pdf/lessons_learned_1.pdf.

National Comprehensive Center for Teacher Quality & Public Agenda. (2008b). *Lessons learned: New teachers talk about their jobs, challenges and long-range plans. Issue No. 3. Teaching in changing times.* Retrieved from http://www.publicagenda.org/files/pdf/lessons_learned_3.pdf.

National Research Council. (2000). *Inquiry and the National Science Education Standards: A guide for teaching and learning.* Washington, DC: National Academy Press.

National Research Council. (2002). *Minority students in special and gifted education* (Committee on Minority Representation in Special Education, M. S. Donovan & C. T. Cross, Eds., Division of Behavioral and Social Sciences). Washington, DC: National Academy Press.

Naughton, C. C., & McLaughlin, T. F. (1995). The use of a token economy system for students with behaviour disorders. *B.C. Journal of Special Education, 19*(2/3), 29–38.

Nebel, M., Jamison, B., & Bennett, L. (2009). Students as digital citizens on Web 2.0. *Social Studies and the Young Learner, 21*(4), 5–7.

Neisser, U. (1976). *Cognition and reality.* San Francisco: W. H. Freeman.

Nesbit, J. C., & Adesope, O. O. (2006). Learning with concept and knowledge maps: A meta-analysis. *Review of Educational Research, 76*(3), 413–448.

Newman, B. M., & Newman, P. R. (2009). *Development through life: A psychosocial approach* (10th ed.). Belmont, CA: Wadsworth/Cengage Learning.

New York Performance Standards Consortium. (2007, October). *The alternative to high-stakes testing.* Retrieved from http://www.performanceassessment.org.

Nichols, S. L. (2007). High-stakes testing: Does it increase achievement? *Journal of Applied School Psychology, 23*(2), 47–64.

Nichols, S. L., & Berliner, D. C. (2005, March). The inevitable corruption of indicators and educators through high-stakes testing (EPSL-0503-101-EPRU). Education Policy Studies Laboratory, Education Policy Research Unit. Retrieved from http://epsl.asu.edu/epru/documents/EPSL-0503-101-EPRU.pdf.

Nichols, S. L., & Berliner, D. C. (2007). *Collateral damage: How high stakes testing corrupts America's schools.* Cambridge, MA: Harvard University Press.

Nichols, S. L., Glass, G. V., & Berliner, D. C. (2006). High-stakes testing and student achievement: Does accountability pressure increase student learning? *Education Policy Analysis Archives, 14*(1). Retrieved from http://epaa.asu.edu/ojs/article/view/72.

Nickerson, R. S. (1994). The teaching of thinking and problem solving. In R. J. Sternberg (Ed.), *Thinking and problem solving.* San Diego, CA: Academic Press.

Nielsen, T., Kreiner, S., & Styles, I. (2007). Mental self-government: Development of the additional democratic learning style scale using Rasch measurement models. *Journal of Applied Measurement, 8*(2), 124–48.

Nieto, S. (2002/2003). Profoundly multicultural questions. *Educational Leadership, 60*(4), 6–10.

Nieto, S. (2008). *Affirming diversity: The sociopolitical context of multicultural education* (5th ed.). Boston: Pearson/Allyn & Bacon.

Nitko, A., & Brookhart, S. (2011). *Educational assessment of students* (6th ed.). Upper Saddle River, NJ: Allyn & Bacon/Pearson.

No Child Left Behind Act of 2001. (2001, January). Retrieved from http://www2.ed.gov/policy/elsec/leg/esea02/107-110.pdf.

Noddings, N. (1984/2003). *Caring: A feminine approach to ethics and moral education* (2nd ed.). Berkeley, CA: University of California Press.

Noddings, N. (2003). *Happiness and education.* Cambridge, England: Cambridge University Press.

Noddings, N. (2008). Caring and moral education. In L. P. Nucci & D. Narvaez (Eds.), *Handbook of moral and character education* (pp. 161–174). New York: Routledge.

Norman, D. A., & Rumelhart, D. E. (1970). A system for perception and memory. In D. A. Norman (Ed.), *Models of human memory.* New York: Academic Press.

Novak, J. D. (2009). *Learning, creating, and using knowledge: Concept maps as facilitative tools in schools and corporations.* New York: Routledge.

Novak, J. D., & Gowin, D. B. (1984). *Learning how to learn.* Cambridge, England: Cambridge University Press.

Oakes, J. (2005). *Keeping track* (2nd ed.). New Haven, CT: Yale University Press.

O'Brennan, L. M., Bradshaw, C. P., & Sawyer, A. L. (2008). Examining developmental differences in the social-emotional problems among frequent bullies, victims, and bully/victims. *Psychology in the Schools, 46*(2), 100–115.

Ochse, R., & Plug, C. (1986). Cross-cultural investigation of the validity of Erikson's theory of personality development. *Journal of Personality and Social Psychology, 50*(6), 1240–1252.

O'Donnell, A. M., Dansereau, D. F., & Hall, R. H. (2002). Knowledge maps as scaffolds for cognitive processing. *Educational Psychology Review, 14*(1), 71–86.

Ogbu, J. U. (2003). *Black American students in an affluent suburb.* Mahwah, NJ: Erlbaum.

Okagaki, L. (2001). Triarchic model of minority children's school achievement. *Educational Psychologist, 36*(1), 9–20.

Okagaki, L. (2006). Ethnicity and learning. In P. A. Alexander & P. H. Winne (Eds.), *Handbook of educational psychology* (2nd ed., pp. 615–634). Mahwah, NJ: Erlbaum.

O'Lone, D. J. (1997). Student information system software: Are you getting what you expected? *NASSP Bulletin, 81*(585), 86–93.

Olson, A. (2002). Technology solutions for testing. *School Administrator, 59*(4), 20–23.

Olson, L. (2003). Legal twists, digital turns. *Education Week, 22*(41), 1, 20–21.

Ophir, E., Nass, C., & Wagner, A. D. (2009). Cognitive control in media multitaskers. *Proceedings of the National Academy of Sciences, 106*(37), 15583–15587.

Ornstein, A. C., Levine, D. U., & Gutek, G. (2011). *Foundations of education* (11th ed.). Belmont, CA: Wadsworth/Cengage Learning.

Ornstein, P. A., Grammer, J. K., & Coffman, J. L. (2010). Teachers' "mnemonic style" and the development of skilled memory. In H. S. Waters & W. Schneider (Eds.), *Metacognition, strategy use, and instruction* (pp. 23–53). New York: Guilford Press.

Osborn Popp, S., Ryan, J., & Thompson, M. (2009). The critical role of anchor paper selection in writing assessment. *Applied Measurement in Education, 22*(3), 255–271.

Osman, M. (2008). Positive transfer and negative transfer/antilearning of problem-solving skills. *Journal of Experimental Psychology: General, 137*(1), 97–115.

Osterman, K. F. (2000). Students' need for belonging in the school community. *Review of Educational Research, 70*(3), 323–367.

Owens, R. F., Hester, J. L., & Teale, W. H. (2002). Where do you want to go today? Inquiry-based learning and technology integration. *Reading Teacher, 55*(7), 616–625.

Owings, W. A., & Kaplan, L. S. (2001). Standards, retention, and social promotion. *NASSP Bulletin, 85*(629), 57–66.

Owston, R., Wideman, H., Sinitskaya, N. R., & Brown, C. (2009). Computer game development as a literacy activity. *Computers and Education, 53*(3), 977–989.

Ozuru, Y., Dempsey, K., McNamara, D. (2009). Prior knowledge, reading skill, and text cohesion in the comprehension of science texts. *Learning and Instruction, 19*(3), 228–242.

Paas, F., & van Gog, T. (2009). Principles for designing effective and efficient training of complex cognitive skills. In F. Durso (Ed.), *Reviews of human factors and ergonomics* (Vol. 5, pp. 166–194). Santa Monica, CA: Human Factors and Ergonomics Society.

Paavola, S., Lipponen, L., & Hakkarainen, K. (2004). Models of innovative knowledge communities and three metaphors of learning. *Review of Educational Research, 74*(4), 557–576.

Pacheco, M., & Gutiérrez, K. (2009). Cultural-historical approaches to literacy teaching and learning. In C. Compton-Lilly (Ed.), *Breaking the silence: Recognizing social and cultural resources students bring to the classroom* (pp. 60–80). Newark, DE: International Reading Association.

Pajares, F. (2007). Motivational role of self-efficacy in self-regulated learning. In B. J. Zimmerman & D. H. Schunk (Eds.), *Motivation and self-regulated learning: Theory, research, and application* (pp. 111–140). New York: Erlbaum.

Pajares, F. (2009). Toward a positive psychology of academic motivation: The role of self-efficacy beliefs. In R. Gilman, E. S. Huebner, & M. J. Furlong (Eds.), *Handbook of positive psychology in schools* (pp. 149–160). New York: Routledge.

Palincsar, A., & Brown, A. L. (1984). Reciprocal teaching of comprehension-fostering and comprehension-monitoring activities. *Cognition and Instruction, 1*(2), 117–175.

Palmer, S. B., & Wehmeyer, M. L. (2003). Promoting self-determination in early elementary school: Teaching self-regulated problem-solving and goal-setting skills. *Remedial and Special Education, 24*(2), 115–126.

Paris, S. G., & Paris, A. H. (2001). Classroom applications of research on self-regulated learning. *Educational Psychologist, 36*(2), 89–101.

Parke, C. S., & Lane, S. (1997). Learning from performance assessments in math. *Educational Leadership, 54*(6), 26–29.

Patrick, H., Ryan, A. M., & Kaplan, A. (2007). Early adolescents' perceptions of the classroom social environment, motivational beliefs, and engagement. *Journal of Educational Psychology, 99*(1), 83–98.

Patterson, B. (2002). Creating two-point perspective on the computer. *Arts & Activities, 131*(4), 52.

Patterson, G. R., DeBaryshe, B. D., & Ramsey, E. (1989). A developmental perspective on antisocial behavior. *American Psychologist, 44*(2), 329–335.

Pea, R. D. (1985). Beyond amplification: Using the computer to reorganize mental functioning. *Educational Psychologist, 21*(4), 167–182.

Pea, R. D. (2004). The social and technological dimensions of scaffolding and related theoretical concepts for learning, education, and activity. *Journal of Learning Sciences, 13*(3), 423–451.

Pedersen, S., & Liu, M. (2002). The effects of modeling expert cognitive strategies during problem-based learning. *Journal of Educational Computing Research, 26*(4), 353–380.

Pedersen, S., & Liu, M. (2002/2003). The transfer of problem-solving skills from a problem-based learning environment: The effect of modeling an expert's cognitive processes. *Journal of Research on Technology in Education, 35*(2), 303–320.

Pekrun, R., Elliot, A., & Maier, M. (2009). Achievement goals and achievement emotions: Testing a model of their joint relations with academic performance. *Journal of Educational Psychology, 101*(1), 115–135.

Pellegrini, A. D. (2009). *The role of play in human development.* Oxford, England: Oxford University Press.

Pellegrini, A. D., & Bohn, C. M. (2005). The role of recess in children's cognitive performance and school adjustment. *Educational Researcher, 34*(1), 13–19.

Pelletier, L. G., Séguin-Lévesque, C., & Legault, L. (2002). Pressure from above and pressure from below as determinants of teachers' motivation and teaching behaviors. *Journal of Educational Psychology, 94*(1), 186–196.

Peltier, G. L. (1991). Why do secondary schools continue to track students? *Clearing House, 64*(4), 246–247.

Peña, C. M., & Alessi, S. M. (1999). Promoting a qualitative understanding of physics. *Journal of Computers in Mathematics and Science Teaching, 18*(4), 439–457.

Penfield, R. D. (2010). Test-based grade retention: Does it stand up to professional standards for fair and appropriate test use? *Educational Researcher, 39*(2), 110–119.

Penfield, W. (1969). Consciousness, memory, and man's conditioned reflexes. In K. Pribram (Ed.), *On the biology of learning.* New York: Harcourt Brace Jovanovich.

Pérez, B. (2004). *Becoming biliterate: A study of two-way bilingual immersion education.* Mahwah, NJ: Erlbaum.

Perkins, D. (1999). The many faces of constructivism. *Educational Leadership, 57*(3), 6–11.

Perry, N. E., VandeKamp, K. O., Mercer, L. K., & Nordby, C. J. (2002). Investigating teacher–student interactions that foster self-regulated learning. *Educational Psychologist, 37*(1), 5–15.

Peters, G. D. (2001). Transformations: Technology and the music industry. *Teaching Music, 9*(3), 20–25.

Peterson, A. C., Compas, B. E., Brooks-Gunn, J., Stemmler, M., Ey, S., & Grant, K. E. (1993). Depression in adolescence. *American Psychologist, 48*(2), 155–168.

Peverly, S. T., Brobst, K. E., Graham, M., & Shaw, R. (2003). College adults are not good at self-regulation: A study on the relationship of self-regulation, note taking, and test taking. *Journal of Educational Psychology, 95*(2), 335–346.

Pewewardy, C. (2002). Learning styles of American Indian/Alaska Native students: A review of the literature and implications for practice. *Journal of American Indian Education, 41*(3), 22–56.

Piaget, J. (1932). *The moral judgment of the child* (M. Gabain, Trans.). New York: Harcourt Brace.

Piaget, J. (1965). *The moral judgment of the child* (M. Gabain, Trans.). Glencoe, IL: Free Press. (Original work published 1932.)

Piaget, J., & Inhelder, B. (1956). *The child's conception of space.* London: Routledge & Kegan Paul.

Pianta, R. C., Belsky, J., Houts, R., Morrison, F., & The National Institute of Child Health and Human Development Early Child Care Research Network. (2007). TEACHING: Opportunities to learn in America's elementary classrooms. *Science, 315*(5820), 1795–1796.

Pintrich, P. R., & Schunk, D. H. (2002). *Motivation in education: Theory, research, and applications* (2nd ed.). Upper Saddle River, NJ: Merrill Prentice Hall.

Planty, M., Hussar, W., Snyder, T., Kena, G., KewalRamani, A., Kemp, J., Bianco, K., & Dinkes, R. (2009, June). *The condition of education 2009* (NCES 2009-081). Washington, DC: National Center for Education Statistics, Institute of Education Sciences, U.S. Department of Education. Retrieved from http://nces.ed.gov/pubs2009/2009081.pdf.

Planty, M., Hussar, W., Snyder, T., Provasnik, S., Kena, G., Dinkers, R., KewalRamani, A., & Kemp, J. (2008). *The condition of education 2008* (NCES 2008-031). Washington, DC: National Center for Education Statistics, Institute of Education Sciences, U.S. Department of Education. Retrieved from http://nces.ed.gov/pubs2008/2008031.pdf.

Pleydon, A. P., & Schner, J. G. (2001). Female adolescent friendships and delinquent behavior. *Adolescence, 36*(142), 189–205.

Podoll, S., & Randle, D. (2005). Building a virtual high school … click by click. *T.H.E. Journal, 33*(2), 14–19.

Pogrow, S. (1990). A Socratic approach to using computers with at-risk students. *Educational Leadership, 47*(5), 61–66.

Pogrow, S. (1999). Systematically using powerful learning environments to accelerate the learning of disadvantaged students in grades 4–8. In C. M. Reigeluth (Ed.), *Instructional design theories and models, Vol. II. A new paradigm of instructional theory.* Mahwah, NJ: Erlbaum.

Pogrow, S. (2005). HOTS revisited: A thinking development approach to reducing the learning gap after grade 3. *Phi Delta Kappan, 87*(1), 64–75.

Pogrow, S. (2008). *Teaching content outrageously: How to captivate and accelerate the learning of all students in grades 4–12.* San Francisco: Jossey-Bass.

Pogrow, S. (2009a). Accelerating the learning of 4th and 5th graders born into poverty. *Phi Delta Kappan, 90*(6), 408–412.

Pogrow, S. (2009b). Teaching content outrageously: Instruction in the era of on-demand entertainment. *Phi Delta Kappan, 90*(5), 379–383.

Polya, G. (1957). *How to solve it* (2nd ed.). Princeton, NJ: Princeton University Press.

Pomerantz, E. M. (2002). Making the grade but feeling distressed: Gender differences in academic performance and internal distress. *Journal of Educational Psychology, 94*(2), 396–404.

Pope, M., Hare, D., & Howard, E. (2002). Technology integration: Closing the gap between what preservice teachers are taught to do and what they can do. *Journal of Technology and Teacher Education, 10*(2), 191–203.

Popham, W. J. (2005). How to make use of PAP to make AYP under NCLB. *Phi Delta Kappan, 86*(10), 787–791.

Popham, W. J. (2006). *Assessment for educational leaders.* Boston: Allyn & Bacon.

Popham, W. J. (2009). Transform toxic AYP into a beneficial tool. *Phi Delta Kappan, 90*(8), 577–581.

Popham, W. J. (2011). *Classroom assessment: What teachers need to know.* Boston: Allyn & Bacon/Pearson.

Portes, P., Dunham, R., & Del Castillo, K. (2000). Identity formation and status across cultures: Exploring the cultural validity of Erikson's theory. In A. L. Comunian & U. Gielen (Eds.), *International perspectives on human development* (pp. 449–459). Lengerich, Germany: Pabst Science.

Postholm, M. (2008). Cultural historical activity theory and Dewey's idea-based social constructivism: Consequences for educational research. *Critical Practice Studies, 10*(1), 37–48.

Premack, D. (1959). Toward empirical behavior laws: 1. Positive reinforcement. *Psychological Review, 66*(4), 219–233.

Pressley, M., & Hilden, K. (2006). Cognitive strategies. In D. Kuhn & R. Siegler (Eds.), *Handbook of child psychology: Cognition, perception, and language* (Vol. 2, pp. 511–556). Hoboken, NJ: Wiley.

Pretz, J. E., Naples, A. J., & Sternberg, R. J. (2003). Recognizing, defining, and representing problems. In J. E. Davidson & R. J. Sternberg (Eds.), *The psychology of problem solving* (pp. 3–30). Cambridge, England: Cambridge University Press.

Psychological Corporation. (2002). *WAIS-III WMS-III technical manual* (updated ed.). San Antonio, TX: Author.

Pugh, K. J., & Bergin, D. (2005). The effect of schooling on students' out-of-school experience. *Educational Researcher, 34*(9), 15–23.

Pullin, D. L., Gitsaki, C., Baguley, M. (Eds.). (2010). *Technoliteracy, discourse and social practice: Frameworks and applications in the digital age.* Hershey, PA: IGI Global.

Purdie, N., & Hattie, J. (1996). Cultural differences in the use of strategies for self-regulated learning. *American Educational Research Journal, 33*(4), 845–871.

Purdie, N., Hattie, J., & Carroll, A. (2002). A review of the research on interventions for attention deficit hyperactivity disorder: What works best? *Review of Educational Research, 72*(1), 61–99.

Puzzanchera, C. (2009, April). Juvenile arrests 2007. *OJJDP Juvenile Justice Bulletin.* Retrieved from http://www.ncjrs.gov/pdffiles1/ojjdp/225344.pdf.

Quenneville, J. (2001). Tech tools for students with learning disabilities: Infusion into inclusive classrooms. *Preventing School Failure, 45*(4), 167–170.

Quihuis, G., Bempechat, J., Jimenez, N. V., & Boulay, B. A. (2002). Implicit theories of intelligence across domains: A study of meaning making in adolescents of Mexican descent. In J. Bempechat & J. G. Elliott (Eds.), *New directions for child and adolescent development, no. 96. Learning in culture and context: Approaching the complexities of achievement motivation in student learning* (pp. 87–100). San Francisco: Jossey-Bass.

Rakes, G. C., Fields, V. S., & Cox, K. E. (2006). The influence of teachers' technology use on instructional practices. *Journal of Research on Technology in Education, 38*(4), 409–424.

Ramirez, A., & Carpenter, D. (2005). Challenging assumptions about the achievement gap. *Phi Delta Kappan, 86*(8), 599–603.

Ramirez, A., & Carpenter, D. (2009). The matter of dropouts. *Phi Delta Kappan, 90*(9), 656–659.

Randi, J., & Corno, L. (2000). Teacher innovations in self-regulated learning. In M. Boekaerts, P. R. Pintrich, & M. Zeidner (Eds.), *Handbook of self-regulation* (pp. 651–685). San Diego, CA: Academic Press.

Rathunde, K., & Csikszentmihalyi, M. (2005). Middle school students' motivation and quality of experience: A comparison of Montessori and traditional school environments. *American Journal of Education, 111*(3), 341–371.

Ratner, C. (1991). *Vygotsky's sociohistorical psychology and its contemporary applications.* New York: Plenum Press.

Raudenbush, S. W. (2009). The *Brown* legacy and the O'Connor challenge: Transforming schools in the images of children's potential. *Educational Researcher, 38*(3), 169–180.

Raugh, M. R., & Atkinson, R. C. (1975). A mnemonic method for learning a second-language vocabulary. *Journal of Educational Psychology, 67*(1), 1–16.

Ravaglia, R., Alper, T., Rozenfeld, M., & Suppes, P. (1998). Successful pedagogical applications of symbolic computation. In N. Kajler (Ed.), *Computer-human interaction in symbolic computation* (pp. 61–88). New York: Springer-Verlag.

Ravaglia, R., Sommer, R., Sanders, M., Oas, G., & DeLeone, C. (1999). Computer-based mathematics and physics for gifted remote students. *Proceedings of the International Conference on Mathematics/Science Education and Technology* (pp. 405–410). Retrieved January 15, 2004, from http://epgy.stanford.edu/research/mset.pdf.

Rawsthorne, L. J., & Elliot, A. J. (1999). Achievement goals and intrinsic motivation: A meta-analytic review. *Personality and Social Psychology Review, 3*(4), 326–344.

Rayner, S. & Cools, E. (Eds.). (2011). *Style differences in cognition, learning, and management: Theory, research, and practice.* New York: Routledge.

Rea, A. (2001). Telementoring: An A1 initiative. *Education Canada, 40*(4), 28–29.

Reardon, S. F. (2008, May). *Thirteen ways of looking at the black–white test score gap* (Working Paper #2008-08). Retrieved from Institute for Research on Education Policy and Practice, Stanford University: http://www.stanford.edu/group/irepp/cgi-bin/joomla/docman/thirteen-ways-of-looking-at-the-black-white-test-score-gap/download.html.

Reardon, S. F., & Galindo, C. (2009). The Hispanic–White achievement gap in math and reading in the elementary grades. *Review of Educational Research, 46*(3), 853–891.

Redl, F., & Wattenberg, W. W. (1959). *Mental hygiene in teaching* (2nd ed.). New York: Harcourt Brace Jovanovich.

Reed, D. S. (2009). Is there an expectations gap? Educational federalism and the demographic distribution of proficiency cut scores. *American Educational Research Journal, 46*(3), 718–742.

Reed, S. K. (2006). Cognitive architectures for multimedia learning. *Educational Psychologist, 41*(2), 87–98.

Reeve, J., & Halusic, M. (2009). How K–12 teachers can put self-determination theory principles into practice. *Theory and Research in Education, 7*(2), 145–154.

Reeve, J., & Jang, H. (2006). What teachers say and do to support students' autonomy during a learning activity. *Journal of Educational Psychology, 98*(1), 209–218.

Reid, C., Romanoff, B., & Algozzine, R. (2000). An evaluation of alternative screening procedures. *Journal for the Education of the Gifted, 23*(4), 378–396.

Reinke, W. M., Lewis-Palmer, T., & Merrell, K. (2008). The classroom check-up: A classwide teacher consultation model for increasing praise and decreasing disruptive behavior. *School Psychology Review, 37*(3), 315–332.

Reis, S. M., & Renzulli, J. S. (1985). *The secondary triad model.* Mansfield Center, CT: Creative Learning Press.

Reis, S. M., & Renzulli, J. S. (2009). Myth 1: The gifted and talented constitute one single homogeneous group and giftedness is a way of being that stays in the person over time and experiences. *Gifted Child Quarterly, 53*(4), 233–235.

Reninger, R. D. (2000). Music education in a digital world. *Teaching Music, 8*(1), 24–31.

Renkl, A., Hilbert, T., & Schworm, S. (2009). Example-based learning in heuristic domains: A cognitive load theory account. *Educational Psychology Review, 21*(1), 67–78.

Renninger, K. A. (2009). Interest and identity development in instruction: An inductive model. *Educational Psychologist, 44*(2), 105–118.

Renninger, K. A., & Hidi, S. (2002). Student interest and achievement: Developmental issues raised by a case study. In A. Wigfield & J. S. Eccles (Eds.), *Development of achievement motivation* (pp. 173–195). San Diego, CA: Academic Press.

Renzulli, J. S. (2002). Expanding the conception of giftedness to include co-cognitive traits and promote social capital. *Phi Delta Kappan, 84*(1), 33–40, 57–58.

Renzulli, J. S., Gentry, M., & Reis, S. M. (2003). *Enrichment clusters: A practical plan for real-world, student-driven learning.* Mansfield Center, CT: Creative Learning Press.

Resnick, L. B. (1987). Learning in school and out. *Educational Researcher, 16*(9), 13–20.

Rest, J., Narvaez, D., Bebeau, M. J., & Thoma, S. J. (1999). *Postconventional moral thinking: A neo-Kohlbergian approach.* Mahwah, NJ: Erlbaum.

Reynolds, T. H., & Bonk, C. J. (1996). Creating computerized writing partner and keystroke recording tools with macro-driven prompts. *Educational Technology Research and Development, 44*(3), 83–97.

Rice, K. L. (2006). A comprehensive look at distance education in the K–12 context. *Journal of Research on Technology in Education, 38*(4), 425–448.

Richard, A. (2005). Supplemental help can be hard to find for rural students. *Education Week, 25*(14), 1, 22.

Rigby, K. (2008). *Children and bullying: How parents and educators can reduce bullying at school.* Malden, MA: Blackwell.

Riggs, E., & Gholar, C. (2009). *Strategies that promote student engagement: Unleashing the desire to learn* (2nd ed.). Thousand Oaks, CA: Corwin Press.

Rikers, R., van Gog, T., & Paas, F. (2008). The effects of constructivist learning environments: A commentary. *Instructional Science, 36*(5–6), 463–467.

Ripley, A. (2010, January/February). What makes a great teacher? *Atlantic,* Retrieved from http://www.theatlantic.com.

Robertson, A. (2001, Sept/Oct). CASE is when we learn to think. *Primary Science Review, 69,* 20–22.

Robertson, J. S. (2000). Is attribution training a worthwhile classroom intervention for K–12 students with learning difficulties? *Educational Psychology Review, 12*(1), 111–134.

Robinson, J. P. (2008). Evidence of a differential effect of ability grouping on the reading achievement growth of language-minority Hispanics. *Educational Evaluation and Policy Analysis, 30*(2), 141–180.

Robinson, J. P. (2010). The effects of test translation on young English learners' mathematics performance. *Educational Researcher, 39*(8), 582–590.

Robledo, M. M., & Cortez, J. D. (2002). Successful bilingual education programs: Development and dissemination of criteria to identify promising and exemplary practices in bilingual education at the national level. *Bilingual Research Journal, 26*(1), 1–21.

Roblyer, M. D. (2006). Virtually successful: Defeating the dropout problem through online school programs. *Phi Delta Kappan, 88*(1), 31–36.

Roderick, M., & Engel, M. (2001). The grasshopper and the ant: Motivational responses of low-achieving students to high-stakes testing. *Educational Evaluation and Policy Analysis, 23*(3), 197–227.

Roediger, H. L., III. (2008). Relativity of remembering: Why the laws of memory vanished. *Annual Review of Psychology, 59,* 225–254.

Roediger, H. L., III., Agarwal, P. K., Kang, S. H. K., & Marsh, E. J. (2010). Benefits of testing memory: Best practices and boundary conditions. In G. M Davies & D. B. Wright (Eds.), *Current issues in applied memory research* (pp. 13-49). New York: Psychology Press.

Roediger, H. L., III., Weinstein, Y., & Agarwal, P. K. (2010). Forgetting: Preliminary considerations. In S. D. Sala (Ed.), *Forgetting* (pp. 1–22). New York: Psychology Press.

Roerden, L. (2001). The Resolving Conflict Creatively Program. *Reclaiming Children and Youth, 10*(1), 24–28.

Rogers, C. R., & Freiberg, H. J. (1994). *Freedom to learn* (3rd ed.). New York: Merrill.

Rogers, W. A., Pak, R., & Fisk, A. D. (2007). Applied cognitive psychology in the context of everyday living. In F. Durso, R. Nickerson, S. Dumais, S. Lewandowsky, & T. Perfect (Eds.), *Handbook of applied cognition* (2nd ed., pp. 3–27). Chichester, England: Wiley.

Rogoff, B. (1990). *Apprenticeship in thinking: Cognitive development in social context.* New York: Oxford University Press.

Rogoff, B., & Chavajay, P. (1995). What's become of research on the cultural basis of cognitive development? *American Psychologist, 50*(10), 859–877.

Rohrbeck, C. A., Ginsburg-Block, M. D., Fantuzzo, J. W., & Miller, T. R. (2003). Peer-assisted learning interventions with elementary school students: A meta-analytic review. *Journal of Educational Psychology, 95*(2), 240–257.

Rohrer, D., & Pashler, H. (2010). Recent research on human learning challenges conventional instructional strategies. *Educational Researcher, 39*(5), 406–412.

Roid, G. (2003). *Stanford-Binet Intelligence Scales: Fifth Edition.* Itasca, IL: Riverside.

Roller, C. M. (2002). Accommodating variability in reading instruction. *Reading & Writing Quarterly, 18*(1), 17–38.

Rolón, C. A. (2002/2003). Educating Latino students. *Educational Leadership, 60*(4), 40–43.

Romance, N. R., & Vitale, M. R. (1999). Concept mapping as a tool for learning: Broadening the framework for student-centered instruction. *College Teaching, 47*(2), 74–79.

Rop, C. (1998). Breaking the gender barrier in the physical sciences. *Educational Leadership, 55*(4), 58–60.

Roscoe, R. D., & Chi, M. T. H. (2007). Understanding tutor learning: Knowledge-building and knowledge-telling in peer tutors' explanations and questions. *Review of Educational Research, 77*(4), 534–574.

Rose, N. S., Myerson, J., Roediger, H. L., III., & Hale, S. (2010). Similarities and differences between working memory and long-term memory: Evidence from the levels-of-processing span task. *Journal of Experimental Psychology: Learning, Memory, and Cognition, 36*(2), 471–483.

Rosen, D., & Nelson, C. (2008). Web 2.0: A new generation of learners and education. *Computers in the Schools, 25*(3–4), 211–225.

Rosen, Y. (2009). The effects of an animation-based on-line learning environment on transfer of knowledge and on motivation for science and technology learning. *Journal of Educational Computing Research, 40*(4), 451–467.

Rosenshine, B. V., & Meister, C. (1994a). Direct instruction. In T. Husen & T. N. Postlewhaite (Eds.), *International encyclopedia of education* (2nd ed., Vol. 3, pp. 1524–1530). New York: Pergamon.

Rosenshine, B., & Meister, C. (1994b). Reciprocal teaching: A review of the research. *Review of Educational Research, 64*(4), 479–530.

Rosenshine, B., Meister, C., & Chapman, S. (1996). Teaching students to generate questions: A review of the intervention studies. *Review of Educational Research, 66*(2), 181–221.

Rosenthal, R. (2002). The Pygmalion effect and its mediating mechanisms. In J. Aronson (Ed.), *Improving academic achievement* (pp. 26–36). San Diego, CA: Academic Press.

Ross, D. D., Bondy, E., Gallingane, C., & Hambacher, E. (2008). Promoting academic engagement through insistence: Being a warm demander. *Childhood Education, 84*(3), 142–146.

Ross, D. D., Bondy, E., & Kyle, D. W. (1993). *Reflective teaching for student empowerment.* New York: Macmillan.

Ross, H. S., & Spielmacher, C. E. (2005). Social development. In B. Hopkins, R. G. Barr, G. F. Michel, & P. Rochat (Eds.), *The Cambridge encyclopedia of child development* (pp. 227–233). Cambridge, England: Cambridge University Press.

Roth, W.-M., & Lee, Y. J. (2007). Vygotsky's neglected legacy: Cultural-historical activity theory. *Review of Educational Research, 77*(2), 186–232.

Rothstein, R. (2004). A wider lens on the black–white achievement gap. *Phi Delta Kappan, 86*(2), 104–110.

Rothstein-Fisch, C., Greenfield, P. M., & Trumbull, E. (1999). Bridging cultures with classroom strategies. *Educational Leadership, 56*(7), 64–67.

Rotter, K. M. (2009). Enhancing memory in your students: COMPOSE yourself. *TEACHING Exceptional Children Plus, 5*(3). Retrieved November 7, 2009, from http://journals.cec.sped.org/cgi/viewcontent.cgi?article=1645&context=tecplus.

Rowan, B. (1994). Comparing teachers' work with work in other occupations: Notes on the professional status of teaching. *Educational Researcher, 23*(6), 4–17.

Rowe, S. M., & Wertsch, J. V. (2002) Vygotsky's model of cognitive development. In U. Goswami (Ed.), *Blackwell handbook of childhood cognitive development* (pp. 538–554). Oxford, England: Blackwell.

Royer, J. M. (1979). Theories of the transfer of learning. *Educational Psychologist, 14,* 53–72.

Royer, J. M., & Cable, G. W. (1975). Facilitated learning in connected discourse. *Journal of Educational Psychology, 67*(1), 116–123.

Royer, J. M., & Cable, G. W. (1976). Illustrations, analogies, and facilitative transfer in prose learning. *Journal of Educational Psychology, 68*(2), 205–209.

Rubin, B. C. (2006). Tracking and detracking: Debates, evidence, and best practices for a heterogeneous world. *Theory Into Practice, 45*(1), 4–14.

Rubin, L. J. (1985). *Artistry in teaching.* New York: Random House.

Ruggiero, V. R. (1988). *Teaching thinking across the curriculum.* New York: Harper & Row.

Ruggiero, V. R. (2009). *The art of thinking: A guide to critical and creative thought* (9th ed.). New York: Pearson/Longman.

Ruhland, S. K., & Bremer, C. D. (2002). Professional development needs of novice career and technical educational teachers. *Journal of Career and Technical Education, 19*(1), 18–31.

Rummel, N., Levin, J. R., & Woodward, M. M. (2003). Do pictorial mnemonic text-learning aids give students something worth writing about? *Journal of Educational Psychology, 95*(2), 327–334.

Russell, N. M. (2007). Teaching more than English: Connecting ESL students to their community through service learning. *Phi Delta Kappan, 88*(10), 770–771.

Russo, A. (2002). Mixing technology and testing. *School Administrator, 59*(4), 6–12.

Rutledge, M. (1997). Reading the subtext on gender. *Educational Leadership, 54*(7), 71–73.

Ryan, A. M., & Patrick, H. (2001). The classroom social environment and changes in adolescents' motivation and engagement during middle school. *American Educational Research Journal, 38*(2), 437–460.

Rycek, R. F., Stuhr, S. L., & McDermott, J. (1998). Adolescent egocentrism and cognitive functioning during late adolescence. *Adolescence, 33*(132), 745–749.

Sadker, D. M., Sadker, M. P., & Zittleman, K. R. (2008). *Teachers, schools, and society* (8th ed.). Boston: McGraw-Hill.

Sadker, D., & Zittleman, K. (2004). Test anxiety: Are students failing tests—or are tests failing students? *Phi Delta Kappan, 85*(10), 740–744, 751.

Sadoski, M., Goetz, E. T., & Rodriguez, M. (2000). Engaging texts: Effects of concreteness on comprehensibility, interest, and recall in four text types. *Journal of Educational Psychology, 92*(1), 85–95.

Sadoski, M., & Paivio, A. (2007). Toward a unified theory of reading. *Scientific Studies of Reading, 11*(4), 337–356.

Saka, Y., Southerland, S., & Brooks, J. (2009). Becoming a member of a school community while working toward science education reform: Teacher induction from a cultural historical activity theory (CHAT) perspective. *Science Education, 93*(6), 996–1025.

Saleh, M., Lazonder, A. W., & De Jong, T. (2005). Effects of within-class ability grouping on social interaction, achievement, and motivation. *Instructional Science, 33*(2), 105–199.

Salmon, M., & Akaran, S. E. (2001). Enrich your kindergarten program with a cross-cultural connection. *Young Children, 56*(4), 30–32.

Salomon, G. (1988). AI in reverse: Computer tools that turn cognitive. *Journal of Educational Computing Research, 4*(2), 123–139.

Salomon, G., Globerson, T., & Guterman, E. (1989). The computer as a zone of proximal development: Internalizing reading-related metacognitions from a reading partner. *Journal of Educational Psychology, 81*(4), 620–627.

Salomon, G., and Perkins, D. N. (1989). Rocky roads to transfer: Rethinking mechanisms of a neglected phenomenon. *Educational Psychologist, 24*(2), 113–142.

Saltzman, J. (2003, July 20). Reinstating two-way bilingual ed is hailed. *Boston Globe* (Globe West section), 1.

Sameroff, A., & McDonough, S. C. (1994). Educational implications of developmental transitions: Revisiting the 5- to 7-year shift. *Phi Delta Kappan, 76*(3), 189–193.

Samuelson, J. (2006). The new rigor: Beyond the right answer. *Academy of Management Learning and Education Archive, 5*(3), 356–365.

Santamaria, L. (2009). Culturally responsive differentiated instruction: Narrowing gaps between best pedagogical practices benefiting all learners. *Teachers College Record, 111*(1), 214–247.

Sapon-Shevin, M. (2003). Inclusion: A matter of social justice. *Educational Leadership, 61*(2), 25–28.

Sarason, S. B. (1993). *The case for change: Rethinking the preparation of educators.* San Francisco: Jossey-Bass.

Sarason, S. B. (2005). *Letters to a serious education president* (2nd ed.). Thousand Oaks, CA: Corwin Press.

Sato, M., Chung Wei, R., & Darling-Hammond, L. (2008). Improving teacher's assessment practices through professional development: The case of National Board Certification. *American Educational Research Journal, 45*(3), 669–700.

Savage, R., Lavers, N., & Pillay, V. (2007). Working memory and reading difficulties: What we know and what we don't know about the relationship. *Educational Psychology Review, 19*(2), 185–221.

Scardamalia, M. (2004). CSILE/Knowledge Forum. In *Education and technology: An encyclopedia* (pp. 183–192). Santa Barbara: ABC-CLIO.

Scardamalia, M., & Bereiter, C. (1991). Higher levels of agency for children in knowledge building: A challenge for the design of new knowledge media. *Journal of the Learning Sciences, 1*(1), 37–68.

Scardamalia, M., & Bereiter, C. (1996). Computer support for knowledge-building communities. In T. Koschmann (Ed.), *CSCL: Theory and practice* (pp. 249–268). Mahwah, NJ: Erlbaum.

Scarr, S., Weinberg, R. A., & Levine, A. (1986), *Understanding development*. San Diego, CA: Harcourt Brace Jovanovich.

Schalock, R., Borthwick-Duffy, S., Bradley, V., Buntinx, W., Coulter, D., Craig, E., Gomez, S., Lachapelle, Y., Luckasson, R., Reeve, A., Shogren, K., Snell, M., Spreat, S., Tassé, M., Thompson, J., Verdugo-Alonso, M., Wehmeyer, M., & Yeager, M. (2010). *Intellectual disability: Definition, classification, and systems of supports* (11th ed.). Washington, DC: American Association on Intellectual and Developmental Disabilities.

Schellenberg, E. G. (2006a). Exposure to music: The truth about the consequences. In G. E. McPherson (Ed.), *The child as musician: The handbook of musical development*. Oxford, England: Oxford University Press.

Schellenberg, E. G. (2006b). Long-term positive associations between music and IQ. *Journal of Educational Psychology, 98*(2), 457–468.

Schlagmüller, M., & Schneider, W. (2002). The development of organizational strategies in children: Evidence from a microgenetic longitudinal study. *Journal of Experimental Child Psychology, 81*(3), 298–319.

Schmidt, L. (2003). Getting smarter about supervising instruction. *Principal, 82*(4), 24–28.

Schmidt, P. (2003). The label "Hispanic" irks some, but also unites. *Chronicle of Higher Education, 50*(14), p. A9.

Schmitz, M. J., & Winksel, H. (2008). Towards effective partnerships in collaborative problem-solving task. *British Journal of Educational Psychology, 78*(4), 581–596.

Schneider, M. (2006, February). *Comments delivered to the American Enterprise Institute for Public Policy Research.* Retrieved from http://nces.ed.gov/whatsnew/commissioner/remarks2006/2_6_2006.asp.

Schneider, W. (2002). Memory development in childhood. In U. Goswami (Ed.), *Blackwell handbook of childhood cognitive development* (pp. 236–256). Malden, MA: Blackwell.

Schneider, W. (2010). Metacognition and memory development in childhood and adolescence. In H. S. Waters & W. Schneider (Eds.), *Metacognition, strategy use, and instruction* (pp. 5–81). New York: Guilford Press.

Schneider, W., Knopf, M., & Stefanek, J. (2002). The development of verbal memory in childhood and adolescence: Findings from the Munich longitudinal study. *Journal of Educational Psychology, 94*(4), 751–761.

Schommer-Aikins, M., Duell, O. K., & Hutter, R. (2005). Epistemological beliefs, mathematical problem-solving beliefs, and academic performance of middle school students. *Elementary School Journal, 105*(3), 289–304.

Schraw, G., Flowerday, T., & Lehman, S. (2001). Increasing situational interest in the classroom. *Educational Psychology Review, 13*(3), 211–224.

Schunk, D. H. (1987). Peer models and children's behavioral change. *Review of Educational Research, 57*(2), 149–174.

Schunk, D. H. (1998). Teaching elementary students to self-regulate practice of mathematical skills with modeling. In D. H. Schunk & B. J. Zimmerman (Eds.), *Self-regulated learning: From teaching to self-reflective practice* (pp. 137–159). New York: Guilford Press.

Schunk, D. H. (2001). Social cognitive theory and self-regulated learning. In B. J. Zimmerman & D. H. Schunk (Eds.), *Self-regulated learning and academic achievement: Theoretical perspectives* (pp. 125–151). Mahwah, NJ: Erlbaum.

Schunk, D. H. (2004). *Learning theories: An educational perspective* (4th ed.). Upper Saddle River, NJ: Merrill Prentice Hall.

Schunk, D. H., & Hanson, A. R. (1985). Peer models: Influence on children's self-efficacy and achievement. *Journal of Educational Psychology, 77*(3), 313–322.

Schunk, D. H., Hanson, A. R., & Cox, P. D. (1987). Peer model attributes and children's achievement behaviors. *Journal of Educational Psychology, 79*(1), 54–61.

Schunk, D. H., & Pajares, F. (2002). The development of academic self-efficacy. In A. Wigfield & J. Eccles (Eds.), *The development of achievement motivation* (pp. 16–31). San Diego, CA: Academic Press.

Schwartz, B. L. (2011). *Memory: Foundations and applications.* Thousand Oaks, CA: Sage.

Schwartz, D., Gorman, A. H., Nakamoto, J., & Toblin, R. L. (2005). Victimization in the peer group and children's academic functioning. *Journal of Educational Psychology, 97*(3), 425–435.

Schwartz, D., Lindgren, R., & Lewis, S. (2009). Constructivism in an age of non-constructivist assessments. In S. Tobias & T. Duffy (Eds.), *Constructivist instruction: Success or failure?* (pp. 34–61). New York: Routledge.

Schwartz, S. J., Zamboanga, B. L., Weisskirch, R. S., & Wang, S. C. (2010). The relationships of personal and cultural identity to adaptive and maladaptive psychosocial functioning in emerging adults. *Journal of Social Psychology, 150*(1), 1–33.

Schweinhart, L. J., Weikart, D. P., & Hohmann, M. (2002). The High/Scope preschool curriculum: What is it? Why use it? *Journal of At-Risk Issues, 8*(1), 13–16.

Scigliano, D. (Ed.). (2010). *Telementoring in the K-12 classroom.* Hershey, PA: IGI Global.

Scott, S., McGuire, J., & Shaw, S. (2003). Universal design for instruction: A new design for adult instruction in postsecondary settings. *Remedial and Special Education, 24*(6), 369–379.

Scriven, M. (1967). The methodology of evaluation. In R. Tyler, R. Gagne, & M. Scriven (Eds.), *Perspectives in curriculum evaluation*. Chicago: Rand McNally.

Seabrook, R., Brown, G. A., & Solity, J. E. (2005). Distributed and massed practice: From laboratory to classroom. *Applied Cognitive Psychology, 19*(1), 107–122.

Seagoe, M. V. (1975). *Terman and the gifted.* Los Altos, CA: Kaufmann.

Seaton, M., Marsh, H. W., & Craven, R. G. (2010). Big-fish-little-pond effect: Generalizability and moderation—two sides of the same win. *American Educational Research Journal, 47*(2), 390–433.

Seddon, F. A., & O'Neill, S. A. (2006). How does formal instrumental music tuition (FIMT) impact on self- and teacher-evaluations of adolescents' computer-based compositions? *Psychology of Music, 34*(1), 27–45.

Seezink, A., Poell, R., & Kirschner, P. (2009). Teachers' individual action theories about competence-based education: The value of the cognitive apprenticeship model. *Journal of Vocational Education and Training, 61*(2), 203–215.

Selman, R. L. (1980). *The growth of interpersonal understanding: Developmental and clinical analyses.* New York: Academic Press.

Shachar, H., & Fischer, S. (2004). Cooperative learning and the achievement of motivation and perceptions of students in 11th grade chemistry classrooms. *Learning and Instruction, 14*(1), 69–87.

Shaffer, D., & Kipp, K. (2010). *Developmental psychology: Childhood and adolescence* (8th ed.). Belmont, CA: Wadsworth/Cengage Learning.

Sharan, S. (1995). Group investigation: Theoretical foundations. In J. E. Pedersen & A. D. Digby (Eds.), *Secondary schools and cooperative learning* (pp. 251–277). New York: Garland.

Sharan, Y., & Sharan, S. (1999). Group investigation in the cooperative classroom. In S. Sharan (Ed.), *Handbook of cooperative learning methods* (pp. 97–114). Westport, CT: Greenwood Press.

Shariff, S. (2008). *Cyber-bullying: Issues and solutions for the school, the classroom, and the home.* New York: Routledge.

Shayer, M. (1997). Piaget and Vygotsky: A necessary marriage for effective educational interventions. In L. Smith, J. Dockrell, & P. Tomlinson (Eds.), *Piaget, Vygotsky, and beyond.* London: Routledge.

Shayer, M. (1999). Cognitive acceleration through science education II: Its effects and scope. *International Journal of Science Education, 21*(8), 883–902.

Shepard, R. N. (1978). Externalization of mental images and the act of creation. In B. S. Randhawa & W. E. Coffman (Eds.), *Visual learning, thinking, and communication.* New York: Academic Press.

Shernoff, D. J., Csikszentmihalyi, M., Schneider, B., & Shernoff, E. S. (2003). Student engagement in high school classrooms from the perspective of flow theory. *School Psychology Quarterly, 18*(2), 158–176.

Sherry, L., & Billig, S. H. (2002). Redefining a "virtual community of learners." *TechTrends, 46*(1), 48–51.

Shin, D. (2009). The evaluation of user experience of the virtual world in relation to extrinsic and intrinsic motivation. *International Journal of Human–Computer Interaction, 25*(6), 530–553.

Shulman, L. S. (2007). Counting and recounting: Assessment and the quest for accountability. *Change, 39*(1), 20–25.

Shure, M. B. (1999, April). Preventing violence the problem-solving way. *OJJDP Juvenile Justice Bulletin.* Retrieved from http://www.ojjdp.gov/jjbulletin/9904_1/contents.html.

Siegel, M. A., & Kirkley, S. E. (1998). Adventure learning as a vision of the digital learning environment. In C. J. Bonk & K. S. King (Eds.), *Electronic collaborators: Learner-centered technologies for literacy, apprenticeship, and discourse* (pp. 341–364). Mahwah, NJ: Erlbaum.

Siegle, D. (2002). Creating a living portfolio: Documenting student growth with electronic portfolios. *Gifted Child Today, 25*(3), 60–63.

Siegler, R. S. (1996). *Emerging minds: The process of change in children's thinking.* New York: Oxford University Press.

Siegler, R. S. (1998). *Children's thinking* (3rd ed.). Upper Saddle River, NJ: Prentice Hall.

Siegler, R. S., & Svetina, M. (2006). What leads children to adopt new strategies? A microgenetic/cross-sectional study of class inclusion. *Child Development, 77*(4), 997–1015.

Sigelman, C. K., & Shaffer, D. R. (1991). *Life-span human development.* Pacific Grove, CA: Brooks/Cole.

Simon, S. (2002). The CASE approach for pupils with learning difficulties. *School Science Review, 83*(305), 73–79.

Simonsen, B., Fairbanks, S., Briesch, A., Myers, D., & Sugai, G. (2008). Evidence-based practices in classroom management: Considerations for research to practice. *Education and Treatment of Children, 31*(3), 351–380.

Simpson, E. J. (1972). *The classification of educational objectives: Psychomotor domain.* Urbana: University of Illinois Press.

Singer, A. (1994). Reflections on multiculturalism. *Phi Delta Kappan, 76*(4), 284–288.

Singer, D. G., & Revenson, T. A. (1996). *A Piaget primer: How a child thinks* (rev. ed.). New York: Plume.

Sipe, R. B. (2000). Virtually being there: Creating authentic experiences through interactive exchanges. *English Journal, 90*(2), 104–111.

Skiba, R., Reynolds, C. R., Graham, S., Sheras, P., Conoley, J. C., & Garcia-Vazquez, E. (2006, February). *Are zero tolerance policies effective in the schools? An evidentiary review and recommendations.* A report by the American Psychological Association Zero Tolerance Task Force. Retrieved from http://www.apa.org/pubs/info/reports/zero-tolerance.pdf.

Skinner, B. F. (1984). The shame of American education. *American Psychologist, 39*(9), 947–954.

Slavin, R. E. (1994). Student teams—achievement divisions. In S. Sharan (Ed.), *Handbook of cooperative learning methods* (pp. 3–19). Westport, CT: Greenwood Press.

Slavin, R. E. (1995). *Cooperative learning: Theory, research, and practice* (2nd ed.). Boston: Allyn & Bacon.

Slavin, R. E. (2002). Evidence-based education policies: Transforming educational practice and research. *Educational Researcher, 31*(7), 15–21.

Slavin, R. E. (2008). What works? Issues in synthesizing educational program evaluations. *Educational Researcher, 37*(1), 5–14.

Slavin, R. E., & Cheung, A. (2005). A synthesis of research on language of reading instruction for English language learners. *Review of Educational Research, 75*(2), 247–284.

Slavin, R. E., Lake, C., & Groff, C. (2009). Effective programs in middle and high school mathematics: A best-evidence synthesis. *Review of Educational Research, 79*(2), 839–911.

Slavin, R. E., Madden, N. A., Chambers, B., & Haxby, B. (2009). *2 million children* (2nd ed.). Thousand Oaks, CA: Corwin Press.

Sleeter, C. E., & Grant, C. A. (2009). *Making choices for multicultural education* (6th ed.). Hoboken, NJ: John Wiley & Sons.

Slotta, J., & Linn, M. (2009). *WISE science: Web-based inquiry in the classroom.* New York: Teachers College Press.

Smith, D. D., & Tyler, N. C. (2010). *Introduction to special education: Making a difference* (7th ed.). Upper Saddle River, NJ: Merrill/Pearson.

Smith, L. (2002). Piaget's model. In U. Goswami (Ed.), *Blackwell handbook of childhood cognitive development* (pp. 515–537). Oxford, England: Blackwell.

Smith, P. K. (2005). Play. In B. Hopkins, R. G. Barr, G. F. Michel, & P. Rochat (Eds.), *The Cambridge encyclopedia of child development* (pp. 344–347). Cambridge, England: Cambridge University Press.

Smoot, B. (2010). *Conversations with great teachers.* Bloomington: Indiana University Press.

Snowman, J. (1986). Learning tactics and strategies. In G. D. Phye & T. Andre (Eds.), *Cognitive classroom learning: Understanding, thinking, and problem solving.* New York: Academic Press.

Sobel, D. M., Taylor, S. V., & Anderson, R. E. (2003). Shared accountability: Encouraging diversity—responsive teaching in inclusive contexts. *Teaching Exceptional Children, 35*(6), 46–54.

Soldier, L. L. (1997). Is there an "Indian" in your classroom? Working successfully with urban Native American students. *Phi Delta Kappan, 78*(8), 650–653.

Solórzano, R. W. (2008). High stakes testing: Issues, implications, and remedies for English language learners. *Review of Educational Research, 78*(2), 260–329.

Sorell, G. T., & Montgomery, M. J. (2001). Feminist perspectives on Erikson's theory: Their relevance for contemporary identity development research. *Identity, 1*(2), 97–128.

Spear-Swerling, L., & Sternberg, R. J. (1998). Curing our "epidemic" of learning disabilities. *Phi Delta Kappan, 79*(5), 397–401.

Spector, J. M. (2006). A methodology for assessing learning in complex and ill structured task domains. *Innovations in Education and Teaching International, 43*(2), 109–120.

Spitz, H. H. (1999). Beleaguered Pygmalion: A history of the controversy over claims that teacher expectancy raises intelligence. *Intelligence, 27*(3), 199–234.

Sprinthall, N. A., & Sprinthall, R. C. (1987). *Educational psychology: A developmental approach* (4th ed.). New York: Random House.

Sprinthall, N. A., Sprinthall, R. C., & Oja, S. N. (1998). *Educational psychology: A developmental approach* (7th ed.). New York: McGraw-Hill.

Stage, S. A., & Quiroz, D. R. (1997). A meta-analysis of interventions to decrease disruptive classroom behavior in public education settings. *School Psychology Review, 26*(3), 333–368.

Standing, L., Conezio, J., & Haber, R. (1970). Perception and memory for pictures: Single trial learning of 2500 visual stimuli. *Psychonomic Science, 19*(2), 73–74.

Starnes, B. A. (2006). What we don't know *can* hurt them: White teachers, Indian children. *Phi Delta Kappan, 87*(5), 384–392.

Stears, M. (2009). How social and critical constructivism can inform science curriculum design: A study from South Africa. *Educational Research, 51*(4), 397–410.

Steinberg, L. (1996). *Beyond the classroom: Why school reform has failed and what parents need to do.* New York: Simon & Schuster

Steinberg, L. (2008). *Adolescence* (8th ed.). New York: McGraw-Hill Higher Education.

Steinberg, L., & Morris, A. S. (2001). Adolescent development. In S. T. Fiske, D. L. Schacter, & C. Zahn-Waxler (Eds.), *Annual review of psychology, 52,* 83–110.

Steinberg, L., Vandell, D. L., & Bornstein, M. H. (2011). *Development: Infancy through adolescence.* Belmont, CA: Wadsworth/ Cengage Learning.

Stemler, S. E., Sternberg, R. J., Grigorenko, E. L., Jarvin, L., & Sharpes, K. (2009). Using the theory of successful intelligence as a framework for developing assessments in AP Physics. *Contemporary Educational Psychology, 34*(3), 195–209.

Stepanek, J., and Peixotto, K. (2009). *Models of response to intervention in the Northwest Region states* (Issues & Answers Report, REL 2009–No. 079). Washington, DC: U.S. Department of Education, Institute of Education Sciences, National Center for Education Evaluation and Regional Assistance, Regional Educational Laboratory Northwest. Retrieved from http://ies.ed.gov/ ncee/edlabs/regions/northwest/pdf/REL_2009079_sum.pdf.

Sternberg, R. J. (1994). Allowing for thinking styles. *Educational Leadership, 52*(3), 36–40.

Sternberg, R. J. (1996). Matching abilities, instruction, and assessment: Reawakening the sleeping giant of ATI. In I. Dennis & P. Tapsfield (Eds.), *Human abilities: Their nature and measurement* (pp. 167–181). Mahwah, NJ: Erlbaum.

Sternberg, R. J. (1997a). Technology changes intelligence: Societal implications and soaring IQ's. *Technos, 6*(2), 12–14.

Sternberg, R. J. (1997b). What does it mean to be smart? *Educational Leadership, 54*(6), 20–24.

Sternberg, R. J. (2002a). Intelligence is not just inside the head: The theory of successful intelligence. In J. Aronson (Ed.), *Improving academic achievement* (pp. 227–244). San Diego, CA: Academic Press.

Sternberg, R. J. (2002b). Raising the achievement of all students: Teaching for successful intelligence. *Educational Psychology Review, 14*(4), 383–393.

Sternberg, R. J. (2003). Construct validity of the theory of successful intelligence. In R. J. Sternberg, J. Lautrey, & T. I. Lubart (Eds.), *Models of intelligence: International perspectives* (pp. 55–77). Washington, DC: American Psychological Association.

Sternberg, R. J. (2008). The answer depends on the question: A reply to Jensen. *Phi Delta Kappan, 89*(6), 418–420.

Sternberg, R. J. (2009). Domain-generality versus domain-specificity of creativity. In P. Meusburger, J. Funke, & E. Wunder (Eds.), *Milieus of creativity: An interdisciplinary approach to spatiality and creativity* (pp. 25–38). Dordrecht, Netherlands: Springer.

Sternberg, R. J., & Grigorenko, E. L. (2004). Successful intelligence in the classroom. *Theory Into Practice, 43*(4), 274–280.

Sternberg, R. J., Grigorenko, E. L., & Zhang, L. (2008). Styles of learning and thinking matter in instruction and assessment. *Perspectives on Psychological Science, 3*(6), 486–506.

Sternberg, R. J., Jarvin, L., & Grigorenko, E. L. (2009). *Teaching for wisdom, intelligence, creativity, and success.* Thousand Oaks, CA: Corwin Press.

Steubing, K. K., Fletcher, J. M., LeDoux, J. M., Lyon, G. R., Shaywitz, S. E., & Shaywitz, B. A. (2002). Validity of IQ-discrepancy classifications of reading disabilities: A meta-analysis. *American Educational Research Journal, 39*(2), 469–518.

Stewart, E. B., Stewart, E. A., & Simons, R. L. (2007). The effect of neighborhood context on the college aspirations of African American adolescents. *American Educational Research Journal, 44*(4), 896–919.

Stier, H., Lewin-Epstein, N., & Braun, B. (2001). Welfare regimes, family-supportive policies, and women's employment along the life-course. *American Journal of Sociology, 106*(6), 1731–1760.

Stiggins, R. J. (2001). The unfulfilled promise of classroom assessment. *Educational Measurement: Issues and Practice, 20*(3), 5–15.

Stiggins, R. J. (2002). Assessment crisis: The absences of assessment FOR learning. *Phi Delta Kappan, 83*(10), 758–765.

Stiggins, R. J. (2007). *An introduction to student-involved assessment for learning* (5th ed.). Upper Saddle River, NJ: Merrill Prentice Hall.

Stiggins, R. J., Arter, J., Chappuis, J., & Chappuis, S. (2007). *Classroom assessment for student learning: Doing it right—using it well.* Upper Saddle River, NJ: Merrill/ Pearson.

Stinson, N., Jr. (2003, August). Working toward our goal: Eliminating racial and ethnic disparities in health. *Closing the Gap, Working Toward Our Goal,* 1–2. Retrieved from http://minorityhealth.hhs .gov/assets/pdf/checked/Working%20Toward%20Our%20Goal —Eliminating%20Racial%20and%20Ethnic%20Disparities%20 in%20Health.pdf.

Stipek, D. (2002). *Motivation to learn: Integrating theory and practice* (4th ed.). Boston: Allyn & Bacon.

Stokes, V. (2005). No longer a year behind. *Learning and Leading with Technology, 33*(2), 15–17.

Strassman, B. K., & D'Amore, M. (2002). The write technology. *Teaching Exceptional Children, 34*(6), 28–31.

Stull, A. T., & Mayer, R. E. (2007). Learning by doing versus learning by viewing: Three experimental comparisons of learner-generated versus author-provided graphic organizers. *Journal of Educational Psychology, 99*(4), 808–820.

Sun, K.-T., Lin, Y., & Yu, C. (2008). A study on learning effect among different learning styles in a web-based lab of science for elementary school students. *Computers & Education, 50*(4), 1411–1422.

Sunderman, G. L. (2006, February). *The unraveling of No Child Left Behind: How negotiated changes transform the law.* Cambridge, MA: The Civil Rights Project at Harvard University. Retrieved from http://civilrightsproject.ucla.edu/research/k-12-education/ nclb-title-i/the-unraveling-of-no-child-left-behind/NCLB_Unravel .pdf.

Suomala, J., & Alajaaski, J. (2002). Pupils' problem-solving processes in a complex computerized learning environment. *Journal of Educational Computing Research, 26*(2), 155–176.

Swalander, L., & Taube, K. (2007). Influences of family based prerequisites, reading attitude, and self-regulation on reading ability. *Contemporary Educational Psychology, 32*(2), 206–230.

Swanson, C. B. (2004). *Who graduates? Who doesn't? A statistical portrait of public high school graduation, class of 2001.* Washington, DC: The Urban Institute. Retrieved from http://www.urban .org/UploadedPDF/410934_WhoGraduates.pdf.

Swanson, H. L., & Hoskyn, M. (1998). Experimental intervention research on students with learning disabilities: A meta-analysis of treatment outcomes. *Review of Educational Research, 68*(3), 277–321.

Tabachnick, S., Miller, R., & Relyea, G. (2008). The relationships among students' future-oriented goals and subgoals, perceived task instrumentality, and task-oriented self-regulation strategies in an academic environment. *Journal of Educational Psychology, 100*(3), 629–642.

Tappan, M. B. (1998). Sociocultural psychology and caring pedagogy: Exploring Vygotsky's "hidden curriculum." *Educational Psychologist, 33*(1), 23–33.

Tappan, M. B. (2005). Mediated moralities: Sociocultural approaches to moral development. In M. Killen & J. Smetana (Eds.), *Handbook of moral development.* Hillsdale, NJ: Erlbaum.

Tappan, M. B. (2006). Moral functioning as mediated action. *Journal of Moral Education, 35*(1), 1–18.

Tauber, R. T., & Mester, C. S. (2006). *Acting lessons for teachers: Using performance skills in the classroom* (2nd ed.). Westport, CT: Praeger.

Taylor, A. Z., & Graham, S. (2007). An examination of the relationship between achievement values and perceptions of barriers among low-SES African American and Latino students. *Journal of Educational Psychology, 99*(1), 52–64.

Taylor, D., & Lorimer, M. (2002/2003). Helping boys succeed. *Educational Leadership, 60*(4), 68–70.

Taylor, P. (1996). Mythmaking and mythbreaking in the mathematics classroom. *Educational Studies in Mathematics, 31*(1–2), 151–173.

Taylor, P. C., & Fraser, B. J. (1998). *The constructivist learning environment survey: Mark 2.* Perth, Australia: Science and Mathematics Education Centre, Curtin University of Technology.

Taylor, P. C., Fraser, B. J., & Fisher, D. L. (1997). Monitoring constructivist classroom learning environments. *International Journal of Educational Research, 27*(4), 293–301.

Tenenbaum, H. R., & Ruck, M. D. (2007). Are teachers' expectations different for racial minority than for European American students? A meta-analysis. *Journal of Educational Psychology, 99*(2), 253–273.

Tennessee Department of Education. (2006, July 20). *Schools to use technology to enhance achievement.* Retrieved from http://tennessee.gov/education/news/nr/2006/07_20_06.shtml.

Thoma, S. J. (1986). Estimating gender differences in the comprehension and preference of moral issues. *Developmental Review, 6*(2), 165–180.

Thomas B. Fordham Institute. (2008, June). *High-achieving students in the era of NCLB.* Retrieved from http://www.nagc.org/uploadedFiles/News_Room/NAGC_Advocacy_in_the_News/Fordham.pdf.

Thomas, J. (2005). Calling a cab for Oregon students. *Phi Delta Kappan, 86*(5), 385–388.

Thomas, M., Barab, S., & Tuzun, H. (2009). Developing critical implementations of technology-rich innovations: A cross-case study of the implementation of Quest Atlantis. *Journal of Educational Computing Research, 41*(2), 125–153.

Thomas, V. G. (2000). Learner-centered alternatives to social promotion and retention: A talent development approach. *Journal of Negro Education, 69*(4), 323–337.

Thomas, W. P., & Collier, V. P. (1997/1998). Two languages are better than one. *Educational Leadership, 55*(4), 23–26.

Thomas, W. P., & Collier, V. P. (1999). Accelerated schooling for English language learners. *Educational Leadership, 56*(7), 46–49.

Thompson, M. S., DiCerbo, K. E., Mahoney, K., & MacSwan, J. (2002, January 25). ¿Exito en California? A validity critique of language program evaluations and analysis of English learner test scores. *Education Policy Analysis Archives, 10*(7). Retrieved from http://epaa.asu.edu/ojs/article/view/286.

Thorn, A., & Page, M. (2009). *Interactions between short-term and long-term memory in the verbal domain.* New York: Psychology Press.

Thrash, T., & Hurst, A. (2008). Approach and avoidance motivation in the achievement domain: Integrating the achievement motive and the achievement goal traditions. In A. Elliot (Ed.), *Handbook of approach and avoidance motivation* (pp. 217–234). New York: Taylor & Francis.

Tieso, C. L. (2003). Ability grouping is not just tracking anymore. *Roeper Review, 26*(1), 29–39.

Tingstrom, D. H., Sterling-Turner, H. E., & Wilczynski, S. M. (2006). The Good Behavior Game: 1969–2002. *Behavior Modification, 30*(2), 225–253.

Tobias, S., & Duffy, T. (2009). The success or failure of constructivist instruction: An introduction. In S. Tobias & T. Duffy (Eds.), *Constructivist instruction: Success or failure?* (pp. 3–10). New York: Routledge.

Toch, T. (2003). *High schools on a human scale.* Boston: Beacon Press.

Tomlinson, C. A. (2002). Invitations to learn. *Educational Leadership, 60*(1), 6–10.

Tomlinson, C. A. (2007/2008). Learning to love assessment. *Educational Leadership, 65*(4), 8–13.

Tomlinson, C. A., Brimijoin, K., & Narvaez, L. (2008). *The differentiated school: Making revolutionary changes in teaching and learning.* Alexandria, VA: ASCD.

Tomporowski, P. D., Davis, C. L., Miller, P. H., & Naglieri, J. A. (2008). Exercise and children's intelligence, cognition, and academic achievement. *Educational Psychology Review, 20*(2), 111–131.

Tong, F., Lara-Alecio, R., Irby, B., Mathes, P., & Kwok, O. (2008). Accelerating early academic oral English development in transitional bilingual and structured English immersion programs. *American Educational Research Journal, 45*(4), 1011–1044.

Toth, K., & King, B. (2010). Intellectual disability (mental retardation). In M. K. Dulcan (Ed.), *Textbook of child and adolescent psychiatry* (pp. 151–172). Arlington, VA: American Psychiatric Publishing.

Trautwein, U., & Lüdtke, O. (2007). Epistemological beliefs, school achievement, and college major: A large-scale longitudinal study on the impact of certainty beliefs. *Contemporary Educational Psychology, 32*(6), 348–366.

Trautwein, U., Lüdtke, O., Köller, O., & Baumert, J. (2006). Self-esteem, academic self-concept, and achievement: How the learning environment moderates the dynamics of self-concept. *Journal of Personality and Social Psychology, 90*(2), 334–349.

Trevisan, M. S. (2002). The states' role in ensuring assessment competence. *Phi Delta Kappan, 83*(10), 766–771.

Triandis, H. C. (1986). Toward pluralism in education. In S. Modgil, G. K. Verma, K. Mallick, & C. Modgil (Eds.), *Multicultural education: The interminable debate.* London: Falmer.

Troyer, L., & Youngreen, R. (2009). Conflict and creativity in groups. *Journal of Social Issues, 65*(2), 409–427.

Trumper, R., & Gelbman, M. (2000). Investigating electromagnetic induction through a microcomputer-based laboratory. *Physics Education, 35*(2), 90–95.

Trumper, R., & Gelbman, M. (2002). Using MBL to verify Newton's second law and the impulse–momentum relationship with an arbitrary changing force. *School Science Review, 83*(305), 135–139.

Tudge, J. R. H., & Rogoff, B. (1989). Peer influences on cognitive development: Piagetian and Vygotskian perspectives. In M. H. Bornstein & J. S. Bruner (Eds.), *Interaction in human development.* Hillsdale, NJ: Erlbaum.

Tudge, J. R. H., & Scrimsher, S. (2003). Lev S. Vygotsky on education: A cultural-historical, interpersonal, and individual approach to development. In B. J. Zimmerman & D. H. Schunk (Eds.), *Educational psychology: A century of contributions.* Mahwah, NJ: Erlbaum.

Tudge, J. R. H., & Winterhoff, P. A. (1993). Vygotsky, Piaget, and Bandura: Perspectives on the relations between the social world and cognitive development. *Human Development, 36*(2), 61–81.

Tukey, L. (2002). Differentiation. *Phi Delta Kappan, 84*(1), 63–64, 92.

Tulving, E., & Pearlstone, Z. (1966). Availability vs. accessibility of information in memory for words. *Journal of Verbal Learning and Verbal Behavior, 5*(4), 381–391.

Turiel, E. (2008). The trouble with the ways morality is used and how they impede social equity and social justice. In C. Wainryb, J. G. Smetana, & E. Turiel (Eds.), *Social development, social inequalities, and social justice* (pp. 1–26). Mahwah, NJ: Erlbaum.

Umar, K. B. (2003, August). Disparities persist in infant mortality: Creative approaches work to close the gap. *Closing the Gap, Working Toward Our Goal,* 4–5. Retrieved from http://minorityhealth.hhs.gov/assets/pdf/checked/Disparities%20Persist%20in%20Infant%20Mortality--Creative%20Approaches%20Work%20to%20Close%20the%20Gap.pdf.

Urdan, T., & Mestas, M. (2006). The goals behind performance goals. *Journal of Educational Psychology, 98*(2), 354–365.

Urdan, T., & Midgley, C. (2001). Academic self-handicapping: What we know, what more there is to learn. *Educational Psychology Review, 13*(2), 115–138.

Urdan, T., Ryan, A. M., Anderman, E. M., & Gheen, M. H. (2002). Goals, goal structures, and avoidance behaviors. In C. Midgley (Ed.), *Goals, goal structures, and patterns of adaptive learning* (pp. 55–83). Mahwah, NJ: Erlbaum.

U.S. Census Bureau. (2008a, August). *Fertility of American women: 2006.* Retrieved from http://www.census.gov/prod/2008pubs/p20-558.pdf.

U.S. Census Bureau (2008b, August). *U.S. population projections: 2008 national population projections.* Retrieved from http://www.census.gov/population/www/projections/ summarytables.html.

U.S. Census Bureau. (2009). *Number in poverty and poverty rates by race and Hispanic origin using 2- and 3-year averages: 2003 to 2005.* Retrieved from http://www.census.gov/hhes/www/poverty/data/incpovhlth/2005/table5.html.

U.S. Department of Education. (2004). *Individuals with Disabilities Education Improvement Act of 2004.* Retrieved October 17, 2006, from www2.ed.gov/policy/speced/guid/idea/idea2004.html.

U.S. Department of Education, National Center for Education Statistics (2008a). *NAEP 2008: Trends in academic progress.* Retrieved from http://nces.ed.gov/nationsreportcard/pdf/main2008/2009479.pdf.

U.S. Department of Education. (2008b, March). *Differentiated accountability: A more nuanced system to better target resources.* Retrieved from http://www.ed.gov/nclb/accountability/differentiated/factsheet.pdf.

U.S. Department of Education, Office of Special Education and Rehabilitative Services, Office of Special Education Programs. (2009a). *28th Annual Report to Congress on the Implementation of the Individuals with Disabilities Education Act, 2006* (Vol. 1). Washington, DC: Author.

U.S. Department of Education, Office of Special Education and Rehabilitative Services, Office of Special Education Programs. (2009b). *28th Annual Report to Congress on the Implementation of the Individuals with Disabilities Education Act, 2006* (Vol. 2). Washington, DC: Author.

U.S. Department of Homeland Security. (2008, September). *2007 yearbook of immigration statistics.* Washington, DC: U.S. Department of Homeland Security, Office of Immigration Statistics. Retrieved from http://www.dhs.gov/xlibrary/assets/statistics/yearbook/2007/ois_2007_yearbook.pdf.

U.S. Department of Labor. (2001, October 16). *Occupational classification system manual.* Retrieved from http://www.bls.gov/ncs/ocs/ocsm/comMoga.htm.

Usher, E. L., & Pajares, F. (2008a). Sources of self-efficacy in school: Critical review of the literature and future directions. *Review of Educational Research, 78*(4), 751–796.

Usher, E., & Pajares, F. (2008b). Self-efficacy for self-regulated learning: A validation study. *Educational and Psychological Measurement, 68*(3), 443–463.

Vallecorsa, A. L., deBettencourt, L. U., & Zigmond, N. (2000). *Students with mild disabilities in general education settings.* Upper Saddle River, NJ: Merrill Prentice Hall.

Valli, L., & Buese, D. (2007). The changing roles of teachers in an era of high-stakes accountability. *American Educational Research Journal, 44*(3), 519–558.

VanDerHeyden, A., Witt, J., & Gilbertson, D. (2007). A multi-year evaluation of the effects of a response to intervention (RTI) model of identification of children for special education. *Journal of School Psychology, 45*(2), 225–256.

Van Overschelde, J. (2008). Metacognition: Knowing about knowing. In J. Dunlosky & R. Bjork (Eds.), *Handbook of metamemory and memory* (pp. 47–72). New York: Taylor & Francis.

Van Wagenen, L., & Hibbard, K. M. (1998). Building teacher portfolios. *Educational Leadership, 55*(5), 26–29.

Varma, S., McCandless, B. D., & Schwartz, D. L. (2008). Scientific and pragmatic challenges for bridging education and neuroscience. *Educational Researcher, 37*(3), 140–152.

Vartanian, L. R. (2000). Revisiting the imaginary audience and personal fable constructs of adolescent egocentrism: A conceptual review. *Adolescence, 35*(140), 639–661.

Veenman, S., Denessen, E., van den Akker, A., & van der Rijt, J. (2005). Effects of a cooperative learning program on the elaborations of students during help seeking and help giving. *American Educational Research Journal, 42*(1), 115–151.

Veermans, M., & Cesareni, D. (2005). The nature of the discourse in web-based collaborative learning environments: Case studies from four different countries. *Computers & Education, 45*(3), 316–336.

Vermont Department of Education. (2009). *New England common assessment program (NECAP).* Retrieved from http://education.vermont.gov/new/html/pgm_assessment/necap.html.

Vernez, G., Naftel, S., Ross, K., Le Floch, K. C., Beighley, C., & Gill, G. (2009). *State and local implementation of the No Child Left Behind Act, Vol. VII. Title 1 school choice and supplemental educational services: Final report.* Washington, DC: U.S. Department of Education. Retrieved from http://www2.ed.gov/rschstat/eval/choice/nclb-choice-ses-final/choice-ses-final.pdf.

Vitz, P. C. (1990). The use of stories in moral development: New psychological reasons for an old educational method. *American Psychologist, 45*(6), 709–720.

Vogel, C. (2009). A call for collaboration. *Direct Administration, 25*(5), 22–25.

Vygotsky, L. S. (1962). *Thought and language* (E. Hanfmann & G. Vakar, Trans.). Cambridge, MA: MIT Press. (Original work published 1934.)

Vygotsky, L. S. (1986). *Thought and language* (A. Kozulin, Trans.). Cambridge, MA: MIT Press. (Original work published 1934.)

Wadsworth, B. J. (2004). *Piaget's theory of cognitive and affective development* (5th Classics ed.). Boston: Allyn & Bacon.

Walberg, H. J. (2006). Improving educational productivity: An assessment of extant research. In R. F. Subotnik & H. F. Walberg (Eds.), *The scientific basis of educational productivity.* Greenwich, CT: Information Age.

Walker, C., & Greene, B. (2009). The relations between student motivational beliefs and cognitive engagement in high school. *Journal of Educational Research, 102*(6), 463–472.

Walker, J. E., Shea, T. M., & Bauer, A. M. (2007). *Behavior management: A practical approach for educators* (9th ed.). Upper Saddle River, NJ: Pearson/Merrill Prentice Hall.

Walker, J. M. T., & Hoover-Dempsey, K. V. (2006). Why research on parental involvement is important to classroom management. In C. M. Evertson & C. S. Weinstein (Eds.), *Handbook of classroom management: Research, practice, and contemporary issues* (pp. 665–684). Mahwah, NJ: Erlbaum.

Wallace-Broscious, A., Serafica, F. C., & Osipow, S. H. (1994). Adolescent career development: Relationships to self-concept and identity status. *Journal of Research on Adolescence, 4*(1), 127–149.

Wang, J., Spalding, E., Odell, S., Klecka, C., & Lin, E. (2010). Bold ideas for improving teacher education and teaching: What we see, hear, and think. *Journal of Teacher Education, 61*(1–2), 3–15.

Wang, M. C., Haertel, G. D., & Walberg, H. J. (1993). Toward a knowledge base for school learning. *Review of Educational Research, 63*(3), 249–294.

Wang, M. J., & Kang, M. (2006). Cybergogy for engaged learning: A framework for creating learner engagement through information and communication technology. In D. Hung & M. S. Khine (Eds.), *Engaged learning with emerging technologies* (pp. 225–253). Dordrecht, Netherlands: Springer.

Wang, S., Jiao, H., Young, M. J., Brooks, T., & Olson, J. (2008). Comparability of computer-based and paper-and-pencil testing in K–12 reading assessments. *Educational and Psychological Measurement, 68*(1), 5–24.

Wasserman, S. (1999). Shazam! you're a teacher: Facing the illusory quest for certainty in classroom practice. *Phi Delta Kappan, 80*(6), 464–468.

Watanabe, M. (2008). Tracking in the era of high stakes state accountability reform: Case studies of classroom instruction in North Carolina. *Teachers College Record, 110*(3), 489–534.

Waterman, A. S. (1988). Identity status theory and Erikson's theory: Communalities and differences. *Developmental Review, 8*(2), 185–208.

Waterman, A. S., & Archer, S. L. (1990). A life-span perspective on identity formation: Developments in form, function, and process. In P. B. Baltes, D. L. Featherman, & R. M. Lerner (Eds.), *Life-span development and behavior* (Vol. 10, pp. 30–57). Hillsdale, NJ: Erlbaum.

Waters, H. S., & Kunnmann, T. W. (2010). Metacognition and strategy discovery in early childhood. In H. S. Waters & W. Schneider (Eds.), *Metacognition, strategy use, and instruction* (pp. 3–22). New York: Guilford.

Watkins, C. (2005). *Classrooms as learning communities: What's in it for schools?* London: Routledge.

Watson, J. B. (1913). Psychology as the behaviorist views it. *Psychological Review, 20*, 158–177.

Watson, M. F., & Protinsky, H. (1991). Identity status of black adolescents: An empirical investigation. *Adolescence, 26*(104), 963–966.

Wayne, A. J., & Youngs, P. (2003). Teacher characteristics and student achievement gains: A review. *Review of Educational Research, 73*(1), 89–122.

Wechsler, D. (1975). Intelligence defined and undefined: A relativistic appraisal. *American Psychologist, 30*(2), 135–139.

Wechsler, D. (1997). *Wechsler Adult Intelligence Scale—Third Edition.* New York: Psychological Corporation.

Wechsler, D. (2003). *Wechsler Intelligence Scale for Children—Fourth Edition.* New York: Psychological Corporation.

Weichold, K., Silbereisen, R. K., & Schmitt-Rodermund, E. (2003). Short-term and long-term consequences of early versus late physical maturation in adolescents. In C. Hayward (Ed.), *Gender differences at puberty* (pp. 241–276). Cambridge, England: Cambridge University Press.

Weiner, B. (2010). The development of an attribution-based theory of motivation: A history of ideas. *Educational Psychologist, 45*(1), 28–36.

Weiss, R. P. (2000). Howard Gardner talks about technology. *Training & Development, 54*(9), 52–56.

Wentzel, K. R. (2002). Are effective teachers like good parents? Teaching styles and student adjustment in early adolescence. *Child Development, 73*(1), 287–301.

Wertsch, J. V. (1998). *Mind as action.* New York: Oxford University Press.

Wertsch, J. V., & Tulviste, P. (1996). L. S. Vygotsky and contemporary developmental psychology. In H. Daniels (Ed.), *An introduction to Vygotsky.* New York: Routledge.

Westwood, P. (2009). *What teachers need to know about students with disabilities.* Victoria, Australia: ACER Press.

Wheelock, A. (1994). *Alternatives to tracking and ability grouping.* Arlington, VA: American Association of School Administrators.

Whitehouse, P., McCloskey, E., & Ketelhut, D. J. (2010). Online pedagogy design and development: New models for 21st century online teacher professional development. In J. O. Lindberg & A. D. Olofsson (Eds.), *Online learning communities and teacher professional development: Methods for improved education delivery* (pp. 247–262). Hershey, PA: IGI Global.

Whittaker, C. R., Salend, S. J., & Duhaney, D. (2001). Creating instructional rubrics for inclusive classrooms. *Teaching Exceptional Children, 34*(2), 8–13.

Wicks-Nelson, R., & Israel, A. C. (2003). *Behavior disorders of childhood* (5th ed.). Upper Saddle River, NJ: Prentice Hall.

Wiechman, B., & Gurland, S. (2009). What happens during the free-choice period? Evidence of a polarizing effect of extrinsic rewards on intrinsic motivation. *Journal of Research in Personality, 43*(4), 716–719.

Wigfield, A., Battle, A., Keller, L. B., & Eccles, J. S. (2002). Sex differences in motivation, self-concept, career aspiration, and career choice: Implications for cognitive development. In A. McGillicuddy-De Lisi & R. De Lisi (Eds.), *Biology, society, and behavior: The development of sex differences in cognition* (pp. 93–124). Westport, CT: Ablex.

Wigfield, A., & Eccles, J. S. (2002). Students' motivation during the middle school years. In J. Aronson (Ed.), *Improving academic achievement* (pp. 159–184). San Diego, CA: Academic Press.

Wigfield, A., Tonks, S., & Klauda, S. L. (2009). Expectancy value theory. In K. Wentzel & A. Wigfield (Eds.), *Handbook of motivation at school* (pp. 55–76). New York: Routledge.

Wiggan, G. (2007). Race, school achievement, and educational inequality: Toward a student-based inquiry perspective. *Review of Educational Research, 77*(3), 310–333.

Wiles, J., Bondi, J., & Wiles, M. T. (2006). *The essential middle school* (4th ed.). Upper Saddle River, NJ: Pearson/Merrill Prentice Hall.

Williams, J. P., Lauer, K. D., Hall, K. M., Lord, K. M., Gugga, S. S., Bak, S.-J., Jacobs, P. R., & deCani, J. S. (2002). Teaching elementary school students to identify story themes. *Journal of Educational Psychology, 94*(2), 235–248.

Willig, A. C. (1985). A meta-analysis of selected studies on the effectiveness of bilingual education. *Review of Educational Research, 55*(3), 269–318.

Willingham, D. (2008). When and how neuroscience applies to education. *Phi Delta Kappan, 89*(6), 421–423.

Willis, J. (2008). Building a bridge from neuroscience to the classroom. *Phi Delta Kappan, 89*(6), 424–427.

Wilson, S. M., Floden, R. E., & Ferrini-Mundy, J. (2002). Teacher preparation research: An insider's view from the outside. *Journal of Teacher Education, 53*(3), 190–204.

Windschitl, M. (2002). Framing constructivism in practice as the negotiation of dilemmas: An analysis of the conceptual, pedagogical, cultural, and political challenges facing teachers. *Review of Educational Research, 72*(2), 131–175.

Winne, P. H. (2001). Self-regulated learning viewed from models of information processing. In B. J. Zimmerman & D. H. Schunk (Eds.), *Self-regulated learning and academic achievement: Theoretical perspectives* (2nd ed., pp. 153–189). Mahwah, NJ: Erlbaum.

Winne, P. H., & Jamieson-Noel, D. (2002). Exploring students' calibration of self reports about study tactics and achievement. *Contemporary Educational Psychology, 27*(4), 551–572.

Winne, P. H., & Jamieson-Noel, D. (2003). Self-regulating studying by objectives for learning: Students' reports compared to a model. *Contemporary Educational Psychology, 28*(3), 259–276.

Winne, P. H., & Stockley, D. B. (1998). Computing technologies as sites for developing self-regulated learning. In D. H. Schunk & B. J. Zimmerman (Eds.), *Self-regulated learning: From teaching to reflective practice* (pp. 107–136). New York: Guilford Press.

Winters, F. I., & Azevedo, R. (2005). High-school students' regulation of learning during computer-based science inquiry. *Journal of Educational Computing Research, 33*(2), 189–217.

Witkin, H. A., Moore, C. A., Goodenough, D. R., & Cox, P. W. (1977). Field-dependent and field-independent cognitive styles and their educational implications. *Review of Educational Research, 47*(1), 1–64.

Wittwer, J., & Renkl, A. (2008). Why instructional explanations often do not work: A framework for understanding the effectiveness of instructional explanations. *Educational Psychologist, 43*(1), 49–64.

Wixted, J. T. (2010). The role of retroactive interference and consolidation in everyday forgetting. In S. D. Sala (Ed.), *Forgetting* (pp. 285–312). New York: Psychology Press.

Wlodkowski, R. J. (1978). *Motivation and teaching: A practical guide.* Washington, DC: National Education Association.

Wlodkowski, R. J., & Ginsberg, M. B. (1995). A framework for culturally responsive teaching. *Educational Leadership, 53*(1), 17–21.

Woodul, C. E., III, Vitale, M. R., & Scott, B. J. (2000). Using a cooperative multimedia learning environment to enhance learning and affective self-perceptions of at-risk students in grade 8. *Journal of Educational Technology Systems, 28*(3), 239–252.

Wouters, P., Paas, F., & van Merriënboer, J. J. G. (2009). Observational learning from animated models: Effects of modality and reflection on transfer. *Contemporary Educational Psychology, 34*(1), 1–8.

Wuthrick, M. A. (1990). Blue jays win! Crows go down in defeat! *Phi Delta Kappan, 71*(7), 553–556.

Yager, R. E. (2000). The constructivist learning model. *Science Teacher, 67*(1), 44–45.

Yamagata-Lynch, L. C. (2007). Confronting analytical dilemmas for understanding complex human interactions in design-based research from a Cultural-Historical Activity Theory (CHAT) framework. *Journal of the Learning Sciences, 16*(4), 451–484.

Yamagata-Lynch, L. C., & Haudenschild, M. (2008). Teacher perception of barriers and aids of professional growth in professional development. *School–University Partnerships, 2*(2), 90–106.

Yamagata-Lynch, L. C., & Haudenschild, M. (2009). Using activity systems analysis to identify inner contradictions in teacher professional development. *Teaching and Teacher Education, 25*(3), 507–517.

Yang, S. C. (2001). Synergy of constructivism and hypermedia from three constructivist perspectives: Social, semiotic, and cognitive. *Journal of Educational Computing Research, 24*(4), 321–361.

Yang, S.-H. (2009). Using blogs to enhance critical reflection and community of practice. *Educational Technology & Society, 12*(2), 11–21.

Yao, Y. (2006). Technology use as a scoring criterion. In C. Crawford, D. A. Willis, R. Carlsen, I. Gibson, K. McFerrin, J. Price, & R. Weber (Eds.), *Proceedings of the Society for Information Technology and Teacher Education International Conference 2006* (pp. 215–219). Chesapeake, VA: Association for the Advancement of Computing in Education.

Yates, F. A. (1966). *The art of memory.* London: Routledge & Kegan Paul.

Yau, R. (2002). High-achieving elementary schools with large percentages of low-income African American students: A review and critique of the current research. In S. J. Denbo & L. M. Beaulieu (Eds.), *Improving schools for African American students* (pp. 193–217). Springfield, IL: Charles C Thomas.

Yelland, N., & Masters, J. (2007). Rethinking scaffolding in the information age. *Computers & Education, 48*(3), 362–382.

Yilmaz-Tuzun, O. (2008). Preservice elementary teachers' beliefs about science teaching. *Journal of Science Teacher Education, 19*(2), 183–204.

Yoerg, K. (2002). Painting patterns with pixels. *Arts & Activities, 131*(4), 50–51.

Yonezawa, S., Wells, A. S., & Serna, I. (2002). Choosing tracks: "Freedom of choice" in detracking schools. *American Educational Research Journal, 39*(1), 37–67.

Young, J. R. (2010). In wired Singapore classrooms, cultures clash over Web 2.0. *Chronicle of Higher Education.* Retrieved from http://chronicle.com/article/In-Wired-Singapore-Classrooms/124328.

Ysseldyke, J. E., Algozzine, B., & Thurlow, M. L. (2000). *Critical issues in special education* (3rd ed.). Boston: Houghton Mifflin.

Zeldin, A. L., & Pajares, F. (2000). Against the odds: Self-efficacy beliefs of women in mathematical, scientific, and technological careers. *American Educational Research Journal, 37*(1), 215–246.

Zellermayer, M., Salomon, G., Globerson, T., & Givon, H. (1991). Enhancing writing-related metacognitions through a computerized writing partner. *American Educational Research Journal, 28*(2), 373–391.

Zhang, J., Scardamalia, M., Reeve, R., & Messina, R. (2009). Designs for collective cognitive responsibility in knowledge building communities. *Journal of the Learning Sciences, 18*(1), 7–44.

Zhang, L. (2005). Validating the theory of mental self-government in a non-academic setting. *Personality and Individual Differences, 38*(8), 1915–1925.

Zhang, L., & Sternberg, R. J. (2001). Thinking styles across cultures: Their relationships with student learning. In R. J. Sternberg & L.-F. Zhang (Eds.), *Perspectives on thinking, learning, and cognitive styles* (pp. 197–226). Mahwah, NJ: Erlbaum.

Zhang, L., & Sternberg, R. J. (2006). *The nature of intellectual styles.* Mahwah, NJ: Erlbaum.

Zhang, L., & Sternberg, R. J. (2009). Intellectual styles and creativity. In T. Rickards, M. Runko, & S. Moger (Eds.), *The Routledge companion to creativity* (pp. 256–266). New York: Routledge.

Zhang, Y. (2009, November). *State high school exit exams: Trends in test programs, alternate pathways, and pass rates.* Retrieved from http://www.cep-dc.org/cfcontent_file.cfm?Attachment=CEP_HSEE09Report_up011310.pdf.

Zhao, Y., & Qiu, W. (2009). How good are the Asians? Refuting four myths about Asian-American academic achievement. *Phi Delta Kappan, 90*(5), 338–344.

Zhu, X., Chen, A., Ennis, C., Sun, H., Hopple, C., Bonello, M., Bae, M., & Kim, S. (2009). Situational interest, cognitive engagement, and achievement in physical education. *Contemporary Educational Psychology, 34*(3), 221–229.

Zientek, L. R. (2007). Preparing high-quality teachers: Views from the classroom. *American Educational Research Journal, 44*(4), 959–1001.

Zimmerman, B. J. (1990). Self-regulating academic learning and achievement: The emergence of a social cognitive perspective. *Educational Psychology Review, 2*(2), 173–200.

Zimmerman, B. J. (2000). Attaining self-regulation: A social cognitive perspective. In M. Boekaerts, P. R. Pintrich, & M. Zeidner (Eds.), *Handbook of self-regulation* (pp. 13–39). San Diego, CA: Academic Press.

Zimmerman, B. J. (2002). Achieving self-regulation: The trial and triumph of adolescence. In F. Pajares & T. Urdan (Eds.), *Academic motivation of adolescents* (pp. 1–27). Greenwich, CT: Information Age.

Zimmerman, B. J. (2008). Investigating self-regulation and motivation: Historical background, methodological developments, and future prospects. *American Educational Research Journal, 45*(1), 166–183.

Zimmerman, B. J., & Kitsantas, A. (2002). Acquiring writing revision and self-regulatory skill through observation and emulation. *Journal of Educational Psychology, 94*(4), 660–668.

Zimmerman, B. J., & Kitsantas, A. (2005). The hidden dimension of personal competence: Self-regulated learning and practice. In A. J. Elliot and C. S. Dweck (Eds.), *Handbook of competence and motivation* (pp. 509–526). New York: Guilford Press.

Zinesky, A., & Sireci, S. G. (2002). Technological innovations in large-scale assessment. *Applied Measurement in Education, 15*(4), 337–362.

Zirkel, P. A., & Thomas, L. B. (2010). State laws and guidelines for implementing RTI. *Teaching Exceptional Children, 43*(1), 60-73.

Zuo, L., & Cramond, B. (2001). An examination of Terman's gifted children from the theory of identity. *Gifted Children Quarterly, 45*(4), 251–259.

Doobay, A., 142
Dooley, S., 206
Doppelt, Y., 79, 257
Dornbusch, S. M., 120
Dorr, N., 101
Doty, D. E., 183
Downing, S. M., 311
Dowson, M., 237
Doyle, W., 169
Doyle-Nichols, A., 366
Drake, F. D., 366
Drew, C., 133, 142
Drier, H. S., 38
Drill, K., 3
Driscoll, M. P., 34, 213
Duckworth, A. L., 84
Duell, O. K., 180, 203
Duff, C., 40, 258
Duffrin, E., 7
Duffy, T., 212
Duffy, T. M., 216
Duhaney, D., 317
Duhaney, D. C., 146, 147
Duhaney, L. M., 146, 147
Duncan, C., 274
Dunham, R., 22
Dunlosky, J., 171
Dupper, D. R., 161
Dweck, C. S., 243, 244, 251

E

Earl, L., 310, 318
Eberstadt, M., 56
Eby, J. W., 14
Eccles, J., 103, 254, 256
Eccles, J. S., 63, 85, 87
Eckert, T. L., 238
Economics and Statistics Administration & National Telecommunications and Information Administration, 100
Efthim, H. E., 110
Egan, M., 133, 142
Einstein, G. O., 193, 198
Eisenberg, N., 54
Eisner, E. W., 10
Elfstrom, J. L., 273, 274
Elkind, D., 25, 29, 33
Elliot, A., 240, 242, 245
Elliot, A. J., 245
Elliott, T., 38
Ellis, A. B., 84
Ellis, A. K., 14
Emmer, E. T., 158, 261, 264, 265–266
Endo, H., 113
Engel, M., 351
Engelhart, M. B., 205, 282
Engeström, Y., 215
Englander, E. K., 274
Engleman, M., 146
Enochs, L., 215
Erdogan, Y., 156
Erickson, D., 67
Ericsson, K. A., 178
Erikson, E. H., 17–23
Ertmer, P., 293
Evans, R., 100
Evertson, C. M., 158, 264, 265–266

F

Fabes, R. A., 50
Fadjukoff, P., 18, 22
Fagley, N., 222
Fairbanks, S., 4, 264
Falk, B., 7, 297
Faloon, S., 178

Fantuzzo, J. W., 109, 300, 302, 303
Fargo, J. D., 317
Farkas, S., 24
Faw, H. W., 285
Fazal, M., 328, 329
Feigenbaum, P., 55
Feiman-Nemser, S., 11
Feist, G. J., 252
Feist, J., 252
Feldman, S. S., 45
Ferrini-Mundy, J., 6
Ferriter, B., 368
Ferster, B., 69
Feyten, C. M., 116
Fields, V. S., 294
Finarelli, M. G., 40
Fine, J., 5
Finnigan, K. S., 352
Fischer, S., 302
Fisher, D. L., 360
Fisk, A. D., 174
Flaspohler, P. D., 273, 274
Flavell, J., 178
Flegg, A., 295
Fleming, J. A. E., 67
Fletcher, J., 127
Flieller, A., 30
Flinders, D. J., 10
Flint, A. S., 5
Floden, R. E., 6
Flora, S. R., 165
Flowerday, T., 245, 246
Flum, H., 253, 254
Flynn, P., 146
Fok, A., 215, 257
Foote, M., 353
Forbes, S., 22
Forbus, K., 216
Foshay, W. R., 357
Fosnot, C. T., 214
Franzke, M., 206
Fraser, B. J., 360
Fredrick, T., 313
Freeman, C. E., 85
Freiberg, H. J., 295, 296, 360, 363
French, S. E., 22
Friedkin, S., 362, 363
Friedlaender, D., 258
Frijters, J., 237
Fromberg, D. P., 50, 57
Fryer, R. G., Jr., 101
Fuchs, D., 124, 127, 130, 138
Fuchs, L. S., 124, 127, 130, 136, 138
Fuller, B., 350
Fulmer, S., 237
Funkhouser, C., 294
Furlong, M. J., 270–271, 274
Furnham, A., 72
Furst, E. J., 205, 282

G

Gable, J., 250
Gable, R. K., 63
Gagné, E. D., 217, 222
Gajdamaschko, N., 215
Galambos, N. L., 67
Galindo, C., 101, 102
Gallagher, J. J., 126, 133, 139, 140, 142
Gallimore, R., 11, 14, 37
Gallingane, C., 264, 267
Gambrell, L., 239, 241
Gamoran, A., 121
Gantner, M., 105
García, E., 96, 97, 106

C

Career choice and gender bias, 85–87

Care theory, Nodding's, 43–44

Caring: A Feminine Approach to Ethics and Moral Education (Noddings), 43

C.AR.ME. *See* Conservation of Area and Its Measurement (C.AR.ME)

Carnegie Corporation, 121–122

CASE. *See* Cognitive Acceleration through Science Education (CASE)

Case in Print: character education programs, 46; constructing knowledge by combining technology and problems, 218–219; cultural diversity, 95; elaborative rehearsal, 171; gender bias, correcting, 86; information-processing/social cognitive theory, 290; joy of being a teacher-artist, 12–13; mainstreaming, 129; middle school anxiety, 64; National Board for Professional Teaching Standards, 366–367; pep rallies for high-stakes tests, 348–349; Positive Behavior Support in schools, 276; remote tracking, 320–321; school as a rewarding experience, 160; self-regulated learners, 200–201; taking an interest in learning, 249

Causal attributions, 193

CBI. *See* Computer-based instruction (CBI)

CBT. *See* Computer-based testing (CBT)

Challenging Assumptions: ability grouping and tracking, 123; bilingual education, 115; on evidence, 10; gender bias, eliminating, 90; intellectual needs of middle school students, selecting, 63; positive reinforcement *vs.* punishment, 164; practice assessment for learning, 318; promoting industry, 20; rigor in teaching and learning, 255; students as learners *vs.* performers, 177; teaching students to be self-regulated learners, 198; transfer of learning, 230; using medical model to guide educational accountability, 354; zero tolerance policies, 277

Character education programs, research on, 45–47

CHAT. *See* Cultural-historical activity theory (CHAT)

Childhood and Society (Erikson), 18

Children: with ADHD, 137; capabilities of, underestimating, 30; elementary school, 55–58; with intellectual disability, 132–133; preschool and kindergarten, 49–52; primary grades, 53–55

Chunking, 170

Cinnamon Tree, The (Flegg), 295

Class participation and gender bias, 87–89

Classroom assessment, 306–332; grading methods for, 324–327; role of, 307–310; of student learning, evaluating, 318–327; of student learning, measuring, 311–318

Classroom assessment, technology in, 327–329; digital portfolios and, 328–329; electronic grade books and programs for, 327–328; performance assessments and, 328; problems associated with, 329

Classroom management, 260–279; approaches to, 261–262; behavior problems and, 266–271; contemporary studies of, 264–265; high school, 265–266; junior high school, 265–266; middle school, 265–266; techniques of, 262–266; technology used to keep students in school, 278–279; violence and, 270–278

Classroom Management for Middle and High School Teachers (Emmer and Evertson), 265

Classroom observation, 360, 361f

Cocaine use, 67

Cognitive ability, 243–245; beliefs about, changes in, 243–244; beliefs about, types of, 244–245

Cognitive Acceleration through Science Education (CASE), 30

Cognitive apprenticeship, 215

Cognitive characteristics: elementary school, 58; high school, 68; middle school, 62–65; preschool and kindergarten, 51–52; primary grades, 54–55

Cognitive constructivism, 214

Cognitive development: conceptual organization and, need for, 241; cooperative learning and, 303; in elementary school, 55t; Erikson's theory of psychosocial development, 16–23; in high school, 65t; in middle school, 59t; Piaget's theory of, 23–31; in preschool and kindergarten, 50t; in primary grades, 53t; Vygotsky's theory of, 31–40

Cognitive development, technology in, 38–40; applied to Piaget, 38; applied to Vygotsky, 39–40; microcomputer-based laboratories and, 38; microworlds and, 38; multiuser virtual environments and, 39–40; telementoring and, 40

Cognitive domain taxonomy, 282–283

Cognitive elaboration in cooperative learning, 303

Cognitive feedback in self-regulated learning, 206–207

Cognitive instructional approach, 288–295, 303t; constructivist approach, 291–293; information-processing/social cognitive approach, 288–291

Cognitive instructional approach, technology in, 293–295; exploratory environments in, 294; guided learning in, 294; problem-based learning in, 294–295; situational learning in, 295

Cognitive needs, Maslow's, 252

Cognitive processes affected by self-efficacy, 190

Cognitive views of motivation, 239–248; attribution theory and, 242–243, 242t; cognitive ability and, 243–245; limitations of, 248; need for achievement and, 241–242; need for conceptual organization and, 241; social, 239–241

Collaborative learning, 304–305

College entrance tests, 83

Commitment in identity attainment, 21

Communication: nonverbal, in ethnicity and learning, 97; verbal patterns in ethnicity and learning, 97

Community, sense of, 298–299

Community of practice, 40

Comorbidity, 137

Complex problems, 315–316

Comprehension-directed learning tactics, 194

Computer-based instruction (CBI), 155–157; defined, 155; evaluation of, 157; programs, types of, 155t; research on effects of, 155–156

Computer-based modeling in SRL, 206

Computer-based testing (CBT), 356

Computer-Supported Intentional Learning Environments (CSILE) project, 232

Concept mapping, 197–198

Conceptual organization, need for, 241

Concrete operational stage, 27

Conditional knowledge, 180

Conduct disorder, 137

Confirmation in ZPD, 37

Conformity in middle school, 60–61

Consequential engagement, 234–235

Conservation of Area and Its Measurement (C.AR.ME), 38

Conservation of continuous quantity, 26

Conservative style, 82t

Consolidation, inadequate, 176

Constructing knowledge, 25

Constructivism, 211–217; claims that frame, 212–214; cognitive, 214; critical, 215; defined, 211; discovery learning and, 212; learning practices in, 215–216; limitations of, 216; social, 214–215; today, 212–217

Constructivist approach, 291–293, 303t; learning by discovery in, 292; multiple viewpoints in, 292–293; problems and tasks emphasized in, 293; scaffolded instruction in ZPD, 292; student autonomy in, 293

Constructivist learning practices, 215–216; cognitive apprenticeship, 215; multiple perspectives, 216; situated learning, 215–216; view of, 167

Constructs, 338

Construct validity evidence, 338

Content standards, 316. *See also* Rubrics

Content validity evidence, 337

Contingency contracting, 159

Contingency management. *See* Behavior modification

Continuous reinforcement schedules, 153

Contributions approach to multicultural education, 106

Control in scientific studies, 7–8

Control processes in information-processing, 168, 168f

Conversations with Great Teachers (Smoot), 11

Cooperative learning, 90, 109, 301–303; achievement effected by, 302; cognitive development effected by, 303; cognitive elaboration effected by, 303; in constructivist approach, 292–293; elements of, 301–302; motivation effect by, 302, 303; in social instructional approach, 304–305; social interaction effected by, 302–303

Cooperative Learning: Theory, Research, and Practice (Slavin), 54

Correlation, 253–254

Course selection and gender bias, 85

Coursework in educational psychology, 5–6

Cramming, 176

Creative ability, 74

Crisis in identity attainment, 21

Criterion-referenced grading, 322–324; definition of, 322; mastery approach to, 324; nature of, 322–323; strengths and weaknesses of, 323–324

Criterion-referenced tests, 339
Critical constructivism, 215
Criticism, 269
Cross-age tutoring, 109
CSILE. *See* Computer-Supported Intentional Learning Environments (CSILE) project
Cultural differences in intellectual development, 31
Cultural diversity: among students, 94f, 95, 96; performance characteristics and, 317
Cultural effects on cognitive development, 32–34
Cultural factors in identity status, 22
Cultural-historical activity theory (CHAT), 215
Cultural pluralism, 94
Culture, defined, 93
Curriculum and high-stakes testing, 352
Cyberbullying, 273
Cybergogy, 83

D

Data, selection and interpretation of, 9
Dave's ESL Cafe, 116
Deaf-blindness, 128, 130
Decentration, 26
Decision-making: social action approach to multicultural education and, 106; in teaching, 10
Decision Point!, 207
Declarative knowledge, 180
Deficiency needs, 248, 256
Defining Issues Test (DIT), 43
Defining limits, 269
Delinquent behavior in elementary grades, 57–58
Demonstrations, 314
Depression, 67–68
Describability as useful test attribute, 312
Detracking, 123
Diabetes, 128
Diagnostic Adaptive Behavior Scale, 133
Dialogue in ZPD, 37
Didion, Joan, 173
Differentiated instruction, 71, 143–144
Digital divide, 90–91, 232
Digital portals for professional development, 367–368
Digital portfolios, 328–329; components and contents of, 328–329; definition of, 328; rubrics for, 329
Direct instruction, 286–288; characteristics of, 286; defined, 286; effectiveness of, 287–288; orientation in, 286–287; practice in, 287; presentation in, 287
Direct writing assessments, 313
Discipline and Group Management in Classrooms (Kounin), 262
Discovery environments. *See* Exploratory environments
Discovery learning, 212, 292
Discrimination in operant conditioning, 153
Disequilibrium, 24–25
Disinhibition, 203
Distance education or learning, 278–279
Distributed practice, 176, 179
DIT. *See* Defining Issues Test (DIT)
Diversity-Responsive Teaching Observation Tool, 360
Domain, 337
Double helix, 225
Drill and practice program, 155t
Dropout rates: high-stakes testing and, 352–353; technology used to reduce, 278–279
Dual coding theory, 174
Dual language. *See* Two-way bilingual (TWB) education

E

Early adolescence, 59
Early-maturing boys, 59–60, 60t
Early-maturing girls, 59–60, 60t
Eating disorders, 67
Educational applications of operant conditioning, 154–165; behavior modification, 157–161, 164–165; computer-based instruction, 155–157, 155t; prescriptions in, 154

Educational psychology, 2–15; behavior and thought processes and, 8–10; defined, 3; learning about, benefits of, 3–6; science and, nature and values of, 6–8; teaching and, 10–15
Educational Psychology: A Cognitive View (Ausubel), 213
Educational-psychology research: to inform teachers, 4–5; limited focus of, 8; neuroscience and, 9–10; scientific basis for artistic teaching provided by, 12–14
Educational Testing Service, 15
Egocentric thought, 27; in middle school, 62
Egocentrism, 27, 29; technology used to reduce, 68–69
Einstein, Albert, 173
Elaborative rehearsal, 168, 171–172
Electronic grade books and programs, 327–328
Electronic portfolios, 328
Electronic read-around, 182
Elementary school, 55–58; cognitive characteristics, 58; emotional characteristics, 57–58; gender differences addressed in, 88; physical characteristics, 55–56; social characteristics, 56–57; theories of development applied to, 55
ELLs. *See* English-language learners (ELLs)
Emerging adolescence, 59
Emotional characteristics: elementary school, 57–58; high school, 67–68; middle school, 61–62; preschool and kindergarten, 51; primary grades, 54
Emotional disturbance, 137–140; *vs.* behavior disorder, 139; characteristics of students with, 139–140; definitions of, 139; estimates of, 137, 139; as IDEA disability, 128, 137; instructing students with, 141
Empirical learning, 35–36
Employment after school, 67
Emulation in self-regulated learning, 202–203, 202t
Encoding specificity principle, 175–176
Encouragement, 269
English-as-a-second-language (ESL), 111, 113, 116
English-language learners (ELLs), 114–115
Enrichment and differentiated instruction, 143–144
Enrichment for gifted and talented learners, 144
Entity theorists, 244
Epigenetic principle, 17–18
Epilepsy, 128
Episodic heavy drinking, 67
Epistemological beliefs, 192
Equal opportunities for success, 301
Equilibration, 24–25
Erikson's stages of psychosocial development, 18–19; autonomy *vs.* shame and doubt, 18; identity *vs.* role confusion, 19; industry *vs.* inferiority, 19; initiative *vs.* guilt, 18; trust *vs.* mistrust, 18
Erikson's theory of psychosocial development, 16–23; applying, 24; criticisms of, 23; epigenetic principle of, 17–18; identity formation and, 20; identity statuses and, 20–22; industry and, developing sense of, 19; psychosocial crisis and, 18; psychosocial moratorium and, 20; stages of (*See* Erikson's stages of psychosocial development)
ESL. *See* English-as-a-second-language (ESL)
Essay tests, 312
Esteem, 248, 252f
Ethnic additive approach to multicultural education, 106
Ethnic factors in identity statuses, 22
Ethnic group, 96–97
Ethnicity and learning, 96–99; instructional formats and, 97–98; learning processes and, 97–98; nonverbal communication and, 97; social values and, 97; teacher expectancy effect and, 102–105; time orientation and, 97; verbal communication patterns and, 97
Ethnocentrism, 96
Evaluation: defined, 308; of standardized tests, 336–339; of student learning, 318–327
Everything Bad Is Good for You (Johnson), 233
Evidence, 10
Exceptional students, technology to assist, 144–147; assistive technologies, 145–147; universal design for learning, 144–145
Executive style, 82t
Exhibitions, 314
Expectancy-value theory, 242
Experience-based knowledge, 13–14
Explicit teaching. *See* Direct instruction

postsituational follow-up, 269; program restructuring, 268–269; proximity and touch control, 268; signals, 268

Information processing: model, 167–177; theory of, 166–184; tools, 182–184; view of learning, 167

Information-processing/social cognitive approach, 288–291; attention-getting devices used in, 288–289; encoding of information into long-term memory, 291; goals and objectives in, 288; organization and meaningfulness in, 289–291, 289f

Inhibition, 203

Initiative vs. guilt stage, 18

Instructional approaches, 280–305; behavioral, 286–288, 303t; cognitive, 288–295, 303t; humanistic, 295–300, 303t; social, 300–305, 303t

Instructional formats in ethnicity and learning, 97–98

Instructional methods in multicultural education, 109–110; cooperative learning, 109; mastery learning, 109–110; peer tutoring, 109

Instructional objectives: assessment aligned with, 284–285; educational goals and, 281–282; effectiveness of, 285; general, 283–284; specific, 283–284; taxonomies of, 282–283; using and devising, 281–283; ways of stating, 283–285

Instructional standards: InTASC, 15; Praxis II, 15

Instruction in cognitive development: in Piaget's theory, 29–30; in Vygotsky's theory, 34–37

Instrumental relativist orientation, 42

InTASC. See Interstate New Teacher Assessment and Support Consortium (InTASC)

Intellectual disability, 132–133; characteristics of children with, 132–133; definition of, 132; mental retardation and, 128

Intellectual Disability: Definition, Classification, and Systems of Supports (AAIDD), 132

Intelligence: contemporary views of, 73–76; multiple, Gardner's theory of, 75–76, 75t, 78; new views of, 77–79; triarchic theory of, Sternberg's, 74, 74f, 77–78, 77t; Wechsler's global capacity view of, 73

Intelligence quotient (IQ): gifted and talented students and, 140; intellectual disabilities and, 132–133; origin of, 71–72

Intelligence testing, 71–73; limitations of, 73; origin of, 71–72; Spearman's two-factor theory and, 72–73; Stanford-Binet Intelligence Scales, 71–72, 77; Wechsler Adult Intelligence Scale, 72; Wechsler Intelligence Scale for Children-Fourth Edition, 72, 77

Interaction, promoting, 301

Interdependence, positive, 301

Interdependent group contingency, 275

Interest, 245–248; boosting, 268; flow and engagement in, 247–248; instructional implications, 247; personal, 245, 246; situational, 245, 246

Intermittent reinforcement schedules, 153–154; fixed interval, 153–154; fixed ratio, 154; variable interval, 154; variable ratio, 154

Internal style, 82t

Interpersonal intelligence, 75t, 88

Interpersonal reasoning, Selman's, 60, 61t

Interpersonal skills, 301

Interpretations or constructions, 176

Interstate New Teacher Assessment and Support Consortium (InTASC), 15

Intrapersonal intelligence, 75t, 88

Intrinsic motivation, 238–239, 239f, 245–248; defined, 238; effect of external rewards on, 239, 239f; vs. extrinsic motivation, 256–257; interest and, 245–248; reinforcement and, 238–239, 239f

Invariant functions, 25

Irreversibility, 26–27

J

Jealousy in preschool and kindergarten, 51

Joplin Plan, 120–121, 122

Judicial style, 82t

Junior high school, classroom management in, 265–266

K

Keyword method, 195t

Kidlink, 69

Knowledge-building explanations and questions, 109

Knowledge construction and problem solving technology, 231–235; CSILE project, 232; mindtools, 231; Quest Atlantis, 232–235

Knowledge-of-person variables, 180

Knowledge-of-strategy variables, 180

Knowledge-of-task variables, 180

Kohlberg's description of moral development, 41–43; criticisms and evaluations of, 42–43; moral dilemmas in, 41; stages of moral reasoning in, 41–42

Kounin's observations on group management, 262–264

L

Language: English-as-a-second-language (ESL), 111, 113, 116; English-language learners, 114–115; preschool and kindergarten skills, 52; two-way bilingual education, 112–114. See also Bilingual education

Language impairments: as IDEA disability, 128; technology for students with, 146

Language use tests, 83

Large muscle development in preschool and kindergarten, 49

Late-maturing boys, 59–60, 60t

Late-maturing girls, 59–60, 60t

Law and order orientation, 42

Learning: about educational psychology, 3–6; adventure, 69; collaborative, 304–305; with computers, 231–235; constructing knowledge and, 25; constructivism and, 167, 215–216; cooperative, 90, 109, 304–305; discovery, 212, 292; empirical, 35–36; equilibration and disequilibrium in, 24–25; ethnicity and, 96–99; evaluating, 318–327; goals, 240; guided, 294; information processing view of, 167; mastery, 109–110, 281; meaningful, 172–173, 213, 220–221; measuring, 311–318; nonmeaningful, 176; peer-assisted, 109; in primary grades, 55; problem-based, 69, 294–295; processes in ethnicity and, 97–98; scaffolding in, 36–37; scientific concepts in, 35; situational, 295; social class and, 99–102; social constructivist, 304; spontaneous concepts in, 34; theoretical, 36; transfer of, 228–231; universal design for, 144–145; ZPD and, 36–37. See also Self-regulated learning (SRL)

Learning disabilities, 133–137; ADHD and, 136–137; characteristics of students with, 133–135; as IDEA disability, 128, 133; identifying students with, 135; instructing students with, 138; psychological processes and, 135–136; technology for students with, 146–147

Learning styles, 79–83; field dependence in, 79–81; field independence in, 79–81; impulsivity in, 79; instruction guided by awareness of, 81–82; mental self-government styles, Sternberg's theory of, 81, 82t; reflectivity in, 79; technology used to accommodate, 82–83

Learning tactics for SRL skills, 194–198; comprehension-directed, 194; concept mapping, 197–198; conclusions regarding, 198; memory-directed, 194; mnemonic devices, 194–196, 195t; rehearsal, 194; self- and peer-questioning, 196–197, 197t

Learning with computers, 231–235; CSILE project, 232; mindtools, 231; Quest Atlantis, 232–235

Least restrictive environment, 125–126

Legislative style, 82t

Lesson study, 362–363, 362f

Level of voice, 88

Liberal style, 82t

Limits, defining, 269

Linguistic intelligence, 75t, 88

Living conditions in social class and learning, 100

Local style, 82t

Loci method, 195t

Logical-mathematical intelligence, 75t, 88

Logical thinking in elementary grades, 58

Long-term memory (LTM), 174–176, 291

Loss of voice, 88

Low-road transfer, 229–230, 231

LTM. See Long-term memory (LTM)

Lying to parents, study on, 45

M

Macromoral issues, 42

Magnet schools, 143

Mainstreaming, 125–126, 129

Maintenance programs in bilingual education, 111–112

Maintenance rehearsal, 170, 171

MAMA. See Moratorium-achievement-moratorium-achievement (MAMA) cycle

Marcia's identity statuses, 20–22

Marijuana use, 67

Maslow's hierarchy of needs, 248, 252, 252f

Operant conditioning, 148–165; applying in the classroom, 162–163; discrimination in, 153; educational applications of, 154–165; extinction in, 152, 152f; generalization in, 152–153; idea of, 149–150; negative reinforcement in, 150–151, 152f; positive reinforcement in, 150, 152f; principles of, 150–154; punishment in, 151, 152f; reinforcement in, 238; schedules of reinforcement in, 153–154; shaping in, 153; time-out in, 151–152

Organization: defined, 23; in information-processing/social cognitive approach, 289–291, 289f; in long-term memory, 174–176; in Piaget's cognitive development theory, 23, 24; in short-term memory, 172, 172f

Orientation in direct instruction, 286–287

Orthopedic impairments: as IDEA disability, 146; technology for students with, 146

Outcome expectations, 191, 240

P

PBS. *See* Positive Behavior Support (PBS)

Pedagogical content knowledge, 6

Peer-assisted learning, 109

Peer-influence: in elementary grades, 56–57; of groups, 61; in high school, 66

Peer-questioning, 196–197, 197t

Peer techniques, 360–367; classroom observation schedules, 360, 361f; guided reflection protocol, 363; lesson study, 362–363, 362f; personal portfolio, 365–367; reflective journal, 363–365, 364f; self-recorded lessons, 363

Peer tutoring, 109

Percentile ranks, 340, 342f

Perceptual centration, 26

Perfectly Valid theory, 338

Performance-approach goals, 240

Performance assessments, 312–318, 315f; characteristics of, 314–317; concerns about, 318; defined, 313; types of, 313–314

Performance-avoidance goals, 240

Performance based assessment, 313

Performance characteristics, 314–317; active responding and, 314; complex problems and, 315–316; cultural diversity and, 317; degree of realism and, 314–315; formative assessment and, 317; scoring rubrics and, 316–317, 316t; teaching and testing relationship as, 316

Performance phase, 192

Performance standards, 316

Permissive parents, 261

Permissive teaching style, 261–262

Personal agency, 187

Personal interest, 245, 246

Physical characteristics of students: elementary school, 55–56; high school, 65–66; middle school, 59–60; preschool and kindergarten, 49; primary grades, 53

Physiological needs, 248, 252f

Piaget's analysis of moral judgment of the child, 40–41; age changes in interpretations of rules, 40; moral realism *vs.* moral relativism, 40–41, 41t

Piaget's stages of cognitive development, 25–29, 25t; concrete operational, 27; formal operational, 27–29; preoperational, 26–27; sensorimotor, 25

Piaget's theory of cognitive development, 23–31; applying, 32–33; criticisms of, 30–31; cultural differences and, 31; instruction and, 29–30; overestimating adolescents' capabilities, 30; principles of, 23–25; social interaction and, 29; stages of (*See* Piaget's stages of cognitive development); technology applied to, 38; underestimating children's capabilities, 30; vagueness in explaining cognitive growth, 30–31

Planful behavior, 25

Planned ignoring, 266, 268

Planning phase of study cycle, 362

Play activities: in elementary grades, 57; in preschool and kindergarten, 50

Political thinking in high school, 68

Portfolios, 313–314, 365–367

Positive Behavior Support (PBS), 276

Positive reinforcement, 150, 152f; *vs.* punishment, 164

Positive transfer, 228

Postsituational follow-up, 269

Practical ability, 74

Practice: in direct instruction, 287; in ZPD, 37

Praise, 250–251, 250t

Praxis II, 15

Predictive validity evidence, 337

Preferences, 79*See also* Learning styles

Premack principle, 158

Preoperational stage, 26–27, 30

Preplacement evaluation, 124–125

Preschool and kindergarten, 49–52; cognitive characteristics, 51–52; emotional characteristics, 51; physical characteristics, 49; social characteristics, 49–51; theories of development applied to, 50t

Presentation in direct instruction, 287

Primary grades, 53–55; cognitive characteristics, 54–55; emotional characteristics, 54; physical characteristics, 53; social characteristics, 53–54; theories of development applied to, 53t

Prior knowledge, 220

Private speech, 55

Problem-based learning, 69, 294–295

Problem framing, 222

Problem recognition, 222

Problem representation, 222

Problem solving, 217–228; compile relevant information, 223–224; defined, 217; evaluation of solutions, 225, 228; formulate and carry out a solution, 224–225; heuristics in, 224–225; nature of, understanding, 222–223; problem recognition in, 222; problem representation in, 222; problem types in, 217–219; steps in, 222–228; techniques, teaching, 226–227

Problem types, 217–219; ill-structured problems, 218; issues, 218–219; well-structured problems, 217–218

Procedural knowledge, 180

Professional Education of Teachers (Combs), 296

Program restructuring, 268–269

Proximity and touch control, 268

Psychological tools, 33–34

Psychometric theory, 308

Psychomotor domain taxonomy, 282, 283

Psychosocial crisis, 18

Psychosocial development: in elementary school, 55t; in high school, 65t; in middle school, 59t; in preschool and kindergarten, 50t; in primary grades, 53t. *See also* Erikson's theory of psychosocial development

Psychosocial moratorium, 20

Pubertal development in middle school, 60

Publication in scientific studies, 7–8

Published tests, 335

Punishment: in behavior modification, 161, 164; in operant conditioning, 151, 152f; *vs.* positive reinforcement, 164

Punishment-obedience orientation, 41–42

Pygmalion effect. *See* Teacher expectancy effect

Q

QA. *See* Quest Atlantis (QA)

Quarrels in primary grades, 54

Quest Atlantis (QA), 39–40, 184, 232–235; consequential engagement in, 234–235; design features of, 233; Project Mission, 234

R

RCCP. *See* Resolving Conflict Creatively Program (RCCP)

Reading, technology tools for, 182–183

Reading Upgrade, 111

Realism, 314–315

Recall in primary grades, 55

Reciprocal effects, 254

Reciprocal teaching, 205

Recognition in information-processing, 168–169

Referrals under IDEA, 130

Reflection phase of study cycle, 362

Reflection skills, 358–368, 360–367; peer and self-assessment techniques for improving, 360–367; student feedback for improving, 360; teaching improved with, 360–367; technology and, 367–368

Reflective journal, 363–365, 364f

Reflective teaching, 14–15

Reflectivity, 79

Reflexes, 25

Regrouping, 120, 122